Contents

IN VOLUME 1:
(pages 1–605)

IN VOLUME 2:
(pages 606–1195)

volume 1

it

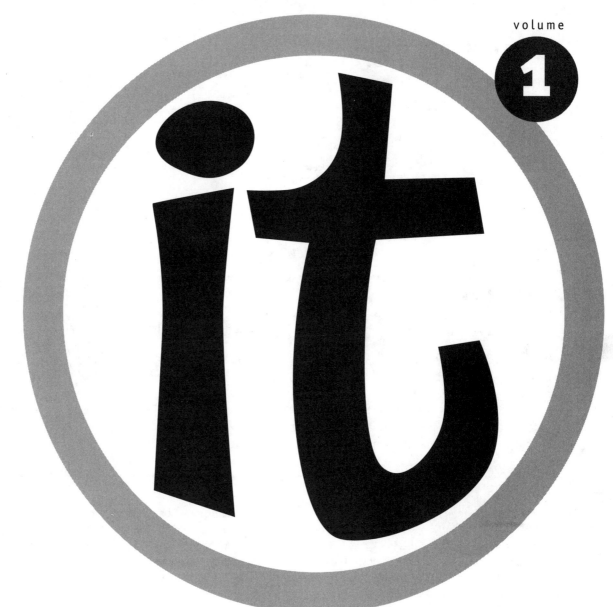

{Innovative Tools} for Children's Ministry

Group
Loveland, Colorado
www.group.com

it: {Innovative Tools} for Children's Ministry

We would like to thank the hundreds of amazing children's workers and freelance writers who've contributed their ideas to our magazines and books for over a decade. *it: Innovative Tools for Children's Ministry* contains some of the best Group-owned ideas and activities we've published—plus great new ideas.

Visit our Web site: **www.group.com**

Credits
Contributing and Compiling Authors: Helen T. Goody, Jennifer Hooks, Jan Kershner, Amy Simpson, Jeff White, and Roxanne Wieman
Editors of Volumes 1 and 2: Tammy L. Bicket and Dawn M. Brandon
Creative Development Editor: Mikal Keefer
Chief Creative Officer: Joani Schultz
Technology Editor: Eli Bernard
Copy Editors: Daniel Birks, Linda Marcinkowski, and Amber Van Schooneveld
Art Director: Jean Bruns
Book and Cover Designer: Sharon Anderson
Production Assistant: Joyce Douglas
Typography: Amnet Systems Private Limited
Print Production Artists: Joyce Douglas and Jan Fonda
Production Manager: Dodie Tipton

LabOra® Software Credits
Duplo Data AS, Forsand, Norway
Managing Director: Per Halvorsen
Vice President–Marketing: Dagfinn Skogøy
Director of Product: Ingve Johnsen
Development Team: Johannes Pettersen, Hans Egil Vaaga, Jorg Dovland

Library of Congress Cataloging-in-Publication Data
It : innovative tools for children's ministry / contributing and compiling authors, Amy Simpson ... [et al.].
p. cm.
Includes bibliographical references and indexes.
ISBN-13: 978-0-7644-3088-6 (v. 1 : pbk. : alk. paper)
1. Church work with children. 2. Religious education of children. I. Simpson, Amy.
BV639.C4I83 2006
259'.22--dc22 2006012869

ISBN 0-7644-3088-2

10 9 8 7 6 5 4 3 2 1 15 14 13 12 11 10 09 08 07 06
Printed in the United States of America.

Welcome to *it*!

This two-volume set is your one-stop-shop for literally thousands of children's ministry ideas. You'll find games, skits, Bible stories, crafts, movie clip illustrations, prayer activities, experiential worship ideas...and the list goes on. Using *it* is like walking through a warehouse piled high with ready-to-use ideas—and each idea is designed to help children grow in their relationship with Jesus.

These program elements are fun—that's true. But it's *purposeful* fun...and that makes all the difference.

it: Innovative Tools for Children's Ministry covers 150 Bible stories with 50 additional topical studies. You'll find teacher training sessions and original skits, too—and we've even integrated 40 songs into Bible lessons! You can use the sessions you find here as complete lessons, or you can pick and choose lesson elements to add a spark to lessons you've already designed. It's up to you!

The programming ideas in *it* are flexible because your ministry is flexible. You can use these lessons and lesson elements in a Sunday school setting, small-group Bible study, children's church, camp, or any other place you program for children.

And you'll love the indexes. They make it easy to find just the right program element whether you're searching by Scripture, topic, or Bible story.

And it's even easier to search when you use the revolutionary LabOra® Children's Ministry Planning Software included in this resource.

The Best of the Best

Where did all these ministry tools come from? Children's Ministry Magazine contributed many from ideas published during the past 14 years. Plus, Group Publishing began creating children's ministry resources over a dozen years ago. That's a lot of great material—but we've added to it fresh, innovative ideas you've never seen before from some of our best children's ministry authors.

What You'll Find

The Bible stories contain enough material for you to easily teach a full-hour lesson. In fact, you'll probably have too *many* ideas to fit in that time frame; you'll need to pick and choose. The topical studies have a bit less material, but enough to design a session for Sunday school or another children's ministry setting.

Once you've decided on a Bible story or a topic, you'll find a variety of lesson elements for your use...

For the Leader

This lesson element provides a Bible background for the Bible stories and topical studies. The background may be interesting facts you can share with your kids, or a bite-sized suggestion for applying the story to the lives of your students. Either way, you'll feel better equipped to lead a life-changing lesson.

Key Scriptures

These Scriptures connect to the Bible Points. You don't have to ask students to memorize verses, but if that's something you value, there's an appropriate verse for each Bible story and topic.

Bible Experience

This lesson element includes fun ways to communicate Bible stories to get kids involved, talking, and applying the Bible Point to their own lives. Application is built right in!

Song & Connect

In about half of the sessions, there's a tie-in to one of the 40 songs you receive with *it*. The songs are on companion CDs and also in the electronic version of *it*. New Testament songs, Old Testament songs—they're both here! And if you want lyrics sheets for your local church, be our guest. The lyrics to all 40 songs are provided—and reproducible.

Children's Message

This lesson element includes engaging, age-appropriate talks that don't just give children information. They also involve children and build in lesson and life application! Use these messages to share Bible truths with children in Sunday school, children's church—anywhere!

Game

Fun and memorable, practical instructions equip you to lead these memorable games quickly and easily. Discussion questions connect the game to the Bible Point being explored.

Craft

Big fun, small preparation—that's a good description of these crafts. Plus, these 150-plus crafts connect to Bible Points!

Snack

Simple, easy, and directly connected to the Bible Point—what could be tastier for teachers?

Science Devotion

Eyes light up and kids say "wow" when they experience these great attention-grabbers that connect to Bible Points.

Discussion Launcher Questions

These insightful, open-ended discussion questions get students talking about the Bible Point or Bible story.

Discussion Launcher

These simple activity ideas will get students thinking and talking about the Bible Point. Each activity comes with discussion questions.

Life Application

These practical suggestions offer specific avenues through which children can apply scriptural truth to their everyday lives.

Movie Clip

These movie clip suggestions from both current and "classic" children's films help you connect culture to spiritual truth. Each entry offers specific start and stop times, a synopsis of the clip, an explanation of how the scene relates to children's faith, and a discussion outline including Scripture.

COPYRIGHT LAW

In general, federal copyright laws do not allow you to use videos or DVDs (even ones you own) for any purpose other than home viewing. Though some exceptions allow for the use of short segments of copyrighted material for educational purposes, it's best to be on the safe side. Your church can obtain a license from Christian Video Licensing International for a small fee. Just visit www.cvli.org, or call 1-888-771-2854 for more information. When using a movie that is not covered by the license, we recommend directly contacting the movie studio to seek permission for use of the clip.

Preschool Story

For each Bible story, you get a separate experience that will engage and delight your preschoolers.

Object Lesson

These fun group devotions creatively use an object as a metaphor to make an unforgettable spiritual point.

Creative Prayer Idea

These prayer prompts include a variety of prayer activities such as using objects in prayer, utilizing the arts in prayer, reciting written prayers, or meditating on Scripture.

Worship Prompt Idea

Usher children into God's presence with these involving worship ideas.

Additional Topics List

This list provides other ways you can use these sessions. For example, a game used to illustrate lying can easily be tweaked to illustrate the concept of integrity. These optional spins you can put on lesson elements are here to get your mental gears turning.

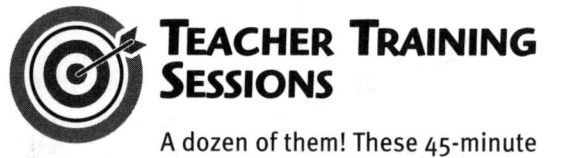

Teacher Training Sessions

A dozen of them! These 45-minute sessions will sharpen your leaders' skills and give your volunteers confidence in working with children.

Skits

These 10 photocopiable scripts are just right for the budding young actors in your midst. The skits assume that you won't be able to pull children together for practice, so they're easy to use after just a quick read-through.

Helpful Labels

Sprinkled throughout these two volumes are labels that highlight a special feature of a programming element or point out a specific way you may want to use an idea. Remember, most of the activities in *it* work great with both big and small groups, both older and younger children, both churched children and non-churched children. Use these labels to help you find what you're looking for, but don't let them limit you. For example, if an activity has the "For Large Groups" label, but your Sunday school class has five students, you can still do the activity—you just need to tweak it.

Here's a quick run-down of the labels you'll find in these pages.

▶ ***NO PREP***

If you're looking for an activity that requires no preparation or supplies, look for activities marked with this label.

▶ ***PREPARE IN ADVANCE***

Activities with this label require advance preparation...but they're worth it!

▶ ***FOR SMALL GROUPS***

If you minister in a small group with 15 or fewer students, this label will point out ideas that work best in that setting.

▶ ***FOR LARGE GROUPS***

Ideas marked with this label work great with 50 or more students.

▶ ***FOR YOUNGER STUDENTS***

If 5- and 6-year-olds are your cup of tea, look for ideas marked with this label.

▶ ***OUTREACH***

If you're working with non-Christian students, ideas marked with this label will help introduce them to Christianity in a non-threatening way.

▶ ***HIGH ENERGY***

Ideas marked with this label involve lots of activity and moving around.

▶ *STUDENT LED*

Looking to develop student leaders? Ideas marked with this label can be easily facilitated by elementary students.

▶ *FAMILY MINISTRY*

This label tells you an activity involves family members or will work especially well if parents are included.

▶ *ALLERGY ALERT*

Be aware that some children have food or animal allergies that can be dangerous. Consult with parents about allergies their children may have. Also be sure to read food labels carefully, as hidden ingredients can cause allergy-related problems.

Indexes

There's not much value in having so many session elements from which to choose if you can't easily find the exact one that will best meet your needs when you're planning a lesson.

Here's good news: the indexes you'll find at the back of Volume 2 will give you the help you need navigating this two-volume set of lessons.

You'll find an index of topics and another of Bible Points, plus an index of Scripture passages. So no matter how you're planning your lesson—by Bible Point, topic, or Scripture reference—you're covered. There are also indexes to search for what kind of activity you want. Crafts, games, movie clips—it's all here.

If you want to search even deeper and quicker, fire up the electronic version of *it*. You'll be able to search by key words and by type of lesson element as well. Want a list of games? crafts? movie clips? It's a snap!

Using the LabOra® Children's Ministry Planning Software

All of the content in these two volumes is also included in the software CD-ROM.

But in addition to being considerably easier to carry around than the two volumes, the CD-ROM has several other things going for it:

It's browsable. If you know you need a great game for a given event or class, you can look up all the games and search through them.

It's flexible. You can copy Group's content and paste it into your own document. That lets you customize any way you wish. You can add specific passages, add notes to volunteer leaders, and generally tweak and tailor to your heart's content.

Please note that this software is compatible with PC only (not Macintosh) and can be used on Windows 98, Second Edition or higher.

INSTALLATION

To begin, install the software by following the prompts that appear when the CD-ROM is inserted into your computer. As part of the installation process, you'll be asked to enter a license number; your license number is printed on the folder that your CD-ROM is packaged in.

> If the installation program doesn't start automatically, just single-click the "Start" button on the Windows task bar. Single-click the "Run" selection. Then enter in the prompt box: [CD-ROM drive letter]:\autorun.exe (for example, d:\autorun.exe). Single-click on "OK" or "Run."

Once you've installed the LabOra Planning Software, you're ready to use it! Here's a quick tour...

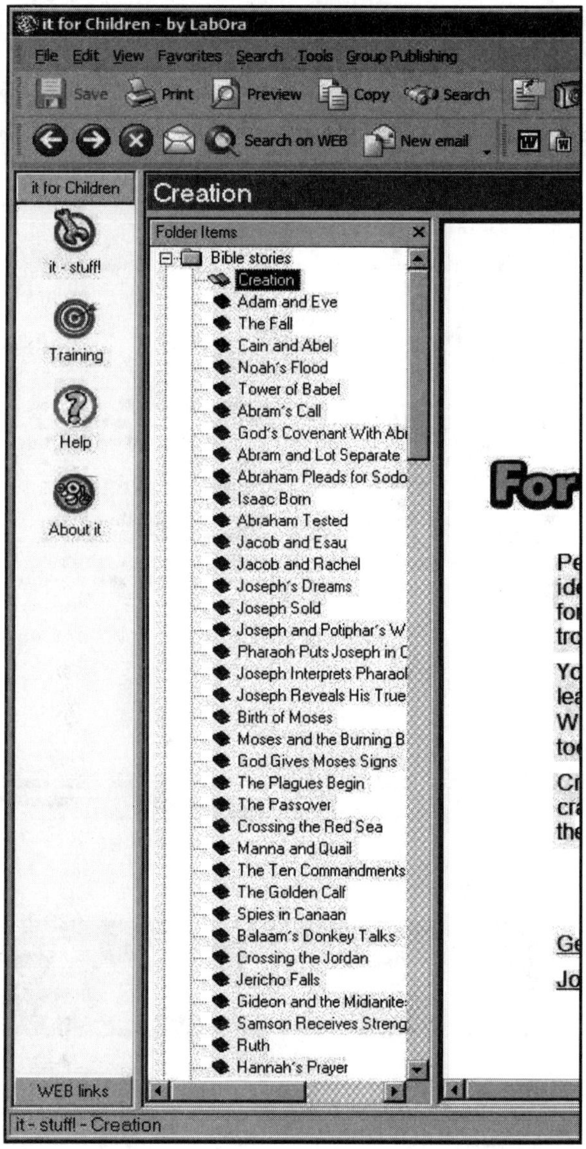

On the left-hand side of the screen, you'll find two bars: "it for Children" and "WEB links." The it for Children bar includes four icons:

About it | it-stuff! | Training | Help

The WEB links bar includes links to all of Group Publishing's online resources for Children's Ministry.

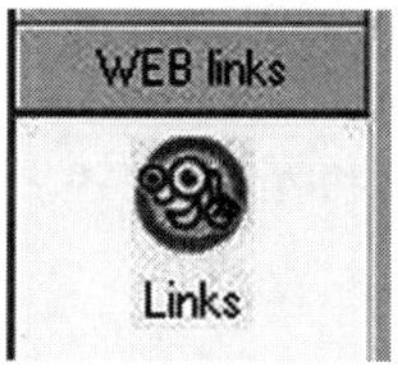

About IT

If you click on the "About it" icon, you'll learn more about...

- This ministry resource and its purpose;
- Group Publishing—our history, mission, and other great Group resources you'll find helpful in your Children's Ministry; and
- Duplo Data, the creators of LabOra Planning Software.

IT-stuff!

This icon takes you to the heart of the software program. This is where you'll find the thousands of ideas that are available to be browsed and searched.

Next to the icons on the left-hand side of your screen is a column called "Folder Items." This folder includes the **Topical Index**, the **Bible Story Index**, and the **Scripture Reference Index**. Simply click on the plus sign in front of each folder to open the folder list.

As the sample page shows, the folder then reveals its contents—*lots* of contents!

When you select a topic or Bible story, the contents will appear in the large window on the right side of your screen. You can scroll through the activities included and decide which if any you want to use.

Occasionally you'll find there are **handouts** as PDF files. Just click on the link to view and print the handouts. When there are references to **music**, you'll see a hot link button that lets you immediately hear the song suggested.

And when there's a **Scripture reference**, you'll be able to click it and immediately see the actual reference on the included New Living Translation of the Bible.

Another way to find topics or Scriptures is to use the **Search** function. To start a search, click on the "Search" icon (with binoculars) at the top of the screen. Enter a word or Scripture passage, and then click "Find." The software will show you a list of all the lesson elements that contain that word.

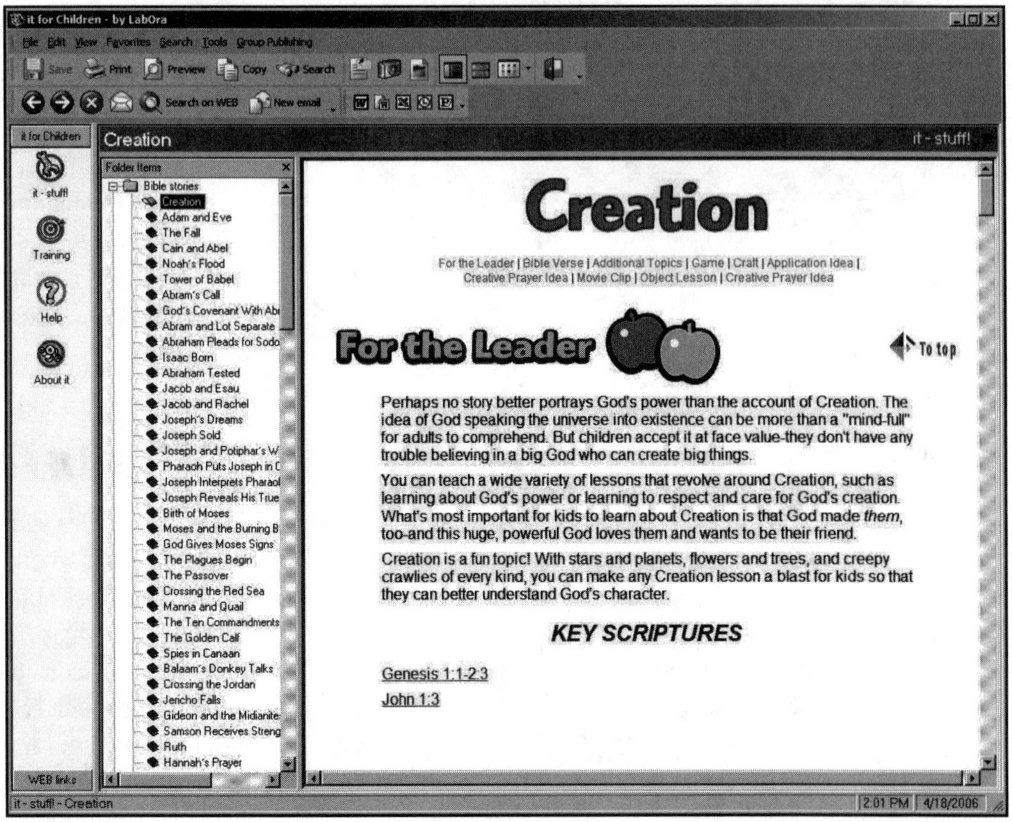

The image at right, for instance, shows the results of a search for the word "Creation." Once a lesson element is selected, the text of that element will appear in the box at the bottom right.

My Stuff in IT-stuff!

Not only will you find thousands of ideas in *it*, you can also add your own ideas from your existing studies, experiences, and resources. it-stuff! is where you can create totally new resources using elements from *it* and any other resource at your disposal.

Simply click on the "Add Your Resource" button on the tool bar...

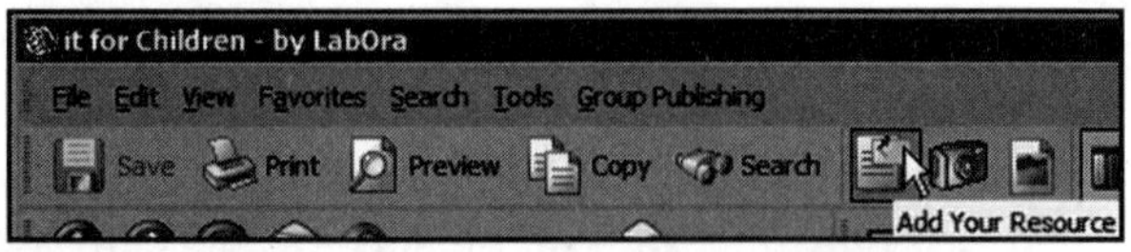

name your resource in the pop-up window...

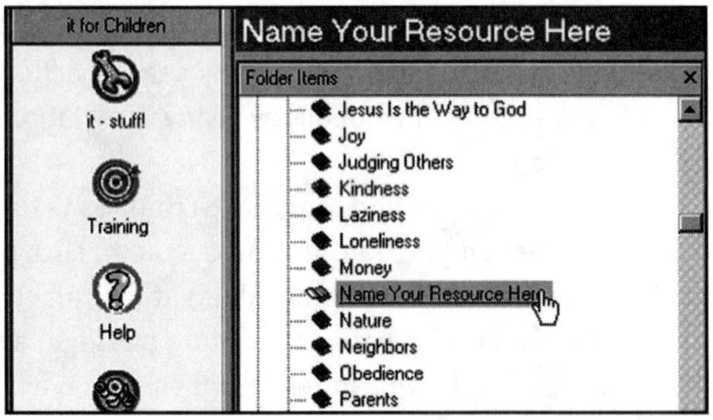

and click OK.

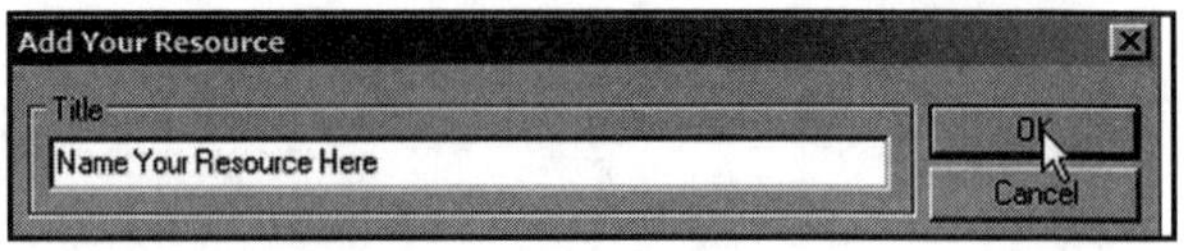

Your new resource will now be included in the list of topical resources, and a blank document will be opened—ready for you to paste and/or create elements for your resource.

You can search for just the right game or song in *it*, copy the text, and then go back to your new resource and paste it in. Or you can open your own existing resource document in a word processing program, select all or any part of it, and then paste that into your new resource. Or start from scratch, and create completely new resources for games, children's messages, and teacher training. You could even include lists of recommended resources or notes about an upcoming event or weekend retreat. Once you're done creating, save the information in your new resource under it-stuff!

A note to technology novices: You won't actually be saving your material onto the CD-ROM itself. Rather, you're creating files on your computer's hard drive. That means if you enter 10 years of children's ministry history and resources and then your hard drive crashes, you're out of luck.

So do this: Occasionally back up your files, and keep them on a disk. If you do encounter a computer meltdown down the road, you'll be able to recover all of the resources you added to it-stuff!

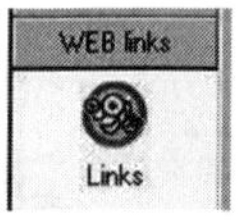

WEB LINKS

Clicking on the Links icon under the WEB links bar will expand this group of resources. You will find here a comprehensive set of quick links to all of Group's online resources for Children's Ministry.

HELP

This icon takes you to a detailed, extensive, and easy-to-use help file that will guide you through the many ways to use this software. If questions do arise, first try clicking on this icon to find answers.

Customer Support

Again—always start with the "Help" file. You're likely to get your answers quickly, and you'll feel so proud when you meet and conquer a challenge yourself. Trust us on this: Self-esteem rises quickly!

But if you should require answers that aren't supplied in the "Help" file, call us for free technical help—we'll be happy to help. Group's technical support hours are Monday through Friday, 8 a.m.

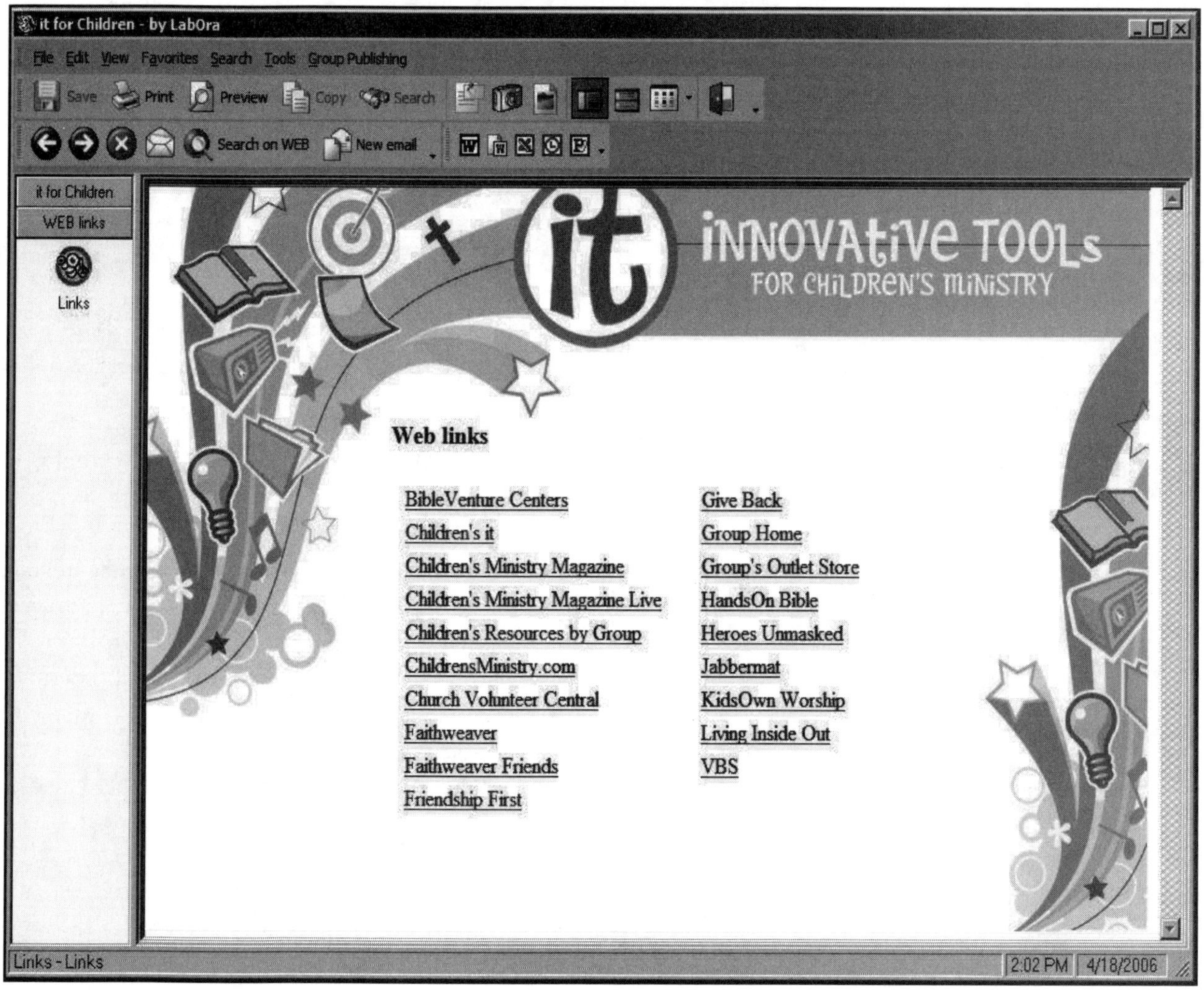

to 5 p.m. Mountain time. Call 970-669-3836 ext. 4414, and leave a message. We'll return your call within one business day.

LabOra®

And in case you were wondering, the name *LabOra* comes from the Latin *ora et labora*, which means "pray and work." LabOra products are created by the team at Duplo Data in Forsand, Norway. To learn more about them, click on the "About" icon in the software.

Ready...Set...Go for it!

You're holding a tremendous resource. Use *it* yourself or hand *it* off to your volunteers. Feel free to dog-ear pages, scribble notes in margins, and customize the material as you use the LabOra Planning Software program.

Make *it* your own as you use and adapt what you find here. We're excited to provide the thousands of ideas and activities you'll find in it—we know you'll make them even better!

Many of the great ideas in this resource come from readers just like you—those with a passion for kids! Children's Ministry Magazine is always looking for the best ideas in children's ministry. Submit your ideas to:

Children's Ministry Magazine
1515 Cascade Avenue
Loveland, CO 80539

or go to

www.cmmag.com

Bible Stories

BIBLE STORY

Creation

For the Leader

Perhaps no story better portrays God's power than the account of Creation. The idea of God speaking the universe into existence can be more than a "mind-full" for adults to comprehend. But children accept it at face value—they don't have any trouble believing in a big God who can create big things.

You can teach a wide variety of lessons that revolve around Creation, such as learning about God's power or learning to respect and care for God's creation. What's most important for kids to learn about Creation is that God made *them*, too—and this huge, powerful God loves them and wants to be their friend.

Creation is a fun topic! With stars and planets, flowers and trees, and creepy crawlies of every kind, you can make any Creation lesson a blast for kids so that they can better understand God's character.

Key Scriptures

Genesis 1:1–2:3

John 1:3

Bible Verse

"God created everything through him, and nothing was created except through him" (John 1:3).

Bible Experience

Bible Point: ▷ **GOD MADE EVERYTHING.**

Children will learn that God created the universe.

Supplies: Bible, globe, black tarp, large light such as a lamp, flashlight

Time: 15 to 20 minutes

Preparation: Set the globe on a table, with the lights underneath the table. Cover the whole thing with the black tarp.

SAY: **Today we're going to talk about God making the world. Look at this black tarp. Before God made the world, there was only darkness. Everyone close your eyes to make it dark. Now cover your eyes with your hands so that it's even darker. That's what God created everything out of!** Take the tarp off the globe, and have children open their eyes. **I'll tell you the things God made each day when he was creating our world. After each one, you say, "And God saw that it was good."** Have kids repeat the phrase.

On the first day, God made light, and he separated the light from the darkness. Have kids open and shut their eyes several times. **He called the light "day" and the darkness "night." And God saw that it was good.** Have kids repeat that phrase.

On the second day, God made the sky. Everyone shade your eyes with your hands as if you're looking up high into the sky. And God saw that it was good. Have kids repeat the phrase.

On the third day, God made the land, trees, and plants. Position a few kids by the globe, and have them spread their arms to represent branches. Have the kids tell you what kind of tree or plant they would like to be, and then SAY: **And God saw that it was good.** Have kids repeat the phrase.

On the fourth day, God made the sun (let someone hold the large light so that it shines on the globe), **the moon** (let someone hold the flashlight so that it shines on the globe), **and the stars.** Place a couple of children by the globe, and have them open and close their hands to imitate twinkling stars. **And God saw that it was good.** Have kids repeat the phrase.

On the fifth day, God made the fish and birds. Ask one child to move his or her hands like a swimming fish and another child to flap his or her arms like a bird. Ask them what kind of fish or bird they would like to be, and then SAY: **And God saw that it was good.** Have the kids repeat the phrase.

On the sixth day, God made people and animals. Choose one child to be Adam, and have the rest be any kind of animal they want. Have them tell you what kind of animal they would like to be, and then SAY: **And God saw that it was good.** Have kids repeat the phrase.

On the seventh day, God rested! Have everyone wipe the sweat off their brows, take a deep breath, and sit down. **God saw all that he had made, and God saw that it was good!** Have the kids repeat the phrase.

Shut off the two lights, gather the children, and read aloud John 1:3.

ASK:

- **Is there anything God didn't create? Explain.**
- **Of all the things God created, what do you like most?**
- **How can we thank God for creating so many wonderful things?**

SAY: ▷ **GOD MADE EVERYTHING! I love all of God's creation, don't you? We can thank God for his creation by praying to him, singing to him, and taking care of the world and all that's in it. Let's thank God for all the things he created. I'll begin, and then you can name anything in God's creation that you're thankful for.** Lead the kids in the prayer.

Additional Topics List

This lesson can be used to help children discover... The Bible, Bodies, God's Power, Nature, and Praise.

Game

▶ *NO PREP*

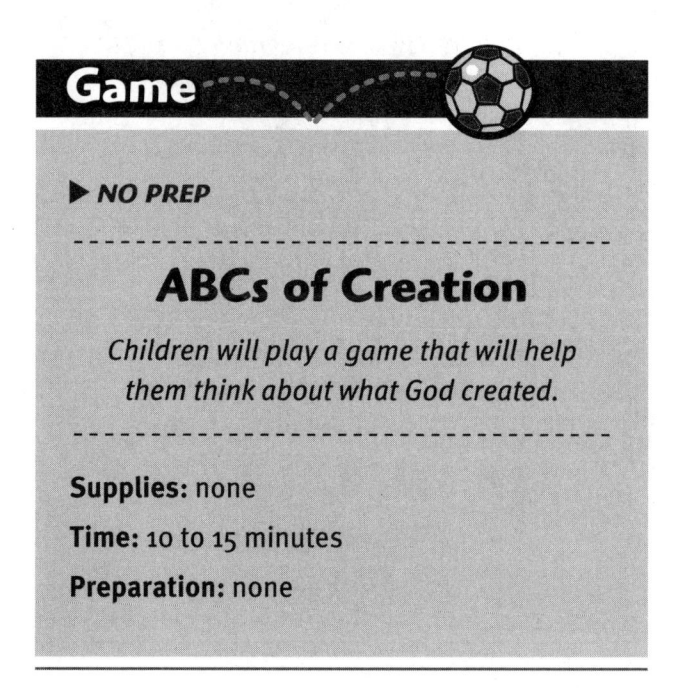

ABCs of Creation

Children will play a game that will help them think about what God created.

Supplies: none

Time: 10 to 15 minutes

Preparation: none

Have the children sit down in a circle.

SAY: **Today we'll think about things God created, using the letters of the alphabet as our guide. I'll begin the game by saying, "God created the earth, and he made Adam." The person next to me will then say, "God created the earth, and he made Adam and** [something that starts with the letter B]**.** Continue around the circle.

After playing this game, ASK:

- **What do you think was the most amazing thing God created? Why?**
- **How can we thank God for his creation?**

SAY: **Let's pray and thank God for all the wonderful things he created.**

Craft

▶ *PREPARE IN ADVANCE*
▶ *FOR YOUNGER CHILDREN*

Creation Shakers

Children will be reminded that creation is evidence of God's love.

Supplies: clean and empty baby food jars or clear plastic soda bottles (one for each child), permanent markers, small items representing creation (such as seashells or small artificial flowers), craft sand or raw white rice, colored electrical tape (optional)

Time: 10 to 15 minutes

Preparation: Create a sample of the craft to show children.

Have kids write the words "The Lord is the Creator" on the outside of their jars with markers. Allow kids to select several of the creation items. Have kids fill the jars about two-thirds full with the sand and then add the creation items. Put the lids on the jars, and help kids tape them in place with colored electrical tape.

After the craft is complete, ASK:

◆ **How does creation show us God's love?**

◆ **How can we use creation to tell others that God loves them?**

SAY: **These Creation Shakers can remind us of God's love and power and help us remember why we're God's children!**

Bible Application

▶ *PREPARE IN ADVANCE*

The Whole World in My Hands

Children will think of ways they can take care of creation.

Supplies: 3- to 4-inch paper circles (1 for each child), blue and green markers

Time: 10 to 15 minutes

Preparation: Cut the paper circles ahead of time. Set aside enough green and blue markers for all the children to use at the same time.

SAY: **In the book of Genesis, we find out that God created everything. And when God made people, he told them to take care of the earth.**

God wants each of us to take care of his creation, too. Think of one thing you can do to take care of God's creation. Ask for volunteers to share their ideas. After three or four have shared, hand out a paper circle to each child.

With a green marker, draw a picture of something you can take care of this week. Give the children a few minutes to draw their green pictures.

After they're finished with their green pictures, SAY: **Now fill in all the rest of the white space on your picture with the blue markers.** When they're finished coloring in the blue, their circles should look like the earth, with the green representing the land and the blue representing the water. Hold up a sample and SAY: **Take this picture with you to remind you to take care of God's creation.**

Creative Prayer Idea

▶ *NO PREP*

Seven Days of Thanks

Children will thank God for each day of Creation.

Supplies: flashlight, cotton ball, leaf or piece of fruit, Christmas-tree light bulb, feather, stuffed animal

Time: 5 to 10 minutes

Preparation: none

Have the children sit in a circle. SAY: **The Bible tells us that God made everything. Let's pray together and thank God for all the things he created.**

Hold up the flashlight, click it on, and SAY: **On the first day, God said, "Let there be light." God, I'm thankful you made light because** [provide your own answer]. Pass the flashlight around the circle, and have kids take turns finishing this sentence: "I'm thankful God made light because..."

Hold up the cotton ball and SAY: **On the second day, God made the sky. This cotton ball represents a cloud in the sky. God, I'm thankful you made the sky because...** Pass the cotton ball around, and have kids SAY: "I'm thankful God made the sky because..."

Hold up the leaf and SAY: **On the third day, God made plants and trees. I'm thankful God made plants because...** Pass the leaf and have kids PRAY: "I'm thankful God made plants because..."

Hold up the Christmas-tree light bulb and SAY: **On the fourth day, God made the stars, sun, and moon. This Christmas-tree light reminds me of the stars. God, I'm thankful you made stars because...** Pass around the bulb, and have kids say: "I'm thankful God made the stars because..."

Hold up the feather and SAY: **On the fifth day, God made the birds and fish. God, I'm thankful you made birds because...** Pass around the feather, and have kids SAY: "I'm thankful for birds because..."

Hold up the stuffed animal and SAY: **On the sixth day, God made all the animals. God, I'm thankful you made animals because...** Pass around the stuffed animal, and have kids SAY: "I'm thankful God made animals because..."

Have all the kids close their eyes. SAY: **On the seventh day, God rested. Let's be quiet for a moment and think about our favorite things that God created.** After a moment of silence, close in prayer.

Movie Clip

Honey, I Shrunk the Kids

Movie Title: *Honey, I Shrunk the Kids* (PG)

Start Time: 18 minutes, 15 seconds

Where to Begin: The kids realize they've been shrunk in size, swept up, and put out with the trash.

Where to End: About a minute later, they head off into the "wilderness."

Plot: During a family scientific experiment gone awry, a group of neighborhood kids are shrunk to the size of small insects. They suddenly find themselves deep within the grass of the backyard, which now looks gigantic and unfamiliar.

Review: You can use this scene to help children look at God's incredible creation in a new and fresh way. This movie clip can help children look past the obvious and discover anew the wonder and intricacy of the world God has set before us.

Discussion

SAY: **Sometimes we get so used to seeing God's creation around us that we don't really pay attention to it. In this movie clip from *Honey, I Shrunk the Kids*, a group of kids suddenly sees creation in a whole new way. Let's watch.**

After showing the clip, ASK:

- **How do you think the kids felt when they saw how little they were?**
- **How did their perspective of God's creation change?**
- **What do you think surprised them most about their new situation?**
- **What can you do to view God's creation in a fresh way?**

Object Lesson

▶ *NO PREP*

Exploding Dictionary

Children will experience how the universe needed a creator for it to exist.

Supplies: Bible, newspaper, paper grocery bags (1 per group), scissors, CD and CD player

Time: about 10 minutes

Preparation: none

Have kids form groups of three or four. Pass out old newspapers, and tell groups to cut out individual letters from a newspaper and drop the letters into a paper grocery bag. Challenge them to cut out as many letters as possible in five minutes. Play a song or two while they're cutting.

After five minutes, have members of each group shake their bags. SAY: **Spill your bags onto the floor. The team that has a dictionary fall on the floor is the winner.**

After they empty their bags, ASK:

- **Why didn't a dictionary fall out?**
- **Some people believe the world came into being in a similar way—that there was a huge explosion and everything just fell into place without any help from God. What do you think of this story?**

Read aloud John 1:3. Have kids arrange the letters to spell their names. SAY: **Just as a dictionary didn't fall out of your paper bag, the world didn't just happen to create itself. Just as you had to put your letters in order, God put the world in order. God is the power behind Creation.**

Preschool Story

▶ *PREPARE IN ADVANCE*

Bible Point: ▷ **GOD MADE EVERYTHING.**

Supplies: Bible, sheet of black construction paper, 3 sheets of white construction paper, scissors, markers, old magazines, glue, large sheet of poster board

Preparation: Cut each piece of construction paper in half. Discard one half of the black construction paper. Write "Creation Card 1" on one side of the half-sheet of black construction paper. Label one half-sheet with "Creation Card 2," the next with "Creation Card 3," and so on through "Creation Card 8." Flip the cards over. On the back of card 2, color one half black and the other half yellow. Color the back of card 3 blue. Cut a picture of a plant from a magazine, and glue it to the back of card 4. Draw the sun, moon, and stars on the back of card 5. Cut a picture of a fish and a bird from a magazine, and glue them to the back of card 6. Cut out pictures of animals and people, and glue them to the back of card 7. Glue or draw a picture of a bed on the back of card 8. Place all the cards in a row on the floor, with the writing facing up.

The Days of Creation

Have all the children form a circle and sit down. Open your Bible to Genesis 1:1, and show children the words.

SAY: **In the beginning there was nothing—only God.** Have a child turn over the first Creation Card. Hold the black card up for the rest of the children to see, and SAY: **The whole world may have been black, just like this card.** Encourage a new child to glue the card to the large sheet of poster board.

But God said, "Let there be light." God separated the light and the dark, and he called the light day and the dark night. Encourage a different child to turn over the second Creation Card. Hold the card up for the rest of the class to see. Point out the light on one side and the dark on the other side. Ask another child to glue the second card to the large poster board next to the first card.

God created the light on day one. On day two, God created the sky. Have another child turn over the third Creation Card to reveal the "sky." Show it to the rest of the class. Ask a child to glue the card to the large poster board.

On day three, God created the land and the plants on the land. Have another child turn over the fourth Creation Card. Point to the plant on the card, and ask kids to name some other plants that God created. Encourage a different child to glue the fourth card to the large poster board.

On day four, God created the sun, moon, and stars. Have a child turn over the fifth Creation Card. Hold it up to show kids the sun, moon, and stars. Encourage children to "twinkle" their fingers like stars. Have another child glue the fifth Creation Card to the large poster board.

On day five, God created the animals in the sea and the birds in the air. Have one child turn over the sixth Creation Card. Point out the sea creatures and birds on the card, and encourage kids to "swim" like fish and flap their arms like birds. Ask another child to glue the sixth card to the large poster board.

On day six, God created all the living things on the earth. He created giraffes, monkeys, lizards, pigs, dogs, and people, too. Have a child turn over the seventh Creation Card. Show the card to the rest of the class. Encourage kids to make animal sounds. Glue the seventh card to the large poster board.

God looked at all that he had made, and he said that it was very good. Encourage children to look at the large poster board and point out the different things that God made. ▷ **GOD MADE EVERYTHING!**

Then, on day seven, God rested. Have a child turn over the final Creation Card. Show children the card, and encourage them to lie down and pretend to sleep. While children are lying down, glue the eighth card to the poster board. Encourage children to "wake up" and shout, "God made everything!" Then ASK:

- **What are some things that God made?**
- **How can you thank God for all the wonderful things he made?**

BIBLE STORY

Adam and Eve

For the Leader

In most public school science classes, there is no such thing as a personal Creator. God is replaced by human reason and the scientific method. There is no such thing as a God who created each one of us, who loves us and knows everything about us. But those who place their faith in science miss out on the amazing knowledge that God made us with a purpose.

Children who never go to church miss out on the chance to learn how much God loves them. The Creation story about Adam and Eve opens the door to a deeper understanding of who God is and why each of us is special.

Use the ideas in this section to help kids understand why God made Adam and Eve as examples of how he has a plan for their lives.

Key Scriptures

Genesis 1:27; 2:4-25

Psalm 89:11

Bible Verse

"So God created human beings in his own image" (Genesis 1:27a).

Bible Experience

Bible Point: ▷ **GOD MADE US.**

Children will reflect on how special humans are among all creation.

Supplies: Bible, modeling clay, plastic bags

Time: about 5 minutes

Preparation: none

ASK:

- **What does a creator do?**
- **How many of you think of yourselves as creators?**

SAY: **I have a small piece of modeling clay for each of you. I'd like you to create something using this modeling clay. But you have only a minute to do it!** Hand out the clay, and allow kids one minute to work. After a minute, have kids hold up their creations for everyone to see.

Look at all the different things you were able to come up with in just one minute! That was really good!

ASK:

- **How does it feel to create something good?**

SAY: **The first story in the Bible tells us that God created the world in six days. He made something out of nothing, and it was all very good.**

ASK:

- **How do you think he did that?**

Read aloud Genesis 1:27 and 2:7-8. SAY: **God created everything in the entire universe! But in the first days of Creation, the most important**

creation was Adam and Eve. When God made humans, he made something extra special. ▷ GOD MADE US! And he placed us in this world to enjoy it and take care of it.

Let's close with a prayer. During the prayer, I'd like you to name a part of God's creation that you enjoy, and we'll thank him for it together. PRAY: **Dear God, thank you for being our creator. You made all things good! We'd especially like to thank you for** (Let kids call out things they are thankful for, and then all together shout...). **Amen!**

Hand out plastic bags for kids to keep their clay in, and remind them to remember that God made them every time they create something with their clay.

Song & Connect

Use "A New Creation" (track 14, *it: Innovative Tools for Children's Ministry: New Testament* CD) to help reinforce the Bible Point, ▷ **GOD MADE US.**

Additional Topics List

This lesson can be used to help children discover... Friends, God's Love, Loneliness, Names, and Self-Esteem.

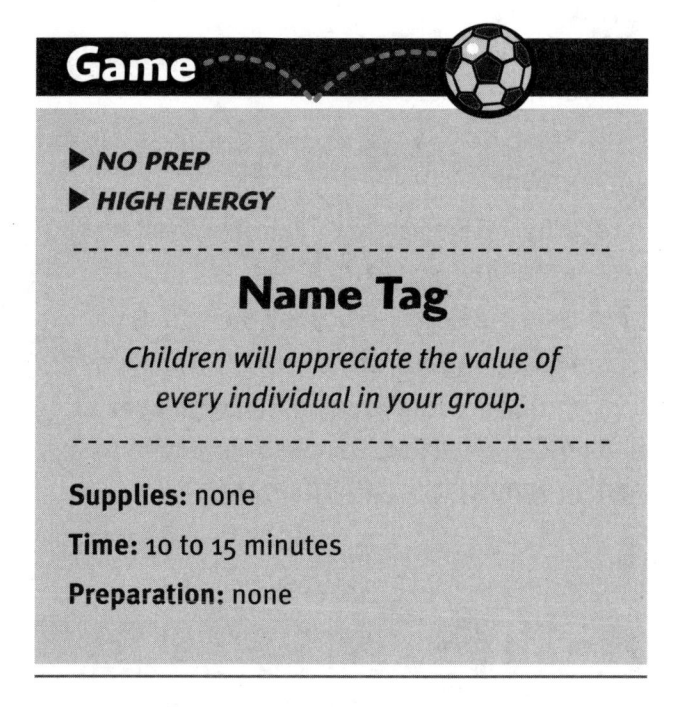

n

o

t

e

s

Game

▶ ***NO PREP***

▶ ***HIGH ENERGY***

Name Tag

Children will appreciate the value of every individual in your group.

Supplies: none

Time: 10 to 15 minutes

Preparation: none

Greet and gather your group, and SAY: **God spent time each day with Adam and Eve, and he knew all their special qualities. Let's spend some time getting to know each other. When your turn comes, please give your name and describe something special about yourself. Listen carefully—you may need to know this information!** Explain that it's easier to remember someone's name if you know something about him or her. Start by introducing yourself so that the kids have an example to follow.

Once everyone has been introduced, SAY: **We're going to play chain tag with a twist.** Explain that as people are tagged by whoever is "It," they join hands with the chain of captives and help tag others.

Here's the twist: In order to keep someone you have tagged, you must say that person's name and declare his or her special quality. For example, if I'm It and I touch Samantha, I grab her hand and say very loudly, "This is Samantha and she has a pet hamster."

If the taggers don't introduce you correctly, introduce yourself again. Next time you're tagged, we'll definitely remember your name!

After playing the game, have kids sit in groups of three and discuss:

- ◆ **What did you learn about the people in our group?**
- ◆ **Why did God create Adam and Eve? How were they special?**
- ◆ **Why did God create you? How did God make you special?**

SAY: **God creates each person with special and unique qualities. He takes time to know us, and he appreciates our differences.**

Craft

▶ *NO PREP*

"Wonderfully Made" Posters

Children will complete a craft that will remind them that God made them unique.

Supplies: Bible, large sheet of newsprint for each child (big enough for the child to lie on), pencils, markers or crayons

Time: about 15 minutes

Preparation: none

Tell kids to do this activity in pairs. Ask one partner to lie down on his or her back on a sheet of newsprint while the other uses a pencil to trace around the child's outline. Then have children switch, using another sheet of newsprint. Have them use markers or crayons to draw a heart in the center of each outline. Ask kids to write the words of Genesis 1:27 inside each heart. Encourage kids to decorate their body outlines to look like themselves. Suggest that they add hair, facial features, and clothes. Have them write their names on their paper people.

After the crafts are complete, discuss these questions:

- ◆ **What does it mean to be "made in God's image"?**
- ◆ **How do you feel knowing that God made you?**
- ◆ **How can you praise God for how he made you?**

SAY: **Think about it—no one except God can create a person. He made each of us who we are. Let's hang our posters along the walls to remind everyone that God made us all special!**

Bible Application

▶ *NO PREP*

God Made Me for a Purpose

Children will understand that God has a purpose for everything he created, including them.

Supplies: Bible, globe or world map, globe stickers (1 per child)

Time: 5 to 10 minutes

Preparation: none

SAY: **Let's talk about some of the wonderful things God has created.** (Place the globe or map in front of you.) **When God made the world** (spin the globe)**, he said that every part of it was good.** Point to places on the globe and ASK:

- **What are some creatures God created in our world?**

Get several responses, and then SAY: **Very good! God made a lot of interesting creatures!**

ASK:

- **How about mosquitoes and spiders—did God create them, too?**

SAY: **God made everything he created good, and everything he created has a purpose.**

ASK:

- **Why do you think God created Adam and Eve?**
- **Why do you think God created mosquitoes and spiders?**

SAY: **Mosquitoes are pretty pesky to us, but even those bugs have a place in the world God made. For one thing, they provide food for bats and birds. God has a plan for everything he created—including you and me. Listen to what the Bible says in Psalm 89:11. I'll read a phrase of this verse, and you repeat it back to me:**

The heavens are yours *(have children repeat the phrase),*
And the earth is yours *(repeat)*;
Everything in the world is yours *(repeat)*—
You created it all *(repeat)*.

This verse reminds us that God has a plan for every single thing he made—especially you and me. He created us. Why? Because he has a purpose for our lives.

ASK:

- **What do you think might be God's purpose for your life?**
- **Why might he have created you just the way you are?**

Pass out the globe stickers and SAY: **Take this sticker as a reminder that God created the world and has a purpose for everything he created, especially you.**

Creative Prayer Idea

▶ ***NO PREP***

In His Image

Children will create something they're thankful for and thank God for it.

Supplies: Bible, 3 chenille wires per child

Time: 5 to 10 minutes

Preparation: none

Read aloud Genesis 1:27.

ASK:

- **What does it mean to be created in the image of God?**
- **How are we like God?**

Give each child three chenille wires. SAY: **You may not be able to create all the amazing things God has created, but God has made you creative. Use your chenille wires to make a model of something you're thankful that God made.**

Once kids are finished, give each a chance to thank God aloud for the things he has made.

Discussion Launcher Questions

Ask children to form trios and discuss:

- **When God made Adam and Eve, what do you think it was like to live in the Garden of Eden?**
- **If you could create humans any way you wanted, how would you make them? Why would you make them that way?**
- **The Bible says God made us in his image. What do you think God's image is like?**

- **Is there anything you wish God hadn't created? Why or why not?**
- **God made each of us unique. What do you think is most unique about you?**

Snack

▶ *PREPARE IN ADVANCE*
▶ *ALLERGY ALERT*

Make Me a Masterpiece

Children will make and eat a snack that demonstrates how each of us is uniquely created by God.

Supplies: a wide variety of natural snack foods, such as sliced fruit, raisins, and nuts; toothpicks

Time: 15 to 20 minutes

Preparation: Clean and slice a variety of fruits and vegetables. Set out the food items and toothpicks in bowls on the table.

SAY: **When God made the world, he made it out of nothing. We don't have that ability, but God did make us creative! Let's see if you can create a sculpture out of the food here on the table. Use the toothpicks to stick the fruits and vegetables together. You'll have 10 minutes to create your own masterpiece. When time's up, you'll have a chance to show your creation to the class. Have fun!**

When kids are finished, have them show their sculptures and tell about them. Affirm each display with kind words and applause. Then ASK:

- **Why do you think these sculptures are all so different?**
- **How is this activity like God creating the world?**

SAY: **When God created the world, he said it was good. Your sculptures are also very good! God made every one of us a special creation, and just like our food sculptures, the world can "taste and see" that God is good because of us. Let's eat our sculptures now to celebrate what an awesome creator God is!**

Preschool Story

▶ *NO PREP*

Bible Point: ▷ **GOD MADE EVERYTHING.**

Supplies: Bible, 1 large ball of moldable clay per child

Time: 15 to 20 minutes

Preparation: none

A Bit of Dust

Have all the children form a circle and sit down. Open your Bible to Genesis 2:3, and show children the words.

SAY: **In the beginning there was nothing—only God. But then God made everything in the world.** Give each child a ball of moldable clay. **God made the water, the sky, the plants, the birds, the fish, and all the animals. God made everything you can see.** Encourage children to use the clay to mold their favorite animal. **God also made a man. God made the man out of the dirt on the ground! This man was the first man in the world, and God named the man Adam.** Have children use a quarter of their clay to form a man.

God put Adam in a garden and told Adam to take care of the garden and all the animals

that lived there. In fact, God gave Adam a job! Adam's job was to name all the animals. Let's name some animals now! Encourage children to shout out the names of as many animals as they can think of.

Adam liked his job, but he was lonely; he needed a friend! One day God made Adam fall asleep, and then God took one bone from Adam's side. From that bone, God made a woman! God named the woman Eve. Encourage children to use some clay from their Adam figure to form a woman so that they have both an Adam figure and an Eve figure. They may need to use some of the extra clay as well to make their Eve figure.

Adam and Eve were happy together! They helped each other name all of the animals and take care of the garden. Tell children to use the rest of their clay to make small animal and plant figures. Encourage kids to bring their animals to Adam and Eve and pretend that Adam and Eve are naming them. Let kids play for several minutes.

▷ **GOD MADE US! God made Adam and Eve, God made you, and God made every single person in the world! Let's sing a song right now to help us remember that God made everyone!**

Lead kids in singing this song to the tune of "This Old Man":

God made you.
God made me.
God made every one of us
With a little bit of dust
And his breath in each of us.
God made us and loves us, too!

ASK:

◆ **Why do you think God made Adam and Eve?**

◆ **How does it make you feel to know that God made you?**

◆ **How can you thank God for making you?**

BIBLE STORY

The Fall

For the Leader

One of the things God gave humans when he created them was the power to choose. Whether we make good or bad choices, we, like Adam and Eve, must live with the consequences. The seemingly minor choices of childhood are actually the prime time for developing the ability to make wise decisions.

These lessons and activities will help kids understand the story of the Fall so that they can avoid their own "fall." They'll explore the importance of the choices they make, and they'll be encouraged to rely on God's wisdom to make good, healthy choices.

Key Scriptures

Genesis 2:16-17; 3:1-24

1 Peter 5:7

1 John 1:9

Bible Verse

"But if we confess our sins to him, he is faithful and just to forgive us our sins and to cleanse us from all wickedness" (1 John 1:9).

Bible Experience

▶ *NO PREP*
▶ *ALLERGY ALERT*

Bible Point: ▷ **GOD CARES FOR US—NO MATTER WHAT.**

Children will understand why Adam and Eve's actions were wrong.

Supplies: Bible; bowl of M&M's candies with a sign that says, "Don't eat! Save for tonight's party"; packets of candy or fruit chews (1 per child)

Time: 10 to 15 minutes

Preparation: none

Hold the bowl of M&M's, and show kids the sign. SAY: **Today we're going to hear a familiar story from the Bible. But first let's read this sign on this bowl of candy: "Don't eat! Save for tonight's party." OK, hmm. I guess we won't eat any candy. We can look at it while I tell you the story.** Open your Bible to Genesis 3, and show kids the words.

This story is about the first two people in the world—Adam and Eve. They lived in the Garden of Eden. God cared for Adam and Eve and gave them all that he created for them to enjoy. "Absentmindedly" reach into the bowl, get a candy, and then eat it. **In the middle of the garden was one tree they weren't supposed to touch. God told them not to eat its fruit. Also in the garden with Adam and Eve was a snake.** Eat another candy, and then SAY: **The Bible tells us that the snake was crafty, or sneaky. And he talked the woman into eating the fruit.** Eat a candy. **Uh-oh! That was wrong. Then Adam ate some fruit. Uh-oh! That was wrong!** Eat a candy. **When Adam and Eve ate the fruit, everything changed for them. They knew they had done wrong. So they hid from God.** Eat a candy. ASK:

- ◆ **How did Adam and Eve disobey God?**
- ◆ **When do we disobey and break rules in our lives?**

While the kids answer, continue to eat candies. If a child points out that you're eating the candy, pause. If no child points it out, pretend that someone noticed and shrug. SAY: **Looks like I've been breaking this rule. But the candies are so good, and there are so many—it's not a problem, is it?** Let children respond, and then SAY: **The rule was, "Don't eat this candy," so it really isn't right for me to eat it, is it? Just because we're tempted, it's not right for us to break a rule. Because they broke God's rule, Adam and Eve had to leave the garden. But God still loved them and cared for them.** ▷ **GOD CARES FOR US—NO MATTER WHAT. Just as he cared for Adam and Eve after they left the garden, he'll always take care of you, too.**

Read aloud 1 John 1:9. ASK:

- ◆ **What can we do when we disobey God?**
- ◆ **How does God take care of us when we do wrong? How about when we do what's right?**
- ◆ **How has God taken care of you this week?**

Close in prayer and surprise kids with the snacks.

Song & Connect

Use "Create in Me a Pure Heart" (track 5, *it: Innovative Tools for Children's Ministry: Old Testament* CD) to help reinforce the Bible Point, ▷ **GOD CARES FOR US—NO MATTER WHAT.**

Additional Topics List

This lesson can be used to help children understand... Confession, Consequences, Obedience, Temptation, and Sin.

Game

▶ ***NO PREP***

Silent Snake Tag

Children will practice listening for trouble and staying away from it.

Supplies: classroom table, 2 clean cloth blindfolds, piece of fruit (real, artificial, or cut from construction paper)

Time: 5 to 10 minutes

Preparation: none

Remove any chairs from around the table. Then have kids stand in a big circle around the table, far enough back so that no one can touch the table. SAY: **The snake tricked Adam and Eve into doing something wrong. He was sneaky and tried to cause trouble! Adam and Eve both should have stayed away from that snake. Let's play a game in which you listen carefully for the "snake" and try not to get caught.**

Choose two volunteers to begin, one as the snake and one as Adam (if a boy) or Eve (if a girl). Blindfold both, and give the fruit to the snake. Both players should stand touching the table on opposite sides.

The child playing the snake will sneak around the table trying to tag Adam or Eve with the fruit, while the child playing Adam or Eve listens carefully to hear when the snake is coming and moves away. Both players must keep at least one hand on the table at all times. They may change direction at any time but may not crawl under the table. The kids watching will impersonate the sound of other animals that might have been in the Garden of Eden. Allow kids to select their own animals to mimic.

Set a time limit, such as 30 seconds, to play. The first round ends when the snake tags Adam or Eve or the time runs out. Then choose two different kids to play. If you have a large group, set up multiple tables at which to play.

After playing, ask kids to sit in small groups and discuss:

- **Was it easy or hard to stay away from trouble in this game? Why?**
- **How is that like real life? How is it different?**
- **Do you think God stopped caring about Adam and Eve after they sinned? Why or why not?**

SAY: **We're going to face many temptations in life. We should try to run away from every one of them. But even if we make a mistake, always remember that ▷ GOD CARES FOR US—NO MATTER WHAT!**

notes

Craft

▶ *PREPARE IN ADVANCE*

He Cares for You

Children will make worry posters to place their worries on.

Supplies: Bible, pencils, 9x12-inch brown and green construction paper, safety scissors, 12x18-inch pieces of blue or white construction paper, crayons, glue, paper clips

Time: about 15 minutes

Preparation: Put all the supplies on a table. Have a couple of sample trees cut out in case some children would like to trace a tree instead of drawing freehand.

SAY: ▷ **GOD CARES FOR US—NO MATTER WHAT. Let's make a craft that reminds us how God cares for us even when we make bad choices.**

Have kids draw a large tree on brown paper. Make sure the trees have at least five big branches. Let the children cut them out. Glue the trees to a larger piece of blue or white construction paper. Have kids cut out five large leaves. On the leaves, have them write or draw pictures of bad choices they've made. Hook the paper clips through the leaves, and then attach the leaves to the branches of the tree. Finally, have children write "God cares for me" on the poster.

After the trees are completed, read 1 Peter 5:7.

ASK:

◆ **What kinds of bad choices do we make?**

◆ **Does God want us to worry when we make bad choices? Why or why not?**

◆ **Instead of worrying about our bad choices, what can we do?**

SAY: **God cares for us and wants to take our worries away, even when we fail and do the wrong thing. Look at your worry tree, and think about the one worry that is the biggest to you. Silently ask God to take that worry away. Then turn your leaf around so that your worry is hidden.** Have kids continue until all leaves are turned around.

If you ever have any other worries, just add them to your tree and ask God to take your worries away.

Bible Application

▶ *FOR SMALL GROUPS*

▶ *PREPARE IN ADVANCE*

Knowing the Difference

Children will see how to avoid the mistake of Adam and Eve.

Supplies: Bible, 2 plates, several apples and potatoes (about the same size)

Time: about 10 minutes

Preparation: Peel the apples and potatoes and cut them into small, similar-looking pieces. Leave them in water so that they don't turn brown. (This can't be done too far in advance.)

Put a plate of the apple pieces and a plate of the potato pieces on a table. Have children come up one at a time to taste one of each while holding their noses. Have them whisper to you which is the potato and which is the apple.

After everyone has tried one of each, have them vote on which is the apple and which is the potato. ASK:

- ◆ **Was it hard to tell the difference? Why or why not?**
- ◆ **Is it hard to tell the difference between right and wrong? Explain.**
- ◆ **Can good and evil sometimes look the same? Explain.**

Read aloud Genesis 2:16-17 and 3:1-7. ASK:

- ◆ **Was it difficult for Adam and Eve to tell the difference between right and wrong? Why or why not?**
- ◆ **When Adam and Eve disobeyed God, did their actions help them become wise, as the serpent had promised?**
- ◆ **How can we know the difference between right and wrong?**

SAY: **God's Word helps us to know the difference between right and wrong. As we believe and obey God, we will be wise.**

notes

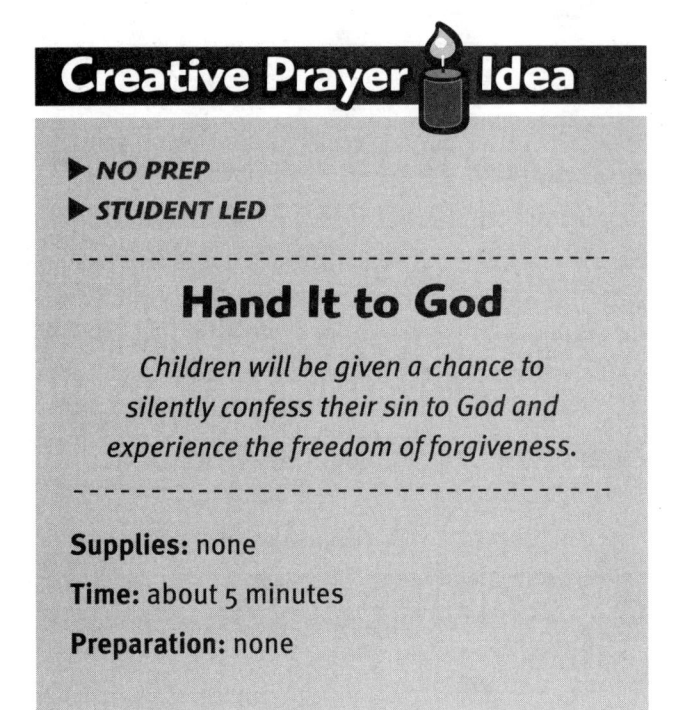

Creative Prayer Idea

▶ ***NO PREP***
▶ ***STUDENT LED***

Hand It to God

Children will be given a chance to silently confess their sin to God and experience the freedom of forgiveness.

Supplies: none
Time: about 5 minutes
Preparation: none

Pretend you're picking a piece of fruit from a tree and SAY: **When Adam and Eve ate the fruit in the Garden of Eden, they disobeyed God and sinned.** Cup your hands in front of you and SAY: **Everything they had was lost.** Slowly pretend to empty your hands, and SAY: **But even though they were no longer in the garden, God still took care of them.** Cross your arms across your chest.

Drop your hands to your side and SAY: **Every one of us has disobeyed God. Maybe we didn't do what our parents told us to do, or maybe we were mean to another person. But all of us have sinned, just like Adam and Eve. ▷ BUT GOD WILL ALWAYS CARE FOR US—NO MATTER WHAT.**

Read aloud from 1 John 1:9. SAY: **This verse tells us that if we tell God about our sin, he'll hear us and forgive us and make us clean again.**

Have kids put their hands over their hearts. SAY: **Think of a sin you'd like to confess to God. Close your eyes and silently tell God about it.** Give kids about 30 seconds, and then SAY: **Hold that sin in your hands.** Demonstrate by cupping your hands in front of you, as if you're hiding a golf ball in your hands. **Silently ask God to forgive you for that sin.** Give kids about 30 seconds, and then SAY: **God has forgiven you! Now you can let it go.** Demonstrate by slowly unfolding your hands and lifting them in the air. Have the kids follow your motions, and then say, with hands upraised: **Let's thank God for making us clean again. Silently thank God for forgiving you and making your heart white as snow.** Give kids a few seconds, and then SAY: ▷ **GOD CARES FOR US—NO MATTER WHAT.**

Discussion Launcher Questions

Ask children to form trios and discuss:

- **Do you think there's anything you could do that might make God stop caring about you? Why or why not?**
- **Even though God will always care for us, what are some consequences we might face for disobeying God?**
- **What are some temptations you face?**
- **What are some things we can do to avoid temptation?**

notes

Movie Clip

I Want More!

Movie Title: *The Little Mermaid* (G)

Start Time: 11 minutes, 30 seconds

Where to Begin: Ariel sings a song about wanting more out of life than her father is willing to permit.

Where to End: Ariel ends her song.

Plot: Ariel, a young mermaid, has been warned by her father, King Triton, not to swim to the surface of the ocean. But Ariel can only think of her own wishes.

Review: Adam and Eve gave in to the temptation of evil and wanted just a little bit more, even though God had forbidden them to. Children will easily be able to make the connection between Ariel disobeying her father's instructions and Adam and Eve disobeying their heavenly Father.

Discussion

After setting up and showing the clip, ASK:

- **Why didn't Ariel want to obey her father?**
- **Think about a time you disobeyed your parents. What happened?**

SAY: **That's a lot like what happened to Adam and Eve in the Bible. God gave them only one rule to obey—not to eat from a particular tree in the garden. But they wanted more and disobeyed, so they had to face the consequences.**

ASK:

- **How do you think Ariel's father felt when she disobeyed?**
- **How do you think God felt when Adam and Eve disobeyed him?**

◆ **How to you think God feels when we disobey him?**

SAY: ▷ **GOD LOVES US AND CARES FOR US—NO MATTER WHAT. Let's all try to obey God this week—and always!**

Preschool Story

▶ *PREPARE IN ADVANCE*

Bible Point: ▷ **GOD CARES FOR US—NO MATTER WHAT.**

Supplies: Bible, long sheet of butcher paper, tape, markers, sock

Time: 15 to 20 minutes

Preparation: Tape a long sheet of butcher paper on your wall. Make sure there's nothing underneath the butcher paper. If you can't tape the paper to your wall, set it out on the floor.

The Off-Limits Tree

Have children form a circle and sit down. Open your Bible to Genesis 3, and show children the words. Remind children that God made Adam and Eve and placed them in a beautiful garden to live.

SAY: **Adam and Eve were very happy living in the garden and enjoying all the wonderful things God made. Let's make a beautiful garden right now!** Have children use markers to draw plants and animals on the butcher paper. Be sure to leave some open space in the middle. As children draw, ask them about their favorite plants and animals and encourage them to make the sounds and movements of different animals. When children are finished, ask them to sit down in a circle.

What a beautiful garden we're in! This garden would be a wonderful place to live! Just like in our garden, there were lots of beautiful plants in the garden where Adam and Eve lived. Adam and Eve could eat the fruit from any plant in the garden except for one. God put one tree in the middle of the garden that he didn't want Adam and Eve to eat from. Use a marker to draw a large tree on the butcher paper. Have kids draw some colorful fruit on the tree.

For a long time, Adam and Eve were happy living in the garden and enjoying the things God made. But then one day a serpent—a snake—came to talk to Eve. The snake lied and told Eve it would be OK to eat from the forbidden tree.

Put a sock on your hand, and use it to talk. As the snake, SAY: **Go ahead and take a piece of fruit. It looks so yummy! God won't *really* care if you eat the fruit. He was probably only joking when he told you not to eat the fruit. Go ahead...go ahead.**

As yourself, SAY: **So Eve listened to the serpent and ate a piece of fruit. She even talked Adam into eating some of the fruit, too! Adam and Even disobeyed God when they ate that fruit. Afterward they felt bad, and they were afraid to see God, so they hid from him. But God knew what they had done. God was sad that they had disobeyed, but God still loved them.**

Because Adam and Eve had disobeyed God, they had to leave the garden. But even though they weren't living in the garden anymore, God still took care of them.

Even when we do bad things and disobey our parents or teachers, God still loves us. ▷ **GOD CARES FOR US—NO MATTER WHAT.**

ASK:

◆ **Why did Adam and Eve eat the forbidden fruit?**

◆ **What did God do when Adam and Eve disobeyed him?**

◆ **When have you done something wrong? What happened?**

BIBLE STORY

Cain and Abel

For the Leader

Just like Cain and Abel, our feelings of anger and jealousy can separate us from our family and friends. You can help kids recognize these feelings in themselves and think of positive solutions. You can also help kids appreciate others and be happy when others experience good things.

The sad story of Cain and Abel is a vivid example of how our hateful emotions can lead us down a dangerous path. Use these sessions to equip kids to identify the roots of sin and empower them to control their feelings.

Key Scriptures

Genesis 4:1-16

Hosea 6:6

Hebrews 11:4

1 John 2:11; 3:12

Bible Verse

"But anyone who hates another brother or sister is still living and walking in darkness. Such a person does not know the way to go, having been blinded by the darkness" (1 John 2:11).

Bible Experience

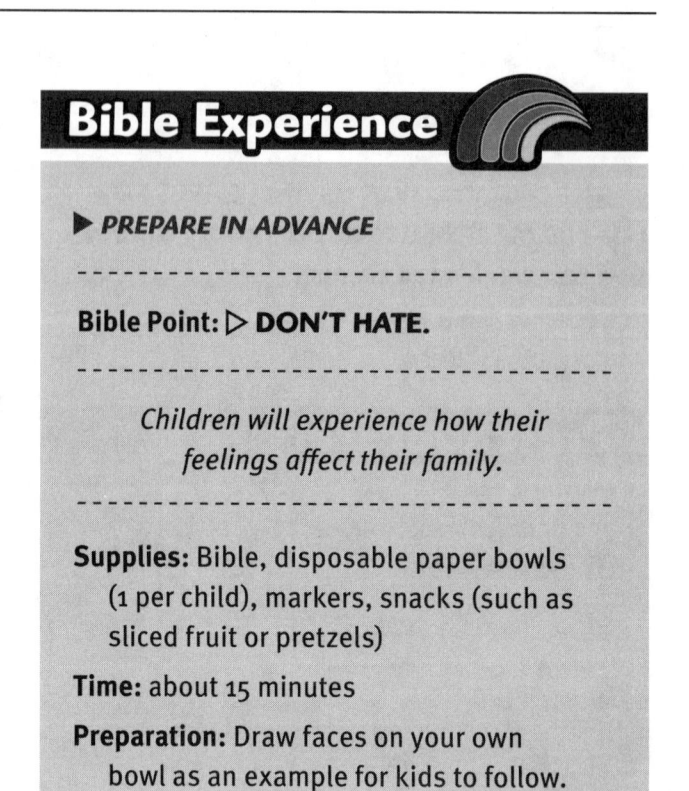

▶ *PREPARE IN ADVANCE*

Bible Point: ▷ DON'T HATE.

Children will experience how their feelings affect their family.

Supplies: Bible, disposable paper bowls (1 per child), markers, snacks (such as sliced fruit or pretzels)

Time: about 15 minutes

Preparation: Draw faces on your own bowl as an example for kids to follow.

Give each child a paper bowl, and have them draw a happy face on the inside of the bowl and an angry face on the bottom side. After their drawings are finished, divide the group into trios. Have kids show either side of the bowl and tell about a time their feelings matched that face. After three minutes, ask for a few volunteers to share their stories.

Read aloud Genesis 4:1-16. As you read, have kids show the side of the bowl that represents Cain or Abel when their names are read. ASK:

- **What attitudes did Cain and Abel have toward God? each other?**
- **What did Cain do wrong?**
- **What would have been a better way for Cain to handle his hatred toward Abel?**
- **How do you handle your bad feelings toward family members?**

Read aloud 1 John 3:12 and then 1 John 2:11. Hold up the angry side of your bowl and SAY: **Cain let his hate and anger control him, and it ended in disaster. The Bible says ▷ DON'T HATE because**

God knows it can only lead to bad things. Turn the bowl over to the happy side, and then SAY: **But when we love others, God can fill us with his love and blessings.** Pour a handful of snacks into the bowl, and then SAY: **It's just like these bowls we made. When we love others and bring them joy, God can fill us. But when we're angry and hateful, God's love does not fill us.**

Say a brief prayer, thanking God for helping us love others. Have the kids line up or form a circle. As you pour some of the snacks into each bowl, SAY: **Love one another.**

Additional Topics List

This lesson can be used to help children discover... Anger, Consequences, Hatred, and Sin.

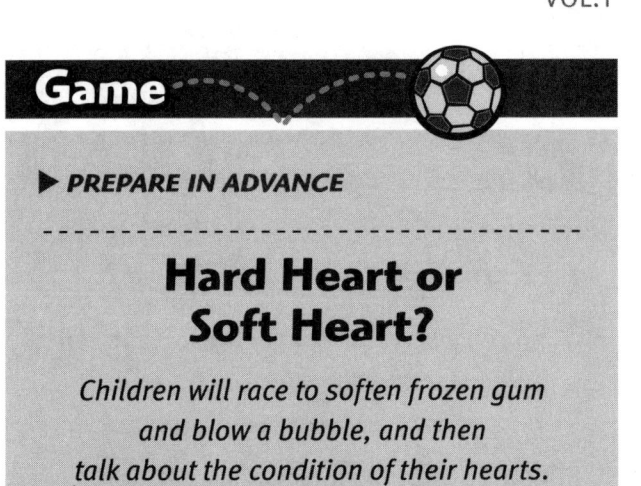

notes

Game

▶ ***PREPARE IN ADVANCE***

Hard Heart or Soft Heart?

Children will race to soften frozen gum and blow a bubble, and then talk about the condition of their hearts.

Supplies: Bible, bubble gum

Time: 5 to 10 minutes

Preparation: Twenty-four hours before the game, freeze the packages of gum.

Read aloud 1 John 3:12, and then SAY: **Let's play a game to show what a cold, hateful heart like Cain's might feel like!** Give each child a frozen piece of bubble gum. As kids try to soften it up, SAY: **When your cold heart gets warm enough, race to blow the first bubble.** After kids have blown bubbles, ASK:

- **How was the cold gum like a cold heart?**
- **What did you have to do to blow a bubble?**
- **What sorts of things are difficult to do if your heart is cold?**
- **What do we have to do to keep our hearts from becoming cold and hateful?**

Craft

▶ *NO PREP*

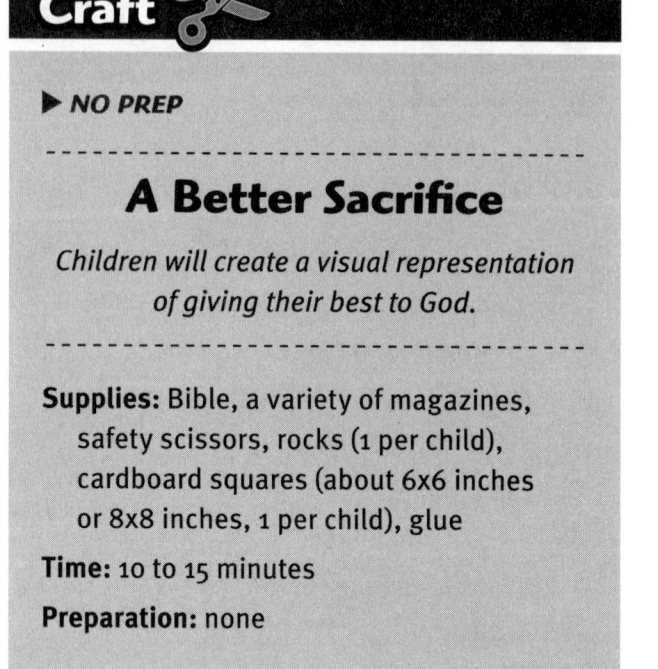

A Better Sacrifice

Children will create a visual representation of giving their best to God.

Supplies: Bible, a variety of magazines, safety scissors, rocks (1 per child), cardboard squares (about 6x6 inches or 8x8 inches, 1 per child), glue

Time: 10 to 15 minutes

Preparation: none

From the magazines, have children cut out pictures of three or four things they value. Then have kids lay their pictures on the table, form pairs, and tell each other about one of their pictures.

After a minute or two of sharing, read aloud Genesis 4:1-16. ASK:

- **Why was Abel's sacrifice better than Cain's?**
- **Does God want our sacrifices? Why or why not?**

Read aloud Hosea 6:6. Explain that Cain's problem was not his sacrifice but rather his attitude. ASK:

- **What can your attitude of giving be this week?**

Give each child a rock, a cardboard square, and glue. Have kids create an altar by gluing the rock in the center of the cardboard and then gluing their pictures around the rock. Explain how this symbolizes putting their most valuable things on God's altar. Lead them in prayer, asking God to help them have the right attitude as they give their best to God.

Bible Application

▶ *NO PREP*

Tied Together

Children will learn that cooperation is one way to show love to others.

Supplies: Bible, 2-foot piece of string for every pair of kids

Time: 10 to 15 minutes

Preparation: none

Form pairs. Have children use the string to join one wrist with their partner's opposite wrist. (Let kids do this on their own.) Once pairs are tied together, give them each a task to accomplish; for example, straighten chairs, pick up trash, move furniture, or hand out books. When the tasks are accomplished, gather kids in a circle and collect the strings. ASK:

- **How is being tied together like having a brother or sister? What ties brothers and sisters together?**

Read aloud Genesis 4:1-11. SAY: **In this story, one brother's anger and jealousy made him kill his brother. When God asked him about it, he said, "Is it my job to take care of my brother?"**

ASK:

- **What should Cain have done differently with his brother?**
- **Can we help our brothers and sisters if we're angry with them or jealous of them?**
- **What does it mean to take care of a brother or sister?**

SAY: **Brothers and sisters are tied together by family ties, like the strings we used. Sometimes it can be helpful, but sometimes it can be hard, too. When we're tied to someone—whether by string or by family—everything's a lot easier when we cooperate.**

Divide the kids into trios, and have them discuss this question:

- **What's one thing you can do to help your brother or sister?**

Close with prayer, asking God to help kids care for their siblings.

notes

Creative Prayer Idea

▶ *PREPARE IN ADVANCE*
▶ *STUDENT LED*

My Best Gift

Children will commit their best to God through a mini altar experience.

Supplies: Bible, several large rocks, palm-sized rock for each child, permanent markers

Time: 5 to 10 minutes

Preparation: Stack the large rocks in the center of a room to make an altar.

Have kids sit in a circle around the makeshift altar. Read aloud Genesis 4:1-7 and 1 John 3:12. SAY: **Throughout the Bible people brought offerings and sacrifices to God. They often used altars that looked similar to this pile of rocks. Cain and Abel brought gifts to God, too. But God wasn't happy with Cain's gift because it wasn't the best he could give.**

Hold up one of the smaller stones and SAY: **Today we're going to give a gift to God. I'm going to give each of you a small stone like this one. On your stone, write or draw a picture of what you think is the best thing about you. For example, I would write** [provide your own response].

Pass out the rocks and markers to kids. Give them a couple of minutes to write on their rocks, and then lead them in the following prayer by saying: **Repeat the following prayer aloud as I pray: Dear God, thank you for your faithfulness.** (Repeat.) **Thank you for the gifts and blessings you've given us.** (Repeat.) **I give you the very**

best of me. (Repeat.) **Help me to use my best to help others love you, God.** (Repeat.) **We praise you, Lord.** (Repeat.) **In Jesus' name, amen.** (Repeat.)

Encourage kids to keep their rocks as a reminder to pray to God and commit the best parts of their lives to him.

Movie Clip

Sibling Quibbling

Movie Title: *The Parent Trap* (1961) (G)

Start Time: 13 minutes

Where to Begin: One of the twin sisters slaps the other, and a fight begins.

Where to End: After they stop fighting, and the counselor says, "Let the punishment fit the crime."

Plot: Identical twins, separated since early childhood, are reunited at summer camp. They form a plan to switch identities in an effort to get their divorced parents back together.

Review: Watching these sisters argue will provide a natural tie-in to the story of Cain and Abel, with its jealousy, anger, and much uglier outcome than the siblings experience in the movie.

Discussion:

After setting up and showing the clip, SAY: **When two people don't get along, the sparks can fly. That's what happened to the sisters in the movie. But the Bible tells about two brothers who really didn't get along.** Read Genesis 4:1-11 or summarize the story. Have partners discuss:

- **How could Cain have handled the situation differently?**
- **What do you think of God's punishment of Cain?**
- **What can you do when you get angry at or jealous of someone?**

Close by leading children as they pray in pairs for each other.

Object Lesson

▶ *NO PREP*

Picture Perfect

Children will learn that God wants us to have attitudes that please him.

Supplies: Bible, a drawing a child drew for you, a color replica of a famous painting (such as found in an art book at the library)

Time: about 10 minutes

Preparation: none

Hold up the picture drawn by a child.

ASK:

- **How much do you think this drawing is worth?**
- **What's so special about this drawing?**
- **Why do you think it means so much to me?**

Hold up the copy of the famous painting. ASK:

- **How much do you think this painting is worth?**
- **What's special about it?**

◆ **Which do you think means more to me: my child's drawing or this painting? Why?**

SAY: **Although the original painting in this book is beautiful and very valuable, I cherish the drawing the child gave me because it was given with love. Let's look at two brothers and the gifts they gave to God.**

Read aloud Genesis 4:1-8. SAY: **Cain brought "some of the fruits of the soil." Abel brought the "fat portions from the firstborn of his flock."**

ASK:

◆ **What was the difference between what the two brothers offered?**

◆ **Why do you think Abel gave his best to God?**

◆ **What do you think Cain thought when he gave his offering to God?**

Read aloud Hebrews 11:4. SAY: **Abel gave to God out of a heart of love, while Cain gave to God because he felt like he had to.**

ASK:

◆ **What are some things you can give to God?**

SAY: **When you give to God because you love him and not because you have to, it makes God happy.**

Preschool Story

▶ *PREPARE IN ADVANCE*

Bible Point: ▷ **DON'T HATE.**

Supplies: Bible, 2 paper plates, wilted vegetables, fresh vegetables, cotton balls, marker, paper, crayons

Time: 15 to 20 minutes

Preparation: Use a marker to make several cotton balls look dirty. Put the dirty cotton balls and several clean cotton balls together on a plate. On another plate, put a few wilted and a few fresh vegetables.

Giving the Very Best

Have all the children form a circle and sit down. Open your Bible to Genesis 4, and show children the words.

SAY: **Adam and Eve had two sons. They named their sons Cain and Abel. Cain was a farmer and grew plants. Let's all pretend we're farmers.** Encourage children to pretend to plant seeds, pull weeds, and harvest and eat the crops. **Abel was a shepherd—he raised sheep. Let's all pretend we're shepherds.** Help children pretend to herd their flocks and care for their sheep.

One day Cain and Abel decided to give gifts to God. Cain decided to give God some of his crops, and Abel decided to give God some of his sheep. Set out the plate of healthy and wilted vegetables and the plate of clean and dirty cotton balls. ASK:

◆ **Which of these vegetables would you give to God?**

◆ **Which of these "sheep" would you give to God?**

SAY: **Cain was selfish. He wanted to keep the best for himself, so he decided to give God the worst of his crops.** Take the healthy vegetables away, and leave the wilted vegetables in the center of the circle. **Abel loved God and wanted to give God the best he could.** Take away the dirty cotton balls, and leave the clean cotton balls. **God was pleased with Abel's gift, but God was not happy with Cain's gift.**

ASK:

- **Why do you think God was happy with Abel's gift and not with Cain's?**
- **If you could give a gift to God, what would it be?**

Give each child a sheet of paper and some crayons. Encourage kids to draw a picture of a gift they would give to God. When kids are finished, have them tell a friend about their picture.

SAY: **Cain was angry that God liked Abel's gift better. Cain was so angry that he started to hate Abel. God warned Cain that hating his brother was wrong, but Cain didn't listen to God.**

One day Cain took Abel to an empty field. While they were in the field, Cain hurt his brother very badly—so badly that Abel died.

Cain tried to hide what he had done, but God knew what Cain had done. God was angry with Cain because Cain had chosen to hate his brother. God doesn't want us to hate each other. God wants us to get along. Let's sing a song and play a game to help us remember that God wants us to love each other.

Sing this song to the tune of "London Bridge." Have two children form a bridge with their arms while the other children walk under the bridge. On the last line, encourage the "bridge" children to drop their arms and hug the child under them.

God wants us to love each other.
Love each other.
Love each other.
God wants us to love each other—
And ▷ DON'T HATE.

ASK:

- **Have you ever been angry with someone? Why?**
- **What does God want us to do when we're angry with someone?**

BIBLE STORY

Noah's Flood

For the Leader

The account of Noah's flood is a beautiful story of how God cares for those who love him. God's promises are as true as God himself. As children grow in their knowledge of God and his Word, they'll discover God's faithfulness and watch his promises come true in their lives.

Use this story as a foundation for children's trust in God because it gives them such a vivid reminder of how much he cares for them. These activities will help kids get a deeper understanding of God's character.

Key Scriptures

Genesis 6:5–7:12; 8:18–9:1, 8-17
1 Peter 5:7

Bible Verse

"Give all your worries and cares to God, for he cares about you" (1 Peter 5:7).

Bible Experience

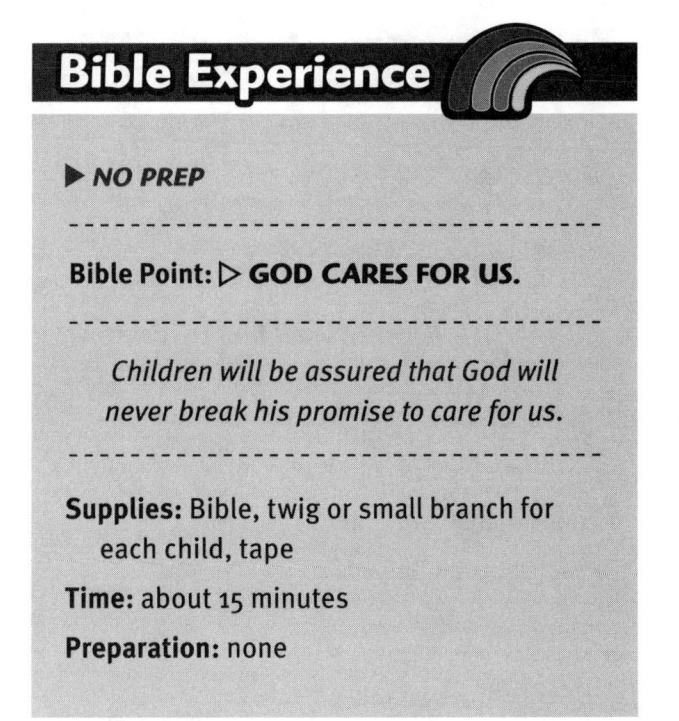

▶ *NO PREP*

Bible Point: ▷ **GOD CARES FOR US.**

Children will be assured that God will never break his promise to care for us.

Supplies: Bible, twig or small branch for each child, tape

Time: about 15 minutes

Preparation: none

Place the twigs at one end of the room. Gather kids in a circle at the opposite end of the room. SAY: **Think for a moment about promises you've made to others or that others have made to you.**

ASK:

- **Who can tell about a promise you've made?**
- **Did you keep your promise? Why or why not?**
- **How does it feel if you break a promise?**

SAY: **The twigs at the other end of the room are pretend promises. When I say "Go," hop to the twigs, break one, and then bring both pieces of the broken twig back to the circle.** When all the kids are back in the circle, pass around the tape, and challenge each child to tape his or her twig back together. When all the twigs are "repaired," ASK:

- **How easy was it to break your twig?**
- **Was it easy or hard to repair? Explain.**
- **Is the repaired twig as strong as it was before it was broken? Why or why not?**

SAY: **These twigs are like promises. If they're broken, the strength is gone—they can never be made as good as new. God knows how important promises are. Let's read about a special promise God made to Noah. Listen carefully and see if you think God has ever broken this promise.**

Let volunteers take turns reading aloud Genesis 8:18–9:1, 8-17. Then ASK:

- **What promise did God make to Noah?**
- **Do you think that promise is for us as well? Why or why not?**

SAY: ▷ **GOD CARES FOR US. That's one promise God has made to you and me that he'll always keep.** Read aloud 1 Peter 5:7. **God always keeps his promises, and just like Noah, he has promised always to take care of us. Let's pray and thank God for promising to take care of us.** Close in prayer.

Song & Connect

Use "All His Promises" (track 9, *it: Innovative Tools for Children's Ministry: Old Testament* CD) to help reinforce the Bible Point, ▷ **GOD CARES FOR US.**

Additional Topics List

This lesson can be used to help children discover... Faithfulness, God's Promises, God's Provision, Nature, and Obedience.

Game

▶ *PREPARE IN ADVANCE*
▶ *FOR YOUNGER CHILDREN*

Rainbow Ball

Children will be reminded that God promises to take care of them.

Supplies: Bible, sock, bag of cotton batting, long strips of rainbow-colored ribbon, string

Time: 5 to 10 minutes

Preparation: Fill the toe of a sock with cotton batting to the size of an orange. Tie a knot in the sock just above the batting. Attach the ribbons with string.

Read Genesis 9:12-16. Have kids form two groups and stand on either side of the room. Show them how the ball creates a rainbow when thrown across the room. Let each child try throwing the ball to the other group, and then

ASK:

- ◆ **What does the Bible tell us a rainbow means?**
- ◆ **What did God promise Noah?**
- ◆ **What does God promise you?**

SAY: **The rainbow is a sign that God always keeps his promises.** ▷ **GOD CARES FOR US—AND THAT'S A PROMISE!**

Craft

▶ *NO PREP*

Forever Rainbows

Children will make "indelible" rainbows.

Supplies: Bible, white paper, crayons, paintbrushes, dark watercolor paint, water

Time: 15 to 20 minutes

Preparation: none

Have the kids sit in a circle. Read aloud Genesis 9:13. SAY: **This verse comes at the end of the story of Noah. Let's see if we can remember what happened in the story.** Start by asking: **What happened first?** Ask the person on your right to begin by telling what he or she thinks happened first. Then ask the next person if anything happened before or after that. Be sure to get around the circle, giving each kid a chance to fill in another detail of the story. Then ASK:

- ◆ **What do you know about the promises God makes?**

SAY: **God has promised always to take care of us, and God never breaks his promises. God gave Noah a rainbow as a sign that he keeps his promises.**

Hand out paper and crayons, and have the children draw rainbows. Make sure they create brilliant rainbows by pressing hard with the crayons. When the rainbows are finished, pass out paintbrushes, dark watercolor paint, and water. Have the kids paint their entire papers with the paint. ASK:

- ◆ **What happened to the rainbow when you painted over it with the dark paint?**

SAY: **Even though the paint is dark, it can't cover up the rainbow. No matter what, God's promises always remain true. ▷ GOD CARES FOR US, AND THAT'S A PROMISE.**

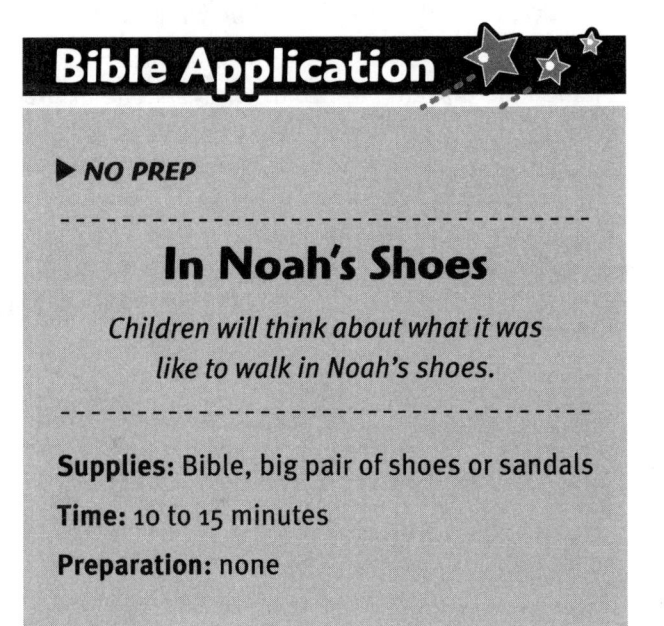

Bible Application

▶ *NO PREP*

In Noah's Shoes

Children will think about what it was like to walk in Noah's shoes.

Supplies: Bible, big pair of shoes or sandals

Time: 10 to 15 minutes

Preparation: none

Place the big shoes in the center of the room, and have kids circle around them. Read aloud Genesis 6:6-17, and then SAY: **Put yourself in Noah's shoes, and think about what happened as this huge boat began to take shape on his property. I'm going to ask a few questions. When you have an answer to a question, go and stand in "Noah's shoes" and give your answer.**

Ask the following questions, allowing a few children to stand in Noah's shoes one at a time to give answers to each question:

- **What do you think Noah's neighbors might have thought?**
- **What would you have said to Noah if you lived back then and didn't follow God?**
- **How would you have felt if you were Noah?**
- **What are some things God asks people to do today that might make others say, "You're crazy for doing that"?**

Read aloud Genesis 6:22. SAY: **Noah did what God told him to do, and God took care of Noah. ▷ GOD CARES FOR US. I'm going to ask some more questions, but this time, go and stand in the center with your shoes off, and give your answer.**

Ask the following questions, allowing children one at a time to stand in the center with their shoes off to give answers to each question:

- **When are some times you've gotten discouraged while trying to do what was right?**
- **What do you think Noah might say to kids today about being faithful to God?**
- **What's one way you can show your faithfulness to God this week?**

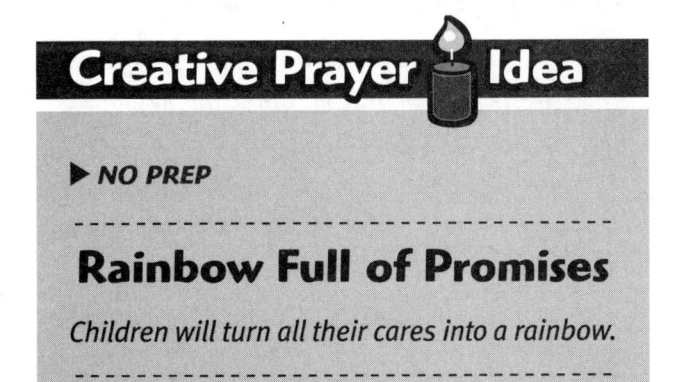

Creative Prayer Idea

▶ *NO PREP*

Rainbow Full of Promises

Children will turn all their cares into a rainbow.

Supplies: Bible, sticky notes in a variety of rainbow colors, pencils, blank wall space

Time: about 10 minutes

Preparation: none

SAY: **The Bible tells us about a time the world was so full of sin that God covered it with water and destroyed every living thing. Only a man named Noah and his family obeyed God. They were kept safe in an ark that God told Noah to build. After the flood was over, God made a promise.**

Read aloud Genesis 9:13 and 16. SAY: **God has also made a promise to us—to always take care of us.** Read aloud 1 Peter 5:7, and then SAY:
▷ **GOD CARES FOR US. Let's take some time to pray and tell God about our cares.**

Have the kids write things they're worried about or want God to take care of on the colored sticky notes. Then have them prayerfully place the notes in the shape of a rainbow on the wall. After the rainbow has been made, SAY: **See our rainbow? It's made of all our cares that we want God to take care of. And this rainbow is a sign of God's promise to take care of every one of those cares.** Close in prayer, thanking God for taking care of us.

Life Application

Children will discover that God cares for them as they participate in these application activities.

Good Measure

Take kids outside the church, and together walk off 450 feet in one direction (either with a pedometer or counting 150 paces). Then have kids turn around and look back. Explain that Noah's ark was 75 feet wide and 45 feet tall, using landmarks to help children understand the distance. ASK:

- **Do you think it made much sense to Noah to make a boat this huge in the middle of dry land? Why or why not?**
- **Do you think it was easy for Noah to obey God's command to build an ark? Why or why not?**
- **In what ways did God take care of Noah?**
- **When has God taken care of you?**
- **How has God taken care of you?**

Noah's Art

Paste a long sheet of butcher paper along the wall, and have kids draw a giant scene of the animals entering Noah's ark. As they draw each different kind of animal, have them tell what they think that animal's cares might be while on the ark. Draw as many animals as possible. Then remind kids that God took care of every one of the animals' cares, just like he takes care of ours.

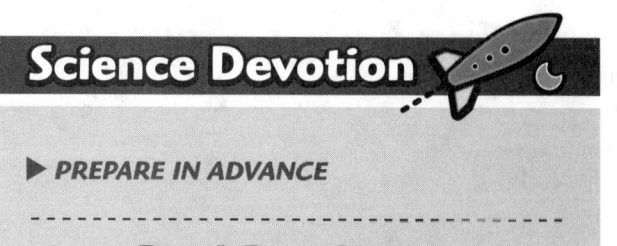

Science Devotion

▶ *PREPARE IN ADVANCE*

Real Rainbows, Real Promises

Children will learn how rainbows are created.

Supplies: Bible, 4x6 card, scissors, transparent tape, drinking glass full of water, sheet of white paper

Time: 15 to 20 minutes

Preparation: Cut a ½ inch vertical slit in the center of the card.

Tell the story of Noah and the ark, or read it from Genesis before the activity. Then read aloud Genesis 9:13-15. SAY: **When we see a rainbow, we can remember that it stands for a promise from God to us. To help us remember God's promise, let's make our own real rainbows.**

Tape the card with the vertical slit to one side of the glass. Set a sheet of white paper on a flat surface near a window, and place the glass of water on it so the sun shines through the water in the glass and onto the white paper. A spectrum of colors should appear on the white paper. You may have to adjust the glass a bit to get the best color spread.

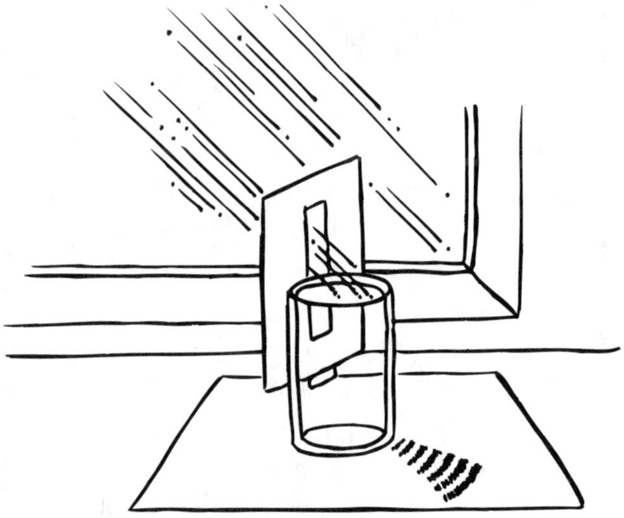

ASK:

- **What caused the sun shining through the glass to form a rainbow?**

SAY: **When the light shines through the glass, it's bent by the water. When light rays are bent, it causes them to separate into their different colors. In the same way, the moisture in the air after a storm causes sunlight to be bent into rainbows in the sky. God uses rainbows as a reminder of the promise he made to us.**

ASK:

- **How do you remember promises you make to others?**
- **Has God ever forgotten his promise to you?**
- **Has God ever not taken care of your needs?**
- **The rainbow also reminds us that God took care of Noah.**
- **What are some promises you can make to God?**

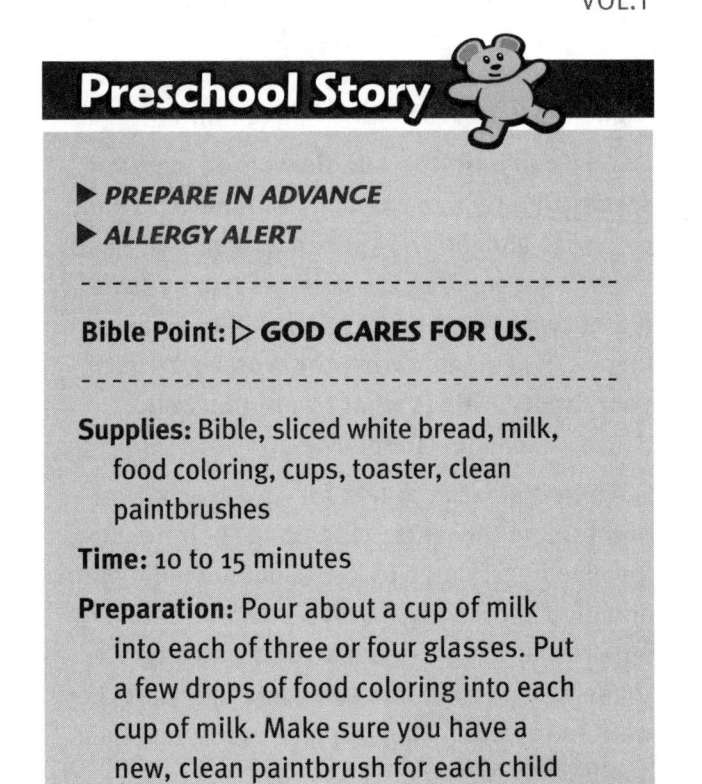

Preschool Story

▶ ***PREPARE IN ADVANCE***

▶ ***ALLERGY ALERT***

Bible Point: ▷ GOD CARES FOR US.

Supplies: Bible, sliced white bread, milk, food coloring, cups, toaster, clean paintbrushes

Time: 10 to 15 minutes

Preparation: Pour about a cup of milk into each of three or four glasses. Put a few drops of food coloring into each cup of milk. Make sure you have a new, clean paintbrush for each child in your class.

A Faithful Man

Have all the children form a circle and sit down. Open your Bible to Genesis 6 and 7, and show children the words. SAY: **Once there was a man named Noah. Noah loved God and trusted God. But he was the only person who did! Let's do an action rhyme now as we hear the story of Noah.**

Lead children in this fun action rhyme about Noah. Say each verse while demonstrating the actions that accompany it. SAY: **Noah was a faithful man who listened to what God said.** (Cup hand to ear.) **Not like the others who pushed God away and did what they wanted instead.** (Push hands away from body, and then put them on hips.)

So God said to Noah, "Please listen to me, this is what you should do. (Cup hand to ear, and hold one finger up.) **Build me an ark. Make it really big because the sky will no longer be blue!** (Pretend to hammer, and then stretch arms wide.) **It's going to rain for a really long time,**

and I want you to be ready." (Twinkle fingers from high to low to imitate falling rain.)

So Noah built the ark. He worked long and steady. (Pretend to hammer, and then cup hand over eyes and look out.) **Then God said to Noah, "See? I am sending the animals two by two.** (Point away from body, and then hold up two fingers, two times.) **Bring them on board with your family. This is what I want you to do."** (Wave hand in toward body.)

Then it started to rain for 40 days and nights, and the water rose up to their heads (twinkle fingers high to low to imitate falling rain, and then show a high level of rain by stretching out one hand high) **because God was angry at those who pushed him away and did what they wanted instead.** (Make an angry face, and push hands away from body.)

When the rain finally stopped, Noah sent out a dove to see if the dove could find land. (Flap arms like a bird.) **The water had dried up, and up in the sky was such a beautiful sight!** (Spread arms out to show God's beauty.) **A rainbow from God, a promise he made, to never cause us such a fright!** (Make a wide arc with hands in the air.)

God saved Noah, his family, and all the animals in the ark. Let's make a rainbow treat right now to help us remember that ▷ GOD CARES FOR US.

Give each child a slice of bread and a paintbrush. Help children dip their paintbrushes into the colored milk and then paint the colors onto their bread. When children are finished, take their bread and toast it. Once the bread is toasted, the rainbow colors will really show up! As children enjoy their rainbow snack, ASK:

- ◆ **How did God take care of Noah and his family?**
- ◆ **How has God taken care of you and your family?**
- ◆ **How can you trust God to take care of you in the future?**

BIBLE STORY

Tower of Babel

For the Leader

In ancient Babylonian cities, ziggurats, or temple towers shaped like pyramids, were thought to be gateways to heaven. *Babel*, the Hebrew form of the name *Babylon*, means "gate of God." In this story, God turns the city of Babel into *balal*, which means "confused in language." What we learn from the tower of Babel story is that when we forget that we need God, we will face a bad end.

These lessons and activities will help kids understand that God is the one responsible for everything we are and everything we have. Without God we're nothing. But with God we are blessed beyond imagination.

Key Scriptures

Genesis 11:1-9

John 15:5

Bible Verse

"Yes, I am the vine; you are the branches. Those who remain in me, and I in them, will produce much fruit. For apart from me you can do nothing" (John 15:5).

Bible Experience

▶ *PREPARE IN ADVANCE*
▶ *FOR SMALL GROUPS*

Bible Point: ▷ **WE NEED GOD.**

Children will consider why it's important to put God first.

Supplies: Bible, large blocks, table

Time: about 10 minutes

Preparation: Place the blocks on the floor by the table.

Read aloud Genesis 11:1-9. SAY: **The Bible tells us about some people who wanted to make a name for themselves. They wanted to be famous. So the people decided to build a tower up to heaven. Let's try to build a tower.** Have everyone take a block and build a tower on the floor.

Hmm. Do you think everyone here can see our tower? Can we build it taller? We want everyone to see it so that people will think we're good builders. Carefully knock down the tower, and have kids take another block. This time, build a tower on top of the table. ASK:

◆ **Why might people want to build a tower that would reach the heavens?**

◆ **How do people try to make themselves important today?**

SAY: **The people in the story wanted to build a tower so that they would be famous. They thought they didn't need God. But God wants everyone to put him first.** Read aloud John 15:5. **God wants us to remember that we need him, that we can't do everything by ourselves.** Knock down the tower. **God stopped the people from building. He made them speak different languages so that they would scatter across the earth, like the way our blocks scattered on the floor.** ▷ **WE NEED GOD!**

Have each child pick up a block and pray together.

Song & Connect

Use "Walk Humbly" (track 15, *it: Innovative Tools for Children's Ministry: Old Testament* CD) to help reinforce the Bible Point, ▷ **WE NEED GOD.**

This song emphasizes the concept of "more of God, less of us," so be sure to keep the mood of this song cheerfully worshipful.

Additional Topics List

This lesson can be used to help children discover... Communication, Jesus Is the Way to God, Popularity, and Pride.

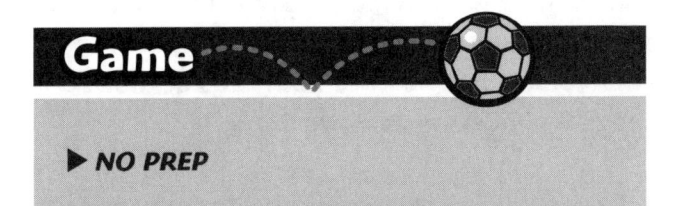

Game

▶ *NO PREP*

What's That You Say?

Children will learn that they need God to accomplish anything worthwhile.

Supplies: Bible, crayons, tape, paper

Time: 10 to 15 minutes

Preparation: none

Help kids form trios, and then give each trio their supplies: 10 crayons, several feet of tape, and three sheets of paper. SAY: **In your trios, take a minute to discuss how you'll make the tallest telephone pole with those supplies.**

Drift around to hear what they're planning. After about a minute, announce these two rules: **Everyone must participate! Each person may say only one word. The person wearing the most red may say only "booga-booga."** Pause for kids to find that person and for the person to repeat the phrase. Then SAY: **The person to the right of that person may say only "oops."** Pause for kids to repeat the phrase, and then SAY: **And the third person may say only "yowza."** Pause for kids to repeat the phrase.

Give trios four minutes to complete their telephone poles as they use their languages. When time has passed, ask kids to show off their creations. ASK:

- **Was it easy or difficult to build your project? Why?**

Read aloud Genesis 11:1-9, and then ASK:

- **Why didn't God want these people to work together?** (See verse 4.)

SAY: **The people decided they didn't need God to do great things. So God confused their language and kept them from accomplishing their plans. But we need God! Let's acknowledge God in everything we do.**

n
o
t
e
s

Craft

▶ PREPARE IN ADVANCE

Towering Needs

Children will create and play a game to understand that we need God.

Supplies: Bible, cardboard tubes from rolls of wrapping paper or paper towels, safety scissors, markers

Time: 15 to 20 minutes

Preparation: Make several copies of the game card sheets (p. 47).

Have kids choose a partner. Have one partner cut the cardboard tubes into different lengths, from 2 to 4 inches. Then have them separate their tubes into two piles. Have the second partner cut out the game cards and mix them up. Instruct the duos to use markers to draw windows and bricks on the tubes. As they work, have them practice saying the different words in German, Spanish, and French.

Have partners take turns being the Reader and the Builder and try building the highest tower using only the cards for directions. To build the towers, the Reader chooses a card from the deck and reads the words in a different language to the Builder (without telling the Builder what the words mean in English). If the Builder guesses the correct move, he or she follows the directions on the card by adding tubes "up" or deleting tubes "down" and then continues with another card. If the Builder guesses incorrectly, the Reader and the Builder switch places.

After a few minutes, gather the kids together and read aloud Genesis 11:1-9. Then ASK:

Game Cards

English one up	***German*** ein auf (English: one up)	***French*** un en haut (English: one up)	***Spanish*** uno arriba (English: one up)
English one down	***German*** ein hinunter (English: one down)	***French*** un en bas (English: one down)	***Spanish*** uno hacia abajo (English: one down)
English two left	***German*** zwei links (English: two left)	***French*** deux gauche (English: two left)	***Spanish*** dos izquierdo (English: two left)
English three left	***German*** drei links (English: three left)	***French*** trois gauche (English: three left)	***Spanish*** tres izquierdo (English: three left)
English four up	***German*** vier auf (English: four up)	***French*** quatre en haut (English: four up)	***Spanish*** cuatro arriba (English: four up)
English two up	***German*** zwei auf (English: two up)	***French*** deux en haut (English: two up)	***Spanish*** dos arriba (English: two up)
English three down	***German*** drei hinunter (English: three down)	***French*** trois en bas (English: three down)	***Spanish*** tres hacia abajo (English: three down)

- **How did you feel trying to pronounce new words?**
- **Was it easy to take directions from your partner? Why or why not?**
- **What happened to the people of Babel who decided they didn't need God?**
- **What happens when God is your partner?**

SAY: **The people of Babel became proud and sinful. They thought they didn't need God. But God wants us to need him. And when God is on our side, we can do everything much better.**

Bible Application

▶ *NO PREP*

Build Up Each Other

Children will learn to do the opposite of the people of the Tower of Babel (bragging) and encourage each other.

Supplies: Bible, pencils, copy paper

Time: about 10 minutes

Preparation: none

Have kids sit in a circle on the floor. Read aloud Genesis 11:1-9. SAY: **The people in this Bible story were proud of themselves. They liked to brag about the amazing things they did. But that's not how God wants us to act. Instead of bragging about ourselves, we're going to build each other up.**

Hand out pencils and paper, and then SAY: **Place your paper on the floor in front of you, and write your name in the center of the paper. Now, everyone rotate one position to the left. Write on the paper in front of you one thing you appreciate about that person—maybe a talent or ability. Make sure that what you write is positive and encouraging.**

Have kids keep rotating until they come back to their original positions and their own handouts. ASK:

- **How does it feel to see what everyone wrote about you?**
- **Do you think it's better to brag about yourself or encourage other people? Why?**

SAY: **The next time you think about telling everyone about all the great things you can do, instead, say something encouraging to someone else. That will make God very happy!**

Creative Prayer Idea

▶ *PREPARE IN ADVANCE*

We Need God

Children will finish statements about themselves, and then finish prayers about God.

Supplies: Bible, strips of paper, 2 paper bags

Time: about 10 minutes

Preparation: On 10 strips of paper, write a variety of open statements (one statement per strip of paper) kids can complete about themselves, such as "One thing I can do really well is..." or "The best thing I ever did was..." Place the statements in a paper bag. On 10 other strips of paper, write a variety of statements kids can complete about God, such as "I need God because..." or "One thing God always does for me is..." Place these God statements in another paper bag.

Have kids form a circle. Pass the bag of kids' statements around the group, and have one child at a time pick a slip of paper and complete the statement aloud. Have them put the slips back in the bag and pass it along.

After everyone has had a chance, briefly tell kids the story of the Tower of Babel. Tell them that these people thought they were something special and that they didn't need God. Read aloud John 15:5. SAY: **God has made each of us special and has given us unique gifts. But without God, we can't do any of these things. ▷ WE NEED GOD. Let's focus on God now and thank him for how special he is.**

Pass the "God" bag around, and repeat the activity. Do this part of the activity as an act of prayer to God.

Life Application

Children will understand that they need God as they participate in these application activities.

Ego-a-Go-Go

Cut from several magazines several pictures of people who are familiar and unfamiliar to the kids. Get pictures with a variety of facial expressions. For each of the pictures, ask kids to respond in one of three ways to this question: How do you think this person views him- or herself? Here are the three responses: (1) as a fairly awesome person, stand up; (2) as only average, sit in a chair; or (3) as a rotten person, sit on the floor. Then talk about how God wants us to view ourselves and how we need God in order to have a healthy self-image.

Say What?

Have a person who speaks a foreign language read the story of the tower of Babel. Ask the kids how it felt to not understand the language. Then reread the story in English. Talk about God confusing the people in the story because of their pride. Discuss ways kids can demonstrate that they need God in their lives.

Stack Attack

Have kids try to stack a variety of odd objects such as shoes and craft supplies, and talk about why we need God to guide us as we build our lives. Tell the kids to think about how the important things in their lives "stack up" next to what God wants them to do.

Snack

▶ ***NO PREP***
▶ ***ALLERGY ALERT***

Leaning Towers of Cheesa

Children will use cheese to build their own Tower of Babel.

Supplies: Bible, small cheese cubes, paper plates, toothpicks

Time: about 5 minutes

Preparation: none

Read Genesis 11:1-9. Have kids use cheese cubes to build towers of Babel. Use toothpicks to help stabilize the towers, which can be gobbled up when kids are finished constructing.

Preschool Story

▶ *NO PREP*

Bible Point: ▷ **WE NEED GOD.**

Supplies: Bible, building blocks

Time: 10 to 15 minutes

Preparation: none

Uh-Oh!

Have all the children form a circle and sit down. Open your Bible to Genesis 11, and show children the words. Tell children to listen for the words *uh-oh* as you tell the story. When they hear those words, they should respond by saying the Bible Point: ▷ **WE NEED GOD.**

SAY: **Long, long ago, in a land far from here, everyone spoke the same language. They lived in a big city. They disobeyed God because they didn't think they needed God. Uh-oh!** Lead children in saying: ▷ **WE NEED GOD.**

Give children several blocks, and encourage them to begin building a big tower. SAY: **These people decided to build a big, big tower so that everyone would talk about their city. But they were going to do it without God's help. Uh-oh!** Lead children in saying: ▷ **WE NEED GOD.**

Then SAY: **God saw that the people were trying to be the very best and build their big tower without him. Uh-oh!** Lead children in saying: ▷ **WE NEED GOD.**

God loved the people, and he wanted them to understand that they needed him. So God made people start talking in different languages. If they couldn't understand each other, they would understand that they needed God, and they would stop building the tower. Have children stop building their tower. Walk around to each child, and whisper one of these words in his or her ear: *Thank you, merci,* or *gracias*. Try to split it up evenly so that about the same number of children hear each of the words. Then encourage children to try to find the other children who heard the same word that they did and form groups. Help children as necessary.

The people found others who could speak the same language, and then they split up and moved to different parts of the world. Encourage each group of children to move to a different part of the room. Give each group several blocks (you can take the blocks from the central tower that was made earlier), and encourage the groups to build their own cities. Once children are finished, have them gather in the center of the classroom again.

ASK:

- **Why didn't God want the people to build the tower?**
- **Why did the people need God?**
- **Why do you need God?**

notes

BIBLE STORY

Abram's Call

For the Leader

Odds are, most of your students have experienced a move. Whether it's been to a new house, a new city, or a new state, leaving one home and starting a new one is tough for kids to handle.

In a lot of ways, moving to a new house is like following Christ. Like Abram, kids may not always find the journey smooth and predictable. But they can take comfort in the fact that God will always be with them, leading them to a better future. Use these sessions to help kids experience what it's like to go where God directs them.

Key Scriptures

Genesis 12:1-9

Psalm 32:8

Hebrews 11:1, 8

Bible Verse

"The Lord says, 'I will guide you along the best pathway for your life' " (Psalm 32:8).

Bible Experience

▶ ***NO PREP***

Bible Point: ▷ **GO WHERE GOD DIRECTS YOU.**

Children will understand that it's best to follow God, even when it seems difficult.

Supplies: Bible, road map, large sheet of paper folded to look like a road map

Time: about 10 minutes

Preparation: none

ASK:

- **How many of you have ever taken a road trip with your family?**
- **Where did you go?**
- **Did anyone use a road map? Why?**

Pull out the map, and show it to the kids. Unfold it and point to a few sites. SAY: **We use a road map to show us the direction we're supposed to go. It tells us if we need to take a different road, and it tells us how far we need to go until we reach our destination.**

Open your Bible to Genesis 12:1-9, and then SAY: **In this Bible story, God talked to Abram about his future. God told Abram to leave his home, his friends, and his parents. God told him to take his wife and just what they could carry and go to another land. Here's a map Abram might have used when God gave him these instructions.** (Unfold the large blank sheet of paper.) **Hmm. What's wrong with this map?** Pause for kids to share, and then SAY: **There's nothing on this map! In fact, Abram didn't have any map at all. He didn't know where he was going. All Abram knew was that God had told him to go, and that's what he did.**

ASK:

◆ **When have you had to follow some difficult instructions?**

◆ **How did God help you?**

SAY: **The next time you have trouble following instructions or don't know whether to trust someone, ask God for faith. Ask God to guide you in the right way because you need to ▷ GO WHERE GOD DIRECTS YOU, just like Abram.** Close in prayer.

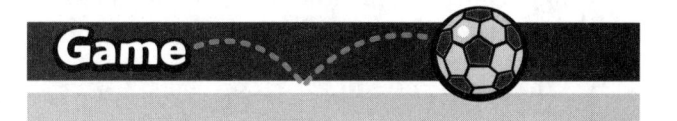

Additional Topics List

This lesson can be used to help children discover... Faith, God's Promises, Guidance, and Obedience.

Game

▶ ***PREPARE IN ADVANCE***

Build It With Blueprints

Children will work together to build something fun as they learn the value of having directions.

Supplies: Bible; 2 or more identical sets of building materials, such as Lincoln Logs, Tinkertoys, or LEGOs; copies of a pictured structure that can be built with the pieces provided (from the toy leaflet); copies of the written directions for building the pictured structure (from the toy leaflet)

Time: 10 to 20 minutes

Preparation: Make copies of the toy leaflet instructions and structure(s).

Based on the size of your class and the number of building sets you have available, have kids form groups. Hold up one of the building sets and SAY: **We're going to work together in groups to build this.** (Show the picture and name the structure you are building.) Explain that you're adding a twist to this project. **God told Abram to leave his home and travel to a new land. Along the way, God gave Abram simple instructions to guide him on the journey.**

I'm providing half of you with a picture of the [name the structure]**. The other group(s) will have a picture and directions.** Encourage kids to have fun building the toy or inventing the steps themselves while looking at the picture.

When the structures are finished, discuss:

◆ **What were the difficulties for the group(s) that built the** [name of the structure] **without directions?**

◆ **How did the directions help the group(s) that had them?**

Read Genesis 12:1-9, and then ASK:

◆ **What directions did Abram receive from God?**

◆ **How might Abram's life have been different if he had been without these instructions?**

SAY: **God always gives us helpful direction when he asks us to do something, and we need to ▷ GO WHERE GOD DIRECTS US.**

notes

Craft

▶ *PREPARE IN ADVANCE*

Mapped Out

Children will be reminded that God has mapped out a perfect plan for each of our lives.

Supplies: Bible, scraps of wood, old road maps or atlas pages, sandpaper, scissors, white craft glue, water, plastic bowl, paintbrushes, plastic tablecloth

Time: 15 to 20 minutes

Preparation: Collect scraps of wood—they don't need to be the same size, but each one must have a side that is at least 3x3 inches. For younger kids, precut old maps or atlas pages into 3-inch squares. Mix 2 parts white craft clue with 1 part water in a plastic bowl. Cover a table with a plastic tablecloth.

Set out all the supplies, and have each child choose a piece of wood and a map. Have kids sand away rough edges. Demonstrate how to brush a light coat of the glue mixture onto the wood, press a map piece into place, and then brush a light coat of the mixture over the map piece.

As kids work, SAY: **We usually have good maps to help us find where we're going.**

ASK:

- **When have you used a map to help you get somewhere?**
- **Can you tell us about a time you got lost because you didn't have a map?**

When kids finish, have them set their map blocks in a sunny place to dry. Then gather kids together and read aloud Genesis 12:1-5. ASK:

- **Who showed Abram and his family where to go?**
- **Do you think God gave Abram a map?**
- **Why do you think Abram obeyed God?**
- **How do you think Abram felt about going to a strange new land?**

SAY: **Use your map block as a reminder that God has a wonderful plan for you and that the best thing you can do is ▷GO WHERE GOD DIRECTS YOU!**

Bible Application

▶ *PREPARE IN ADVANCE*

True Clues

Children will experience what it's like to follow God.

Supplies: Bible, strips of colored paper, pen

Time: 15 to 20 minutes

Preparation: Set up the clue hunt in your church building. Write clues that describe specific locations. Place the clues where kids will find each one and be led to the next clue. For example, start the hunt with a clue such as "Look in the place where the Good News is preached," and place the second clue where your minister stands to preach. Place at least four or five different clues. The last clue should lead kids back to your meeting place.

Have kids form groups of about four. Give each group the first clue, but allow about a minute between groups' departures. Tell kids to leave the clues in place so that the next group can see them. When all the groups have returned, ASK:

- **How did you find your way back here?**

Read aloud Genesis 12:1-9. ASK:

- **How is what we did similar to what Abram did?**
- **What clues did Abram follow?**
- **How was Abram faithful to God?**
- **How can we be faithful in following God?**

SAY: **Abram followed God faithfully, even when he didn't know where God was leading him. You can ▷GO WHERE GOD DIRECTS YOU one step at a time, just as you did in the clue hunt.**

ASK:

- **Where can you get the clues that teach you how to ▷GO WHERE GOD DIRECTS YOU?**
- **How can you follow God this week?**

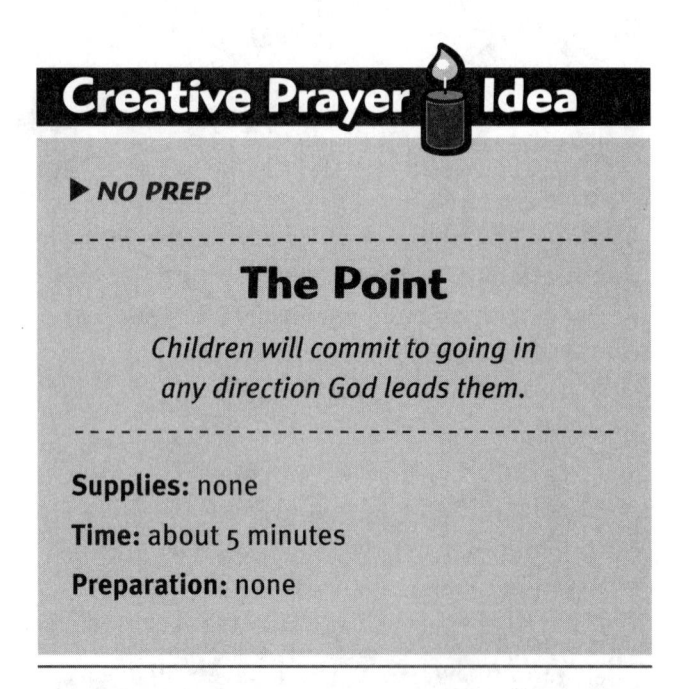

Creative Prayer Idea

▶ ***NO PREP***

The Point

Children will commit to going in any direction God leads them.

Supplies: none

Time: about 5 minutes

Preparation: none

Gather in a circle, and ask kids a variety of questions that require them to answer by pointing in a certain direction. For example, ask them all to point in the direction of their home, and then pray together about following God when they're at home. Then ask them to point in the direction of their school, their favorite restaurant, or other locations. Close by having kids point to the ceiling as they commit to following God wherever he directs them.

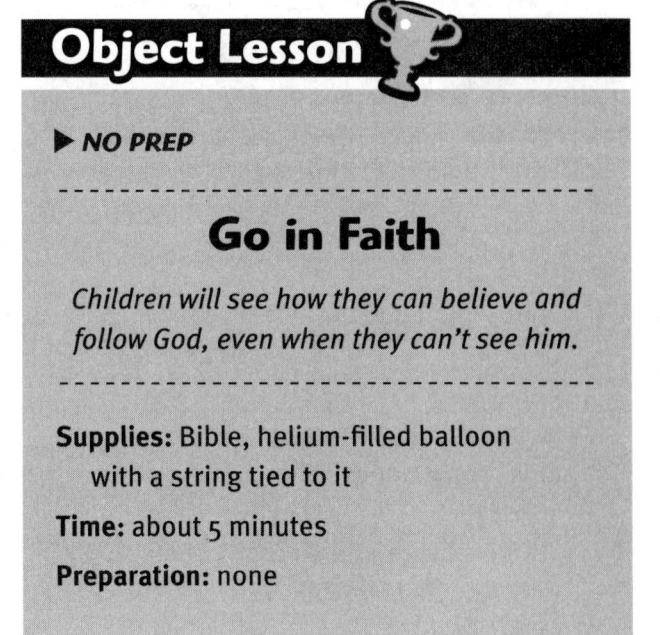

Object Lesson

▶ ***NO PREP***

Go in Faith

Children will see how they can believe and follow God, even when they can't see him.

Supplies: Bible, helium-filled balloon with a string tied to it

Time: about 5 minutes

Preparation: none

Hold the string so the balloon is floating high.

ASK:

- **Who knows what makes this balloon float?**
- **How do you know the helium is in there? Can you see it?**

Bring the balloon down, and then let it float up again. SAY: **Even though we can't see it, we know the balloon has helium in it. The helium makes the balloon float.**

Read aloud Hebrews 11:1 and 11:8. Then turn to Genesis 12 and show the children the words. SAY: **The Bible tells us about a man named Abram who had that kind of faith. Abram didn't even know where he was going, but he had faith in God to lead him. Even though Abram couldn't see God, he knew God was real. Abram had faith to ▷GO WHERE GOD DIRECTED HIM.**

ASK:

- **Why do you think Abram had faith in God?**
- **How do we show others our faith in God?**

SAY: **Abram trusted in God to lead him, even though he couldn't see God. Even though we can't see God, we know he's real. We go where he directs us by obeying him, treating others kindly, telling others about Jesus, and following God's Word—the Bible.**

Bring the balloon down and hold it. SAY: **As we pray, I want you to imitate what I do with the balloon. Right now, crouch down low, and when I let the balloon fly up high, stand and stretch up high.**

PRAY: **Dear God, even though we can't see you, we have faith and trust that you are real.** (Let the balloon float high.) **Thank you for Abram, who trusted you and had faith to go where you directed him. Help our faith to grow so that we can go where you direct us to go. In Jesus' name, amen.**

notes

Snack

▶ *NO PREP*
▶ *ALLERGY ALERT*

Blessings Overflowing

Children will be reminded that God blesses us when we follow him.

Supplies: Bible, bowl with a few pieces of candy or packs of fruit chews, large bag of candy or packs of fruit chews containing enough for each child to have two pieces or packs

Time: 5 to 10 minutes

Preparation: none

Read aloud Genesis 12:1-9. SAY: **God told Abram he would bless him if he would go where God directed him. God said he would make Abram a great nation, and lots of people would be blessed because of him. Let me show you an example of what this blessing looks like.**

Ask a child to take the bowl of candy and go around giving a piece to each child. Each time the child gives away a piece of candy, put several more pieces into the bowl. Keep doing this until the child has given several pieces away and you have filled the bowl until it overflows.

ASK:

- **What did I want the helper to do?**
- **What happened because the helper obeyed?**
- **What did God want Abram to do?**
- **What did God say he'd do for Abram?**

SAY: **Because** [name of child] **did what I asked and gave away candy,** [name of child] **was blessed with even more candy. In fact, the**

bowl overflowed! When we obey God and ▷ GO WHERE HE DIRECTS US, God always blesses us back.

Have enough snacks available so that each child can have one more. As they receive another snack, have them pray, "Thanks, God, for blessing me so much."

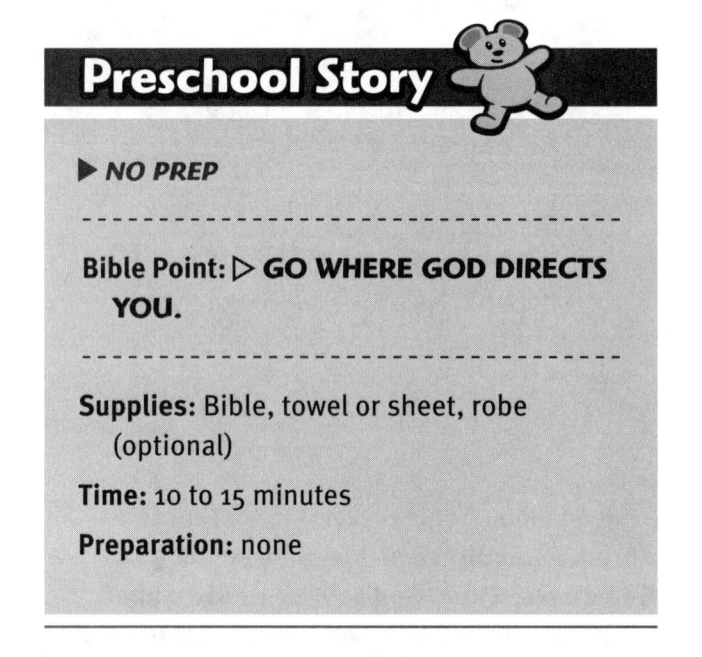

Preschool Story

▶ ***NO PREP***

Bible Point: ▷ **GO WHERE GOD DIRECTS YOU.**

Supplies: Bible, towel or sheet, robe (optional)

Time: 10 to 15 minutes

Preparation: none

Follow Me!

Have kids form a circle and sit down. Open your Bible to Genesis 12, and show children the words.

ASK:

- ◆ **Have you ever had to move away from your home to a new home?**
- ◆ **How did it feel to have to move?**

SAY: **It can be really hard to move away from your home and your friends. Just ask Abram! Shh...I hear him coming now!** Turn around and put a towel or sheet around your head. If you can, put on a robe as well. Turn back around and speak to the kids in a deep voice.

Hello there! My name is Abram. I'm getting ready to move to a new land. I'm a little worried about leaving my home and all my friends, but God has asked me to move to a new place, and I want to follow God. My wife, Sarai, and my nephew, Lot, are coming with me, but I could sure use some more help. Will all of you come along? You can pretend to be my servants and come on this journey with me. We'll leave early in the morning. For now, you will all want to get some sleep. Have kids lie on the ground and pretend to sleep.

Then SAY: **Wake up, everyone! We're going to get started on our journey. We'd better pack up our things.** Have kids pretend to pack up a tent, some food, and clothes. **Let's start marching.** Lead children in marching around the room. Make comments about the heat, the long walk, and the surrounding countryside. Then SAY: **Here, I think this is a good place to stop.** Have kids pretend to set up camp, eat dinner, and then lie down to sleep. After a few minutes, wake the children and go through a day's march again.

Wait! God has told me that we should stop here! God has told me that this is my land, my children's land, and my grandchildren's land. Oh, God is such a wonderful God! Let's pray and thank God right now!

PRAY: **God, thank you for taking care of us on our journey. Thank you for helping us to follow you. You are a wonderful God! Amen.**

SAY: **Thank you, everyone, for coming with me on this journey! You have been a wonderful help! I'm excited that God has led me to this beautiful land. I'm glad that I followed God. You can ▷ GO WHERE GOD DIRECTS YOU, too! Goodbye, everyone!** Turn around and take off your costume. When you're finished, turn around again and have kids sit down in a circle on the floor. ASK:

- ◆ **What did God want Abram to do?**
- ◆ **How did Abram follow God?**
- ◆ **How can you follow God in your life?**

BIBLE STORY

God's Covenant With Abram

For the Leader

Abram's story of faith is perhaps the most remarkable in the Bible. Again and again God told Abram about his grand plans for Abram's future, but that plan seemed to fly in the face of all the facts of Abram's life. It would be like telling a bird it was going to fly even though it had no wings. But God made a promise, and God promised to keep it.

Kids need to know that God has a plan for their lives. Yet they also need to have the faith and courage to follow God's plan, even when it doesn't seem like that plan is coming together very well. These activities help kids understand how to discover God's plan for each of them.

Key Scriptures

Genesis 15

Jeremiah 29:11

Bible Verse

"'For I know the plans I have for you,' says the Lord. 'They are plans for good and not for disaster, to give you a future and a hope'" (Jeremiah 29:11).

Bible Experience

▶ ***PREPARE IN ADVANCE***

Bible Point: ▷ GOD HAS GOOD PLANS FOR US.

Children will experience what it's like to include God in their plans.

Supplies: Bible, copies of a blank calendar page for the upcoming month, pencils, paper

Time: 15 to 20 minutes

Preparation: Make copies for each child of a blank calendar page for the upcoming month.

Have kids form two groups, creating a path down the center of the two groups. Stand at one end of the path, and read aloud Genesis 15:1-10. Then slowly walk down the path between the kids as you read verses 17 and 18. ASK:

- **When God promised Abram he would have many descendants, why did Abram have a hard time believing God?**
- **Do you sometimes think it's hard to believe that God has great plans for you? Why or why not?**

SAY: **God made a covenant, or promise, with Abram by sacrificing the animals. Back in Bible times, when two people made a covenant like this, they would stand between the sacrificed animal and call a similar fate upon themselves if they didn't uphold their part of the covenant. When the flames passed between the dead animals, that was God saying he would keep his promise to fulfill his plans for Abram, no matter what.**

Give each child a pencil and a copy of the blank calendar page. SAY: **Everybody has plans for their lives. Write down all the plans you already know about for the month to come. Be sure to include all your sports practices, doctor appointments, lessons, activities, school, birthdays, holidays, and everything else you can remember.**

Allow a few minutes for children to think and write. Then give each child a sheet of blank paper and SAY: **Now let's think about more long-term plans. Write down these questions, and spend the next few minutes answering them:**

- **What would you like your life to be like in high school?**
- **What would you like your life to be like 10 years after high school?**

Have kids form groups of two or three and jot down words that show the plans they'd like to make for their own future, such as driving a car, going to college, or becoming a baseball player. When they're finished, ask for volunteers to share their future plans. ASK:

- **What were you thinking as you wrote down your plans for the month and as you considered your future?**

SAY: **Sometimes it can be really hard to think about what's going to happen in the future. And while we know a lot of good things are going to happen to us, there will also be sad things. But ▷GOD HAS PLANS FOR EACH OF US, and he promises to help us with our future.**

Read aloud Jeremiah 29:11. ASK:

- **How does this verse affect how you feel about your future?**

Pray that every child will remember that God has a plan for him or her.

Song & Connect

Use "The Plans I Have for You" (track 14, *it: Innovative Tools for Children's Ministry: Old Testament* CD) to help reinforce the Bible Point, ▷ **GOD HAS GOOD PLANS FOR US.**

Additional Topics List

This lesson can be used to help children discover... Faith, God's Love, Obedience, Patience, and Plans.

Game

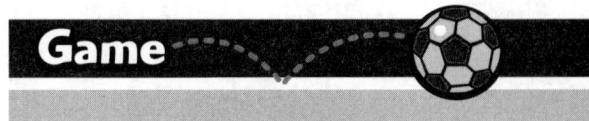

▶ ***PREPARE IN ADVANCE***
▶ ***FOR SMALL GROUPS***

Everyone Fits

Children will learn that everyone has a place in God's plans.

Supplies: Bible, different 10-to-15-piece puzzle (created for young children) for every 3 or 4 kids, prizes (such as stickers or candy)

Time: 10 to 15 minutes

Preparation: Place the pieces for each puzzle in its box, but take one piece from each puzzle and place it in one of the other puzzle boxes.

ASK:

◆ **Have you ever felt out of place or like you didn't belong?**

◆ **How do you feel when other kids are playing but you're left out?**

SAY: **God has a plan for every one of us. And we each have a place to fit in God's master plan.**

Read aloud Jeremiah 29:11. Form groups of three or four. Give each group a puzzle and SAY: **The first group to complete its puzzle gets a prize.** When the kids comment about the misfit piece in their box, SAY: **Even though that piece may not seem valuable to you, it's very important to the completion of another group's puzzle.**

Have kids figure out which group needs the misfit pieces. When the puzzles are finished, have the kids sit in a circle. ASK:

◆ **What was easy or hard about this activity?**

◆ **How is this activity like knowing that we have a purpose in God's plan?**

Give every child a prize and SAY: **We're all winners in God's eyes! He loves us and ▷ HAS GOOD PLANS FOR EACH OF US.**

notes

Craft

▶ ***PREPARE IN ADVANCE***

Inheriting a Galaxy

Children will make jars of stars to remind them to believe God's promises.

Supplies: Bible, baby-food jars with lids, corn syrup, blue food coloring, water, aluminum foil, star hole punch, construction paper, silver glitter, ½-inch masking tape, scissors, glue, blue foil star stickers, silver ribbon

Time: about 15 minutes

Preparation: Provide two work areas: one for filling the jars and another for decorating the outside of the jars. Have warm, soapy water and towels handy to rinse off the corn syrup.

Have kids fill a small glass jar a little more than half full with corn syrup. Add one drop of blue food coloring and water, leaving about ½ inch of air at the top. Have each child punch 10 to 15 stars out of the aluminum foil and drop them in the jar. Sprinkle in silver glitter. Screw the lid on tightly, and seal it with masking tape. Cut out a 3-inch circle from construction paper, shape it to cover the lid, trim the edges, and glue it on. Place blue foil stickers on the top of the lid, and tie a 15-inch piece of silver ribbon into a bow around the neck of the jar, covering any masking tape.

When finished, gather the kids together and read aloud Genesis 15:5-6. Explain why God made this promise to Abram and how he kept his word.

ASK:

- **What promise did God give to Abram?**
- **What promises has God made that you can believe?**
- **How will your mini-galaxy remind you to believe God's promises?**

Have kids shake their jars, and then SAY: **God planned great things for Abram, but Abram needed to obey and trust God. We can't count how many stars are in the sky, but we can always count on God to have good plans for us. We can believe God's promises to us.**

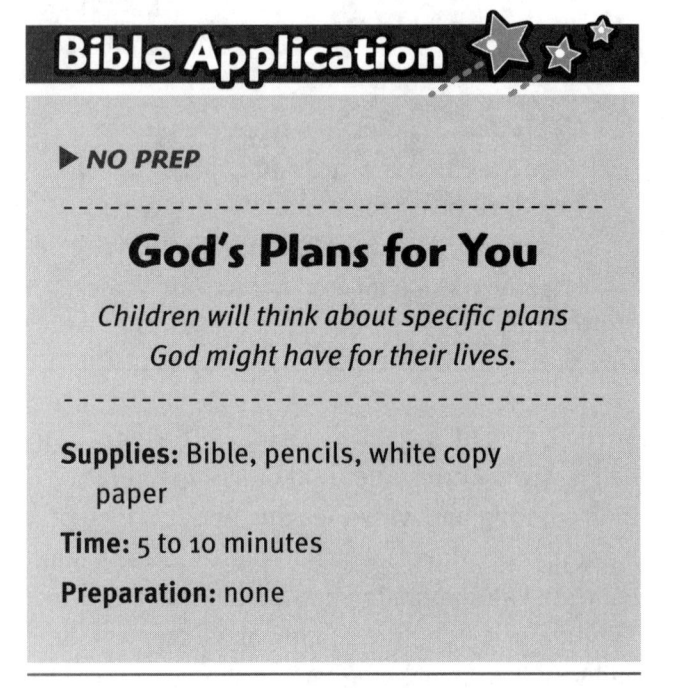

Bible Application

▶ *NO PREP*

God's Plans for You

Children will think about specific plans God might have for their lives.

Supplies: Bible, pencils, white copy paper

Time: 5 to 10 minutes

Preparation: none

Give children pencils and identical sheets of paper. Have them trace around their left hands on their papers. Then have them write their names lightly on the back of the paper. Collect the papers and mix them up. Then hold up the papers one at a time, and have children guess which handprint is theirs.

SAY: **Many of you recognized your handprint by some special mark. God not only knows every part of you, he also has special plans for the way he created you.** Read aloud Jeremiah 29:11, and then

ASK:

- **What does this verse mean to you?**
- **How does this make you feel about God?**
- **What's one thing you think God has planned for your life?**

Give kids back their papers, and have each write one thing in the middle of the handprint that they believe God might have planned for them. SAY: **God knows your handprint and everything about you. God knows your future, too. ▷ GOD HAS GOOD PLANS FOR US!**

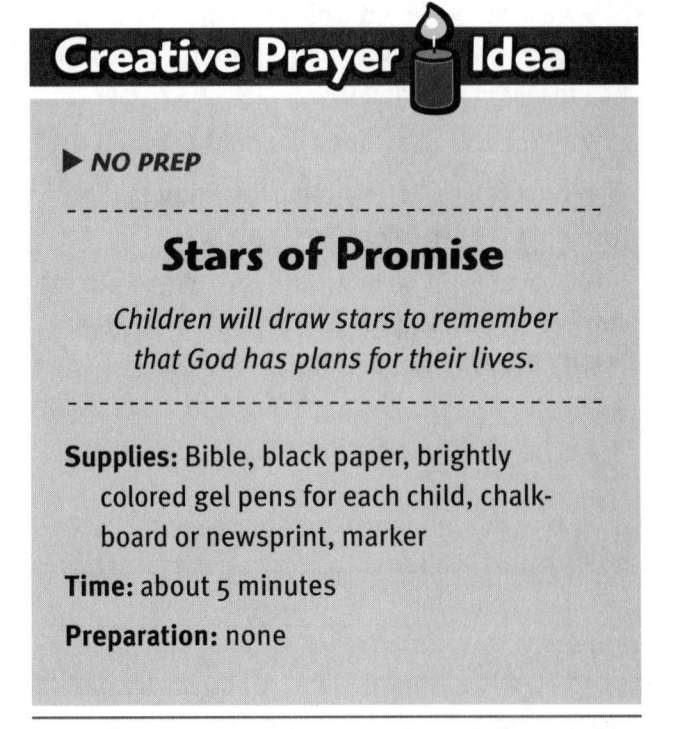

Creative Prayer Idea

▶ *NO PREP*

Stars of Promise

Children will draw stars to remember that God has plans for their lives.

Supplies: Bible, black paper, brightly colored gel pens for each child, chalkboard or newsprint, marker

Time: about 5 minutes

Preparation: none

Read aloud Genesis 15:1-6. SAY: **God promised Abram that he would give him a family so big that no one would be able to count all his descendants. God had good plans for Abram, and he kept his promise. ▷ GOD HAS GOOD PLANS FOR US, too. Let's do a quick activity that will help us remember that.**

Give each child a sheet of black paper and a gel pen. Use the chalkboard to show them how to draw a simple, five-line star. As you draw each line of the star, say the Bible Point: ▷ **GOD...HAS...GOOD...PLANS...FOR...US.** Have kids practice drawing the stars as they repeat the Bible Point aloud.

Abram couldn't count the stars, but he could believe that God would keep his promise. ▷GOD HAS GOOD PLANS FOR US, too. Lead kids in a prayer as they draw their stars and repeat God's promise.

Life Application

Children will discover that God has good plans for them as they participate in these application activities.

Interviews With the Stars

Have kids create pretend microphones and conduct interviews with family members or church members about God's plans for their lives. Do a couple of sample interviews in front of the class to give them an example to follow.

Mission Statements

Show kids samples of logos from companies, sports teams, and restaurants they would recognize. Talk about how those companies have mission statements about their plans for the future. Encourage kids to talk with their parents about a mission statement or God's plans for their family.

Role Reversal

Have kids pair up and think of various professions, such as a dentist, baker, or pastor. Instruct them to role-play those jobs and talk about the plans those people might make for the future. Have some of them share with the rest of the class, and then talk about how God has plans for each of their lives.

Worship Prompt Idea

▶ ***NO PREP***

Crowning the Future

Children will praise God for his plans for their lives.

Supplies: Bible, chair draped with fabric to form a throne, 12-inch length of tinsel garland taped in a circle to form a crown

Time: about 5 minutes

Preparation: none

Have children form a circle around the throne. SAY: **The Bible has exciting news for you!** Read aloud Jeremiah 29:11. **Isn't that great? We don't know how our lives will turn out, but God does. Let's praise God for the wonderful plans he has for us.**

Have the child to your left sit on the throne. As you place the crown on his or her head, SAY: [Name], **God has good plans for you!** Then have the rest of the kids say, "Search for God with all your heart!" and give that child a standing ovation. Have that child give you the crown and join the circle as the next child sits on the throne. Repeat the affirmation for all the kids in the class.

notes

Preschool Story

▶ *PREPARE IN ADVANCE*

Bible Point: ▷ **GOD HAS GOOD PLANS FOR US.**

Supplies: Bible, glow-in-the-dark stars, paper, pencils or crayons, dress-up clothes (optional)

Time: 15 to 20 minutes

Preparation: Stick several glow-in-the-dark stars on your ceiling or on another high point in your room.

When I Grow Up

Have kids form a circle and sit down. Open your Bible to Genesis 15, and show children the words. Then turn off the lights in the classroom, and have children lie down on the floor. (If some children are afraid, you may want to leave the door open or leave a small light on.) Point out the stars on the ceiling.

SAY: **Abram had trusted God and followed God to a new land. Abram loved God and was very happy in the new land. But there was one thing that was still making Abram sad—Abram didn't have any children!**

ASK:

- **Have you ever been sad? What made you sad?**
- **What made you feel better?**

SAY: **One night God told Abram to go outside and look at the stars in the sky. God told Abram to count the stars. Abram probably thought that was kind of silly. Who can count the stars? There are way too many stars to count! But God told Abram that someday his family would have as many people in it as there are stars in the sky. Wow, that's a really big family!** Turn on the lights, and give each child a piece of paper and a pencil (or crayons). Encourage children to draw a picture of their family and to tell a partner about their family.

God has given all of us wonderful families that love and care for us. God promised Abram that he would also have a family. This was part of God's good plan for Abram's life. ▷ GOD HAS GOOD PLANS FOR US!

God cares for us and wants us to have a wonderful life and do wonderful things.

ASK:

- **What are some things you'd like to do?**
- **What do you think you want to be when you grow up?**
- **What are some good plans God might have for your life?**

SAY: **Let's play a game now to show each other some of the good plans God might have for our lives.** Have kids stand up one at a time and act out what they want to be when they grow up. If you have dress-up clothes, let children use them to complete their charade.

We don't know exactly what God's plans are for us, but we do know that ▷ GOD HAS GOOD PLANS FOR EACH ONE OF US, just as God had a good plan for Abram! Let's pray together right now and ask God to help us trust his plans.

PRAY: **Dear God, we know that you have wonderful plans for us. Help us to trust your plans and to follow you. Amen.**

BIBLE STORY

Abram and Lot Separate

For the Leader

Fairness is a huge issue with kids. And conflict is inevitable as they grow up. Teaching them to treat others fairly in the midst of conflict can be a challenge.

So it was for Abram, when he and Lot realized they could no longer live together in harmony. Abram provides a memorable example of a person who handled conflict the way God wants us to—by treating others fairly. In fact, Abram was more than fair, and God blessed him for it.

Help kids see that God has a higher standard for Christians. These activities will give children a chance to experience the blessing that comes from considering the interests of others.

Key Scriptures

Genesis 13:1-18

Philippians 2:4

Bible Verse

"Don't look out only for your own interests, but take an interest in others, too" (Philippians 2:4).

Bible Experience

▶ ***PREPARE IN ADVANCE***

Bible Point: ▷ **TREAT OTHERS FAIRLY.**

Children will experience why it's important to treat others fairly.

Supplies: Bible, paper, markers or crayons

Time: 10 to 15 minutes

Preparation: Fold all the sheets of paper in half vertically.

Have kids sit in the center of the room. Point to one side of the room and SAY: **Over here is a big area of wilderness. It's rocky, the ground is kind of hard, it has a few patches of grass here and there, maybe a few trees, and a little trickling stream runs down the hill.**

Point to the other side of the room and SAY: **Over here is a beautiful area of land that's lush and green, with lots of fruit trees, flowing rivers, plenty of cool shade, and lots of room to run around and have fun. Which area would you pick?**

Have the kids move to the side of the room they would prefer. Most, if not all, will move to the lush land. SAY: **Oh, but wait, there's not enough room for all of you over here, so some of you will have to move to the other side. Those with stripes on their clothing, move to the other side.**

Once the kids are divided up about evenly, read them the story of Abram in Genesis 13:6-18. As you read verses 10 and 11, have the kids on the lush side stand. As you read verses 15 through 17, have the kids on the other side stand. After reading the scriptures, SAY: **When Abram built an altar to the Lord, he was honoring God. When Abram let Lot choose the land, he was honoring God.**

Read aloud Philippians 2:4. SAY: **Abram did exactly what this verse says. God wants us to ▷ TREAT OTHERS FAIRLY—just like Abram did. We make God happy when we do that. We must not always think only of ourselves; God wants us to think about others before ourselves.**

Give each child a sheet of the folded paper, and instruct them to draw *half* of a self-portrait, with their nose, mouth, and eyes split down the middle on the creased side of the page. Show them an example so that they understand. When they're finished with their half-portrait, one side of the folded paper should show half of a face. Then have them exchange papers with a partner. Tell the partners to unfold the papers and complete the drawing of their friend. When they're finished, tell them that this portrait is a reminder that we must not always think only of ourselves—that's just half the picture. God wants us to think of others, too.

Song & Connect

Use "Do to Others" (track 7, *it: Innovative Tools for Children's Ministry: New Testament* CD) to help reinforce the Bible Point, ▷ **TREAT OTHERS FAIRLY.**

Additional Topics List

This lesson can be used to help children discover... Friends, Giving, Greed, Neighbors, and Selfishness.

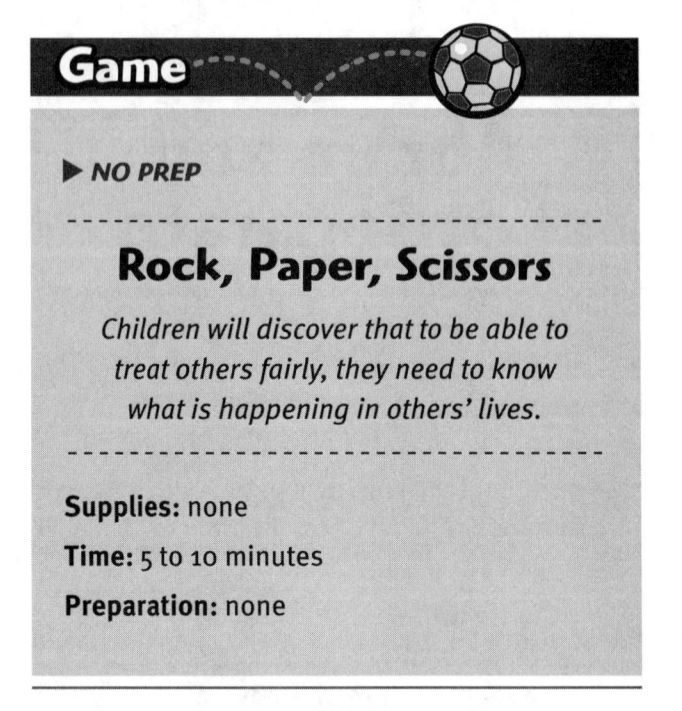

Game

▶ ***NO PREP***

Rock, Paper, Scissors

Children will discover that to be able to treat others fairly, they need to know what is happening in others' lives.

Supplies: none

Time: 5 to 10 minutes

Preparation: none

SAY: **The Bible tells us, "Don't look out only for your own interests, but take an interest in others, too"** (Philippians 2:4)**. We're going to play a game called Rock, Paper, Scissors.**

Explain the rules of Rock, Paper, Scissors. In pairs, kids make a fist with one hand. At the same time, on the count of three, both kids will make a sign with their hand: a closed fist for "rock," a hand flat for "paper," and two fingers in the shape of a V for "scissors." Rock beats scissors, paper beats rock, and scissors beat paper.

Have kids find partners. Then SAY: **After each round of Rock, Paper, Scissors, the winner must tell the other person his or her name, favorite food, and favorite television show.** Have kids change partners after each round. Play long enough so that students have introduced themselves at least three times.

After playing the game, have students sit in groups of three and discuss:

- **Which did you think was the most fun: telling the other person about yourself or learning something about the other person? Why?**

- **Why is it important to learn the likes and dislikes of your friends?**
- **Why does God want us to care about our friends?**

SAY: **The Bible makes it clear that we should be interested in others. The more you know about your friends, the easier it is to treat them fairly.**

Craft

▶ *PREPARE IN ADVANCE*

Fair Flowers

Children will make coupons to help them treat others fairly.

Supplies: Bible, colored construction paper, scissors, markers, tape, green chenille wire

Time: 10 to 15 minutes

Preparation: Cut the construction paper into 3-inch circles (one per child). Also cut petal-shaped pieces (about 5 per child). Create a sample to show the kids.

Read aloud Philippians 2:4. Have kids write, "Look out for the interests of others" onto one side of the circle. Ask them to think of things they'd enjoy doing, eating, or receiving. Talk about how other people might enjoy those things, too. Have them create "care coupons" with the petals by writing on each petal something they could do for someone else that they would also enjoy. After each child has created five petal coupons, have them tape the petals to the circle.

Tape the chenille wire onto the circle to make a stem. Again, read aloud Philippians 2:4. ASK:

- **What does it mean to be selfish?**
- **Why should we think of others more than ourselves?**
- **How can you look out for the interests of others?**

SAY: **Sometimes we only care about what we want to do. But God wants us to be fair and think about others, too. Use these coupons to treat others the way you would like to be treated. This week you can look out for the interests of others and have some fun, too!**

Bible Application

▶ *NO PREP*

Care to Be Fair

Children will experience how difficult it is to be completely fair.

Supplies: Bible, cookies or crackers

Time: 5 to 10 minutes

Preparation: none

Open your Bible to Genesis 13, and show kids the words. SAY: **In this Bible story, Abram and Lot were living in the same area, but they had so many animals that it was too crowded for both of them to stay there. So, to settle their problem, Abram offered to let Lot choose which part of the land he wanted to live in. Of course, Lot took the land that was lush and green and had lots of water. Abram could have taken whatever land he wanted because he was Lot's uncle. But he decided to treat Lot fairly.**

ASK:

- ◆ **Why do you think Abram let Lot take the better land?**
- ◆ **Do you think it was hard for Abram to do that?**

Give each child a cookie or cracker. Instruct them to try to break the snack *exactly* in half. Then

ASK:

- ◆ **Was it hard or easy to break your cookie exactly in half?**
- ◆ **What are some things in life that are hard to do exactly evenly?**

Read aloud Philippians 2:4. SAY: **When it comes to settling conflicts with other people, God tells us to consider the interests of others, just like Abram did.**

ASK:

- ◆ **What are some examples of conflicts you have with other kids?**
- ◆ **How could you follow Philippians 2:4 in those situations?**

Creative Prayer Idea

▶ *NO PREP*

Prayer Gift

Children will write prayers for others and see how thinking of others and praying for them pleases God.

Supplies: Bible, a variety of colored sticky notes, pencils

Time: 5 to 10 minutes

Preparation: none

Have kids read aloud together Philippians 2:4. Then SAY: **One of the ways we can consider the interests of others is to pray for them. Think about some people you can pray for.**

Distribute the sticky notes and pencils, and have kids write a brief phrase indicating something they want to pray about for another person. Ask each child to write one to three prayer notes. As they finish each one, collect them one at a time and post them to a blank wall. Place all the notes on the wall in the shape of a wrapped present (such as a large square with ribbon and a bow). When everyone is finished, explain that our prayers are a gift we can give to others. Lead them in prayer for some of the requests on the wall.

Discussion Launcher Questions

Ask children to form trios and discuss:

- ◆ **Describe a time you thought you were treated unfairly. How did that feel?**
- ◆ **If you could change something that you thought was unfair, what would it be? Why would you change it?**
- ◆ **In what ways do you treat other people unfairly sometimes? Why do you think you do that?**
- ◆ **What are good things that can happen when we treat others fairly?**

notes

Worship Prompt Idea

▶ *NO PREP*

Abram Attitude

Children will learn that treating others fairly shows an attitude of worship toward God.

Supplies: Bible, chalkboard and chalk or newsprint and marker

Time: 5 to 10 minutes

Preparation: none

Write out the words from Philippians 2:4 on a chalkboard or newsprint. Lead kids in reading the verse several times. Then read aloud Genesis 13:6-11. Explain that Abram had the right to take the better land, but he had the right attitude that Philippians 2:4 is talking about. SAY: **Abram let Lot choose first, and he treated Lot fairly. God wants us to treat others fairly, too. We need to have an attitude like Abram.**

Write the word "worship" vertically down the side of the chalkboard. For each letter of the word, have the kids think of a word that names an attitude or action that shows God we treat others fairly. For example, you might write: W—wait your turn, or O—open your heart. Explain that when we act this way toward others, we honor God with an attitude of worship. Lead the kids in a prayer in the end to commit to worshipping God through our actions.

n ______

o ______

t ______

e ______

s ______

Preschool Story

▶ *PREPARE IN ADVANCE*

▶ *ALLERGY ALERT*

Bible Point: ▷ **TREAT OTHERS FAIRLY.**

Supplies: Bible, masking tape; 1 to 2 houseplants; pitcher of water; bucket of sand; plates and bowls; several kinds of snacks, such as pretzels, raisins, small candies, dried fruit, and sunflower seeds

Time: 15 to 20 minutes

Preparation: Use masking tape to make a circle or box on the floor. The circle or box needs to be big enough to just fit all of the children—but make sure it's small enough that you'll be a little crowded. Place the houseplant and water on one side of your room, and place the bucket of sand on the other side of the room. Fill one bowl per child with one of the snacks. Some of the bowls can have the same things, but be sure that each bowl only has one kind of snack.

You First!

Have kids stand in the masking-tape circle. Open your Bible to Genesis 13, and show children the words. SAY: **God called Abram to leave the home where his family lived and go to a place that God would show him. So Abram packed his bags, took his wife, Sarai, and his nephew Lot, and followed God on a journey to a new place.**

Along the way Abram and Lot became very rich and had lots of animals and people to serve them. Soon it was too crowded for all of the people and animals to live together in

one place—kind of like how we're crowded into this little space. In fact, they were so crowded that they started to argue with each other. Abram knew that it wasn't right for them to be arguing, so he decided that they should separate.

Abram knew that God wants us to ▷ TREAT OTHERS FAIRLY, so he pointed out across all the land they could see and asked Lot to choose where he would like to live. Abram let Lot choose first!

ASK:

- **Have you ever let someone else choose first? When? What happened?**

SAY: **Lot looked out across the land. He saw one side that was beautiful, green, and full of plants.** Lead children to the potted plants and water on one side of your room. Talk about how beautiful and lush the land is. Then SAY: **On the other side, Lot saw a dry and ugly land.** Lead children to the bucket of sand. Talk about how hot and boring this land is. **Lot could choose either the beautiful, green land, or Lot could choose the drier area.**

ASK:

- **Which side would you choose?**

SAY: **Lot chose the beautiful, green land, and Abram went to the drier land. God was happy with Abram because Abram had chosen to treat Lot fairly. Let's have a snack now that will help us practice treating others fairly.**

Give each child one plate and one bowl of snacks. Point out that everyone has a different kind of snack. Encourage children to share their snacks with each other so that everyone has some of each kind of snack. Once all the children have a variety of snacks, have them sit down and eat their treats.

SAY: **If you hadn't shared your snacks, you would have had only one kind. God knows that it's better when we share with each other and when we get along. God wants us to ▷ TREAT OTHERS FAIRLY, just as Abram treated Lot.**

ASK:

- **When can you share with others?**
- **How does it make you feel when you share with someone?**
- **Why does God want us to treat others fairly?**

SAY: **We can always share with others. We can share our snacks, our toys, our books, our crayons, and lots of other things. It makes us feel happy when we share, and it makes God feel happy, too! God wants us to ▷ TREAT OTHERS FAIRLY.**

n
o
t
e
s

BIBLE STORY

Abraham Pleads for Sodom

For the Leader

Abraham's prayers for Sodom in Genesis 18:16-33 stand in stark contrast to Jonah's prayers for Nineveh. Both cities were full of evil people. Jonah couldn't have cared less if God judged Nineveh and destroyed it. But Abraham pleaded for God to save Sodom, and God promised not to destroy the city if Abraham could find at least 10 "innocent" people.

Of course, Abraham couldn't find even 10 people in all of Sodom who were faithful to God. But this Bible passage provides a great story of God's compassion and patience for people. God wanted Abraham to pray for Sodom, and God wants us to pray for those who need him. Pass along that humble attitude of compassion to children with these experiences.

Key Scriptures

Genesis 18:16-33

1 Timothy 2:1-4

Bible Verse

"Pray for all people" (1 Timothy 2:1).

Bible Experience

▶ ***PREPARE IN ADVANCE***

▶ ***ALLERGY ALERT***

Bible Point: ▷ **PRAY FOR THOSE WHO NEED GOD.**

Children will understand that it's important to pray for others.

Supplies: Bible, large bag of M&M's, plastic bag, clear jar, table, index cards, markers, glue

Time: about 15 minutes

Preparation: Take out all of the yellow M&M's, put them in a plastic bag, and set them out of sight. Pour the rest of the M&M's into a jar. Put one yellow M&M's candy into the middle of the other M&M's so that it's hidden.

Have an adult helper carry in the jar of M&M's into the room and improvise a dialogue with you, similar to the following:

Helper: Here are the M&M's you asked for.

Teacher: *(Take the jar and scrutinize it.)* I don't see any yellow ones in here. Throw it in the trash. *(Hand the jar back to the helper.)*

Helper: *(Look carefully at the jar.)* Will you keep these M&M's if there are 50 yellow ones in the jar?

Teacher: Yes, I'll keep them if there are 50 yellow ones.

Helper: How about if there are 45? Will you keep the M&M's then?

Teacher: I suppose I'll keep them if there are 45 yellow ones.

Helper: Well, what if there are only 30 yellow ones? Will you throw away the whole jar if there are 30?

Teacher: No, I won't throw it away if there are 30 yellow ones in there.

Helper: *(Once again, examine the jar slowly and speak hesitantly.)* Maybe there are only 20 yellow ones in here. Will you trash this jar if there are only 20?

Teacher: No, I guess not. I'll keep it if there are 20.

Helper: *(Inspect the jar further, shaking it a little.)* Just one more question, and then I'll stop. What if we find only 10 yellow M&M's?

Teacher: For the sake of the 10 yellow ones, I won't throw away the rest of them.

Helper: *(Set the jar down on a table, and walk out of the room.)*

SAY: **Today we're going to talk about one of the most interesting stories in the Bible. Remember this jar of M&M's as we begin.**

Read aloud Genesis 18:20-32. Pour the jar of M&M's onto the table, and pick out the yellow one. ASK:

- ◆ **How many innocent people do you think God found?**
- ◆ **Why do you think Abraham prayed that God would save the people?**
- ◆ **What can we do for people who need God?**

Hand out markers and index cards, and set out the glue. Have kids write the word "pray" in big capital letters on their cards. Read aloud 1 Timothy 2:1. SAY: **God wants us to ▷ PRAY FOR THOSE WHO NEED HIM—and that means everyone! God listens when we pray for people, and he gives everyone a fresh start when they trust in Jesus.**

Hold up the bag of yellow M&M's and SAY: **Think of people who need God's help and forgiveness. For each person you think of, glue a yellow candy onto your card.** Encourage kids to keep their cards for a week to remind them every day to pray for those who need God.

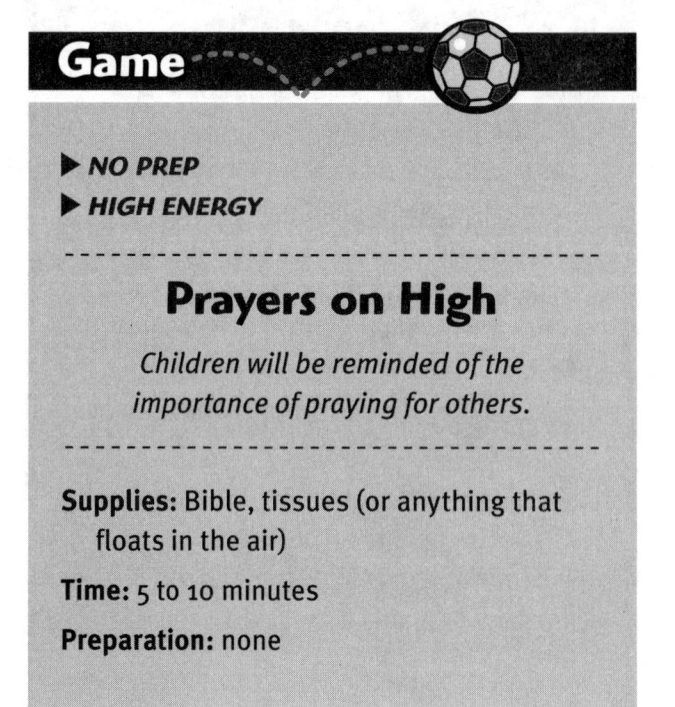

Additional Topics List

This lesson can be used to help children discover... Caring for Others, Faithfulness, Justice, Prayer, and Sin.

Game

▶ ***NO PREP***
▶ ***HIGH ENERGY***

Prayers on High

Children will be reminded of the importance of praying for others.

Supplies: Bible, tissues (or anything that floats in the air)

Time: 5 to 10 minutes

Preparation: none

Form teams of four to six kids. SAY: **The Bible talks about our prayers "rising up" to God. Let's see what upward floating prayers might look like.** Give each team a tissue, and tell kids to work together to get it to touch the ceiling. They can't use their hands; they must make the tissue rise by blowing it.

After kids have tried, have them catch their breath and sit down. ASK:

- ◆ **How are the floating tissues like prayer? How are they different?**

Read aloud 1 Timothy 2:1-4. SAY: **Some people can't help us pray because they don't know God. So we need to pray for them.**

ASK:

- ◆ **Why is it important to pray for people who need God?**

◆ **What happens to our prayers when we pray for other people?**

Encourage kids to pray for people who need God.

Tell kids to keep their prayer pockets in a safe place and move the cards to the "Answers" pocket when they see God working in that person's life.

Craft

▶ ***NO PREP***

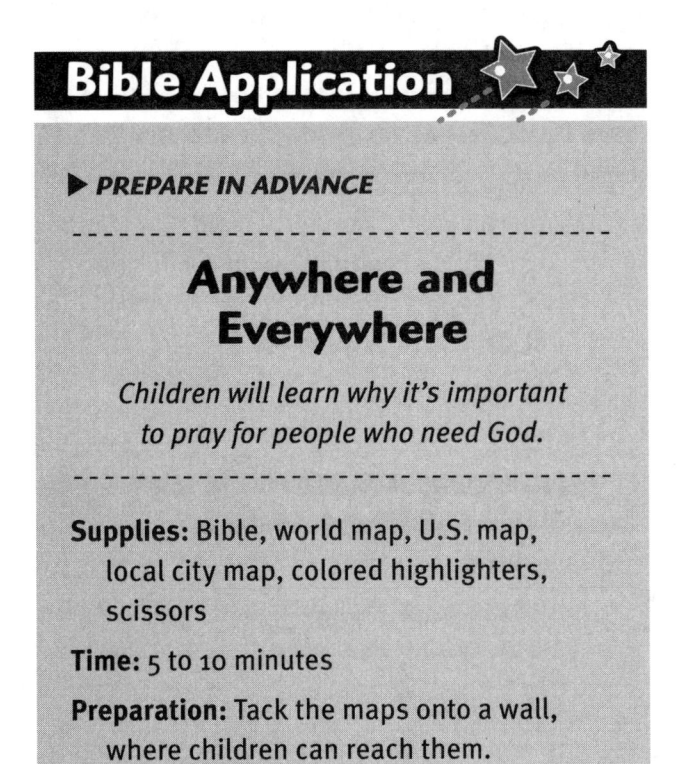

Pocket Full of Prayers

Children will create a "prayer pocket" to remind them to pray for others.

Supplies: Bible, 5½ x11-inch piece of vinyl wallpaper for each child, stapler, markers or crayons, 6 index cards per child

Time: 15 to 20 minutes

Preparation: none

Give each child a piece of wallpaper, and instruct them to fold the pieces in half, making squares. Have kids open the squares and make a 2-inch fold on both ends to create the pockets. Help kids staple the sides of the pockets close to the edges. Tell kids to open the wallets and neatly write "Prayers for People Who Need God" on one pocket of the wallet. On the other pocket, have them write "Answers."

Read aloud 1 Timothy 2:1-4. ASK:

◆ **What do these verses tell us about people who need God?**

◆ **What can you do to help those people?**

Have kids write "I urge you to pray for all people" on the outside of their wallets. Direct kids to write names of people who need God on the cards and put them into the "Prayers" pocket.

Bible Application

▶ ***PREPARE IN ADVANCE***

Anywhere and Everywhere

Children will learn why it's important to pray for people who need God.

Supplies: Bible, world map, U.S. map, local city map, colored highlighters, scissors

Time: 5 to 10 minutes

Preparation: Tack the maps onto a wall, where children can reach them.

Have kids gather around the maps on the wall. Point to the world map, and ask if any kids have been to other places around the world. If any have, tell them to mark the spot on the map with a highlighter. You may want to point out a few places on the map that the kids might have heard about. Next, point to the U.S. map and do the same thing. You should have more kids who have visited different spots around the country. Point out some locations kids might be familiar with, like Disney World or the Grand Canyon.

Finally, point to the local map of your community. Have kids point to their homes, their schools, and other places they know. Help them identify locations if they have trouble understanding the map. Again, use highlighters to mark landmarks around town.

SAY: **Everywhere we go, whether it's in our town, across the country, or around the world, people need God. Every place we've marked on the maps is a place where people need God.**

Read aloud 1 Timothy 2:1-4, and then have kids repeat verse 4 with you. SAY: **God wants everyone to be saved. No matter where you go, you'll always find people who need God. God loves them, just as he loves you and me.**

Take the local map down, and cut it into pieces so that you can give one to each child. Encourage kids to keep the map with them for a week and pray for the people in that part of town who need God.

Creative Prayer Idea

▶ *NO PREP*
▶ *STUDENT LED*

Lists of Love

Children will learn that they can pray for those who need God.

Supplies: Bible, several sheets of newsprint, markers

Time: about 5 minutes

Preparation: none

Gather children and ASK:

◆ **What things do you pray for?**

◆ **How important is it for Christians to pray for other people?**

SAY: **God always hears our prayers, and he answers them. Many prayers we pray are for ourselves, but did you know that we're supposed to pray for others, too? The Bible tells us a story about a man who prayed for people who needed God.**

Read aloud Genesis 18:20-32. Have a child read 1 Timothy 2:1-4. ASK:

◆ **Who are we to pray for?**

◆ **Have you ever prayed for someone who needed God? What happened?**

SAY: **Today we're going to think of people who need God. Then we'll pray for them.**

Have children form groups of four or five. Hand each group a piece of newsprint and a marker. Give kids a few minutes to list the names of people who need God. Tell them they can list anyone. Then direct kids to put their prayer list in the center of the group so that each person can see it. Say the following prayer, leaving room for people's names, and have kids quietly whisper the names on their list: **Dear God, we're glad that we can pray for others and that you hear those prayers. Today we'd like to pray for** (pause). **These people need you, God. Please show them how much you love them, and help us to love them, too. Thank you for hearing our prayer. In Jesus' name, amen.**

notes

Discussion Launcher Questions

Ask children to form trios and discuss:

- **Talk about people who have been really mean or unfriendly. Do you think God loves them as much as he loves you? Why or why not?**
- **God wants us to pray for people who need him. What are some other things we can do for people who need God?**
- **Sodom was so full of wicked people that Abraham couldn't even find 10 innocent people. Do you think there are any places in the world today that are like Sodom? Explain.**

Science Devotion

▶ *PREPARE IN ADVANCE*
▶ *ALLERGY ALERT*

Turning Up the Heat

Children will compare the need for heat to make popcorn to the need people have for God.

Supplies: Bible, hot-air popcorn popper, unpopped corn, tablecloth, paper cups

Time: about 10 minutes

Preparation: Spread the tablecloth on the floor, and set the popper in the center.

Read aloud 1 Timothy 2:1, 3-4. SAY: **God loves everyone in the world, but not everyone knows it. So God wants us to pray for those people. This experiment might help us understand why this is important.**

Have kids sit around the edges of the tablecloth. Pour the unpopped corn into the popcorn popper, and turn on the machine. (Leave the lid off.) As the machine warms up,

ASK:

- **What do you think is happening to the popcorn right now?**
- **Why does corn pop?**
- **Can you think of a time you needed someone to pray for you or needed God's help? Explain.**

Once the corn starts popping, it will pop all over the tablecloth. Keep kids at a safe distance from the popper so that kernels won't hit them. They will be hot!

After all the corn has popped, turn off the machine and SAY: **There's a scientific word to explain why the corn pops: *pressure*. Pressure is a pushing force. Each of these corn kernels has moisture inside. As the kernel heats up, steam is created inside the kernel. The steam puts pressure on the outside layer of the kernel, and eventually it bursts. Not all of the kernels pop open, though.**

When we pray for people who need God, it's kind of like putting the heat on their hearts. Just like the popcorn needs heat and pressure to open up, God wants us to pray for people who need to open up to God. God wants everyone to be saved, and God wants us to pray for people who don't know him yet.

Give each child a paper cup, and let kids each take some popcorn to eat. You might even salt the popcorn and talk about how we can be like salt to people who want to know God.

Preschool Story

▶ *NO PREP*

Bible Point: ▷ **PRAY FOR THOSE WHO NEED GOD.**

Supplies: Bible

Time: 10 to 15 minutes

Preparation: none

Who's Left?

Have kids form a circle and sit down. Open your Bible to Genesis 18, and show children the words. Then lead children in doing this action rhyme as they learn how Abraham prayed for the people of Sodom.

SAY: **God beckoned Abraham to come** (motion toward yourself with your hand),

And take a look at the city of Sodom. (Point off in the distance.)

God told Abraham that the people living in Sodom were bad. (Make a thumbs-down sign.)

The evil and mean things that they were doing made God sad. (Make a sad face, and point to your mouth.)

God told Abraham that he would destroy the city of Sodom. (Slap your hands together.)

But Abraham begged God not to. He asked if there were some (get on your knees)—

Even just fifty—who were still good, and kind, and nice (shrug your shoulders),

Then would God still make them pay the price? (Shake your head.)

"No," God said, "if there are just 50 left (shake your head),

Then I will spare the rest." (Hug yourself.)

"But what if there are only 45, or 40, or 30?" Abraham said. (Stretch your arms out wide, and then bring them in closer and closer.)

Even for 30, God said he would spare the city instead. (Hug yourself.)

"Well, what about for 20 or for 10 (shrug your shoulders)—

What if there are only 10 left without sin?" (Hold up 10 fingers.)

God said, yes, he would spare that city (nod your head);

If there were just a few, he would take pity. (Hug yourself.)

SAY: **Abraham prayed for the city of Sodom and for all the people who lived there. Abraham knew that the people in Sodom needed God. We can also ▷ PRAY FOR THOSE WHO NEED GOD.**

ASK:

- **Do you know anyone who needs God?**
- **How can you pray for that person?**

SAY: **Everyone needs God, but some people don't know about God. We can pray that those people will get to know God, and we can also help them to find out about God.**

ASK:

- **What can you tell others about God?**

SAY: **We can tell people that God loves them and will take care of them. And we can pray for people who need God, just as Abraham prayed for the people of Sodom.**

notes

BIBLE STORY

Isaac Is Born

For the Leader

Some miracles in the Bible can seem easier to believe than others. Parting the Red Sea? Sure, we can believe that. A donkey talking? No problem. The sun and moon standing still? God can handle it.

A barren woman older than most great-grandmothers having a baby? Yikes! Even Sarah laughed at that one. But God was true to his promise, and Sarah laughed again when her baby Isaac was born. Her joy was overflowing!

Children, too, can experience the joy God wants to give them. These activities will help make the point real to kids and will fill their hearts with joy in the process!

Key Scriptures

Genesis 18:10-14; 21:1-7

John 15:11

Bible Verse

"I have told you these things so that you will be filled with my joy. Yes, your joy will overflow" (John 15:11)!

Bible Experience

▶ *PREPARE IN ADVANCE*

▶ *FOR LARGE GROUPS*

Bible Point: ▷ **GOD GIVES US JOY.**

Children will explore why God wants to give them joy.

Supplies: Bible, smiley-face self-inking stamp or marker

Time: about 10 minutes

Preparation: Select three people with strong laughs—an adult, a teenager, and an older woman. Cue them ahead of time on their role during the lesson.

SAY: **Today we're going to talk about some things that may seem impossible to us. Sometimes there are things in our lives that seem so unbelievable that people laugh when they hear them.** [Name of adult], **will you please stand up?** (Pause.) **What would you say if I told you I was going to give you 10 million dollars?** (Wait for the adult to laugh loudly and the rest of the room to join in.) [Name of teenager], **will you please stand up?** (Pause.) **What would you say if I told you that you were someday going to be the leader of our country?** (Wait for the teenager to laugh loudly and the rest of the room to join in.) [Name of older woman], **will you please stand up?** (Pause.) **What would you say if I told you that you were going to have a baby?** (Wait for the older woman to laugh loudly and the rest of the room to join in.)

ASK:

◆ **Why do you think those people laughed when I asked them those questions?**

SAY: **I think they didn't believe what I told them. Most of us know that usually only younger women have babies. That's the way our bodies are made.** Open your Bible to Genesis 21 and SAY: **The Bible tells us about a woman named Sarah, who was older than most of your great-grandmothers. God told her she was going to have a baby, and she laughed because she thought she was too old to have a baby. But then...** Read aloud Genesis 21:1-7.

God wanted to bring joy into Sarah's life, so he gave her a son named Isaac. The name *Isaac* means "he laughs." What a great name! Read aloud John 15:11. **▷GOD GIVES US JOY, too! Tell me something God has done to give you joy.**

As each child tells you something, stamp or draw a smiley face on the back of his or her hand, and have the child repeat John 15:11 with you.

Additional Topics List

This lesson can be used to help children discover... Faith, God's Love, God's Promises, Patience, and Praise.

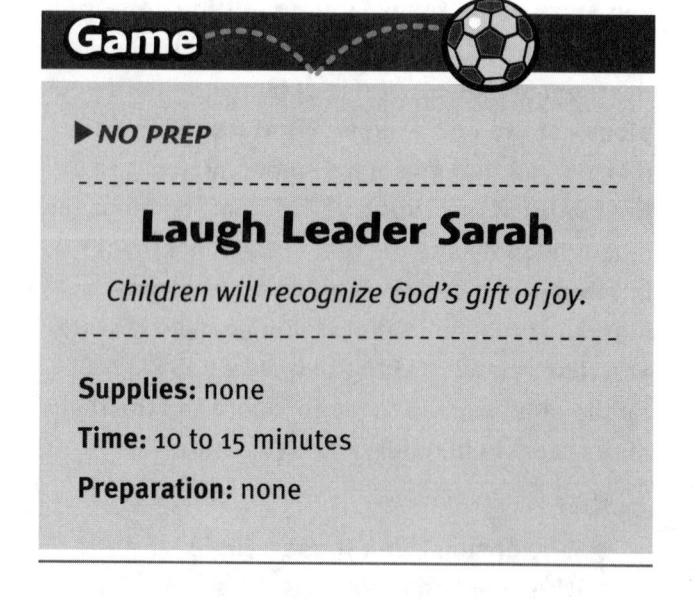

Game

▶*NO PREP*

Laugh Leader Sarah

Children will recognize God's gift of joy.

Supplies: none

Time: 10 to 15 minutes

Preparation: none

Send a few students out of the room to wait quietly until you call them back inside. After they've left, pick one person to be "Sarah the Laugh Leader." Instruct kids who've remained in the room to walk around, laughing. They've got to secretly watch Sarah because when Sarah stops laughing, everyone must stop laughing—though they'll all continue walking around the room.

Ask the other students to come back into the room and walk around with the laughing students, watching everyone carefully. When all the students stop laughing because Sarah has stopped, ask the students observing to each guess which child is Sarah. Each child the students choose must tell whether he or she is Sarah and then share one thing that makes him or her laugh. Play several rounds, as time allows, sending different children out of the room and choosing a new Sarah each time.

After playing the game, read aloud Genesis 21:1-7. Then ask students to sit down and discuss:

- **How did you know who Sarah was?**
- **What are some other ways besides laughter that we can tell someone is happy?**
- **Why do you think ▷GOD GIVES US JOY?**

notes

Craft

▶ *PREPARE IN ADVANCE*

Faces of Joy

Children will experience joy and share it with others as they paint their faces.

Supplies: face paint and paintbrushes

Time: 10 to 15 minutes

Preparation: You may want to have paint shirts on hand to protect kids' clothes.

Ask kids how they can tell if someone is joyful. When a child's answer has anything to do with the face or smile, SAY: **Yes! We can always see joy on someone's face!**

Read aloud John 15:11. SAY: ▷**GOD GIVES US JOY!**

ASK:

- **What are some things we can be joyful about?**

SAY: **Let's show everyone the joy that's in our hearts...by putting it on our faces!**

Have children join with partners. (Pair up younger kids with older kids.) Have kids paint joyful symbols on each other's cheeks. Suggest that they paint hearts, smiley faces, suns, or other joyful images.

Bible Application

▶ *NO PREP*

Joy in the Hard Times

Children will learn why they need God's joy.

Supplies: Bible; several pictures of people doing difficult jobs, such as being a doctor, an astronaut, a soldier, or a teacher

Time: 10 to 15 minutes

Preparation: none

ASK:

- **What's something you think would be difficult to do?**
- **What makes a job hard?**
- **What makes a job easy?**

Hand out the pictures of people doing difficult jobs, and ask kids if they think those jobs are hard or easy, and why. Then SAY: **Some things in life are easy, and some are hard. Sometimes things can even seem impossible. But that's never true with God.**

ASK:

- **Can you think of anything that's too hard for God?**

Read aloud Genesis 18:10-14 and 21:1-7. SAY: **Even though it was hard to believe, Sarah had a baby when she was more than 90 years old. It seemed impossible for Sarah, but it wasn't too hard for God. God gave Sarah joy even though she didn't think it was possible.**

Sometimes it's hard for us to have joy in our lives.

ASK:

- **What are some things in life that are easy for you?**

- **What are some things in life that are hard for you?**
- **Is it easier to have joy during easy times or hard times? Why?**

Read aloud John 15:11. SAY: **God wants to give us joy in the easy times and in the hard times. In fact, he wants our joy to overflow! When things in your life seem hard, remember that ▷GOD GIVES US JOY, and God's joy gives us strength.**

Lead the kids in prayer, asking that God would give them joy.

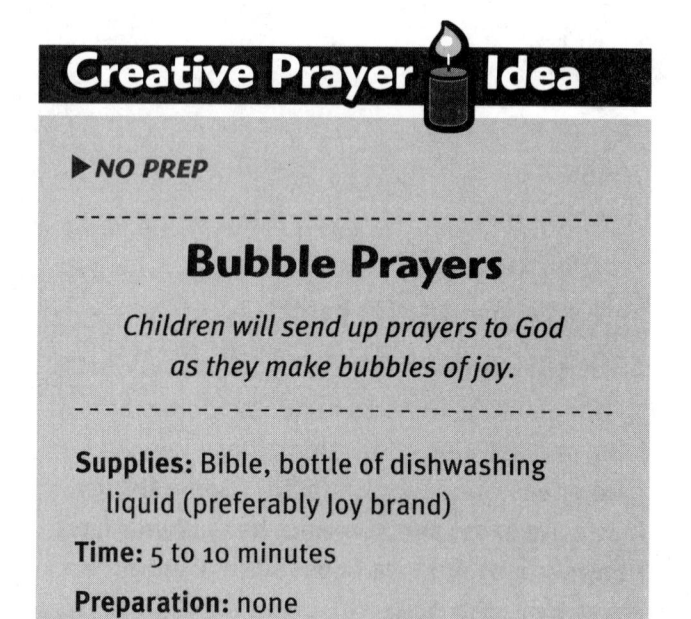

Creative Prayer Idea

▶*NO PREP*

Bubble Prayers

Children will send up prayers to God as they make bubbles of joy.

Supplies: Bible, bottle of dishwashing liquid (preferably Joy brand)

Time: 5 to 10 minutes

Preparation: none

Read aloud John 15:11. Tell kids that God has given us all much to be joyful about, and you're going to lead them in joyful prayers to thank God for all those blessings.

Gently tip the bottle of Joy liquid detergent upside down, and then upright again. Open the cap, and quickly squeeze the bottle to make a bubble float out. As the bubble floats, offer thanks to God for something joyful he's brought into your life. Then give each child a chance to squeeze a bubble and say a quick prayer of thanks to God for the joy he gives us.

Snack

▶*NO PREP*

▶*ALLERGY ALERT*

Joy Inside

Children will create a snack that reminds them why they should be joyful.

Supplies: mini pretzel twists, jumbo marshmallows

Time: about 5 minutes

Preparation: none

Give the kids two or three pretzels each, and challenge them to nibble out the center of the pretzel, leaving just the outer, heart-shaped section. After the kids have created their pretzel hearts, ASK:

- **What are some things that steal your joy?**
- **How does it make you feel when you don't have any joy?**

SAY: **Sometimes things in life try to steal our joy, but God wants us to be filled with joy. These pretzels remind me of how our hearts feel empty without any joy.** Read aloud John 15:11. ASK:

- **What are some things that give us joy?**
- **How does it make you feel when you're filled with joy?**

Hand out a jumbo marshmallow to each child, and have the kids stuff the marshmallows into their heart-shaped pretzels. Hold one up as an example and SAY: **When God gives us joy, our hearts are filled with joy!** Have the kids repeat after you, "God fills my heart with joy!" and then have them pop the pretzels into their mouths.

Worship Prompt Idea

▶ *NO PREP*

Rhythms of Joy

Children will learn a rhyme that reminds them that God gives joy.

Supplies: Bible; 7 sheets of construction paper, each with a letter of the word *promise* written on it boldly

Time: 5 to 10 minutes

Preparation: none

Hand each of seven kids a letter sheet, and have these Card Kids stand in front of the group.

SAY: **Let's praise God with some rhythm and rhyme! We'll shout out the words to a rhyme about one of God's good promises: that ▷ GOD GIVES US JOY. As we spell out the word *promise,* the Card Kids will hold out the letters. The rest of us will provide the rhythm and say the rhyme.**

Teach the kids the following rhyme:

P-R-O-M-I-S-E!

God gives joy to you and me!

P-R-O-M-I-S-E!

The Lord's joy will set us free!

SAY: **Now let's start dropping letters. When we repeat the rhyme, clap instead of saying the letter P. The next time through, we'll clap on P and R. We'll keep going until we've clapped out the word *promise* without saying a letter.** When you've finished, have a volunteer read aloud Genesis 21:1-7.

ASK:

- **Why did Sarah doubt God's promise at first?**
- **Do you think Sarah ever doubted God again? Why or why not?**

SAY: **When God makes a promise, he always keeps it!** Have another volunteer read aloud John 15:11. God promises to gives us joy! Have the kids repeat the rhyme again.

Preschool Story

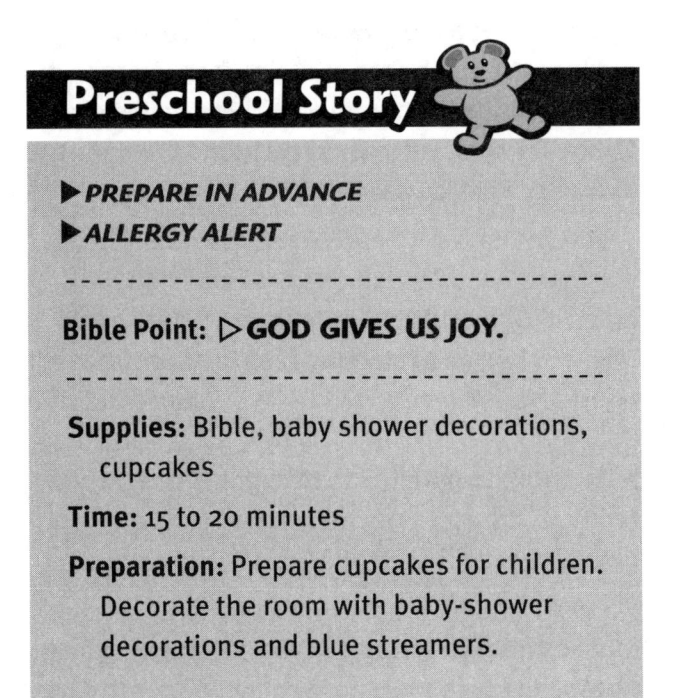

▶ *PREPARE IN ADVANCE*
▶ *ALLERGY ALERT*

Bible Point: ▷ **GOD GIVES US JOY.**

Supplies: Bible, baby shower decorations, cupcakes

Time: 15 to 20 minutes

Preparation: Prepare cupcakes for children. Decorate the room with baby-shower decorations and blue streamers.

A Shower of Joy!

Have children form a circle and sit down. Open your Bible to Genesis 21, and show children the words. SAY: **Look at all these fun decorations! I wonder what they're for? Let's listen to our story to find out.**

Abraham was very old—much older than any of your grandpas. His wife, Sarah, was very old, too. For years and years, they had wanted a baby more than anything, but now they were way too old. No one had babies when they were as old as Abraham and Sarah. God knew they wanted to have a baby, and he wanted to bless them with a baby. Have children cradle their arms as you sing "Rock-a-Bye, Baby."

One day some visitors from far away came to talk to Abraham. Abraham and Sarah lived far away from people and didn't get very many visitors. Abraham noticed that the three

visitors looked very important, so he bowed to them (have children stand up, bow, and then sit down) **and asked Sarah to make a big feast especially for them.** Have children stand, pretend to stir, and then sit down.

Sarah stayed inside their tent-house to prepare the meal. One of the visitors from God said Abraham and Sarah would have a baby of their very own! Have children cradle their arms and sing "Rock-a-Bye, Baby."

But in the tent, Sarah was listening. (Have kids put a hand behind one ear and listen quietly.) **She couldn't believe what she heard! She laughed and thought, *I could never have a baby now. I'm way too old!*** Have children cradle their arms and sing "Rock-a-Bye, Baby," and then SAY: **Sarah laughed. She thought it was very funny to think that an old woman would have a baby.** Let each of the children take turns making their funniest laugh.

One of the visitors heard Sarah laughing and wanted to know why she laughed. After all, God could do that. Didn't she believe him? Sarah realized that she had been caught listening, and she was afraid. Instead of telling the truth, she lied and said she hadn't laughed. But God knew. The visitor told her that nothing is too hard for God to do. Just wait and see! Have children cradle their arms and sing "Rock-a-Bye, Baby."

A whole year went by, and guess what! Sarah did have a baby—a baby boy. Abraham and Sarah named this wonderful surprise of a baby *Isaac*, which means "laughter." Baby Isaac brought laughter to his mom and dad and to all who saw him. Have children laugh all at once, and then SAY: **God gave Abraham and Sarah joy, and ▷GOD GIVES US JOY, too! Nothing is impossible for God.**

Now I know what these decorations are for! They're for a baby shower! Bring out the cupcakes and SAY: **Here are some treats for us to eat while we celebrate the birth of Isaac and the joy God gave Abraham and Sarah.** As children enjoy their treats,

ASK:

- **How did God give Abraham and Sarah joy?**
- **When have you felt joy?**
- **How can you thank God for giving you joy?**

SAY: **Abraham and Sarah had to wait a very long time before Isaac was born, but God kept his promise and gave them a baby of their own. God gave them great joy, and ▷GOD GIVES US JOY, too!**

notes

BIBLE STORY

Abraham Tested

For the Leader

For parents the story of Abraham's faith in Genesis 22 can be rather unsettling. The mere thought of sacrificing one's child as an act of obedience can send a chill up the spine. Yet Abraham obeyed, never doubting for a second that God would somehow spare his beloved son, or even raise him from the dead.

For kids this story might also be a little frightening. How far does God want us to go to obey him? Will God ever ask me to make that kind of sacrifice? These activities will help children understand that God loves them and wants only the best for them. And they'll experience God's best when they obey him.

Key Scriptures

Genesis 22:1-19

Deuteronomy 5:10

Hebrews 12:1-3

Bible Verse

"But I lavish unfailing love for a thousand generations on those who love me and obey my commands" (Deuteronomy 5:10).

Bible Experience

▶ *NO PREP*

Bible Point: ▷ **OUR OBEYING GOD GIVES GOD JOY.**

Children will understand that their obedience to God always pleases him.

Supplies: Bible, several colored index cards for each child, markers

Time: 10 to 15 minutes

Preparation: none

As you read the story from Genesis 22, you'll be asking questions about feelings. Each time you ask a question about feelings, have each child write a specific feeling on his or her card and hold it up to show you.

SAY: **In today's story God asked Abraham to do a very hard thing, something Abraham couldn't understand. As we read the story from the Bible, imagine what Abraham and Isaac must have been feeling.** Read Genesis 22:1-2, and then ASK:

◆ **How do you think Abraham felt?**

Make sure the kids write their responses on a card. Then read verses 3-8.

ASK:

◆ **Isaac wasn't a little child anymore. How do you think he felt?**

Read verses 9-10. Ask how Abraham felt, and then how Isaac felt.

Read verses 11-13, and ask how Abraham and Isaac felt then.

Read verses 14-18, and ask how Abraham and Isaac felt. Then ASK:

- **How do you think God felt after Abraham obeyed him?**

Have kids write their answers on their cards.
SAY: **God was very pleased with Abraham for having faith and obeying God, even though it was very hard.** Read aloud Deuteronomy 5:10.
▷ **OUR OBEYING GOD GIVES GOD JOY! All the feelings we experience when we obey God can be very different, just like with Abraham. Sometimes we're unsure, sometimes we're confident, and sometimes we're really scared. But our obeying God always makes God happy.**

Have kids bring their cards to the center of the room. Together, have everyone use all the cards to spell out the word *joy* on the floor. Then join hands around the cards and pray that God will give kids strength to obey.

Additional Topics List

This lesson can be used to help children discover...Faith, God's Love, God's Promises, Obedience, and Sacrifice.

n
o
t
e
s

Game

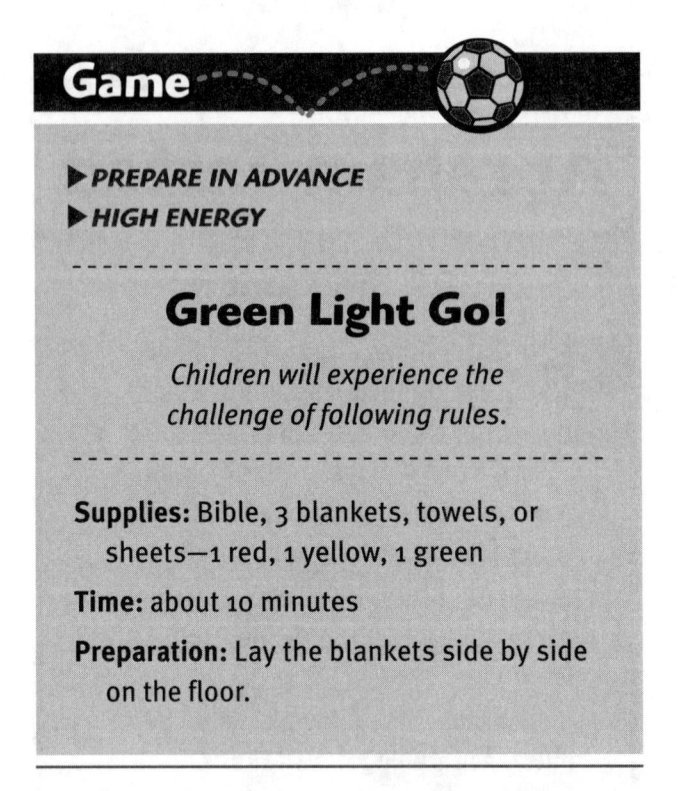

▶ *PREPARE IN ADVANCE*
▶ *HIGH ENERGY*

Green Light Go!

Children will experience the challenge of following rules.

Supplies: Bible, 3 blankets, towels, or sheets—1 red, 1 yellow, 1 green

Time: about 10 minutes

Preparation: Lay the blankets side by side on the floor.

Tell kids the colors represent a traffic light. Have all the children stand on the yellow (middle) blanket. When you shout out another color, have kids quickly move to the appropriate blanket. The last child to get both feet on the correct blanket is eliminated from the game.

To make the game more challenging, occasionally call out the color on which the children are already standing. Anyone who steps off the blanket is eliminated. For a change of pace, call out "traffic accident" and have everyone vacate all blankets. The last child to get off is eliminated.

Keep the pace quick, and vary the colors called. The winner is the last person to remain in the traffic light. Play several rounds if time allows.

SAY: **We often don't like to obey rules, especially other people's rules!** Read aloud Deuteronomy 5:10.

ASK:

- **What's a rule you have to obey as a kid? Why?**
- **What's one of God's rules that you want to obey? Why?**

- **Why do you think it makes God happy when we obey him?**
- **What's a rule you don't like to obey that you'll obey this week?**

Craft

▶ ***PREPARE IN ADVANCE***

Heroes Who Obey

Children will consider the examples of Bible heroes who obeyed God.

Supplies: Bible, shiny white fabric, scissors, 1-inch square sponges, newspapers, shallow bowls of black tempera paint, tape, fine-tipped markers, straws

Time: about 15 minutes

Preparation: Create a sample of the craft to show children. Cut the white fabric to 5x9-inch rectangles. Cut sponges to make 1-inch squares. Cover the workspace with newspapers, and then set out shallow bowls of black paint.

Have kids put tape around the edges of fabric to keep it from fraying. Stamp black squares on the fabric to make a checkered flag. As the flags dry, read aloud Genesis 22:1-19.

ASK:

- **What are some things that are hard for you to do?**
- **What does God think when you do the right things even though they're hard?**

SAY: **We're servants of God, just like Abraham was. God wants us to obey him, just like the heroes in the Bible did. And just like Abraham, God wants us to go all the way and finish the race.**

Read aloud Hebrews 12:1-3. Have kids write the names of obedient heroes from the Bible on the white spaces of their checkered flags. Roll a straw into the edge of one side of the fabric, and tape it closed.

Bible Experience

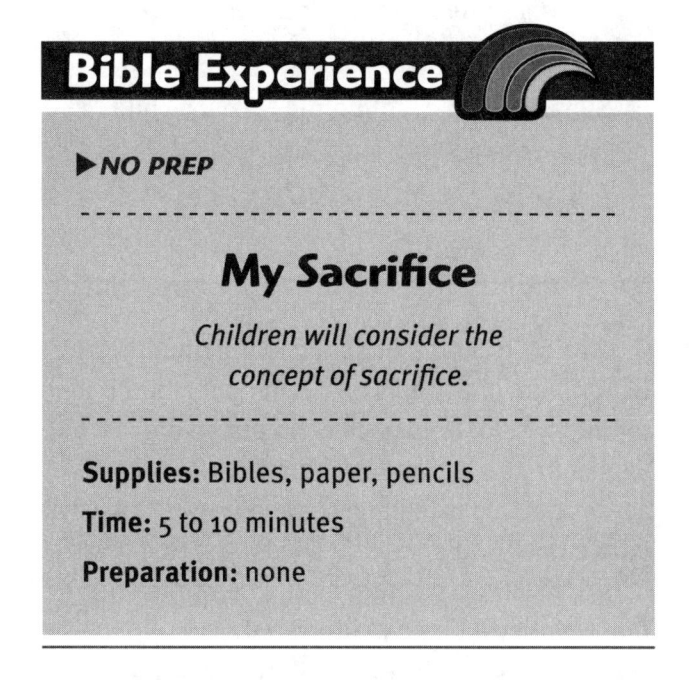

▶ ***NO PREP***

My Sacrifice

Children will consider the concept of sacrifice.

Supplies: Bibles, paper, pencils

Time: 5 to 10 minutes

Preparation: none

Hand out paper and pencils. In trios, have kids read Genesis 22:1-19 and then share something that would be hard for them to give to God. That something might be a possession, a hobby or sport, an activity, an emotion, or a person. Have kids write what they shared on a piece of paper. Place a chair or table at one end of the room.

SAY: **God may never ask you to give up the one thing that's most important to you. But if you really trust God and want to follow him, you need to be willing to give your precious thing to him—just as Abraham was willing to give up Isaac. This chair is like an altar to God. Let's put our papers on the chair as a symbol of turning over our treasures to God.**

Have kids silently and prayerfully lay their papers on the chair.

Creative Prayer Idea

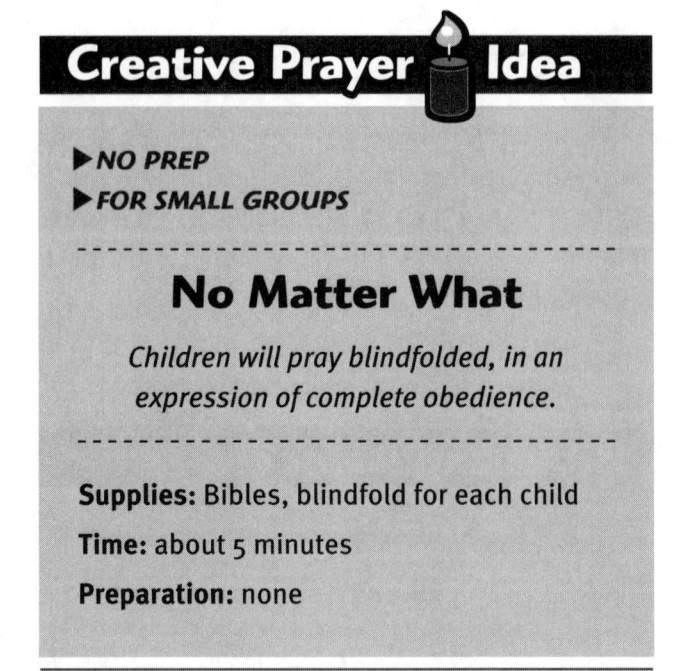

▶ *NO PREP*
▶ *FOR SMALL GROUPS*

No Matter What

Children will pray blindfolded, in an expression of complete obedience.

Supplies: Bibles, blindfold for each child

Time: about 5 minutes

Preparation: none

Give each child a Bible. Read together the story of Abraham in Genesis 22. Then read aloud Deuteronomy 5:10. Help each child put on a blindfold. Explain that, just like Abraham, we can't always see where God is leading us, and we don't always understand God's ways. Tell kids that God loves us and always takes care of us—he wants only that we obey him, no matter what.

SAY: **With your Bibles in your laps and blindfolds on, pray together, either one by one or silently, that God will help you all obey—no matter what.**

notes

Movie Clip

Whom Do You Trust?

Movie Title: *Peter Pan* (1953) (not rated)

Start Time: 1 hour, 2 minutes, 35 seconds

Where to Begin: The pirates are dancing in a circle around the Lost Boys and Wendy, who are tied up.

Where to End: Captain Hook mocks Wendy when she says that Peter Pan will save them.

Plot: Captain Hook has captured the Lost Boys and ordered them to become pirates or walk the plank. Wendy challenges the boys to hold fast and trust Peter Pan to help them.

Review: The Lost Boys were scared and in a bad situation. Wendy reminded them that they could trust Peter Pan to help. Abraham trusted God, even when he could have run away from his bad situation.

Discussion

After setting up and showing the clip, ASK:

◆ **How do you think the Lost Boys felt when Captain Hook captured them?**

◆ **Why would it have been hard for the Lost Boys and Wendy to trust Peter Pan to help them?**

Read aloud Genesis 22:1-19, and then SAY: **God wants us to trust him with everything we have and in everything we do. Abraham may have been scared or worried, but he knew he could trust God, even in a bad situation.**

ASK:

◆ **Why can we trust God?**

Object Lesson

▶ ***PREPARE IN ADVANCE***
▶ ***ALLERGY ALERT***

Don't Be a Dough-Dough

Children will make cookie dough to see how obedience brings joy.

Supplies: Bible, cookie recipe, ingredients for the cookies, measuring utensils, glass mixing bowl, mixing spoon, plastic bag, photocopy of the recipe card, batch of cookies already made

Time: 15 to 20 minutes

Preparation: Have all the ingredients and supplies ready and set out on a table so all the kids can see you. Have pre-made cookies ready to hand out.

Read aloud the story of Genesis 22:1-19, or tell the story in your own words. Then SAY: **When Abraham and Isaac got back from their experience on the mountain, they must have been hungry and tired. I'm feeling kind of hungry myself. Let's whip up a batch of cookies!**

Hand the copy of the recipe to a child, and ask him or her to read it to you. As the child reads the ingredients, intentionally ruin the cookies by ignoring the amounts given in the recipe, saying things like, "I really think it needs a lot more of this" and "We don't need *that* much." Try to make the dough as watery and messy as possible. Make sure all the kids can see your mess.

SAY: **Yuck! These cookies look horrible. Why did they turn out so badly?** Ask kids to give their opinions about why the cookie dough was ruined. Then SAY: **OK. I guess we'd better start over.**

Pour the ruined dough into a plastic bag. Ask for another student to read the recipe. This time have kids take turns carefully helping you measure and mix each ingredient. Set the dough aside. SAY: **There! That's better. This dough will make cookies that someone will enjoy, won't it?**

ASK:

- **Why is it important to follow the directions in recipes?**
- **How is following the directions in a recipe like following the directions God gives us in the Bible? How is it different?**
- **Why was it important for Abraham to follow God's directions, even if he didn't understand them?**

SAY: **We need to remember that God can see and understand many things we can't. God knew about the angel he would send to stop Abraham from sacrificing Isaac. Abraham didn't know about that, but he did know he could trust God. And God was happy with Abraham because he obeyed.**

Bring out the batch of cookies you already made and SAY: **When we obey God, it brings God joy. It's kind of like these cookies—when we follow the directions in the recipe, it will bring us joy.** Hand out the cookies and enjoy!

notes

Preschool Story

▶ *PREPARE IN ADVANCE*
▶ *ALLERGY ALERT*

Bible Point: ▷ **OUR OBEYING GOD GIVES GOD JOY.**

Supplies: Bible, cookies, toilet tissue rolls, chenille wires, cotton balls, glue sticks, googly eyes (optional)

Time: 15 to 20 minutes

Preparation: Cut toilet tissue rolls into 2-inch sections. You'll need one section for each child. You'll also need one chenille wire, cut in half, for each child.

A Hard Choice

Have all the children form a circle and sit down. Open your Bible to Genesis 22, and show children the words. Give each child a cookie. Tell children they can have one bite of their cookie right now. Let kids hold their cookies as you begin your story.

SAY: **Abraham was very happy when his son Isaac was born. But one day God told Abraham that he wanted Abraham to give Isaac back to God. Abraham didn't understand why God wanted Isaac back, but he knew it was important to obey God—no matter what.** Have children give you back their cookies. Place the cookies on a plate beside you for the rest of the story.

So Abraham took Isaac on a long walk up a mountain. They climbed and climbed and climbed that mountain. Have children stand up and pretend to climb a mountain.

Abraham planned to give Isaac back to God when they reached the top of the mountain. But just as Abraham was about to give Isaac back to God, God stopped him! God was pleased that Abraham was willing to obey God no matter what, so he told Abraham to give him a ram instead of giving Isaac. God even showed Abraham right where the ram was! Give children back their cookies, and let them eat the rest of the cookies.

Let's make a ram right now to remind us that God was pleased when Abraham chose to obey God. Give each child one section of a toilet tissue roll, one chenille wire cut in half, and several cotton balls. You'll also need glue sticks for children to share.

Show children how to bend and attach their chenille wires to the toilet roll to make legs for their ram. Then have them stick cotton balls to the tissue roll to make soft, furry rams. For extra fun, provide googly eyes for children to attach. As children work, ask them about times they've had to obey their parents or teachers.

ASK:

◆ **How did Abraham obey God?**

◆ **Have you ever had to obey your parents or teachers even when you didn't want to?**

SAY: **Sometimes it's hard to obey our parents and teachers, but when we obey them, we're also obeying God, and ▷ OUR OBEYING GOD GIVES GOD JOY.**

BIBLE STORY

Jacob and Esau

For the Leader

This Bible story takes the phrase *sibling rivalry* to a new level. Isaac and Rebekah knew, even before their twin sons, Esau and Jacob, were born, that they were going to be trouble. They wrestled in Rebekah's womb, and Jacob had Esau by the ankle when they were born. Even though God had a grand plan for Jacob and his heirs, Jacob chose to do things his own way—with deception and lies. In fact, the name *Jacob* means "he deceives."

Kids are sometimes tempted to shade the truth and manipulate people to achieve their own goals. These activities show kids that lies always bring trouble in the end, while honesty and patience bring lasting rewards.

Key Scriptures

Genesis 25:19-34; 27:1-40
Exodus 23:1
Psalm 120:2
Proverbs 19:5
Zechariah 8:16
John 8:31-32
Romans 2:8
Ephesians 4:15, 25
1 Timothy 2:4
3 John 4

Bible Verse

"But this is what you must do: Tell the truth to each other. Render verdicts in your courts that are just and that lead to peace" (Zechariah 8:16).

Bible Experience

▶ ***NO PREP***

Bible Point: ▷ **GOD WANTS US TO TELL THE TRUTH.**

Children will act out a modern version of Jacob and Esau's trade and learn to make better choices.

Supplies: props for the skit (see next page)

Time: 10 to 15 minutes

Preparation: none

In this Bible experience, you'll engage children in the Bible story through a skit and debriefing questions that help children discover that ▷ **GOD WANTS US TO TELL THE TRUTH.**

Cast the following characters: Jessica, Blake, and Jared.

Esau Slurped the Soup

SCENE:
A boy makes an important choice at a lemonade stand.

PROPS:
You'll need a table, a table cloth, a napkin, two chairs, a pitcher, paper cups, and a bike.

Jessica: *(Sitting with Blake at lemonade stand)* Get your lemonade here!

Blake: Just 25 cents to cool off!

Jared: *(Comes up to the stand, pushing his bike.)* It sure is hot! *(Licks lips.)* I'd give anything for a glass of lemonade.

Jessica: All we're asking is a quarter.

Jared: You don't understand, Jessica. I just rode 10 blocks in 100-degree heat. I'm dying here. I'll pay you a quarter tomorrow, OK?

Jessica: You already owe me 75 cents!

Jared: How about you, Blake? How about giving me a break?

Blake: Sorry, Jared, if you want a glass of ice-cold lemonade, you're going to have to cut us a deal.

Jared: What kind of deal?

Blake: How about trading us something for our lemonade?

Jared: Man, I'm so thirsty. I'd give you everything I own for a sip!

Blake: Everything? How about just your bike?

Jared: *(Looks at bike, stunned.)* My ride?

Blake: You said you were willing to give us everything. And we've got freshly squeezed lemonade. Do you want some or not?

Jared: *(Eyes the lemonade greedily.)* It does sound tempting...

Jessica: Jared, you wouldn't trade us your new bike for a glass of lemonade, would you?

Jared: I don't know, Jessica. I'm so thirsty I might die!

Jessica: *(Shakes her head.)* Jared, you remind me of Esau.

Jared: Who?

Jessica: Let me show you. *(She removes the tablecloth from the table—taking care to not spill the pitcher or glasses—and drapes it over her head.)* It's like this. The Bible tells a story about twin brothers named Esau and Jacob. One day Jacob was cooking a pot of stew.

Jared: It's too hot for stew!

Jessica: Anyway *(kneels down and pretends to be stirring a big pot over a campfire),* Esau had been hunting all day and hadn't had a bite to eat.

Blake: I remember what happens. *(Grabs the napkin and holds it to his chin like a beard, and then acts out the part of Esau.)* Give me a bowl of that soup, Jacob—I'm starving!

Jessica: Sorry, Esau. You'll have to cook your own stew.

Blake: But I'm starving! If you give me a bowl, I'll give you everything I own!

Jessica: You'll give me all the money Dad is saving for you?

Blake: Quit fooling around, Jacob. I told you I was starving. I'll give you all you want—just give me that stew!

Jared: *(Interrupting)* That seems like a pretty silly thing for Esau to do.

Jessica: He was pretty silly, if you ask me. He gave up everything he owned for something he could have made himself.

Blake: Now about that bike, Jared.

Jared: No deal, Blake. I'm going home to make my own pitcher of lemonade.

SAY: **Great job, actors! Give yourselves a hand!**

Jacob did more than steal Esau's inheritance from their father. Later on, Jacob lied to his father to steal Esau's blessing, too. Jacob deceived Esau over and over. But ▷ GOD WANTS US TO TELL THE TRUTH. The Bible tells us in Zechariah 8:16, "Tell the truth to each other." Have the kids repeat the verse back to you, and then ASK:

- **Why would it have been foolish for Jared to trade his bike for lemonade?**
- **God had big things planned for Jacob, but Jacob tried to do things his own way. Why do you think that is?**
- **Esau later threatened to kill Jacob, so Jacob ran away and never saw his family again. What are other consequences of deceiving people?**

Song & Connect

Use "Do to Others" (track 7, *it: Innovative Tools for Children's Ministry: New Testament* CD) to help reinforce the Bible Point, ▷ **GOD WANTS US TO TELL THE TRUTH.**

Additional Topics List

This lesson can be used to help children discover... Consequences, Giving, Honesty, Jealousy, Selfishness, and Siblings.

Game

▶NO PREP

No Lie!

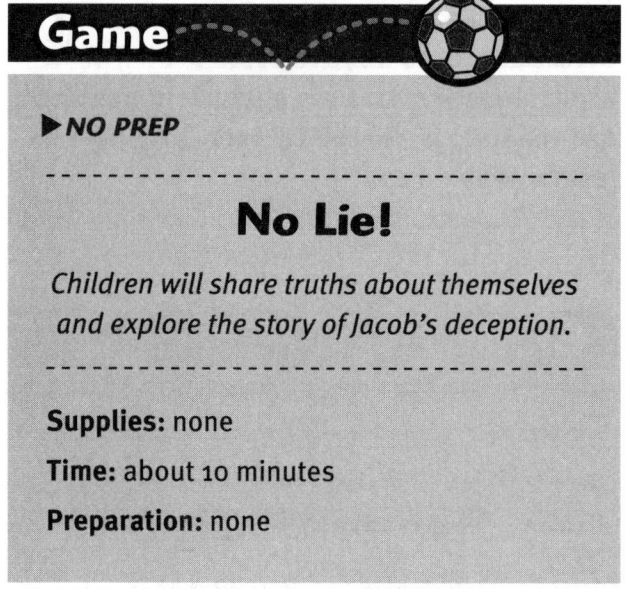

Children will share truths about themselves and explore the story of Jacob's deception.

Supplies: none

Time: about 10 minutes

Preparation: none

Gather kids into a circle and SAY: **Let's share some interesting facts about ourselves.** Explain to the kids that a fact is something that is true. **For example, I was born in** [name your birthplace]. Give students a moment to think of a fact they might share. Encourage them to pick something that others probably don't know.

Let's add a twist to our game. Have the students imagine an untruth—or lie—about themselves. **For example, I once visited** [name a destination to which you've never been]. When everyone is ready, take turns sharing facts and lies. As each person shares, allow the group to guess which statements are true and which are false.

When the game is finished, recount the story of Jacob from Genesis 25:27-34 and 27:1-40.

ASK:

- **How did you feel as you told the lie about yourself? Why?**
- **How could you tell whether someone was lying or telling the truth?**
- **What lies did Jacob tell his father about himself?**
- **Why did Jacob lie?**

SAY: **God wants us to tell the truth all the time. Sometimes we're tempted to bluff or lie about ourselves. Lies can get us into trouble. And the truth is, God and others appreciate us just the way we are.**

Craft

▶ *NO PREP*

Stop-or-Go Signs

Children will understand how to choose to tell the truth.

Supplies: Bible, red and green construction paper, safety scissors, glue sticks, craft sticks, black markers

Time: 10 to 15 minutes

Preparation: none

Have each child cut one circle from the red paper and one from the green paper; put them together to make sure they're the same size. Show children how to glue the two sheets together, placing the craft stick at the bottom as a handle. Then have kids write "STOP" on the red side and "GO" on the green side.

Read aloud the story of Jacob's tricking and deceiving Esau in Genesis 25 and 27. Let the children take turns naming situations in which they could choose to tell the truth or tell a lie. Let others respond with their signs to show which actions they would choose.

Bible Application

▶ *NO PREP*

The Truth and Nothing but the Truth

Children will look up Scriptures on truth and discuss ways to apply them.

Supplies: Bibles

Time: 15 to 20 minutes

Preparation: none

Read aloud the story of Jacob and Esau in Genesis 25:27-34 and 27:1-40. Ask children to form trios. Assign them each one of these Scriptures: Ephesians 4:25; Psalm 120:2; Proverbs 19:5; John 8:31-32; Zechariah 8:16; Exodus 23:1; Ephesians 4:15; Romans 2:8; 1 Timothy 2:4. Instruct kids to think of a brief, real-life situation that would force them to choose to lie or tell the truth. Then have each trio share their story with the group about what would happen if they lied and what would happen if they told the truth. Then have them read their assigned Scripture. Finally, SAY: **We don't have to tell lies to get blessings. The Bible is full of truths that will bless us if we just live them out!**

n
o
t
e
s

Creative Prayer Idea

▶ *NO PREP*
▶ *STUDENT LED*
▶ *ALLERGY ALERT*

Sour Lies, Sweet Truth

Children will pray to God, thanking him for his truth.

Supplies: Bible, lemon and orange wedges

Time: about 5 minutes

Preparation: none

Talk to the kids about truth and lies—lies are sour, but the truth is sweet. Read aloud Zechariah 8:16 and 3 John 4. Give each child a lemon wedge, and as they taste its bitterness, have them pray silently to ask God to forgive them for telling any lies. Then give each child an orange wedge, and as they taste its sweetness, have them pray silently to thank God for his truth.

Discussion Launcher Questions

Ask children to form trios and discuss:

◆ **Is it possible to be dishonest and truthful at the same time? Why or why not?**

◆ **Is it hard or easy to fool people into believing something that's not true? Why?**

◆ **Do you think God is sometimes fooled when we say things that aren't true? Why or why not?**

◆ **Why do you think God wants us to avoid telling lies?**

◆ **Even though God has a great plan for each of our lives, why do you think we still lie to try to make things better for ourselves?**

Movie Clip

Deceived

Movie Title: *Aladdin* (G)

Start Time: 1 hour, 9 minutes

Where to Begin: Aladdin says, "I've got to tell Jasmine the truth."

Where to End: Iago flies away with the lamp.

Plot: Iago, trying to steal the lamp from Aladdin, tricks Aladdin into thinking Jasmine is calling him.

Review: Use this scene to help kids understand that God wants us to do what's right, including tell the truth. Just as Iago pretended to be Jasmine to get the lamp from Aladdin, so Jacob pretended to be Esau to get Isaac's blessing. Jacob's actions were selfish and deceitful. God doesn't want us to lie to get something that belongs to someone else.

Discussion

After setting up and showing the clip, ASK:

◆ **How do you think Aladdin felt about having deceived Jasmine into thinking he was a prince?**

◆ **How do you think Iago felt about deceiving Aladdin into thinking he was Jasmine?**

◆ **Was either character doing the right thing? Why or why not?**

SAY: **God wants us to tell the truth. In the Bible are two brothers, Jacob and Esau. Esau was the firstborn son and, therefore, entitled to his father's blessing. Jacob deceived his father into giving him the blessing by pretending to be Esau. This hurt everyone involved. The Bible tells us in Zechariah 8:16, "Tell the truth to each other."**

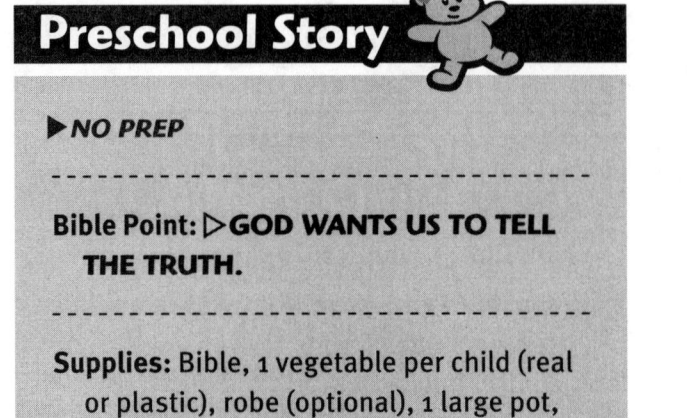

Preschool Story

▶ ***NO PREP***

Bible Point: ▷**GOD WANTS US TO TELL THE TRUTH.**

Supplies: Bible, 1 vegetable per child (real or plastic), robe (optional), 1 large pot, 1 large spoon, 3 towels, tape

Time: 15 to 20 minutes

Preparation: none

Truth Not Tricks

Have kids form a circle and sit down. Open your Bible to Genesis 25, and show children the words. Give a vegetable to each child. (Be sure the vegetables are too large for accidental swallowing.) If you have a Bible-times robe, put it on. Tell children that you will pretend to be a young man named Jacob.

SAY: **My name is Jacob. You know, ▷ GOD WANTS US TO TELL THE TRUTH. Let me tell you about a time I *didn't* tell the truth—it wasn't a very happy ending. You see, my dad, Isaac, told my brother, Esau, to go hunting for some meat to make a special stew for a celebration. Dad told us that it was time to give Esau his special family blessing. That meant that because Esau was the oldest son, he would get most of Dad's money and land and be in charge of the family.**

Mom and I didn't like that. Mom wanted the blessing for me. She came up with a plan to trick my dad into giving me the blessing instead.

Let me show you what happened. You can use your vegetables to help me make the stew. First, I set the pot on the fire. Place the pot on the floor and SAY: **When I point to you, bring your food and put it in the pot. Don't forget to stir the vegetables in the pot, and be careful of my fire!** Have the children come one at a time to put their vegetables in the pot and stir.

Smells yummy! Now I have to make Dad think that I'm my brother, Esau. Dad can't see very well, so he won't see my face. But if he touches me, he'll know I'm Jacob. Hmm. What can I do to feel and smell like Esau? Let's put fur on my arms and neck so that my skin will feel more like Esau's hairy skin. Have children wrap towels around your arms and neck. Secure the loose ends with tape.

I'm ready! Oh, good! My brother isn't back from hunting yet, so I'll take this stew in to my dad. Carry the pot of "stew" to a far corner of the room. Hold out a spoon of stew, and pretend to talk. Return to the children, looking sad.

I did a great job of tricking Dad. He really thought I was Esau! Dad gave me the family blessing, which included most of his money and land. When Esau came back, he was very angry! I made Dad sad when I lied to him. I made Esau so mad that he wanted to hurt me. I had to run away and stay away for a long time before I finally became sorry for my lie. I got what I wanted, but it didn't make me happy. And no one else was happy either. Children, always remember that ▷ GOD WANTS US TO TELL THE TRUTH.

ASK:

◆ **Have you ever told a lie? What happened?**

◆ **Why is it important to tell the truth?**

SAY: **Let's sing a song now to remind us that the truth is always best!**

Lead children in singing "Tell the Truth" to the tune of "If You're Happy and You Know It." Each time you sing the verse, have children repeat different sounds—such as clapping twice, stomping twice, or clacking their tongues twice—at the end of each line. Sing:

Oh, God is happy when we tell the truth.
(Clap hands twice.)

Oh, God is happy when we tell the truth.

God is happy when we're truthful; when we lie it makes him sad.

Oh, God is happy when we tell the truth.

notes

BIBLE STORY

Jacob and Rachel

For the Leader

God had made a promise to Abraham. He made the same promise to Abraham's son Isaac. Then God made the same promise to Isaac's son Jacob. But Jacob decided to rely on his own cleverness to ensure that God's promise would be fulfilled. As a result, he was sent away from his family and the land God had promised him. But even after all of Jacob's mistakes, God continued to help him, providing him with a job, wealth, and the love of his life.

God had a master plan for all three men, and he was true to his word to each of them. The same holds true for the children you're teaching. God has a plan for them, and he will always help them. Use these sessions to reassure kids that they can always count on God's help.

Key Scriptures

Genesis 28:10-22; 29:1-14

Psalm 111; 121:2

Matthew 7:7-8

Bible Verse

"My help comes from the LORD, who made heaven and earth" (Psalm 121:2).

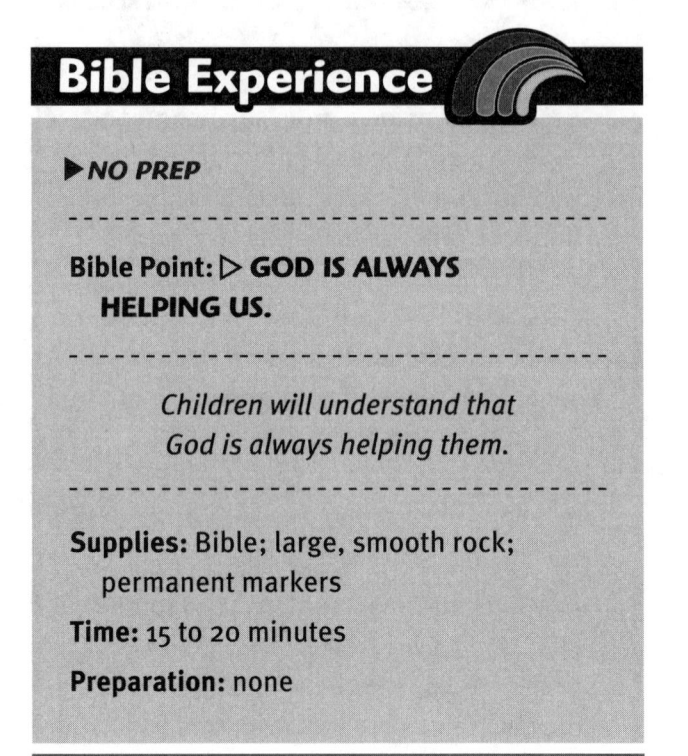

Bible Experience

▶ *NO PREP*

Bible Point: ▷ **GOD IS ALWAYS HELPING US.**

Children will understand that God is always helping them.

Supplies: Bible; large, smooth rock; permanent markers

Time: 15 to 20 minutes

Preparation: none

Place the large rock where all the kids can see it.

ASK:

◆ **Who thinks they can move this rock?**

Firmly place one of your feet on top of the rock, and allow one or two kids to try moving the rock by themselves. (They shouldn't be able to move it.) SAY: **I have a plan for someone to move this rock. But you'll need help to move this rock, and you can't move it until I'm ready for you to move it.**

ASK:

◆ **How many of you know that God has a plan for your life?**

Hold up the Bible to Genesis 28 and 29, and show kids the words. SAY: **God had big plans for Jacob's life. But instead of trusting God to let his plans work out, Jacob tried to make those plans work out his own way. He tricked his brother, Esau, out of his inheritance. Then later he tricked his father into giving him Esau's blessing. He made some big mistakes.**

ASK:

◆ **How many of you have ever made a mistake?**

SAY: **Because of Jacob's mistakes, he had to leave his family and even leave his country. He was an outcast! He left home with nothing but a walking stick. He walked and walked and walked until the sun went down. Then he found a rock for a pillow and lay down to sleep.**

Lie down on the floor, and rest your head on the rock. Pretend to sleep for a moment, and then SAY: **As Jacob slept, he dreamed of a stairway that went all the way to heaven. At the top of the stairway was God, and here's what God said.**

Have a child loudly read Genesis 28:13-15. Then SAY: **Jacob woke up and was amazed. He remembered that God was always helping him and had special plans for his life. So he took the stone he had used as a pillow and set it up as a memorial. He made a vow to God.** Read aloud Genesis 28:20-22.

ASK:

◆ **Even though Jacob had made mistakes, do you think God was still helping him?**

SAY: **Jacob kept walking and walking.** (Walk in place.) **He was headed for the faraway land of his uncle, whose name was Laban. He hoped to get a job with Laban and work on his ranch. When he got to the land, Jacob found a well where shepherds gave water to their sheep.** (Point to the rock.) **On top of the well was a rock that kept the water fresh. The shepherds had a custom of not moving the rock until all the sheep had come. Jacob couldn't wait to see if this was Laban's well. Soon a woman named**

Rachel arrived with the rest of the sheep, and Jacob was very excited.

ASK:

- **Does anyone know why Jacob was excited?**

SAY: **Jacob was excited for two reasons: First, Rachel was Laban's daughter, so he knew he had made it to his destination. Second, Rachel was beautiful, and Jacob immediately fell in love with her. Jacob rolled the rock away so she could water her sheep.** (Roll the rock over a little.) **Later, Laban gave Jacob a job, and Jacob married Rachel. Even though Jacob didn't always know it, God was always helping him.**

I told you I had a plan for this rock. Have three strong children help you carefully lift the rock onto a table. **No matter what we do or where we go, ▷ GOD IS ALWAYS HELPING US.**

Read aloud Psalm 121:2. SAY: **Just as Jacob used a stone to make a memorial of God's help, we're going to make this stone a memorial to remember how God helps us.** Have all the children come up to the table and write their names on the rock with the marker. Close in prayer, thanking God for always helping us.

Song & Connect

Use "God Is Our Help"(track 4, *it: Innovative Tools for Children's Ministry: Old Testament* CD) to help reinforce the Bible Point, ▷ **GOD IS ALWAYS HELPING US.**

Additional Topics List

This lesson can be used to help children discover... God's Plan, God's Provision, Friends, and Loneliness.

Game

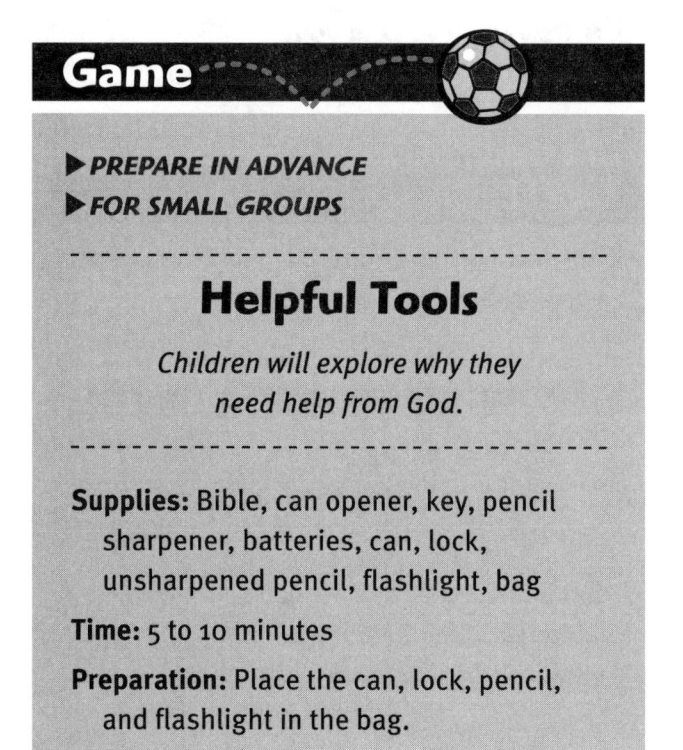

▶ *PREPARE IN ADVANCE*
▶ *FOR SMALL GROUPS*

Helpful Tools

Children will explore why they need help from God.

Supplies: Bible, can opener, key, pencil sharpener, batteries, can, lock, unsharpened pencil, flashlight, bag

Time: 5 to 10 minutes

Preparation: Place the can, lock, pencil, and flashlight in the bag.

Pass the can opener, key, pencil sharpener, and batteries to different children. SAY: **We're going to play a short game. I'd like one of you who isn't holding something to pull something out of the bag. Then find the person who has what you need to be able to use your item.** Ask a child to pull out one item and find the partner who is holding the tool he or she needs. ASK:

- **Why shouldn't you go to** [name a child who is holding the wrong tool] **to help you use your item?**

Proceed in the same way until all the objects are matched. ASK:

- **What's the message in this game?**

SAY: **When you need help, you go to the person who has the right tools to help you.**

Read aloud Psalm 121:2. **In this Psalm we learn that ▷ GOD IS ALWAYS HELPING US.**

ASK:

- **Can you give me some examples of people in the Bible whom God helped? How did he help him or her?**
- **How can God help you?**

Craft

▶ *NO PREP*

Bumper-Sticker Slogans

Children will think of catchy phrases that convey how God helps them.

Supplies: Bible, 4¼x11-inch sheets of construction paper, markers

Time: 10 to 15 minutes

Preparation: none

Have kids form pairs. Hand out construction paper and markers. Read aloud Psalm 121:2. SAY: **Work with your partner to write a bumper-sticker slogan that tells people how God helps you. You can use products you know about for inspiration, like your favorite cereal, soda, or commercial. Then write your slogan on your bumper sticker.**

After a few minutes, have kids display their bumper stickers. Then have kids discuss the following questions with their partners:

- **What do these bumper-sticker slogans tell you about God?**
- **How do these slogans help you to understand God better?**

Snack

▶ *NO PREP*

▶ *ALLERGY ALERT*

Take Good Care

Children will experience what it's like to take care of something and think about how God helps them.

Supplies: individually wrapped chocolate mints for each child, markers

Time: 5 to 10 minutes

Preparation: none

Give each child a wrapped chocolate mint and a marker. Ask kids to gently draw faces on their wrappers. SAY: **Psalm 121:2 talks about God as our ultimate helper. He takes care of us through thick and thin. Your challenge this week is to take care of this mint the way God takes care of us.**

ASK:

- **What are some ways God helps us?**
- **What are some things you could do this week that would show that you were a good helper for this mint?**

SAY: **Every time you look at this mint this week, remember that ▷ GOD IS ALWAYS HELPING US, no matter where we go.**

If possible, be sure to ask how kids did with their challenges and how God helped them during the week.

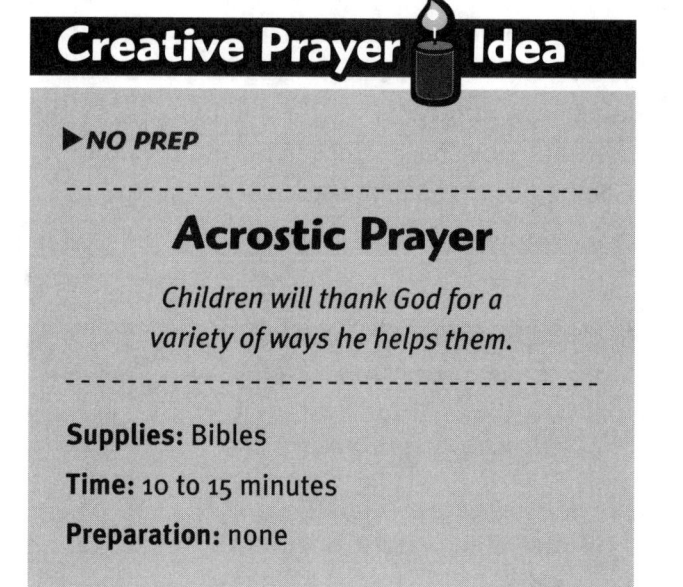

Creative Prayer Idea

▶ *NO PREP*

Acrostic Prayer

Children will thank God for a variety of ways he helps them.

Supplies: Bibles

Time: 10 to 15 minutes

Preparation: none

Psalm 111 is an acrostic, which means that the lines of the psalm begin with successive letters of the Hebrew alphabet. Have children read Psalm 111 aloud with you. Then ASK:

- **In what ways has God helped us?**
- **How does God help us in ways we can't see?**
- **How can we thank God for helping us so much?**

Create a litany of thanks for the ways God helps us. Assign a letter of the alphabet to each child. You may want to assign more than one letter to some children, and you may need to offer suggestions for letters like Q and X. Have children think of things God can help them with that begin with the letters they've been assigned. For example, someone might say "homework" for H. Write down kids' suggestions as they list them.

After all the letters have been listed, read aloud the following litany, having children name how God has helped them as indicated.

LEADER: **God who helps us, we thank you for helping us with** [items A, B, C, D, and E]. **We praise your name.**

CHILDREN: God helps us! *(Raise arms high.)*

LEADER: **For** [items F, G, H, I, and J], **we praise your name.**

CHILDREN: God helps us! *(Raise arms high.)*

LEADER: **For** [items K, L, M, N, and O], **we praise your name.**

CHILDREN: God helps us! *(Raise arms high.)*

LEADER: **For** [items P, Q, R, S, and T], **we praise your name.**

CHILDREN: God helps us! *(Raise arms high.)*

LEADER: **For** [items U, V, W, X, Y, and Z], **we praise your name.**

CHILDREN: God helps us! *(Raise arms high.)* Amen!

Discussion Launcher Questions

Ask children to form trios and discuss:

- **What kinds of things can you do only if someone helps you?**
- **What kinds of things can you do only if God helps you?**
- **Why do you think it's hard sometimes to let God help us?**
- **Describe a time God helped you. How did that feel?**

Snack

▶ *ALLERGY ALERT*

▶ *NO PREP*

Ask and You'll Receive

Children will see that if they need God's help, they need only ask.

Supplies: Bible, snacks for all the kids (like pretzels or cookies)

Time: 5 to 10 minutes

Preparation: none

Before class, place the snacks in a prominent place, but do not refer to them. Have the children stand shoulder to shoulder at one end of the room while you stand at the other end. Play a game of "Father, May I?" with the children, giving them permission to take baby steps, giant steps, scissors steps, bunny steps, crab steps, or bear steps.

After the game, have children sit in a circle with you.

ASK:

- **When were you allowed to move during this game?**
- **Why did some of you have to go back to the starting line?**

As children answer your questions, help yourself to small portions of the snack. If any of the kids ask to share the snack, offer them a portion without making a comment. Offer the snack to anyone who asks. Then read aloud Psalm 121:2 and Matthew 7:7-8.

ASK:

- **What does the Bible say happens to those who ask for God's help?**

SAY: **I brought this snack today for all of us to share. I've just been waiting for you to ask. Is anyone hungry?** When the children ask, freely distribute the snack. Close in prayer, thanking God for always helping us.

Preschool Story

▶ *PREPARE IN ADVANCE*

Bible Point: ▷ GOD IS ALWAYS HELPING US.

Supplies: Bible, boy doll, building blocks, flashlight or nightlight

Time: 15 to 20 minutes

Preparation: Use the blocks to build a staircase in one part of the room. You will also need several extra blocks for kids to use during the story.

God's Help

Have kids form a circle and sit down. Open your Bible to Genesis 29, and show children the words.

Hold up the boy doll, and tell children that the doll is Jacob. SAY: **Jacob tricked his brother, Esau, so Jacob had to leave his home and move far away. Even though Jacob had done something wrong when he tricked his brother, God still loved Jacob and took care of him.**

Jacob left his home and his family, and he walked all day. Encourage children to stand up and march around the room. Be sure to stop near the block staircase. **When the sun had set and it was dark outside, Jacob stopped to sleep for the night.** Turn out the lights in the classroom.

(Be sure to have a nightlight or flashlight for kids who might be afraid.) **He used a stone for a pillow, and he lay down on the sand.** Encourage kids to lie down, and then SAY: **While he was sleeping, Jacob had a dream. He dreamed about a stairway that started on earth and went all the way up to heaven.** Shine the flashlight on the block staircase you built before class. **There were angels on the stairway, and they were going up and down the stairs. Jacob looked up and saw the Lord standing at the very top of the stairway. The Lord said** (stand up and begin to talk in a very loud, deep voice):

I am the Lord, the God of your grandfather and your father. I will give this land to you and to all of your children and your children's children. You will have as many people in your family as there are specks of dust on the earth. Your family will grow and spread out in all directions—to the east and the west, the north and the south. I will bless everyone in the world through your family. I am with you and will watch over you no matter where you go. And I will bring you back to this land. I won't leave you until I've done what I promised.

Sit back down and begin speaking in a normal voice again. SAY: **After that, Jacob woke up from his dream. He was so excited about the things God had said to him that he built a pillar for God and promised God that he would always believe in God and always give God part of everything he had. Jacob knew that ▷ GOD IS ALWAYS HELPING US.**

Have kids sit up and gather in a circle. Give each child a block. Encourage children to name one way God has helped them and then place their blocks in the center of the circle. Tell kids that Jacob built a pillar so he would remember the ways God had helped him. Remind children that **▷ GOD IS ALWAYS HELPING US, too.**

SAY: **The next day Jacob began walking again, and God led Jacob to a man named Laban, who was Jacob's uncle. Laban asked Jacob to come and live with his family. That was good news for Jacob—God had given him a new family to live with! God was helping Jacob.**

Jacob stayed with Laban and his family for 14 years. He worked hard for Laban, and God helped Jacob while he was with Laban. Jacob married Laban's daughter Rachel, and Jacob started his own family. God was helping Jacob, and ▷ GOD IS ALWAYS HELPING US, too.

ASK:

- **How did God help Jacob?**
- **How has God helped you in the past?**
- **How can you trust God to help you in the future?**

SAY: **Even though Jacob had done something wrong when he tricked his brother Esau, God still loved Jacob and helped him. ▷ GOD IS ALWAYS HELPING US, too.**

notes

BIBLE STORY

Joseph's Dreams

For the Leader

We don't know for sure if Joseph's coat was actually Technicolor, but we do know it caused quite an amazing stir. Joseph was only 17 years old, and he was his father's most beloved son. God had given him some remarkable dreams, and the naive Joseph couldn't help remarking about them.

This part of the story reveals that God had long-term plans for Joseph and his family, just as he'd had for Abraham, Isaac, and Joseph's father, Jacob. Joseph's brothers didn't know Joseph was giving them a glimpse of the future, so they became angry and hateful toward him.

Kids need to learn and remember that families need to show love to each other at all times, no matter what the circumstances. We never know what God is doing in each other's lives, and we never know what's in store for us in the future. But we do know that God commands us to love one another.

Key Scriptures

Genesis 37:1-11

Romans 12:10

2 John 5-6

Bible Verse

"Love each other with genuine affection, and take delight in honoring each other" (Romans 12:10).

Bible Experience

▶ ***NO PREP***

Bible Point: ▷ **FAMILIES NEED TO SHOW LOVE.**

Children will be reminded to show love to their families.

Supplies: Bible, whiteboard and marker or chalkboard and chalk

Time: 10 to 15 minutes

Preparation: none

Read aloud Genesis 37:1-11. SAY: **Joseph had a dream that one day his brothers and whole family would bow down to him. Joseph was telling his brothers that he would become more important than them. His brothers didn't like that; in fact, they hated him for it. But that's not the way God wants families to treat each other. ▷ FAMILIES NEED TO SHOW LOVE to each other. The brothers didn't understand that the dream was a way of showing the plans God had for Joseph and his family.**

Ask kids to tell you what chores they do, what chores their brothers or sisters do, and things their parents do. Make three columns on the whiteboard or chalkboard—one column titled "My Chores," another column titled "My Brothers' and

Sisters' Chores," and the last one labeled "My Parents' Chores."

After listing all the chores, SAY: **A modern-day story of Joseph telling his dreams might go like this: "Hey family. I had a dream that all of you had to do my chores as well as your chores!"** Draw a big X through the "My Chores" column. Draw big arrows from the "My Chores" column to the other ones.

ASK:

- **How would you feel if a brother or sister told you this?**
- **How do you think the brothers felt when Joseph told them his dreams?**

SAY: **In a family, sometimes bad feelings happen. But ▷ FAMILIES NEED TO SHOW LOVE to each other.**

Song & Connect

Use "Brotherly Love" (track 11, *it: Innovative Tools for Children's Ministry: New Testament* CD) to help reinforce the Bible Point, **▷ FAMILIES NEED TO SHOW LOVE.**

Additional Topics List

This lesson can be used to help children discover... Anger, Dreams, Family, Guidance, Judging Others, and Love.

Game

▶ ***NO PREP***

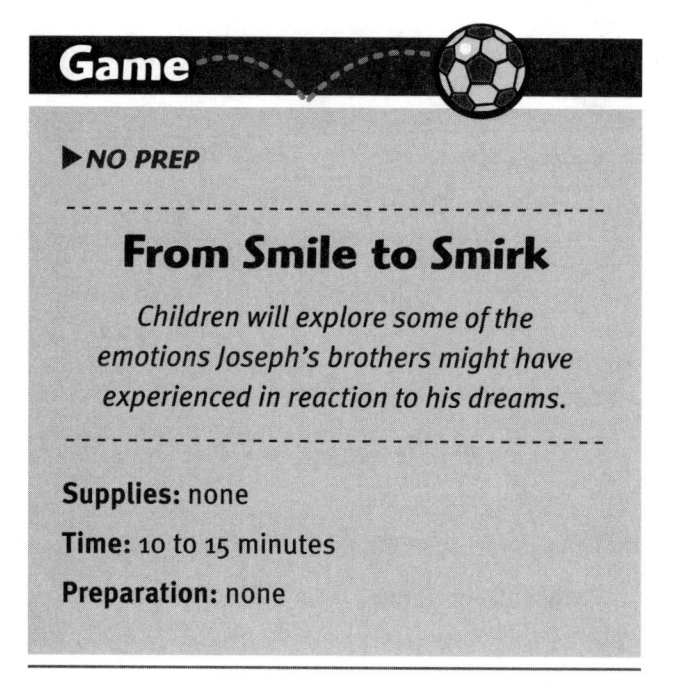

From Smile to Smirk

Children will explore some of the emotions Joseph's brothers might have experienced in reaction to his dreams.

Supplies: none

Time: 10 to 15 minutes

Preparation: none

Have students form a circle. Their goal is to keep frowns on their faces while, one by one, chosen students come up to them and say, "Listen to this dream I had. I dreamed that..." The student in the middle must finish the sentence and use only his or her voice to try to draw out the desired smile. If the "target" student smiles, then the two students trade places. If there's no smile after 30 seconds, the student must move on to tell another student about a different dream. The game ends when all have had a chance at both Frowner and Dream-Teller or when time runs out.

After playing the game, have kids sit down in groups of three and discuss:

- **Joseph's brothers weren't very happy about his dreams; how do you react when people tell you their dreams?**
- **What was the funniest dream you ever had?**
- **Have you ever had a dream come true? Tell about it.**
- **Joseph's brothers were angry and jealous of Joseph; how can you love your family when you're angry with them?**

Craft

▶ *NO PREP*

Walk in Love

Children will think about what it means to love their families.

Supplies: Bible, markers, paper grocery bags, safety scissors

Time: 10 to 15 minutes

Preparation: none

Tell kids the story of Joseph in Genesis 37:1-11. Then read aloud 2 John 5-6. SAY: **God wants us to walk in love, especially with our families.**

ASK:

- **What does it mean to walk in love?**
- **Why does God want us to do those things?**

Give each child a marker and a paper grocery bag. Tell kids to put their feet on the paper, trace around them, and then cut out the footprints.

Form groups of no more than five. SAY: **On each footprint, write ways you can love your family.** When each child has finished writing, have each group lay its footprints out to form a trail.

Take turns walking along your group's trail of love. Read and think about each action of love as you step on it. Allow kids to take home their footprints as a reminder that ▷ **FAMILIES NEED TO SHOW LOVE.**

Bible Application

▶ *PREPARE IN ADVANCE*

Love Your Family

Children will learn how to love God and their family as they love themselves.

Supplies: Bibles, construction paper, pink and yellow sticky notes, pens

Time: 10 to 15 minutes

Preparation: Make a large construction-paper cross to hang on one wall of your classroom. Hang the cross so the crossbeam is within kids' reach.

Ask a volunteer to read aloud Genesis 37:1-11. Have another volunteer read aloud Romans 12:10. SAY: **Sometimes it can be hard to love our families, just like it was hard for Joseph's brothers to love him.**

ASK:

- **How can we love God?**
- **How can we love our families?**

SAY: **Let's think of specific actions we can do to obey God's command to love God and love our families.**

Have kids brainstorm about how to love God and their families. Write each of their ideas for loving God on a pink sticky note. Write each of their ideas for loving their families on a yellow sticky note. Attach the pink notes to the vertical beam of the cross and the yellow notes to the horizontal beam of the cross. Give kids pens, and have them write their names on the actions they'd like to try during the coming week. Leave the cross up for a few weeks. When children finish a task, they can initial and date the actions beside their names.

Creative Prayer Idea

▶ *PREPARE IN ADVANCE*

Sweet Hearts

Children will pray and focus on the love their families share.

Supplies: Bible, red finger gelatin, heart-shaped cookie cutter, napkins

Time: about 10 minutes

Preparation: Prepare the finger gelatin, and cut it into heart shapes.

Gather children into a circle. Read aloud Genesis 37:1-11. ASK:

- **Why were Joseph's brothers angry with him?**
- **If you had been one of Joseph's brothers, would you have been jealous of him? Why or why not?**
- **Have you ever been jealous of someone? Explain.**

SAY: **Sometimes things don't seem fair in our families, and sometimes we wonder if our brothers and sisters are loved more than we are. But God wants family members to show love to each other. We're all part of God's family, and God loves each of us.**

ASK:

- **How can you show the people in your family that you love them?**

Hand each child a gelatin heart on a napkin. SAY: **Let's go around the circle and say the names of the people in your families. As you peek through your gelatin heart, say their names and end by saying, "I love you."** Close in prayer, thanking God for our families.

Movie Clip

Mine, All Mine

Movie Title: *Cinderella* (1950) (not rated)

Start Time: 40 minutes, 52 seconds

Where to Begin: Cinderella yells, "Wait! Please wait for me!" as she comes down the steps in her new dress.

Where to End: Cinderella runs out of the house and collapses on a bench.

Plot: Cinderella's jealous stepsisters take back their discarded items from the dress Cinderella was planning to wear to the ball. The stepmother takes her daughters and leaves Cinderella in a mess.

Review: Jealousy can cause us to look at people in a negative way, just as Cinderella's family looked at her. The same thing happened to Joseph when his brothers became jealous of him.

Discussion

After setting up and showing the clip, ASK:

- **How do you think Cinderella felt?**

Read aloud Genesis 37:1-11. SAY: **Joseph may have felt as Cinderella did. Joseph's older brothers didn't like Joseph or the attention he got from his father. They didn't show Joseph love; they were only worried about themselves.**

God says ▷ FAMILIES NEED TO SHOW LOVE. Jealousy and anger keep us thinking only about ourselves.

ASK:

- **How can we show our families that we love them?**

Worship Prompt Idea

▶*NO PREP*
▶*HIGH ENERGY*

Special Messages

Supplies: Bible
Time: 5 to 10 minutes
Preparation: none

Form two groups: Group A and Group B. Ask each group to huddle, explaining that each will soon receive a special message from Jesus.

In a whisper, say to Group A: **Your message is: "Love God with all your heart." Now whisper it back to me. Pause. Keep practicing your message until we begin.**

Go to Group B and whisper: **Your message is: "Love your families as yourself." Whisper the message back to me.** Pause. **Keep practicing your message until we begin.**

After a few moments, have both groups stand, facing each other, about 7 feet apart. SAY: **Group A, tell Group B your message.** Pause for Group A to repeat its message, and then SAY: **Now, Group B, tell Group A your message.** Go back and forth, repeating the messages and getting a little louder with each round. Continue until each group ends with one last, rousing retort.

Have the kids sit down to rest their voices. SAY: **You remembered your special messages very well!** Read aloud Genesis 37:1-11 and Romans 12:10. Talk about the importance of honoring and worshipping God through loving our families. End with a challenge to see if Group A can repeat Group B's message and vice versa.

Preschool Story

▶*NO PREP*

Bible Point: ▷ **FAMILIES NEED TO SHOW LOVE.**

Supplies: Bible, paper or poster board, crayons or markers
Time: 15 to 20 minutes
Preparation: none

Sweet Dreams

Begin your story time by singing "Joseph Went to Sleep" to the tune of "A Sailor Went to Sea, Sea, Sea."

Joseph went to sleep, sleep, sleep. (Place hands alongside face as if using them as a pillow.)

He had a dream so deep, deep, deep. (Squat down a little each time you say "deep.")

And when he woke, he shared his dream. (Stretch arms and pretend to yawn.)

It made his brothers scream, scream, scream. (Pretend to be angry, and get a little louder each time you say "scream.")

Have kids form a circle and sit down. Open your Bible to Genesis 37, and show children the words.

SAY: **Let's listen to our story to find out about Joseph's dreams. As you listen, I want you to draw a picture of our story.** Give each child a sheet of paper or a piece of poster board and several crayons.

Hi, I'm Joseph, I have *10* older brothers and one little brother. Can you believe that? What a lot of boys in one family! Encourage children to draw 12 boys on their papers. SAY: **Sometimes my brothers and I don't get along very well. I know God wants us show his love to**

our families, but we weren't always so good at doing that. Let me tell you about a time I made my brothers really mad.

It all started when my dad gave me a very colorful coat. I know my dad loves me a lot, and he always makes me feel important. But when he gave me that fancy coat, my brothers were jealous and angry. They couldn't understand why Dad didn't give them coats, too. Encourage children to draw a colorful coat on one of the brothers in their pictures.

One night when I went to sleep, I dreamed that all of my brothers and I were working in a field. Suddenly my plant grew straight and tall—much taller than my brothers' plants. Then all of my brothers' plants gathered around my plant and bowed down to it. Encourage kids to stand up and bow down. Then tell them to draw several plants bowing down to another plant.

I told my brothers about my dream, and it made them really mad! "No way will we ever bow down to you!" they said.

But then on another night, I had another dream. In this dream I saw the sun, moon, and eleven stars bowing down to me. The sun and moon were my mother and father. And the eleven stars? Well, guess who they were—my brothers, of course!

When I told my brothers about the second dream, they were *really* mad. Encourage kids to draw the sun, moon, and eleven stars. **My brothers and I weren't very good at showing each other love. I wish we had been better.**

ASK:

- ◆ **What do you think Joseph's dreams meant?**
- ◆ **Why didn't Joseph and his brothers show love to each other?**
- ◆ **How can you show love to your family?**

SAY: **Joseph's brothers were really jealous of him, but they still should have shown love to him. ▷ FAMILIES NEED TO SHOW LOVE.**

BIBLE STORY

Joseph Is Sold

For the Leader

We all know the story has a good ending. But selling their brother into slavery and then telling their dad he died? What were they thinking?!

It's hard to imagine this kind of scenario in today's society, especially in your students' families. But kids still face the same kinds of emotions that led to Joseph's being sold: jealousy, anger, and hatred, for starters. Dealing with those feelings is important to building strong character. But perhaps even more important is learning to persevere through hard times in life. Kids need to know that God uses those hard times to shape them into something special.

These sessions give kids a firsthand look at Joseph's amazing story and how they, too, can let God build their faith through difficult situations.

Key Scriptures

Genesis 37:12-36

1 Peter 1:6-7

Bible Verse

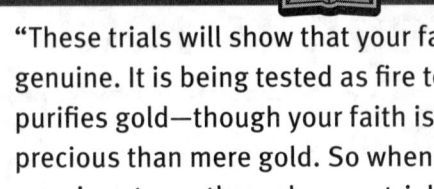

"These trials will show that your faith is genuine. It is being tested as fire tests and purifies gold—though your faith is far more precious than mere gold. So when your faith remains strong through many trials, it will bring you much praise and glory and honor on the day when Jesus Christ is revealed to the whole world" (1 Peter 1:7).

Bible Experience

▶ *NO PREP*

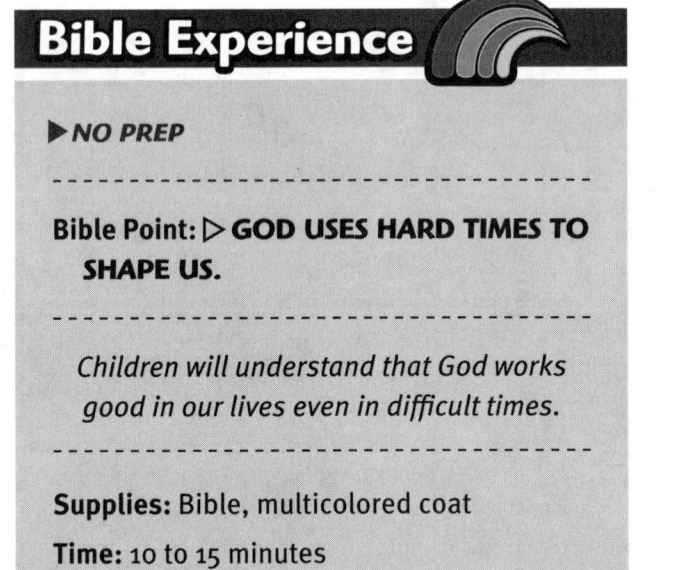

Bible Point: ▷ **GOD USES HARD TIMES TO SHAPE US.**

Children will understand that God works good in our lives even in difficult times.

Supplies: Bible, multicolored coat

Time: 10 to 15 minutes

Preparation: none

SAY: **Let's talk about how God can make good things come out of bad.** Share a personal story or a story you know about how a bad situation ended up good. Ask if one or two volunteers can share a similar story.

Open your Bible to Genesis 37:12-36, and show children the words. SAY: **The Bible tells us about Joseph. He had lots of brothers, who were jealous of him. His brothers thought their dad loved Joseph more than he loved them. One day their father gave Joseph a beautiful coat with lots of colors. Kind of like this one!** Ask a volunteer to put on the coat and stand in front of the others. Lead all the kids in SAYING: **Wow, Joseph! You look great in that beautiful coat! Have "Joseph" turn around and model the coat for everyone. But this made Joseph's brothers even more angry and jealous of Joseph.**

ASK:

◆ **When have you been jealous?**

◆ **When has someone been jealous of you?**

SAY: **You know what the brothers did? They made a plan to get rid of Joseph. When their father wasn't looking, they took Joseph's coat.** (Take the coat from the volunteer.) **Then they put Joseph in a deep hole until they could decide what to do with him.** Ask Joseph to sit on the floor. Then have everyone form a tight circle around him and raise their arms high, like a high wall of a hole. ASK:

◆ **How do you feel down there, Joseph?**

SAY: **The brothers took Joseph out of the well and sold him to some travelers going to Egypt.** Have all the children sit down. ASK:

◆ **What do you think Joseph was feeling when he became a slave?**

◆ **What do you think Joseph thought about his future?**

◆ **Have you ever been through a hard time? Explain.**

SAY: **You know what? ▷ GOD USES HARD TIMES TO SHAPE US. God was watching out for Joseph and had a plan for him. Eventually Joseph got a job with Pharaoh, and he helped thousands and thousands of people live through a famine, which is a time there's no rain and little food.**

Read aloud 1 Peter 1:7. ASK:

◆ **What are some ways God can use hard times to shape you and me?**

Ask everyone to gather around so they can hold onto the coat as you pray and thank God for the hard times in our lives.

Song & Connect

Use "Persevere!" (track 21, *it: Innovative Tools for Children's Ministry: New Testament* CD) to help reinforce the Bible Point, ▷ **GOD USES HARD TIMES TO SHAPE US.**

Additional Topics List

This lesson can be used to help children discover... Anger, Consequences, God's Plans, Jealousy, and Trials.

Game

▶ ***PREPARE IN ADVANCE***
▶ ***ALLERGY ALERT***

Obstacles, of Course

Children will navigate an obstacle course to reach a reward.

Supplies: Bible, obstacles, cookies or doughnuts

Time: 10 to 15 minutes

Preparation: Set up a simple obstacle course outside or in a large room or gym. You might include a slide, sawhorses, or tires for kids to run through.

Gather kids together, and show them how to run through the obstacle course. SAY: **We'll take turns going through this obstacle course of "troubles." At the end, you'll each receive a tasty prize!** After each child has finished the obstacle course, distribute the snack. As children eat, ASK:

- **What was the hardest part of the obstacle course?**
- **What kept you going when the course was difficult?**

Tell kids about the story of Joseph's trials in Genesis 37, and then have a volunteer read aloud 1 Peter 1:6-7.

ASK:

- **What troubles do we face in real life?**
- **What good things come from hard times?**
- **What can we look forward to when we're going through hard times?**

SAY: **When the obstacle course was difficult, you kept going because you knew a terrific prize was waiting for you. When life gets tough, we can keep going because we know that ▷ GOD USES HARD TIMES TO SHAPE US into something wonderful.**

Craft

▶ ***NO PREP***

Perseverance Prizes

Children will remember that they can trust God in hard times.

Supplies: Bible; aluminum foil; 1 juice-can lid per child; paper clips; 1-foot lengths of 1-inch, heavyweight blue or red ribbon; tacky glue

Time: about 15 minutes

Preparation: none

Give each child a 6-inch length of aluminum foil and a juice-can lid. Have them wrap the foil around the lids. Prompt kids to think of something that has been hard for their families to go through. Give each child a paper clip, and instruct them to use a bent end of the clip to etch pictures in the foil that represent their hard times. For example, they could etch a broken heart or a sad face. Ask kids to place their "medals" facedown in front of them and to each choose a piece of ribbon. Help each child tie the ribbon into a loop with a knot. Show kids how to attach the ribbon to the medal by applying a dot of tacky glue to the top of the medal and pressing the ribbon firmly onto the glue. Have them pinch the lids and ribbons together between their fingers until they dry.

Discuss the following questions with your kids:

◆ **What is an award you've won?**

◆ **What did you have to do to win that prize?**

Tell kids briefly about Joseph's hardships in Genesis 37. Read aloud 1 Peter 1:6-7.

ASK:

◆ **Why should we have joy when we face hard times?**

◆ **What kind of "prize" can we earn by going through hard times?**

Encourage kids to wear their medals to remind them that facing hard times will get them a prize only God can give them.

notes

Bible Application

▶ *NO PREP*

Nothing Compares to Joy

Children will consider possible tough times and possible outcomes.

Supplies: Bible, whiteboard and markers or chalkboard and chalk, erasers

Time: 15 to 20 minutes

Preparation: none

Read aloud 1 Peter 1:6-7.

ASK:

◆ **What is a trial?**

SAY: **Let's take a look at one example of a trial in the Bible.** Tell kids the story of Joseph in Genesis 37. Have them brainstorm a list of possible trials they might go through, and write them in a column on a whiteboard or chalkboard. Start a corresponding column with possible outcomes for each of the trials.

Have kids form trios, and assign each trio one or two trials on the board. Have them recite 1 Peter 1:7 together, and then discuss what good things might result from persevering through the trial.

After a few minutes, have each group share the good things that could come from their trials. In a third column on the board, list all the good things that could happen from the trials. Then erase all the trials and outcomes columns, and have kids consider all the good things. Repeat the memory verse together.

Creative Prayer Idea

▶ *NO PREP*
▶ *STUDENT LED*

Needful Hands

Children will commit their hard times to God in prayer.

Supplies: Bible, disposable non-latex plastic gloves, permanent markers

Time: 5 to 10 minutes

Preparation: none

Have a volunteer read aloud 1 Peter 1:6-7. Give each child a pair of disposable plastic gloves. Ask them to think about the trials, or hard times, they're going through or have gone through. Have them write those hard times on their gloves. Then instruct kids to put the gloves on their hands and fold their hands in prayer. Lead the kids in prayer, asking God to help them through their hard times and to bring them joy during the hard times.

notes

Movie Clip

Blessings in Disguise

Movie Title: *Harriet the Spy* (PG)

Start Time: 24 minutes, 30 seconds

Where to Begin: Harriet and Mr. Waldenstein are having a stare-down at the dinner table.

Where to End: Harriet, Miss Gully, and Mr. Waldenstein sit down at the movie.

Plot: Miss Gully has invited Mr. Waldenstein for dinner. Harriet isn't sure about this man. When Miss Gully burns the bratwurst, Mr. Waldenstein calls it a blessing in disguise because now they can all go out to dinner and a movie.

Review: Use this clip to show how God can take bad things in our lives and make something good out of them. Joseph could have given up when his brothers sold him into slavery. Instead, he let God use him for greater things.

Discussion

After setting up and showing the clip, ASK:

- **Have you ever had a blessing in disguise, which is something that went wrong at first but ended up being good? What happened?**
- **How did it make you feel?**

SAY: **When Joseph's brothers sold him into slavery, it was a terrible time. Joseph had no idea what God had in store for him. But God turned that situation into a blessing in disguise. Because of what happened to him, Joseph was able to help his family and his whole nation! God always knows what is best for us.**

Read aloud 1 Peter 1:6-7.

ASK:

- **Do you trust God to work things out? Why or why not?**
- **What would help you trust God when things are hard?**

Object Lesson

▶ ***PREPARE IN ADVANCE***

▶ ***ALLERGY ALERT***

No Slammin' the Salmon

Children will see how God helps us persevere through hard times.

Supplies: Bible, index cards, markers, several skeins of yarn in enough colors so there is 1 color for every 2 children, tape, small plastic bags, fish-shaped crackers, picture of a salmon

Time: about 15 minutes

Preparation: Before class, write the following directions on the cards, one direction per card. Make one complete set of directions for every two children. Wrap the different-colored lengths of yarn around objects in the classroom, such as chairs, table legs, and doorknobs, so that the yarns are tangled. As you wrap the yarn, tape a set of directions onto each color of yarn in four places. At the end of each length of yarn, tape a plastic bag with fish-shaped crackers in it. Try to hide the end of the yarn to keep the crackers out of view at the beginning of the game.

(Directions: 1. Hungry, fish-eating birds are nearby; do four jumping jacks. 2. The water is polluted, and it's hard to swim; hop on one foot six times. 3. The journey is long, and you're tired; jump up and down for 10 seconds. 4. A hungry bear is splashing in the water; spin around three times.)

Have kids find partners, and then have partners sit together in a semicircle. SAY: **We're going to learn about a fish that teaches us about persevering through hard times.** Show the picture of the salmon and SAY: **Salmon have to take a treacherous journey from the ocean to the rivers to lay their eggs. This journey takes them through many obstacles and hard times. Imagine you're a salmon and it's time to swim to the river to lay your eggs.**

Give each pair of kids an end of yarn, and have them follow it. Tell them there's a prize at the end of the yarn. After all the kids have found the crackers, have them sit in a circle. SAY: **God gave salmon the ability to persevere through hard times. God gives us the ability to persevere through hard times, too.** Read aloud 1 Peter 1:6-7.

ASK:

- **How did you feel when you continued to meet obstacles in your path as a salmon?**
- **What are some difficult tasks in your own life?**
- **What can you do to encourage yourself to persevere through hard times?**

notes

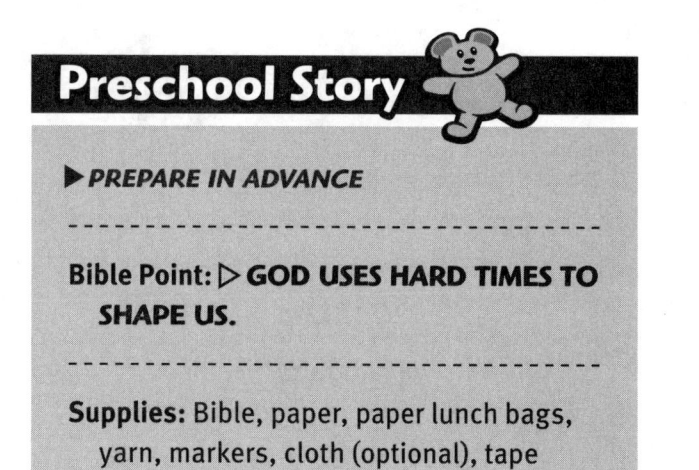

Preschool Story

▶ *PREPARE IN ADVANCE*

Bible Point: ▷ GOD USES HARD TIMES TO SHAPE US.

Supplies: Bible, paper, paper lunch bags, yarn, markers, cloth (optional), tape

Time: 15 to 20 minutes

Preparation: Create a simple Joseph puppet for each child in class. For each puppet, stuff a paper wad inside a small paper lunch bag, and use yarn to tie off the bag beneath the paper wad to make the head. Make a puppet for yourself, also.

A Happy Ending

Have kids form a circle and sit down. Open your Bible to Genesis 37, and show children the words. Give each child one of the puppets you prepared and several markers. Lead kids in the following actions.

SAY: **Jacob lived in the land of Canaan. He had many sons, but Joseph was his favorite.** Have each child draw a face on his or her puppet as you SAY: **Jacob loved Joseph so much that he gave him a beautiful coat of many colors to wear. Joseph's brothers were jealous.** Let each child use markers to decorate a sheet of paper or a cloth square as Joseph's coat. Help kids wrap the coats around the puppets. Secure the coats with tape.

One day Joseph went to visit his brothers, who were watching over their sheep. (Make your puppet walk.) **Joseph's brothers took his coat and threw him down into an empty well.** (Remove the puppet's coat, and place the puppet on the floor.) **Then they sold him as a slave to people who were traveling to Egypt.** (Wave goodbye.) **They put animal blood on Joseph's coat.** (Crumple up the coat.) **Then they went home and told their father that a wild animal had killed Joseph. Jacob was very sad.** (Rub your eyes as if crying.)

What Joseph's brothers did was wrong. Let's do an action rhyme to remind us that God wants us to be nice. Lead children in the following action rhyme:

Joseph's 10 brothers were jealous.

And jealousy is not very nice. *(Wag puppet back and forth.)*

Just stop and think twice *(hold hand up in front of you to make "stop" motion)*

When you're not feeling right *(wag puppet back and forth),*

And God will help you all day and all night. *(Bow puppet's head so it looks as if the puppet is praying.)*

SAY: **God wants us to be kind and to get along with others. Joseph's brothers meant harm for Joseph, but God turned the bad thing they did into a good thing. God took care of Joseph in Egypt and made him very powerful. In fact, he was in charge of all the food in the land.** (Hold your puppet up high.) **God told Joseph about Pharaoh's dream: Soon there wouldn't be enough food to eat.** (Rub your tummy.) **Joseph's brothers were very hungry, and they came to Egypt to ask for food for their family. They were afraid when they saw that it was Joseph who was in charge of the food.** (Cover your eyes.) **But Joseph forgave his brothers and gave them all the food they wanted. And the family lived together again!** (Wave the puppet in the air.) **Even though the brothers meant for bad to happen, God used what they did for the good. ▷ GOD USES HARD TIMES TO SHAPE US.**

ASK:

- **What bad things happened to Joseph?**
- **How did God use those bad things for good?**
- **Has God ever turned something bad into something good in your life?**

BIBLE STORY

Joseph and Potiphar's Wife

For the Leader

Paul summed it up well when he said that he always wanted to do the right thing but just couldn't: "When I want to do good, I don't. And when I try not to do wrong, I do it anyway" (Romans 7:19). If one of the greatest Christians of all time had trouble, how's a kid supposed to do what's right?

These activities are a great place to start. Joseph, though not perfect, chose to do what was right when he was tempted by Potiphar's wife. You can help kids learn how to rely on God to do what's right by taking a close-up look at Paul's words and Joseph's example.

Key Scriptures

Genesis 39:1-23
Psalm 119:105
Romans 6:12-13; 7:19

Bible Verse

"Do not let any part of your body become an instrument of evil to serve sin. Instead, give yourselves completely to God, for you were dead, but now you have new life. So use your whole body as an instrument to do what is right for the glory of God" (Romans 6:13).

Bible Experience

▶ *NO PREP*

Bible Point: ▷ **DO WHAT'S RIGHT.**

Children will recognize that they can use their minds and bodies to avoid temptation and do what's right.

Supplies: Bible, paper, markers, safety scissors

Time: 10 to 15 minutes

Preparation: none

Gather the kids together and ASK:

◆ **Who here has ever been accused of doing something you didn't do? Explain.**

SAY: **The Bible tells us about a man who was accused of something he didn't do. His name was Joseph. You might have heard about him and his coat of many colors. Well, after his brothers sold him as a slave, he was taken to Egypt and sold to a man named Potiphar.** Read aloud Genesis 39:2-6a. **Joseph really made his mark in Potiphar's house. He worked hard and made a strong impression on his master. Let's make a mark right now.** Have kids trace their foot on a piece of paper with a marker.

Potiphar's wife was a bad person. She liked to do wrong things. She kept trying to get Joseph to do wrong things, too. But Joseph chose to ▷ DO WHAT'S RIGHT, again and again. Read aloud Genesis 39:8-9. **Joseph told her to "cut it out!" Let's do the same thing!** Have kids use scissors to cut out their footprints.

But Potiphar's wife was wicked, and she wouldn't give up. One day she tried to make

Joseph do the wrong thing, but he said no again. So she stole his shirt and started screaming. And what did Joseph do? The Bible says he ran away.

Read aloud Romans 6:13. Have kids use markers to write the following verse on their footprints: "Use your whole body as an instrument to do what is right."

SAY: **Well, Joseph got thrown into prison. But even in prison, God blessed Joseph for doing what's right.** Read aloud Genesis 39:19-23. **The Bible says, "The Lord was with him and caused everything he did to succeed." When we ▷ DO WHAT'S RIGHT, we're successes because we're honoring and obeying God.**

Song & Connect

Use "We Should Do Good" (track 16, *it: Innovative Tools for Children's Ministry: New Testament* CD) to help reinforce the Bible Point, ▷ **DO WHAT'S RIGHT.**

Additional Topics List

This lesson can be used to help children discover... Armor of God, Choices, Holiness, Sin, and Temptation.

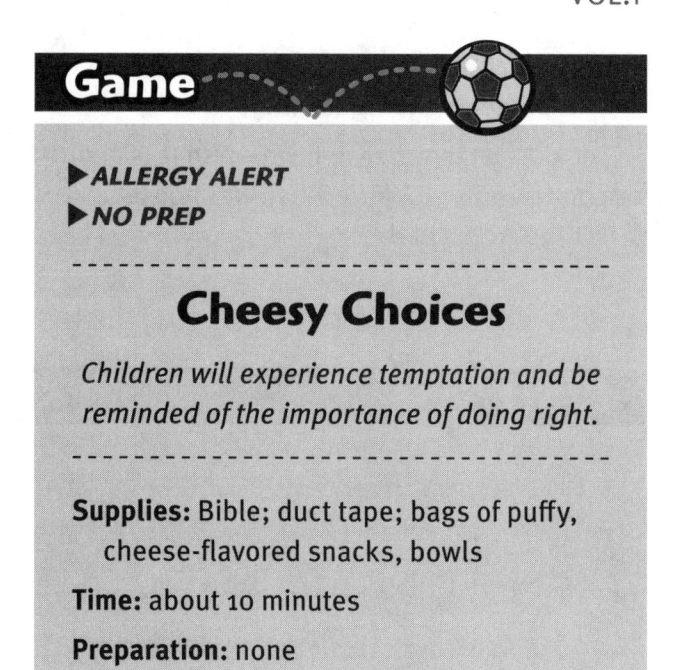

n

o

t

e

s

Game

▶ ***ALLERGY ALERT***

▶ ***NO PREP***

Cheesy Choices

Children will experience temptation and be reminded of the importance of doing right.

Supplies: Bible; duct tape; bags of puffy, cheese-flavored snacks, bowls

Time: about 10 minutes

Preparation: none

Have kids form teams of five, and have each team designate one participant to "grow a head of hair." Have players carefully wrap duct tape, STICKY SIDE OUT, around their chosen player's head. (It should look like a helmet.) Warn children to avoid ensnaring the hair of the helmet-wearers!

When each team has wrapped its "head case," hand out a bowl of puffy, cheese-flavored snacks to each group. SAY: **When I say, "Say 'cheese,'" begin applying cheese puffs to the sticky head, trying to build the fullest head of hair. No eating the cheese puffs! Think of them as supplies. Say "cheese"!**

After four minutes, call time and compare the hair. Kids can take off the cheese-puff helmets and then discuss the following questions:

- **Were you tempted to eat the cheese puffs as you played the game? Why or why not?**
- **How is that like the temptation to sin that we face?**

Ask a volunteer to read aloud Romans 6:13, and then ASK:

- **How do we know how to do what's right?**

◆ **In what ways can we use our bodies as tools to do the right thing?**

Let kids eat the cheese-flavored snacks and celebrate God's guidance when we choose to ▷ **DO WHAT'S RIGHT.**

Craft

▶ ***PREPARE IN ADVANCE***

No-Nos and Yo-Yos

Children will be reminded to do what's right no matter how people treat them.

Supplies: Bible, craft foam, blank index cards, safety scissors, colored markers, brass fasteners, 3-foot pieces of string, 8 pennies per child, stapler, mailing tape

Time: about 15 minutes

Preparation: Cut the craft foam into two 2½-inch squares for each child.

Give each child two pieces of craft foam. Show kids how to cut off the corners of the craft foam to form circles. Direct kids to cut two identical circles out of the cards, using the foam circles as a pattern. Have each child use a marker to mark the middle of the foam circles and slide a brass fastener through one circle at that marked midpoint. Tell kids to tie one end of their string into a knot around the brass fastener ends. Then help kids tie a 1-inch loop on the other end of the string. Show kids how to slide the fastener through the second foam circle at its midpoint and fold down the fastener ends tightly against the second circle.

Instruct kids to tape four pennies flat to the face of one foam circle, keeping the pennies as close as possible without overlapping them. Have them repeat the process on the other side. Help each child staple the two paper circles to the foam circles around the edges, using at least four staples each. Make sure any staple ends along the inside are pushed flat against the foam. Have kids decorate the yo-yos with markers.

Tell kids the story of Joseph and Potiphar's wife in Genesis 39:1-23. Read aloud Romans 6:13. Discuss these questions:

◆ **What's so special about a yo-yo?**

◆ **Can doing the wrong thing come back to hurt us? How?**

◆ **Can doing what's right come back to help us? How?**

SAY: **The Bible tells us that we should ▷ DO WHAT'S RIGHT. When we do, it will always come back to bless us.**

Bible Application

▶ ***NO PREP***

Virtue Reality

Children will figure out how to do what's right in real situations.

Supplies: Bible

Time: 10 to 15 minutes

Preparation: none

Read the following scenarios, and have children pair up and act out the situations. Then read aloud the question following each scenario, and allow a few minutes for pairs to discuss and decide on the best solution.

SCENARIO 1: **You're at a friend's house, and he wants you to watch a movie your parents told you not to watch. How do you do what's right?**

SCENARIO 2: **You're at school and notice that your best friend is cheating on a test. How do you do what's right?**

SCENARIO 3: **You're walking to school and notice that your elderly neighbor's dog is loose. If you help, you might be late for school. How do you do what's right?**

SCENARIO 4: **You find a 50-dollar bill on the floor at a grocery store. How do you do what's right? What do you do if it's a 1-dollar bill?**

SCENARIO 5: **You get your math test back and notice that the teacher forgot to mark three answers wrong. If you tell her, your grade will drop. How do you do what's right?**

SCENARIO 6: **You told your friend you'd sit with her on the field trip. Now you want to sit with someone else, even though you know it will hurt your friend's feelings. How do you do what's right?**

After all the scenarios have been acted out and discussed, ASK:

◆ **What do you think God would say about our decisions?**

◆ **Why is it important to do the right thing?**

Have a volunteer read Romans 6:12-13.

ASK:

◆ **What can you do when you're faced with tough decisions?**

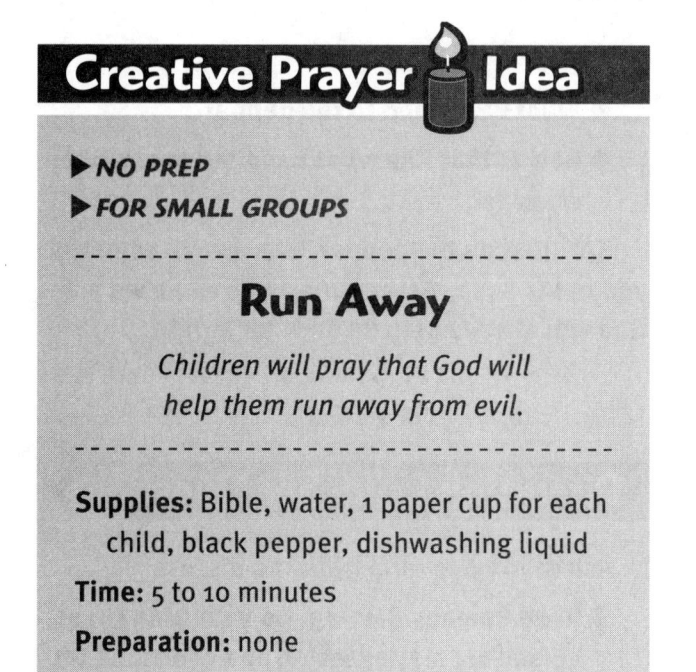

Creative Prayer Idea

▶ *NO PREP*

▶ *FOR SMALL GROUPS*

Run Away

Children will pray that God will help them run away from evil.

Supplies: Bible, water, 1 paper cup for each child, black pepper, dishwashing liquid

Time: 5 to 10 minutes

Preparation: none

Have children form pairs, and give each pair a cup of water. Read aloud Romans 6:13. SAY: **When we do what's right, it's like a cup of fresh water. We're clean and pure when we do what's right.** Have all the kids take a sip of water and thank God for helping us do what's right.

But sometimes we're tempted to do what's wrong. Things like lying, cheating, stealing, or disobeying come along. Sprinkle a little pepper onto the surface of each cup.

ASK:

◆ **How does the water look now?**

Tell kids how Joseph fled from Potiphar's wife when she tempted him to do the wrong thing. SAY: **Sometimes we need a bit of extra strength when we're tempted to do wrong.** Read aloud James 4:7-8. **When we pray, we're calling on God's power to help us do what's right. The power of God is strong enough to send all those bad things running away. Pray with your partner, and ask God to forgive you for the bad things you've done.**

After kids have prayed, SAY: **When we pray, God gives us strength to do what's right.** Pour a drop of dishwashing liquid into each child's cup.

ASK:

- **What happened to the pepper?**
- **How is that like what happens to sin when we pray?**

SAY: **Just as the pepper "ran away" when we added the soap, Satan runs away when we pray. God will always help us do what's right.**

Discussion Launcher Questions

Ask children to form trios and discuss:

- **Read Romans 6:12-13. Do you think these verses are a suggestion or a command for Christians? Why?**
- **Describe the hardest time you ever had choosing to do what's right.**
- **Do you think it's possible for a person to do the right thing for an entire day? a week? Why or why not?**
- **Why do you think it's difficult to always do the right thing?**

Life Application

Children will discover that they can do what's right as they participate in these application activities.

From Guess to Yes

Conceal a piece of candy in one hand, and let kids guess which hand is hiding the candy. If they get it right, they get the candy. Play the game enough times to let each child get a piece of candy. Talk about how the guessing game is different from real life. Discuss ways kids don't have to guess when to do the right thing.

God's Bright Light

Shine a flashlight on your Bible as you read aloud Romans 6:13 and Psalm 119:105. Lead kids in a discussion about why it's important to do what's right. Explain how the Bible is like a bright light in the darkness and how God's Word can help kids choose the right thing. Shine the light in each of their faces and say one thing they can choose to do right during the week.

Preschool Story

▶ *NO PREP*

Bible Point: ▷ **DO WHAT'S RIGHT.**

Supplies: Bible

Time: 10 to 15 minutes

Preparation: none

The Right Way

Have kids form a circle and sit down. Open your Bible to Genesis 39, and show children the words. SAY: **When Joseph lived in Egypt, he worked for a man named Potiphar. Joseph had to do lots of chores for Potiphar.**

ASK:

- **What chores do you do at your house?**

Encourage children to act out the chores that they do at home.

SAY: **Even though Joseph had to do all those chores, he didn't complain because he wanted to ▷ DO WHAT'S RIGHT. Joseph chose to do the chores and to serve God as he worked. We can serve God when we do the chores at our homes, too!**

But then one day, Potiphar's wife tried to make Joseph do something that was wrong. Joseph didn't want to do the wrong thing because Joseph knew that God would want him to ▷ DO WHAT'S RIGHT.

ASK:

◆ **Has anyone ever tried to get you to do the wrong thing? What did you do?**

SAY: **Potiphar's wife was mad at Joseph because he wouldn't do the wrong thing, so she did something really mean to Joseph. She told Potiphar something that wasn't true about Joseph and made Potiphar put Joseph in prison.** Have children pretend to hold onto bars and look out.

ASK:

◆ **Have you ever gotten in trouble for something you didn't do? How did that make you feel?**

SAY: **Even though Joseph was in prison, he still chose to ▷ DO WHAT'S RIGHT. God was pleased with Joseph for doing the right thing, and God took care of Joseph while he was in prison.**

Let's sing a song now to help us remember that God wants us to do the right thing.

Sing the following song to the tune of "The Mulberry Bush." Encourage children to hold hands and skip in a circle as you sing. Change directions during the second and third verses.

God wants us to do what is right,
Do what is right,
Do what is right.
God wants us to do what is right,
Even when it's hard.

Joseph chose to do what is right,
Do what is right,
Do what is right.
Joseph chose to do what is right,
And to please God.

God wants us to do what is right,
Do what is right,
Do what is right.
God wants us to do what is right,
Even when it's hard.

ASK:

◆ **When can you choose to do the right thing?**

◆ **When is it hard to do what's right?**

◆ **How can God help you do what's right even when it's hard?**

n
o
t
e
s

BIBLE STORY

Pharaoh Puts Joseph in Charge

For the Leader

Talk about rags to riches! When Joseph's brothers stole his colorful coat and turned it to shreds, Joseph's future appeared to be nothing more than tatters. And it only went downhill from there: sold into slavery, taken far from home, thrown into jail, and forgotten. No one—except God—would have guessed that Joseph would eventually become the second most powerful man in the world.

It's easy for kids to think their lives are tough. Even small setbacks can make some kids dizzy with doubt. But Joseph is a hero every kid can look up to. His key to success was something we all can do: serve God. Use the activities in this section to help kids explore the blessings that come from serving God.

Key Scriptures

Genesis 39:20-41:49

Romans 12:11

Bible Verse

"Never be lazy, but work hard and serve the Lord enthusiastically" (Romans 12:11).

Bible Experience

▶ *PREPARE IN ADVANCE*

Bible Point: ▷ **WE CAN SERVE GOD.**

Children will discover many ways in which Joseph served God and in which they can serve God, too.

Supplies: Bible, 4 sheets of newsprint, tape, markers

Time: 20 to 25 minutes

Preparation: Tape the sheets of newsprint to the wall where kids can reach them. From left to right, label the first sheet "Prison," the second "Cupbearer and Baker," the third "Prisoner Dreams," and the fourth "King Dream."

SAY: **The Bible tells us to "serve the Lord enthusiastically" (Romans 12:11). Let's look at Joseph's life and see how he served the Lord throughout his life.**

Have kids form four groups. Read Genesis 39:20-23 from a kid-friendly version of the Bible. SAY: **The story starts with Joseph being thrown into prison by his master.** Have Group 1 sit under the newsprint labeled "Prison."

Read Genesis 40:1-23. SAY: **Two of the king's servants have been thrown into prison with Joseph because they had done something to make the king mad.** Have Group 2 sit under the newsprint labeled "Cupbearer and Baker."

Read Genesis 41:1-40. SAY: **Two years later Pharaoh had some dreams he didn't understand. He needed someone to help him. The cupbearer finally remembered Joseph and told Pharaoh about him. Then Pharaoh sent for**

Joseph. Have Group 3 sit under the newsprint labeled "Prisoner Dreams," and send Group 4 to the newsprint labeled "King Dream."

Read Genesis 41:41-49. Have Group 1 draw a picture on their newsprint of how they think Joseph may have felt when he was thrown into prison. Tell Group 2 to draw a picture of what they think the cupbearer and baker may have done to make the king mad. Have Group 3 draw a picture of what the cupbearer and baker dreamed. Tell Group 4 to draw a picture of what the king dreamed. Give teams 10 minutes to work. Have volunteers from each group share what they've drawn. Then gather kids in a circle and ASK:

- ◆ **What are all the ways you saw God use Joseph in this story?**
- ◆ **How was Joseph's waiting to get out of prison like your wondering what God wants you to do for him?**

SAY: **The Bible tells us in Romans 12:11 to "serve the Lord enthusiastically."**

ASK:

- ◆ **What does it mean to be enthusiastic?**
- ◆ **How can you serve God enthusiastically?**

SAY: **Joseph served God in many ways. And**
▷ ***WE CAN SERVE GOD, too.***

Additional Topics List

This lesson can be used to help children discover... Faith, God's Plans, Patience, Perseverance, and Respect.

Game

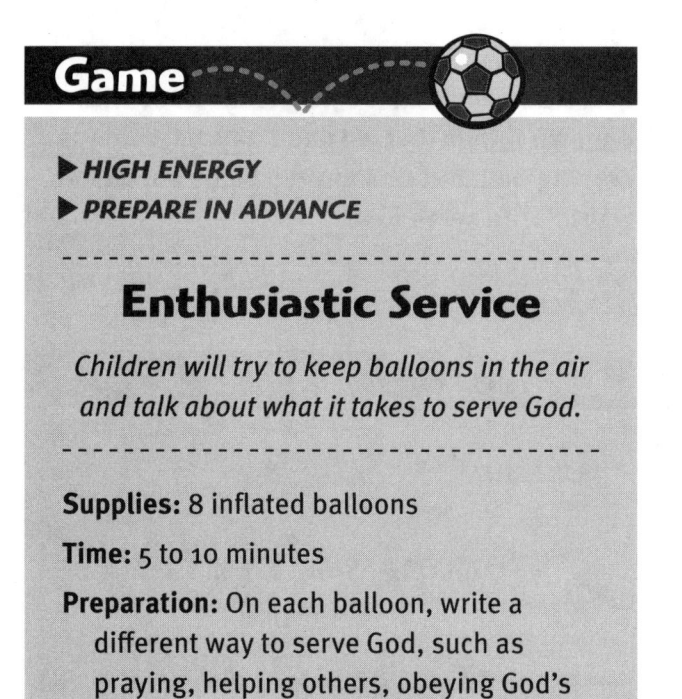

▶ ***HIGH ENERGY***
▶ ***PREPARE IN ADVANCE***

Enthusiastic Service

Children will try to keep balloons in the air and talk about what it takes to serve God.

Supplies: 8 inflated balloons

Time: 5 to 10 minutes

Preparation: On each balloon, write a different way to serve God, such as praying, helping others, obeying God's Word, or giving an offering.

Have children stand with you in a circle and SAY: **God wants us to serve him! There are many ways we can serve him. For example,** [read the service words written on your balloons]. **Joseph served God in a lot of ways. He helped others, he stayed faithful, and he used his gifts. Even when times were hard, he continued to serve. Joseph didn't give up and let others down. Don't let the balloons fall now!** Begin serving each balloon volleyball-style into the circle until all eight balloons are being bopped in the air. Encourage kids to keep the balloons from touching the ground.

After a couple of minutes, set the balloons aside and SAY: **You were very enthusiastic in that game! Romans 12:11 says, "Serve the Lord enthusiastically." I think you can do that!**

ASK:

- ◆ **Do you think it's always easy to serve God? Why or why not?**
- ◆ **Who can tell about a time you helped or served someone?**

SAY: **Sometimes it can be a challenge to serve God. Sometimes we get too busy with our own things that we don't pay attention to serving God. But God always helps us, and he wants us to serve him.**

Craft

▶ ***NO PREP***

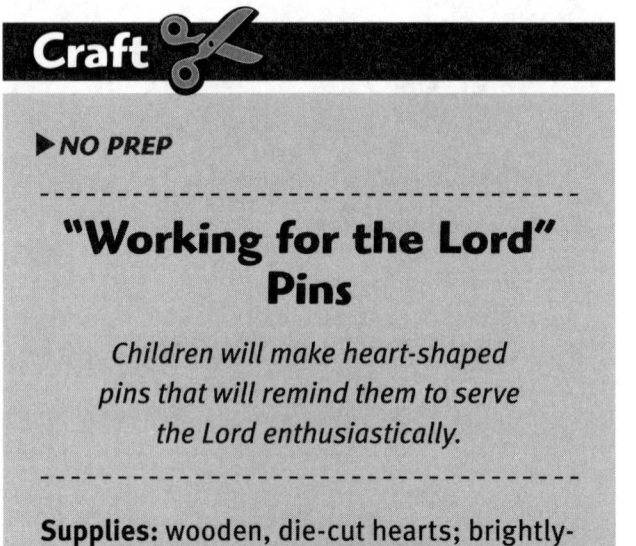

"Working for the Lord" Pins

Children will make heart-shaped pins that will remind them to serve the Lord enthusiastically.

Supplies: wooden, die-cut hearts; brightly-colored markers; brightly colored puffy paint; self-adhesive pin clasps

Time: about 15 minutes

Preparation: none

Distribute one die-cut heart to each child, and have kids decorate the wooden hearts with markers. Help kids write "I'm working for the Lord" on the front with puffy paint and decorate as desired. Have kids attach a pin clasp to the back of each heart.

ASK:

- ◆ **What does it mean to serve the Lord with all our hearts?**
- ◆ **When we serve the Lord with all our hearts, how do you think God feels?**
- ◆ **What can each of us do to serve God?**

Bible Application

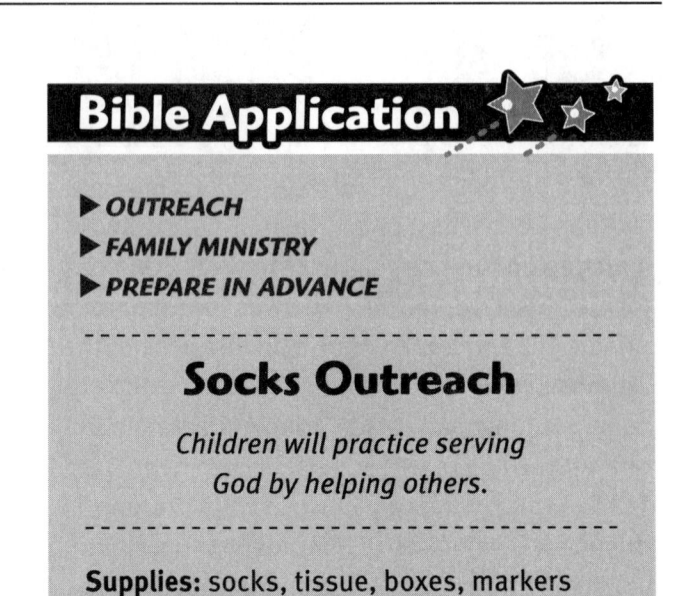

▶ ***OUTREACH***
▶ ***FAMILY MINISTRY***
▶ ***PREPARE IN ADVANCE***

Socks Outreach

Children will practice serving God by helping others.

Supplies: socks, tissue, boxes, markers

Time: 15 to 20 minutes

Preparation: Encourage kids to work with the church to organize an outreach to collect socks for people who need them.

Gather kids to organize socks collected in the drive. Have fun while you do it! Ask kids to put a pair of socks on their hands. Set out the supplies, and have kids wear the socks as they do the following:

- **Divide the socks according to size.**
- **Place tissue paper in the boxes.**
- **Place the socks in each box.**
- **Count the number of socks in each box.**
- **Take off the socks they're working on, and place them in the right box.**
- **Label each box with the number and type of socks inside.**

At the end of the organizing, discuss the following questions:

- ◆ **What was easy or hard about this activity?**
- ◆ **How might that be like being in need?**

SAY: **The Bible tells us in Romans 12:11 to "serve the Lord enthusiastically." When we serve others, we're also serving God. It doesn't matter who we are, how old we are, or how much money we have; we all can serve God.**

Ask kids and parents to help you deliver the socks to an outreach center.

Creative Prayer Idea

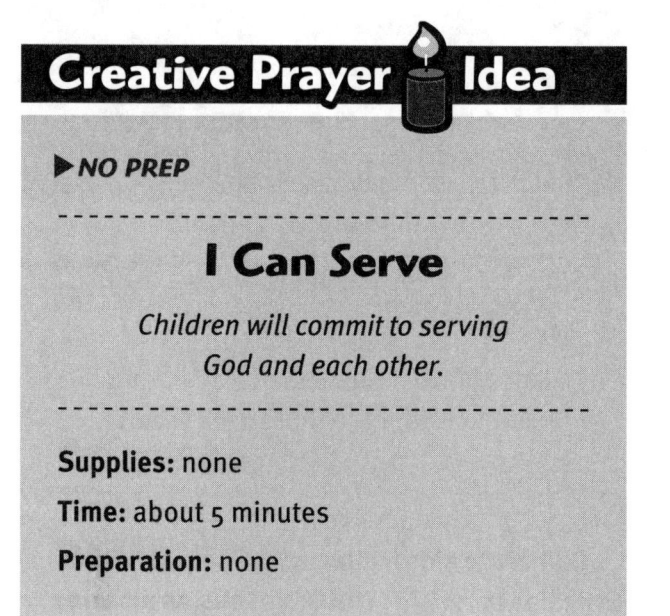

▶ *NO PREP*

I Can Serve

Children will commit to serving God and each other.

Supplies: none

Time: about 5 minutes

Preparation: none

Have kids sit in a circle.

ASK:

◆ **What are some ways we can serve God?**

SAY: **In all we say and do, we want to serve God first. When we serve God first, we can use our hands and hearts to serve others.**

Stand alone, bow your head, and PRAY: **Lord, I can serve you by praying.** Then turn and hold out your hand to the child on your left and SAY: **I can help you, too.** Help the child stand up. That child will bow his or her head and say a quick prayer to God about how he or she can serve God. Then the child will offer his or her hand to the next child on the left and say, "I can help you, too." Repeat this all the way around the circle.

When everyone is standing, join hands and close in prayer, asking God to help you find new ways to serve him.

Object Lesson

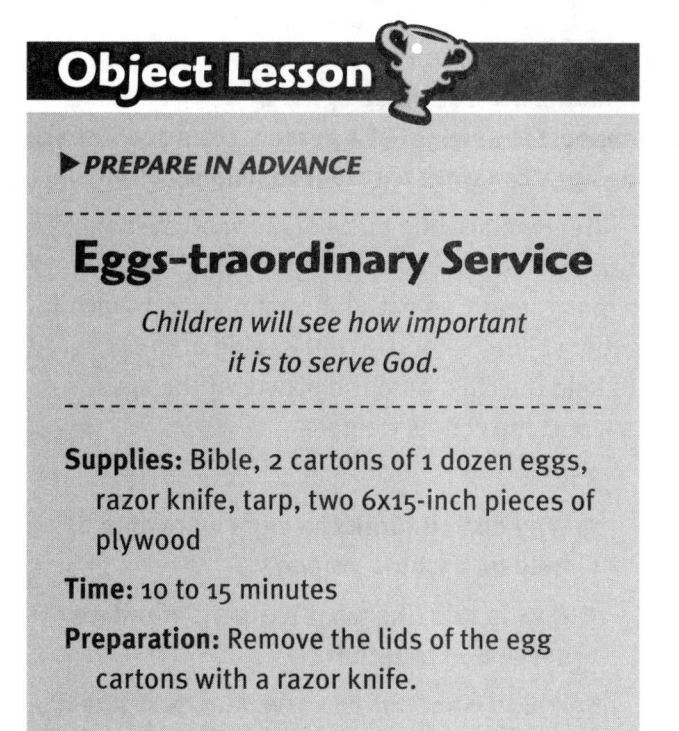

▶ *PREPARE IN ADVANCE*

Eggs-traordinary Service

Children will see how important it is to serve God.

Supplies: Bible, 2 cartons of 1 dozen eggs, razor knife, tarp, two 6x15-inch pieces of plywood

Time: 10 to 15 minutes

Preparation: Remove the lids of the egg cartons with a razor knife.

Lay the tarp on the ground (just in case). Set the two cartons of eggs on the ground, parallel to each other, with about 6 inches between them. Remove one egg from a carton, and hold it up.

ASK:

◆ **What would happen if I tried to place all my weight on this one egg?**

SAY: **One egg, all by itself, can't hold a lot of weight. The shell is fragile and cracks when it's given a job to do that's too big for it.**

ASK:

◆ **Have you ever had a job that was too big for you to handle? Did you ask for help?**

◆ **Can you think of any jobs that need to be done in the church that are too big for one person to do alone?**

Open your Bible to Genesis 39 and SAY: **God gave Joseph the job of organizing all the food for Egypt. But it was too big of a job for Joseph to do by himself. Joseph wanted to serve God, but he needed help.**

Pick up the egg carton, and return the egg to its place. SAY: **Pharaoh gave Joseph all the help**

he needed. Joseph served God, but he didn't do it alone. Look at these eggs. One egg couldn't support the weight of a person. Let's see if these 24 eggs can work together to hold someone up.

Gently place one piece of plywood over each carton. Select a younger, lighter child to place a foot gingerly on each piece of plywood. Have other children stand on either side of the eggs to help the child onto the plywood. The eggs will support the child's weight.

ASK:

- **Why do you think the eggs were able to hold up a whole person?**
- **How is this like what happens when we serve God together?**

SAY: **God wants us to serve him. Just like Joseph, God wants us to do some amazingly big jobs—jobs we can't do on our own. But together we can serve in ways that we never thought possible.**

n
o
t
e
s

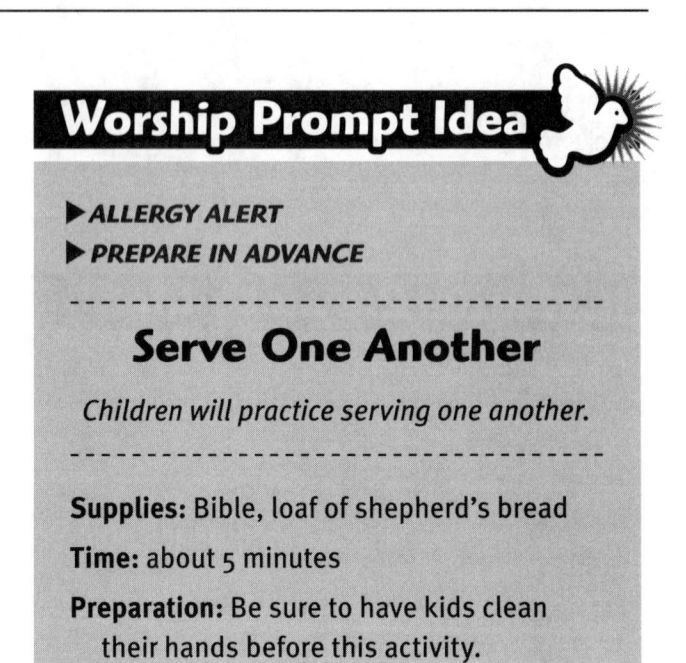

Worship Prompt Idea

▶ *ALLERGY ALERT*
▶ *PREPARE IN ADVANCE*

Serve One Another

Children will practice serving one another.

Supplies: Bible, loaf of shepherd's bread

Time: about 5 minutes

Preparation: Be sure to have kids clean their hands before this activity.

Gather the kids into a circle. Open your Bible to Genesis 41 and SAY: **The Bible tells an amazing story about Joseph. Joseph's life was hard, but all along the way, he chose to serve God. Because he was so faithful, Joseph eventually became second-in-command over all of Egypt—second only to Pharaoh. Joseph was in charge of gathering enough food to last for all the people for seven years of famine.** Read Genesis 41:47-49 aloud. **Because of Joseph's faithful service to God, all the land had plenty of food. They had enough grain to make all the bread they needed. God wants us to serve him, too. And when we do, God promises to be with us and take care of us.**

Take the loaf of bread, and hold it up. PRAY: **Lord, we're here today to worship you and to serve you with our hearts.** Tear off a small piece of bread, and feed it to the child sitting to your right. As you put the bread in his or her mouth, SAY: **I serve you because I serve God.** Pass the bread to that child, and have him or her repeat the action, feeding a small piece of bread to the next child, saying, "I serve you because I serve God." Repeat all around the circle.

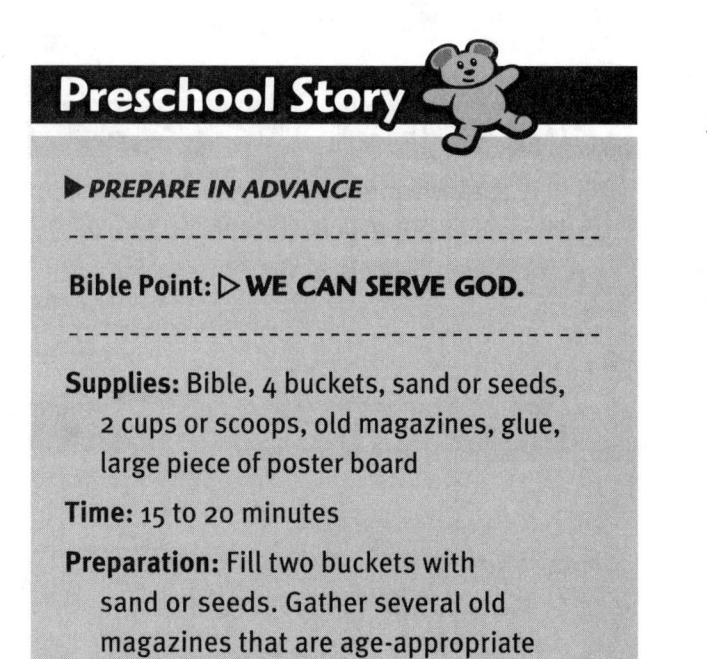

Preschool Story

▶ ***PREPARE IN ADVANCE***

Bible Point: ▷ **WE CAN SERVE GOD.**

Supplies: Bible, 4 buckets, sand or seeds, 2 cups or scoops, old magazines, glue, large piece of poster board

Time: 15 to 20 minutes

Preparation: Fill two buckets with sand or seeds. Gather several old magazines that are age-appropriate for preschoolers.

Rewarding Work

Have kids form a circle and sit down. Open your Bible to Genesis 39, and show children the words. SAY: **God gave Joseph wisdom and helped him understand that Pharaoh's dreams meant there would be seven years with lots of food and then seven years with very little food. When Pharaoh heard this news, he decided to put Joseph in charge of saving up food during the years with plenty so that everyone would have enough food during the hard years.**

ASK:

- **Are you in charge of any jobs at your house?**

SAY: **Joseph's job was very important, and he was in charge of many things and many people. While Joseph was doing his important job, he always worked hard because he knew that he was serving God. ▷ WE CAN SERVE GOD in all of the chores and jobs that we do, too!**

Joseph helped people save their grain and meat during the years with plenty of food. He stored all of the extra food in big buildings.

Let's play a game to help us remember how Joseph saved the extra food.

Have kids form two groups. Have each group line up at one end of the room, and give each group an empty bucket. At the other end of the room, place two buckets filled with seeds or sand.

Give the first child in each line an empty cup or scoop. Encourage the first child to run—or walk quickly—to the other end of the room and fill the cup or scoop with the sand or seeds. The child will then walk back and dump the sand or seeds into the team's empty bucket.

The child should then hand the empty cup or scoop to the next child in line. That child will repeat the same steps. Play the game until each child has gone or, if you have extra time, until all the sand or seeds have been moved.

SAY: **Good job, everyone! You moved all the grain and put it into storage so there would be plenty during hard years. That's kind of like what Joseph did when he was in charge of all the food in Egypt.**

Joseph served God while he worked in Egypt. Joseph knew that it doesn't matter where you are or what job you're doing—you can serve God while you work.

ASK:

- **How can you serve God while you do your chores at home?**

Distribute the old magazines, and encourage children to find pictures that show people working hard. Tell kids to tear out the pictures. Then have each child tell the rest of the class how he or she could serve God while doing the task in the picture. Have kids glue all of the pictures to a large piece of poster board to make a mural.

ASK:

- **How did Joseph serve God in Egypt?**
- **How can you serve God this week?**

BIBLE STORY

Joseph Interprets Pharaoh's Dreams

For the Leader

During Old Testament days, God frequently used dreams to send messages to people. Kids will undoubtedly wonder if God will speak to them through dreams. Of course, Christians have different views about this. Some say God doesn't need to speak to us through dreams anymore because now we have the Holy Spirit. But others maintain that God still uses dreams to send messages and certain revelations.

Help kids understand the real point of this story: Joseph asked for God's wisdom to help him in the situation, and God gave it to him. God also promises to give all of us wisdom; all we have to do is ask. Use these sessions to give kids the opportunity to ask for God's wisdom, and then see God provide the wisdom the children need.

Key Scriptures

Genesis 41:1-40

Proverbs 2:1-6

James 1:5-8

Bible Verse

"If you need wisdom, ask our generous God, and he will give it to you. He will not rebuke you for asking" (James 1:5).

Bible Experience

▶ *FOR YOUNGER CHILDREN*

▶ *NO PREP*

Bible Point: ▷ **GOD GIVES US WISDOM.**

Children will understand that God was the source of Joseph's wisdom and can give them wisdom, too.

Supplies: Bible

Time: about 10 minutes

Preparation: none

Have kids sit on the floor.

ASK:

◆ **Can you tell me about some of the dreams you've had?**

SAY: **The Bible tells about a king who had a dream. This king was the Pharaoh of Egypt, and he had two dreams that he couldn't figure out. In the first dream, he saw seven fat and healthy cows standing by the Nile River.** Have kids make "mooing" sounds. **Then he saw seven skinny, ugly cows come along and eat the fat cows.** Have kids pretend to eat, making loud "gobble" noises, and then SAY: **In the second dream, Pharaoh saw seven heads of grain that were growing really well and looked good to eat.** Have kids stand up really tall, point their arms straight up in the air, and wave them back and forth as if they are blowing in the wind. **Then he saw seven skinny heads of grain that looked really bad come and eat the seven good heads of grain.** Have kids pretend to eat again, making "gobble" noises.

When Pharaoh told his magicians about the dreams, no one could tell him what they meant. Have all the kids look around and shrug. **Then one of Pharaoh's servants remembered that a Hebrew man named Joseph had interpreted his dream when they were both in prison. He told Pharaoh about Joseph, and Pharaoh asked for Joseph to come.**

Joseph didn't know how to interpret dreams either. Have all the kids shrug again, and then SAY: **But Joseph knew that God could do it. And God used Joseph to help Pharaoh understand the dreams. He told Pharaoh that both dreams meant the same thing. There would be seven good years in the land, when there would be plenty of food for everyone.** Have kids rub their stomachs and say, "Mmm, I'm so full!" Then SAY: **But the dreams also meant that seven really bad years with no food were going to follow.** Have kids rub their stomachs and say, "I'm so hungry!"

So Joseph warned Pharaoh to save up food during the seven good years so people would have enough food during the seven years with no food. Pharaoh saw that God had made Joseph wise, so he put Joseph in charge of all of Egypt.

ASK:

- **How did God help Joseph?**
- **How can God give us wisdom?**

Read James 1:5. SAY: **Just like Joseph, ▷ GOD GIVES US WISDOM. When you need God's help, just pray and ask him for wisdom.**

Additional Topics List

This lesson can be used to help children discover... Faith, The Future, God's Plans, Guidance, and Reputation.

Game

▶ *PREPARE IN ADVANCE*
▶ *FOR SMALL GROUPS*

Be My Guess

Children will guess a wrapped object and discuss God's wisdom.

Supplies: Bible, a variety of common objects (such as a crayon, a pencil, scissors, a spoon, a fork, a bottle of glue, or a ruler), wrapping paper

Time: 10 to 15 minutes

Preparation: Wrap the objects in wrapping paper in such a way that the objects keep their shape and can be felt through the wrapping paper.

Form groups of six, and direct groups to sit in a circle. Set aside seven wrapped objects for each group. Hand the first object to the youngest child, and give that child 30 seconds to feel the object and try to guess what it is. If the guess is incorrect, have that child pass the item to the child to his or her right, who also will get 30 seconds to feel the object and take a guess. Go around the circle until the object is guessed, and then have that person unwrap the object for everyone to see. Then give a new wrapped object to the next child in the circle.

After all the objects have been guessed and opened,

ASK:

- **How did you figure out what the objects were?**

SAY: **It would have been easier to tell what the objects were if you could have seen them. In our lives, there are a lot of things we can't see or understand.** Read aloud Genesis 41:15-16 and verse 39.

ASK:

- **What kinds of dreams have you had?**
- **Do you think it would be easy or hard to tell everybody what their dreams mean? Why?**
- **How was Joseph able to interpret Pharaoh's dreams?**

Read aloud James 1:5. SAY: **God's wisdom is a gift. But unlike the wrapped gifts we guessed about earlier, God says all we have to do to get his gift of wisdom is to ask for it.** ASK:

- **What's one thing you would like God to give you wisdom for?**

Set out the supplies and the "Treasure Box" copies. Open your Bible to Proverbs 2:1-6 and SAY: **This Scripture passage talks about hunting for hidden treasure. Listen carefully and see if you can discover what that hidden treasure is.** Read the passage aloud, and then

ASK:

- **What is the hidden treasure?**
- **Why is wisdom such a great treasure?**
- **How can you get this treasure?**

SAY: **The Bible tells us that all we have to do to find this hidden treasure is to ask God for it.**

ASK:

- **Who can tell about some of the wise things the Bible teaches us?**

SAY: **To celebrate God's gift of wisdom, we're going to make treasure boxes.** Show the sample box. Have kids cut out the box pattern on the heavy lines, fold on the dotted lines, and tape the tabs to the inside of the box. Then let each child choose a few craft jewels to glue to the top of his or her box.

Craft

▶ *PREPARE IN ADVANCE*

Wisdom Treasures

Children will learn that God's wisdom is a treasure.

Supplies: Bible; safety scissors; craft jewels in different colors, sizes, and shapes; tape; tacky craft glue; photocopies of the "Treasure Box" pattern (p. 128) on heavy paper

Time: 10 to 15 minutes

Preparation: Make a sample treasure box to display for the kids.

Bible Application

▶ *NO PREP*

From Whys to Wise

Children will experience how and why to ask God for wisdom.

Supplies: Bible, copies of the "Question Mark" pattern (p. 127), safety scissors, pens

Time: about 10 minutes

Preparation: none

Form trios. Give each child a copy of the "Question Mark" pattern. Have them cut out the question mark with scissors. SAY: **Each of us has skills and talents to do special things. But there are a lot of things we can't do. Tell your group members about a job or activity you don't know how to do. For example, I don't know how to** [name a job or activity you're not familiar with].

Give kids a minute or two to discuss, and then SAY: **On your question mark, write a question you might ask someone who could help you do that job or activity. For example, since I don't know how to** [name activity], **I would ask an expert in** [name the field], **"How can I learn to** [name activity]**?"**

After kids write down their questions, read aloud Genesis 41:15-16, 39. SAY: **Joseph didn't know how to interpret people's dreams. But he knew that God knew how to interpret dreams. So Joseph asked God for the wisdom to do it.**

ASK:

- **What's one thing you'd like God to help you do?**
- **What would you say to ask God to help you?**

Instruct kids to turn their question marks over to the other side and upside down. SAY: **Now the question mark looks like a J. J stands for *Jesus*. When we need God's help with something, all we have to do is ask him, and he'll give us wisdom.**

Read aloud James 1:5, and then have kids write down their question for God on the J side of the paper. Encourage them to pray that question to God in the coming week.

Treasure Box

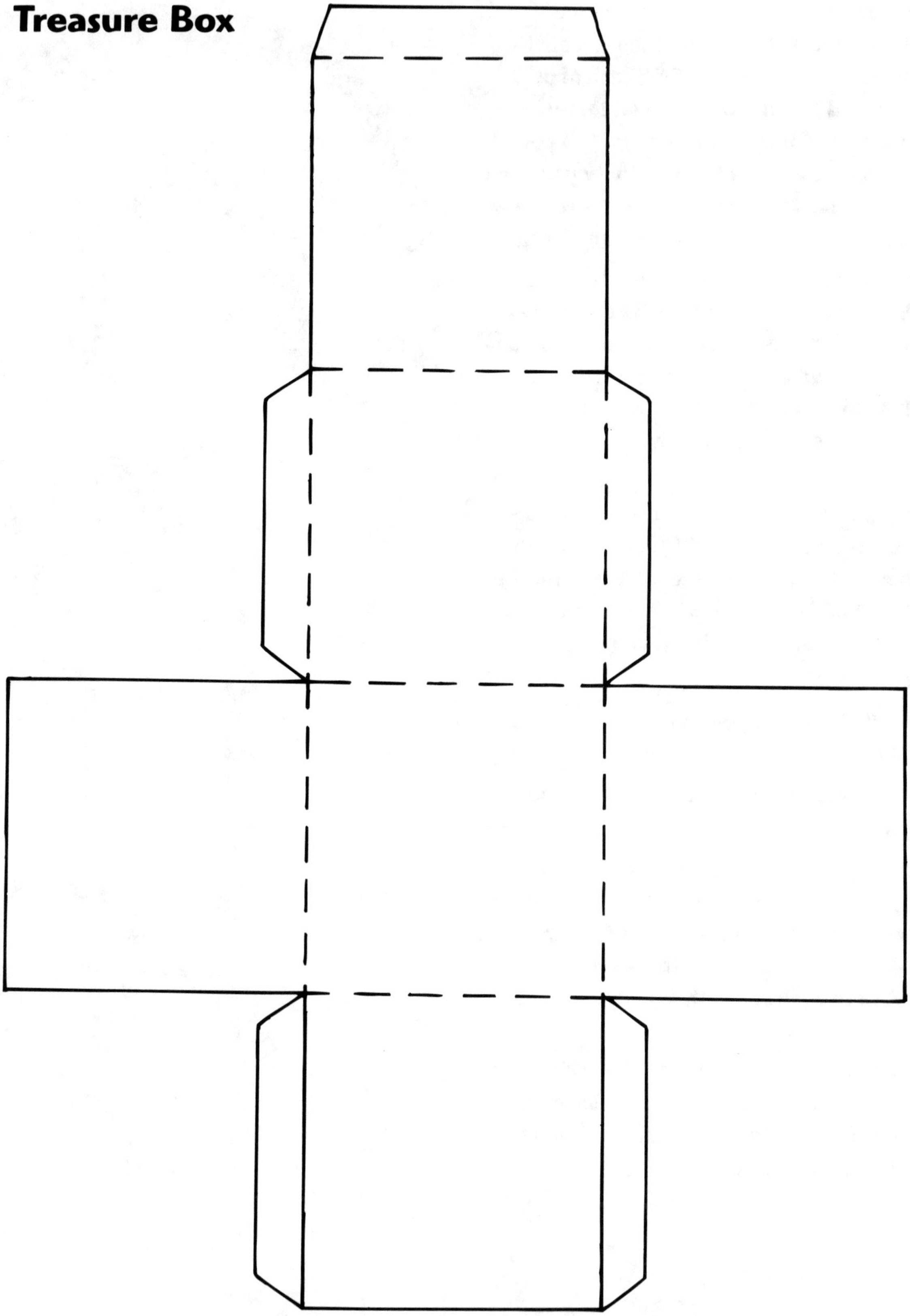

Creative Prayer Idea

▶ *FOR YOUNGER CHILDREN*
▶ *NO PREP*

W is for Wisdom

Children will be reminded to ask God for wisdom in daily situations.

Supplies: none

Time: about 5 minutes

Preparation: none

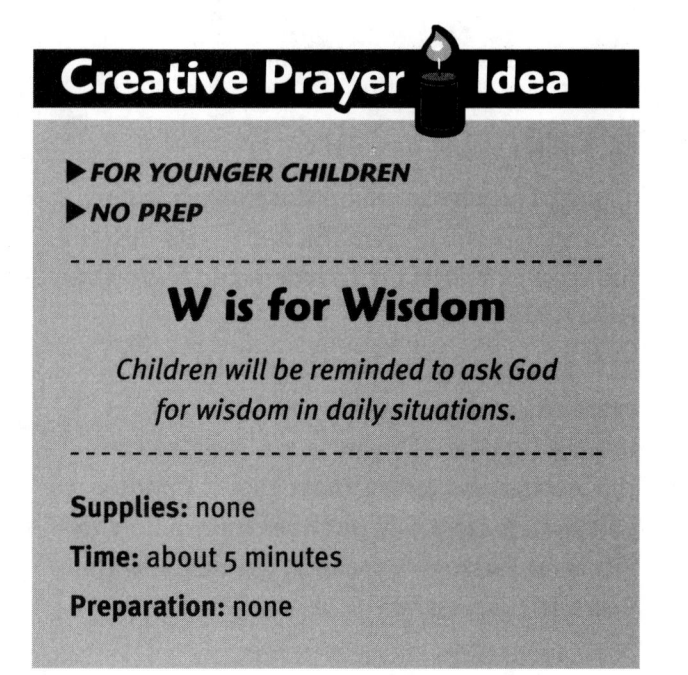

Have kids sit in a tight circle on the floor. Briefly tell them about how Joseph relied on God's wisdom to interpret Pharaoh's dreams. Ask kids about the kinds of things they might need God's help with that start with the letter W (like waiting their turn or working on homework). Read aloud James 1:5, and tell kids that God's wisdom can help them when they aren't sure how to do something. Have kids make a W shape with their fingers by placing their hands in front of them, touching the tips of their thumbs, and pointing their index fingers out and up.

SAY: **W stands for *wisdom*. When we want wisdom, all we have to do is pray and ask God for it.** Have all the kids connect their W's around the circle by connecting their index fingers. Then pray together for wisdom.

Life Application

Children will discover that God gives them wisdom as they participate in these application activities.

Crazy Definitions

Select a few unusual-sounding words from the dictionary, and have kids make up crazy definitions for the words. Then hold up the dictionary and SAY: **It would be hard to know the definitions for all these words. But God knows them because he is wise.** Then have kids write their own definitions for the word *wisdom* as it applies to their lives at home or at school.

Hot Seat

Set a chair at the front of the room, and designate it the "hot seat." One at a time, have kids sit in the hot seat and complete the following sentence: "I am the wisest person in the world because I can..." Then have each successive volunteer try to outdo the previous hot-seat sitter with his or her "wisdom." After everyone has had a turn in the hot seat, talk about how our wisdom will never match God's wisdom. In fact, our wisdom looks silly when we compare it to his.

Wise Up

Form groups of five. Give each group a rope and four blindfolds. Have four members of the group put on the blindfolds. Instruct each seeing group member to hold one end of the rope, and then have the other group members grab the rope. Tell the seeing group members to lead their groups around the room for three minutes. After they're finished, read aloud James 1:5-8. Talk about how trusting God is like following our leaders around the room. Challenge kids to think of one thing they can ask God to give them wisdom for during the week.

Science Devotion

▶ *PREPARE IN ADVANCE*

Wisdom Solvers

Children will explore how we can use God's wisdom to solve our problems.

Supplies: Bible, 6 clear plastic cups for each group of 5 kids, newspaper, pitcher of water, permanent marker

Time: 10 to 15 minutes

Preparation: Around each cup, draw a line about an inch from the bottom to show how full to fill it.

Tell the story of Joseph in Genesis 41:1-15. Then read aloud Genesis 41:16. SAY: **Joseph had a big challenge, didn't he? We're going to do an experiment today that shows how Joseph solved his problem.**

Have kids get into groups of five, and give each group six cups and some newspaper. SAY: **I'd like you to spread your newspaper on a table and set your cups out on top of it. I'll come around and fill three of your cups with water.** Fill three of each group's cups with water to the lines you drew before class, and leave three of each group's cups empty. **Place your cups in a straight line in this pattern: two empty cups, three full cups, and one empty cup. Now I'd like you to try to change the order your cups are in to make this pattern: one full, one empty, one full, one empty, one full, and one empty. The only rule is that you can only move one cup.**

Let groups work for a few minutes to try to solve the problem, and then ASK:

- **Did anyone figure it out?**

SAY: **The way to create the pattern is by pouring the water from the fourth cup into the first cup and putting the fourth cup back where it was.**

It was difficult to find the solution to this problem. I could see that some of you were feeling frustrated because you didn't know the answer and didn't know how to find the solution. Joseph may not have known how to interpret Pharaoh's dreams, but he knew that God had the answer.

ASK:

- **When we have a problem we can't solve, how can God help us?**

Read aloud James 1:5.

ASK:

- **What problems have you faced in life?**
- **How has God given you wisdom to solve your problems?**

SAY: **God wants to help us solve our problems with his wisdom. All we have to do is ask!**

Preschool Story

▶ *NO PREP*

Bible Point: ▷ **GOD GIVES US WISDOM.**

Supplies: Bible

Time: 10 to 15 minutes

Preparation: none

A Wise Guy

Have kids form a circle and sit down. Open your Bible to Genesis 41, and show children the words. SAY: **When Joseph was living in Egypt, someone told a lie about him that got him into trouble. Because of the lie, Joseph ended up in prison—even though he hadn't done anything wrong.** Encourage children to stand up and pretend they're in prison.

SAY: **But Joseph loved God and knew that God could use him even in prison, so Joseph chose to serve God while he was in prison. Soon the prison guard put Joseph in charge of everything at the prison because he knew he could trust Joseph.**

ASK:

- **What would you do if you were in charge of a prison?**

SAY: **One day two prisoners asked Joseph to tell them what their dreams meant. Joseph didn't know if he would understand their dreams, but he did know that ▷ GOD GIVES US WISDOM, so he agreed to listen to their dreams. God did give Joseph wisdom and helped him understand the dreams.** Have kids turn to a partner and tell each other one dream they've had before.

SAY: **Many days later, one of those prisoners was set free and went to work for the king, called Pharaoh. But the prisoner never forgot how Joseph had helped him understand his dreams. So one day, when Pharaoh had some strange dreams, the man told him about Joseph. He said that Joseph could tell what the dreams meant. So Pharaoh sent for Joseph and asked him to tell what the dreams meant. Joseph knew that ▷ GOD GIVES US WISDOM, so he agreed to listen to Pharaoh's dreams.**

Have kids form four groups: fat cows, skinny cows, fat heads of grain, and skinny heads of grain. Then SAY: **These were Pharaoh's dreams:**

Seven fat cows came out of the Nile River. Have the first group act like cows. **Then seven skinny cows came out of the Nile River.** Have the second group also act like cows. **The skinny cows swallowed the fat cows! But the skinny cows were still just as skinny as before!** Tell the second group to "swallow" the first group by hugging them. Have the first group sit down, but leave the second group standing.

In the second dream, there were seven plump heads of grain on a stalk. Have the third group stand and wave in the wind like grain. **Then seven skinny heads of grain grew out of the same stalk.** Have the fourth group stand and wave in the wind also. **Then the skinny heads of grain swallowed the plump heads of grain!** Tell the fourth group to "swallow" the third group by hugging them. Have the third group sit down, but leave the fourth group standing with the second group.

Kids will love pretending to swallow each other. If you have extra time, let kids swap roles and act out the dreams again.

SAY: **God gave Joseph wisdom and helped him understand that Pharaoh's dreams meant there would be seven years with lots of food and then seven years with very little food. Joseph told Pharaoh that it would be wise to save food during the first seven years so there would be enough food for the second seven years. God gave Joseph wisdom to know these things, and ▷ GOD GIVES US WISDOM, too.**

ASK:

- **How did God give Joseph wisdom?**
- **Has God ever given you wisdom? What happened?**
- **When can you trust God to give you wisdom?**

BIBLE STORY

Joseph Reveals His True Identity

For the Leader

Forgiveness can be tough for kids. It's hard to see how letting someone off the hook for hurting us can be good for us. Sometimes forgiveness doesn't seem fair.

Joseph had every right in the world to be mad at his brothers. They turned his life into a living nightmare. For 22 years Joseph suffered the consequences of his brothers' actions. But somehow Joseph was able to dig deep into his heart and forgive them. And when he did, the nightmare ended for everyone.

Use these activities to help kids understand how important it is to forgive others. If God can forgive us for all the things we've done, surely we can find a way to forgive others, too.

Key Scriptures

Genesis 42–44; 45:1-28; 50:19-21

Colossians 3:13

1 John 1:9

Bible Verse

"Make allowance for each other's faults, and forgive anyone who offends you. Remember, the Lord forgave you, so you must forgive others" (Colossians 3:13).

Bible Experience

▶ *NO PREP*

Bible Point: ▷ **FORGIVE OTHERS.**

Children will explore Joseph's example of forgiving those who hurt us.

Supplies: Bibles, paper, pencils

Time: 15 to 20 minutes

Preparation: none

ASK:

◆ **What would you do if most of your family turned against you?**

SAY: **That's what happened to Joseph. I'd like you to discover what he did.** Have kids form four groups, and assign each group one of the following passages: Genesis 42; 43; 44; 45:1-28. Tell them their research will be used by the other groups, so they should work carefully. Have students answer the following questions for their sections:

◆ **What did Joseph do?**

◆ **Why did he do it?**

◆ **What were the results?**

Allow several minutes for groups to read and research their passages. When groups are finished, have them get together with another group and share their findings. When they're finished sharing their findings, have groups rotate so all groups have a chance to share their findings with the other groups.

ASK:

◆ **Why do you think Joseph waited so long before he told his brothers who he was?**

◆ **Why do you think Joseph waited before he forgave his brothers?**

◆ **What did it mean for Joseph to forgive his brothers?**

SAY: **Can you imagine the moment at the end of this passage? In Genesis 45:3-4 Joseph revealed his identity to his brothers. It must have been an incredible moment! Joseph showed us an example of forgiveness. He thought about it before he did it. We, too, should think about what we're forgiving and why we're forgiving it. God wants us to ▷ FORGIVE OTHERS.**

Additional Topics List

This lesson can be used to help children discover... God's Plans, God's Provision, Gratitude, Patience, and Respect.

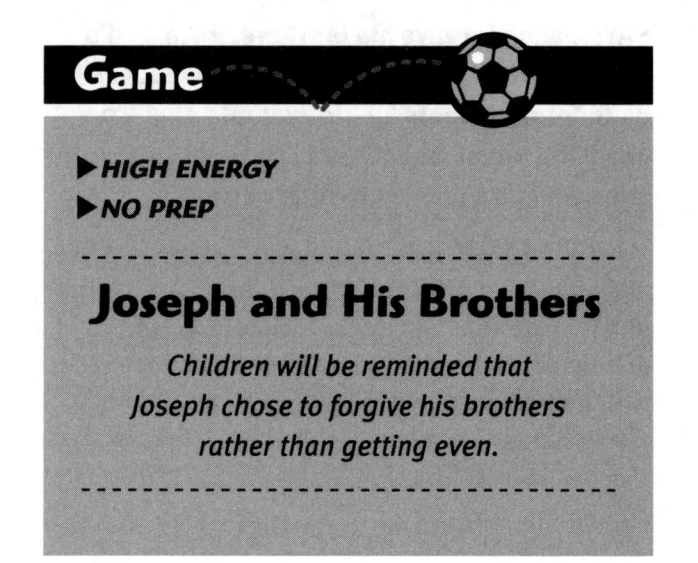

Game

▶ *HIGH ENERGY*

▶ *NO PREP*

Joseph and His Brothers

Children will be reminded that Joseph chose to forgive his brothers rather than getting even.

Supplies: none

Time: about 10 minutes

Preparation: none

Form two groups: Joseph and the brothers. Have groups line up, facing each other, about 4 feet apart, in the middle of the play area. Tell kids the story of Joseph's jealous brothers who "got" him first and threw him in a pit (Genesis 37). Later Joseph had a chance to "get" his brothers (Genesis 42-45).

Explain that you'll call out either "Joseph" or "brother." If you call out "Joseph," that team chases the other back to its home base (the wall behind them). Any kids who are tagged will join the Joseph team for the next round. Those who make it back to the wall will remain a brother for the next round.

Call out either "Joseph" or "brother," and let the chase begin. Then gather kids in the starting formation, and have them play again. Vary the name you call so kids won't know what to expect.

After a few rounds, gather kids in a circle. Tell them how Joseph had the chance to go after his brothers, but he didn't. Joseph was kind and forgave them. Discuss the following questions:

◆ **Why is it hard to be kind and forgiving to people who aren't kind and forgiving to us?**

◆ **How can you be forgiving when others aren't?**

Craft

▶PREPARE IN ADVANCE

Forgiveness Bracelets

Children will make bracelets that demonstrate the process of forgiveness.

Supplies: colored masking tape, permanent markers

Time: 10 to 15 minutes

Preparation: Cut the masking tape into 6-inch strips, two per child.

Give each child a strip of masking tape. Tell kids the story about Joseph being sold into slavery by his brothers. Have kids roll the masking tape across various surfaces, such as linoleum, carpet, or cloth. Bring kids together and look at their lint and dirt collections.

ASK:

- **What's on your tape?**
- **Were you surprised to find so much dirt and stuff around here?**

SAY: **Joseph's brothers treated him like dirt. He became a slave and lived in prison for a long time. Those things made Joseph's life look really bad, just like our tape.**

Tell the rest of the story of Joseph, how he was put in charge of Egypt and forgave his brothers. Give each child another strip of masking tape. Show them how to place that tape on top of the dirty strip of tape, sticky side to sticky side, leaving ½ inch exposed on each end. Have them write the word "forgive" on the tape. Then tell them to help each other wrap the strips around their wrists, connecting the exposed ends to make a bracelet.

ASK:

- **What happened to the dirt on our tape?**
- **How is covering up the dirt on our bracelets like forgiving others?**

SAY: **Joseph forgave his brothers for the terrible thing they did to him. It didn't change what happened, but it turned into something good. Let these bracelets remind you that we need to ▷ FORGIVE OTHERS, and when we do, God can turn it into good.**

Bible Application

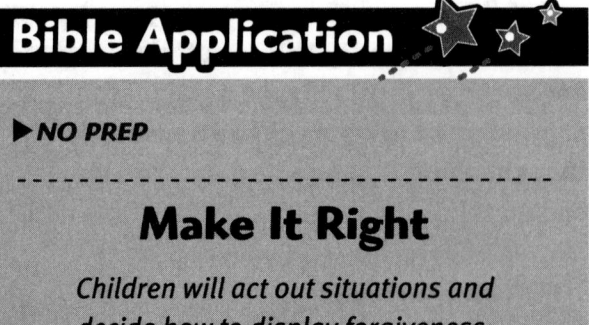

▶NO PREP

Make It Right

Children will act out situations and decide how to display forgiveness.

Supplies: Bible

Time: 10 to 15 minutes

Preparation: none

Read or summarize Genesis 45:1-28; 50:19-21.

SAY: **Joseph forgave his brothers. With God's help we can forgive others, too. God teaches us to forgive others by his example of always forgiving our sins. Let's act out times in our lives when we needed to forgive others.**

Form pairs. Give each pair a scene to act out, and select a character for each child. Let one pair at a time pantomime the scene using words and actions. Encourage children to end each scene with a display of forgiveness.

SCENE 1:

Your friend borrowed your favorite book and lost it.

SCENE 2:

Your sister took one of your toys without asking.

SCENE 3:

Your brother called you a crybaby when you stubbed your toe and cried.

SCENE 4:

Your friend said she wouldn't be your friend anymore unless she got to be the first on the swing.

After each scene, ask the questions below:

- **What wrongdoing took place in this scene?**
- **How did our characters make the situation right?**
- **What do you do when you have wronged a friend?**

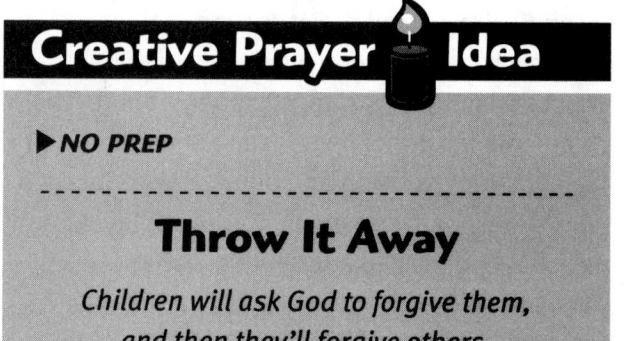

Creative Prayer Idea

▶ *NO PREP*

Throw It Away

Children will ask God to forgive them, and then they'll forgive others.

Supplies: Bible, lots of scrap paper, pencils, large trash can

Time: 5 to 10 minutes

Preparation: none

Give each child a piece of paper and a pencil. Read aloud 1 John 1:9. Ask kids to think about something they need to ask God to forgive them for, and have them write it on a piece of paper. One by one, have kids line up in front of the trash can and pray, asking God to forgive them. Then have children quietly wad up the paper and drop it into the can.

After every child has done this, give each child another piece of paper. Ask kids to think about something bad another person has done to them and write it on a piece of paper. Read aloud Colossians 3:13. One by one, have kids line up in front of the trash can again and pray that God will help them forgive that person. Then have kids quietly wad up that paper and drop it in the can.

Movie Clip

Totally Forgiven

Movie Title: *Tarzan* (Animated Disney Version) (G)

Start Time: 1 hour, 27 minutes, 55 seconds

Where to Begin: Tarzan comforts an injured Kerchak and asks for his forgiveness.

Where to End: Tarzan, the new leader of the gorilla family, walks away with the gorillas following him.

Plot: After Tarzan's parents were killed by a cheetah, the infant boy is raised by a pack of gorillas. Tarzan struggles for acceptance and always feels out of place. The gorilla leader, Kerchak, doesn't accept Tarzan until moments before he dies.

Review: Just as Joseph forgave his brothers for selling him into slavery, Tarzan and Kerchak forgave each other for their wrongdoings. This will help kids understand our need to forgive others.

Discussion

After setting up and showing the clip,

ASK:

- **How do you think Tarzan felt about what happened to Kerchak?**
- **What did Tarzan say to Kerchak?**
- **Did Kerchak forgive Tarzan?**

SAY: **Tarzan felt badly about causing harm to his gorilla family. He asked forgiveness from Kerchak. Kerchak forgave Tarzan, and Tarzan forgave Kerchak.** Read or summarize Genesis 45:1-28; 50:19-21. **Joseph forgave his brothers. With God's help, we can forgive others also. When we wrong someone, we should ask for that person's forgiveness. And in turn, when someone wrongs us and asks for forgiveness, we should forgive him or her.** Close by reading aloud Colossians 3:13.

Snack

▶ ***PREPARE IN ADVANCE***
▶ ***FOR YOUNGER CHILDREN***
▶ ***ALLERGY ALERT***

Bad to Good

Children will play a snack game to help them understand how bad turned into good when Joseph forgave his brothers.

Supplies: Bible, cereal, large containers, 1-cup measuring cups, quart-sized resealable bags

Time: about 15 minutes

Preparation: Pour cereal into one large container for every four or five children. Put a measuring cup into each container.

Read Genesis 45:1-28; 50:19-21, or tell the story in your own words.

ASK:

- **How do you think Joseph felt when he saw his brothers?**
- **How do you think Joseph's brothers felt when they recognized Joseph?**

SAY: **Even though Joseph's brothers sold him into slavery, God had a plan for his life. In time, the Pharaoh of Egypt put Joseph in charge of Egypt. Because of his job, Joseph was able to help all of his family and many other people during the great famine. And because Joseph forgave his brothers, God was able to use that situation for good.**

Let's do an activity to remind us that God worked good when Joseph forgave his brothers. Have children form groups of four or five. Choose one person in each team to be "Joseph." Give each Joseph a container of cereal. Give the remaining team players a resealable bag. Those players will be "Joseph's Brothers." Have all the Josephs stand at one end of the room and Joseph's Brothers at the other end of the room. Have each Joseph scoop a cup of cereal from the container and race to a Brother, pouring the cereal into his or her bag. Joseph should return to the container to scoop and pour cereal until each teammate's bag has cereal. Continue playing until each person has had a turn being Joseph.

notes

Preschool Story

▶ *NO PREP*

Bible Point: ▷ **FORGIVE OTHERS.**

Supplies: Bible, paper plates, red and blue crayons

Time: 10 to 15 minutes

Preparation: none

An Emotional Roller Coaster

Before you begin, give each child two paper plates, a red crayon, and a blue crayon. Tell kids to draw a bright happy face with the red crayon on both sides of one paper plate and a sad face with the blue crayon on both sides of the other plate.

Have kids bring their plates and sit in a circle on the floor. Open your Bible to Genesis 45, and show children the words. SAY: **At different times during our Bible story, I'm going to ask you how you might feel if something happened to you. Then you can hold up the face that shows how you would feel if you were that person. God wants us to ▷ FORGIVE OTHERS. Let's see if Joseph forgave.**

Joseph had 10 older brothers who laughed at his dreams.

ASK:

- **How would you feel if people laughed at you?** (Have kids hold up the plate they choose.)
- **Would you forgive people who laughed at you?**

SAY: **The brothers were jealous of the beautiful coat Joseph got from their dad.**

ASK:

- **How would you feel if someone were jealous of you?** (Encourage kids to hold up one of their plates.)
- **Would you forgive someone who was jealous of you?**

SAY: **Joseph's brothers even sold him to be a slave. Joseph had to live far, far away and couldn't see his family.**

ASK:

- **How would you feel if that happened to you?** (Have kids hold up the plate they choose.)
- **Would you forgive someone who did that to you?**

SAY: **One night Pharaoh had a scary dream, so he sent for Joseph. God showed Joseph what Pharaoh's dream meant. Pharaoh believed him and put Joseph in charge of all the food in Egypt.**

ASK:

- **How would you feel if you were Joseph now?** (Encourage kids to hold up one of their plates.)

SAY: **Joseph's family lived a long way from Egypt, but when there was no rain to grow food, they had to travel all the way to Egypt to get more food.**

ASK:

- **How would you feel if you had no food?** (Have kids hold up one of their plates.)

SAY: **Joseph's brothers had forgotten all about Joseph and didn't know who he was when they met him. But when Joseph saw his brothers, he knew them right away. He remembered that they had sold him to be a slave.**

ASK:

- ◆ **How would you feel if you were Joseph?** (Encourage kids to hold up one of their plates.)
- ◆ **Would you forgive?**

SAY: **Joseph knew that God had made all the bad things his brothers did to him into something good. Joseph had become a leader in Egypt, and people bowed down to him. Joseph could help his brothers now, or he could get back at them for all the mean things they had done to him.**

ASK:

- ◆ **What would you do?**

SAY: **Joseph chose to forgive his brothers for all the mean things they had done to him. God wants us to ▷ FORGIVE OTHERS just as Joseph did.**

ASK:

- ◆ **Has someone hurt you?**
- ◆ **Will you forgive that person?**

notes

BIBLE STORY

Birth of Moses

For the Leader

What would you do if a baby you loved was faced with a death sentence? Because the king of Egypt was afraid the enslaved Hebrews would rebel, he issued a command to throw all Hebrew baby boys into the Nile River. Moses' mother hid her baby in a basket and placed him among the reeds at the edge of the river. There Pharaoh's daughter found him. Amazingly, the princess adopted Moses, and even more amazingly, Moses' mother was hired as a nurse to help raise him.

Just as Moses was adopted, those who accept Jesus as Lord of their lives are adopted into God's family. These activities will help kids understand the depth of God's love for them. God protected Moses, and God promises to protect them, too.

Key Scriptures

Exodus 2:1-10

Psalm 61:1-4; 121:8

Bible Verse

"The Lord keeps watch over you as you come and go, both now and forever" (Psalm 121:8).

Bible Experience

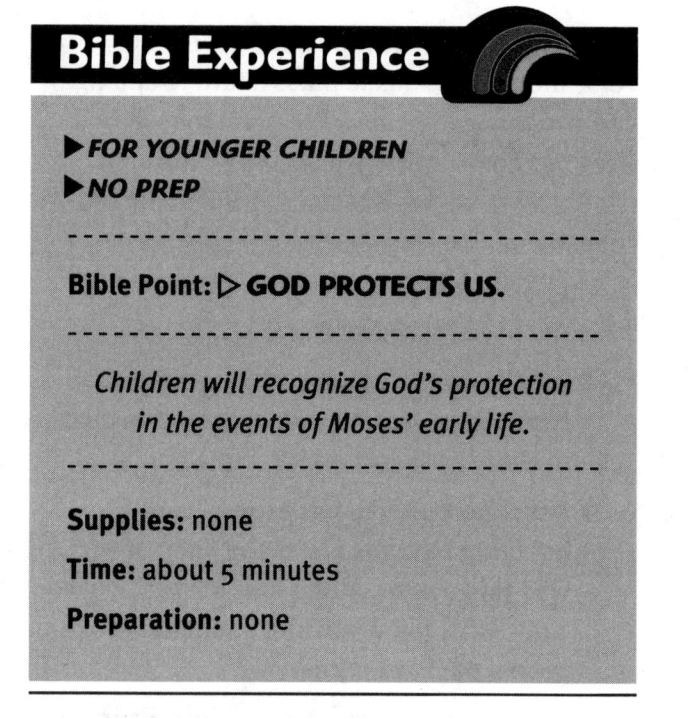

▶ *FOR YOUNGER CHILDREN*
▶ *NO PREP*

Bible Point: ▷ **GOD PROTECTS US.**

Children will recognize God's protection in the events of Moses' early life.

Supplies: none
Time: about 5 minutes
Preparation: none

As you tell this story, have kids listen for the following cue words and do the accompanying motions when they hear the words.

Israelite—Hold up a fist.

God—Clap twice and say, "The Lord!"

Pharaoh—Boo.

Baby—Rock a pretend baby, and say, "Wah."

SAY: **An *Israelite* woman and her family lived in Egypt. The woman loved *God* very much, but the wicked ruler of Egypt didn't love *God* at all. The wicked ruler was *Pharaoh*. *Pharaoh* decided there were too many *Israelites* in the land. He decided to have all the *baby* boys killed.**

The *Israelite* woman had a *baby* boy. She hid the *baby* for three months. But then she couldn't hide him anymore, so she wove a basket and laid the *baby* inside. She carefully placed the basket at the edge of the Nile River. The *baby* floated in his basket while his sister watched to see what would happen.

Soon *Pharaoh*'s daughter came down to the river to take a bath. The princess saw the floating basket and told one of her slave girls to bring it to her. What do you think happened then? The princess peeked in the basket and saw the *baby*! She felt sorry for him. "This baby belongs to the *Israelites*," she said.

Just then the *baby*'s sister ran up and offered to find someone to take care of him. "Yes, go!" said the princess. So the girl brought the *baby*'s own mother to the princess. "Take care of him until he's older," the princess commanded.

When the *baby* grew older, the *Israelite* woman gave him back to the princess, and from that day on, he grew up in the palace. The princess named him Moses. When Moses grew up, he helped set the *Israelites* free from cruel *Pharaoh*.

ASK:

◆ **Has God ever protected you from anything? Explain.**

SAY: **God has plans for each of us, just like he had for Moses. God will protect us and make his plans come true. Psalm 121:8 says, "The Lord keeps watch over you as you come and go, both now and forever." This was true of Moses, and it's true for each one of us today. ▷ GOD PROTECTS US!**

Song & Connect

Use "Wherever You Go (track 1, *it: Innovative Tools for Children's Ministry: Old Testament* CD) to help reinforce the Bible Point, ▷ **GOD PROTECTS US.**

Additional Topics List

This lesson can be used to help children discover... Caring for Others, Faith, God's Plans, Joy, and Trusting God.

Game

▶ *NO PREP*

▶ *FOR YOUNGER CHILDREN*

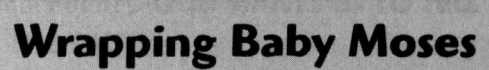

Wrapping Baby Moses

Children will discover the incredible act of faith that Moses' mother showed in hiding her baby in the river to save him from death.

Supplies: baby doll, basket or box large enough to hold the doll, baby blanket or bath towel, stopwatch

Time: 10 to 15 minutes

Preparation: none

SAY: **Let's play a game that will help us understand what Moses' mother must have gone through when she hid baby Moses at the edge of the Nile River to save him from Pharaoh.**

Have kids form two parallel lines, facing each other, on opposite sides of the room. Designate one line the "Wrappers" and the other line the "Unwrappers." Lay the doll, a blanket, and the basket next to each other in the middle of the space between the two lines.

SAY: **The first person in the Wrappers line will run out to the baby, wrap it tightly in the blanket, place it in the basket, and run back to the line. Then the first person in the Unwrappers line will run out to where the baby is lying, unwrap the doll, and place the blanket, doll, and basket where you see them right now. Whenever someone returns to his or her line, the next person in the other line may go. We're racing against the clock!**

After giving the instructions, start the lines running. Make sure each child has a turn. You may wish to have each child say the memory verse aloud as he or she takes a turn wrapping or unwrapping the baby. Once everyone in both lines has gone, switch which line wraps and which unwraps. See if teams can complete the second round in less time.

After playing the game, divide the kids into trios and have them discuss:

- **How do you think Moses' mother must have felt when Pharaoh ordered the death of every newborn male? Explain.**
- **Describe how you felt as you were hurrying to take care of the baby. How was this like or unlike how Moses' mother must have felt when she had to let Moses go in a basket in the river?**
- **God protected baby Moses. How does God protect us today?**

Craft

▶ *PREPARE IN ADVANCE*

Little Moses

Children will create a miniature baby Moses to remind them of God's protection.

Supplies: Bible, kitchen sponges, scissors, small wooden ice-cream spoons, markers, tissues

Time: about 10 minutes

Preparation: Cut each sponge in half, forming two squares.

Read or summarize the story of baby Moses in Exodus 2:1-10. SAY: **God protected Moses. God kept Moses safe and gave him an Egyptian**

home to grow up in so he wouldn't be killed as a baby. ▷ GOD PROTECTS US, too. Let's make a take-home basket to remind us that God will protect us, just as he protected Moses.

Give all children a sponge square. Have them draw a face on the wooden spoon and wrap it in a tissue. Show kids how to lay "baby Moses" on the sponge "basket." While kids are working, ASK:

- ◆ **How did God protect Moses in order for his plans to take place?**
- ◆ **What kinds of things does God protect you from?**
- ◆ **Who can you tell the story of Moses to?**

SAY: **Take your Moses basket home, and place it in your bedroom or bathroom. It can remind you that God will protect you.**

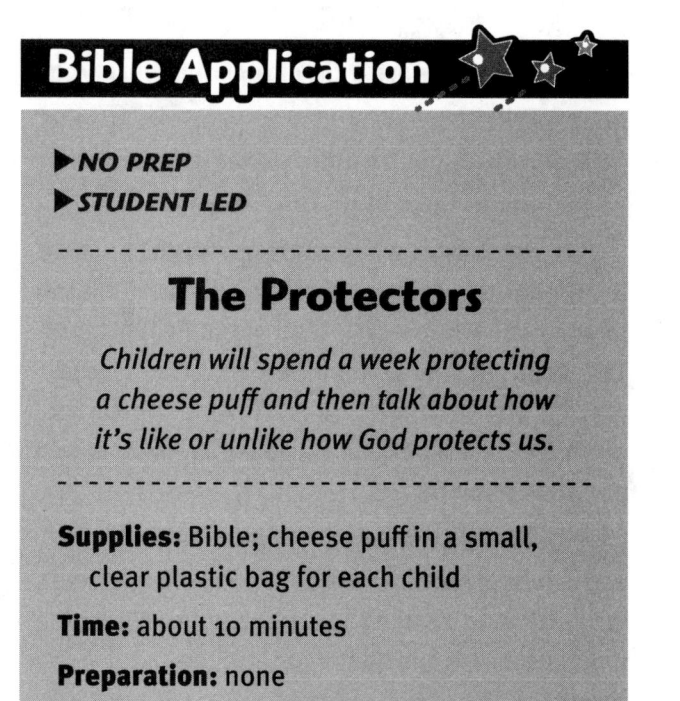

Bible Application

▶ *NO PREP*
▶ *STUDENT LED*

The Protectors

Children will spend a week protecting a cheese puff and then talk about how it's like or unlike how God protects us.

Supplies: Bible; cheese puff in a small, clear plastic bag for each child

Time: about 10 minutes

Preparation: none

Read the story of God protecting Moses in Exodus 2:1-10. Talk to kids about how God protects us, too. Give each child a cheese puff in a bag, and instruct kids to take care of their cheese puffs for a week. Tell them it's very important that they take care of their cheese puffs and return them safely the following week.

When kids return a week later, ASK:

- ◆ **How well did you protect your cheese puff from being smashed or being eaten?**
- ◆ **Was it hard or easy to protect your cheese puff? Why?**
- ◆ **How is this like how God protects us? How is it different from how God protects us?**
- ◆ **How do you think God will protect you as you grow up?**
- ◆ **Aren't you glad you're not a cheese puff?**

Creative Prayer Idea

▶ *NO PREP*
▶ *FOR SMALL GROUPS*

God, Our Fortress

Children will build a fortress and then pray inside and thank God for his protection.

Supplies: Bible, chairs, tables, blankets and sheets, clothespins

Time: 10 to 15 minutes

Preparation: none

Encourage kids to build a "fortress" from the materials you've provided. Have them make the fortress large enough for everyone to fit inside. When the fortress is complete, crawl inside with the kids and ASK:

- ◆ **Why do people build fortresses?**
- ◆ **When do you feel especially safe and protected?**

Read aloud Psalm 61:1-4, and then ASK:

- ◆ **Who was David's fortress?**
- ◆ **Who was Moses' fortress? Explain.**
- ◆ **Can God be our fortress today? Explain.**
- ◆ **When do you need God's protection?**

Lead the kids in prayer inside the fortress, thanking God for his protection.

Discussion Launcher Questions

Ask children to form trios and discuss:

- ◆ **Describe a time you knew God was protecting you. How did that feel?**
- ◆ **Do you think there's ever a time God doesn't protect somebody? Why or why not?**
- ◆ **When God says he'll protect us, does that mean we'll never get hurt? Why or why not?**
- ◆ **What's something you hope God will always protect you from?**

notes

Object Lesson

▶ *NO PREP*
▶ *ALLERGY ALERT*

Powerful Protection

Children will use birthday candles to help them understand God's protection.

Supplies: Bible, sheet cake, birthday candle, matches, taper candle in a holder with a glass hurricane shade

Time: about 10 minutes

Preparation: none

ASK:

- ◆ **When you were a tiny kid, what were you afraid of?**
- ◆ **Now that you're older, what's the scariest thing in the whole world to you?**

SAY: **No matter what our fears might be, God is bigger and stronger than any of them. Listen to what the Bible says.** Read aloud Psalm 121:8. **The writer of this psalm knew that God would protect him because God is the most powerful of all. Let's see how God's power compares with people's power.**

Set out the cake and birthday candles. Have each child place a candle on the cake. Light the birthday candles and the taper candle. Replace the glass hurricane shade around the taper candle.

SAY: **The birthday candles represent the power we have. Sometimes scary things happen, and the winds of trouble blow in our lives. Blow at these candles on the cake.** When all the candles have been blown out, SAY: **We're not very strong, are we? But God is like this**

candle. Point to the taper candle. **Blow at this candle the same way you blew at the birthday candles.** Don't allow the children to blow down the top of the hurricane shade.

ASK:

◆ **Why didn't this candle go out?**

SAY: **God is more powerful than anything that can hurt us. ▷ GOD PROTECTS US now and forever!**

Preschool Story

▶ ***NO PREP***

Bible Point: ▷ **GOD PROTECTS US.**

Supplies: Bible

Time: 15 to 20 minutes

Preparation: none

Water Baby

Have kids form a circle and sit down. Open your Bible to Exodus 2, and show children the words. Instruct children to cradle their arms as if rocking a baby every time they hear the word *baby* during the Bible story.

SAY: **Once there was a *baby*** (pretend to rock a baby) **boy who was very small. His mommy had to keep him safe from the mean king, called Pharaoh, who wanted to hurt him. So Moses' mommy made a special basket that wouldn't sink in the water. She wrapped him in a blanket and laid him in the basket.**

Parents like to pray and ask God to help their children because ▷ GOD PROTECTS US, even when we're not with our moms or dads.

The mommy then placed her *baby* (pretend to rock a baby) **in the water to float safely down the river. But the *baby*** (pretend to rock a baby) **wasn't alone. God was watching over him, and so was his big sister, Miriam. She followed the floating basket a long way down the river. She wanted to make sure her little brother was safe from the mean Pharaoh.**

Miriam saw the basket floating near an area where many women were in the water. Miriam heard a woman say she saw the basket. It was the princess, the mean Pharaoh's daughter. A few of the servants went to get the basket.

ASK:

◆ **What do you think the princess did when she found out what was inside the basket?**

SAY: **As the basket got closer, the princess could hear a small sound coming from inside. When she opened the basket, she saw the *baby.*** (Pretend to rock a baby.) **She wasn't mean like Pharaoh. She felt sorry for the *baby*** (pretend to rock a baby). **He was crying, and she wanted to make him feel better. But she couldn't take care of a hungry *baby*** (pretend to rock a baby). **Miriam came out of the bushes because she knew that her mother could feed the hungry *baby*** (pretend to rock a baby) **until he grew older.**

The princess named the *baby* (pretend to rock a baby) **Moses. Little Moses grew up with his mother and then went to live with the princess in a big palace. God protected *baby*** (pretend to rock a baby) **Moses, and ▷ GOD PROTECTS US, too.**

ASK:

◆ **How did God protect Moses?**

◆ **When can you trust God to protect you?**

SAY: **Let's say a prayer now to thank God for protecting us.** Lead children in the following action prayer.

PRAY:

Dear God,

I know that Moses' mom was worried and hid baby Moses in the river. (Wring your hands.)

You helped her to know what to do. (Point up.)

Baby Moses was crying. (Rub your eyes.)

You helped him to be safe. (Point up.)

Big sister Miriam was scared. (Cover your eyes.)

You helped her to be brave. (Point up.)

You will help us, too. (Hug self.)

You protect us and help us when we're scared. (Point up.)

Thank you, God. Amen. (Hug self.)

notes

BIBLE STORY

Moses and the Burning Bush

For the Leader

It's pretty likely that none of your students have had burning-bush experiences. Well, neither had Moses. "Amazing!" Moses said to himself. "Why isn't that bush burning up?" When God spoke to Moses, the Bible says "he was afraid."

One of the most common questions kids ask about God is why he doesn't talk to us directly, like he did in the Bible stories. That's what these lessons and activities are for: to help children experience how God really can speak to them—how they can hear his voice and, as Moses ultimately did, follow.

Key Scriptures

Exodus 3:1-22

Joshua 2:1-17; 6:1-25

1 Samuel 17

Hebrews 3:15

Bible Verse

"Remember what it says: 'Today when you hear his voice, don't harden your hearts as Israel did when they rebelled'" (Hebrews 3:15).

Bible Experience

▶ *NO PREP*

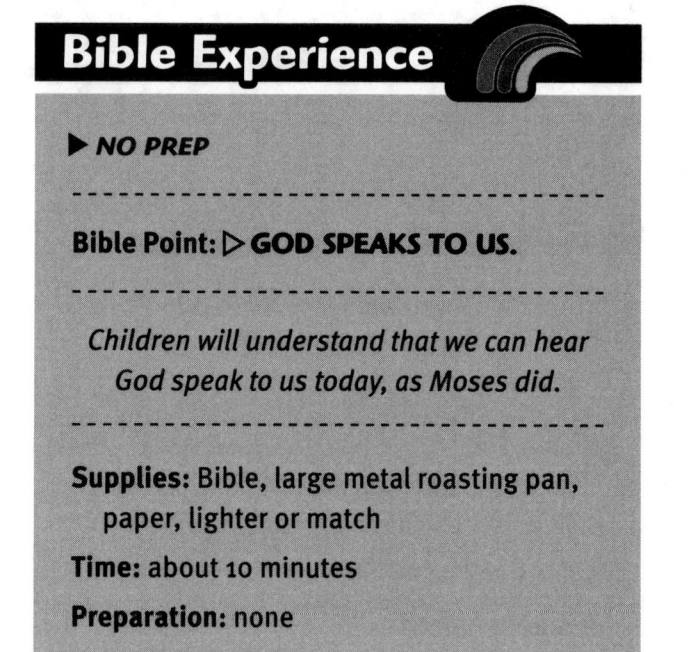

Bible Point: ▷ GOD SPEAKS TO US.

Children will understand that we can hear God speak to us today, as Moses did.

Supplies: Bible, large metal roasting pan, paper, lighter or match

Time: about 10 minutes

Preparation: none

Gather the kids and ASK:

◆ **When you're watching TV or playing a game and your parents want you for something, what do they do to get your attention?**

SAY: **What a lot of ways to get your attention! Well, the Bible tells us that one time God wanted to get Moses' attention. And God did it in an amazing way.**

Read aloud Exodus 3:1. Start a piece of paper on fire, and hold it over the roasting pan as it burns. Then drop it in the pan. SAY: **Do I have your attention? I'm sure you didn't expect me to start a fire here today!**

Read Exodus 3:2-4. SAY: **God got Moses' attention, all right. Not only did God use an amazing burning bush, God also spoke to Moses in a voice he could hear. Moses couldn't believe it!**

ASK:

◆ **What would you have done if you had seen the burning bush?**

Read Exodus 3:5-6. Have kids take off their shoes. SAY: **When God talks to us, it's a special thing. Even though probably none of us have ever seen a burning bush like that, ▷ GOD SPEAKS TO US, too.**

ASK:

◆ **How does God get your attention?**

◆ **What are some of the ways God can speak to us?**

Read Exodus 3:7-9. SAY: **God needed to get Moses' attention because he had a special job for Moses to do. God wanted him to lead his people out of Egypt and into the Promised Land!**

ASK:

◆ **What does God want us to do?**

Read Exodus 3:10. SAY: **Just like Moses, God has a plan and a purpose for each of us.**

ASK:

◆ **What's one thing you know God wants you to do for him this week?**

As the children give their responses, have them put their shoes back on and say, "God speaks to me, and I will go and do what he says."

SAY: **God speaks to us today, and we must listen. Hebrews 3:15 says, "Today when you hear his voice, don't harden your hearts."**

Close in prayer, asking God to help each of us hear his voice and give us the strength to follow him.

Additional Topics List

This lesson can be used to help children discover... God's Power, God's Voice, Holiness, Obedience, and Weakness.

Game

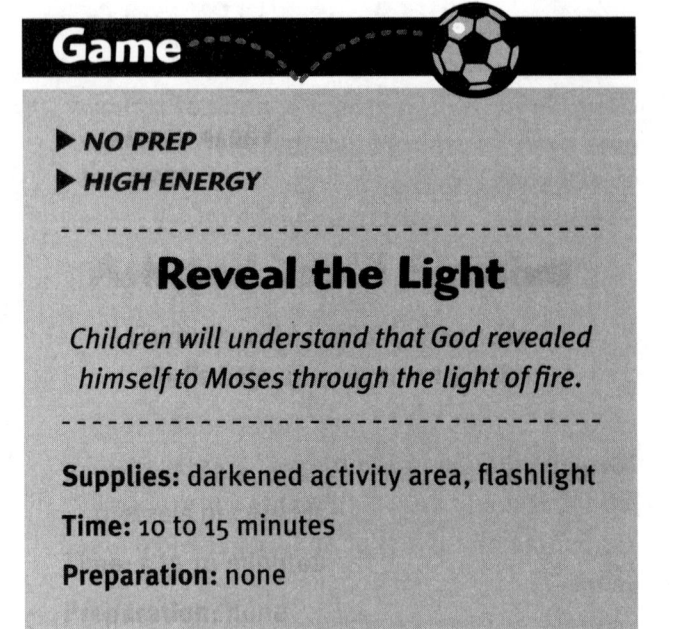

▶ *NO PREP*
▶ *HIGH ENERGY*

Reveal the Light

Children will understand that God revealed himself to Moses through the light of fire.

Supplies: darkened activity area, flashlight

Time: 10 to 15 minutes

Preparation: none

Play this game in a large, dark room or in a large outdoor area after dark. To begin, ask kids to brainstorm some ideas about what it *means* to follow God and what it's *like* to follow God. Give one student a flashlight, and explain that he or she is "It." Don't use a high-powered flashlight—a smaller or weaker one will actually work better for this game. The group will play a game of tag in which the person who is It tries to tag others by shining the flashlight on them. Give the group to the count of five to scatter, and then begin the game. When a person is tagged, he or she should "freeze" and call out one of the ideas about following God and then continue to play. Continue until It becomes tired, and then choose a new It.

After playing the game, have kids sit in a circle and discuss:

- **How did you feel when you saw the light coming for you? Explain.**
- **How do you think Moses felt when he saw the burning bush? Why?**
- **How does God reveal himself to you?**
- **How can you follow God?**

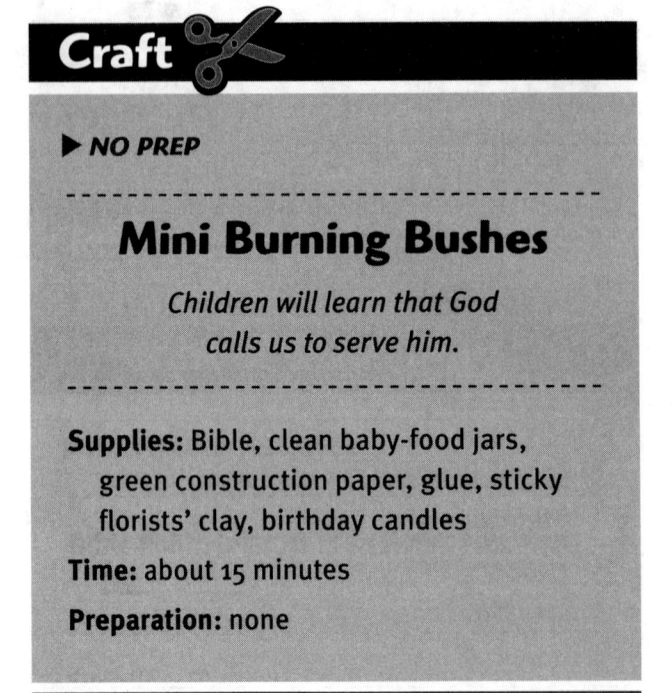

Craft

▶ *NO PREP*

Mini Burning Bushes

Children will learn that God calls us to serve him.

Supplies: Bible, clean baby-food jars, green construction paper, glue, sticky florists' clay, birthday candles

Time: about 15 minutes

Preparation: none

Hand each child a baby-food jar, and set out the supplies. Show kids how to tear small leaves from the construction paper and glue them to the jar in layers to resemble a bush. When each jar is covered with paper leaves, have each child stick a walnut-sized lump of florists' clay in the bottom of the jar. Be sure the clay is centered in the jar. Then help each child stick a candle securely into the clay.

When the mini burning bushes are finished, read aloud Exodus 3:1-10. Then ASK:

- **What was special about the burning bush?**
- **What did God want Moses to do?**
- **How do you think Moses felt as God talked to him? How would you feel?**
- **How does God talk to you?**

Bible Application

▶ *PREPARE IN ADVANCE*

I Will Follow

Children will think of ways they can follow God with this hands-on, "feet-on" paint project.

Supplies: Bible; 4 large pieces of newsprint; markers; red, yellow, and orange tempera paint; 3 pie pans; paintbrushes; towels and water; large plant

Time: 15 to 20 minutes

Preparation: Tape the four pieces of newsprint to the floor to form a square. Place a large plant in the center of the square to represent the burning bush.

Have children sit along the edges of the square. SAY: **Let's learn about how God spoke to Moses in a special way.** Read aloud Exodus 3:1-8a.

ASK:

◆ **Why did Moses have to remove his shoes?**

Ask children to consider ways God could talk to them. Then encourage each child to share, in one to three words, a way they can follow God. After everyone has shared, have kids write their responses with markers on the newsprint. Pour red, yellow, and orange paint into the pie pans, and have kids use paintbrushes to completely cover the bottom of one of their feet with paint. Have each child make a footprint beside his or her written way to follow God.

ASK:

◆ **Which of these ways to listen to and follow God can you do?**

◆ **Which ones don't you understand?**

◆ **What can you do to hear what God has to tell you?**

Be sure children's feet are completely clean and dry before they put their shoes back on.

Creative Prayer Idea

▶ *NO PREP*

▶ *FOR LARGE GROUPS*

Step Up to the Microphone

Children will tell God they will listen for his voice.

Supplies: Bible, microphone hooked up to a loudspeaker

Time: about 5 minutes

Preparation: none

Gather kids together and ASK (without the microphone):

◆ **What are some ways we try to get each others' attention?**

SAY: **Sometimes when we're speaking in front of a lot of people, the only way we can be heard is to use a microphone.** Hold up the microphone. (Make sure it's on.) Speaking into the microphone, SAY: **Can you hear me better now? Do I have your attention?**

ASK:

◆ **What are some ways God might try to get our attention?**

SAY: **Thankfully, we don't need a microphone to talk to God. But today we're going to**

remember what it says in Hebrews 1:15: "Today you must listen to God's voice." Let's pray right now and tell God we'll listen when he speaks to us.

Turn off the microphone. Bring kids together in a circle, and one at a time, have kids quietly say the following prayer into the microphone: "Today I will listen to your voice."

Life Application

Children will discover that God speaks to them as they participate in these application activities.

God's Mega-Voice

Have each child make a mini megaphone by rolling a piece of construction paper into a cone and taping it. Give them a chance to practice speaking to each other through their megaphones. Then have them place the megaphone to their ears (wide side facing out) to practice listening to God's voice. Talk about how speaking and listening are different.

That's Impossible!

Form trios and have kids do a job or activity that they think would be impossible to do but that God might tell them to do. Then have them think of a way to act out how God would help them do what he has told them to do. For each idea, have the rest of the group rank the job or activity on their imaginary "impossibility meter." Have them fold their arms across their chests and then raise one arm like a noise-level gauge. Talk about how God can help us do anything he asks us to do.

Worship Prompt Idea

▶ ***PREPARE IN ADVANCE***

Flames of Praise

Children will worship God as they remember Moses' encounter with God at the burning bush.

Supplies: red, orange, and yellow crepe paper

Time: about 5 minutes

Preparation: Cut the crepe paper into 4- to 5-foot lengths, two per child.

Tell kids the story of Moses and the burning bush. Give each child two strips of crepe paper. As you sing praises to God, have kids wave and twirl the crepe paper to mimic the flames of the burning bush.

Preschool Story

▶ ***PREPARE IN ADVANCE***

▶ ***ALLERGY ALERT***

Bible Point: ▷ **GOD SPEAKS TO US.**

Supplies: Bible; red, orange, and yellow construction paper; paper-towel rolls; red, yellow, and orange tissue paper; plastic plates; pretzel sticks; shredded cheese; microwave oven (optional)

Time: 15 to 20 minutes

Preparation: Place paper-towel rolls in a pile in the center of the room to simulate a bush that will later "burn."

On Fire!

Have kids form a circle and sit down. Open your Bible to Exodus 3, and show children the words. Invite kids to stand in a circle. Have a piece of construction paper ready for each of the children to use during the story.

SAY: **Moses did something bad in Egypt and then ran away and hid.** Let kids quickly pretend to hide in the room, and then SAY: **He walked and walked until he was sure he was far away.** Have kids walk in a circle a few times.

He made some friends. He got married. He was happy every day. Have children find a partner and walk arm in arm in a circle.

As Moses watched his sheep one day (have kids crawl around and say, "Baa!"), **he saw a burning bush.** Point to the pile of paper-towel rolls. Give kids red, orange, and yellow construction paper to throw onto the pile of paper-towel rolls to create a "burning bush." **He took off his shoes and listened to God, and God gave him a push.** Let kids take off their shoes and then sit quietly, with their fingers in front of their mouths, and be silent for about 10 seconds. Then SAY: **God sent Moses back to Egypt. God wanted Moses to obey.**

God loved the Israelites, it's true. But Moses said, "No way!" Have kids point to their hearts. **"I can't talk to Pharaoh! I'll make mistakes. I don't know what to say!"** Have kids place their hands over their mouths.

"That's all right," God said, "Your brother will talk for you." Have kids shake their hands with a friend next to them. **"Now go, and I will use *you* to set my people free!"** Let kids walk in a small circle, holding hands. **So Moses left and walked and walked, until the Pharaoh he could see.** Encourage kids to put one of their hands over their eyes and scan the horizon.

ASK:

- **How did God speak to Moses?**
- **Has God ever spoken to you?**
- **What are some ways God speaks to us?**

Have kids form two groups. Lead one group to the craft station and the other group to the snack station. If you have enough time, be sure kids rotate and do both activities.

At the craft station, give each child half of a paper-towel roll and several pieces of red, yellow, and orange tissue paper. Have kids push the tissue paper through the roll until it comes out the other side. Let kids make the flames disappear and reappear several times. Remind kids that God spoke to Moses through a burning bush, and ▷ **GOD SPEAKS TO US, too.**

At the snack station, give kids plastic plates, several pretzel sticks, and some shredded cheddar cheese. Encourage kids to make a pile of pretzel sticks on their plates and then sprinkle the shredded cheese on top of the sticks so it looks like a burning bush. If you have a microwave, heat each child's snack to melt the cheese. Remind children that God spoke to Moses, and ▷ **GOD SPEAKS TO US, too.**

notes

BIBLE STORY

God Gives Moses Signs

For the Leader

Moses just didn't want to do it. He tried every excuse to duck the assignment. "I'm not the right guy." "They won't believe me." "I'm not talented enough." His excuses sound *exactly* like the excuses most of us use today to get out of doing what God wants us to do. But God wouldn't have it. He wanted Moses.

God wants your students, too. His plans for each of them are different, but his desire is the same: He wants to use them for his good purposes. Each of them represents God's body to the rest of the world, and only by casting the excuses aside can we begin to let him use us freely.

Use these experiences to give kids a firsthand look at the amazing things God did in Moses' life. Let your students see that Moses was no more special or unique than they are and that God indeed wants to use them to do wonderful things.

Key Scriptures

Exodus 3:1-22; 4:1-17

Ephesians 3:20

Bible Verse

"Now all glory to God, who is able, through his mighty power at work within us, to accomplish infinitely more than we might ask or think" (Ephesians 3:20).

Bible Experience

▶ ***NO PREP***
▶ ***FOR YOUNGER CHILDREN***
▶ ***FOR SMALL GROUPS***

Bible Point: ▷ **GOD USES US.**

Children will learn that God can help them do mighty things for him.

Supplies: Bible, kazoos

Time: 10 to 15 minutes

Preparation: none

Gather kids together and ASK:

◆ **What are some of the most annoying things people do?**

Divide the group into pairs, and discuss the following questions:

◆ **When you need someone to help you with something, how does it make you feel when people make excuses not to help you?**

◆ **Describe a time you made up an excuse to get out of doing something.**

SAY: **Every one of us has made excuses at one time or another to get out of doing something. One of the greatest people in the Bible did the same thing. In fact, he did it over and over again.**

Hand out kazoos to children and SAY: **On the count of three, let's all try our kazoos to make sure they work. Then, when we're finished, keep them quiet until I tell you to use them again.** After they blow their kazoos, SAY: **We're going to read about the time God wanted Moses to do something very important. But Moses kept making excuses why he couldn't do it. Every time I read one of Moses' excuses, let's all blow our kazoos in each others' faces.**

Read the story of Moses in Exodus 3:9-14 and 4:1-17. Have kids blow their kazoos after verses 3:11; 3:13; 4:1; 4:10; and 4:13. After the story, ASK:

- ◆ **How would it feel to get a kazoo blown in your face every time you asked someone to help you?**
- ◆ **How do you think God felt when Moses made excuses?**

SAY: **Even though Moses gave God a bunch of annoying excuses, God took all of those excuses and turned them into ways he could help Moses. ▷ GOD USES US. And he'll help us do what he asks us to do. Ephesians 3:20 says, "Now all glory to God, who is able, through his mighty power at work within us, to accomplish infinitely more than we might ask or think." Nothing God asks of us is too difficult for us to do. Instead of giving God excuses, we should say yes to God.**

Lead the kids in playing a praise song, such as "God Is Our Help" (track 4, *it: Innovative Tools for Children's Ministry: Old Testament* CD) on their kazoos.

Song & Connect

Use "God Is Our Help" (track 4, *it: Innovative Tools for Children's Ministry: Old Testament* CD) to help reinforce the Bible Point, ▷ **GOD USES US.**

Additional Topics List

This lesson can be used to help children discover... Bodies, God's Purpose, God's Will, Great Commission, and Obedience.

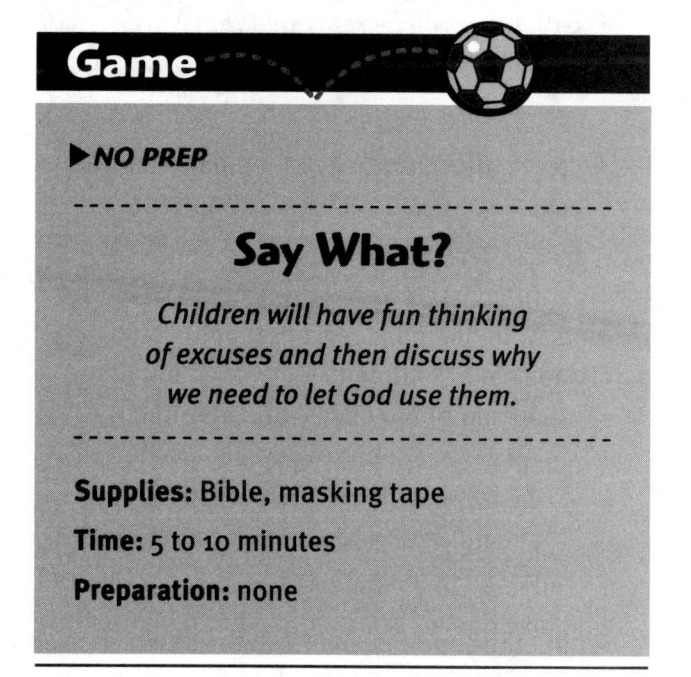

Game

▶ ***NO PREP***

Say What?

Children will have fun thinking of excuses and then discuss why we need to let God use them.

Supplies: Bible, masking tape

Time: 5 to 10 minutes

Preparation: none

Give kids masking tape, and ask them to tape one side of their mouths shut. SAY: **I'm going to give you 10 seconds to think of a joke.** After 10 seconds have passed, call time and SAY: **With one-half of your mouth taped, tell your joke to two or three people.** Give kids a minute or two to talk to others. Then have them remove the tape and throw it away. ASK:

- ◆ **What was it like to think of a joke so quickly?**
- ◆ **What was it like to tell your joke with half your mouth taped shut?**
- ◆ **What do you do when you're asked to do tasks that seem too hard?**

SAY: **Sometimes we try to talk our way out of hard jobs. But God wants to use us, just as he wanted to use Moses.** Read aloud Exodus 3:9-11 and 4:10-12. Encourage kids to let God give them strength so he can use them.

Craft

▶ *PREPARE IN ADVANCE*

"I Can" Can

Children will be reminded that with God's help, they'll always say, "I can!"

Supplies: Bible, duct tape, colored construction paper, small slips of plain paper, safety scissors, markers, clear tape, 1 clean aluminum can for each child

Time: 15 to 20 minutes

Preparation: Collect and rinse out aluminum cans. Cover any sharp edges with duct tape.

Set out the supplies, but keep the small slips of paper for later. Hand each child a can. Tell kids to cut paper labels to fit around their cans and then write the words, "I can't, but God can!" on the labels. Invite kids to decorate the labels any way they wish and then tape the labels around the cans. SAY: **Sometimes we're asked to do things we're not sure we can do.**

ASK:

◆ **Can you tell us about a time you said, "I can't"?**

SAY: **It's easy to say, "I can't." Sometimes we say those words before we've even tried. Let's read about a man in the Bible who said, "I can't" to God.** Have volunteers read aloud Exodus 3:11-12 and 4:1-17.

ASK:

◆ **What was Moses afraid of?**

◆ **How did God help Moses?**

◆ **How can God help you this week?**

Hand out the slips of paper. SAY: **Write down something you think you can't do.** When kids are finished, SAY: **Now drop your papers in your cans and say, "I can't, but God can!"** Pause for kids to respond, and then SAY: ▷ **GOD USES YOU. Sometimes you'll be tempted to say, "I can't." When you do, write your fear on a piece of paper and drop it into your can. Then say, "I can't, but God can!"**

Bible Application

▶ *NO PREP*

No More Excuses

Children will explore why we make excuses and how we can let God use us.

Supplies: Bible, sheets of newsprint, markers, small trash can

Time: 5 to 10 minutes

Preparation: none

Ask students to think about excuses they've made to avoid difficult tasks. Form three teams, and give each team a sheet of newsprint and some markers. Ask teams to write as many excuses on their newsprint as they can in three minutes. Call time after three minutes. Ask a volunteer from each group to read the group's excuses aloud. Then

ASK:

◆ **Why do people make excuses?**

◆ **Who can tell about a time you made an excuse to get out of a hard job?**

Encourage kids by telling about an excuse you made to avoid something difficult. SAY: **Sometimes even Bible heroes made excuses to get**

out of doing difficult things. Tell kids the story about Moses from Exodus 3 and 4. **God wanted to use Moses, and God helped Moses do everything Moses thought he couldn't do. ▷ GOD WANTS TO USE US, too! And he'll help us do everything he wants us to do.**

Have kids each tear a long strip from the newsprint they used to write down their excuses. Have kids stand with their newsprint strips on the far side of the room while you stand holding a trash can on the opposite end of the room. Tell them to wad up their excuses and throw them in the trash can—but make sure they're too far away. After they object that it's impossible, walk right up to them and let them drop their excuses in the can. Point out that, just as you helped them accomplish the task, God will help them when he wants to use them, too. Encourage them by reading Ephesians 3:20.

Creative Prayer Idea

▶ *NO PREP*

God's Power to Use Us

Children will pray that God will use their mouths to say the right words.

Supplies: Bible, colored masking tape, permanent markers

Time: about 5 minutes

Preparation: none

Read or summarize the story in Exodus 3 and 4 of how Moses was used by God. Tell kids that ▷ **GOD USES US, too,** whether or not they can think of the right words to say. SAY: **We're going to pray right now that God will use us with his power, not ours.** Give each child a piece of colored masking tape, and have them tape it over their mouths. Invite them to pray silently, asking for God's strength to help them obey him. Then read aloud Ephesians 3:20. Have kids remove the tape from their mouths and write the words "Ephesians 3:20" on the tape. Then have them place the tape on the back of their hand to remind them that God wants to use them to do good things.

Life Application

Children will discover that God uses them as they participate in these application activities.

Found in Translation

Find a variety of Bible versions and translations. Divide them up among the kids in groups of two or three. Have kids look up Ephesians 3:20. Have each child share his or her version of the verse with the rest of the class, and then have kids talk about which ones they liked the best and why. Have kids write the verse in their own words, applying it to a specific situation in their lives.

Want Ads

Tell kids that God wants to use them and that he has a job for each of them. Instruct them to form groups of three and find verses that tell how God wants us to live. Have students create want ads such as they might find in a newspaper. Display the ads on a bulletin board, or have students take them home to hang in their rooms.

Signs

Divide students into three groups. Give each a piece of poster board, and assign one of the following passages: Exodus 4:1-5; 4:6-8; and 4:9.

Have each group make a sign describing in words or illustrating in pictures the sign God gave to show that he was using Moses. Challenge teams to brainstorm signs in their own lives that God can use them, too (such as specific talents he has given them, opportunities, Scripture verses, and so on). Ask them to write a list of these "signs" on the back of their sign.

Movie Clip

God Calls Moses

Movie Title: *The Princess Diaries* (G)

Start Time: 10 minutes, 11 seconds

Where to Begin: The Queen welcomes Mia to tea and says, "Amelia, I'm so glad you could come."

Where to End: Mia storms off after telling her grandmother that she doesn't want to be a princess.

Plot: Mia has been asked to tea by her grandmother, whom she has never met. She surprises Mia by announcing that Mia is a princess.

Review: Use this lesson to help kids understand that when God wants to use us in a way we may not think we're capable of, he will give us the strength, courage, and wisdom to accomplish it. God guides us when we say yes to him.

Discussion

After setting up and showing the clip, ASK:

- **How would you react if someone told you that you were the only living heir to the throne of a country you had never been to?**
- **How do you feel when someone asks you to do something you don't think you can do?**

SAY: **Many leaders in the Bible felt that they weren't the right people for the job God had given them. In fact, in Exodus 4, God called Moses to be a leader, and Moses argued that he couldn't do it. But with God's help, Moses accomplished wonderful things. Likewise, if we say yes to God and let him work in us, we can do great things.**

ASK:

- **What kinds of things would you like to do for God?**
- **How do you feel when you do something you never thought you could?**
- **How do you think God feels when we say yes to him?**

Preschool Story

▶ ***PREPARE IN ADVANCE***

Bible Point: ▷ **GOD USES US.**

Supplies: Bible, chenille wire, white finger paint, black construction paper, moist towels, cup of water, red food coloring, shallow dish or plate

Time: 15 to 20 minutes

Preparation: Pour some white finger paint into a dish.

Signs

Have kids form a circle and sit down. Open your Bible to Exodus 4, and show children the words. Give each child a chenille wire to use as you instruct them throughout the story.

SAY: **God had spoken to Moses through the burning bush, and God had told Moses to go to Egypt and free God's people, the Israelites. But Moses wasn't so sure about this plan. "What if they don't believe me or listen to me?" Moses asked God.**

ASK:

- **Have you ever been afraid to do something? What happened?**

SAY: **God told Moses to throw his staff on the ground.** Tell children to throw their chenille wires on the ground. **Then God turned the staff into a snake!** Encourage children to form their chenille wires into wiggly snakes. Let kids play with their "snakes" for a few minutes. **Only God could turn a staff into a snake. God told Moses to turn his staff into a snake in front of Pharaoh so that the Egyptians would believe that God had sent him.**

But Moses still wasn't so sure. So God told Moses to put his hand inside his robe. When Moses pulled his hand out, it had turned white as snow! Have kids dip one hand into the white finger paint and then press their palm onto a black sheet of paper to make a white handprint. **When Moses put his hand back under his coat, all the white went away.** Help kids use a moist towel to wipe the paint off of their hands. **Only God could do that to a hand! God told Moses to show Pharaoh his hand so that the Egyptians would believe.**

But still Moses didn't know if he wanted to go. So God told him that if the Egyptians didn't believe the first two signs, to try a third one. God told Moses to take some water from the Nile River and pour it on the ground, and it would turn to blood! Help kids put several drops of red food coloring in the cup of water and then pour the water into a shallow container or onto a plate. **Only God could turn water into blood!**

But Moses was still afraid! "God, I can't speak very well," Moses said. "Why can't you send someone else?" Have kids shake their hands and say, "Not me, not me!"

That made God mad! After all, God is more powerful than anything else. God wanted Moses to trust him. God wanted to use Moses to save his people!

God told Moses that he would send Moses' brother, Aaron, with Moses as a helper. Have kids form pairs and put their arms around one another. **This made Moses feel better, so he *finally* agreed to go to Egypt.**

ASK:

- **Why didn't Moses want to go to Egypt?**
- **Have you ever been afraid to do something you were supposed to do? What happened?**
- **How can God help you when you're afraid?**

SAY: **God was able to use Moses to help his people—but only after Moses agreed to go. ▷ GOD USES US, too, but we have to be ready to help him.**

ASK:

- **Have you ever had to help someone do something important? How did you feel?**
- **How do you think God can use you?**

SAY: **God can use us in many ways. We can be nice to others, help others, and tell others about God. When we do those things, we are helping God!**

notes

BIBLE STORY

The Plagues Begin

For the Leader

You'd think that just one plague would have been enough to convince Pharaoh to free the Hebrews from slavery. After all, the first one was rather remarkable—the Nile River, along with the canals, marshes, reservoirs, and everywhere else there was water, turned to blood. Yuck! But "Pharaoh's heart remained hard," even through another nine plagues.

God continued to demonstrate his power—his dominating, matchless power—in helping Moses give the Hebrew people their freedom. Time after time, God's power proved too much for Pharaoh to overcome.

Kids need to know all about that power because God's power still reigns supreme today. These activities can help your students explore that power and understand that God's power is on their side.

Key Scriptures

Exodus 6:8–7:24

Exodus 7–11

Psalm 147:5-6

Bible Verse

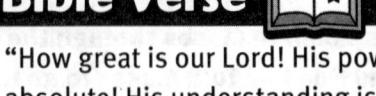

"How great is our Lord! His power is absolute! His understanding is beyond comprehension!" (Psalm 147:5).

Bible Experience

▶ *NO PREP*

Bible Point: ▷ **NOTHING MATCHES GOD'S POWER.**

Children will consider God's great power from the perspective of some who saw it displayed miraculously.

Supplies: Bibles, paper, pencils

Time: 15 to 20 minutes

Preparation: none

Divide the class into five groups, and assign each group one of the following perspectives: God, Moses, Pharaoh, the Egyptians, and the Israelites. Have groups read the story of Moses in Exodus 6:8–7:24. Give them about eight to 10 minutes to read the passage and discuss their answers to the following questions from the perspective of their character or group.

ASK:

- **How was this person or group feeling when this part of the story began?**
- **What was the biggest problem this person or group had to face?**
- **What did this person or group think about the plague of blood?**

◆ **Who displayed the most power during this passage?**

Summarize the story again briefly for everyone to hear. Then have each group assign one person to be the "voice" of the group. Ask the "voices" to answer the questions above for the entire group to hear. Then ASK:

◆ **Why didn't Pharaoh listen to Moses?**

◆ **How do you think Moses felt when Pharaoh didn't change his heart after the first plague?**

◆ **Egypt suffered through nine more plagues before Pharaoh changed his mind. Why do you think it took him so long?**

◆ **Could Pharaoh do anything that would match God's power? Why or why not?**

◆ **Is there anything that can match God's power? Why or why not?**

Have kids return to their groups and read Psalm 147:5-6 together. Then have each group write their own four-line psalm praising God for his power. Remind them that the psalm doesn't need to rhyme; it just needs to talk about how powerful God is compared with anything else. Then have the groups select a new "voice," and instruct those "voices" to read each group's psalm to the rest of the class.

SAY: ▷ **NOTHING MATCHES GOD'S POWER. And God's power can help us do wonderful things.** Close in prayer.

Additional Topics List

This lesson can be used to help children discover... Attitudes, Consequences, Nature, and Stubbornness.

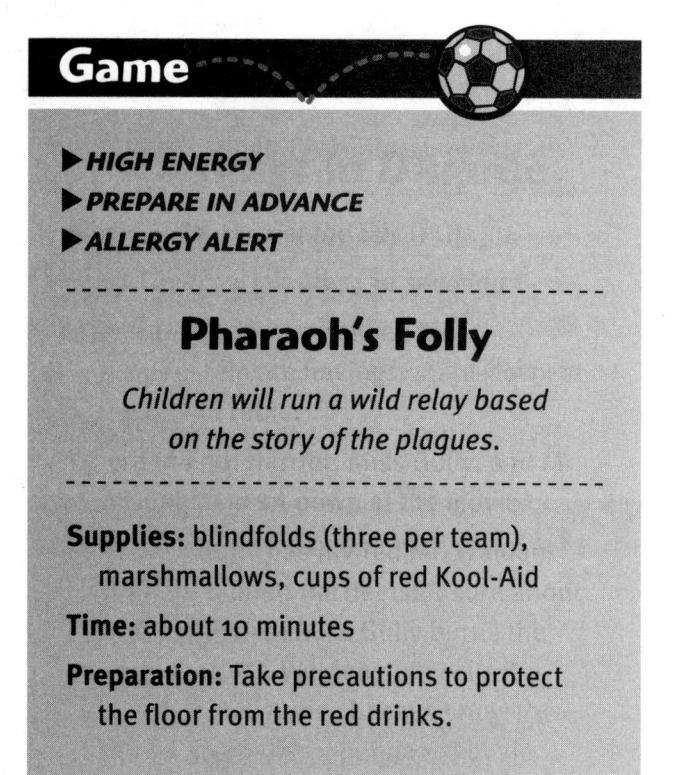

Game

▶ ***HIGH ENERGY***

▶ ***PREPARE IN ADVANCE***

▶ ***ALLERGY ALERT***

Pharaoh's Folly

Children will run a wild relay based on the story of the plagues.

Supplies: blindfolds (three per team), marshmallows, cups of red Kool-Aid

Time: about 10 minutes

Preparation: Take precautions to protect the floor from the red drinks.

Teach kids about the plagues in Exodus 7–11, and then play this relay.

Form teams of four. At one end of the room, blindfold three members of each team (to illustrate the plague of darkness). The fourth member of each team will stand at the other end of the room. Place some marshmallows and a cup of red Kool-Aid near the child.

On "Go," the blindfolded players will begin leapfrogging (plague of frogs) toward their teammate, who may only "moo" like a cow (plague on livestock) to give directions. Teams might want to work out a code beforehand, such as two "moos" mean "turn left."

When leapfroggers have reached their teammate, one blindfolded player must find the marshmallows (plague of hail) and red Kool-Aid (plague of blood). He or she will then feed the marshmallows to the second player and give the Kool-Aid to the third player. Have the fourth teammate go to the other end of the room. The three blindfolded teammates will then turn around and leapfrog back to where they began, as the fourth teammate guides them with more "moos."

At the end of the game, discuss these questions:

- ◆ **What do you remember about the Bible story?**
- ◆ **How did these plagues make Pharaoh let the Israelites go?**
- ◆ **What do these plagues say about God's power?**

Craft

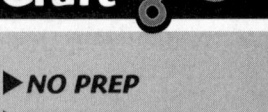

▶ *NO PREP*
▶ *FOR YOUNGER CHILDREN*

Bouncy Bugs

Children will make bugs like the locusts God sent to show his power.

Supplies: Bible, colored yarn, safety scissors, florists' wire, chenille wire, wiggly eyes

Time: 10 to 15 minutes

Preparation: none

Briefly review the story of the 10 plagues, especially the part about the locusts. Have volunteers read aloud Exodus 10:3-20. Then read aloud Psalm 147:5. Tell kids that the plagues showed how powerful God is and that ▷ **NOTHING MATCHES GOD'S POWER.**

Give each child at least 6 feet of yarn. Have each child hold one hand horizontally so the thumb is on top and the palm is facing in. Show kids how to wrap the yarn around their hands, keeping their fingers together. (The more yarn kids use, the puffier their bugs will be.) When kids reach the end of their yarn, help them carefully pull the wound yarn off of their hands and pinch it in the middle to form figure eights. Then hand out 5-inch sections of yarn, and show students how to tie them around the middle of their bundles. Have kids cut off the leftover strands.

Distribute 9-inch lengths of florists' wire, and show kids how to wrap one end of the wire around their knots a few times. When kids have secured one end of the florists' wire to the yarn, have them cut the looped ends of their figure eights and fluff up the loose strands of yarn. Allow kids to decorate the bugs using wiggly eyes and chenille wire. The bugs will bounce on their stems!

Bible Application

▶ *NO PREP*
▶ *FOR SMALL GROUPS*

Power Surge

Children will consider how they need God's power every day.

Supplies: Bible, light bulb

Time: about 10 minutes

Preparation: none

Gather kids in a circle, and read aloud Psalm 147:5. SAY: **God's power was demonstrated in an unforgettable way when he sent the plagues on Egypt. God's power also comes to us in big and small ways every day.**

Have kids talk to a partner and brainstorm areas where we need God's power every day. Encourage them to each come up with one idea. After a couple of minutes, hold up a light bulb and name one area where you need God's power every day in your own life. Then pass the light bulb to the child to your left, and have each child share one area where we need God's power every day.

After everyone has a chance to hold the bulb and share an idea, ASK:

- **Is anything that concerns you too big for God's power to take care of? Explain.**
- **Is anything that concerns you too small for God to care about?**
- **How does God use his power to help us?**

SAY: **Just as nothing matched God's power for Moses in Egypt, so God's power is strong enough for any situation. He's strong enough to take care of any need we have—big or small.**

Creative Prayer Idea

▶ *NO PREP*
▶ *FOR YOUNGER CHILDREN*

God's Never-Ending Power

Children will use wind to think about and pray for God's power.

Supplies: Bible, fan

Time: 5 to 10 minutes

Preparation: none

Talk with kids about the different sources of energy we use to power our televisions, cars, radios, bicycles, and so on. Then talk about how different the power of wind is from all the others—it doesn't cost any money, and it never runs out.

Read aloud Psalm 147:5. Have kids close their eyes and think about God's power. As they sit with their eyes closed, tell them to ask God to give them power in their lives. Then turn on your fan, and slowly run it across each child's face as he or she prays. Leave the fan on, and set it to the side. Allow kids to sit in front of the fan and pray again if they choose.

Discussion Launcher Questions

Ask children to form trios and discuss:

- **What's the most powerful thing you can think of?**
- **In what areas would you like to see God use his power?**

- **Do you think God uses his power to protect you from bad things today? If so, what kinds of bad things? If not, why not?**
- **If God always protects us, then why do you think we still get hurt sometimes?**
- **Can you think of anything that might be almost as powerful as God? Explain.**

Object Lesson

▶ *PREPARE IN ADVANCE*

Real Power

Children will consider that no other power compares with God's.

Supplies: Bible, 4 empty plastic film canisters, 2 pennies, rubber band

Time: 5 to 10 minutes

Preparation: Wear long sleeves. Place 2 pennies in one of the film canisters. Hold the film canister next to your right forearm, and place the rubber band around the canister and your forearm so the rubber band holds the canister next to your arm. Have your sleeve cover the canister completely. Practice the trick before performing it in front of kids.

Set out the three empty film canisters in a row. Have children sit so they can see the canisters. SAY: **I have a really cool trick to show you. I've placed a couple of pennies in one of these film canisters.** Pick up one of the canisters with your right hand. Shake the film canister. To your audience, the sound will seem to come from the film canister you're holding up. Keep the canister attached to your arm hidden. After you shake the canister, set it back down.

I'm going to move these three film canisters around. Watch closely so that when I've finished moving them around, you can tell me which canister has the pennies in it. Move the canisters around slowly, so kids can easily keep up with the canister they think contains the pennies. Ask them to pick which canister contains the pennies. Pick up that canister with your LEFT hand, and shake the canister so that no sound is heard; then set down the canister.

Are you sure it was that one? Let's try again. With your right hand, pick up a different canister and shake it so it seems the sound is coming from that canister. Set it down and repeat the trick.

Pretty amazing, huh? Do you think I have amazing powers? Actually, a trick means I can do something that looks powerful, when really I just have a secret. At first glance it might seem that the devil is as powerful as God, but he's not! Read aloud Psalm 147:5, and then pray, thanking the Lord for his real, unmatched power.

Preschool Story

▶ *NO PREP*

Bible Point: ▷ **NOTHING MATCHES GOD'S POWER.**

Supplies: Bible

Time: 15 to 20 minutes

Preparation: none

Powerful Persuasion

Have kids form a circle and sit down. Open your Bible to Exodus 6 and 7, and show children the words. SAY: **Pharaoh kept God's people, the Israelites, in Egypt for a very long time. He made them build beautiful palaces and tall pyramids and wouldn't let them leave. He thought he was the strongest king ever, but there was someone even stronger—God!** Lead children in shouting: ▷ **NOTHING MATCHES GOD'S POWER!**

The mean Pharaoh made God's people slaves and worked them harder and harder all the time. Every day the people cried to God to set them free. Then one day God said, "That's enough of that mean Pharaoh! I'll send Moses to set you free."

Moses prayed to God for help. Encourage children to fold their hands and pray, "Dear God, help me set your people free."

So God turned all of Egypt's water red. (Run fingers back and forth like water.)

It looked as if the water was dead. (Flip hands over so they're palms up.)

After God turned the water red, Moses went to Pharaoh and asked, "Will you let my people go?" But mean Pharaoh still wouldn't change his mind. Have kids shout, "No way!" as they shake their index finger.

Moses prayed to God for help. Encourage children to fold their hands and pray, "Dear God, help me set your people free."

So God sent a bunch of frogs to cover all the land. (Hop like a frog.)

There were so many, you couldn't even see the sand! (Keep hopping.)

Moses went to Pharaoh and asked, "Will you let my people go now?" But even the frogs didn't change his mind. Have kids shout, "No way!" as they shake their index finger.

Moses prayed to God for help. Encourage children to fold their hands and pray, "Dear God, help me set your people free."

So God sent little gnats and flies (twinkle fingers like bugs.)

That got in people's hair, nose, and eyes. (Touch hair, nose, and eyes.)

Moses went to Pharaoh and asked, "Will you let my people go now?" But even with all those flies, Pharaoh didn't change his mind. Have kids shout, "No way!" as they shake their index finger.

Moses prayed to God for help. Encourage children to fold their hands and pray, "Dear God, help me set your people free."

God gave the people sores and made the animals sick. (Rub arms and belly.)

He sent hail and locusts to kill the plants—there was nothing left to pick! (Look around and shrug shoulders.)

Moses went to Pharaoh and asked, "Will you let my people go now?" But even with all that had happened, Pharaoh wouldn't change his mind. Have kids shout, "No way!" as they shake their index finger.

Moses prayed to God for help. Encourage children to fold their hands and pray, "Dear God, help me set your people free."

So God made the daytime into night (cover eyes)

And gave all the people quite a fright! (Put hands over mouth.)

God showed Pharaoh that ▷ **NOTHING MATCHES GOD'S POWER!**

ASK:

◆ **How do you know God is powerful?**

◆ **How can you thank God for his power?**

BIBLE STORY

The Passover

For the Leader

The annual feast called the Passover began on the day of the final plague in Egypt, when the Hebrews were still slaves. God commanded them to smear the blood of a lamb on their doorposts as a sign for God to pass over their homes when he brought death to all the firstborn sons in Egypt. The purpose of the blood wasn't just to leave a mark but to be a substitution for their own blood.

The Passover offers a beautiful and deeply meaningful parallel to the coming of Christ and his death for our sins. Jesus, a Jew himself, celebrated Passover on the evening he was taken prisoner.

Help kids learn the importance of celebrations that help us remember the great things God has done for us. These experiences will give kids a chance to understand Passover and its rich meaning.

Key Scriptures

Exodus 11:4-8; 12:1-20

Psalm 103:2-5

Bible Verse

"Let all that I am praise the Lord; may I never forget the good things he does for me" (Psalm 103:2).

Bible Experience

▶ *PREPARE IN ADVANCE*

Bible Point: ▷ **GOD WANTS US TO REMEMBER HIM.**

Children will understand the importance of remembering the great things God has done.

Supplies: Bibles, butcher paper or newsprint, tape, containers of red tempera paint, 2 pie tins, small branches of a shrub to use as brushes

Time: 15 to 20 minutes

Preparation: Tape two large pieces of butcher paper to the wall, and draw a door on each sheet. Set the two "doors" at least 10 feet apart.

SAY: **Moses tried many ways to convince the Pharaoh of Egypt to free the Hebrews.**

ASK:

◆ **What are some of the things Moses tried?**

SAY: **Pharaoh refused over and over again. But God had a plan to make Pharaoh set his people free. Let's see what God planned.**

Help kids find Exodus 11 in their Bibles. Ask a volunteer to read Exodus 11:4-8. Then SAY: **God**

knew Pharaoh was stubborn. Can you show me what a stubborn Pharaoh might look like? Pause. **This Pharaoh was even more stubborn than that! In fact, he was so mean and stubborn that God planned something terrible to make him let the Hebrews go: The firstborn son of every household in Egypt would die. But God had a different plan for the Hebrew people. Let's read about that plan.**

Have a volunteer read Exodus 12:21-23. SAY: **God's people painted the doorframes of their houses with lambs' blood. This showed that they loved and obeyed God. Let's paint a doorframe, like the Hebrew people did.**

Hand out small branches for brushes, and set out the tempera paint in the pie tins. Invite kids to take turns painting the top and sides of one of the paper doorframes. Have half the kids gather near the painted doorframe and the other half near the unpainted doorframe.

Have volunteers read Exodus 12:12-13 and 12:29-30. Invite kids in front of the unpainted door to fall to the ground dramatically to show that some of the Egyptian people died. Invite the rest of the kids to act the way they think the Egyptians acted when they discovered their firstborn sons had died.

ASK:

- **What would you have thought that night if you were an Egyptian? if you were a Hebrew?**
- **Why did God let this happen?**

Have volunteers read Exodus 12:24-27.

ASK:

- **Why did God want the Hebrews to remember the Passover instructions?**
- **What are some other things God wants us to remember about him?**

SAY: **See the blood on the doorposts? The reason they put that blood there was not just to mark their homes. The lambs' blood was a substitute for their own blood.**

ASK:

- **Who else shed his blood as a substitute for us?**

SAY: **Jesus, God's Son, was sacrificed as a substitute for us. ▷ GOD WANTS US TO REMEMBER HIM and the wonderful things he did. That's why the Jews continue to celebrate Passover to this day, to remember how God saved their people.** Close by reading Psalm 103:2.

Additional Topics List

This lesson can be used to help children discover... Celebrations, Communion, God's Provision, Gratitude, and Jesus.

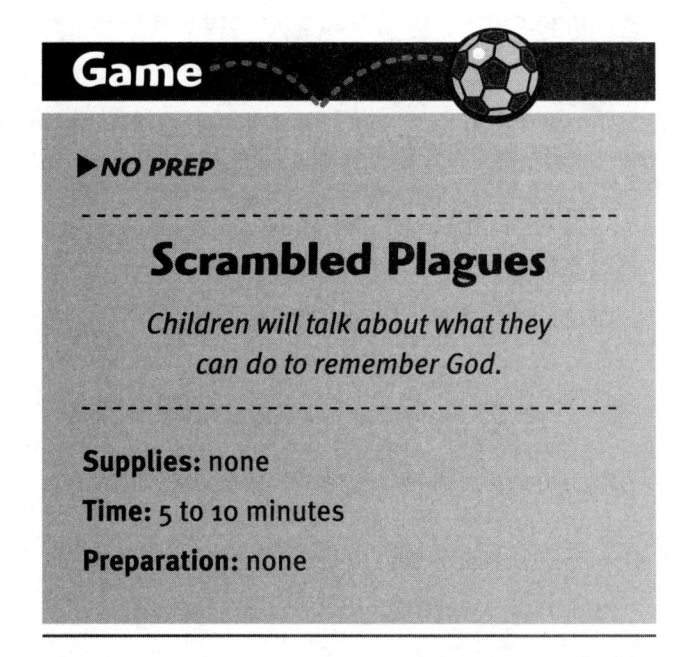

Game

▶ *NO PREP*

Scrambled Plagues

Children will talk about what they can do to remember God.

Supplies: none

Time: 5 to 10 minutes

Preparation: none

Have kids sit in a circle. Start with the youngest child. Have that child name the first plague of Egypt. (The 10 plagues are: [1] river turned to blood, [2] frogs, [3] gnats, [4] flies, [5] disease that killed the livestock, [6] boils/sores, [7] hail, [8] locusts, [9] darkness for three days, and [10] death of the firstborn.) Then have the child on his or her left say the first plague and the second plague. Continue around the circle, adding one plague for each child. See if kids can remember them as you go around the circle. Challenge children to go around the circle until they can name all 10 plagues. If they can't, tell them they did a great job anyway, and provide the information. All the children should leave this experience feeling good about themselves!

After the game, ASK:

- **Was it hard or easy trying to remember all 10 plagues? Why?**
- **What are some other things you have trouble remembering? Why?**
- **What are some things God has done for us?**
- **How can we remember what God has done for us?**

Close by reading aloud Psalm 103:2. If you have time, see if the circle of kids can go around the circle memorizing that verse one word at a time.

Craft

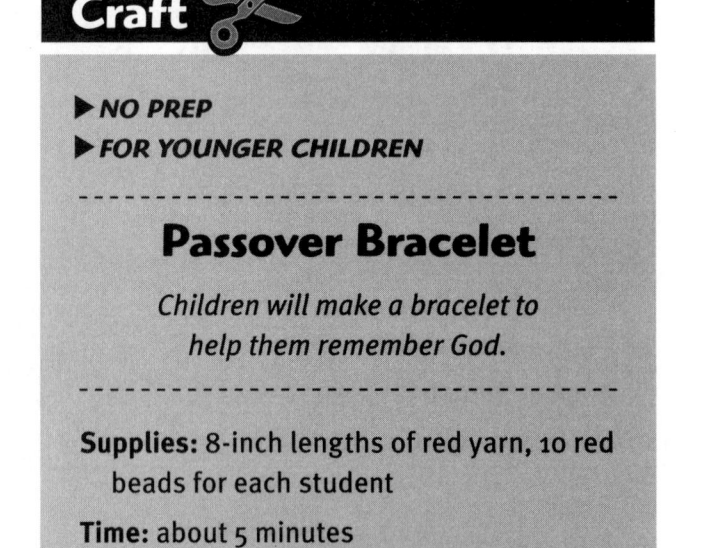

- *NO PREP*
- *FOR YOUNGER CHILDREN*

Passover Bracelet

Children will make a bracelet to help them remember God.

Supplies: 8-inch lengths of red yarn, 10 red beads for each student

Time: about 5 minutes

Preparation: none

SAY: **When the 10th plague came to Egypt, God kept the Israelites safe that night. God said to always remember how he protected the Israelites from death. That's why people still have a celebration called Passover every year, even today! We're going to make bracelets to remind us of the Passover. The 10 beads will remind us that God sent 10 plagues to the Egyptians. And the red color will help us remember the blood of the lamb the Israelites used.**

Show each child how to tie a knot in one end of the yarn, thread the beads onto the yarn, and knot the other end. Loosely tie the bracelets on kids' wrists so they can be easily removed. ASK:

- **What do our beads stand for?**
- **How important is it to trust in God?**
- **How important is it to remember God?**

SAY: **When you wear your Passover bracelets, remember that God wants us to have faith, just as the Israelites did.**

Bible Application

- *FOR SMALL GROUPS*
- *PREPARE IN ADVANCE*
- *ALLERGY ALERT*

Always Remember

Children will get a small taste of a Passover meal and talk about why they should remember God.

Supplies: Bible, crackers or matzos, cups of water

Time: 5 to 10 minutes

Preparation: Set out crackers or matzos and cups of water on a table.

Have kids gather around the table. Briefly review the story of Moses and the 10 plagues, emphasizing the 10th plague of death. Tell kids that God instructed the Hebrew people to make a special meal so they would be "passed over" when God killed all the firstborn sons in Egypt. SAY: **God told the people to get dressed as if they were going on a trip and then eat the special Passover meal that night. God told the people to have a special meal every year to remember how he had protected them. We can remember that special time, too.**

Invite kids to eat the crackers and enjoy the cups of water. As they eat and drink, read Exodus 12:8-17, 24-27. ASK:

- **How did eating the meal this way help the people remember God?**
- **Why is it good to have special times to remember what God has done?**
- **What's something you could do today to remember God?**

SAY: **God wants us to remember him so we'll never forget all the wonderful things he's done for us.**

Creative Prayer Idea

▶ ***NO PREP***

Remembrance Prayer

Children will remember God through prayer.

Supplies: Bible

Time: about 5 minutes

Preparation: none

Gather children around the Bible. SAY: **People in Bible times and people today remember God through their prayers. Let's use a psalm in the Bible to help us remember all the things God has done for us.**

As you slowly read Psalm 103:2-5, have kids pray silently as you direct them following each verse:

After verse 2, SAY: **Remember a good thing God has done for you.** Pause. After verse 3, SAY: **Remember something God has forgiven you for.** Pause. **Remember something God has healed you from.** Pause. After verse 4, SAY: **Remember something God has protected you from.** Pause. After verse 5, SAY: **Remember something God has given you to make you strong.** Pause. **Amen.**

Snack

▶ ***FOR SMALL GROUPS***
▶ ***PREPARE IN ADVANCE***
▶ ***ALLERGY ALERT***

Quick Passover Bread

Children will make and eat unleavened bread just like the unleavened bread Jewish people make today.

Supplies: Bible, flour, measuring cups, mixing bowls, water, rolling pins, forks, a kitchen timer, greased baking sheets, oven, napkins (Note: This recipe will make enough matzo bread for 8 children.)

Time: about 20 minutes

Preparation: Preheat oven to 450 degrees.

Before you begin, make sure kids have washed their hands.

Tell kids the story of the 10th plague in Egypt and about the Passover. Read aloud Exodus 12:17.

SAY: **When Jewish people make this kind of bread for the Passover feast, they make it in less than 18 minutes to remind them of how quickly their ancestors had to leave Egypt. Let's make this same kind of bread together.**

Have one child measure 3 cups of flour into a mixing bowl while another child measures 1½ cups of water into another bowl. Choose one or two kids who will mix the dough later. Give everyone else rolling pins and forks, and explain that they'll be rollers and pokers.

Set the kitchen timer for 18 minutes and begin. Pour the water into the flour, and have the mixers mix the dough with their hands. Add flour as needed so the dough is pliable—neither crumbly nor sticky. When the dough is mixed, have kids divide it into eight sections and give one section to each of the rollers. Have them roll the dough until it's thin, about 1/16 to 1/8 inch thick. Carefully place the rolled-out dough on the greased baking sheets, and have kids use their forks to prick holes in the dough.

Bake for 10 to 12 minutes. When the matzo is done, have children hurriedly wrap it in napkins and take it outside to eat. If you want, you may ask the kids to try to name all 10 plagues while the bread is baking.

Worship Prompt Idea

▶ *NO PREP*

I'll Remember You

Children will remember God's blessings and worship God.

Supplies: Bible, red string or thread

Time: about 5 minutes

Preparation: none

After telling kids the story of the first Passover in Exodus 12, read aloud Psalm 103:2. Ask kids how they can remember all the things God has done for them. After they give you a few ideas, tell them that some people used to tie a string around their finger to help them remember something they didn't want to forget. Give each child a 4-inch piece of red string. Ask kids to think about one thing God has done for them. Help kids tie the strings around one of their index fingers (make sure it's not too tight). Then spend some time praying and worshipping together, remembering God's blessings.

Preschool Story

▶ *ALLERGY ALERT*

▶ *PREPARE IN ADVANCE*

Bible Point: ▷ **GOD WANTS US TO REMEMBER HIM.**

Supplies: Bible, red finger paint, poster board, moist towels, chocolate frosting, plastic knives or spoons, plastic plates, graham crackers, red licorice ropes

Time: 15 to 20 minutes

Preparation: Set out red finger paint, moist towels, and pieces of poster board in your story-time area. Set up a separate snack area with graham crackers, chocolate frosting, plastic knives and plates, and red licorice ropes.

Remember Me

Have kids form a circle and sit down. Open your Bible to Exodus 12, and show children the words. SAY: **Remember all of the plagues and**

bad things God sent to the mean King Pharaoh of Egypt to show that nothing matches God's power?

ASK:

- **What were some of the bad things God sent?**

Let kids act out the plagues they remember.

SAY: **Well, even after all those plagues and bad things, Pharaoh *still* wanted to keep God's people, the Israelites, and use them as slaves forever. Pharaoh was really stubborn!** Have kids shake their fingers and say, "No way!"

Moses asked Pharaoh one more time to let God's people go, but that mean Pharaoh still said no.

Moses prayed to God and asked God to set the Israelites free. Encourage children to get on their knees and fold their hands in prayer. **God told Moses that this would be the last and the worst plague of all. God would send the plague of death on the Egyptians. But God would keep the Israelites safe.**

In order to be safe, the Israelites had to paint a red stripe on their doors so the plague of death would pass by their houses without harming them. Set out the red finger paint and the poster board. Encourage children to finger-paint several red stripes on the poster board. When kids are finished, use a moist towel to clean their fingers.

The plague of death made the Egyptians very sad. Pharaoh finally understood God's power. This time Pharaoh finally agreed to let God's people go.

Pharaoh said, "Yes! Get out of here and don't come back!"

The Israelites had to go on a long journey, but they knew that they could trust God.

Lead the children from your story-time area to the snack area you set up before class.

SAY: **The Israelites always remembered how God kept them safe from the plague of death and how he freed them from the mean Pharaoh. Every year the Israelites celebrate the way God saved them. They remember God and his power during this celebration. ▷ GOD WANTS US TO REMEMBER HIM, too.**

Let's make a snack right now to help us remember the way God saved the Israelites.

Give each child a graham cracker, a spoonful of chocolate frosting, and one red licorice rope. Encourage kids to frost their graham cracker with the chocolate frosting. Then help kids use their licorice rope to make a stripe on top of their graham cracker "door." Remind kids that the Israelites painted a red stripe on their doors so that the plague wouldn't harm them.

ASK:

- **How did the Israelites remember God?**
- **What good things has God done for you?**
- **What are some ways you can remember the good things God has done for you?**

n

o

t

e

s

BIBLE STORY

Crossing the Red Sea

For the Leader

In the ancient Middle East, very hot, dry winds could blow across the desert landscape, blowing water away. These sirocco winds could dry land, but they could not have caused walls of water to pile up, leaving dry land beneath.

Help kids understand that while God caused a strong wind to blow, he used supernatural force as well. This was evident in walls of water that piled up. It also was evident in God's protection of the Israelites as they crossed the Red Sea in the face of a wind strong enough to blow water out of its path.

Key Scripture

Exodus 14:5-31; 15:1-18

Bible Verse

"But Moses told the people, 'Don't be afraid. Just stand still and watch the Lord rescue you today. The Egyptians you see today will never be seen again' " (Exodus 14:13).

Bible Experience

▶ *PREPARE IN ADVANCE*

▶ *HIGH ENERGY*

Bible Point: ▷ **GOD HELPS US WHEN WE'RE AFRAID.**

Children will reenact the crossing of the Red Sea.

Supplies: Bible, large vacant room, 2 bedsheets, masking tape, fans

Time: 15 to 20 minutes

Preparation: Find a large, vacant room, and make a "Red Sea" out of two sheets, masking tape, and fans. Lay the sheets on the floor, about a foot apart. Tape the sheets to the floor, and then set a fan at the end of each sheet. The fans should be facing the sheets. You'll be using the fans to "billow" the "sea." Make sure you don't stretch the sheets too tightly, or they won't blow. Enlist four or five adults to play Pharaoh's army and one to play Moses.

Have children gather around the Red Sea you set up with sheets.

SAY: **The Bible tells us some amazing stories of things God has done. We can find one of those amazing stories in Exodus 14:5-31. This story tells about a time God helped his people when they were afraid.**

Read aloud Exodus 14:5-31.

SAY: **We're going to act out the amazing story of how the Israelites crossed the Red Sea when God parted the waters. We'll see what this experience might have been like for God's people.**

Cue the adults you recruited to play Pharaoh's army. Have the volunteers pound on the door and yell, "We'll get you Israelites!" or "You can't escape!"

As you stand at the edge of the Red Sea, have kids each turn to a partner and answer the following questions. Pause after each question. ASK:

- **How do you feel right now?**
- **How do you think the Israelites felt as the Egyptians came after them?**

After pairs have discussed the last question, open the door. Your volunteers should step into the room, yelling things like, "We're going to get you!" Tell volunteers to chase the kids from a safe distance. Kids should feel like they're being pursued, but volunteers shouldn't be close enough to catch them.

Turn on the fans so the sheets billow up. Have your Moses guide kids through the sea. Just as the Egyptians enter the sea, rip up the outside tape and turn the fans toward the Egyptians so the sheets blow all over them. The Egyptians will be swallowed up. Watch until the Egyptians are lying on the floor.

ASK:

- **How did you feel as you crossed the Red Sea?**
- **How did it feel to see the Egyptian army covered by the sea?**

Read Exodus 14:13 aloud. ASK:

- **How do you think the Israelites felt when Moses told them God would fight for them?**
- **How do you think the Israelites felt after this experience?**

SAY: **Just as God helped the Israelites cross the Red Sea, ▷ GOD HELPS US WHEN WE'RE AFRAID. God may not always do amazing things we can see, such as parting the waters of the Red Sea. But God does amazing things to help us every day!**

Song & Connect

Use "All His Promises" (track 9, *it: Innovative Tools for Children's Ministry: Old Testament* CD) to help reinforce the Bible Point, ▷ **GOD HELPS US WHEN WE'RE AFRAID.**

Additional Topics List

This lesson can be used to help children discover... Courage, Faithfulness, God's Power, and Guidance.

Game

▶ ***HIGH ENERGY***
▶ ***ALLERGY ALERT***
▶ ***PREPARE IN ADVANCE***

Crossing the Red Sea

Children will encounter obstacles as they cross the "Red Sea."

Supplies: tape, newsprint, marker, water, paper cups, honey-graham crackers

Time: 10 to 15 minutes

Preparation: Tape a long sheet of newsprint on the floor—as large as the room allows. Draw five large rock shapes in different areas of the newsprint. On each rock, write one of the following directions: "hop on one foot," "turn around three times," "go back and begin again," "bark like a dog," and "take one shoe off."

Remind children about the story of the Red Sea parting as the Israelites fled from Pharaoh and his soldiers (Exodus 14:5-31).

SAY: **This newsprint is the Red Sea, and you must flee from Pharaoh. But just as a river has rocks, there are some obstacles along the way. As you come to one of the paper rocks in the Red Sea, do what it says.**

As kids finish crossing, give them water and honey-graham crackers.

SAY: **Just as you did in this game, the Israelites encountered a lot of hardships in their journey to the Promised Land. They faced fear as soon as they left Egypt and reached the Red Sea. By parting the waters of the Red Sea, God did something amazing to help them when they were afraid. ▷ GOD HELPS US WHEN WE'RE AFRAID, too!**

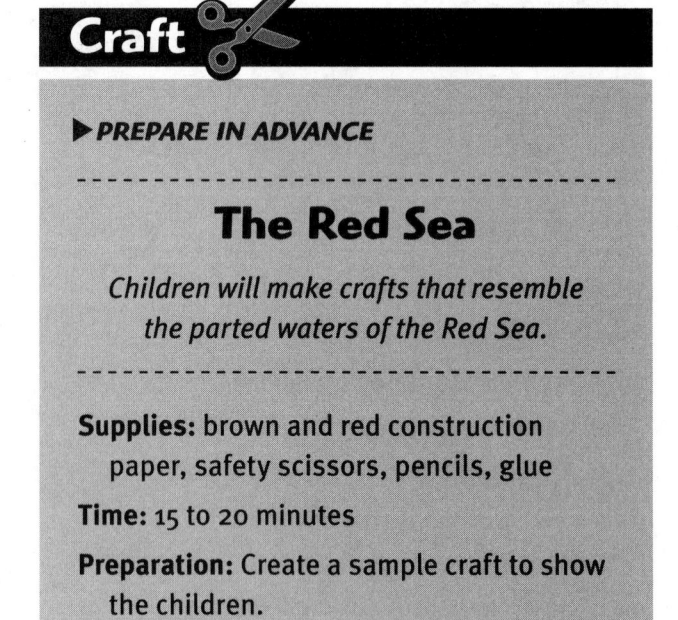

Craft

▶ PREPARE IN ADVANCE

The Red Sea

Children will make crafts that resemble the parted waters of the Red Sea.

Supplies: brown and red construction paper, safety scissors, pencils, glue

Time: 15 to 20 minutes

Preparation: Create a sample craft to show the children.

Give each child a brown sheet and a red sheet of construction paper. Have children fold the red sheets in half widthwise and cut on the fold. Then have them cut 1-inch-wide strips widthwise. Have children roll each strip tightly around a pencil until the whole strip is rolled up.

Have kids each fold their brown sheet in half. Then have them unfold the papers and glue half of their curls on the right side of the brown paper at least 1 inch from the center fold. Have them glue the other curls to the other half of their paper at least 1 inch from the center fold.

SAY: **Remember that just as God helped the Israelites cross the Red Sea, ▷ GOD HELPS US WHEN WE'RE AFRAID.**

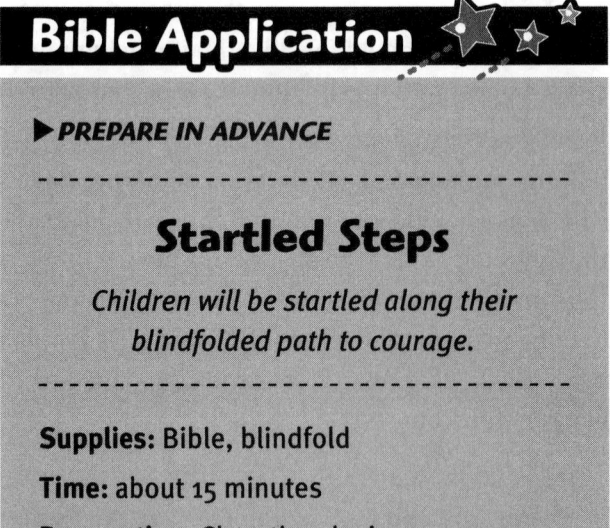

Bible Application

▶ PREPARE IN ADVANCE

Startled Steps

Children will be startled along their blindfolded path to courage.

Supplies: Bible, blindfold

Time: about 15 minutes

Preparation: Clear the playing area.

Choose one person to be "It." Blindfold this person, and take him or her to one side of the room. Scatter the remaining children. When you give the signal, the blindfolded child will slowly begin to move to the other side of the room. His or her goal is to touch the opposite wall as quickly as possible, while bumping into the fewest people possible along the way.

The remaining children should stand silent and motionless. Whenever the blindfolded person bumps another player, the seeing player must shout, "Hey!" Continue until the blindfolded person has reached the other side of the room.

Ask It to give the blindfold to another child and then join the others as potential obstacles. Take turns until everyone has a chance to cross the room. Then ASK:

- **What was it like to be blindfolded and play this game?**
- **How was this game similar to the challenges we face each day?**

Read aloud Exodus 14:13-14; then ASK:

- **How can you remember that ▷ GOD HELPS US WHEN WE'RE AFRAID?**

Ask kids to form pairs and share with their partners why they need God's help when they're afraid this week. Encourage them to share ideas for ways to trust God to help them. After a few minutes, ask partners to pray for each other.

Then participate in this experience again, having a sighted person walk alongside the blindfolded person, repeating, "Courage, God will protect you."

SAY: **God helped the Israelites when they were afraid, and ▷ GOD HELPS US WHEN WE'RE AFRAID, too. Think about something that makes you afraid. Maybe you're afraid of a bully at school, a class that seems hard, a fight your parents had, or a scary movie you watched.**

Give kids a few minutes to think about things that make them afraid. Then SAY: **Now we're going to pray, asking God to help us when we're afraid. As you pray, walk between the lines of people, just as the Israelites walked down the middle of the Red Sea.**

Have kids take turns walking between the lines of students. As they do so, have them pray aloud if they're comfortable, "God, please help me when I'm afraid." As each child is finished, ask him or her to stand at the end of the line while other kids make their way through.

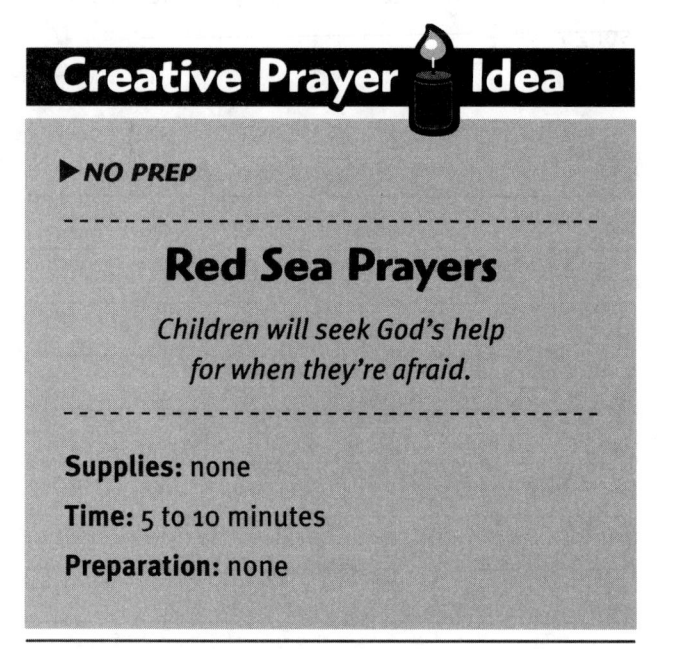

Creative Prayer Idea

▶ *NO PREP*

Red Sea Prayers

Children will seek God's help for when they're afraid.

Supplies: none

Time: 5 to 10 minutes

Preparation: none

Ask children to form two lines by standing shoulder to shoulder, with the lines facing each other. Be sure you have room for a person to walk between the lines.

Snack

▶ *PREPARE IN ADVANCE*

▶ *ALLERGY ALERT*

Red Sea Split

Children will make sundaes to commemorate the way God helped the Israelites.

Supplies: bowls, ice cream scoop, vanilla ice cream, plastic knives, bananas, strawberry syrup, spoons

Time: about 15 minutes

Preparation: Slice some bananas—enough so that each child will have a few banana slices. Set out all the supplies on a table where kids can create their snacks. You may want to put a cloth or tarp on the floor in case of spills.

Give each child a bowl, and help kids scoop some vanilla ice cream into their bowls. Show kids how to use plastic knives to split their ice cream into two parts and place them on either side of the bowl.

Give each child a few banana slices to place on top of both sides of their ice cream. Then allow children to top their creations with strawberry syrup.

As kids are eating their snacks, ASK:

- **How does this snack remind you of what God did at the Red Sea?**
- **How can knowing that ▷ GOD HELPS US WHEN WE'RE AFRAID change your life?**

Worship Prompt Idea

▶ *NO PREP*
▶ *FOR FAMILY MINISTRY*

Music's Message

Supplies: Bible, newsprint, markers

Time: about 30 minutes

Preparation: none

Form two teams. Have teams race to write the most kinds of music on a sheet of newsprint. When teams are finished, read both lists. Then have kids tell the purpose of each kind of music. For example, marching band music makes it easier for military or band units to walk in time together.

SAY: **Sometimes music can tell a story. Listen to how Moses and his sister, Miriam, sang to God after God led the Israelites through the Red Sea.** Read aloud Exodus 15:1-18.

ASK:

- **What did Moses and Miriam's music say about how they felt?**
- **How can we tell God thanks for helping us when we're afraid?**

SAY: **Let's try one way of showing thanks to God for the ways ▷ GOD HELPS US WHEN WE'RE AFRAID. Let's use music to worship God.**

Form four groups. A group can be one person. Have groups each choose a different musical style from the lists kids created earlier. Have groups each prepare a song about how God helps us when we're afraid, using their style of music. After groups are ready, have them present their songs.

notes

Preschool Story

▶ *ALLERGY ALERT*

▶ *PREPARE IN ADVANCE*

Bible Point: ▷ **GOD HELPS US WHEN WE'RE AFRAID.**

Supplies: Bible, small teddy bear cookies, small paper muffin cups, blueberry gelatin, knife, paper, crayons or markers

Time: 15 to 20 minutes

Preparation: Make a batch of blue gelatin squares by following the directions on the box to make the gelatin. Cut the gelatin into enough squares so that each child can have one.

Parting the Way

Have kids form a circle and sit down. Open your Bible to Exodus 14, and show children the words. SAY: **Moses obeyed God by leading his people out of slavery and into a new land.** Select one teddy bear cookie to represent Moses. Put the rest of "God's people" into a muffin cup.

But Pharaoh was angry about losing his slaves, so he started after them as they crossed the desert! Select another teddy bear cookie to represent Pharaoh, and put his "army" into another muffin cup.

Moses led the people away from Pharaoh and across the desert. But then they came to a gigantic sea and didn't know what to do! Slide the muffin cup with Moses and his people up to the blue gelatin square.

Moses trusted God and knew he would help, so he raised his staff into the air and told the sea to part! Break your gelatin square in half.

Moses and God's people quickly crossed the split sea. Move Moses and his people between each half of the gelatin.

When God's people were safely across, Moses lowered his hands, and the sea went back together, covering Pharaoh's army! The muffin cup with Moses and his people should be on one side of the gelatin, while Pharaoh and his people are in between the halves. Bring the two halves together so they cover the muffin cup with Pharaoh's army.

God helped the Israelites when they were afraid, and ▷ GOD HELPS US WHEN WE'RE AFRAID, too.

Encourage kids to enjoy their snacks as they retell the Bible story to one another. After kids finish their snacks, have them gather in a circle and do this finger play together.

Pharaoh let the people go. *(With thumbs up, throw your hands over your shoulders.)*

The Israelites were free! *(Stretch out arms.)*

Through the desert they did go *(walk fingers up arm),*

And then camped out by the sea. *(Interlock fingers, and make rolling motion with hands.)*

Pharaoh changed his mind, you know.

The people were afraid. *(Show scared face.)*

But God did make the sea to part *(place hands together over head, and then separate them),*

And gave them a new start. *(Place hands on heart.)*

ASK:

- **How did God help the Israelites when they were afraid?**
- **How has God helped you when you were scared?**
- **How can you trust God to help you when you're scared in the future?**

Before kids leave, give them each a piece of paper, and have them draw a picture of something they're afraid of. Then tell kids to draw how they can trust God to help them in that scary situation.

BIBLE STORY

Manna and Quail

For the Leader

As the Israelites traveled through the desert, they grumbled and complained on many occasions. They complained when they were thirsty, hungry, tired, afraid, or sick of traveling. God didn't appreciate their grumbling—but God took care of them and provided for them anyway.

It's easy to judge the Israelites, thinking they were a bunch of whiners. But most of us complain for all the same reasons—and more. In fact, most of us complain when we're traveling a few hours in an air-conditioned car, two hours after our most recent meal!

Remind kids that even though complaining and grumbling are not good choices, God still provides for us, just as he provided for the Israelites.

Key Scriptures

Exodus 16:1-35

Matthew 6:33

Bible Verse

"Seek the Kingdom of God above all else, and live righteously, and he will give you everything you need" (Matthew 6:33).

Bible Experience

▶ *PREPARE IN ADVANCE*

▶ *ALLERGY ALERT*

Bible Point: ▷ **GOD PROVIDES.**

Children will reenact the Israelites' journey.

Supplies: Bible, tablecloth, saltine crackers, graham crackers

Time: 15 to 20 minutes

Preparation: Lay out a tablecloth on the floor.

Have children sit on the floor around the tablecloth. Open your Bible to Exodus 16. SAY: **Today's Bible story comes from Exodus 16:1-35. God's people had been slaves in Egypt. Moses led them out of Egypt. Before they left, they baked some bread to eat on the way.**

Give each child a saltine. Ask children to wait until you tell them to eat it. SAY: **God told them to leave in a hurry because the Egyptians would come after them. Let's pretend we're on the run.** Lead children in running around the room. If your room is small, have children run in place. Return to your original spot and SAY: **That was tiring! I'm hungry. Let's eat.** Have the children eat their saltines. **God's people had a long way to travel to get to the good place he wanted them to live. It's time to travel again. Let's go.** Lead the children in walking around the room.

It's been a long couple of days of traveling through the desert. Let's eat. Let the children point out that they're out of crackers. ASK:

- **How do you think God's people felt when they ran out of food?**
- **What would you do if you thought you might starve in the desert?**

SAY: **God loved the people and knew that they needed food. God had Moses tell the people to go to sleep, and when they woke up, they would see that God could provide for their needs.**

Have kids pretend to sleep. While their eyes are closed, place pieces of graham crackers all over the tablecloth. Have the children "wake up."

SAY: **When they woke up, the ground was covered with a special type of bread. The Israelites called it *manna*, which means, "What is it?"**

Let children pick up the graham cracker pieces and eat them.

SAY: **The people were happy with their new food for a while. Then they began to get tired of eating the same food week in and week out. They began complaining. Let me hear what they probably sounded like.** Pause.

Moses prayed and asked God to provide for their needs. God sent a flock of quail. The people caught, cooked, and ate the quail.

ASK:

- **How do you think the people felt when they realized God had provided for their needs?**
- **How does God provide for your needs?**

Read Matthew 6:33 aloud. SAY: **God loves to take care of our needs. We don't need to be worried or complain to have our needs met. ▷ GOD PROVIDES for our needs. All we have to do is ask!**

Song & Connect

Use "He Is Good" (track 16, *it: Innovative Tools for Children's Ministry: Old Testament* CD) to help reinforce the Bible Point, ▷ **GOD PROVIDES.**

Additional Topics List

This lesson can be used to help children discover... Equipping, God's Provisions, Thankfulness, and Trust.

Game

▶ PREPARE IN ADVANCE

▶ ALLERGY ALERT

Manna From Heaven

Children will flip and catch some tasty "manna."

Supplies: butcher paper, plastic spoons, mini marshmallows

Time: 5 to 10 minutes

Preparation: Ask children to wash their hands before playing.

Have kids form pairs and sit on the butcher paper. Give each pair a plastic spoon and eight mini marshmallows (manna). Ask partners to take turns flipping manna at each other. Kids can't use their hands to catch it, only their mouths.

At the end of the game, discuss the following questions:

- **How would you feel if you had to rely on food falling from the sky?**
- **How do you think God's people felt relying on God for their food?**
- **How is that like or unlike your relying on God to provide for you?**

Craft

▶ *FOR YOUNGER CHILDREN*
▶ *NO PREP*
▶ *ALLERGY ALERT*

Breakfast Flakes

Children will consider what manna might have been like and how God still provides for our needs.

Supplies: bowl of frosted-flake cereal, construction paper, crayons, white glue

Time: 15 to 20 minutes

Preparation: none

Pass the bowl around the circle, and let kids taste a piece of cereal. SAY: **Manna might have looked a little bit like this cereal. ▷ GOD PROVIDES for our needs. Let's decorate these pictures to remind us that we can ask God to provide for all of our needs.**

Give each child a piece of construction paper, and set out crayons. Have kids draw pictures of the Israelites gathering manna. Show them how to glue the frosted flakes to the ground areas of the picture to remind them of manna.

Bible Application

▶ *PREPARE IN ADVANCE*

Picture This

Children will evaluate the difference between what they want and what they need and understand that God provides what they truly need.

Supplies: old magazines or catalogs, safety scissors, poster board, marker, glue stick

Time: about 15 minutes

Preparation: Set out the magazines, catalogs, and scissors.

SAY: **Let's look through these magazines and catalogs to find and cut out pictures of things we can ask God for.**

Give children five minutes to find and cut out their pictures, and then collect the pictures. Have kids sit in a circle, and set the poster board in the middle of the circle. Use the marker to divide the poster board into two columns. Write "Wants" at the top of one column and "Needs" at the top of the other.

SAY: **▷ GOD PROVIDES the things we need. But God doesn't promise to give us everything we want. Let's go through our pictures and decide whether these are things we want or things we need.**

Hold up each picture, and let the children decide if it's a picture of a want or a need. Let a volunteer apply glue to the back of the picture and place it on the correct side of the poster board. Repeat the process with every picture. Then ASK:

- **What are other things you might put in the "need" column that we didn't have pictures of? in the "want" column?**
- **Why doesn't God always give us what we want?**
- **What's the best part of knowing we can ask God for what we need?**

SAY: **There's nothing wrong with asking God for things we want. But God knows what things would be good for us to have and what things we'd be better off without. ▷ GOD PROVIDES what we need.**

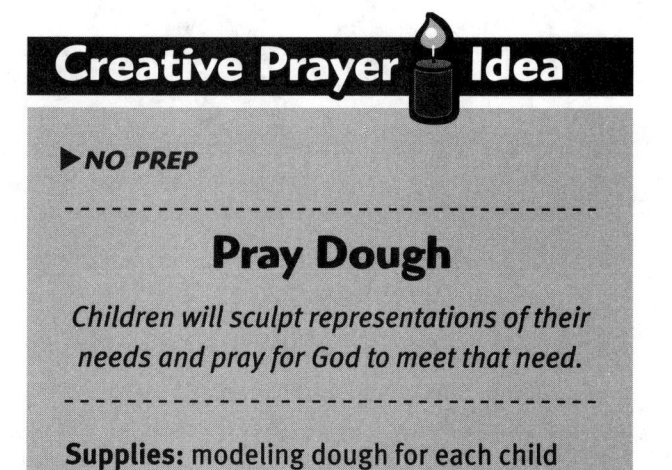

Creative Prayer Idea

▶ *NO PREP*

Pray Dough

Children will sculpt representations of their needs and pray for God to meet that need.

Supplies: modeling dough for each child

Time: 5 minutes

Preparation: none

Have kids sit in a circle, and give each child a piece of modeling dough.

SAY: **Mold your dough into something you need God to provide for you, just as he provided manna and quail for the Israelites.**

Give children two minutes to shape their dough. Explain that you'll pray aloud and then pause, during which time they may silently pray for what their dough represents.

PRAY: **Dear God, thanks so much for loving us and *wanting* to provide for our needs. We will ask you for everything we need. Right now we ask you to provide** (pause for a minute for children to pray silently). **Amen.**

Discussion Launcher

▶ *NO PREP*
▶ *FOR SMALL GROUPS*

Got the Gripes?

Children will discuss the importance of turning to God with our needs.

Supplies: old pots and pans or aluminum pie tins

Time: 5 to 10 minutes

Preparation: none

Distribute pots and pans.

SAY: **Let's find out what things turn us into complainers. I'm going to read a list of things that might make you want to complain. If what I read would make you complain a whole lot, bang your pot a lot. If you would complain a little bit, just make a little bit of noise. If you don't think you would complain at all, don't make any sounds with your pot.**

Read the following list, and pause between items.

- **You find out you're having Brussels sprouts for dinner.**
- **Your sister ate the last piece of cake.**
- **Your teacher gave you extra homework.**
- **Your brother is sick, and your dad asked you to do his chores.**
- **Your mom signs you up for the football team.**
- **Your dad grounds you from video games for a week.**
- **Your mom signs you up for ballet classes.**

Collect all the pots and pans, and set them aside. ASK:

◆ **How is complaining like the sound of pots and pans?**

◆ **How do you feel when you're around a complainer?**

◆ **What should we do when we need something we don't have?**

SAY: **Sometimes it's easy to complain when we can't have things we want. But as the Israelites learned, ▷ GOD PROVIDES for our needs.**

Snack

▶ *ALLERGY ALERT*
▶ *NO PREP*

What We Need

Children will get a "taste" for God's divine provision and be reminded to thank God for the food he provides.

Supplies: mini marshmallows, 6 tablespoons of honey, large plastic bowl, spoons, microwave oven, graham crackers, cookie sheet, access to a refrigerator

Time: 20 to 30 minutes

Preparation: none

Have kids help you pour a bag of mini marshmallows and 6 tablespoons of honey into a large bowl. Melt in a microwave set on medium. Stop every few seconds, and let children take turns stirring the mixture until smooth.

While some children stir, have others line a cookie sheet with graham-cracker halves—one for each child. Help children dribble the marshmallow mixture over the graham crackers, and then place the "manna" in a refrigerator.

After a few minutes, bring the snack from the refrigerator and SAY: **Before we eat our make-believe manna, let's say a prayer of thanks for all the food ▷ GOD PROVIDES for us.**

Before kids enjoy their snacks, PRAY: **Dear God, thank you for being the perfect provider. We know you give us everything we need, and we give you our thanks. In Jesus' name, amen.**

Preschool Story

▶ *PREPARE IN ADVANCE*
▶ *ALLERGY ALERT*

Bible Point: ▷ **GOD PROVIDES.**

Supplies: Bible, large blanket, package of marshmallows, plates, assorted lunchmeats

Time: 15 to 20 minutes

Preparation: Place assorted lunchmeats on two plates.

A Divine Dinner

Have kids form a circle and sit down. Open your Bible to Exodus 16, and show children the words. SAY: **God had helped Moses and the people escape the Egyptians, and now they were no longer slaves. When they left Egypt, they began to walk in the desert. They walked and walked and walked.** Encourage kids to march together in a circle for a few minutes. Then stop and begin to complain.

I'm so tired. We've been walking forever. Wipe your brow and act very tired. **I'm hungry, too. Does anyone have any food? There's no food here! We're going to starve to death. This isn't any fun. We were better off in Egypt. At least in Egypt we had food!** Encourage kids to sit back down.

The Israelites were angry with God and with Moses because there was no food. They complained and complained and complained. They whined and whined and whined. Then one day God finally said, "Enough!" God told the Israelites that he would provide for them.

Spread a large blanket on the floor, and direct kids to sit on the blanket. Then open a package of marshmallows, and empty the marshmallows over kids' heads. Encourage each child to pick up one marshmallow and eat it.

SAY: **Every morning God sent bread to the Israelites. The bread was white and tasted sweet. God told the Israelites to pick up just enough bread—not too much—for each person in their family.**

Hold up two plates of assorted lunchmeats and "fly" the two plates down to the blanket. Encourage kids to snack on the lunchmeats.

SAY: **Every evening God sent birds so the Israelites would have meat to eat. God sent the bread and birds to the Israelites so they wouldn't be hungry and so they'd remember that ▷ GOD PROVIDES everything we need.**

When you're finished telling the story, lead children in this simple action rhyme:

God's people were tired and hungry; they'd walked and walked and walked. (Rub tummy and march in place.)

"We had more food in Egypt," they grumped and whined and talked. (Point over your shoulder, and then cross arms over your chest.)

They yelled at God; they complained and whined. (Shake your finger, and stick your bottom lip out in a pout.)

Then God sent bread and meat on which they dined. (Twinkle hands down from above to imitate falling rain, and then pretend to eat.)

"Don't worry or fret, I'll provide for you," God said. (Shake your head, and then hug yourself.)

And God provides for us, too, from morning till bed. (Point to yourself, spread your fingers open wide like a sun, and then put hands under your head to look as if you're sleeping.)

ASK:

- **How did God help the Israelites when they were hungry?**
- **How can you trust God to provide for you?**

BIBLE STORY

The Ten Commandments Given and Received

For the Leader

It's hard to imagine what this scene was like: A nation purified and waiting to hear from God. Thousands of people surrounding a mountain in the desert. Thunder and lightning and fire on the mountain. A loud, mysterious trumpet blast. Sounds like a scene from a great movie...oh, I guess that's been done.

God made clear that what he had to share was important. And the Israelites listened. They received the Ten Commandments, a wonderfully simple but extremely challenging set of rules that became the basis of law in countries, communities, and households around the world and across time. The wisdom of God, applied to daily human life—it was revolutionary.

Help kids understand the importance of these 10 rules and their relevance to their lives today. God gave those Ten Commandments not only to the ancient Israelites but to all people, everywhere, in all generations.

Key Scriptures

Exodus 20:1-17

Psalm 103:1

Bible Verse

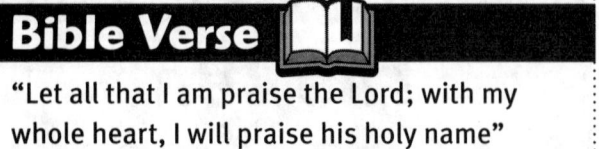

"Let all that I am praise the Lord; with my whole heart, I will praise his holy name" (Psalm 103:1).

Bible Experience

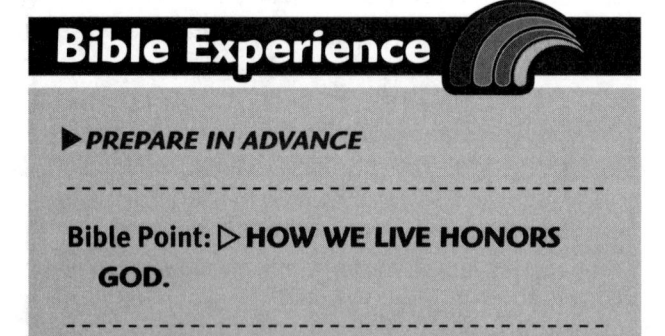

▶ ***PREPARE IN ADVANCE***

Bible Point: ▷ **HOW WE LIVE HONORS GOD.**

Children will navigate an obstacle course that teaches the importance of obeying the Ten Commandments.

Supplies: Bible, markers, construction paper, tape, colored dot stickers, scissors

Time: 15 minutes

Preparation: Write the numbers 1 through 10 on separate sheets of construction paper. On another sheet of paper, write "home." Create an obstacle course by taping the papers to the floor, close enough together so children can step from one numbered paper to another. Have the obstacle course end at "home."

Count out 10 colored dot stickers for each child, and number the stickers 1 through 10 with a marker. Place all the "1" stickers near the "1" paper on the obstacle course. Place all the "2" stickers near the "2" paper, and so on. Finally, cut a 1x10-inch strip of construction paper for each child.

SAY: **After the Israelites left Egypt, while they were traveling to the land God had promised them, God gave Moses some special rules he wanted his people to follow. These rules are called the Ten Commandments. They're special rules to help us show our love for God and one another. Let's find out what those commandments are.**

Let's count the Ten Commandments on our fingers.

Open your Bible to Exodus 20:1-17, and say aloud this simplified version of the Commandments. Have children repeat each one after you've said it.

SAY:

1. **Don't worship other gods.**
2. **Don't have idols.**
3. **Don't misuse God's name.**
4. **Keep the Sabbath day holy.**
5. **Honor your mom and dad.**
6. **Don't kill.**
7. **Be true to your husband or wife.**
8. **Don't steal.**
9. **Don't lie about others.**
10. **Don't wish you had what others have.**

Good job! Now that we know what the Ten Commandments are, let's see how they can help us follow God.

Tape a strip of paper around each child's wrist. SAY: **These Top-10 Bands will help you remember the Ten Commandments on an obstacle course. You're going to step on each number, making sure you don't touch the ground, and try to make it all the way to "home."** Point out where "home" is.

As you stop at each number, take a sticker and stick it on your wristband. But watch out—there are traps out there that will try to keep you from getting home. Be careful! Ready? Let's go!

Lead kids through the obstacle course, making sure each child stops to place a sticker on his or her wristband at each number. As children move, shout out comments such as, "Careful, don't step on that pile of lies" or, "Oh no—some people want you to steal; don't listen to them!" Then have kids sit down.

SAY: **Great job! It's a good thing we had those numbers to walk on to help us get safely home.**

Read Psalm 103:1 aloud.

SAY: **The Ten Commandments are a great reason to praise God. God's rules help us live good lives. Those numbers on your stickers are kind of like the Ten Commandments. When we follow God's rules, ▷ HOW WE LIVE HONORS GOD.**

Song & Connect

Use "Create in Me a Pure Heart" (track 5, *it: Innovative Tools for Children's Ministry: Old Testament* CD) to help reinforce the Bible Point, ▷ **HOW WE LIVE HONORS GOD.**

Additional Topics List

This lesson can be used to help children discover... Faith, Following God, Righteousness, Trust, and Worship.

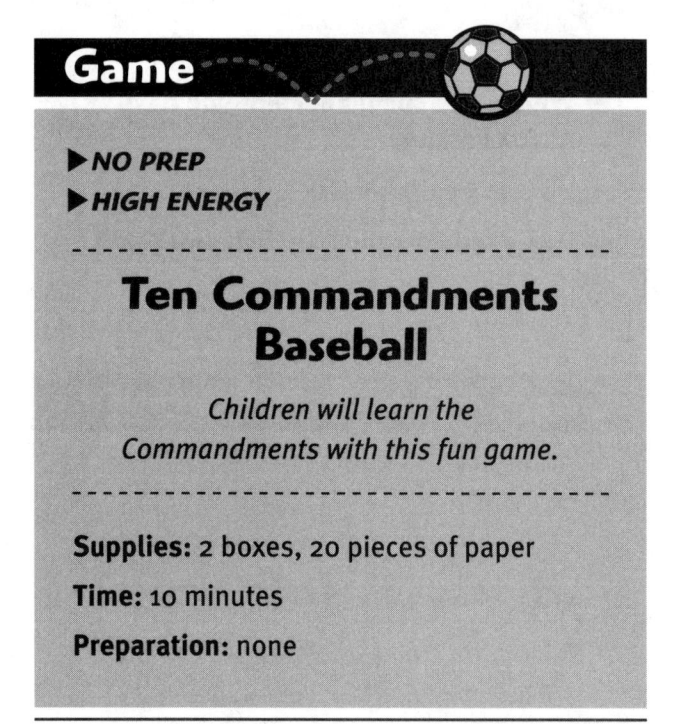

n ______
o ______
t ______
e ______
s ______

Game

▶ ***NO PREP***
▶ ***HIGH ENERGY***

Ten Commandments Baseball

Children will learn the Commandments with this fun game.

Supplies: 2 boxes, 20 pieces of paper
Time: 10 minutes
Preparation: none

Form two teams. Have each team choose a pitcher. Give each pitcher 10 pieces of paper. Then have each team choose a catcher. This should be a person who writes quickly. Also have each team designate an outfielder, who will retrieve pitches that don't hit the mark and give them back to the pitcher.

The rest of the team members will be basemen. Their job is to help the pitcher and catcher remember the Ten Commandments.

Place two boxes at least 15 feet away from each team. Station the two outfielders near the boxes. On each team, as the basemen remember each commandment, the catcher writes it on a sheet of paper, wads it up, and gives it to the pitcher, who throws it into the box.

Each team's outfielder gathers all the balls that don't go inside the box and tosses them back to the catcher. The catcher hands them to the pitcher, who must try again to get them in the box. The first team to get all Ten Commandments into its box is the winner.

At the end of the game, talk about ▷ **HOW WE LIVE HONORS GOD.**

ASK:

- **What's one commandment you have obeyed today?**
- **How do you think that honors God?**
- **How would disobeying dishonor God?**

Craft

▶ *NO PREP*

Hidden in Your Heart

Children will make pictures as reminders to honor God's commandments.

Supplies: Bibles, brightly colored construction paper, paint pens or glitter markers, safety scissors, transparent tape, spray bottle filled with 2 parts bleach and 1 part water, safety goggles, painting smocks

Time: about 20 minutes

Preparation: none

Give each child two pieces of brightly colored construction paper. Stick with darker colors—yellow, pink, and light blue won't work well for this activity.

Have children look up Exodus 20:1-17 and use paint pens or glitter markers to write one of the Ten Commandments in the middle of their colored paper. Then have kids each cut a large heart from another sheet of construction paper. Help children make small transparent tape rolls to place on the back of their cut-out heart shapes. The tape rolls will hold the hearts in place over the written commandments. Have children gently tape their paper hearts over the written commandments. The hearts must completely cover the commandments.

Take the pictures outside, and allow kids to spray them with the bleach and water solution. Be sure kids are wearing safety goggles and paint smocks or shirts and are spraying away from all other students. Leave the papers in the sun for a minute or two. Kids will enjoy watching the paper fade.

When the paper is dry, allow kids to remove the hearts, being careful not to tear the paper. All areas of the paper that were exposed will have faded.

SAY: **Just as the commandment looks like it's inside the heart, we should keep God's commandments in our hearts by remembering that they're important and asking God to help us obey them.**

n
o
t
e
s

Bible Application

▶ *NO PREP*

God Gives Moses the Ten Commandments

Children will learn to honor God by keeping his commandments.

Supplies: child car seat, bike helmet

Time: about 15 minutes

Preparation: none

SAY: **Rules, rules, rules—they're everywhere! Don't run in church, be quiet when Dad is taking a nap, chew with your mouth closed, no gum in school, and wash your hands before you eat.** Hold up the car seat and then the bike helmet. For each one, ask these questions:

- **What rule does this item remind you of?**
- **Why do we have that rule?**

SAY: **Rules show us how to live, and they keep us safe. God knew that long ago, when he gave Moses the Ten Commandments. When Jesus was on earth, he talked about the greatest commandments. He said we are to love God above all else, and our neighbor as ourselves.**

ASK:

- **What's it mean to love God above all else?**
- **What's it mean to love our neighbor as ourselves?**

SAY: **If we love God above all else, we make him number one in our lives. We focus on him, pray to him, and trust him completely. When we love our neighbors as ourselves, we treat them kindly and care for them. And when we follow those rules, ▷ HOW WE LIVE HONORS GOD.**

Creative Prayer Idea

▶ *NO PREP*

Commandments Prayer

Children will pray for God's help in following God's rules.

Supplies: none

Time: up to 5 minutes

Preparation: none

SAY: **As Jesus said when he lived on earth, all Ten Commandments help us follow these two basic rules: Love God above all else, and love our neighbor as ourselves. Knowing that ▷ HOW WE LIVE HONORS GOD, let's pray and ask God to help us honor him by following these rules.**

Ask kids to each hold up a pointer finger as "number one." PRAY: **Dear God, please help us keep you number one in our lives.** Then ask kids to hug a neighbor. PRAY: **Help us love our neighbor as ourselves. In Jesus' name, amen.**

notes

Movie Clip

A Little Sin

Movie Title: *Veggie Tales: Larry-Boy and the Fib From Outer Space* (G)

Start Time: 13 minutes, 23 seconds

Where to Begin: Laura and the others find Junior. Laura says, "There he is."

Where to End: Fib says, "A little fib couldn't hurt anybody."

Plot: When Junior breaks his father's collector's plate, a little blue fib from outer space ends up in Junior Asparagus's living room. The fib encourages Junior to tell a little lie, Junior agrees, and the fib grows out of control.

Review: Use this clip to help children see that God gives us rules for our good. Junior thought that a little lie wouldn't really matter, but eventually the lie grows out of control. Even "little" sins can grow into destructive forces that ruin our lives.

Discussion

After setting up and showing the clip, ASK:

- ◆ **Why do you think God wants us to always tell the truth?**
- ◆ **What do you think life would be like without rules?**
- ◆ **Why do you think God gives us rules?**

SAY: **When we follow the Ten Commandments, ▷ HOW WE LIVE HONORS GOD.**

Snack

▶ ***ALLERGY ALERT***

▶ ***NO PREP***

Mount Sinai

Children will make and eat a snack that represents the mountain where Moses received the Ten Commandments.

Supplies: Bible, ice-cream scoop, bowls, ice cream, hot fudge, wafer cookies, spoons

Time: about 10 minutes

Preparation: none

Read Exodus 19:10-25 aloud. ASK:

- ◆ **What was the mountain like where Moses received the Ten Commandments from God?**
- ◆ **What do you think it looked like to the people of Israel?**

SAY: **Let's make snacks that will remind us of the mountain where God gave the people his commandments.** Scoop a "mountain" of ice cream into each child's bowl. Let kids smother their mountains in hot fudge and top them with two wafer "stone tablets."

n ______

o ______

t ______

e ______

s ______

Preschool Story

▶ *NO PREP*

Bible Point: ▷ **HOW WE LIVE HONORS GOD.**

Supplies: Bible

Time: 15 to 20 minutes

Preparation: none

Ten Good Rules

Have kids form a circle and sit down. Open your Bible to Exodus 19, and show children the words. SAY: **This was a big day for the Israelites! God was going to give some special rules to his people that we still use today. Moses had walked a very long way up the mountain, and down below, the people waited. They saw fire and smoke way up on top. They knew God was on that mountain.**

All of a sudden, there was thunder. Lead kids in stomping their feet. **Then there was lightning.** Flip the lights on and off, and have kids clap their hands. **Next there may have been a trumpet blast.** Lead kids in putting their hands over their mouths and pretending to blow on trumpets.

God wanted his people to listen! He was giving Moses 10 good rules to make their lives happier. (Have children cup their hands around their ears to show they are listening closely.)

The first good rule was to love God more than anything or anyone else. Have kids hold up one finger and then hug themselves.

The second rule was to worship only God. Have kids hold up two fingers and then hold up both their hands to heaven.

The third was to speak nicely when using God's name. Have kids hold up three fingers and then make talking signs with both their hands.

The fourth was to rest on the Sabbath day. Have kids hold up four fingers and then put their hands under their heads as if they're sleeping.

The fifth rule was to love your mommy and daddy. Have kids hold up five fingers and then hug themselves.

The sixth rule was to never hurt anyone. Have kids hold up six fingers and then hug a friend.

The seventh rule was to love one husband or one wife. Have kids hold up seven fingers and then hold up one index finger.

The eighth rule was to never steal. Have kids hold up eight fingers and then hold both hands forward, palms up.

The ninth rule was to never lie and always tell the truth. Have kids hold up nine fingers and then shout, "Tell the truth!"

And the 10th and last good rule was to be happy and thankful for all you have. Have kids hold up 10 fingers and then turn to a partner and tell one thing they are thankful for.

Then, one more time, God sent thunder, lightning, and a trumpet blast. Have kids stomp their feet, clap their hands, and then pretend to blow on a trumpet.

God loved his people, and God loves us. He knows what's best for us. God gave these 10 rules so we can do what's best and honor him. ▷ **HOW WE LIVE HONORS GOD.**

ASK:

- **Is it easy or hard to follow these rules? Why?**
- **Why is it important to follow God's rules?**
- **What are some ways you can follow God's rules this week?**

BIBLE STORY

The Golden Calf

For the Leader

Those ancient Israelites...so easy for us to judge. Why were they so fickle? How could they turn their backs on God so easily, to worship a statue made from their own gold? But the Israelites had been living in Egypt, where idol worship was commonplace. They were used to being able to see something that represented their object of worship.

Moses had been up on Mount Sinai for almost six weeks, and the Israelites didn't know if he would ever come back. They had lost their own visible reminder of God's presence—Moses himself. So they reverted to what they knew, what was easy, what felt good.

Before we judge the Israelites for their fickle choices, we should remember how easy it is to give in to the world around us. How easy it is to "worship" heroes in our culture and to forget God. Maybe we're not so different after all.

Key Scriptures

Exodus 32:1-35; 34:14

Isaiah 9:6

Psalm 24:7; 80:1

Bible Verse

"You must worship no other gods, for the Lord, whose very name is Jealous, is a God who is jealous about his relationship with you" (Exodus 34:14).

Bible Experience

▶ ***NO PREP***

Bible Point: ▷ **WORSHIP GOD ALONE.**

Children will consider why we should worship only God.

Supplies: Bible, several broken toys or household items (without sharp edges), broken pencil, pencil sharpener, 1 unsharpened pencil for each child

Time: about 15 minutes

Preparation: none

Place the broken items where the children can see them.

ASK:

- ◆ **What do these items have in common?**
- ◆ **When have you broken something?**
- ◆ **What happens after someone breaks something?**

Open your Bible to Exodus 32. SAY: **God had written his special laws on big slabs of stone that we call stone tables. The Bible tells in Exodus 32 about a time Moses broke the stone**

tablets—on purpose! While Moses was getting God's commandments, the people were already disobeying by worshipping a statue instead of God. Moses broke the tablets out of anger because the people of Israel were disobeying God's laws and worshipping a golden calf.

ASK:

- **Do you think God was angry with Moses for breaking the tablets?**
- **Why was God angry with the people?**

Hold up some of the broken objects.

ASK:

- **How do you think these got broken?**
- **How do you feel when something important gets broken?**
- **What happens when you break an important rule?**

SAY: **One of God's important rules is that people shouldn't worship anything or anyone besides God. When we worship something other than God—making that thing more important in our lives than God is—we sin against God. We should ▷ WORSHIP GOD ALONE.**

Read Exodus 34:14 aloud.

ASK:

- **What do you think this verse means?**
- **Why does God want us to worship only him?**
- **What do you think happens when people break this rule?**

SAY: **I'm going to give you each a new pencil to keep. When you write with it, I'd like you to think of how God has written his laws for you in the Bible. When you break the point or need to sharpen this pencil, remember that we shouldn't break God's rules, and we should worship only God.** Hand out the pencils.

Song & Connect

Use "Let Us Worship" (track 6, *it: Innovative Tools for Children's Ministry: Old Testament* CD) to help reinforce the Bible Point, **▷ WORSHIP GOD ALONE.**

Additional Topics List

This lesson can be used to help children discover... Glorifying God, Honor, Praising God, and Reverence.

Game

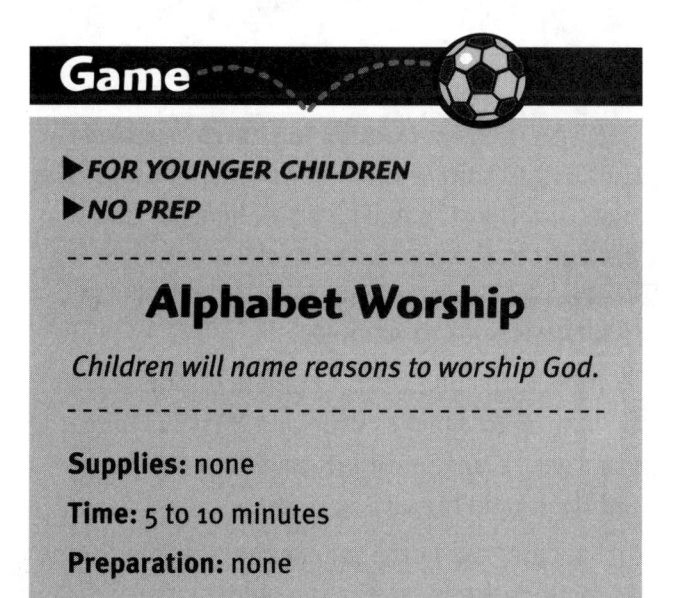

▶ ***FOR YOUNGER CHILDREN***
▶ ***NO PREP***

Alphabet Worship

Children will name reasons to worship God.

Supplies: none
Time: 5 to 10 minutes
Preparation: none

Ask kids to form a circle. SAY: **The Bible says we should ▷ WORSHIP GOD ALONE. Worshipping God is easy—there are so many different reasons to worship God! Let's think of some of those reasons now. Let's go around the circle and name the letters of the alphabet. For every letter, we'll name a reason to worship God.**

Have kids take turns around the circle, with each child naming a letter of the alphabet and a reason to worship God that begins with that letter.

Craft

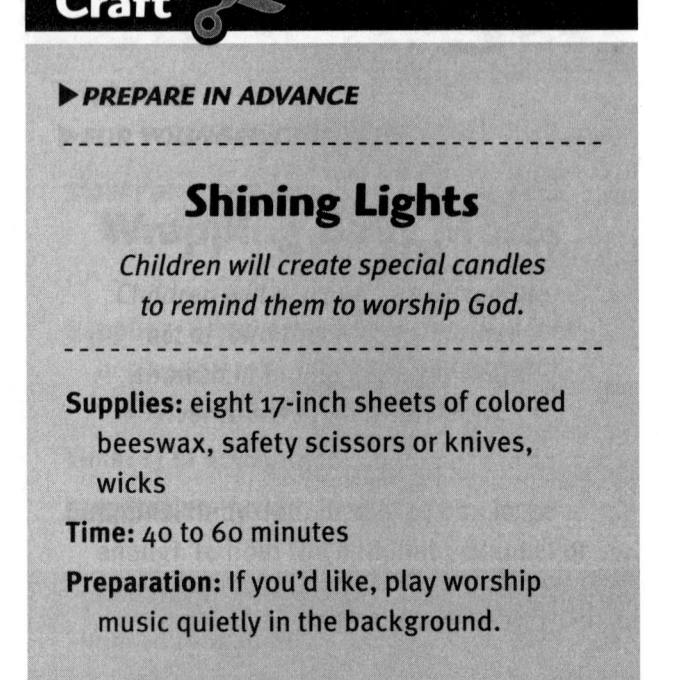

▶ *PREPARE IN ADVANCE*

Shining Lights

Children will create special candles to remind them to worship God.

Supplies: eight 17-inch sheets of colored beeswax, safety scissors or knives, wicks

Time: 40 to 60 minutes

Preparation: If you'd like, play worship music quietly in the background.

SAY: **When we worship in church, we sometimes light candles to remind us that God is the light and that those who know him can shine his light in the world. Let's take some time for everyone to create a candle as a reminder to ▷ WORSHIP GOD ALONE.**

Help each child cut a rectangular strip of beeswax 3 to 4 inches wide and 8 inches long. Lay a wick along one edge, and then roll the wax tightly around the wick.

Encourage children to take their candles home as reminders to worship God, who shines light into darkness.

Bible Application

▶ *NO PREP*

Worship Leaders

Children will lead one another in worshipping God.

Supplies: none

Time: about 30 minutes

Preparation: none

Have kids form groups of four to six. SAY: **The Bible tells us to ▷ WORSHIP GOD ALONE. There are many ways to worship God. Let's make a list of some of those ways.**

Lead kids in making a list of ways to worship God. Examples include singing, praying, serving others, reading the Bible, talking about God's Word, offering our time and money to God, and others.

SAY: **These are great ways to worship God at church, at home, and everywhere we go. In your groups, pick one of these ways to worship, and lead the rest of us in it. You'll have 10 minutes to plan your worship.**

After 10 minutes, have groups take turns leading each other in worship.

n
o
t
e
s

Creative Prayer Idea

▶ *NO PREP*

Make a Joyful Noise

Children will learn that prayer is a way we can worship God.

Supplies: paper, pens or pencils

Time: 10 to 15 minutes

Preparation: none

Have children form groups of four or five. Encourage older children to partner with younger ones. SAY: **One way to worship God is by praying to him. Let's practice worshipping God through prayer. A prayer of worship should tell God how great he is, just as a cheer for your favorite sports team would. A prayer of worship is not a prayer where we list all the things we need. It's a way of telling God we think he's the best!**

Explain that each group will write a prayer of worship and then share it with one or more other groups. Encourage kids to be creative. Suggest that they consider setting their prayer to music, creating a rap or cheer, or writing a prayer they would all whisper together. Remind children that they can use some of the names of God in their prayers, too.

After several minutes, have each group partner with another group, and let them share their prayers. Remind kids that even though they're letting others hear their prayers, they're really speaking to God.

Discussion Launcher Questions

Ask children to form trios and discuss:

- **What does it mean to worship God?**
- **Why do you think God cares whether we ▷ WORSHIP GOD ALONE?**
- **How can you remember to worship God every day?**

Worship Prompt Idea

▶ *PREPARE IN ADVANCE*

A Name Worthy of Praise

Children will learn and use various names of God to worship him.

Supplies: pencils, "Worship Your Name" handouts (p. 190)

Time: about 5 minutes

Preparation: Make a copy of the handout for each student.

Distribute pencils and "Worship Your Name" handouts. On the handouts, have each child read the names of God and draw a symbol or small picture to illustrate this name. If you have time, children can look up the verses.

When kids are finished with their handouts, have all the children stand in a circle and hold hands or link elbows.

SAY: **As the Bible tells us, we should ▷ WORSHIP GOD ALONE. There are many reasons to worship God. The Bible gives us many names for God, and those names can remind us of reasons to worship God. Let's**

Worship Your Name

A Few Names of God:

Prince of Peace	King of Glory	Shepherd of Israel
(Isaiah 9:6)	(Psalm 24:7)	(Psalm 80:1)

worship God now by using some of God's names that we've learned.

Explain that you will pray, and when you pause, you'll squeeze the hand (or elbow) of the child on your right. This child will then call out one of God's names and squeeze the hand or elbow of the next child, and so on until everyone has had a turn. Then you will complete the prayer.

PRAY: **Dear God, we praise you and worship you because you are holy. Your names tell us how special you are and how much we should honor you. You are** (pause for children to respond)**. Your name is worthy of all our praise. Help us remember to worship you alone. Amen.**

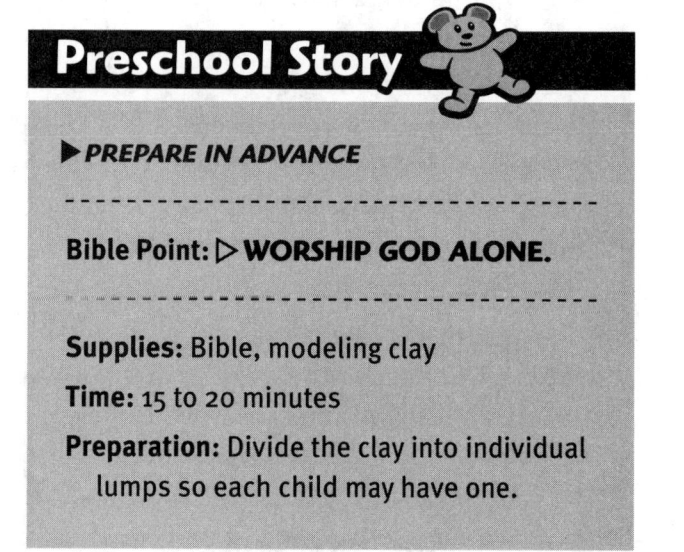

Preschool Story

▶ ***PREPARE IN ADVANCE***

Bible Point: ▷ **WORSHIP GOD ALONE.**

Supplies: Bible, modeling clay

Time: 15 to 20 minutes

Preparation: Divide the clay into individual lumps so each child may have one.

A Silly Plan

Have kids form a circle and sit down. Open your Bible to Exodus 32, and show children the words. SAY: **One day Moses was up on the mountain talking to God. He stayed up there for a very long time, and the Israelites started to think he'd left them forever! They forgot all of the wonderful things God had done for them, and they started to believe God had left them.**

The Israelites decided they needed a new god, so they decided to make one themselves. They threw gold and jewelry into a big fire and then formed the melted gold into the shape of a calf. Give children each a handful of clay, and encourage them to mold their clay into the shape of a calf.

Once the Israelites had made a calf, they decided to worship it. They gave gifts to the calf, bowed down to the calf, and started to tell each other that it was the calf that had saved them from Egypt. Isn't that silly? A calf made of gold couldn't have saved them from Egypt! But that's what they pretended.

They worshipped their calf as if it were God! Isn't that silly? God is alive. Is your clay statue alive? Allow children time to respond. **God is powerful and strong. Is your clay statue powerful and strong?** Let children respond. **God can do amazing things, such as heal people, send powerful storms, and turn the day into night. Can**

notes

your clay statue do any of those things? Give children time to respond. **God loves us. Does your clay statue love you?** Let children respond.

Our clay statues can't do any of the amazing things God can do. Our clay statues aren't even alive! And it was just like that with the Israelites. Their golden statue wasn't alive, it wasn't powerful and strong, it couldn't do amazing things, and it didn't love them. Yet the Israelites still decided to worship that silly statue.

It made God very angry that the Israelites were worshipping a fake god. He sent Moses back down the mountain, and Moses told the Israelites not to worship the calf any longer. God forgave the Israelites because he loved them, just as God forgives us because he loves us. But God wants us to worship him alone.

Encourage kids to play a game like "Simon Says." Have the leader stand up and say, "Worship God," as he or she leads the other children in doing one thing to worship God, such as sing, twirl, or hop. Tell kids that if the leader doesn't say, "Worship God" before he or she does the actions, then they shouldn't follow the actions. If a child follows the actions when the words aren't said, that child becomes the next leader. Remind children that there are many ways to worship, but we should ▷ **WORSHIP GOD ALONE.** When finished, ASK:

- **Why did the Israelites worship the golden calf?**
- **Why should we worship God alone?**
- **How can you worship God this week?**

BIBLE STORY

Spies in Canaan

For the Leader

It's interesting that after spying out the land of Canaan, the spies didn't care about the giant grapes or the land flowing with milk and honey. They had heard about the big, strong people and their fortified cities, and they panicked. It's also interesting that after reaching their destination, the people would want to turn around and go back to Egypt—where they were slaves.

Like all of us, the Israelites were trusting in their own strength and were overwhelmed by their sense of weakness. They apparently forgot what they had experienced since leaving Egypt. They forgot about God's promises.

And their consequences were fitting. God allowed them to stay in the desert rather than enter the land he had promised—for the rest of their lives.

Key Scriptures

Numbers 13:1–14:45

1 Corinthians 16:13

Bible Verse

"Be on guard. Stand firm in the faith. Be courageous. Be strong" (1 Corinthians 16:13).

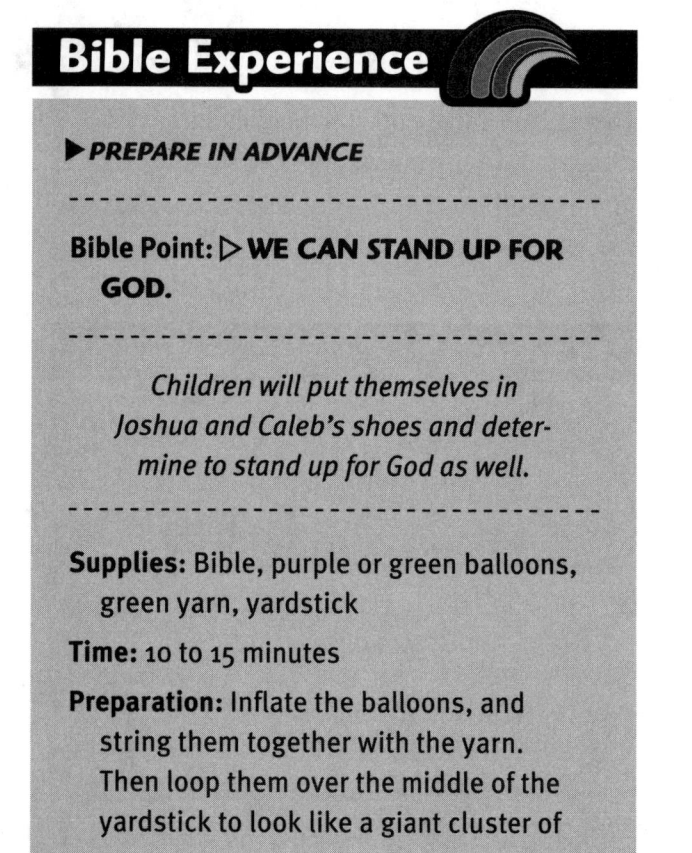

Bible Experience

▶ ***PREPARE IN ADVANCE***

Bible Point: ▷ **WE CAN STAND UP FOR GOD.**

Children will put themselves in Joshua and Caleb's shoes and determine to stand up for God as well.

Supplies: Bible, purple or green balloons, green yarn, yardstick

Time: 10 to 15 minutes

Preparation: Inflate the balloons, and string them together with the yarn. Then loop them over the middle of the yardstick to look like a giant cluster of grapes.

SAY: **After the Israelites left Egypt, God promised he'd give them a special place to live, a good land for food and everything they'd need to raise their families. God told Moses to send someone to check out the new land. So Moses sent Caleb and Joshua and 10 other men to be spies and see what the land was like. They saw some amazing things.**

Have two kids hold up the yardstick of "grapes" at each end. SAY: **When the men came back, they brought some samples of the fruit they found. The fruit was so huge that one cluster of grapes had to be carried on a pole between two people! They couldn't believe all the food that was there.**

But there were some big problems. The land was filled with giant people! This terrified the rest of the Israelites, who felt the giants were too strong for them. They didn't trust God to help them.

The Israelites were scared and didn't want to fight, so they grumbled instead. Let's all mumble and grumble the way they did. Pause. **But Caleb and Joshua weren't afraid. They reminded the people that God always keeps his promises. If God said they could take the land, they could! God would help them. They stood up for God.**

The Israelites thought it would be better to go back to Egypt, where they had been slaves. But their lives in Egypt had been terrible—they were slaves. Let's moan and groan like sad slaves. Pause. **Someone called out, "Let's pick a new leader and go back to Egypt!"**

Moses and Aaron got very upset. They bowed down to the ground in front of everyone. Have kids put their faces down to the floor. **Joshua and Caleb tore their clothes to show how sad they were.** Have kids make ripping sounds. **They wanted to move into the new land.**

notes

But the people were so afraid and angry that they thought about throwing rocks at Moses and Aaron and Joshua and Caleb. Then God's glory started shining from the Meeting Tent—the big tent where they worshipped God. Have kids shield their eyes. **It scared all the people. Moses went into the Meeting Tent, and God talked to him. God told Moses that because the people refused to trust in God, they would not get to go into the Promised Land of Canaan. But because Joshua and Caleb had stood up for God, they would get to enter the land someday.**

ASK:

- **How do you think Joshua and Caleb felt when everyone else refused to trust God?**
- **Why did Joshua and Caleb have courage to stand up for God?**

Read 1 Corinthians 16:13 aloud.

ASK:

- **How did Joshua and Caleb follow this Bible verse?**
- **How can you have the courage to stand up for God, too?**

SAY: **Like Joshua and Caleb, ▷ WE CAN STAND UP FOR GOD, too. God will give us courage to stand up for him.**

Song & Connect

Use "The Battle Is the Lord's" (track 2, *it: Innovative Tools for Children's Ministry: Old Testament* CD) to help reinforce the Bible Point, ▷ **WE CAN STAND UP FOR GOD.**

Additional Topics List

This lesson can be used to help children discover... Fearlessness, Honor, Service, and Strength.

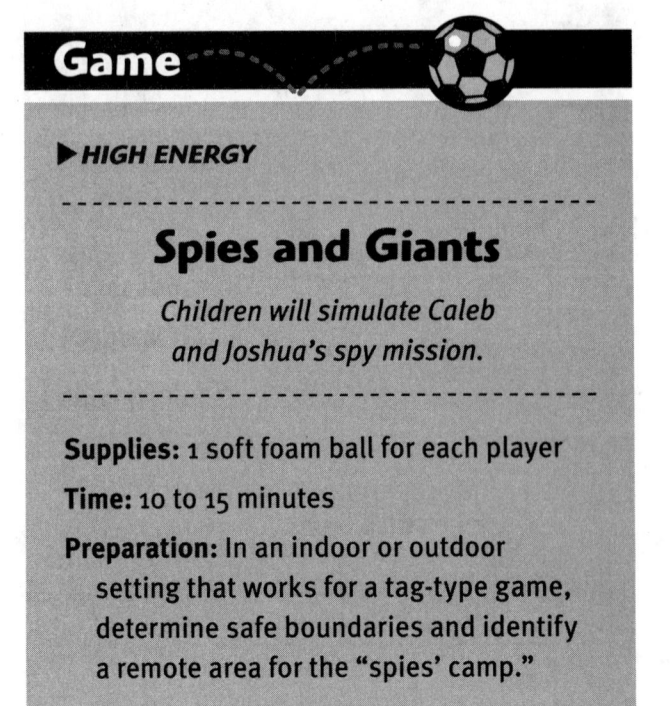

Game

▶ ***HIGH ENERGY***

Spies and Giants

Children will simulate Caleb and Joshua's spy mission.

Supplies: 1 soft foam ball for each player

Time: 10 to 15 minutes

Preparation: In an indoor or outdoor setting that works for a tag-type game, determine safe boundaries and identify a remote area for the "spies' camp."

Explain that half of the group will be "spies" and the other half "giants." The giants have two minutes to go out in pairs and hide from the spies.

SAY: **Spies, after two minutes, try to capture the giants by tossing foam balls at them. If a giant is touched by a foam ball, you can take the giant back to the spies' camp. Giants can be freed from "prison" if another giant reaches the camp and hits a captured giant with a foam ball.**

Send the spies to their camp and the giants off to hide. After two minutes, let the game begin. When all the giants are captured, or after a certain amount of time, have kids switch roles and play again.

Craft

▶NO PREP

Spy Cups

Children will make their own spies to remind them to stand up for God.

Supplies: Bibles, small paper cups, craft sticks, markers, scissors

Time: 15 to 20 minutes

Preparation: none

Give each child a paper cup and a craft stick, and set out markers. SAY: **When the Israelites wanted to know what the Promised Land was like, they sent spies into the land. Let's make our own spies.**

Instruct children to use markers to decorate their craft sticks to look like the spies who went into the land of Canaan. Encourage them to decorate their paper cups with objects that remind them of the Bible story: clusters of grapes, giant people, walled cities, or a Bible verse from Numbers 13:1–14:45.

Help kids cut a slit in the bottom of their paper cups and insert their craft stick people through the slit from the bottom of the cup. Show them how to raise the sticks so their spies will peek out from above the cup and then pull them back when they want the spies to hide.

Bible Application

▶NO PREP

▶FOR SMALL GROUPS

Stand Up

Children will learn how to stand up for God as they trust in him.

Supplies: binoculars

Time: about 10 minutes

Preparation: none

SAY: **Joshua and Caleb trusted and stood up for God. Joshua and Caleb were allowed to enter the land, but the other Israelites weren't.**

ASK:

- **How did Joshua and Caleb show that they trusted God?**
- **How can we trust and stand up for God?**

SAY: **Joshua and Caleb trusted God, and their trust gave them courage to stand up for God. We can trust God and stand up for him.**

ASK:

- **When do you really need to trust God?**
- **How can trusting in God help you stand up for God?**

Allow each child an opportunity to look through binoculars and share one way he or she will trust God and stand up for him.

n

o

t

e

s

Creative Prayer Idea

▶ *NO PREP*

Stand-Up Prayers

Children will stand up for God as they pray.

Supplies: none

Time: about 5 minutes

Preparation: none

SAY: **Just as Joshua and Caleb stood up for God, ▷ WE CAN STAND UP FOR GOD. As we pray, let's show that we will stand up for God.**

Tell kids that you'll lead them in prayer to ask God for courage to stand up for him. When you pause and invite them to pray, they should stand up. Be sure kids know it's OK not to pray or to stand if they don't feel comfortable doing so.

PRAY: **Dear God, we want to stand up for you. Please give us courage to do so. We need courage in these situations:** Pause for children to pray and stand. **Thanks for listening and helping us stand up for you. Amen.**

n

o

t

e

s

Science Devotion

▶ *PREPARE IN ADVANCE*

Jiggle, Shake, Quake

Children will experience miniature "earthquakes" as they explore how they can stand up for God.

Supplies: two 9x12-inch pans, 4 boxes of flavored gelatin, 2 cups of marshmallows, box of toothpicks

Time: 10 to 15 minutes

Preparation: Prepare two pans of flavored gelatin. Chill overnight.

ASK:

- **Have you ever been in an earthquake or seen the results on TV?**
- **What causes earthquakes?**

SAY: **Earthquakes are caused when the tectonic plates under the surface of the earth shift. Sometimes they run into each other, and this causes the ground above the plates to shift and shake. We're going to experience miniature earthquakes today.**

Have children form two groups, and have kids sit in their groups at a long table. Give each group a pan of flavored gelatin and a cup of marshmallows.

SAY: **Your gelatin represents the earth, and the marshmallows are your building materials. Using the marshmallows, build a house that can stand up by itself.** Give one group the box of toothpicks, and SAY: **I'm giving toothpicks to this group to use along with the marshmallows.**

After groups have built their houses, test them by shaking the table.

ASK:

◆ **Which building didn't fall** (or didn't fall as easily)? **Why?**

◆ **What kinds of situations in your life might feel like an earthquake?**

◆ **How do you think Joshua and Caleb felt?**

◆ **What can we do to become stronger so ▷ WE CAN STAND UP FOR GOD, even when we feel like everything around us is shaking?**

SAY: **Just as the toothpicks helped our marshmallow "buildings" stand up, God wants us to let him help us stand up for him.**

Snack

▶ *ALLERGY ALERT*
▶ *PREPARE IN ADVANCE*

Pita Spies

Children will eat a snack that reminds them of the spies who went into Canaan.

Supplies: pita bread, cream cheese, plastic knives, shredded carrots, plates, napkins

Time: 5 to 10 minutes

Preparation: Shred enough carrots so that each child will have a small handful.

Give each child half a piece of pita bread. Help kids spread cream cheese in their pitas and then tuck shredded carrots inside the pitas so they're barely visible.

SAY: **These snacks can remind us of the spies who went into Canaan to see what the land was like. They had to be sneaky and hide, just as our carrots are hiding inside.**

Preschool Story

▶ *ALLERGY ALERT*
▶ *PREPARE IN ADVANCE*

Bible Point: ▷ **WE CAN STAND UP FOR GOD.**

Supplies: Bible, disguises (hats and/or sunglasses), plate or bowl, grapes, knife, fig bars

Time: 15 to 20 minutes

Preparation: Slice several grapes. Then place the sliced grapes and fig bars on a plate or bowl.

But They're Only Giants!

Have kids form a circle and sit down. Open your Bible to Numbers 13, and show children the words. SAY: **God had saved the Israelites from the Egyptians and promised them a wonderful new land to live in. One day God told Moses to have some Israelite leaders sneak into the land of Canaan to see what it would be like to live there.**

The 12 leaders of Israel went exploring in the land of Canaan. Let's pretend we're exploring, too! The men who went to Canaan were called spies, and they had to sneak very quietly into Canaan so no one would hear or see them. Let's pretend we're spies. Let's put on our spy masks and start sneaking around and exploring. Lead children in putting on hats or sunglasses and sneaking quietly around the room. Encourage kids to look through toys, peek under tables, open up cabinets, and generally explore the room. Tell kids they can whisper quietly to each other about what they discover.

The Israelite spies found good food in the land of Canaan. They even carried some of the food back with them. Pick up the bowl of snacks. **But they found something else, too. They found lots of giant people who were very strong! Most of the explorers were afraid of those giants.**

Encourage children to sit down and enjoy the snacks as you continue the story.

SAY: **When the 12 leaders came home, all the Israelites talked with the spies about what they'd found.** Ask children to take turns telling the others about what thing they found while they were exploring.

Ten of the spies said the land was no good because they were afraid of the giants. Because of what those men said, the other Israelites were afraid of the new land.

But two of the spies, Joshua and Caleb, remembered that God had promised to give the Israelites the land of Canaan. Joshua and Caleb stood up for God. They believed God would be with them and help them. They told everyone that the land was good, and they asked everyone to remember all God had done for them.

God is more powerful than giants or giant problems. God wants us to stand up for him and believe in him, just as Joshua and Caleb stood up for God and believed that God would take care of them in the new land. ▷ WE CAN STAND UP FOR GOD by telling others about him, by showing people his love, and by doing the right thing.

ASK:

- **Why were most of the spies afraid to move to the new land?**
- **Why did Joshua and Caleb want to go the new land?**
- **How can you stand up and show people that you believe in God?**

BIBLE STORY

Balaam's Donkey Talks

For the Leader

Some believe Balaam was a fortune-teller and pagan priest who lived in ancient Assyria and was also known as Pitru. He probably worshipped many gods, predicted the future, cast spells, and interpreted dreams. He would have turned to God as just another deity he thought he could use to increase his power and influence over others.

But God had other plans. God spoke to Balaam and made clear that Balaam could not curse the people of Israel. God then used an angel and a donkey to show Balaam who really had power and influence. And Balaam had no choice but to obey God.

Key Scriptures

Numbers 22:1-38

Job 36:22

Bible Verse

"Look, God is all-powerful. Who is a teacher like him?" (Job 36:22).

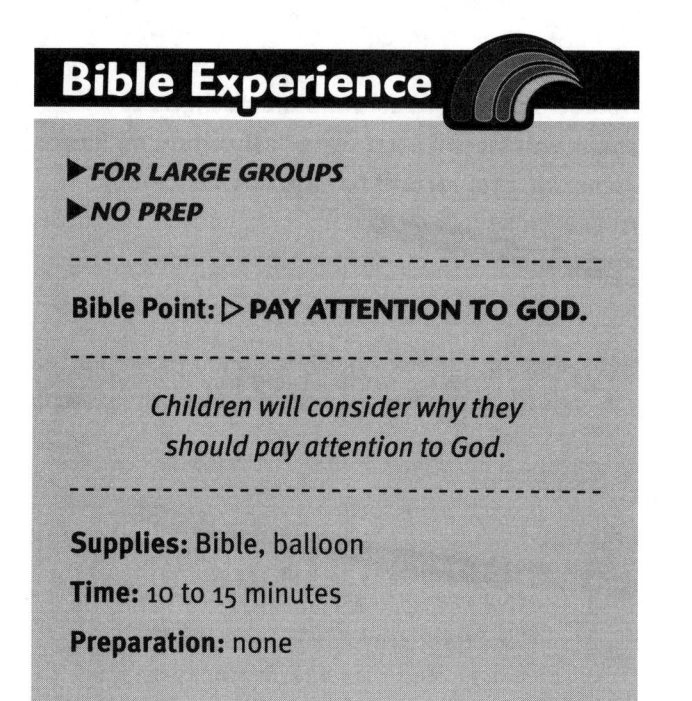

Bible Experience

▶ *FOR LARGE GROUPS*
▶ *NO PREP*

Bible Point: ▷ **PAY ATTENTION TO GOD.**

Children will consider why they should pay attention to God.

Supplies: Bible, balloon
Time: 10 to 15 minutes
Preparation: none

Blow up a balloon in front of kids. Hold the end tightly so air doesn't leak out. SAY: **I have a message for you today.** Stretch the opening of the balloon, letting the air out so the balloon squawks loudly. **Did anyone understand the message? Of course not; I was being silly! But one time God spoke to a man in a stranger way than that.**

Open your Bible to Numbers 22:1-38, and show the kids the words. SAY: **God made a donkey talk to a man one time! I'm not kidding you; it's in the Bible. The man's name was Balaam, and he wasn't listening to God, so God used Balaam's donkey to speak to him. Strange, huh? Let's back up.**

You see, there was a king in a certain country who considered Balaam a prophet, someone who speaks with God. He wanted Balaam to pray and curse the Israelites so they wouldn't be able to fight successfully against his people. The king promised Balaam lots of gold and silver. Balaam said he wouldn't curse the Israelites because they were God's people. But he got on his donkey and rode to meet the king anyway. That made God angry. He knew what was in Balaam's heart: Balaam cared more about money than about doing what pleased God.

On the road to the king's palace, God sent an angel to stop Balaam. Balaam couldn't see the angel, but his donkey could. The donkey stopped and refused to move. Balaam began to beat the donkey. Then the Lord opened the donkey's mouth, and it spoke!

Release more air from the balloon, making it squawk lightly while you say the donkey's words.

SAY: **It said, "Don't hurt me. Am I not your faithful donkey that you've always ridden? Have I ever done this to you before?" Then Balaam saw the angel. If the donkey hadn't stopped him, the angel would've killed Balaam. Not only did the donkey speak, but it also saved Balaam's life. Balaam was sorry, and after that he tried to do what God told him.**

ASK:

◆ **What surprised you about this story?**
◆ **Why do you think God cared so much whether Balaam paid attention to God?**

Read Job 36:22 aloud.

ASK:

◆ **What does *all-powerful* mean?**
◆ **Why is God all-powerful?**
◆ **Why should we pay attention to God?**

SAY: **Let's make sure we ▷ PAY ATTENTION TO GOD and do what God tells us to do—just as Balaam's donkey did.**

Additional Topics List

This lesson can be used to help children discover... Hearing God, Listening, Obedience, Observance, Reverence, and Wisdom.

Game

▶ *NO PREP*

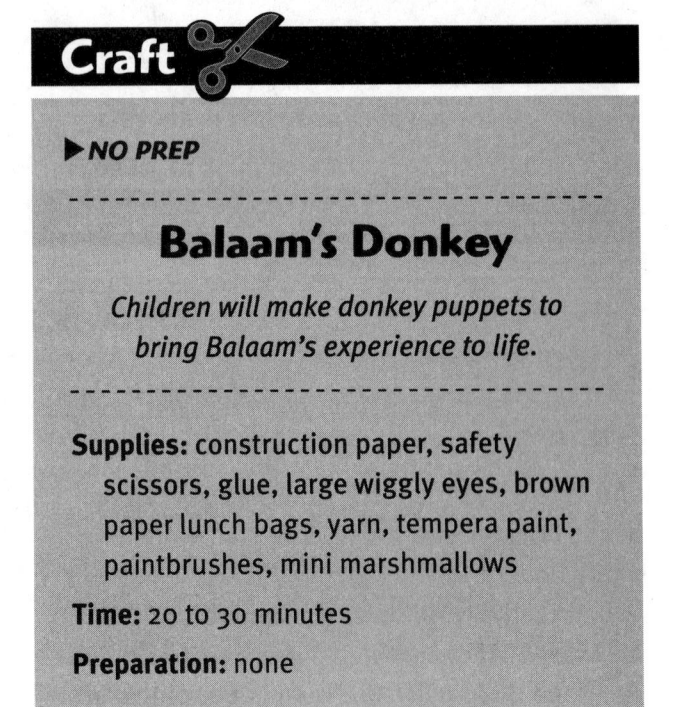

Furry Friends and Friendly Faces

Children will describe important people in their lives and appreciate God's creative power.

Supplies: none

Time: 5 to 15 minutes

Preparation: none

SAY: **It's fun to discover how creative God is in the ways he designs and communicates with his creation. This game will help us celebrate God's creativity.** Explain that each person will have a turn to describe the good qualities of a family member or close friend. Once the description is complete, other children can ask questions about the person.

SAY: **Once we've heard about your loved one, we'll think of an animal that symbolizes this person. For example, a strong, brave person reminds us of a horse, whereas a fun, playful person resembles an otter.** It's fun to offer several suggestions, narrowing the discussion until the person is excited about an animal that represents his or her family member or friend.

Encourage students to offer positive descriptions and flattering animal associations.
After everyone has had a turn, discuss these questions:

- **How has God used these people to teach you about him?**
- **Why would God use a donkey to communicate with Balaam?**

SAY: **Everything on earth belongs to God. Sometimes God uses unusual methods to communicate with us, especially when he has something important to say. Always ▷ PAY ATTENTION TO GOD.**

Craft

▶ *NO PREP*

Balaam's Donkey

Children will make donkey puppets to bring Balaam's experience to life.

Supplies: construction paper, safety scissors, glue, large wiggly eyes, brown paper lunch bags, yarn, tempera paint, paintbrushes, mini marshmallows

Time: 20 to 30 minutes

Preparation: none

Have kids cut the donkey's muzzle and ears from construction paper. Attach wiggly eyes, muzzle, and ears to the paper bag with glue. Use yarn to make the donkey's reins and mane. Paint the inside of the donkey's mouth with pink tempera paint, and then glue on marshmallow teeth.

n

o

t

e

s

Bible Application

▶ *NO PREP*

God Can Do Amazing Things

Children will consider God's power and creativity.

Supplies: live, tame animal; animal stickers

Time: about 15 minutes

Preparation: none

Show the animal to the children. If the animal is trained to respond to commands, demonstrate these to the children.

SAY: **Have you ever heard an animal talk? You've probably heard a cat meow, a bird chirp, or a dog bark. Some birds can even be trained to copy our voices, but those birds aren't really telling us their thoughts; they're just copying.**

In the Bible, Balaam's donkey really talked out loud in words Balaam could understand! What do you think Balaam thought when he heard his donkey talking?

I've never heard of any other time God made an animal talk. But I have heard of other amazing things God has done.

ASK:

- **Can you think of Bible stories in which amazing things happened?**
- **When has God taken care of you in an amazing way?**
- **How can we remember to ▷ PAY ATTENTION TO GOD and the amazing things God does?**

Give each child an animal sticker. SAY: **Take this animal sticker home as a reminder that God can do amazing things and that we should ▷ PAY ATTENTION TO GOD—just as Balaam learned!**

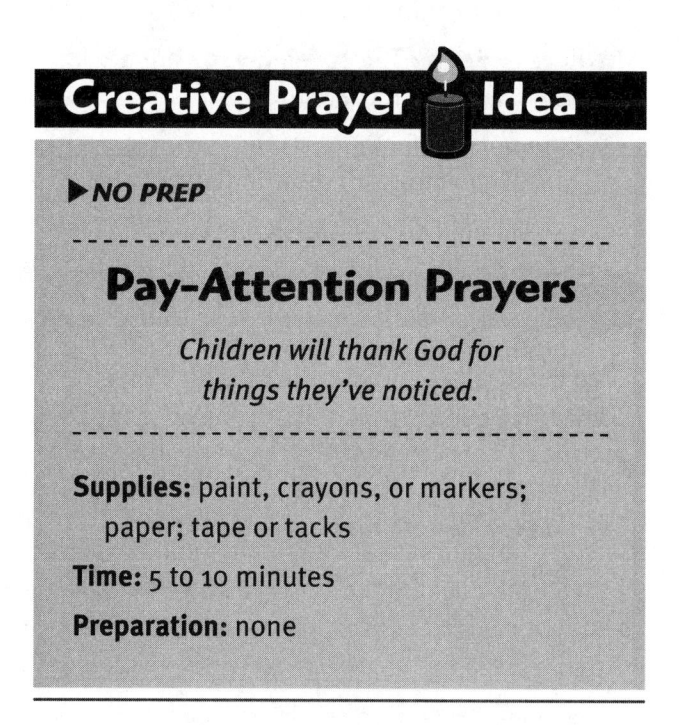

Creative Prayer Idea

▶ *NO PREP*

Pay-Attention Prayers

Children will thank God for things they've noticed.

Supplies: paint, crayons, or markers; paper; tape or tacks

Time: 5 to 10 minutes

Preparation: none

SAY: **We're going to pray and thank God for some of the things we notice as we ▷ PAY ATTENTION TO GOD. But first let's take some time to create pictures of some of those things.**

Have kids spend a few minutes creating pictures of what they notice when they pay attention to God. For example, they might draw God's creation, their families or friends, people God has healed, or things God has provided.

When the pictures are finished, hang them on the wall and gather in a line, holding hands and facing the pictures.

PRAY: **Dear God, thank you so much for the ways you remind us to pay attention to you. And thank you for the things we notice when we pay attention to you. You do amazing things, such as...**Pause for kids to call out descriptions of the pictures they created. **Thank you, God! Amen.**

Movie Clip

Talking Donkey

Movie Title: *Shrek* (PG)

Start Time: 4 minutes, 56 seconds

Where to Begin: The seven dwarfs are being carted off in chains.

Where to End: Donkey falls out of the sky.

Plot: A woman tries to sell her talking donkey, but he refuses to talk because he doesn't want to be taken away. When the people realize he really can talk, they're amazed.

Review: Even though they were rounding up all kinds of strange creatures, the people still were amazed to hear a donkey talk. It must have been even more amazing in real life, when Balaam's donkey talked to him!

Discussion

After setting up and showing the clip, SAY: **When the donkey talked, people were surprised—even more surprised than they were to see Pinocchio or the Three Little Pigs.**

ASK:

- **How do you think Balaam felt when his donkey talked to him?**
- **What do you think other people thought when Balaam told them what had happened?**
- **Why do you think God chose to make Balaam's donkey talk?**

SAY: **Just as Balaam learned, we should ▷ PAY ATTENTION TO GOD, too. He may not surprise us by making animals talk to us, but he does other amazing things every day.**

Object Lesson

▶ PREPARE IN ADVANCE

Pay Attention!

Children will have to pay attention to figure out how you make a card disappear.

Supplies: deck of cards, handkerchief with a hem, toothpick, scissors

Time: about 5 minutes

Preparation: Cut a toothpick so its length matches the width of one of your cards. Slide the toothpick into the hem of the handkerchief. Practice the trick a couple of times.

Spread out the cards on a table where kids can see them. SAY: **I'm going to make one of these cards disappear. Watch and see if you can figure out how I do it.**

Cover the cards with the handkerchief, with the toothpick on the bottom. Use one hand to pick up the toothpick in a way that looks like you're holding one of the cards. Then show kids the underside of the handkerchief and wave it around so they can see you're not holding a card.

ASK:

- **How do you think I made the card disappear?**
- **How can paying attention help you figure out what I did?**
- **Why is it important to ▷ PAY ATTENTION TO GOD?**

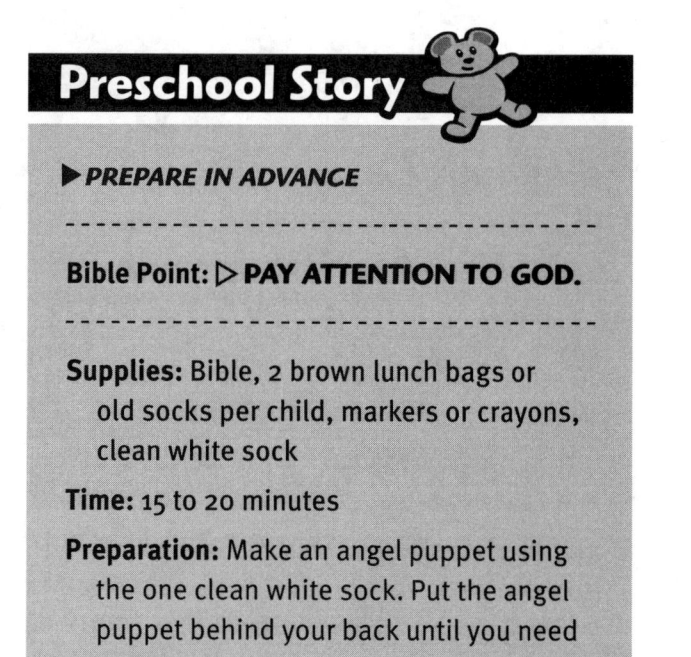

Preschool Story

▶ *PREPARE IN ADVANCE*

Bible Point: ▷ **PAY ATTENTION TO GOD.**

Supplies: Bible, 2 brown lunch bags or old socks per child, markers or crayons, clean white sock

Time: 15 to 20 minutes

Preparation: Make an angel puppet using the one clean white sock. Put the angel puppet behind your back until you need it during the story.

A Stubborn Streak

Have kids form a circle and sit down. Open your Bible to Numbers 22, and show children the words.

Before you begin the Bible story, give each child two old socks or two brown paper lunch bags and crayons or markers. Help children make the socks or bags into puppets by decorating one to look like a man and one to look like a donkey. Encourage kids to use their puppets to act out the story as you tell it.

SAY: **Today's Bible story tells us to ▷ PAY ATTENTION TO GOD.**

ASK:

- **What does it mean to pay attention?**
- **Can you show me how you listen carefully?**

SAY: **When we listen and watch carefully, we're paying attention. Let's hear what happened to a man in the Bible who didn't pay attention to God.**

Balaam was a man who didn't pay attention to God. Encourage children to hold up their man puppet. **A bad king wanted Balaam to come to see him and pray that bad things would happen to God's people. God told Balaam not to pray for bad things, but Balaam didn't listen.** Lead children in making their Balaam puppet shake its head back and forth.

Balaam got on his donkey and rode to see the king. Show children how to move both their puppets up and down and forward as if they're walking on a journey. **God was angry with Balaam, and he sent an angel to talk to him. Balaam didn't see the angel, but his donkey did. The donkey walked into a field and lay down.** Have children walk their donkey puppet away from their Balaam puppet and then have it pretend to lie down. **Balaam was angry, and he hit the donkey with a stick.** Encourage children to make their Balaam puppet act very angry. **Then God let the donkey talk.**

"Why are you hurting me? I'm the same donkey you ride every day. You know I always obey you." Have children make their donkey puppet say these words.

Finally Balaam realized that there must be a reason his donkey wouldn't obey, and *there it was*! Pull out the angel puppet you prepared. **Now Balaam could see the angel standing in front of them, blocking their way.**

Balaam remembered that he had prayed and asked God what he should do. Show children how to make their Balaam puppet bow and pray. **Balaam said, "I will do only what the Lord tells me to do." So Balaam said only good things about the Israelites!** Give children a round of applause for their puppet play.

Balaam didn't pay attention to God at first, but then God got Balaam's attention by making his donkey talk and by sending the angel. We can ▷ PAY ATTENTION TO GOD by praying, listening to our parents, and learning more about God.

ASK:

- **Why didn't Balaam pay attention to God?**
- **How can you pay attention to God this week?**

BIBLE STORY

Crossing the Jordan

For the Leader

This Bible story is reminiscent of God's parting the Red Sea for the previous generation of Israelites as they left Egypt. But this time God's presence was represented by the Ark of the Covenant going before the people.

Without God's miraculous intervention, the people would not have been able to cross. This was no lazy river—the Jordan River at flood stage was 10 to 12 feet deep in some places. And the Israelites recognized this. They readily obeyed God's command to build a stone altar as a reminder of what God had done for them.

Key Scriptures

Joshua 3:14–4:24

Psalm 107:1

Bible Verse

"Give thanks to the Lord, for he is good! His faithful love endures forever" (Psalm 107:1).

Bible Experience

▶ ***PREPARE IN ADVANCE***

Bible Point: ▷ **REMEMBER TO THANK GOD.**

Children will reenact the crossing of the Jordan and be reminded to be thankful.

Supplies: Bible; paper; masking tape; 2 boards, pieces of cardboard, sections of plywood, or carpet samples for each group of 6 to 8 children

Time: 20 to 30 minutes

Preparation: Tape several pieces of paper to the floor of your meeting area. The papers should be spaced apart by about the length of your boards, cardboard, plywood, or carpet samples. Your boards, cardboard, plywood, or carpet samples should be large enough for three kids to stand on uncomfortably (at least 2 feet long). Make sure kids will have to (and can!) use the boards, cardboard, plywood, or carpet samples to travel between the papers.

Open your Bible to Joshua 3:14–4:24, and show children the passage. SAY: **Today's Bible story comes from the book of Joshua in the Bible. The Israelites were getting ready to take over their new land—the land of Canaan—as God had promised them. But to get there they had to cross the Jordan River. And the river was running at flood stage—which means it was completely full of swiftly running water!**

Tell kids to pretend that your meeting area is the Jordan River and that they need to get from one side to the other without being swept away by the water. Have kids form groups of six or eight, and give each group two boards, cardboard, plywood, or carpet samples. Instruct each group to find a way across the "river" by stepping only on the pieces of paper and on the boards, cardboard, plywood, or carpet samples.

As groups make their way across the room, read aloud Joshua 3:14–4:7.

ASK:

- **What was it like to try to cross without stepping on the floor?**
- **How did your group work together?**
- **How do you think the Israelites felt as they crossed the Jordan River on dry land?**
- **Why do you think Joshua had people gather rocks from the river?**

Read Psalm 107:1 aloud, and then SAY: **Just as you needed help from each other to cross the room, the Israelites needed God's help to get them across the river. You probably felt thankful when your group worked together, just as the Israelites felt thankful to God for helping them. They gathered rocks so they could set them up in a pile to help them remember to be thankful for what God had done. God helps us, just as he helped the Israelites. Let's ▷ REMEMBER TO THANK GOD.**

Song & Connect

Use "Praise the Lord" (track 10, *it: Innovative Tools for Children's Ministry: Old Testament* CD) to help reinforce the Bible Point, ▷ **REMEMBER TO THANK GOD.**

Additional Topics List

This lesson can be used to help children discover... God's Provision, Praise, Thanksgiving, and Trust.

Game

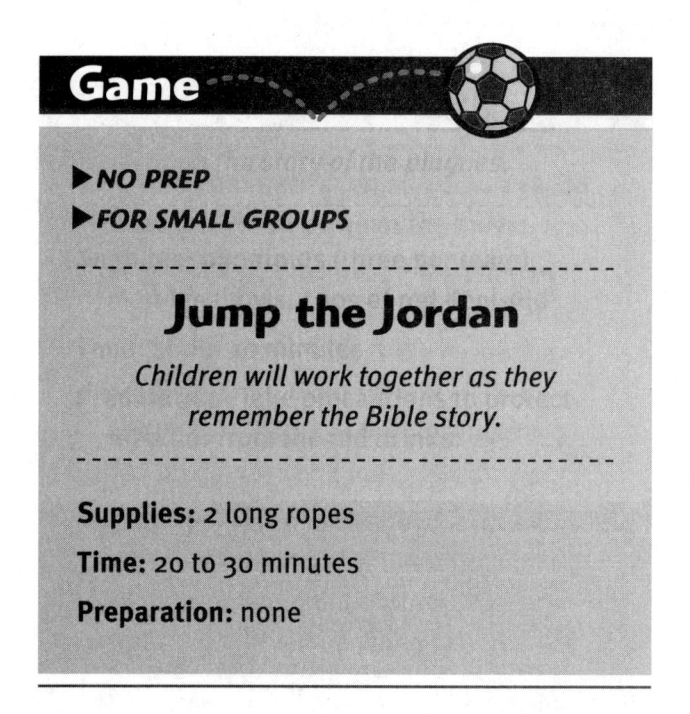

▶ ***NO PREP***
▶ ***FOR SMALL GROUPS***

Jump the Jordan

Children will work together as they remember the Bible story.

Supplies: 2 long ropes

Time: 20 to 30 minutes

Preparation: none

Stretch out the two ropes across your game area, parallel to each other and a few inches apart. Tell kids that this is the Jordan River, and have them all stand on one "shore." At your signal, ask all the kids to jump across the river, being careful not to get their toes "wet" by touching the space in between the ropes. Widen the river a little by moving the ropes a couple of inches farther apart. Then have all the kids jump back over to the first side. Continue to widen the river, a little at a time, having kids jump over it after each widening. Play until no one can jump as wide as the river, and then ASK:

- **How did you feel as you tried to cross the river?**

SAY: **The Israelites may have felt nervous and anxious as they crossed the Jordan River with water threatening to crash down on them. But they felt thankful, too, because God took care of them.**

Craft

▶ *PREPARE IN ADVANCE*

Pet Rock Memorials

Children will create reminders of all God has done for them.

Supplies: Bible, acrylic paint, paintbrushes, wiggly eyes, glue, 1 rock per child

Time: about 20 minutes

Preparation: Wash and dry the rocks.

Have volunteers read aloud Joshua 4:1-9.

ASK:

- **Why did God want the people to collect rocks?**
- **What was special about the rocks?**

SAY: **Let's make our own special pet rocks. As you take care of your pet rocks, they can remind you that God takes care of you every day, just as he took care of the Israelites.**

Set out the supplies. Have each child choose a rock. Invite kids to decorate the rocks to look like silly creatures. As kids work, encourage them to tell about times God has taken care of them.

Bible Application

▶ *NO PREP*

▶ *ALLERGY ALERT*

Thirsty Thanks

Children will talk about things to thank God for.

Supplies: bowls of pretzels, chips, or other salty snacks; cups of water

Time: about 15 minutes

Preparation: none

Have kids form groups of four or five. Give each group a bowl of pretzels. SAY: **Let's talk about some reasons to thank God. In your group, talk about what makes you thankful to God. Think of as much as you can.**

After about five minutes, ask groups to share what they talked about. Then SAY: **Is anyone thirsty? I'll bet you'll be thankful to get a drink of water after eating those salty snacks!**

Distribute cups of water, and then ASK:

- **How did you feel before you got to drink some water?**
- **How can we ▷ REMEMBER TO THANK GOD?**

SAY: **Cups of water can help us remember to thank God. Every time you drink water from now on, try to ▷ REMEMBER TO THANK GOD.**

Creative Prayer Idea

▶ *PREPARE IN ADVANCE*
▶ *FOR FAMILY MINISTRY*

Thanksgiving Stones

Children will use stones to create a monument to thank God.

Supplies: small rocks, permanent markers

Time: 5 to 10 minutes

Preparation: Wash and dry the rocks.

Give each child a small rock, and set out permanent markers. SAY: **Just as the Israelites did after God helped them cross the Jordan River, we are going to make a monument of stones to show that we want to ▷ REMEMBER TO THANK GOD. On your rock, write or draw a reminder of something you want to remember to thank God for.**

After a few minutes, have students use their rocks to build a pile on the floor. Then have kids form a circle around the rocks and hold hands.

PRAY: **Dear God, we thank you for all these reasons and more. Thank you for helping us, just as you helped the Israelites. Help us to remember to thank you every day! Amen.**

n
o
t
e
s

Science Devotion

▶ *PREPARE IN ADVANCE*

We Live Through Him

Children will see that God's blessings are constant.

Supplies: newspaper, water in a small pitcher with a spout, wide-mouth container, 3-foot piece of cotton string

Time: 5 to 10 minutes

Preparation: Spread newspaper over a table or on the floor. Place the pitcher of water and the wide-mouth container on the newspaper.

ASK:

- ◆ **What kinds of blessings does God give to his children?**

SAY: **We're going to do an experiment today that will help us see more about how God wants to bless his children.**

Have kids gather around the newspaper. Dip the piece of string into the water in the pitcher, and tie one end of the string to the pitcher's handle. Pull the wet string through the pitcher's spout and over to the empty container. Let the free end drop into the container. (See the illustration.)

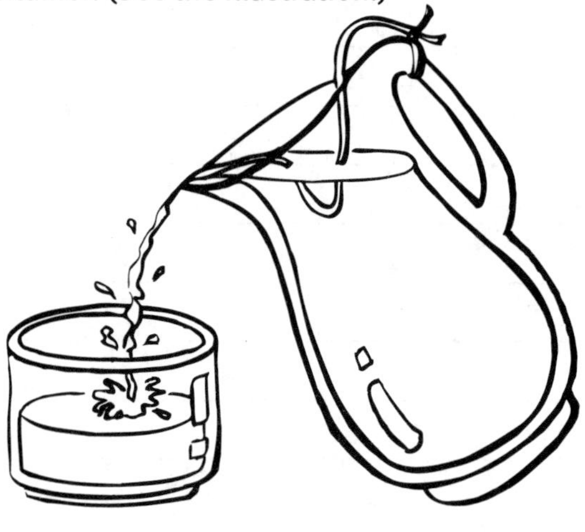

Carefully pour the water into the container so it runs down the string.

ASK:

- **Why do you think the water slides down the string?**

SAY: **The water slides down the string because the molecules that form water are attracted to each other. This makes them stick together. The force of gravity makes them move down the string together. And as long as I'm pouring water from the pitcher, the water will travel down the string this way.**

ASK:

- **How is this like what God does when he gives you blessings?**

SAY: **Just like the water continues to flow down the string, God gives you blessings constantly because he loves you.**

ASK:

- **What do you think will happen if I pour the water too fast?**

Pour the water faster, and see what happens.

ASK:

- **Does God ever give you too many blessings?**
- **How can we thank God for the blessings he gives us?**

notes

Worship Prompt Idea

▶ FOR LARGE GROUPS
▶ NO PREP

Significant Symbols of God

Children will be reminded that God is their rock and will worship and thank God through prayer.

Supplies: paper, pencils, rock
Time: about 20 minutes
Preparation: none

Have kids form groups of four or five. Give each group paper and a pencil. Then SAY: **One of the things we do when we come to church is worship God.**

ASK:

- **What are some of the ways we worship God at church?**

Hold up the rock and ASK:

- **What characteristics of a rock are also true of God?**
- **In what ways do you think God is a rock to his people?**
- **In what specific ways has God been a rock in your life?**

SAY: **One look around this room shows that God has given us many reasons to worship him. Just as the Israelites used a pile of rocks to help them remember to thank God, this rock can remind us of many reasons to thank God. So let's close by worshipping God in a prayer of thanks for all he has done for us.**

Invite members of each group to pray together for 30 seconds, thanking God for being a rock in their lives.

Preschool Story

▶ *PREPARE IN ADVANCE*

▶ *ALLERGY ALERT*

Bible Point: ▷ **REMEMBER TO THANK GOD.**

Supplies: Bible, 12 pieces of paper, 2 blue blankets or sheets, snack

Time: 15 to 20 minutes

Preparation: Crumple 12 pieces of paper and set them on the floor—these represent the stones the Israelites picked up. Cover the stones with two blue blankets or sheets, representing the Jordan River. Set a snack on a table in a far corner of the room.

A Night to Remember

Have kids form a circle and sit down. Open your Bible to Joshua 3, and show children the words. SAY: **The Israelites had been living in the desert for a very long time, but it was time to go the land God had promised them. Joshua told all the people to pack their things and get ready to go. Let's pretend we're packing our things right now.**

Lead children in pretending to pack backpacks full of clothes, toys, and other necessities. Then tell kids to pretend to put their backpacks on their backs and get ready to go on a journey.

SAY: **Joshua told the people to follow him.** Motion for children to follow you and SAY: **Let's start marching toward the Promised Land.** Lead children in a march around your room, but be sure to end up at the "river" you prepared before class. Then stop.

Joshua led the people straight to the Jordan River. Then it didn't seem like they could go any farther. The Promised Land was just on the other side; they could see it and even though they were tired, they smiled big, big smiles. Shade your eyes with your hand, and squint to look across the river. Then point at the snacks

n
o
t
e
s

you've set out on the other side of the river. **If they could just get across, then they'd be in the Promised Land. But the river was very long and very wide. They couldn't jump over the river.** Lead children in jumping up and down. **They couldn't crawl under the river.** Lead children in getting down on all fours and trying to get very small. **They couldn't go around the river.** Look around and point at how long the river is.

They didn't know what to do. But God had a plan for the Israelites. He told them he would stop the river so they could walk right through it! So that's what they did. When they started across the river, God stopped the water on both sides. Spread the blankets apart to make a path and to uncover the paper stones. Lead children in walking through the blankets.

Once they got to the other side, Joshua told the people he wanted them to make something special so they would remember what God had done for them. He told the people to go back into the river and pick up 12 stones. Encourage children to go back and pick up the 12 paper stones. Then help kids make a pile with the rocks on their side of the river. Once the pile is finished, encourage each child to say one thing he or she is thankful for. Then lead kids to the snacks you set out. As they eat, discuss the story together.

The Israelites remembered to thank God for the way he helped them cross the Jordan River. God helps us all the time, too, and we need to ▷ REMEMBER TO THANK GOD for his help.

ASK:

- **How did God help the Israelites?**
- **How has God helped you?**
- **How can you thank God for the ways he's helped you?**

BIBLE STORY

Jericho Falls

For the Leader

It's interesting to note that at the beginning of this Bible passage, Jericho was shut up tight–no one left or entered the city. This, the Bible says, was because of the Israelites. Their presence must have made the inhabitants nervous in spite of the fortified city walls.

The Bible records none of the grumbling and fear the previous generation of Israelites had expressed as they approached the Promised Land. Perhaps the consequences of their grumbling had led them to teach their children to anticipate God's gift and to be bold in taking it. This generation seemed poised to follow God's commands and their leader, Joshua, in courageously conquering Canaan, no matter how ridiculous their method may have seemed.

This story is a classic example—one of many in the Bible—that shows God using obedient people to accomplish his purposes, while still making clear that God was in control. Help kids understand that God will work in their lives as well as they are obedient to God. God will show his power!

Key Scriptures

Joshua 5:13–6:21

Psalm 147:5

Bible Verse

"How great is our Lord! His power is absolute! His understanding is beyond comprehension!" (Psalm 147:5).

Bible Experience

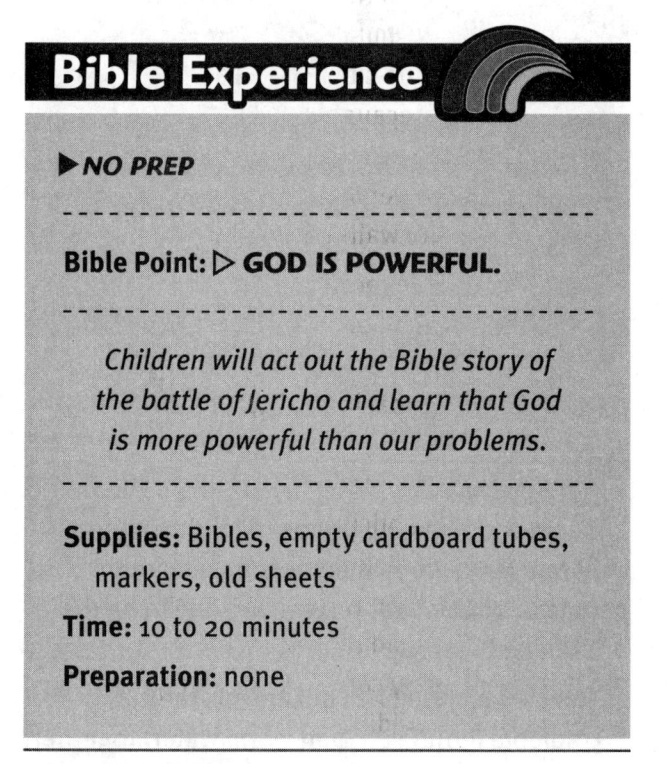

▶ *NO PREP*

Bible Point: ▷ **GOD IS POWERFUL.**

Children will act out the Bible story of the battle of Jericho and learn that God is more powerful than our problems.

Supplies: Bibles, empty cardboard tubes, markers, old sheets

Time: 10 to 20 minutes

Preparation: none

Form two groups, and have them sit on opposite sides of the room. Explain that Group 1 is the Israelites and Group 2 is the Walls of Jericho. Distribute Bibles, and have groups take turns reading aloud Joshua 6:1-20.

Give Group 1 cardboard tubes and markers. Instruct kids to make rams' horns "trumpets" by decorating the cardboard tubes.

Hand out the old sheets and markers to Group 2. Encourage kids to draw large stones on the sheets to make them look like the walls of a city.

When groups are finished decorating, have the Walls stand up and hold their sheets around them. Instruct the Israelites to form a line and march around the Walls. Tell children to pretend that it's the seventh day in the story and to count out loud as they march around the Walls seven times, blowing their trumpets. When they complete the final time around, have them shout. Then signal the Walls to fall down.

Let groups trade roles and repeat the enactment. Then ASK:

- **How do you think the Israelites felt as they went around the walls?**
- **How did they see God's power on the seventh day?**

Read Psalm 147:5 aloud.

ASK:

- **What makes God great and mighty?**
- **When have you seen God's power in your life?**

SAY: ▷ **GOD IS POWERFUL, and he can "knock down" the problems we face just as he knocked down the walls of Jericho.**

Song & Connect

Use "So Do Not Fear" (track 13, *it: Innovative Tools for Children's Ministry: Old Testament* CD) to help reinforce the Bible Point, ▷ **GOD IS POWERFUL.**

Additional Topics List

This lesson can be used to help children discover... God's Will, Omnipotence, Strength, and Trust.

Game

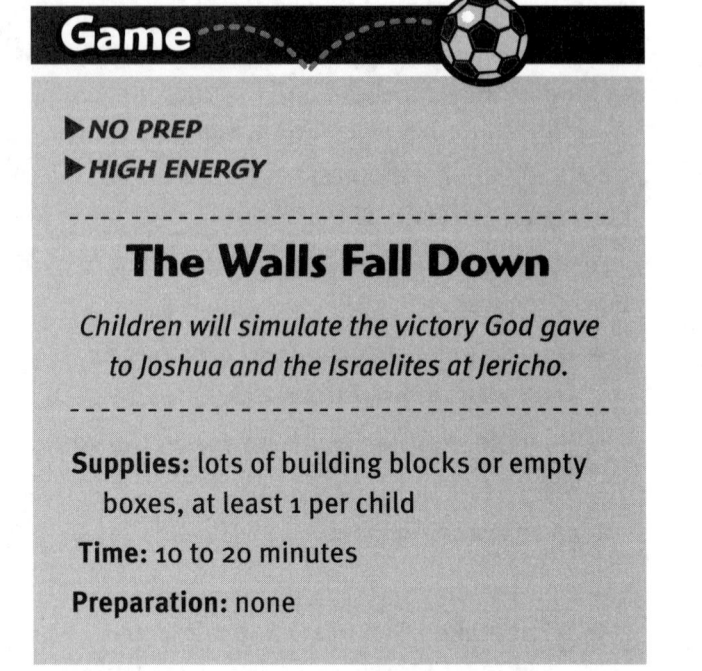

▶ *NO PREP*
▶ *HIGH ENERGY*

The Walls Fall Down

Children will simulate the victory God gave to Joshua and the Israelites at Jericho.

Supplies: lots of building blocks or empty boxes, at least 1 per child

Time: 10 to 20 minutes

Preparation: none

Have students stand in a circle and number off. Place the pile of blocks in the center of the circle, and designate an area where students will build the wall. Explain that you will call out numbers and every child with one of those numbers should run to the blocks, pick up one block, and add it to the wall.

When you're out of blocks and all the children have had a turn, noisily march around the wall together. Then allow the children to knock down the wall with cheers and shouts.

n
o
t
e
s

Craft

▶ *PREPARE IN ADVANCE*

And They All Came Tumbling Down

Children will make reminders of God's power.

Supplies: for each group of 4 to 5 kids: 4 cups flour, 1 cup salt, 1½ to 1¾ cups warm water; 2 mixers; cookie sheets; oven

Time: about 40 minutes

Preparation: Have ingredients separated and ready to mix.

Form brick-making groups of four or five children. Have group members designate three people to be the brick mixers and one to be the brick baker.

Have two of the brick mixers mix the clay ingredients (flour, salt, and warm water) together. Then instruct the other brick mixer to knead the dough for several minutes. When the dough is mixed sufficiently, have all group members mold it into small rectangular bricks approximately 2x3 inches and no more than ¾ inch thick. Instruct the brick baker to assemble the bricks on a cookie sheet. With adult supervision, children should bake bricks at 300 degrees for about 20 minutes. If you do not have access to a kitchen oven, let the bricks air-dry until your next class time.

When the bricks have baked and cooled, show kids how to work together to create a wall with their bricks. Then simulate the fall of Jericho. Children can take turns being Joshua and giving the signal to knock down the wall.

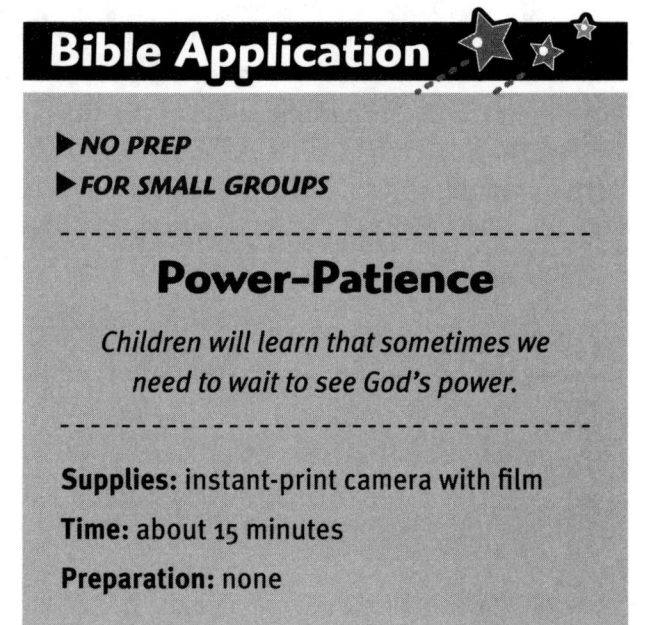

Bible Application

▶ *NO PREP*
▶ *FOR SMALL GROUPS*

Power-Patience

Children will learn that sometimes we need to wait to see God's power.

Supplies: instant-print camera with film
Time: about 15 minutes
Preparation: none

Take an instant-print picture of the group, and place it on the floor.

SAY: **Let's stand and march around the picture. We have to keep marching until the picture develops.** Lead kids in marching slowly.

Is it ready yet? No? Let's keep marching. Still not ready? We've got to keep going. It's hard to wait, isn't it? Does it help time go faster if we're marching? Keep marching until the picture is fully developed.

Allow the children to sit and pass the picture around as they respond to these questions.

ASK:

- **How did it feel to keep marching around our picture?**
- **How do you think the Israelites felt as they marched day after day?**
- **When have you had to wait for God to show his power?**
- **What are some ways to show that you trust God while you wait?**

SAY: **God made sure the people were willing to obey him by giving them a task to do. God answers our prayers in his time and in his way. He asks us to trust him and obey him. We need to obey God and trust that ▷ GOD IS POWERFUL.**

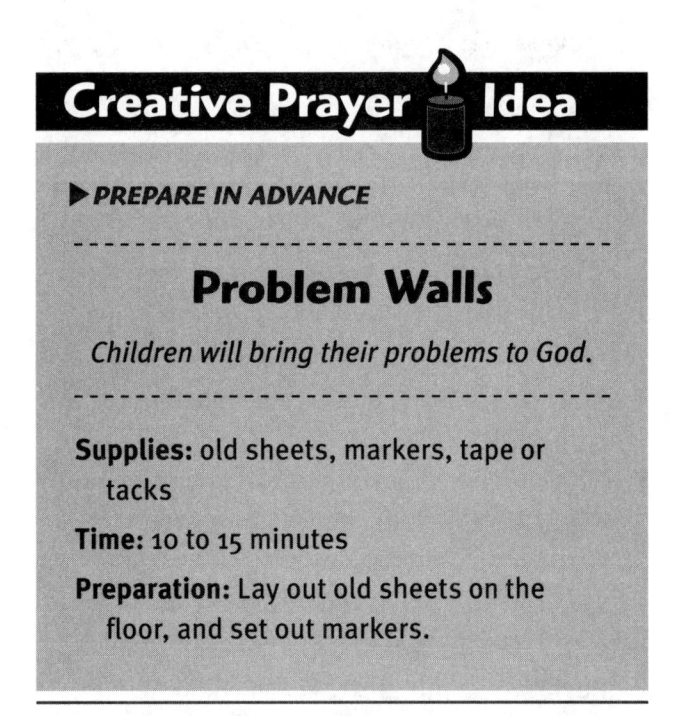

Creative Prayer Idea

▶ *PREPARE IN ADVANCE*

Problem Walls

Children will bring their problems to God.

Supplies: old sheets, markers, tape or tacks
Time: 10 to 15 minutes
Preparation: Lay out old sheets on the floor, and set out markers.

Invite kids to write on the sheets descriptions of problems they face. When they're finished, hang the sheets on the wall in your meeting area.

SAY: **The Israelites might have been afraid of the people in the mighty, walled city of Jericho. But when they followed God's instructions, they saw that ▷ GOD IS POWERFUL!** Point to the wall sheets. **God is more powerful than our problems, too. Let's pray about these problems and then shout and watch them fall down.**

PRAY: **Dear God, we know that you are more powerful than any problem we face. We bring these problems before you today, knowing that you will help us.** Pause to allow children to pray silently. **Amen.**

Lead children in shouting, and then pull the sheets off the wall.

Movie Clip

The Fall of Jericho

Movie Title: *Veggie Tales: Josh and the Big Wall* (PG)

Start Time: 19 minutes, 48 seconds

Where to Begin: The narrator says, "Those are very interesting instructions."

Where to End: The narrator says, "Oh no, it looks like they are going to disobey God again."

Plot: The children of Israel have been following God's seemingly odd instructions for the siege of Jericho. God has told them to simply march around the wall for days. The army comes back to the camp. Dissension breaks out, and several alternate plans are discussed.

Review: Use this clip to teach children that we should trust God even when his will doesn't seem to make sense. We constantly have to choose whether to trust in God's power or to go our own way.

Discussion

After setting up and showing the clip, ASK:

- **Why do you think people were coming up with plans that were different from God's plan?**
- **Have you ever been tempted to do something God did not want you to do because God's ways didn't seem to make sense?**
- **Can you think of some of God's rules that are hard to understand?**

SAY: **Joshua and his people did choose to follow God's plan. They listened to God's plan instead of their own plans—and God's power came through. On the seventh day, they marched around the wall seven times. They blew their trumpets, and the walls of the city came falling down! We can trust that ▷ GOD IS POWERFUL!**

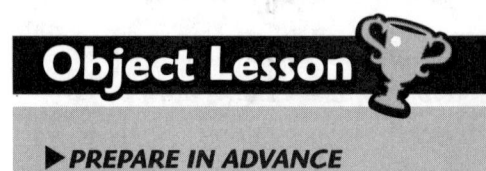

Object Lesson

▶ *PREPARE IN ADVANCE*

Obey God

Children will see the fruit of obedience.

Supplies: 2 balloons, transparent tape, straight pin

Time: about 10 minutes

Preparation: Inflate two balloons three-fourths full, and tie them off.

Hold up one of the balloons and the pin, and then ASK:

- **Who thinks I can push this pin into the balloon without popping it?**
- **Would any of you like to try?**

Have a volunteer try it.

SAY: **Many things in our lives seem impossible. Joshua felt that he had something impossible to do, too. But Joshua trusted God and obeyed him, and God's power knocked down the walls of Jericho.**

I read in a book how to put a pin in a balloon without making it pop. So it might be possible after all, if we follow the instructions. Let's try.

Make an X on the balloon with two pieces of tape. Hold the balloon firmly, and carefully insert the pin through the center of the tape. Hold up the balloon, and show kids the pin.

SAY: **It worked! I followed the instructions and had success. That's how it was for Joshua at Jericho. He obeyed God's instructions, and everything turned out as God said it would. God can do anything.**

ASK:

- **Why do you think Joshua obeyed God?**
- **How can knowing ▷ GOD IS POWERFUL help us obey him?**

Preschool Story

▶ ***PREPARE IN ADVANCE***

Bible Point: ▷ **GOD IS POWERFUL.**

Supplies: Bible, building blocks or small cardboard boxes, paper

Time: 15 to 20 minutes

Preparation: Build a wall using building blocks or small cardboard boxes. Roll up pieces of paper into the shape of cones to create trumpets for children.

They're Coming Down!

Have kids form a circle and sit down around the wall. Open your Bible to Joshua 5, and show children the words.

Help kids practice saying the CHILDREN lines with the motions, and then begin the Bible story.

CHILDREN: God is going to do it! God is going to win! *(Pump fist in the air.)*

SAY: **God was going to give Jericho to his people, but the city of Jericho had a big wall around it. It was very, very wide. What were they going to do?**

ASK:

- **How do you think they could get past the tall wall?**

CHILDREN: God is going to do it! God is going to win! *(Pump fist in the air.)*

SAY: **God had a plan. He told the Israelites to march around the wall once each day, and then on the seventh day, they marched around the wall seven times.**

Have children stand up in a circle and walk around the block wall seven times, counting each time they pass the starting point. When you say number seven, have them stop and stand in place.

CHILDREN: God is going to do it! God is going to win! *(Pump fist in the air.)*

SAY: **On the seventh day, God told the Israelites to blow their trumpets as loud as they could.** Give children the paper trumpets, and let them march around the wall one more time, blowing their trumpets as they march.

CHILDREN: God is going to do it! God is going to win! *(Pump fist in the air.)*

Knock down the block wall with your feet or hands. Lead children in shouting and cheering together.

SAY: **Guess what God did! The walls fell down, just as God said they would! ▷ GOD IS POWERFUL!**

CHILDREN: God is going to do it! God is going to win! *(Pump fist in the air.)*

Lead children in singing "Oh, When We March" to the tune of "When the Saints Go Marching In":

Oh, when we march around that wall
(march in place),
Oh, when we march around that wall
(march in place),

We know that God will give us the victory
(point to heaven)
When we march around that wall
(march in place).
Oh, when we blow our trumpets loud
(pretend to blow trumpet),
Oh, when we blow our trumpets loud
(pretend to blow trumpet),
We know that God will give us the victory
(point to heaven)
When we blow our trumpets loud
(pretend to blow trumpet).

ASK:

- **How did God use his power to help the Israelites?**
- **How do you know that God is powerful?**
- **How can you thank God for his power?**

notes

BIBLE STORY

Gideon and the Midianites

For the Leader

Gideon's army is another example of how God's ways sometimes don't make sense to us. A *smaller* army? Why would God keep shrinking the army?

This story presents another way God shows his power through weakness. He called Gideon—the least significant son in an insignificant family, in an insignificant tribe. He used 300 men with empty jars. And God got all the glory.

Key Scriptures

Judges 7:1-25

Proverbs 3:5

Bible Verse

"Trust in the Lord with all your heart; do not depend on your own understanding" (Proverbs 3:5).

Bible Experience

▶ *NO PREP*
▶ *FOR LARGE GROUPS*

Bible Point: ▷ **WE CAN TRUST GOD.**

Children will participate in telling the Bible story.

Supplies: Bible
Time: 15 to 20 minutes
Preparation: none

Open your Bible and SAY: **Our Bible story comes from Judges 7:1-25.** Go over the following cue words and actions. Encourage kids to listen closely for these cue words and do the accompanying motions:

- *Gideon*—Fold hands in prayer.
- *drink*—Pretend to drink.
- *ram's horn trumpet*—Blow a pretend trumpet.
- *Lord*—Raise a fist and say yes!

SAY: **Long ago the Israelites lived close to the Midianites, who were their enemies. The Lord promised Gideon that the Israelites would beat the Midianites in a big battle. So Gideon got an army ready. He had 32 thousand men. That was a pretty big army! But the Lord said to Gideon, "You have too many men." The Lord didn't want the Israelites to brag about how they could win on their own. He wanted them to trust in him.**

So the Lord told Gideon to let everyone go home who felt afraid. Twenty-two thousand men left; 10 thousand stayed. Gideon thought that was OK. He still had a big army. But the Lord thought the army was too big. He told Gideon to have the men get a drink of water from the river—the Lord would choose men for the army by the way they got a drink.

The men who got down on their knees to drink were sent away. The Lord chose 300 men who got a drink by using their hands to bring water to their mouths, lapping it as a dog does. Only 300 men. That was a tiny army! How would they ever fight the big, strong Midianites?

The Lord let Gideon go near the camp of Midian. Gideon overheard two Midianite soldiers talking. One soldier had dreamed about Gideon and the Israelites winning the battle. So Gideon went back to tell the 300 men that the Lord had prepared a victory for them.

Gideon gave each man an empty jar, a torch, and a trumpet. On his signal, the men broke the jars, held the torches high, and blew the trumpets. When the trumpets sounded, the Midianites began fighting each other. Then they got scared and ran away! Gideon and the 300 men stood on the hills around the camp. The Lord had won the battle!

ASK:

◆ **How do you think Gideon felt as his army got smaller and smaller?**

◆ **Why do you think God shrunk Gideon's army?**

Read Proverbs 3:5 aloud.

ASK:

◆ **What does it mean to lean on our own understanding?**

◆ **When is it hard to remember that ▷ WE CAN TRUST GOD?**

SAY: **Just as God reminded Gideon, ▷ WE CAN TRUST GOD, even when we're terrified! God is never scared, and he's always in control. God took away many things that would have made Gideon powerful. But he made Gideon and his men victorious anyway. God wanted Gideon's army and their enemies to know that true power comes only from trusting God.**

Song Connect

Use "God Is Our Help" (track 4, *it: Innovative Tools for Children's Ministry: Old Testament* CD) to help reinforce the Bible Point, ▷ **WE CAN TRUST GOD.**

Additional Topics List

This lesson can be used to help children discover... Belief, Faith, Imperfection, Loyalty, Trustworthiness, and Weakness.

Game

▶ ***NO PREP***

Power Building

Children will learn that true power and victory come from God.

Supplies: 10 small building blocks for each student, playing cards without jokers

Time: 5 to 10 minutes

Preparation: none

Give each student 10 blocks. Tell students that the object of this game is to build the tallest tower. Explain that they'll take turns drawing cards. If a person draws a black card, he or she can take that number of blocks from other players and use them to make his or her tower taller. If a person draws a red card, he or she must give away that number of blocks to other players. Point out that face cards (jacks, queens, and kings) are worth 10 points, and aces are worth one point. Choose a person to go first; play goes clockwise.

Continue until everyone has had at least two turns. If someone runs out of blocks, he or she can still draw a card and take blocks from other people if the card drawn is black.

After playing the game, discuss these questions:

- **How did it feel to try to build your tower? Why?**
- **How do you think Gideon felt when God kept taking soldiers away?**
- **How do you think he felt when God used them to bring victory?**
- **When is it easy or difficult to trust God?**

Craft

▶ ***PREPARE IN ADVANCE***

An Angel Messenger

Children will create message holders to remind them of God's Word.

Supplies: Bibles, index cards, permanent markers, plastic spoons, glue, 5-inch lengths of white or silver ribbon, yellow yarn

Time: 20 to 30 minutes

Preparation: Set out all the supplies.

Explain that kids will be making a messenger angel like the one who brought an important message to Gideon. Give each student a card, and have him or her write a favorite verse on it. Then instruct students to hold the index cards horizontally and glue a spoon to the back of each card so the rounded side of the spoon faces the front (see diagram).

While the glue is drying, give two lengths of ribbon to each child. Help kids glue one end of each ribbon to the spoon handle and then wrap the other ends around to the sides of the cards. Have students use the permanent markers and yarn to decorate the "faces" of the spoons to look like angel faces. Then show kids how to gather the ends of the ribbons and glue them to the cards.

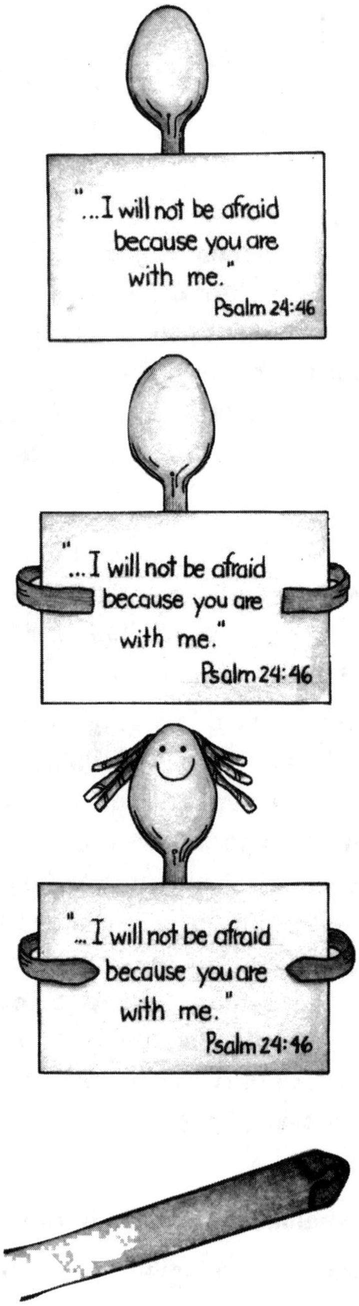

Bible Application

▶ ***PREPARE IN ADVANCE***

Tug of Warrior

Children will learn that trusting God gives us peace.

Supplies: masking tape, long length of cotton rope, pair of gloves for each child

Time: about 10 minutes

Preparation: Place a line of tape in the middle of the floor.

Organize kids into two groups. Place all the bigger and stronger kids on one team and the younger children on the other. SAY: **We'll play Tug of War. The team that drags any member of the other team across the line wins.** Tell kids they're *not allowed* to wrap the rope around their arms, and give each child a pair of gloves so there are no rope burns.

ASK:

- **Who do you think will win? Why?**

Join the team with the younger children, begin the game, and help your team win. Make certain you pull slowly so no one gets hurt.

ASK:

- **Why didn't the game turn out the way you expected?**
- **How did you feel when you've faced problems too big for you?**
- **How is God's being on our side like my joining one of the teams?**

Have each child tell a partner one way he or she will trust God this week.

SAY: **Sometimes we get worried when a problem seems too big for us. We may panic if we forget that God is on our side. But things look a lot different when we remember that ▷ WE CAN TRUST GOD.**

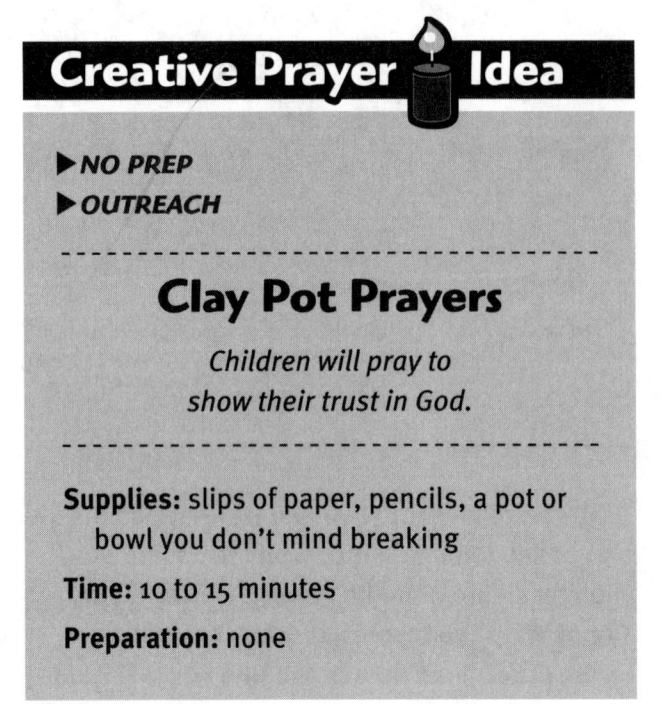

Creative Prayer Idea

▶ *NO PREP*
▶ *OUTREACH*

Clay Pot Prayers

Children will pray to show their trust in God.

Supplies: slips of paper, pencils, a pot or bowl you don't mind breaking

Time: 10 to 15 minutes

Preparation: none

SAY: **Let's show trust by praying about ways we need God's help.**

Give each person a slip of paper and a pencil, and allow kids a few minutes to write prayer needs on their papers. Be sure to tell them not to sign their names. Then pass around a breakable pot or bowl, and have kids put their slips of paper in it. When the pot or bowl comes back to you, break it. Then pray aloud for all the prayer needs on the slips of paper.

n ______

o ______

t ______

e ______

s ______

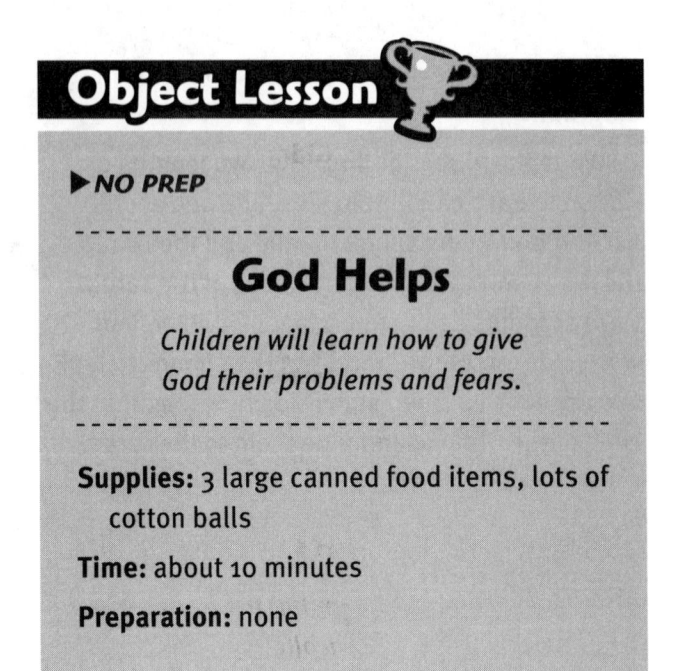

Object Lesson

▶ *NO PREP*

God Helps

Children will learn how to give God their problems and fears.

Supplies: 3 large canned food items, lots of cotton balls

Time: about 10 minutes

Preparation: none

SAY: **God told Gideon to save the Israelites from their enemies. But Gideon didn't think he could do it. The enemies were big, and he was small.** Set the three cans of food in a row and SAY: **These cans are the big enemies.** Place a cotton ball next to the cans. **Imagine that this cotton ball is Gideon.**

ASK:

- **Who's bigger, stronger, and tougher?** Have a child cover the cotton ball with one of the cans, smashing it.

Have another child dump a big pile of cotton balls out on the table. SAY: **Gideon's army was big—32 thousand men! But God said, no, that's too many—make it 300.** Have a couple of children help you clear away all but three of the cotton balls, and stand them facing the large cans. **It seemed impossible. And that's just how God wanted it. God wanted everyone to know that he was the reason the Israelites would defeat their enemies. Gideon trusted and obeyed God. Gideon and his men beat their enemies.**

ASK:

- **What seemed impossible in the story?**
- **What seems impossible in your life?**

SAY: **Sometimes we might be afraid to face something, just as Gideon was afraid to face the enemies. God helped Gideon, and God helps us.**

Science Devotion

▶*NO PREP*

Look!

Children will learn that they can choose to automatically trust God.

Supplies: several flashlights, large mirror (or hand mirror for each child)

Time: 5 to 10 minutes

Preparation: none

Have kids form pairs. SAY: **Look into each other's eyes, at the black circle, or the pupil, in the middle. The pupils let in just the right amount of light so we can see clearly. In bright light, pupils get smaller to keep the light from hurting our eyes. If we turn off the light, our pupils get bigger to let in more light so we can see better.**

Turn off the lights, and have kids look at their partners' eyes. Then give each child a small flashlight, and have children stand in front of a mirror.

SAY: **Quickly turn on your flashlight and shine it across your face while you look into the mirror. You can't see your pupils change because we can't make our eyes do this. It happens automatically.**

In the same way, we can choose to automatically trust God. Whenever we're feeling lonely or afraid, we can remember that God is always with us. We have nothing to fear when God is with us

Preschool Story

▶*ALLERGY ALERT*

▶*PREPARE IN ADVANCE*

Bible Point: ▷ **WE CAN TRUST GOD.**

Supplies: Bible, small bowl, large bowl, teddy bear cookies

Time: 15 to 20 minutes

Preparation: Place at least six bear cookies per child in one bowl, and place a noticeably larger amount in the larger bowl.

Blow, Trumpet, Blow!

Have kids form a circle and sit down around the wall. Open your Bible to Judges 7, and show children the words. SAY: **The people in the land where the Israelites lived were very mean to the Israelites, so God sent Gideon to help them.** Point to the bowl that has more bear cookies, and tell children that this bowl of bear cookies is the mean people's army. **God called Gideon a mighty warrior, and Gideon asked many men to join his army.** Point to the second, smaller bowl, and tell the children that they will pretend that these bears are Gideon's army.

ASK:

◆ **How many soldiers does it take to make a big, *huge* army?**

SAY: **Well, Gideon thought he had a big army—he had 32 thousand men! But Gideon knew the people they had to fight had an even bigger army** (point to the larger bowl)**, so Gideon's army would never win. But God said Gideon had too many men. "Trust me," God said again and again. "Ask the brave men to stay, and see how many are left."**

Each time men left, the army got smaller. Have the children take turns coming up and taking two bear cookies from the smaller bowl back to their seats to eat while they listen.

Gideon's army was much smaller now, but God said his army was *still too big*. This time God told Gideon to take the men down to the river to see how they drank. If they got down on their knees to drink, they had to leave the army and go home. Have kids pretend to drink water while on their knees, and then SAY: **But if they lifted the water to their mouths in their hands, they could stay.** Have kids pretend to lift the water to their mouths, lap up water like dogs, and then SAY: **Lots more men left this time!** Have children come up, take three bear cookies each from the smaller bowl, and then return to their seats to eat them.

Now Gideon only had 300 men left! Point out the difference between the amounts of bear cookies in the bowls.

ASK:

◆ **Do you think Gideon's army will win with a smaller army? Why or why not?**

SAY: **God was happy with Gideon's tiny army. Now Gideon's army was ready. Gideon and all the Israelites had to trust God for the victory now! But God hadn't finished. He told Gideon that the army should carry rams' horn trumpets and clay jars instead of swords! That's the craziest thing. How could anyone win a battle without fighting with weapons?**

ASK:

◆ **Would you trust God to win a battle without any weapons? Why or why not?**

SAY: **The battle plan was finally set. The Israelites were to sneak up on the army during the night with trumpets and clay pitchers in their hands. The army blew their trumpets.** Have kids pretend to blow trumpets and make trumpet sounds, and then SAY: **The army shouted and broke the clay pitchers.** Have kids clap their hands and yell. **And God gave Gideon's army the victory! They won the battle that day with only a small amount of men and no weapons.**

▷ **WE CAN TRUST GOD to take care of us, too!**

ASK:

◆ **How did Gideon trust God?**

◆ **How can you trust God?**

n

o

t

e

s

BIBLE STORY

Samson Receives Strength From God

For the Leader

Before Samson was born, God told his parents that Samson would be a Nazirite. A Nazirite was someone completely dedicated to God and who showed that dedication visibly. A Nazirite was not allowed to consume grape products, eat non-kosher foods, get haircuts, or come into contact with dead bodies.

At face value, the secret of Samson's strength appears to have been in his hair. But as a Nazirite, his uncut hair was an outward symbol of his special dedication to God. When Samson allowed his hair to be cut, he was visibly renouncing his vow as a Nazirite to be dedicated to God. His strength left him because it had been a result of God's special blessing on Samson's life.

Even after Samson turned away from God and his Nazirite commitment, God loved Samson and used him to accomplish God's will. As Samson's hair regrew, so did evidence of hope in God's care for Israel. And God showed this care in a powerful way as Samson gave up his life.

Key Scriptures

Judges 15:9-16; 16:4-30

Romans 12:6

Bible Verse

"In his grace, God has given us different gifts for doing certain things well. So if God has given you the ability to prophesy, speak out with as much faith as God has given you" (Romans 12:6).

Bible Experience

▶ ***NO PREP***

▶ ***FOR LARGE GROUPS***

Bible Point: ▷ **GOD GIVES US GIFTS TO USE.**

Children will learn where Samson's strength came from.

Supplies: Bible, several current superhero action figures

Time: about 10 minutes

Preparation: none

Show children some superhero action figures. For each action figure,

ASK:

- **Who is this superhero?**
- **What makes this superhero strong?**
- **What is this superhero's weakness?**

Open your Bible to Judges 15, and show children the words. SAY: **The Bible tells about a real superhero named Samson. Samson was a leader of God's people. God gave Samson the gift of strength. And wow, was Samson strong! Samson was so strong that he picked up a bone**

of a donkey and struck down one thousand men. Compare that number to the number of people who are in your room.

Samson fell in love with Delilah. She wanted to trick Samson and find out why he was so strong. Some people who wanted to capture and hurt Samson said they'd pay Delilah a lot of money if she'd trick him. Samson told Delilah that God had given him the gift of strength. He told her that if someone cut his long hair short, he would lose his strength. Delilah led Samson's enemies to cut his hair. Ask kids to touch their hair.

His enemies captured Samson, and then they blinded him. Ask kids to close their eyes. **Then they took him to prison. Samson was in prison for a while and had to work very hard. His hair grew back, and his heart was sorry for what he had done. Samson's enemies wanted him to entertain them. So his enemies brought Samson to where everyone was gathered. They stood him between two pillars that held up the building. Samson asked God to give him the gift of strength one more time, and God did. Samson pushed on the pillars that were holding up the area where all his enemies were.** Have kids push their arms out as if pushing over two pillars.

The wall toppled on top of all of Samson's enemies. Samson used his gift of strength to conquer his enemies.

ASK:

- **How did Samson use his gift of strength for God?**
- **How else could Samson have used his gift of strength?**

Read aloud Romans 12:6.

ASK:

- **What kinds of gifts does God give people to use in serving God?**
- **What gifts has God given you?**

SAY: **▷GOD GIVES US GIFTS TO USE—to serve God and other people, just as Samson did.**

Song & Connect

Use "Wherever You Go" (track 1, *it: Innovative Tools for Children's Ministry: Old Testament* CD) to help reinforce the Bible Point, **▷GOD GIVES US GIFTS TO USE.**

Additional Topics List

This lesson can be used to help children discover... Body of Christ, Church, God's Will, Strength, and Wisdom.

Game

▶***NO PREP***
▶***HIGH ENERGY***

Super Strength

Children will realize that God gives us strength.

Supplies: 2 CD players ready to play 2 different, upbeat songs

Time: 10 to 20 minutes

Preparation: none

Gather your group in a large open space, and choose an "It." SAY: **We're going to spread out and play a game of freeze tag. If you're tagged**

by It, freeze until someone touches and frees you.

Explain that you'll be playing music during the game. Play an excerpt from the first song and SAY: **When this song is playing, It will have normal strength to tag and freeze people.** Now play the second song and SAY: **When this song is playing, It will have super strength, like Samson. When It has super strength, everyone except It must play the game on one foot!**

Once the instructions are clear, begin the normal-strength song. As the game progresses, switch between the songs. Change who is It by stopping the music and calling out the name of a new child. Try to play until everyone has experienced being It. If your group is large, use several taggers in each game.

After playing the game, ask students to discuss these questions:

- **How did it feel to be It with normal strength? Why?**
- **What was it like with super strength? Explain.**
- **Why was Samson stronger than other men?**
- **Where did Samson get his strength?**

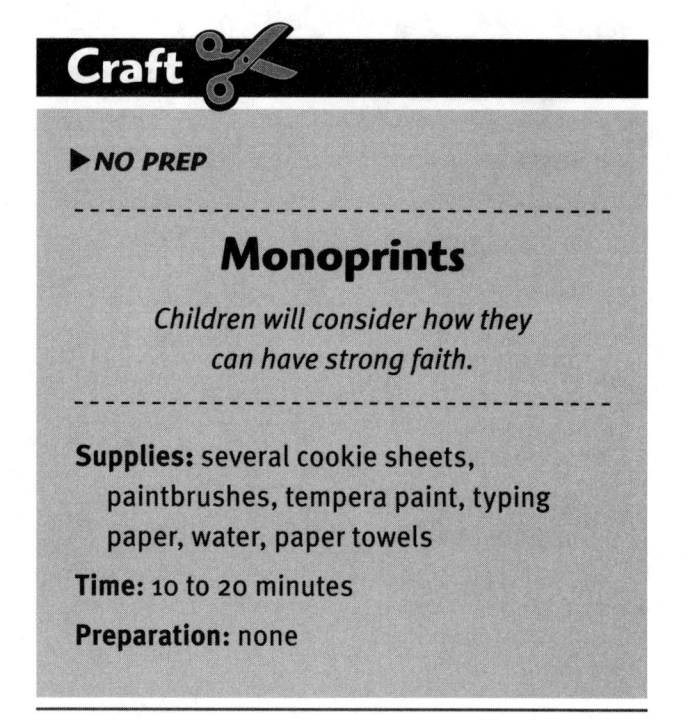

Craft

▶ *NO PREP*

Monoprints

Children will consider how they can have strong faith.

Supplies: several cookie sheets, paintbrushes, tempera paint, typing paper, water, paper towels

Time: 10 to 20 minutes

Preparation: none

Have children each paint a picture of how they can show strong faith, such as praying or going to church. Have children each paint their picture on their cookie sheet. Immediately after painting, have children each place a sheet of typing paper on their painting, press gently, and lift the paper slowly. Set paintings aside to dry. Between paintings, have children wash and dry the cookie sheet for the next child's turn.

notes

Bible Application

▶ *NO PREP*

Gifts to Serve

Children will learn that God provides what we need to do his work.

Supplies: sports-drink bottle, wrapped protein bar, small weight, straight-back chair with no armrests

Time: about 10 minutes

Preparation: none

ASK:

- **How strong are you?**
- **What do people do to become stronger?**

SAY: **I have some things that might help us become stronger.** Allow kids to pass around the sports-drink bottle, protein bar, and weight.

ASK:

- **Do these things make us stronger? How?**
- **What would you want to do if you were stronger?**

SAY: **Let's flex our arm muscles to see how strong they are. We can try an experiment to see how strong we are, too.**

Place a chair in the middle of the group. Have a child sit in the chair with his or her back against the chair back, feet firmly on the floor, arms folded, head back, and chin up. Choose another child to come forward and press just an index finger against the seated child's forehead, making sure to keep the child's head toward the back of the chair. Ask the child in the chair to stand, keeping arms folded. The child in the chair will be unable to stand. Let the other children try this as time allows. This works best with children who are about the same size.

SAY: **The person who is sitting is unable to shift his or her center of gravity, which is necessary in order to stand up. That's a great trick to make us look strong. The Bible tells us about Samson, who didn't need any tricks.**

ASK:

- **How do you think Samson got his strength?**
- **What special gifts has God given you?**
- **How can you use your gifts to serve God?**

SAY: **Remember that our gifts come from God and should be used for God's work. Even as children, you can be strong enough to do God's work.**

Creative Prayer Idea

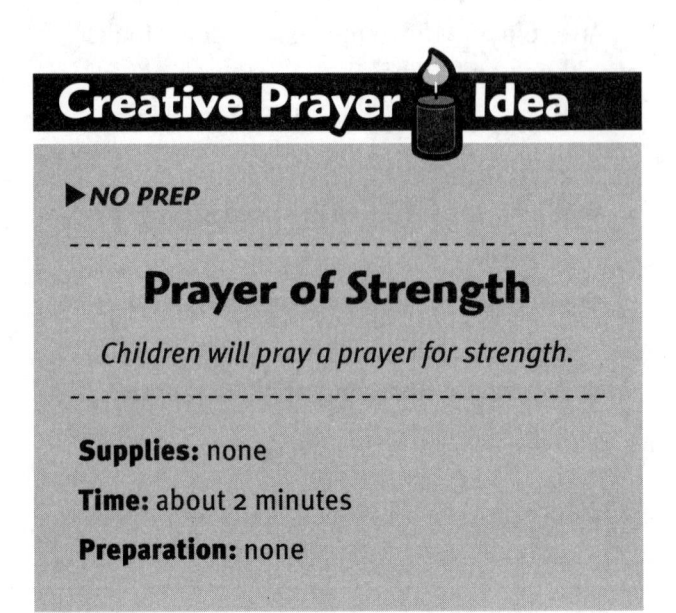

▶ *NO PREP*

Prayer of Strength

Children will pray a prayer for strength.

Supplies: none

Time: about 2 minutes

Preparation: none

Have the children make strong-arm muscles while you PRAY: **Dear God, thanks for all the wonderful gifts you give us. Help us learn how to use those gifts the way you want us to. We love you and want to help others know you. In Jesus' name, amen.**

Movie Clip

Hidden Strength

Movie Title: *The Princess Bride* (PG)

Start Time: 21 minutes, 33 seconds

Where to Begin: Westley prepares to duel, saying, "You've been more than fair."

Where to End: Westley wins the duel.

Plot: Buttercup has been kidnapped by a group of talented criminals. Her masked love, Westley, comes to her rescue and must face each criminal along the way. Westley's first challenge is a duel with master swordsman Inigo Montoya. Both men start the duel using their weaker hands, and Westley wins the fight.

Review: Both Inigo and Westley are master sword fighters. Inigo begins the duel using his left hand to make the fight interesting. During the fight, he's amazed to learn that Westley was using his weaker hand also. Like Samson, Westley had amazing power.

Discussion

After setting up and showing the clip, ASK:

- **What special talent did the two men have?**
- **How did they try to hide their talents?**

SAY: **There was a man in the Bible named Samson who had a special talent.**

ASK:

- **Does anyone know what his special talent was?**
- **What was the secret of Samson's strength?**

Briefly summarize the story of Samson.

SAY: **We all have special gifts and abilities. Our talents come from God, just as Samson's strength came from God. ▷ GOD GIVES US GIFTS TO USE. Let's use those gifts to glorify God.**

Object Lesson

▶ *NO PREP*

▶ *ALLERGY ALERT*

Food for Thought

Children will consider how God can help them use their gifts.

Supplies: thick licorice twists

Time: 5 to 10 minutes

Preparation: none

Have children each try to break the licorice with their hands. Then

ASK:

- **How easy or difficult was it to break the licorice?**
- **How easy is it to use your gifts to serve God instead of yourself?**
- **How can God make us strong to help us serve him with our gifts?**
- **What's one way God can help you not to break when the pressure's on?**

Preschool Story

▶ *NO PREP*

Bible Point: ▷ **GOD GIVES GOOD GIFTS.**

Supplies: Bible

Time: 15 to 20 minutes

Preparation: none

A Bad Haircut

Have kids form a circle and sit down. Open your Bible to Judges 15, and show children the words. SAY: **God gave a man named Samson a secret strength that made him stronger than anyone else in the land.**

Samson was an Israelite who promised to serve God from the time he was very little. One thing he promised God was that he would never cut his hair. I'm sure he had very long hair by the time he was a grown man.

Let the children who wish come stand by you and line up in order of hair length. Starting with the person who has the shortest hair, SAY: **Do you think Samson's hair was shorter or longer?** Continue doing the same with each of the children in line. Then SAY: **Everyone wanted to know what made Samson strong, but he wouldn't tell. The Israelites' enemies especially wanted to know what made Samson so strong because they wanted to stop him. They were always trying to think up ways to trick him into telling them.**

Samson's girlfriend, Delilah, tried to trick him into telling her the secret of his mighty strength. Many times Delilah tied up Samson, and every time Samson broke the ropes.

Help children form trios for this fun game. Have two of the trios form a bridge with their arms, and let the third child stand in the center, pretending to be Samson. Tell the two children forming the bridge to "lock" their arms around "Samson" so he or she can't get away. At the end of the following song, tell Samson that he or she can break out of the locked arms. Sing the following song to the tune of "London Bridge." Be sure to give everyone a chance to be Samson.

What's the secret of your strength,

Of your strength, of your strength?

What's the secret of your strength?

Tell me now.

SAY: **Delilah begged and pleaded, but Samson wouldn't tell her the secret of his mighty strength.** Have children pretend to beg and plead.

Finally, one night when Delilah was begging and pleading with Samson to tell her the secret of his strength, Samson finally gave up. "Stop! Enough! I'll tell you already! The secret is my long hair. If I cut my hair, my strength will be gone."

So that night, Delilah tied up Samson again and this time had a man cut his hair while he was asleep. When she yelled, Samson's enemies came running in.

Samson had lost his strength. He couldn't get away.

Samson was sorry he had trusted Delilah and broken his promise to God. He asked God to forgive him and use him again.

God forgave Samson and gave him back his mighty strength, and Samson won a victory for all of Israel.

God gave Samson the gift of strength. ▷ **GOD GIVES GOOD GIFTS to us, too.**

ASK:

- **What gifts has God given you?**
- **How can you use your gifts for God?**

BIBLE STORY

Ruth

For the Leader

Ruth's decision to go with Naomi was more than a whimsical choice. By following Naomi to her homeland, Ruth was leaving behind her family, her own homeland, and her culture. She also left behind her family's religion.

Because Ruth was from Moab, she would have been a second-class citizen in Judah. The Moabites were considered distant relatives of the Israelites because they were descended from Abraham's nephew Lot. As such, they were allowed to live among the Israelites, but they were not allowed in the tabernacle.

When she committed to go with Naomi, Ruth also committed to follow Naomi's God. This amounted to a conversion to the Israelites' religion. And it put Ruth in a place of great honor—as an eventual ancestor of Jesus himself!

Key Scriptures

Ruth 1:1-18

Proverbs 17:17; 18:24; 27:10

John 15:13-17

Bible Verse

"Never abandon a friend—either yours or your father's. When disaster strikes, you won't have to ask your brother for assistance. It's better to go to a neighbor than to a brother who lives far away" (Proverbs 27:10).

Bible Experience

▶ ***NO PREP***
▶ ***FOR LARGE GROUPS***

Bible Point: ▷ **GOD WANTS US TO BE LOYAL.**

Children will learn how to be a true friend.

Supplies: Bibles, pencils, paper

Time: 15 to 25 minutes

Preparation: none

Form three groups of one to six people. If your class is large, form six groups, assigning two groups to the same passage of Scripture. Instruct students to choose two people to read, one person to tell the class what happened in the Scripture or what it means, one to ask questions, one to encourage everyone in the groups to participate in answering the questions, and one to report the group's findings to the rest of the class. The jobs can be combined to accommodate the number of students in your groups and in your class.

Group 1's Scripture: *Ruth 1:1-18*

Group 1's questions:

- **What problem did Ruth and Naomi face?**
- **How do you know they were friends?**

Group 2's Scripture: *Proverbs 17:17; 18:24; 27:10*

Group 2's questions:

- **What does a friend do at all times?**
- **What should you never do to a friend?**

Group 3's Scripture: *John 15:13-17*

Group 3's questions:

- **How did Jesus show us that he is a true friend?**
- **How can we show our friendship with Jesus?**

After groups have finished, allow each group to report their findings to the whole group. Then read Proverbs 27:10 aloud.

ASK:

- **What does *abandon* mean?**
- **How can we show loyalty to our friends?**

SAY: **Ruth and Naomi proved their friendship even when things got tough. Ruth could have gone back to her family and her country as Naomi told her to. But Ruth loved Naomi and knew that Naomi needed her. Ruth and Naomi promised to stick together, and that's what they did. They were loyal, just as ▷ GOD WANTS US TO BE LOYAL.**

Song & Connect

Use "Those Who Hope" (track 12, *it: Innovative Tools for Children's Ministry: Old Testament* CD) to help reinforce the Bible Point, **▷ GOD WANTS US TO BE LOYAL.**

Additional Topics List

This lesson can be used to help children discover... Dedication, Fairness, Friendship, Loyalty, and Trustworthiness.

Game

▶ *NO PREP*

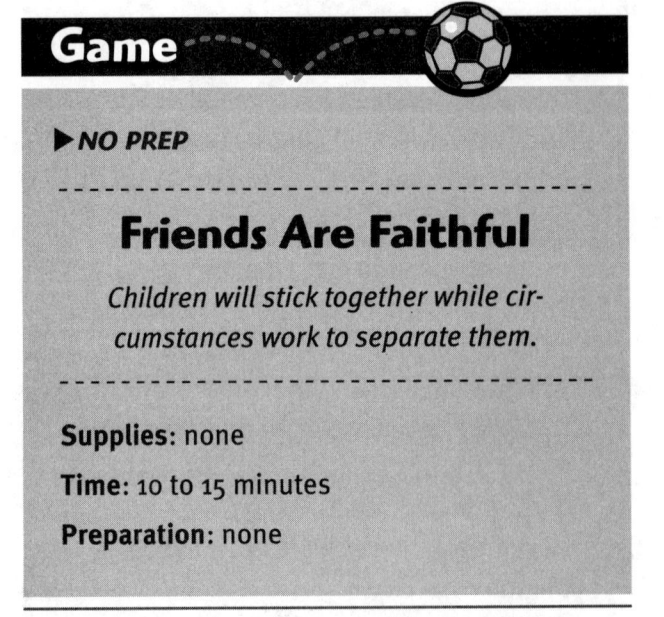

Friends Are Faithful

Children will stick together while circumstances work to separate them.

Supplies: none

Time: 10 to 15 minutes

Preparation: none

Form two groups, and send them to opposite sides of the room. Have Group 1 form two lines facing each other, about 5 feet apart. Tell kids that this is the Tunnel of Troubles and they are the Troublemakers. Instruct members of Group 2 to find partners to be their Best Buddies. Have the Best Buddies link arms and line up at one end of the Tunnel of Troubles.

SAY: **These Buddies will try to walk through the Tunnel of Troubles without being pulled apart. Each Troublemaker in the tunnel may use two fingers of one hand to try to pull the Buddies apart. Troublemakers, be careful not to poke or scratch—just tug with two fingers. If you succeed in pulling the Best Buddies apart, they'll join your group. Ready? Go!**

Send the Best Buddies through the tunnel. Remind the Troublemakers to be gentle. When all the Best Buddies have had a turn, have groups trade roles and play again. Then ask kids to discuss these questions:

- **What made it hard to go through the tunnel?**
- **What kinds of troubles pull real friends apart?**
- **How can you be a faithful friend?**

Craft

▶ *NO PREP*

Grain Painting

Children will learn to share with others.

Supplies: unpopped popcorn, paper cups, plastic spoons, construction paper, tempera paint, large shallow boxes, trash can, paper towels

Time: 10 to 15 minutes

Preparation: none

Ask kids to form four groups. One group is in charge of all the popcorn, one of all the paper, one of all the boxes, and one of all the paint.

SAY: **Use your supplies to make grain paintings with popcorn. You'll need to share your supplies to do this. Each of you needs a cup and spoon. Fill each cup one-fourth full of unpopped popcorn. Add one spoonful of paint to each cup, and stir until the kernels are coated. Then place one sheet of paper in each box. Pour the paint-coated kernels onto the paper, and shake the box gently to create a design. Remove your paper, and pour your used kernels into a trash can. Continue until everyone has made a painting.**

After painting,

ASK:

- **How did it feel to work with other groups to accomplish your goal?**
- **Could you have made your picture if groups hadn't shared? Why?**
- **How can you show generosity at home or at school?**

SAY: **Whenever you see or eat grain, remember that ▷ GOD WANTS US TO BE LOYAL, just as Ruth was.**

Bible Application

▶ *NO PREP*
▶ *STUDENT LED*

Friends Forever

Children will learn attributes that will help them form lasting friendships.

Supplies: copies of the "Forever Friends" worksheet (p. 232), pencils

Time: about 20 minutes

Preparation: none

SAY: **Ruth and Naomi were true friends. How good a friend are you?**

Distribute the "Forever Friends" worksheets, and give kids a few minutes to complete them. Assure them that nobody needs to see their answers and that they can answer using pictures or symbols if they prefer to ensure their privacy.

Forever Friends

How good a friend are you? Are you loyal, like Ruth? Think about the following questions to evaluate how you could be a better friend:

- ▶ When was the last time you ditched a friend or "stood up" a friend?
- ▶ When was the last time you stood up *for* a friend?
- ▶ When was the last time you insisted on your own way with a friend?
- ▶ When was the last time you did what your friend wanted to do, even though you had other ideas of your own?
- ▶ When was the last time you turned down spending time with a friend in order to do something else?
- ▶ When was the last time you chose to spend time with a friend rather than doing something else?
- ▶ How can you be a better friend?

Creative Prayer Idea

▶ *NO PREP*

Friendly Thoughts

Children will thank God for the friends God has given them.

Supplies: old magazines, safety scissors, glue, poster board

Time: 25 to 40 minutes

Preparation: none

Have students form groups. SAY: **Ruth and Naomi shared a special friendship. Each person should look through the magazines and find five words and/or pictures that remind you of your friends. Cut them out and glue them to the poster board to make a collage.**

After kids finish the collages, ask volunteers to share why they chose their words or pictures. Hang the collages around the room. Ask kids to join hands and look at the collages as they pray, thanking God for giving them good friends.

notes

Discussion Launcher

Protect Me

Children will be "workers," trying to get things done while "bodyguards" protect them from paper wads.

Supplies: paper, recycling bin

Time: about 20 minutes

Preparation: Think of a job the kids can help with.

Have kids form three groups: "workers," "bodyguards," and "throwers." Assign one bodyguard to each worker, and give the paper to the throwers.

Explain a task you need the workers to accomplish. Say that the throwers will wad up papers and toss them at the workers, and the bodyguards will bat away the paper wads so the workers can work. Encourage the workers to trust their bodyguards instead of paying attention to the throwers. Each time workers get hit, they have to freeze for 10 seconds before they continue their work.

When everyone understands how to play, have throwers begin making and throwing paper wads, and have workers begin working. After about a minute, stop the play and have groups switch roles. After a minute, switch roles again.

After everyone has played each role, discuss these questions:

◆ **What was it like to play each role in this game?**

◆ **When has someone been unkind to you, as when the throwers were trying to "get you" while you worked?**

◆ **How has someone showed loyalty to you, as the bodyguards did?**

◆ **When have you showed loyalty, as Ruth did?**

◆ **How can you remember to be kind to your family? your friends?**

Ask everyone to assume the role of the workers, complete the work, and gather the paper balls to put into a recycling bin.

Snack

▶ ***PREPARE IN ADVANCE***

▶ ***ALLERGY ALERT***

Bread and Honey

Children will eat a snack that reminds them of the story of Ruth.

Supplies: bread machines, bread-recipe supplies, honey, butter, plates, knives

Time: about 10 minutes

Preparation: Start baking bread in bread machines before kids arrive.

As kids arrive, they will smell the bread baking. The aroma will help children understand how the grain Ruth gleaned was used.

Serve warm bread with butter and honey as you remind the children of Ruth's loyalty to Naomi, gathering grain in the fields to feed herself and Naomi.

ASK:

◆ **Why does bread remind us of Ruth's friendship with Naomi?**

◆ **Next time you smell bread baking, will you remember Ruth and Naomi and how important it is to be loyal to our friends?**

Preschool Story

▶ ***PREPARE IN ADVANCE***

▶ ***ALLERGY ALERT***

Bible Point: ▷ **GOD WANTS US TO BE LOYAL.**

Supplies: Bible; plates; 1 heart-shaped cookie cutter per 2 children; 2 slices of bread, 1 slice of cheese, and 1 slice of lunchmeat per child

Time: 15 to 20 minutes

Preparation: Prepare a plate with four slices of bread, two slices of cheese, and two slices of lunchmeat for each pair of children.

I'm Stickin' With You

Have kids form a circle and sit down around the wall. Open your Bible to Ruth 1–4, and show children the words. SAY: **There was a lady named Ruth who lived in a land far away from God's people. Her husband had died, and she lived with her husband's mother, Naomi. She loved Naomi. Take turns with your partner cutting out a heart shape from one slice of your bread to show that Ruth loved Naomi.** Give children time to complete this.

Naomi's husband had also died. She was glad she had Ruth with her because she loved Ruth. Cut another heart shape from the other piece of bread you have to show that Naomi loved Ruth. Be sure to share with your partner. Allow time for children to do this.

Naomi wanted to go back to her family in the land of Judah, the land of God's people. Ruth loved Naomi so much that she decided to go

with her. Make a heart from the cheese to show that Ruth was willing to leave her country to follow Naomi. Encourage children to cut a heart from the cheese.

When they finally reached the land of Judah, Ruth knew she would have to work hard out in the fields to find food to feed both of them. The owner of the fields was a man named Boaz. He saw what a kind and good person Ruth was and fell in love with her. Cut a heart shape from the lunchmeat to show how Boaz loved Ruth. Encourage children to cut a heart from the lunch-meat.

Ruth and Boaz got married and had a little baby. So Naomi had a grandchild. They all made a happy family. Now put all of your things together to show that Ruth and Boaz and Naomi and the baby were all together in a family. Let's eat our happy snack together.

When children finish eating their snack, lead them in the following song to the tune of "My Bonnie Lies Over the Ocean":

Wherever you go, I will follow.
Wherever you stay, I will, too.
Your people will all be my people.
And your God I'll worship with you.
Fol-low, fol-low,
I'll follow you and there I'll stay.
Fol-low, fol-low,
I'll follow you and there I'll stay.

ASK:

- **How did Ruth show love to her friends and family?**
- **How can you show love to your friends and family?**

SAY: ▷ **GOD WANTS US TO BE LOYAL and show love to our friends and families just as Ruth showed love to Naomi.**

BIBLE STORY

Hannah's Prayer

For the Leader

Hannah was desperately sad—even depressed. The Bible says she cried and was unable to eat. Why? Anyone who desires a child and is unable to conceive may feel sad and even depressed. But in Hannah's time a woman's whole purpose and sense of value were based on her ability to bear children.

Instead of merely feeling sorry for herself or cursing God, Hannah turned to God in her sorrow. She not only recognized that God could give her a child, but she also promised that she would commit her child to the Lord's service.

What a powerful legacy Hannah's faith produced: Samuel, one of the boldest and most important prophets in Israel!

Key Scriptures

1 Samuel 1:1-20; 2:1-10

Psalm 34:18

Bible Verse

"The Lord is close to the brokenhearted; he rescues those whose spirits are crushed" (Psalm 34:18).

Bible Experience

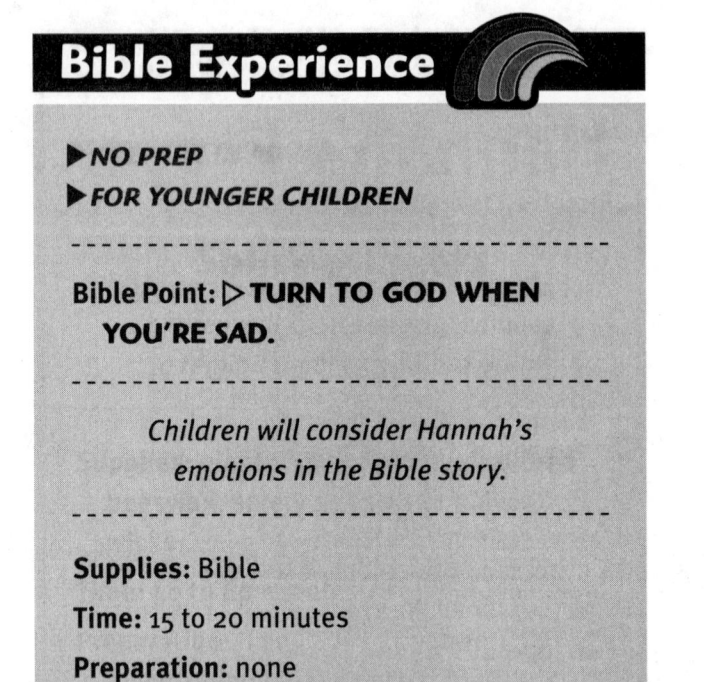

▶ *NO PREP*
▶ *FOR YOUNGER CHILDREN*

Bible Point: ▷ **TURN TO GOD WHEN YOU'RE SAD.**

Children will consider Hannah's emotions in the Bible story.

Supplies: Bible
Time: 15 to 20 minutes
Preparation: none

Open your Bible to 1 Samuel 1:1-20 and SAY: **Today's story comes from 1 Samuel in the Bible. This is the story of a woman named Hannah. As I tell the story, I want you to make sounds to show how you think Hannah sounded.**

Hannah was very sad. She really wanted to have a baby. She cried and she cried. She got so sad that she couldn't even eat.

Then one day Hannah and her husband went to worship God at the temple, in another town. While they were there, Hannah went to the temple to pray and ask God to give her a baby. She cried while she prayed very quietly. She promised God that if he would give her a son, she would bring the boy to the temple to serve God all his life.

After Hannah prayed, she felt better. She didn't look so sad, and she was even able to eat again!

After a while, God answered Hannah's prayer in the way she had hoped—she had a baby boy! She was very happy, and she remembered that her son was a gift from God. In fact, she named him Samuel because his name reminded her that God answered her prayer.

ASK:

- **Why did you make such different sounds throughout the story?**
- **How did praying help Hannah?**

Read Psalm 34:18 aloud, and then

ASK:

- **What does God do when we're sad?**
- **When have you been as sad as Hannah was?**
- **Why do you think God wants us to turn to him when we're sad?**

SAY: **Hannah was really, really sad. After she turned to God, God helped her feel better. God also answered her prayer. If you ▷ TURN TO GOD WHEN YOU'RE SAD, God will do the same for you. Even if God doesn't give you what you ask for, he will always answer your prayers. And he will help you feel better when you turn to him.**

Additional Topics List

This lesson can be used to help children discover... Comforter, Graciousness, Holy Spirit, Peace, Prayer, and Protection.

n
o
t
e
s

Game

▶ *PREPARE IN ADVANCE*

Hannah's Hot Seat

Children will find a heart and give thanks.

Supplies: Bible, CD player, upbeat Christian music, chairs (1 per person), red construction paper, scissors, tape

Time: 15 to 20 minutes

Preparation: Arrange chairs in a circle. Cut three hearts from the construction paper, and tape them underneath the seats of three chairs.

Read 1 Samuel 2:1 and SAY: **Hannah was so thankful when God answered her prayer that she gave her son back to God. We can express our praise to God in lots of ways. Let's play a game to tell a few things we're thankful for.**

Play upbeat Christian music, and instruct kids to move around the circle of chairs in a wacky way, such as hopping, skipping, walking backward, tiptoeing, or taking giant steps. Have everyone move in the same fashion.

After a few seconds, stop the music and instruct everyone to take a seat quickly. Kids might be surprised to discover enough seats for everyone.

SAY: **Look under your seat. If you see a paper heart, you're in a "hot seat." Shout out one thing you're thankful for.** Pause while kids share their thanks. Then SAY: **Now, everyone close your eyes and stay seated while the people in the hot seats move the hearts to different chairs.** Pause while kids move the hearts. When they've returned to their seats, play the music and have kids play again. Continue until all the kids have had a chance to share.

God helps us to be thankful. Sometimes it's good to stop and remember all the terrific things God does for us.

Craft

▶ *PREPARE IN ADVANCE*

Feelings Mobiles

Children will create reminders to turn to God with their feelings.

Supplies: coat hangers, construction paper, safety scissors, markers, hole punch, yarn

Time: 15 to 20 minutes

Preparation: Cut the yarn into pieces of varying lengths—about 6 to 18 inches.

Give each child a coat hanger and some construction paper. Set out scissors and markers. Instruct kids to cut out several circles of various sizes.

When kids are finished, have them draw faces that show various emotions. They can draw on both sides of the circles.

When kids are finished drawing, help them punch a hole in the top of each face, tie yarn through it, and tie it onto the coat hanger. Make sure the yarn is cut into different lengths so the faces will hang to various lengths.

SAY: **Take your mobile home and hang it in your room. It can remind you to ▷ TURN TO GOD WHEN YOU'RE SAD or when you have other feelings. God will always listen and help you.**

Bible Application

▶ *PREPARE IN ADVANCE*
▶ *FOR SMALL GROUPS*

Friend Acrostic

Children will learn about themselves.

Supplies: pencils, paper

Time: about 15 minutes

Preparation: On a piece of paper, write a word or phrase spelled out vertically down the left margin. You can use the name of your group, a greeting, or any appropriate word or phrase that has fewer total letters than the number of participants. Make a copy for each child in your class.

Have each child go to other children and get them each to write something about themselves that starts with a letter in the word or phrase. For example:

Has three sisters.

Elephants—She collects them.

Loves music.

Long hair.

Ordinarily skips breakfast.

The first person who gets his or her acrostic completely filled out and can match each fact with the appropriate child is the winner.

SAY: **We just learned some things about each other, but God already knew these things. In fact, God knows all about us. He even knows when we're happy or sad or feeling anything else at all. So there's no point in trying to hide our feelings from God. The very best thing to do is to ▷ TURN TO GOD WHEN YOU'RE SAD.**

Creative Prayer Idea

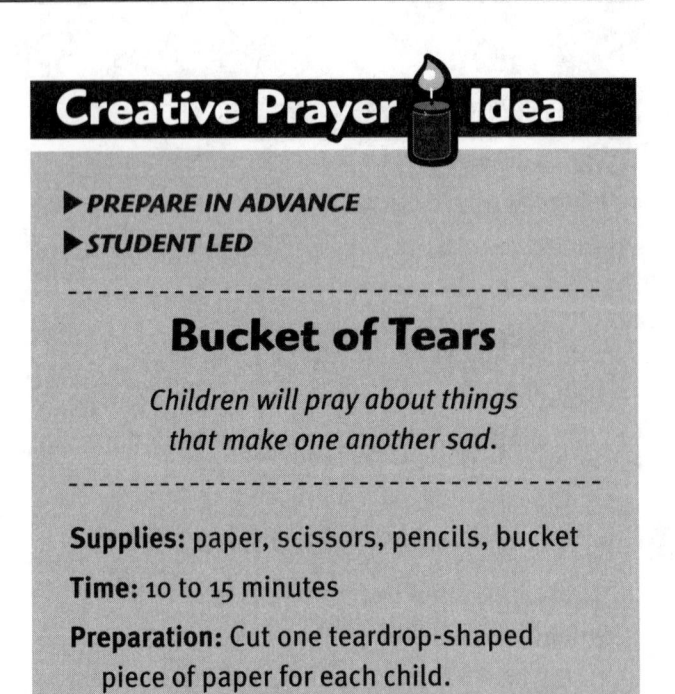

▶ *PREPARE IN ADVANCE*
▶ *STUDENT LED*

Bucket of Tears

Children will pray about things that make one another sad.

Supplies: paper, scissors, pencils, bucket

Time: 10 to 15 minutes

Preparation: Cut one teardrop-shaped piece of paper for each child.

Give each child a paper teardrop and a pencil. Have kids scatter so they can have some privacy. Encourage kids to spend a few minutes writing about something that makes them sad and that they would like to bring to God. Make sure kids know that they should not write their names on their papers and that someone else will be reading what they write.

After five to 10 minutes, ask kids to drop their teardrops in a bucket. Then gather everyone in a circle. SAY: **This bucket of tears represents the things that make us sad. We're going to turn to God with these things now by praying for each other. As we pass this bucket around, each person should draw a teardrop. Then we'll spend a few moments with each person praying silently for what's written on his or her teardrop.**

Pass the bucket around the circle, and then ask kids to pray silently for the prayer needs on the teardrops they drew from the bucket.

Object Lesson

▶ *ALLERGY ALERT*

Sad Fruit

Children will be reminded of what happens when we turn to God.

Supplies: citrus fruit, knife, juicer (if possible) or bowl, washcloth, cups (optional), water and sugar (optional)

Time: about 10 minutes

Preparation: Make sure you have a clean working surface.

On a table where everyone can see, cut open at least one orange, lemon, or other citrus fruit. Begin to either squish the fruit on a juicer or squeeze the juice out of the fruit and into a bowl. As you squeeze out the fruit juice, SAY: **When Hannah was sad, she cried so much that she couldn't even eat. Then she turned to God, and he helped her feel better. He also answered her prayer and gave her a baby boy. God made something beautiful out of Hannah's sadness, and God can do the same for us.**

Show kids the juice you've made. Point out that even though we may "cry" like the fruit when we're sad, when we turn to God, he turns our tears into something good.

If you have enough, allow kids to sample the juice you made. If you used lemons, be sure to add a little water and sugar.

Snack

▶ *NO PREP*

▶ *ALLERGY ALERT*

Prayer Necklaces

Children will make and eat a snack that reminds them to turn to God in prayer.

Supplies: colored loop cereal, red licorice whips

Time: about 5 minutes

Preparation: none

Have kids string colored loop cereal on red licorice whips. Have kids tie the ends of the licorice whips together and then put on the prayer necklaces.

Encourage kids to eat a piece of cereal as each prayer request or praise is shared during class prayer time, or encourage kids to take home their prayer necklaces and pray at home. Remind them to turn to God with their feelings.

SAY: **Just as Hannah did, you can ▷ TURN TO GOD WHEN YOU'RE SAD. These necklaces can help you remember to turn to God with your feelings.**

n

o

t

e

s

Preschool Story

▶ *NO PREP*

Bible Point: ▷ **TURN TO GOD WHEN YOU'RE SAD.**

Supplies: Bible, baby doll or folded towel

Time: 15 to 20 minutes

Preparation: none

A Simple Prayer

Have kids form a circle and sit down. Open your Bible to 1 Samuel 2, and show children the words. Have children form trios to act out the following simple drama. Designate a child in each group to be Hannah, a child to be Eli, and a child to be Elkanah. Then read the story and have children follow your directions.

SAY: **There once was a man named Elkanah and a woman named Hannah. Elkanah loved his wife Hannah. But they had no children, and Hannah wanted a baby very badly. Elkanah and Hannah went to the temple to worship.** Have the children portraying Elkanah and Hannah hold hands and skip or jump to the front of the room.

Elkanah and Hannah prayed. Instruct Elkanah to kneel and fold his hands in prayer, and ask Hannah to stand, fold her hands in prayer, and move her lips as though praying.

Eli, the priest, saw Hannah's great faith as she prayed to the Lord. Hannah told him (have Hannah repeat after you), **"I would like to have a baby." Then Eli said to Hannah** (have Eli repeat after you), **"May God give you what you wish."**

Hannah was very happy. Have Hannah jump for joy and clap hands. **She had faith that the Lord would answer her prayer. Elkanah and Hannah went back home.** Allow Elkanah and Hannah to hold hands and skip away.

Soon Hannah and Elkanah had a baby boy. Have Elkanah pick up a baby doll or a folded towel and hand it to Hannah. **Hannah and Elkanah were very happy.**

Instruct Hannah and Elkanah to say together: **"His name is Samuel."** Then SAY: **Hannah and Eli gave their son to God so that one day, Samuel would grow up and serve God.**

After you tell the story, have kids sing the following song to the tune of "The Mulberry Bush." Encourage kids to hold hands and move in a circle as they sing.

A lady named Hannah wanted a child,
Wanted a child,
Wanted a child.
A lady named Hannah wanted a child.
So she prayed to God.

God said, "Yes, you will have a child,
Have a child,
Have a child."
God said, "Yes, you will have a child."
His name was Samuel.

Hannah took Samuel to the church,
To the church,
To the church.
Hannah took Samuel to the church.
She took him to the temple.

Hannah showed how she loved God,
She loved God,
She loved God.
Hannah showed how she loved God.
She gave her son to God.

BIBLE STORY

God Calls Samuel

For the Leader

First Samuel 3:1 says, "In those days the word of the Lord was rare; there were not many visions." It's easy to miss this subtle setup for what follows: God chose to reveal himself powerfully and audibly to a boy.

God knew he had a servant in Samuel; his life was dedicated to God's service from the beginning. And he proved a faithful prophet.

Samuel chose to listen to God when he first heard God's voice, and he never stopped listening. He proclaimed God's word from that day on, and the Israelites listened.

Key Scriptures

1 Samuel 3:1-14

Deuteronomy 30:20

Bible Verse

"You can make this choice by loving the Lord your God, obeying him, and committing yourself firmly to him. This is the key to your life. And if you love and obey the LORD, you will live long in the land the LORD swore to give your ancestors Abraham, Isaac, and Jacob" (Deuteronomy 30:20).

Bible Experience

▶ *NO PREP*

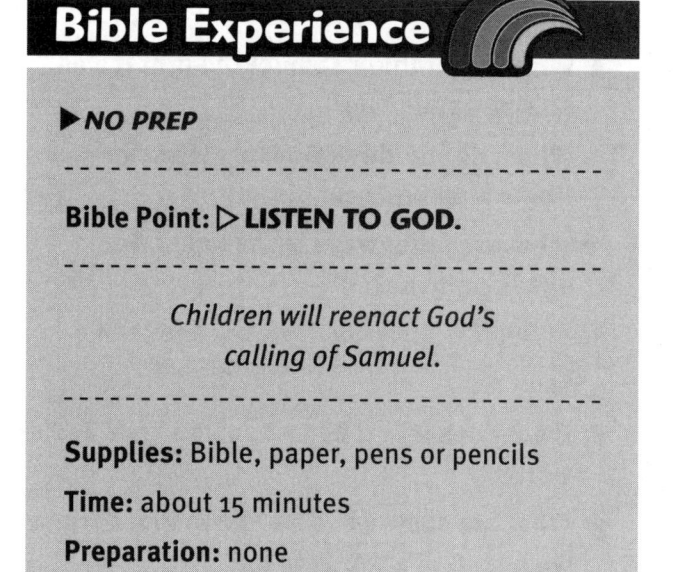

Bible Point: ▷ **LISTEN TO GOD.**

Children will reenact God's calling of Samuel.

Supplies: Bible, paper, pens or pencils

Time: about 15 minutes

Preparation: none

Give each child a piece of paper, and ask them to tear their paper into four pieces. Have children write their names on each piece, fold the papers, and give them back to you. Ask all the children to lie down on their backs as if they were sleeping. As they "sleep," draw a child's name from the pile and put it aside. Tell the children that when they hear their names, they are to come to you and say, "Here I am; you called me."

As each child comes to you, SAY: **I did not call; go back and lie down.** Do this until every child's name has been called.

After a name has been drawn three times, SAY: **Go and lie down, and if he calls you, say, "Speak, Lord, for your servant is listening."** Children may need to be coached on their lines.

Then SAY: **What we have just done is a lot like what happened to a young boy in the Bible.** Open your Bible to 1 Samuel 3:1-11. Paraphrase or read the passage directly from your Bible. To help children connect the experience to the story, ask them to raise their hands when they hear something that happened to Samuel that was similar to something they just experienced.

ASK:

- ◆ **Why do you think Samuel thought it was Eli who called him?**
- ◆ **Whom do you think God might use in your life to help you hear his voice?**
- ◆ **What are other ways we can hear God speaking to us?**

Read Deuteronomy 30:20 aloud, and then

ASK:

- ◆ **What does it feel like when you hear God's words?**
- ◆ **What are some ways we can respond when we hear God's words to us?**
- ◆ **How does God want us to respond to him?**

SAY: **Samuel heard and listened to God's voice. Even though we may not hear with our ears God speaking to us, we can hear and ▷ LISTEN TO GOD'S WORDS, too.**

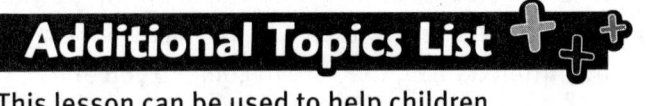

Additional Topics List

This lesson can be used to help children discover... Bible, Calling, God's Will, Holy Spirit, Prayer, and Wisdom.

notes

Game

▶ ***ALLERGY ALERT***

Look and Listen

Children will discover the value of careful listening as they work together and explore the story of Samuel's hearing God.

Supplies: button, penny, or other small object; CD player and CD or radio; healthy snacks or other simple surprises (optional)

Time: 10 to 15 minutes

Preparation: Hide a small object in the meeting area.

SAY: **I've hidden a button** [or other object] **in the room, and your job is to find it. The button won't be easy to find, and you may need clues. You must listen carefully to hear the clues because music will be playing and no one will know when I'm going to offer the clues.**

Help kids form pairs or small teams, and encourage them to cooperate as they search. For example, someone might want to concentrate on hearing the clues while his or her partner searches intently.

Give general—not specific—clues. For instance, if the button is near a clock, you might say, "I've got to *hand* it to you, you're good searchers."

Provide the students with a goal. You might say, "Our goal is to find the button within three clues." Play the game until the children succeed, and celebrate with a simple surprise to enjoy as students debrief.

After playing this game, ask kids to discuss these questions:

- ◆ **How did the noise affect your ability to hear the clues?**

- **How did you overcome the noise?**
- **How did Samuel know when God was speaking to him?**
- **How can we learn to hear God's voice?**

SAY: **God speaks to people in quiet and creative ways. When we tune out earthly noise, it's easier to ▷ LISTEN TO GOD.**

Craft

▶ *NO PREP*
▶ *FOR SMALL GROUPS*

A Walk in Samuel's Shoes

Children will learn to be servants, as Samuel did.

Supplies: for each child: 10x10-inch felt square, 12 jewel-like stones, 18-inch piece of red yarn, glue; stapler
Time: about 20 minutes
Preparation: none

SAY: **The Bible says that Samuel wore an ephod as the priests did, even though he was only a boy. An ephod was a very special piece of clothing that only those who worked in the house of God could wear. Our ephods won't look exactly like the ones the priests wore, but they will be close enough to remind us that we are servants of God, too, even though we don't live in the tabernacle or work with priests.**

Give each child a felt square, 12 jewel-like stones, an 18-inch piece of red yarn to hang the ephod around the child's neck, and some glue. Show children how to glue the jewels in three rows with four gems in each row. Then have them turn the ephods over, and show them how to put glue around the edges of three sides of the smaller pieces of felt. Have children staple the yarn to the upper corners of the breastplates so they can wear the ephods.

Have kids put on their ephods, and then

ASK:

- **How do you think Samuel felt when he put on his ephod?**
- **How do you feel when you think of yourself as a servant of God?**

SAY: **All servants have to be especially good at one thing. They have to know how to listen and respond to the voice of the one they serve. We can ▷ LISTEN TO GOD, just as Samuel did.**

Bible Application

▶ *NO PREP*

Following the Footsteps

Children will learn how to respond to God's voice.

Supplies: index cards, pens or pencils
Time: about 5 minutes
Preparation: none

Give each student a card and a pen or pencil. Have children sit in a semicircle on the floor. SAY: **Samuel heard God's voice and made a choice to listen and obey. God is speaking to each one of us as well. Sometimes God speaks in a small voice that we almost hear, but most of the time God speaks through the Bible and through leaders in our lives, such as parents, teachers, and pastors.**

Most of us know of things God has told us to do—but not all of us are listening and obeying. Sometimes we're too busy to listen; other times we have heard but not obeyed. Let's take some time right now to stop being busy and listen to God.

Ask kids to close their eyes, bow their heads, and relax. Encourage them to listen with their hearts and to each think of one thing they know God has asked them to do. It may be something God told them through their parents, a teacher, or a pastor. It may be to obey their parents and clean their rooms; it may be to share Jesus with a friend at school; it may be to spend time each day reading the Bible and praying to God. You can offer some suggestions to get kids thinking, but challenge them to think of something personal.

After a few minutes, have kids write what they thought of on their cards. No one is to look at what others write—this is just between God and each student. Explain that not even the teacher will read their cards.

notes

Creative Prayer Idea

▶ *PREPARE IN ADVANCE*
▶ *FOR SMALL GROUPS*

Samuel Speaks to God

Children will speak to God in a creative way.

Supplies: 2 clean soup cans, awl, string, duct tape

Time: about 5 minutes

Preparation: Make a play telephone by poking a hole in the bottom of each can, threading the string through the holes, and tying each end of the string in a knot. Cover the cans' edges with duct tape to avoid cuts.

Let kids practice using the play phone to whisper "God loves you" to each other. Then have them pray by speaking into the play phone. PRAY: **Hello, God. I am so glad that you hear my prayers no matter how I try to talk to you. I want to hear what you want to tell me. Help me to listen to you in the Bible, when I pray, and when other Christians talk to me. Remind me to tell others they can know you and hear from you, too. In Jesus' name, amen.**

Discussion Launcher Questions

Ask children to form trios and discuss:

- **Have you ever heard God speaking to you? How?**
- **Why do you think God chooses not to speak to most people the way he spoke to Samuel?**
- **How can we ▷ LISTEN TO GOD?**

Object Lesson

▶ *PREPARE IN ADVANCE*
▶ *OUTREACH*

Samuel Listens to God

Children will learn that God will hear their prayers.

Supplies: 2 clean soup cans, awl, string, duct tape

Time: about 15 minutes

Preparation: Make a play telephone by poking a hole in the bottom of each can, threading the string through the holes, and tying each end of the string in a knot. Cover the cans' edges with duct tape to avoid cuts.

Show children the play phone of two soup cans connected by string. SAY: **I need a volunteer to take one end of our play phone and stand as far away from me as possible, with the string tight.** Wait for the child to get into position, and then SAY: **Place the can to your ear, and repeat what I'm about to say into this end of the phone.** As softly as possible, say into the can: **God loves you.** Do this several times, each time speaking a little louder until your message is finally heard. Then ask the child to return to the group.

Sometimes we have to repeat what we say so others can hear and understand. When Samuel was a boy, God talked with him and told him many important things.

ASK:

- **How does God speak to us?**
- **What are things God tells us to do?**

SAY: **God spoke to Samuel at night and called his name. God speaks to us through worship, Christian friends, prayer, songs, and the Bible. Let's ▷ LISTEN TO GOD and tell others about him, too.**

Preschool Story

▶ *NO PREP*

Bible Point: ▷ LISTEN TO GOD.

Supplies: Bible, standard-size envelopes, napkins, markers

Time: 15 to 20 minutes

Preparation: none

A Voice in the Night

Have kids form a circle and sit down. Open your Bible to 1 Samuel 3, and show children the words. Show students how to make Samuel puppets out of standard-size envelopes: Seal the empty envelopes, and then cut the envelopes at the bottom, when held vertically, so children's hands slide up inside. Then help each child draw a simple sleeping face (a smile with closed eyes) on one side of the envelope and a happy face (with eyes open) on the other side. Each child will also need a napkin.

Have children slide their hands up into the envelopes with Samuel's sleeping face looking at them. Help children place the napkins on their arms for Samuel's blanket. As you read the following Bible-story rhyme, use a deep voice when God speaks and a higher voice for young Samuel.

SAY: **Samuel, Samuel tucked in tight, sweetly dreaming in the night.** *(Show sleeping Samuel.)*

GOD: Samuel! Samuel!

SAMUEL: Here I am. *(Show Samuel awake and raise arm. Blanket will fall off.)*

SAY: **Over to Eli Samuel ran.** *(Eyes-open face moves toward other arm.)*

SAMUEL: You called me, sir.

ELI: No, I didn't. Go to bed. *(Other hand points to Samuel.)*

(Repeat the first part of the rhyme two more times.)

ELI: Oh, wait, I know whom you heard. The Lord called you. *(Point finger at Samuel.)* If one more time God calls, say to him, "Speak, and I will hear." *(Place free hand behind your ear.)*

SAY: **Samuel, Samuel tucked in tight, sweetly dreaming in the night.** *(Show sleeping Samuel.)*

GOD: Samuel! Samuel!

SAMUEL: Here I am. *(Show Samuel awake and raise arm. Blanket will fall off.)*

SAY: **The Lord came and stood by Samuel's bed.** *(Wave hand over Samuel.)*

GOD: Samuel! Samuel!

SAMUEL: Speak, Lord, I'll hear. *(Cup hand to Samuel's ear.)*

SAY: **God spoke to Samuel very clear.**

God spoke and Samuel heard. Samuel grew up with God's Word.

ASK:

◆ **What are some ways we can hear God speak to us?**

SAY: **We can ▷ LISTEN TO GOD, just as Samuel did.**

BIBLE STORY

Israel Wants a King

For the Leader

The people of Israel came to a crossroads. Since leaving Egypt, they had followed God as their king, and God had revealed himself through prophets and other leaders. But now they wanted a king–a man to rule over them.

So what was the big deal? Why was Samuel upset, and why did God warn them against submitting to a king? It was because they were rejecting God as their king. They were no longer content to follow God and the authorities God appointed; they wanted to be like the nations around them. God let them have their way, but he made clear what they were getting themselves into.

And it turns out God was right. The Israelites, like all people, suffered at the hands of leaders who were unjust, unwise, and selfish.

Key Scriptures

1 Samuel 8:1-22

Leviticus 18:4

Bible Verse

"You must obey all my regulations and be careful to obey my decrees for I am the Lord your God" (Leviticus 18:4).

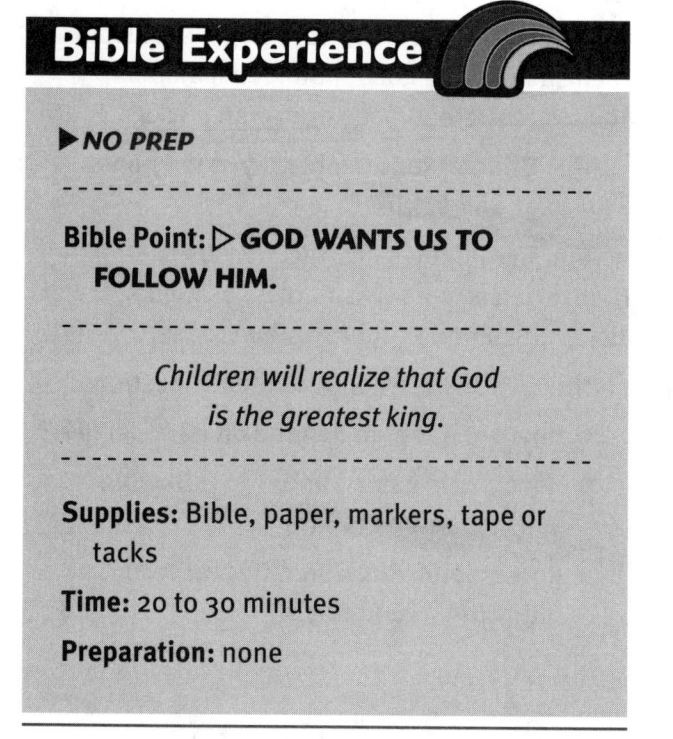

Bible Experience

▶ *NO PREP*

Bible Point: ▷ **GOD WANTS US TO FOLLOW HIM.**

Children will realize that God is the greatest king.

Supplies: Bible, paper, markers, tape or tacks

Time: 20 to 30 minutes

Preparation: none

Distribute paper and markers. SAY: **It's time to elect a leader for our group. All of you are good candidates, so let's make campaign posters to show why people should vote for each of you.**

Give kids a few minutes to create their campaign posters. As they work, walk around and encourage individual students to either write or draw about specific characteristics that would make them class leaders or campaign promises to help them get elected.

After a few minutes, ask children to wrap up their work. Display the campaign posters on the walls. As a class, review some of the characteristics and promises highlighted on the posters. Then

ASK:

- **What do you like about the posters the class created?**
- **If God were to create a campaign poster to show why we should choose him as our class leader, how would God's poster compare with the ones our class created?**
- **If you were going to choose a class leader, would you want to choose God or someone in our class? Why?**

SAY: **Our Bible story is about some people who made that choice.**

Read aloud the Bible story from 1 Samuel 8:1-22. Then

ASK:

- **Why do you think the people decided they wanted a king?**
- **Why didn't God want to give them a king?**
- **Why did God decide to give the people a king after all?**
- **What kind of person was the best king for the Israelites? Why?**

SAY: **Sometimes people want things that aren't the best for them. For instance, sometimes I want a cookie instead of fruit, or sometimes I want to spend all my money instead of saving some.**

Read aloud Leviticus 18:4, and then SAY: **God lets us make choices, just as he let the Israelites make choices. But ▷ GOD WANTS US TO FOLLOW HIM, and following God is always best for us.**

Song & Connect

Use "Wonderful" (track 11, *it: Innovative Tools for Children's Ministry: Old Testament* CD) to help reinforce the Bible Point, ▷ **GOD WANTS US TO FOLLOW HIM.**

Additional Topics List

This lesson can be used to help children discover... Faith, Glorifying God, Honor, Loyalty, Service, and Trust.

Game

▶ *PREPARE IN ADVANCE*

Leading the Blind

Children will guide their blindfolded partners to create an object.

Supplies: paper lunch bags, marker, craft sticks, glue or tape, yarn, scissors, O-shaped cereal, blindfold

Time: 15 to 20 minutes

Preparation: Label half the paper bags "A" and the other half "B." In each bag A, place four craft sticks and either a roll of tape or a bottle of glue. In each bag B, place a piece of yarn 3 feet long and 10 pieces of O-shaped cereal.

Create a sample of object A by gluing or taping four craft sticks together to form a cross. Create a sample of object B by stringing together 10 pieces of cereal on yarn to create a cereal necklace. Set these samples aside where no one will see them.

Have players form pairs. Give each pair a blindfold, one paper bag A, and one paper bag B. Don't allow players to look inside the bags yet. Explain that blindfolded players will be making something with their hands by relying on their partners' instructions. The nonblindfolded partners will see an object, and it's their job to guide their partners in making that object. Partners can communicate freely, but the ones giving instructions cannot use their hands or touch the materials in any way, and the blindfolded person cannot peek at any time.

Have one partner from each pair securely blindfold the other and set bag A directly in front of him or her (have them keep bag B set aside). Then show all the nonblindfolded members object A, the cross made from craft sticks.

SAY: **Blindfolded members, you may open your bags and begin.**

After five minutes, instruct players to stop. Then have partners switch roles, using bag B and displaying object B, the cereal necklace.

After five minutes, discuss these questions:

- **How did it feel to depend on your partner?**
- **How is this game similar to following another person in life?**
- **How is following God different from following other people?**

Craft

▶ *NO PREP*

▶ *STUDENT LED*

Clay Thrones

Children will create thrones to remind them that God is their king.

Supplies: modeling clay; small items such as buttons, beads, and pins

Time: 10 to 15 minutes

Preparation: none

Give each child a lump of modeling clay. SAY: **The Israelites wanted a king they could follow instead of just following God. Let's make some thrones like kings sit on. These thrones can remind us that no matter who our leaders are, God is always our king.**

Encourage children to be creative in making their clay thrones. Set out a variety of small items such as buttons, beads, and pins. Show kids how to press the items into their clay to decorate their thrones.

SAY: **Your empty throne can remind you that God is our real king. ▷ GOD WANTS US TO FOLLOW HIM. Let's make sure we remember to let God be king of our lives.**

Bible Application

▶ *PREPARE IN ADVANCE*

▶ *ALLERGY ALERT*

Winding Paths

Children will explore why following God is best.

Supplies: masking tape or string; various "good reward" items, such as healthy snacks, small toys, and stickers; various "bad reward" items, such as empty candy wrappers, unsharpened pencils, and plastic silverware

Time: 20 to 30 minutes

Preparation: Use masking tape or string to create a few winding paths on the floor of your meeting area. Each path should start at the entrance kids will be using. At the end of each path, place a few items for kids to find. Some paths should have treats at the end, and others should have disappointing items.

As kids arrive, tell each person to select a path and follow it to receive a reward. After kids get their rewards, ASK:

- **How did you decide which path you were going to follow?**
- **How was choosing a path in this game similar to choices you have to make in real life?**
- **How did you feel when you found your reward?**
- **If you had known what reward was at the end of each path, would you have chosen a different path? Why or why not?**

SAY: **Life is full of choices, and we have to pick which path we'll follow each day. We have plenty of guides available to tell us which way to go; unfortunately, they don't always point us down the right path.**

Have kids help you make a list of some of the various "guides" available for them to follow in real life. For example, they might name God, parents, friends, movie stars, teachers, pastors, musicians, athletes, politicians, grandparents, and the Holy Spirit. Then ASK:

- **How do you choose which guide to follow?**
- **Why do you think ▷ GOD WANTS US TO FOLLOW HIM?**

SAY: **Only God knows for sure what is at the end of each path we might choose. And only God knows what is best for us. Let's follow God.**

Creative Prayer Idea

▶ *NO PREP*

Bow to the King

Children will bow to God, our King, as they pray.

Supplies: none

Time: 5 to 10 minutes

Preparation: none

Have kids gather in a circle, facing outward. SAY: ▷ **GOD WANTS US TO FOLLOW HIM. As we pray today, let's show that God is our king and that we want to follow him. We're going to bow as we pray, just as we might bow when talking to a king.**

Tell children that during the prayer, you'll pause to let them pray silently.

Ask all the kids to bow before God, and then PRAY: **God, our king, thank you for being our perfect leader and for always showing us the right way to live. We want to follow you. Help us to treat you as our king. Here are some ways we need to treat you as the king of our lives...**Pause for kids to pray silently about ways they need to live to treat God as their king. **Thank you for helping us to follow you. Amen.**

Snack

▶ ***PREPARE IN ADVANCE***

▶ ***ALLERGY ALERT***

Crown Cake

Children will decorate and eat a snack that will remind them of Israel's first king.

Supplies: cake mix to make a 9x13-inch sheet cake, 15x30-inch piece of cardboard, aluminum foil, yellow frosting, decorator's sugar, assorted candies, plastic knives, plastic forks, paper plates

Time: 15 to 20 minutes

Preparation: Bake the cake, and cover the cardboard with aluminum foil to make a base for the finished cake.

SAY: **Let's make a cake to remind us of King Saul, Israel's first king.**

Carefully remove the cake from the cake pan, and place it on the base you prepared earlier. Cut a zigzag lengthwise down the center of the cake. Lay the two halves of the cake side by side, with the zigzag edge at the top to create a crown shape.

Have kids frost the cake, starting by frosting between the two cake halves to hold them together. Once the entire cake is frosted, have kids decorate the crown with decorator's sugar and assorted candies for jewels. Then serve the cake and let kids enjoy eating it.

Worship Prompt Idea

▶ ***NO PREP***

Committed to the King

Children will make a personal commitment to follow God.

Supplies: poster board or newsprint, markers, tape or tacks

Time: about 15 minutes

Preparation: none

SAY: ▷ **GOD WANTS US TO FOLLOW HIM. As a way to worship God, let's make a commitment to follow God as our king. Kings and other leaders of countries can make new laws. Let's write a law for our lives.**

Work as a class to write on a piece of poster board or newsprint a commitment to follow God, such as "No matter what leaders God puts in authority over us, we want to follow God. We will follow God as our true king."

Set out markers, and gather around the poster. SAY: **We're going to sing in worship. While we're singing, sign your name to the new law if you're ready to show that you want to follow God as your king.**

Sing a worship song or two (such as "Shout to the Lord" or "King of Majesty"), and allow kids to sign the poster. Then hang it on a wall in your meeting area or somewhere else in the church where it can inspire others.

Preschool Story

▶ *NO PREP*

Bible Point: ▷ GOD WANTS US TO FOLLOW HIM.

Supplies: Bible

Time: 15 to 20 minutes

Preparation: none

We Want a King!

Have kids form a circle and sit down around the wall. Open your Bible to 1 Samuel 8, and show children the words. Before you begin the story, have children practice the CHILDREN lines a few times.

SAY: **When Samuel grew old, the people of Israel decided they wanted a king, like all the other nations around them. Samuel tried to tell the people that God was their king and they didn't need another king, but the Israelites didn't care what God wanted. They only wanted their own way.**

CHILDREN: We want a king, yes we do! We want a king, yes that's true! We want a king, strong and tall! We want a king to rule us all! *(Pump arms in the air and stomp feet.)*

SAY: **Samuel knew that a king was a bad idea, so he prayed and asked God what to do. God told him to let the people have their way, but he said to warn them that a king would not make them happy.**

So Samuel went to the people and told them about God's warning. *(Stand up tall, and act as if you were Samuel about to make a proclamation.)* **A king will rule over you. He will take your sons and make them fight in his army.** *(Gather the boys on one side of the room, and make them line up and march in place.)* **They will also have to work for him and plow his fields.** *(Lead the boys in pretending to plow a field.)* **The king will take your daughters away from you and make them cook and work hard for him.** *(Gather the girls on the other side of you, and make them pretend to cook.)* **The king will take away your best fields and crops. He will take some of everything that you have. He will take the people that work for you and make them work for him instead. He will take your cows and donkeys for himself.** *(Encourage kids to pretend to be cows and donkeys.)* **When the king does all these things, you will wish that you had not wanted a king.** *(Sit back down and begin speaking to the kids in your normal voice again.)* **But the people didn't listen to Samuel or God. They still wanted a king.**

CHILDREN: We want a king, yes we do! We want a king, yes that's true! We want a king, strong and tall! We want a king to rule us all! *(Pump arms in the air and stomp feet.)*

SAY: **The Israelites chose not to follow God's way—even though God's way is always best. ▷ GOD WANTS US TO FOLLOW HIM.**

ASK:

- **Why didn't the Israelites follow God's way?**
- **How can you choose to follow God's way?**

BIBLE STORY

Samuel Anoints David

For the Leader

When the Israelites rejected God as their king and demanded a human king instead, God gave them what they asked for. But he didn't abandon them. He still put authorities in place over them, just as he does today.

Samuel's anointing of David made this clear. God was choosing the king, and he had a set of criteria quite different from what people would have had. Rather than choosing the man who looked the part, he chose the boy with the right heart.

Key Scripture

1 Samuel 16:1-13

Bible Verse

"People judge by outward appearance, but the Lord looks at the heart" (1 Samuel 16:7).

Bible Experience

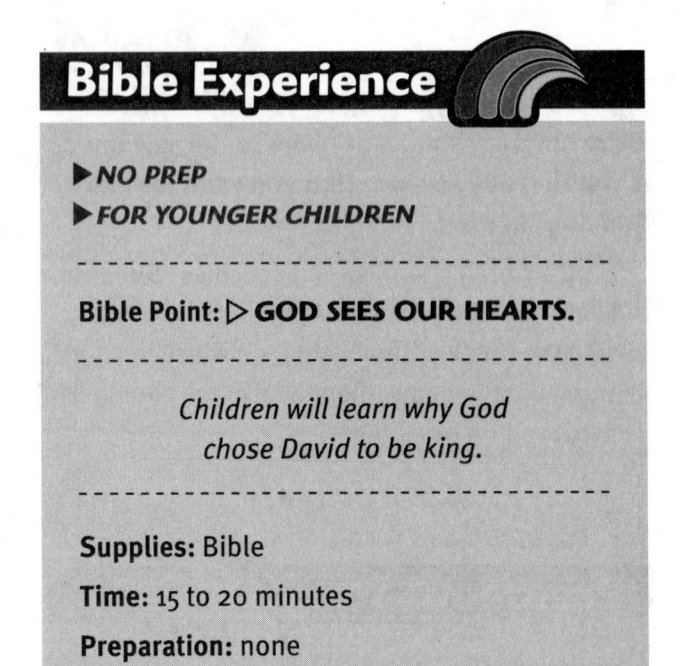

▶ *NO PREP*
▶ *FOR YOUNGER CHILDREN*

Bible Point: ▷ **GOD SEES OUR HEARTS.**

Children will learn why God chose David to be king.

Supplies: Bible
Time: 15 to 20 minutes
Preparation: none

Open your Bible to 1 Samuel 16:1-13, and show the children the words. SAY: **Today's Bible story is about God choosing a person to be king!**

ASK:

◆ **If you were choosing someone to lead our country, what kinds of things would you look for?**

SAY: **Let's pretend we're looking for a leader for our country. We'd want the leader to be** [use characteristics the children mentioned when you asked the previous question]. With each word, ask kids to stand taller and taller. After everyone is standing tall, SAY: **Yes! That's what we'd want for a leader!**

Let kids sit down again. SAY: **In our Bible story, God sent Samuel to find a new king for God's people. God sent Samuel to Jesse, the father of many sons. When Samuel looked at the sons, it seemed like any one of them would be fit to be a king.** Ask kids to stand tall. **Samuel looked at all these sons, but he knew that the one God wanted to be king wasn't there. So as he looked at each son, he said, "No, this isn't the one."** Have children get in a line; look at each one and SAY: **No, this isn't the one.** Have children sit down one at a time.

Samuel asked if Jesse had any other sons. Jesse said there was only the youngest son, who wasn't there because he was taking care of the family's sheep. Samuel asked to see the youngest son. Ask kids to crouch down as small as they can get and say, "I'm little David."

When Samuel saw David, he said, "Yes! This is our new king!"

ASK:

- **What surprised you about our Bible story?**
- **Did you think God would pick young David? Why or why not?**

SAY: **David was a boy, maybe even your age. But God told Samuel that David was the one he wanted to lead his people. God wanted the youngest son.**

Read aloud 1 Samuel 16:7, and then SAY: **This verse tells us why God chose David. God didn't look at how old David was. God didn't look at how small David was. ▷ GOD SEES OUR HEARTS. God knows what we're like on the inside. God knew David had a good heart and loved God.**

Song & Connect

Use "The Work of His Hands" (track 3, *it: Innovative Tools for Children's Ministry: Old Testament* CD) to help reinforce the Bible Point, ▷ **GOD SEES OUR HEARTS.**

Additional Topics List

This lesson can be used to help children discover... Character, Faithfulness, Humility, Omniscience, and Unconditional Love.

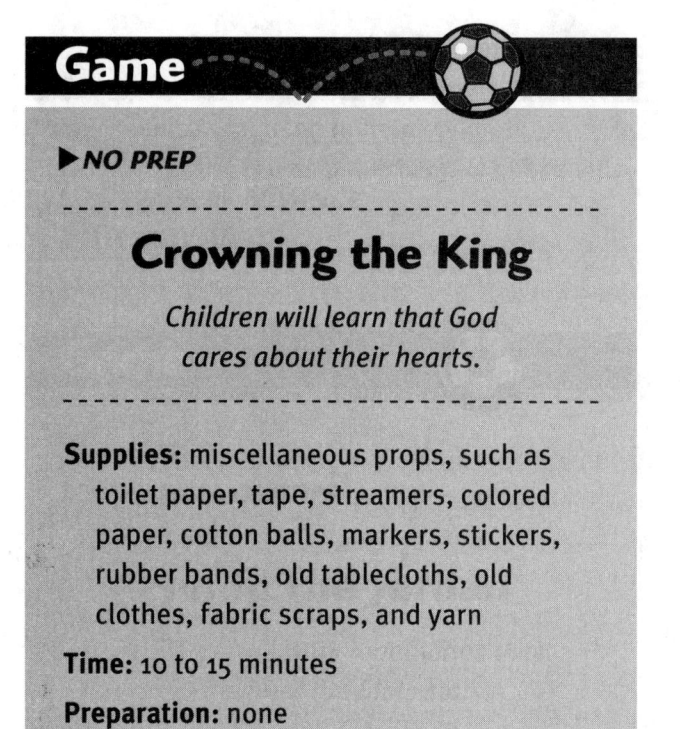

Game

▶ ***NO PREP***

Crowning the King

Children will learn that God cares about their hearts.

Supplies: miscellaneous props, such as toilet paper, tape, streamers, colored paper, cotton balls, markers, stickers, rubber bands, old tablecloths, old clothes, fabric scraps, and yarn

Time: 10 to 15 minutes

Preparation: none

Form groups of five or six. SAY: **Today we'll crown a king—or queen—for each of our teams. Each team should choose its royalty now.**

Allow a minute or so for each team to select one king or queen. Then show children your props. Explain that each group must decorate its royalty using those supplies. Their task is to make the king or queen look as regal as possible by using what they have available. Give them ample space and about five minutes.

Have a parade of kings and queens. Then ask students to discuss:

- **Why did you choose the person you did to become king or queen?**
- **Now that you have completed the task, would someone else have made a better king or queen for your group? Explain.**
- **Why do you think God wanted Samuel to anoint David as king of Israel?**

Craft

▶PREPARE IN ADVANCE

Container Creatures

Children will make containers to hold important things.

Supplies: Bible, cylinder-shaped cardboard containers (from oatmeal or cornmeal), construction paper, glue or tape, markers, pompoms, hole punch, 12-inch pieces of yarn, large wooden beads, wooden spools

Time: about 30 minutes

Preparation: Have kids each bring a cylinder-shaped cardboard container (such as an empty oatmeal or cornmeal container) to class.

Read aloud 1 Samuel 16:1-13. SAY: **We're going to make a fun storage container that will help us remember this scripture. It doesn't matter what it looks like on the outside, but we'll store things inside that are important.**

Give each child a cardboard container. Have children wrap their containers with construction paper. Then have them make faces on the containers with markers and paper, using pompoms for noses. To make the legs, help each child punch two small holes about $3/4$ inch from the bottom edge and about $2\frac{1}{2}$ inches apart under the face. Thread a 12-inch piece of yarn in one hole and out the other, pulling it through until equal amounts hang out of each hole. Tape the yarn on the inside of the container to secure it. Tie a large wooden bead or spool at each end for feet.

Bible Application

▶NO PREP
▶FOR SMALL GROUPS

Wonderfully Made

Children will begin to develop a positive body image.

Supplies: Bible, fashion magazines, safety scissors, construction paper, glue

Time: 20 to 30 minutes

Preparation: none

Have kids cut out pictures of how the world thinks we should look and act. Then let students glue the pictures onto construction paper so each child has a collage. Have several children show their collages and explain what the messages are. Then ASK:

- **What messages did you find about how people should look or act?**
- **What do these say about how the world thinks people should look?**

SAY: **Society is obsessed with physical perfection, and the message is, "If you look like this, you'll be happy." Each day we're bombarded with advertisements from magazines, billboards, television, and newspapers.** Read aloud 1 Samuel 16:7. ASK:

- **Why do you think God focuses on looking at our hearts?**
- **Does God want us to compare ourselves with each other? Why or why not?**
- **What's the difference between how God sees people and how the media see people?**

Creative Prayer Idea

▶ *NO PREP*

David Becomes King

Children will reveal their hearts to God.

Supplies: none

Time: 5 to 10 minutes

Preparation: none

Have kids stand as tall as they can. PRAY: **Dear God, we might be tempted to focus on how people look on the outside—tall, strong, and talented.**

Have kids crouch.

PRAY: **You look at our hearts and how much we love you. Thank you! It's the inside that counts!**

Have kids stand tall again.

PRAY: **Help us love you with our whole hearts, just as David did. Amen.**

notes

Object Lesson

▶ *PREPARE IN ADVANCE*

▶ *ALLERGY ALERT*

On the Inside

Children will learn that outsides don't always match insides.

Supplies: Bible, caramel apple for each child, red onion, caramel, wet wipes

Time: 10 to 15 minutes

Preparation: Cover the red onion with caramel to look like a caramel apple.

Give each child a caramel apple, and give the caramel onion to a child with a good sense of humor. Have children stand in a circle.

SAY: **I've brought a treat for you to enjoy today. Let's eat!**

Have kids bite into their snacks. Watch to see the reaction of the child who has the caramel onion. After the commotion has cleared, give that child a real caramel apple. Then

ASK:

- **How was the outside of the caramel onion similar to or different from the caramel apples? How about the inside?**

Read aloud 1 Samuel 16:7.

ASK:

- **How are people sometimes great on the outside but not so great on the inside?**
- **How are people sometimes not very appealing on the outside but really great on the inside?**
- **How can you discover what's on the inside of a person?**

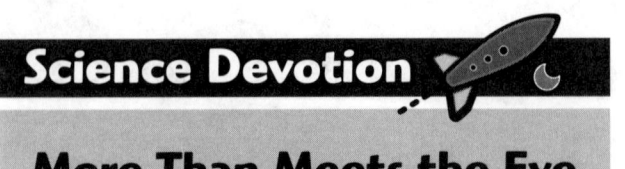

Science Devotion

More Than Meets the Eye

Children will understand that God sees what's in our hearts.

Supplies: Bible, newspaper, black felt-tip pens with water-soluble ink, cone-shaped coffee filters, small clear plastic cups, pitcher of water

Time: 10 to 15 minutes

Preparation: Spread newspaper on a table or on the floor.

Have kids gather around the newspaper. Read aloud 1 Samuel 16:7 and SAY: **Let's try to understand this verse.** Hold up a felt-tip pen and

ASK:

- **What color is this pen? Are you sure?**
- **Does everyone agree that the pen is black?**

Give each child a coffee filter, a plastic cup, and a felt-tip pen. Pour about ½ inch of water in each child's cup. Have each child draw a stick figure about 1 inch tall near the bottom edge of the large side of the coffee filter. Then have kids place their filters in their cups with the tips pointing up.

SAY: **Let's pretend that putting our stick figures into the water is like God looking at us to see what we're like.**

Wait until the colors begin to separate. SAY: **The scientific word for the water climbing up the filter is *adhesion*. This means the water is being pulled up the filter when, normally, gravity would make the water fall down.**

ASK:

- **What do you notice about your black stick figure?**
- **How many different colors do you see?**

SAY: **When you try to get to know someone, you can see only what's on the outside. It's like when you looked at your stick figure: All you could see was one color. But God looks in your heart and sees everything.**

Preschool Story

▶ *PREPARE IN ADVANCE*

Bible Point: ▷ **GOD SEES OUR HEARTS.**

Supplies: Bible, magazines, scissors, paper crown

Time: 15 to 20 minutes

Preparation: Cut from magazines seven pictures of young men and one picture of a younger boy.

The Smallest One

Have kids form a circle and sit down. Open your Bible to 1 Samuel 16, and show children the words. Give each of the magazine pictures to a child—give the youngest boy's picture to the youngest child in your class. Have students say the CHILDREN lines below at the appropriate times.

SAY: **It was Samuel's job to lead the people. The Lord said to Samuel, "I have chosen a new king. Go to the home of Jesse. He has eight sons. I'll show you which of his sons I have chosen to be the king."** *(Hold up the crown.)*

Samuel went to Jesse's house. He saw the first son. While this young man walked by *(have a child hold up the first picture)*, **Samuel thought, "Wow! This young man must surely be the king. He is tall and handsome."**

CHILDREN: No. God has not chosen him!

SAY: **God said, "He may be handsome, smart, and tall, but his love for me is just too small."**

A second young man walked by. *(Have a child hold up another picture.)* **Samuel thought, "This young man must surely be the king. He is tall and handsome."**

CHILDREN: No. God has not chosen him!

SAY: **God said, "He may be handsome, smart, and tall, but his love for me is just too small."**

A third young man walked by. *(Have a child hold up another picture.)* **Samuel thought, "This young man must surely be the king. He is tall and handsome."**

CHILDREN: No. God has not chosen him!

SAY: **God said, "He may be handsome, smart, and tall, but his love for me is just too small."**

A fourth, fifth, sixth, and seventh young man walked by. *(Have children hold up each picture.)* **Each time Samuel thought, "This young man must surely be the king. He is tall and handsome."**

CHILDREN: No. God has not chosen him!

SAY: **Each time God said, "He may be handsome, smart, and tall, but his love for me is just too small."**

Samuel asked Jesse, "Are these all the sons you have?"

Jesse said, "Well, there's one more. But he's little, and he's busy watching the sheep."

Samuel said, "Go and get him." *(Have the child with the young boy's picture stand up.)*

Samuel said, "Yes. This is David. He'll be the king. He loves the Lord with all his heart. *(Put the crown on "David's" head.)*

▷ **GOD SEES OUR HEARTS, big or small, young or old, short or tall.**

ASK:

- ◆ **Why did God choose little David to be king?**
- ◆ **What do you want God to see in your heart?**

notes

BIBLE STORY

David and Goliath

For the Leader

First Samuel 17 tells us that Goliath was tall—at least 9 feet tall.

Assuming you don't have anyone that height to introduce, consider leaning a board that length against a wall. On the board mark the heights of several professional basketball players and the height of Robert Wadlow, the world's tallest man (8 feet 11.1 inches).

Goliath's spearhead was heavy—estimated at about 15 pounds. So provide a 15-pound bucket of stones for children to attempt to hold at arm's length.

These tactile reminders of Goliath's size will help connect the Bible story to your children's experience.

Key Scriptures

1 Samuel 17:45-51

Romans 12:10

Romans 14:13

Romans 16:16

Ephesians 4:32

Bible Verse

"I come to you in the name of the Lord of Heaven's Armies" (1 Samuel 17:45).

Bible Experience

Bible Point: ▷ **GOD GIVES US STRENGTH.**

Children will act out a skit and learn about God's strength in David's life.

Time: 15 to 20 minutes

In this Bible experience, you'll engage children in the Bible story through a skit and through debriefing questions that help children discover that ▷ **GOD GIVES US STRENGTH.**

Cast the following characters: David, King Saul, Eliab, Goliath, Lion, Bear, Guard 1, Guard 2, Guard 3, Taunting Philistines, Shivering Israelites. If you have fewer than 11 children, cast the roles in the order above. One child can, if necessary, play the part of the Lion, Bear, Taunting Philistines, and Shivering Israelites. Your goal: Get everyone involved!

Goliath Meets a Rock

Scene: David comes to Israel's camp and defeats Goliath.

Props: You'll need an adult, a full-length coat, and a strong nonfolding chair. You'll also need to make a harp, sword, and slingshot from cardboard.

David: *(Strums cardboard harp and sings to the tune of "Heigh-Ho" from* Snow White and the Seven Dwarfs.*)* Heigh-ho, heigh-ho, it's off to camp I go—to bring some mail and wish them well, heigh-ho, heigh-ho...

Eliab: *(In hiding)* Who goes there?

David: It is I, David the shepherd boy, coming to bring my brothers chocolate chip cookies and news from home.

Eliab: Little bro! *(Hugs David.)* How's the family?

David: Fine, Eliab. *(Wiggles eyebrows.)* Cindy Lou says hi.

Eliab: *(Digs his foot in the ground and looks bashful.)* Aw, shucks, tell her hi, too.

David: What's the news at camp? Are we beating the Philistines?

Eliab: No, the battle isn't going well. In fact, it's not going at all. It seems we have a little... well...a *big* problem.

David: What's too big for God?

Eliab: I don't think you understand the situation.

David: I understand God is strong. What could be stronger than God?

Eliab: It's almost time...you'll see.

Goliath: *(Stands on chair, wearing long coat that covers the chair, adding to the appearance of Goliath's height. Holds the cardboard sword. Shouts in a deep voice.)* Fe fi fo fum! I smell the blood of a Hebrew man. If he can fight me, let him come. Fe fi fo fum!

David: So who's going to fight him?

Guard 1: *(Quakes.)* Not I.

Guard 2: *(Quakes.)* Not I.

Guard 3: *(Quakes.)* Not I.

David: Then I'll do it myself! Take me to the king!

Eliab: *(Scoffing)* Right—like he'll let you fight Goliath. You're just a kid! Did you see the size of that giant? He's a lean, mean, fighting machine! *(Takes David to King Saul.)*

David: *(Stands at attention.)* I know I'm just a kid, sir. I tend my father's sheep. But God gave me the strength to...

Lion: *(Springs at David; David drops him with a fake karate chop.)*

David: I killed a lion. And God gave me the strength to...

Bear: Growl! *(Stands on hind feet and attacks David; David drops him with another martial arts move.)*

David: And a bear. *(Wipes the sweat off his brow.)* If I can kill a lion and a bear, I know God will give me strength to kill that giant.

King Saul: Here's my armor and sword!

David: *(Tries to lift sword, but it's too heavy. Pulls slingshot out of back pocket.)* Thanks, King. But if you don't mind, I'll use this instead.

Goliath: *(In deep voice)* Fe fi fo fum! I smell the blood of a Hebrew man. If he can fight me, let him come. Fe fi fo fum! I'm waiting! *(Taunting)* Are you men, or are you mice?

Taunting Philistines: *(Waving)* Yeah! Come on out! Are you men, or are you mice?

Shivering Israelites: *(Cowering)* Send over some cheese!

David: *(Pretends to pick up stones.)* Prepare to die, you large and very nasty person!

Goliath: Ha! Why, if it isn't an itsy-bitsy slingshot...carried by an itsy-bitsy little boy. *(Grinds his fist into his palm.)* I'll make mincemeat out of you, boy!

David: *(Shouts)* You come to me using a sword, a spear, and a javelin, but I come to you in the name of the Lord All-Powerful, the God of the armies of Israel! The battle is the Lord's!

Goliath: *(Taunting)* Like I'm scared! Na-na, na-na-na!

David: *(Pretends to sling stone at Goliath.)*

Goliath: *(Grabs forehead, carefully jumps off chair, staggers a few steps, and falls down.)*

David: *(Raises arms in victory.)* The victory is the Lord's!

SAY: **Great job, actors! Give yourselves a hand!**

You know, David understood that he was able to kill Goliath not just because he was good with a slingshot. He was able to do it because God gave David strength. ▷ GOD GIVES US STRENGTH, too!

The first time David fought wasn't with Goliath. God had put David in situations where the young man could practice with his slingshot. He'd fought a lion and a bear, and he'd won. He'd obviously also "fought" lots of times with targets as he perfected his aim with his slingshot.

But facing Goliath took concentration, confidence, and strength that David didn't have on his own. It took God's strength!

Ask children to form pairs and discuss:

- ◆ **What's something you've done that was really, really hard to do?**
- ◆ **How did preparing before you did that hard thing help you accomplish it?**
- ◆ **What's a situation in your life where you could see God's strength working through or in you?**

SAY: **Our God is strong! His name is powerful, and so is his love. As David said, "I come to you in the name of the Lord All-Powerful."**

One last question for you to talk over with your partner:

- ◆ **What's something hard you have to do? How can God's strength help you accomplish it?**

Song & Connect

Use "The Battle Is the Lord's" (track 2, *it: Innovative Tools for Children's Ministry: Old Testament* CD) to help reinforce the Bible Point, ▷ **GOD GIVES US STRENGTH.**

This is a wonderful song for marching. Consider singing it twice and marching during the second round!

Additional Topics List

This lesson can be used to help children discover... Courage, God's Power, Trust, and Faithfulness.

notes

Game

▶ *PREP IN ADVANCE*

Small and Mighty

Kids will toss soft "stones" at a high target to get an idea of what David's battle with Goliath might have been like.

Supplies: Bible, paper plate, newspapers, masking tape, trash bags

Time: 5 to 10 minutes

Preparation: Use tape to mount the paper plate on a wall. For younger kids, place the plate at eye level; for older children, mount it about 9 feet off the floor. Use masking tape to mark a line about 15 feet away from the wall for the kids to stand behind. Note: As kids play the game, vary the line's position to make it closer to or farther from the wall to decrease or increase the difficulty.

Open your Bible to 1 Samuel 17, and briefly summarize the story of David and Goliath. Then let kids have some target practice. Demonstrate how to wad up newspaper pages into "stones," stand behind the line, and throw the paper at the target.

SAY: **OK! Now it's your turn to make your stones and throw them at the target. Pretend you're David aiming for Goliath's forehead.**

Have all the kids line up and fire their stones at the paper plate at the same time. (If you let kids go one at a time, at least one child will move at a snail's pace and frustrate the other children.)

At the end of the game, have kids sweep the stones into a pile and form a circle around it.

Hold a trash bag. As kids answer the following questions, have them toss the newspaper "stones" into the bag. ASK:

- **What was it like for you to throw paper stones at the paper Goliath?**
- **How did God help David beat Goliath?**
- **How does God give you strength in your daily life?**

Lead children in a brief prayer thanking God for giving David strength and giving us strength, too.

Craft

▶ *PREP IN ADVANCE*

Stop-Action Goliath Slaying

Kids will put themselves in the place of David during his encounter with Goliath.

Supplies: Bible, index cards, fine-tipped markers, string, hole punch

Time: 10 to 15 minutes

Preparation: Create a sample of the craft to show children.

Read 1 Samuel 17:45-51 aloud.

SAY: **Consider how this must have looked to David. He's looking up at a 9-foot giant who's wearing armor and carrying a 15-pound spear. And the giant is definitely *not* happy.**

Hold up the sample you created, and then continue.

SAY: **We're going to create a "Stop-Action Goliath Slaying" comic by showing the story from David's point of view. Each of you will**

receive 10 cards. You can use all of them or fewer—it's up to you.

On the first card, draw Goliath from David's perspective. David would be looking up at the giant. Then use the rest of the cards to sketch what David would have seen as he placed a rock in his sling, drew a bead on Goliath, and smacked Goliath with a rock. Goliath then fell, and David beheaded the giant. You can show that in as much or as little detail as you wish.

Don't worry if you're not a great artist. You'll have just eight minutes to create your cards, so make sure you draw quickly.

When you've finished, put your cards in order. Then punch a hole in the left upper and lower corners of your completed stack. Tie string through each hole. Then flip through the pages, and watch the action develop.

Once you've done that, exchange your cards with someone else so you can see a different version of the same event.

Bible Application

▶ *NO PREP*

You Want Me to *What?*

Children will depend on God to give them strength to apply biblical teaching.

Supplies: Bibles

Time: about 5 minutes

Preparation: none

Ask your children to form pairs.

SAY: **God gives us strength to do what God wants done in the world. He'll use us to do great things so long as we let him lead us. That means we have to be willing to go where he sends us and do what he tells us to do. We won't always be comfortable, and we have to try new things.**

We're going to practice that right now!

In a moment I'm going to ask volunteers to read aloud some verses and then ask you to do things based on those verses. Some of what I ask you to do may make you feel uncomfortable. If you're *way* too uncomfortable to do what I ask, that's OK—but please stretch. Give these activities a try.

Ask a volunteer to read Romans 12:10 aloud.

SAY: **I want you to honor your partner by shaking your partner's hand and then applauding for your partner. God gives us strength to honor others!**

Ask a volunteer to read Romans 14:13 aloud.

SAY: **Please look your partner in the eye and say, "God loves you just as you are. I accept you, too." And no laughing! God gives us strength to accept others!**

Ask a volunteer to read Ephesians 4:32 aloud.

SAY: **We need to forgive others. Turn to your partner, and if there's anything you need to forgive, do so now. God gives us strength to forgive others!**

Ask a volunteer to read Romans 16:16 aloud.

SAY: **Give your partner a high five and say, "You've been greeted!"**

Creative Prayer Idea

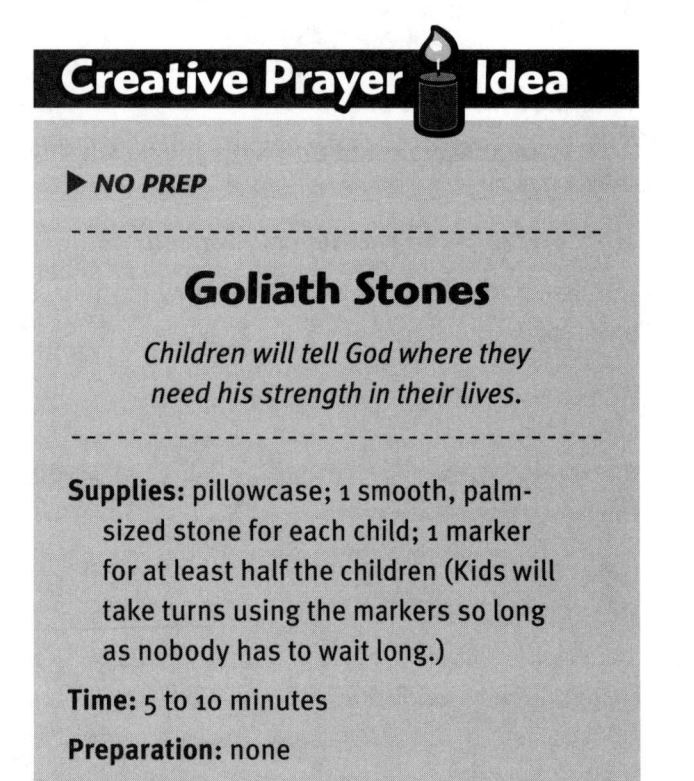

▶ ***NO PREP***

Goliath Stones

Children will tell God where they need his strength in their lives.

Supplies: pillowcase; 1 smooth, palm-sized stone for each child; 1 marker for at least half the children (Kids will take turns using the markers so long as nobody has to wait long.)

Time: 5 to 10 minutes

Preparation: none

Distribute one stone to each child, and make markers available.

SAY: **God gave David strength when he had to go face a giant. We have "giants" we're facing, too.**

Maybe something at school frightens us. Or something at home. Or a bully who hangs out halfway between school and home. Whatever we have to do, God can give us wisdom to tackle the problem the right way and strength to see it through.

On your stone, write one or more "Goliaths" in your life. Just a word or two describing each is fine. We'll take a few moments to quietly write—and share markers—and then I'll ask you to do something with your stone. I won't ask you to share what you wrote with anyone, so you can be completely honest. Even I won't read what you wrote.

After children write on their stones, ask kids to set aside the markers and form a circle around where you've placed the pillowcase. Lead children in sentence prayers, asking God for the strength to do what he wants us to do and to overcome the giants in our lives. As children pray, ask them to place their stones in the pillowcase.

After your meeting, dispose of the stones by burying them or tossing them into running water where they won't be seen.

Discussion Launcher

Goliath's Point of View

For this activity you'll need a sturdy stepladder and an adult or teenage spotter for every 10 children.

Let children go up the ladder until they're viewing the room from about 9½ feet in the air. Tell kids this is how Goliath looked at the world and specifically at David.

After children have looked at each other from 9½ feet in the air, have children form trios and discuss:

- **Why do you think Goliath didn't fear David?**
- **How might Goliath's jeering have changed if Goliath knew God was helping David?**
- **In what ways do you feel like David in your own life?**

notes

Movie Clip

The Big Green

Movie Title: *The Big Green* (PG)

Start Time: 1 hour, 30 minutes, 45 seconds

Where to Begin: The coach is announcing with a megaphone that his son will play the final part of the soccer game.

Where to End: The Big Green team wins the final championship, and the crowd erupts.

Plot: A team of soccer misfits become local heroes when the goalie gathers his strength and blocks the goal, and the smallest boy on the team scores a goal to win the game.

Review: The crowd didn't think the two boys could defeat their opponent, but the small boys found the strength to win the game. In 1 Samuel 17, David faced a similar problem when he fought Goliath. Despite his size and age, David trusted God and God's strength and was victorious.

Discussion

After setting up the clip and showing it, SAY: **David had to do something that seemed impossible. He fought a giant named Goliath whom many people were afraid of. David knew that God would be with him, and when God is with us, we can do things that are hard to do.**

Our impossible situations aren't impossible for God. God can solve them!

Turn to a neighbor and discuss:

- **What's something that seems hard to do that you need to do?**
- **In what ways could God help you do what's hard?**
- **How can your partner pray for you?**

Close by leading children as they pray in their pairs for each other.

Preschool Story

▶ ***PREP IN ADVANCE***

Bible Point: **GOD GIVES US STRENGTH.**

Supplies: Bible, 5 pieces of paper per child, transparency, overhead projector, marker, 1 paper bag per child, pillows or cotton fiberfill

Time: 15 to 20 minutes

Preparation: Draw a picture of a man on a transparency sheet. Shine the overhead projector against a blank wall and adjust it so that the man is as tall as your ceiling—this is "Goliath." Put several pillows or bunches of cotton fiberfill in one corner of your room opposite of Goliath—these are David's "sheep." Near the sheep, scatter several wadded up pieces of paper (you will need five for each child)—these are the "stones" that David picked up.

The Big, Mean, Scary Giant

Have all the children form a circle and sit down. Open your Bible to 1 Samuel 17, and show children the words.

Tell children that when you say the name *Goliath*, they should stand up on their tiptoes and use deep voices to say, "I'm big and mean and scary," and when you say, "Israelite soldiers," they should shake their heads and wave their arms as they say, "Oh no, Goliath is too big and mean and scary." Tell kids that when you say the name "David," they should point to the sky and say, ▷ **"GOD GIVES ME STRENGTH."** Practice this with the children several times before you begin your story.

SAY: **The Israelites were fighting a war with the bad Philistines. But God told the Israelites that he would help them win against the bad Philistines. There was just one *big* problem—Goliath!** Lead kids in standing on their tiptoes and saying, "I'm big and mean and scary." **Goliath** ["I'm big and mean and scary"] **was a giant Philistine; in fact, he was 1, 2, 3, 4, 5, 6, 7, 8, *9* feet tall! That's really tall!** Turn on the overhead projector and point to the giant Goliath on the wall. **Goliath** ["I'm big and mean and scary"] **was taller than any of the other soldiers. He had a huge pointy spear, a strong helmet, and a sharp sword. He wore armor and carried a giant shield that was bigger than you are. And Goliath** ["I'm big and mean and scary"] **was really, really mean! He wanted to fight one of the Israelite soldiers.** Lead kids in shaking their heads and waving their hands as they say, "Oh no, Goliath is too big and mean and scary!" **Goliath** ["I'm big and mean and scary"] **stood up tall and shouted in his big, scary voice, "Choose a man to fight me! Come on, just try and fight me!" But all the Israelite soldiers** ["Oh no, Goliath is too big and mean and scary"] **were so scared of the giant that they ran away and hid.** Cover your face and encourage kids to cover their faces as well.

Let's go see what David is up to. Lead kids in pointing to the sky and saying, ▷ **"GOD GIVES ME STRENGTH."** Encourage children to follow you to the area where you set out the pillows or fiberfill sheep. Let kids pet the sheep as you continue with the story. **David** ▷ ["GOD GIVES ME STRENGTH"] **was still just a little boy, and he was taking care of the sheep. But when he heard the news that none of the Israelite soldiers** ["Oh no, Goliath is too big and mean and scary"] **would fight the giant, he decided that he would fight the giant. David** ▷ ["GOD GIVES ME STRENGTH"] **said, "You come against me with your spear and sword. But there is nothing for me to fear because I have the strength of the Lord!"**

Give children each a paper bag, and encourage them to pick up five of the paper stones that you set out. SAY: **David** ▷ ["GOD GIVES ME STRENGTH"] **picked up one, two, three, four, five smooth stones. He marched over to Goliath** ["I'm big and mean and scary"]. Lead children in marching over to the image of Goliath on the wall. Tell children to get out one stone. **David** ▷ ["GOD GIVES ME STRENGTH"] **put one stone in his sling, and he swung it around and around. The stone came flying out of his sling and hit that big, mean giant right smack in the middle of his forehead!** Encourage children to throw their stones at the image of Goliath. **Goliath** ["I'm big and mean and scary"] **fell to the ground with a big boom.** Turn the transparency of Goliath sideways so it looks as if he's lying on the ground. Encourage kids to cheer and give each other hugs. **Goliath wasn't so big and mean and scary anymore. Little David** ▷ ["GOD GIVES ME STRENGTH"] **had trusted God to help him win against that big giant. And God had helped him. If we trust God, God will give us strength, too—just as God gave David strength.**

ASK:

- **Why wasn't David afraid of Goliath?**
- **How did God help David?**
- **How can you trust God to help you be strong?**

BIBLE STORY

Saul's Jealousy

For the Leader

After David killed Goliath, Saul was his number-one fan. He took David in and appointed him to a position of leadership in the army. But how quickly things changed.

When Saul heard the people of Israel praising David's accomplishments (and perhaps when he saw his own son's devotion to David), Saul's jealousy spread like a disease. He became so jealous of David that he tried to have him killed in battle. When this plan failed, he actually tried to pin David against the wall with a spear.

Saul suspected that David might take the throne of Israel. It's interesting that Saul thought he could kill David and usurp God's appointing. Although he didn't realize that David already had been anointed the next king of Israel, he should have known that he couldn't stop David from becoming king if God had appointed him.

Key Scriptures

1 Samuel 18:1-16

Proverbs 14:30

Bible Verse

"A peaceful heart leads to a healthy body; jealousy is like cancer in the bones" (Proverbs 14:30).

Bible Experience

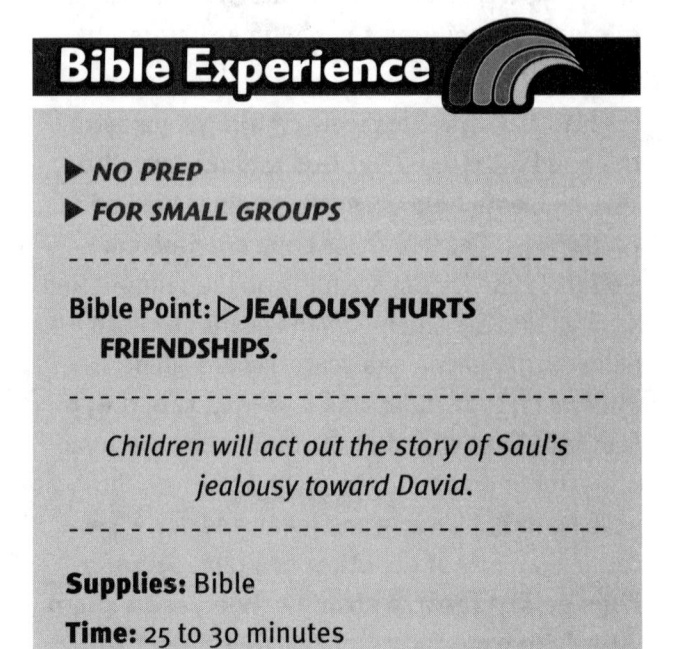

▶ *NO PREP*

▶ *FOR SMALL GROUPS*

Bible Point: ▷ **JEALOUSY HURTS FRIENDSHIPS.**

Children will act out the story of Saul's jealousy toward David.

Supplies: Bible

Time: 25 to 30 minutes

Preparation: none

SAY: **We're going to act out today's Bible story. I'll be the narrator, and I'll tell the story. You'll be the actors, and you'll act out what I say. Our story comes from 1 Samuel 18:1-16 in the Bible.**

Assign the roles of David, Saul, Jonathan, a group of women, and a group of soldiers. If you have enough kids, assign the roles of a harp, a spear, a wall, tambourines, Saul's throne, and other furnishings in Saul's palace. Read this story while kids act it out.

SAY: **After David defeated the giant, Goliath, David became friends with King Saul. Saul was so impressed with David that he brought David back to his palace with him and let him live**

there. David also became best friends with the king's son Jonathan.

Saul gave David some jobs to do. He sent him out to do the king's work. And everything David did, he did very well. Saul made David an important leader in his army. David led soldiers in battle. Everyone was happy because David was doing a great job.

But then it happened. As the army came back from battle, some women ran out to greet the soldiers and welcome them home. They sang and danced and shook their tambourines. They sang a song that said, "Saul has killed his thousands, and David his ten thousands."

Saul got really jealous and angry at David. He didn't like to hear people singing about what a great job David was doing. In fact, he became so jealous and angry that he tried to kill David. While Saul was sitting on his throne and David was playing his harp in the palace, Saul threw a spear at David. David got out of the way, and the spear hit the wall instead.

Then Saul thought of a new plan. He made David a leader over thousands of soldiers, and he sent him away to lead the soldiers into dangerous battles. He hoped David would get killed by Israel's enemies. But God protected David, and all the people loved him.

Congratulate kids on a job well done. Then

ASK:

◆ **Why was Saul jealous of David?**

◆ **What do you think happened to Saul's and David's friendship?**

◆ **What do you think happened to King Saul himself?**

Read aloud Proverbs 14:30, and then SAY: **This verse describes what happens when people become jealous. King Saul's jealousy destroyed his friendship with David, and it also destroyed him as a person. He was so jealous of David that he forgot to be the good king God wanted him to be. And eventually David became king.** ▷**JEALOUSY HURTS FRIENDSHIPS, and it also hurts people.**

Additional Topics List

This lesson can be used to help children discover... Desires, Forgiveness, Jealousy, Patience, Sin, and Wisdom.

Game

▶ ***HIGH ENERGY***

Field of Protection

Children will learn that God used David's best friend to protect David from Saul and that it's better to help than hurt others.

Supplies: none

Time: 15 to 20 minutes

Preparation: Find a large playing area.

Choose three volunteers—one to be "David," one to be "Jonathan," and one to be "Saul." Have the rest of the group be the field boundaries by forming a circle around David, standing about a foot apart, facing outward, and holding hands tightly. Jonathan and Saul should be on the outside of the circle.

SAY: **King Saul was jealous of David.** Point to your Saul and David volunteers. **God blessed David because David had a pure heart and was right with God, which is why Saul was jealous of him. But Saul's son Jonathan was David's**

best friend. Point to your Jonathan volunteer. **When David hid from Saul in a field, Jonathan protected him from King Saul.**

Explain that when you tell Saul and Jonathan "go," Saul will try to crawl under the hands of the kids in the circle to tag David but Jonathan will try to tag Saul. David needs to try to stay away from Saul inside the circle, but he can't leave the circle. Tell the kids in the circle to hold on tightly so Saul can't get to David.

The goal of the game is to protect David. When someone gets tagged, find new volunteers for each part and play the game again. Try to play enough times so each person has a turn to be David, Jonathan, or Saul.

After the game, ask students to discuss these questions:

- ◆ **What was it like to protect David during this game? Why?**
- ◆ **How did God protect David from Saul in real life?**
- ◆ **How does God protect us in our lives?**

SAY: **God protected David from Saul because God had a special plan for David. God has a special plan for our lives as well.**

notes

Craft

Joyful Noisemakers

Children will make instruments of praise like the ones David might have used.

Supplies: variety of boxes (shoe boxes, cereal boxes, tissue boxes), safety scissors, tempera paint, liquid soap, crayons, glitter, paper scraps, glue, rubber bands

Time: 20 to 30 minutes

Preparation: Mix a few teaspoons of liquid soap into your tempera paint. This will help it adhere to boxes with waxy surfaces.

Let each student choose a box. Have each one cut a 4-inch hole in the middle of one of the large sides of the box. Set out tempera paint, crayons, glitter, and paper scraps, and allow a few minutes for kids to decorate their boxes as they wish. Place the boxes in a sunny place to dry.

While boxes are drying, sing lively praise songs to set the stage for kids to celebrate with their own instruments.

When boxes have dried, distribute five rubber bands to each person. Show kids how to wrap the rubber bands around the boxes so they stretch across the holes. Demonstrate how to strum the instruments lightly to produce a twanging sound. Sing a few praise songs, encouraging kids to make joyful noises with their new instruments.

Bible Application

▶ *NO PREP*
▶ *FOR SMALL GROUPS*

A Jealous Mess

Children will draw pictures that symbolize jealousy's effects.

Supplies: paper, pencils, dry-erase board or newsprint, marker

Time: 15 to 20 minutes

Preparation: none

Give each child paper and a pencil. Set up a dry-erase board or newsprint. SAY: **I'm going to draw a picture, and I want you to copy what I'm drawing. I want to make sure you copy me exactly, so you aren't allowed to look at your paper. You must keep your eyes on my drawing as you draw.**

Draw a simple picture, such as a house or a stick-figure family. Be sure to pick up your marker several times to make the picture somewhat hard for kids to follow without looking at their papers.

Have several kids display their drawings, and then ASK:

- **Are you happy with your drawing? Why or why not?**
- **What might have made your drawing better?**
- **What was it like to keep your eyes on my drawing the whole time?**
- **How was this like or unlike what happens when we're jealous of others?**

SAY: **When we're jealous of other people, we look at what they have instead of the ways God has blessed us. And we often forget to be the kind of people God wants us to be. We're too busy watching other people!**

ASK:

- **How has jealousy affected your friendships?**
- **How can we get rid of jealousy in our friendships?**
- **How can God help you resist jealousy?**
- **How can thankfulness help you overcome jealousy?**

Have kids form pairs and share with partners one way they'll try to overcome jealousy this week, with God's help.

Creative Prayer Idea

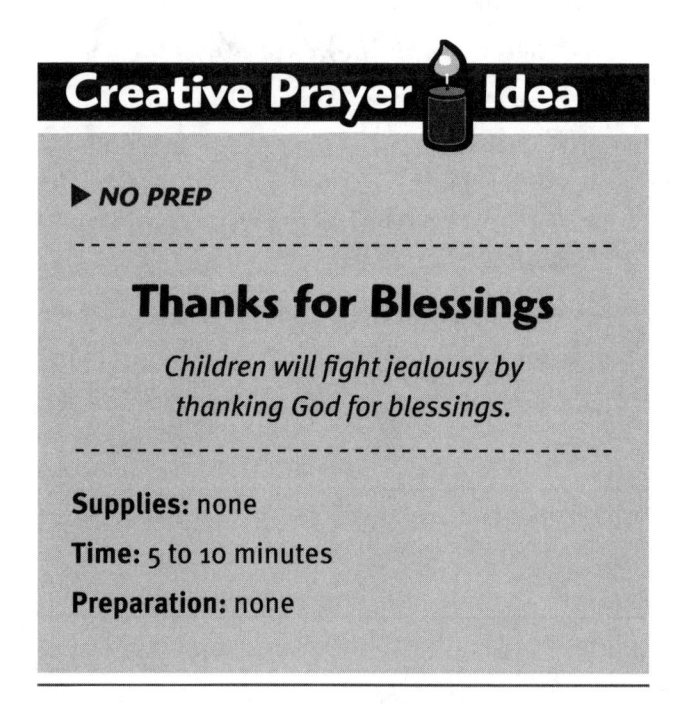

▶ *NO PREP*

Thanks for Blessings

Children will fight jealousy by thanking God for blessings.

Supplies: none

Time: 5 to 10 minutes

Preparation: none

Have kids form a circle and put their arms around each other. SAY: **One way to fight jealousy in our hearts is to keep our eyes on the ways God has blessed us. Let's pray, thanking God for some of the wonderful blessings in our lives. As we pray, let's keep our arms around each other to show that we want strong friendships without jealousy.**

PRAY: **Dear God, thank you for the many blessings you give us. Help us to remember these...** Pause for kids to call out blessings. **Please help us to keep our eyes on your blessings instead of being jealous of other people. And please help us to have strong friendships. Amen.**

Discussion Launcher

▶ *SMALL GROUPS*
▶ *NO PREP*

Ask children to form trios and discuss:

- **What kinds of things or situations make you jealous?**
- **Why is it so easy to become jealous of other people?**
- **Why does ▷ JEALOUSY HURT FRIENDSHIPS?**
- **Why does God want us to stop being jealous?**
- **How can we overcome jealousy?**

notes

Movie Clip

Ugly Jealousy

Movie Title: *Toy Story* (G)

Start Time: 0 hours, 17 minutes, 15 seconds

Where to Begin: Woody tells Bo Peep, "It's like they've never seen a new toy before."

Where to End: Woody glares at Buzz as the other toys crowd around him.

Plot: Andy has received a new toy for his birthday: Buzz Lightyear. Woody, who has always been Andy's favorite toy, is jealous.

Review: Jealousy got Woody and Buzz off to a bad start. They could have been great friends (and eventually they were), but Woody's jealousy prevented them from getting along at first. Jealousy does the same thing in our friendships.

Discussion

After setting up and showing the clip, SAY: **Jealousy kept Woody and Buzz from becoming friends right away. In real life, ▷ JEALOUSY HURTS FRIENDSHIPS.**

ASK:

- **Why is jealousy so harmful?**
- **Why is it so easy to become jealous?**
- **Why do you think God wants us to stay away from jealousy?**

SAY: **Just as Woody learned and David experienced, ▷ JEALOUSY HURTS FRIENDSHIPS. Let's celebrate the ways God blesses us and stay away from jealousy.**

Preschool Story

▶ *NO PREP*
▶ *ALLERGY ALERT*

Bible Point: **JEALOUSY HURTS FRIENDSHIPS.**

Supplies: Bible, variety of snacks

Time: 10 to 15 minutes

Preparation: none

Jealous Saul

Have kids form a circle and sit down against one wall of your classroom. Open your Bible to 1 Samuel 18, and show children the words. SAY: **After David killed Goliath, Saul and David became friends. David stayed with Saul and helped Saul fight battles. God blessed David and helped him win the battles. After a while Saul became jealous of all the wonderful things David was doing.**

ASK:

◆ **Have you ever been jealous of someone? Why?**

◆ **Why do you think it's wrong to be jealous?**

Pass out all the different snacks you brought. Wait to see if kids begin to complain about their snack or wish they had someone else's snack.

SAY: **I gave each of you a snack, and yet some of you are jealous of the snacks I gave to your friends.** Encourage kids to share their snacks with each other. **That's what happened with Saul and David. God had given Saul many wonderful things, but Saul was still jealous of the things God had given to David. Saul was so jealous that he started to get really mad. Saul got so mad that he wanted to hurt David!**

One day David was playing his harp for Saul. Let's all pretend we're playing a harp. Lead kids in pretending to play a harp. **Saul sneaked up on David and then threw a spear at him!** Lead kids in pretending to throw a spear. **God helped David escape from the spear.** Lead kids in ducking low and then running to the other side of the room.

After that day Saul was even more jealous of David because he knew that God was helping David. So Saul sent David far away to lead his soldiers. Lead children in marching to the other side of the room.

David was a very good soldier, and God helped him to win battles and lead the soldiers. But because of Saul's jealousy, David and Saul were never friends again. ▷ JEALOUSY HURTS FRIENDSHIPS.

ASK:

◆ **What can you do instead of being jealous?**

◆ **How can you love your friends?**

notes

BIBLE STORY

David and Jonathan

For the Leader

The book of 1 Samuel shows a sharp contrast between King Saul and his son Jonathan. Saul was obsessed with killing David because he could not accept the thought that the throne of Israel would pass to David rather than to Jonathan. Yet Jonathan himself seems to have been unconcerned about this reality. Not only was he best friends with David, but he also protected David from the king.

Jonathan was a loyal friend, even in the midst of what may have felt like a personal rejection from God. Instead of becoming jealous of David, Jonathan embraced God's choice and was a true friend.

Key Scriptures

1 Samuel 20:1-13, 18-42

Proverbs 17:17

Bible Verse

"A friend is always loyal, and a brother is born to help in time of need" (Proverbs 17:17).

Bible Experience

▶ *PREP IN ADVANCE*

▶ *FOR YOUNGER CHILDREN*

Bible Point: ▷ **FRIENDS ARE LOYAL.**

Children will consider what makes friends loyal.

Supplies: Bible, red poster board, paper, scissors

Time: 15 to 20 minutes

Preparation: Cut the poster board into a large heart, and cut hearts from the paper (one heart per sheet of paper per child).

SAY: **When young David beat the giant Goliath, the man who ruled over Israel at that time was King Saul. The king had a son, Jonathan, who became best friends with David. Jonathan and David were loyal friends.** Hold up the poster-board heart and SAY: **Hearts are a symbol of love. One way to show love is by being loyal—sticking by your friends no matter what.**

ASK:

◆ **In what ways do best friends show that they love each other?**

When children answer, hand each child a paper heart.

SAY: **Those are all great ways to show friends that you love them. I love all of you, so I'll give each of you a paper heart.** Hand out the rest of the paper hearts.

Another way friends show that they love

each other is by giving each other presents. I love presents!

Open the Bible to 1 Samuel 18, and point to it. SAY: **The Bible says that Jonathan gave his robe and sword to David. Think about it: Jonathan (who was a king's son) gave David (who was a servant) good presents! What a great way for friends to show that they love each other!** Have kids make heartbeat sounds by using one hand to hold the paper hearts on their chests and then patting them with the other hand.

Read aloud 1 Samuel 20:1-13, 18-42. Then SAY: **Another way Jonathan showed how much he loved David was by protecting him from his father, King Saul. King Saul wanted to hurt David because he was jealous of David. David was loved by the people of Israel more than Saul was. Jonathan was loyal and protected his friend David. Wow! What a great way for friends to show they love each other!** Make heartbeat sounds.

Read aloud Proverbs 17:17, and then ASK:

- **What does this verse say friends do for each other?**
- **How can we show our friends that we love them?**

SAY: **Let's show our friends here that we love them!** Ask children to hug someone close to them. Afterward, make heartbeat sounds. Ask kids to hug someone else, and then make heartbeat sounds. Finally, ask them to help someone sitting near them to stand up and then make heartbeat sounds.

Tell students to keep their paper hearts.

SAY: ▷ **FRIENDS ARE LOYAL. Each time you see your paper heart, pray for a friend. Ask God to help you love your friends and be loyal to them as Jonathan was to David.**

Additional Topics List

This lesson can be used to help children discover... Commitment, Forgiveness, Friendship, Love, Loyalty, and Support.

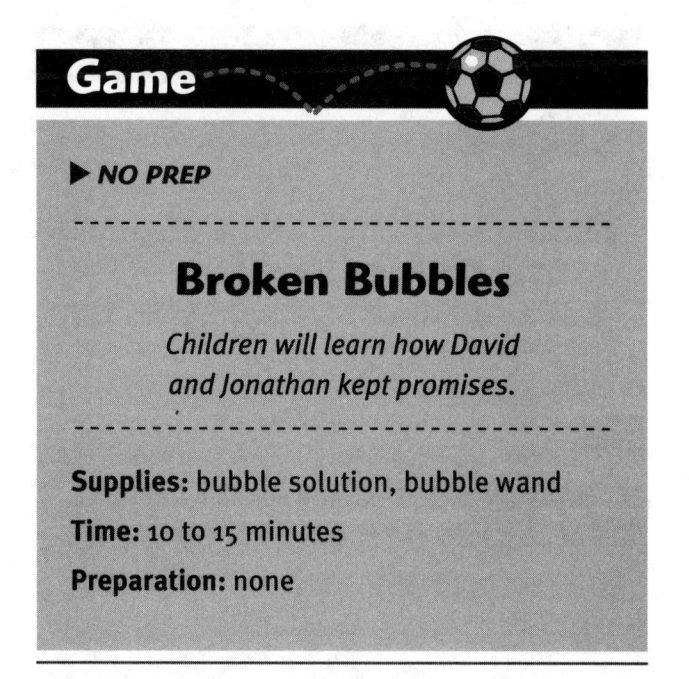

Game

▶ *NO PREP*

Broken Bubbles

Children will learn how David and Jonathan kept promises.

Supplies: bubble solution, bubble wand

Time: 10 to 15 minutes

Preparation: none

Have kids form two groups, and ask them to line up at opposite sides of the room, facing each other. Give the first person in one group a container of bubble solution and a bubble wand.

SAY: **This child will blow a bubble. Then** [he or she] **will blow the bubble across the room to the first person in the next line, give that person the bubble solution, and then stay on that side. The new person will blow the *same* bubble, if it still exists, back to the next person standing in line on the opposite side. Continue until everyone has blown the bubble and traded sides. It the bubble pops, blow a new one and keep going. Ready? Go!**

Play until everyone has had a turn to blow a bubble across the room. After the game, discuss the following questions:

- **What did you notice about the bubbles?**
- **What helped you successfully move the bubbles?**

◆ **In what ways do these bubbles remind you of promises?**

◆ **How can keeping promises show that we're loyal?**

Craft

▶ ***NO PREP***

Between You and Me

Children will make friendship bracelets to give away.

Supplies: various colors of cross-stitch floss in 12-inch strands, safety scissors, tape

Time: 30 to 45 minutes

Preparation: none

Explain that children will make friendship bracelets as reminders of the gifts Jonathan gave to David. Allow each student to choose six strands of cross-stitch floss, two of each color. Have students adjust strands so the ends line up evenly, and then tie a knot at one end. Be sure they leave a tail of 1½ inches at the end.

Instruct kids to tape the knotted end to the edge of a table. Lead them through the following instructions, helping those who are having trouble.

1. Arrange the two strands of color A together, the two strands of color B together, and the two strands of color C together.

2. Wrap the strands of color A over, and then under, color B. Pull down on color B as you tighten color A. Then wrap color A over and under color B and tighten.

3. Wrap color A over and under color C and tighten. Repeat.

4. Wrap color B over and under color C and tighten. Repeat. Wrap color B over and under color A and tighten. Repeat.

5. Wrap color C over and under color A and tighten. Wrap color C over and under color B and tighten. Repeat.

Have children continue in this sequence until the bracelets are the desired length, and then have them tie all the strands together. Have them trim and leave a 2- to 3-inch tail.

When students are tying their bracelets, have them state three characteristics they like about the person they're going to give the bracelet to. Children can also state how God has used their friend to bless them.

Bible Application

▶ ***NO PREP***

Friendship Commitment

Children will commit to developing friendship-building qualities.

Supplies: balloons, slips of paper, pencils

Time: about 45 minutes

Preparation: none

Give each person a balloon, a slip of paper, and a pencil. SAY: ▷ **FRIENDS ARE LOYAL. There are lots of other qualities of good friends. On your slip of paper, write one quality you want to develop or strengthen.**

Have kids each place their slip of paper inside their balloon, inflate the balloon, and tie it off. Tell kids to take the balloons home. SAY: **When your balloon loses its air, cut it open and read the paper as a reminder of your desire to improve a friendship-building quality.**

Close by having kids each say something positive to at least one person about that person's ability to be a friend.

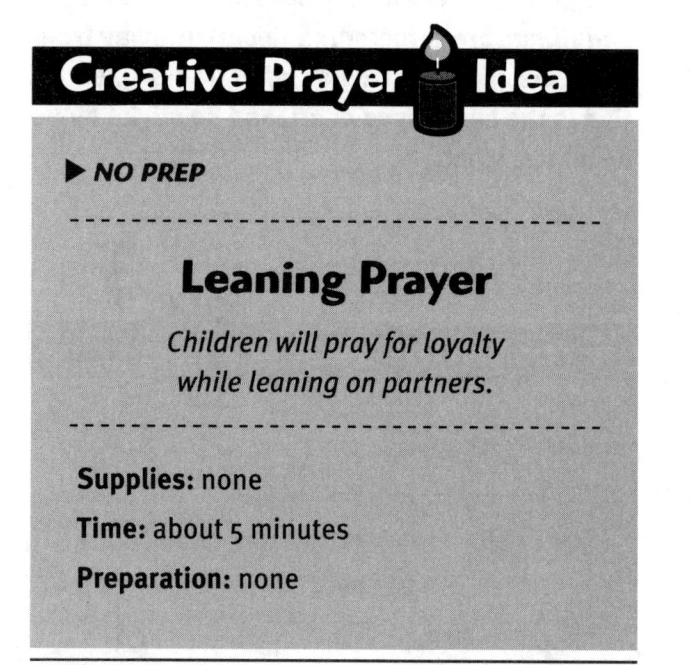

Creative Prayer Idea

▶ *NO PREP*

Leaning Prayer

Children will pray for loyalty while leaning on partners.

Supplies: none

Time: about 5 minutes

Preparation: none

One of the best ways children can learn to be loyal is through praying for one another's needs. During the prayer, have kids choose buddies to put their arms around and to gently lean on.

PRAY: **Dear Lord, thank you that we can always lean on you. As we lean on each other, help us remember to be loyal friends. Help us to remember to pray for each other and to be loyal. Amen.**

Discussion Launcher

▶ *NO PREP*
▶ *FOR SMALL GROUPS*

Sticking Together

Children will find someone to stick to and will consider how to be a better friend.

Supplies: 1 piece of Velcro (at least 1x1-inch, with a self-adhesive back) for every 2 people

Time: about 10 minutes

Preparation: none

Have kids count off by fours. Hand the Ones and Twos the top part of the Velcro and the Threes and Fours the bottom part of the Velcro. Tell kids to stick their Velcro on their hands, shoulders, knees, or feet.

SAY: **Don't take off your Velcro until the game is over. When I say go, the Ones will have two minutes to find all the Threes and stick together. The Twos will have two minutes to stick to the Fours. Go!**

After two minutes, call time. After kids get "unstuck," ASK:

- **How was this game like friendship?**
- **How can we be more loyal friends?**
- **What kinds of people make the best friends?**
- **How can you become a better friend?**

Science Devotion

▶ *NO PREP*

Friends Stick Together

Children will see that they should stick by their friends.

Supplies: 2 pieces of paper per child, pens, a few spray bottles full of water, various stackable plastic containers, paper plates, stackable plastic drinking glasses

Time: 10 to 15 minutes

Preparation: none

Give each child two pieces of paper and a pen and SAY: **I'd like you to draw pictures of some things a friend has done or said that made you angry.** Give kids a few minutes to do this, and then SAY: **See if you can get your two pieces of paper to stick together without folding them.** Pause. **It doesn't work, does it? Sometimes when a friend says or does mean things to us, we don't want to be that person's friend anymore.**

Give a few kids the spray bottles and SAY: **Now I'd like you to take turns spraying a little water on your pieces of paper. After you've done that, try to get them to stick together.** Give kids a few minutes to do this, and then invite them to repeat the experiment with the plastic containers, the plastic drinking glasses, or the paper plates.

ASK:

- **Why do you think these things stuck together when they were wet?**

SAY: **The molecules in water are very attracted to each other, so they stick together really well.**

ASK:

- **When have you had to stick by a friend?**
- **What are some things you could do to stick by a friend?**
- **What could happen if you don't stick by a friend?**

SAY: **When we stick by our friends even when bad things are threatening to pull us away from them, we show our friends what God is like. God is the best friend of all, and he sticks by us no matter what.**

Preschool Story

▶ *PREP IN ADVANCE*

Bible Point: ▷ FRIENDS ARE LOYAL.

Supplies: Bible, 3 foam cups per child, crayons, tape, yellow and brown construction paper, scissors, toothpicks

Time: 15 to 20 minutes

Preparation: Cut out a small crown for each child from yellow construction paper, and cut out a circular rock shape out of brown construction paper for each child.

The Smallest One

Have kids form a circle and sit down against a wall in your classroom. Open your Bible to 1 Samuel 20, and show children the words. Give each child three foam cups. Instruct kids to turn the cups upside down and make three puppets by drawing the following simple faces on the front: *mean* King Saul, *nice* Jonathan, and *nice* David. Be sure to make puppets for yourself. Have the children tape the yellow crown to King Saul, line their puppets up in front of them, and follow the actions of your puppets as you tell the Bible story.

<u>SAY</u>: **Jonathan was the son of King Saul.** Move "Jonathan" out in front of the other puppets. Lift up "King Saul," and then place him back down. **He liked being friends with David** (move "David" next to Jonathan), **and David liked being friends with Jonathan. Jonathan even gave David his special robe and his sword.** Move the puppets back into line. Then move King Saul forward.

King Saul grew jealous and began to hate David. Hold up King Saul, tilt him back and forth, and lead the children in saying the following line in an angry voice: **I don't like David! David must go!** Then set him back down.

Hold up Jonathan, tilt him back and forth, and lead the children in saying the following line: **But David is my friend.** Then set him back down.

Hold up King Saul and <u>SAY</u>: **As long as David is alive, people will want *him* to be king. I'm going to get rid of him.** Then set him down.

David trusted God, and God protected him. David went into a field and hid behind a rock so King Saul couldn't find him. Bring David out front, and lean the brown rock in front of David.

Jonathan knew where David was, and Jonathan wanted to help his friend. So Jonathan sneaked out of the palace to warn David that it was too dangerous to come back home because King Saul wanted to hurt David. Move Jonathan toward David.

Jonathan shot three arrows past the rock where David was hiding. Lead children in counting to three as you toss the three toothpicks past David. Then <u>SAY</u>: **The arrows were a signal that King Saul was still angry, and David needed to run away and not come back until King Saul had calmed down.**

David came out from behind the rock. Set the rock aside and <u>SAY</u>: **David bowed three times to Jonathan because he was the prince. They cried because they knew that David would stay away a long time.** Make the David puppet bow three times to the Jonathan puppet. Have the two puppets "hug" and pretend to cry as they say goodbye. **They promised to be friends forever!**

<u>ASK</u>:

- ◆ **How was Jonathan a loyal friend to David?**
- ◆ **How can you be a loyal friend?**

<u>SAY</u>: ▷ **FRIENDS ARE LOYAL to each other. God wants us to be loyal friends, just as David and Jonathan were loyal friends.**

n
o
t
e
s

BIBLE STORY

David Spares Saul

For the Leader

David showed great kindness and incredible restraint when he spared Saul's life as Saul slept in a cave. Saul was hunting for David, and he meant to kill David if he got the chance.

But David also showed true respect for God. Rather than seeing Saul merely as an enemy to be conquered or a threat to be neutralized, he still saw Saul as God's choice for king of Israel. And he knew it would be wrong to defy God's choice by killing Saul.

In fact, David felt guilty even for cutting off the hem of Saul's robe. This act held more significance than simply taking a souvenir. It was a symbolic way to show rebellion or disloyalty. By cutting off a piece of Saul's robe, he was insulting Saul and rejecting his authority.

Key Scriptures

1 Samuel 24:1-22

1 Samuel 26

Proverbs 17:17

Galatians 5:22-23

Bible Verse

"But the Holy Spirit produces this kind of fruit in our lives: love, joy, peace, patience, kindness, goodness, faithfulness, gentleness, and self-control" (Galatians 5:22-23).

Bible Experience

▶ ***NO PREP***

▶ ***FOR YOUNGER CHILDREN***

Bible Point: ▷ **GOD HELPS US TO BE KIND.**

Children will learn about David's kindness and want to be kind themselves.

Supplies: Bible, small piece of cloth with a ragged edge

Time: 15 to 20 minutes

Preparation: none

SAY: **It's not always easy to be kind to others.** Open your Bible to 1 Samuel 24 and SAY: **The Bible tells us in 1 Samuel 24 about King Saul, who was chasing David and trying to kill him. King Saul knew that God wanted David to be the next king. This made King Saul very angry. He was so angry that he wanted to get rid of David.**

David followed God and wanted to do what was right, even though he had to run away and hide to keep from being killed. At one point, David and the men who traveled with him hid in a cave. Let's pretend we're with David and his

men and huddle very close together. Squeeze everyone close together as if you were hiding. Begin talking softly, but still loud enough so children can hear you. **We'll have to whisper or talk very quietly so no one will know we're in here! David hid from King Saul in a cave.**

ASK:

- **What do you think it might have been like in the cave?**

SAY: **While King Saul was looking for David, King Saul went into the very same cave where David was hiding! Now we really have to be quiet! King Saul didn't know David was in the cave, but David and his men knew that King Saul was in the cave. Let's read what the men and David did.**

Read aloud 1 Samuel 24:4, and then SAY: **David sneaked up on King Saul and used his sword to cut off a small piece of King Saul's robe.** Hold up the cloth. **Even though he hadn't hurt Saul, David later felt bad for even cutting Saul's robe. After King Saul left the cave, David called to him and showed him the piece of cloth. King Saul knew that David could have killed him while he was in the cave but that David had spared his life. David knew it would be wrong to kill the king, even though the king was trying to kill David. David wanted to be kind. ▷ GOD HELPS US TO BE KIND, too.**

Read Galatians 5:22-23 aloud. ASK:

- **What does this verse say about kindness?**
- **Where does kindness come from?**

SAY: **David had the chance to kill King Saul and keep the king from chasing him. But God helped David to be kind. David cut off a small part of King Saul's robe but did not harm King Saul. ▷ GOD HELPS US TO BE KIND, too. Even when it's hard, let's remember David and be kind.**

Song & Connect

Use "Walk Humbly" (track 15, *it: Innovative Tools for Children's Ministry: Old Testament* CD) to help reinforce the Bible Point, ▷ **GOD HELPS US TO BE KIND.**

Additional Topics List

This lesson can be used to help children discover... Choices, Forgiveness, Goodness, Holy Spirit, and Mercy.

Game

▶ ***NO PREP***
▶ ***FOR YOUNGER CHILDREN***

Kindness Coins

Children will learn how to give and receive compliments.

Supplies: coins
Time: 10 to 15 minutes
Preparation: none

Give each child three coins. Have kids walk around the room and each say something kind to another person. The child who receives the comment will then "pay back" with a kind comment and a coin. Kids will continue playing until they have given away all their coins and received three new coins from others.

For the second part of the game, ask for a volunteer to be grouchy. Remind kids that we're instructed to be kind to others, even if they're unkind. Have the grouchy child approach each child, one at a time, and make a grouchy comment. Some examples are "Boy, what a yucky day! I hate the rain!" "This sandwich tastes horrible! I wish my mom would have made me a peanut butter sandwich instead!" or "Math is so boring!" When the grouchy child makes an unkind comment, the other child should respond by speaking kindly and giving the grouchy person a coin. After each child has a turn repaying the grouchy person with kind words, point out that the grouchy person is now "rich" with kind words. Then have the grouchy person end with a kind comment or kind act.

SAY: **Just as David was kind to King Saul, so ▷ GOD HELPS US TO BE KIND. And when we're kind, we really help other people feel good.**

Craft

▶ ***PREP IN ADVANCE***
▶ ***STUDENT LED***

Kindness Brings a Smile

Children will learn that being kind produces happiness.

Supplies: "Kindness Brings a Smile" handouts (p. 281), black and yellow crayons

Time: 5 to 10 minutes

Preparation: Photocopy one "Kindness Brings a Smile" handout (p. 281) for each child.

Give each child a copy of the handout "Kindness Brings a Smile." Instruct each child to use a black crayon to circle the pictures that show kids doing unkind things and to completely color over the picture with a black crayon. Next, have each child color in the rest of the large circle with the yellow crayon. When kids are finished, their pages will resemble smiling faces. SAY: **When we show kindness to others, it makes us happy and it makes others happy.**

Bible Application

▶ ***PREP IN ADVANCE***

David and Saul

Children will discuss what it means to be kind to others.

Supplies: Bible, newsprint, safety scissors, markers or crayons, construction paper, tape, glue

Time: about 15 minutes

Preparation: Cut out a paper "robe" using the newsprint.

Have children use markers or crayons to decorate the robe you cut out before class. Then tape the robe to the wall with the hem at floor level.

Read 1 Samuel 24:1-22. Then have each child sneak up quietly, as David sneaked up on Saul, and cut off a small piece from the bottom of the robe. Trace around each child's hand on construction paper. Then have them each glue their robe remnant to their outlined hand. Using an easy-to-understand translation, write the

Kindness Brings a Smile

words to 1 Samuel 24:11 on each child's sheet of construction paper. ASK:

- **Has anyone ever made you mad? Tell us about it.**
- **Did you ever want to hurt someone who hurt you?**

SAY: **King Saul wanted to hurt David. King Saul was an enemy to David, but David treated King Saul kindly.**

ASK:

- **Why does God want us to be kind to all people?**
- **How can we be kind to people who are mean to us?**
- **What will you do this week to be kind to someone when it's hard?**

Close in prayer, asking God for help to be kind to people when they're mean to us.

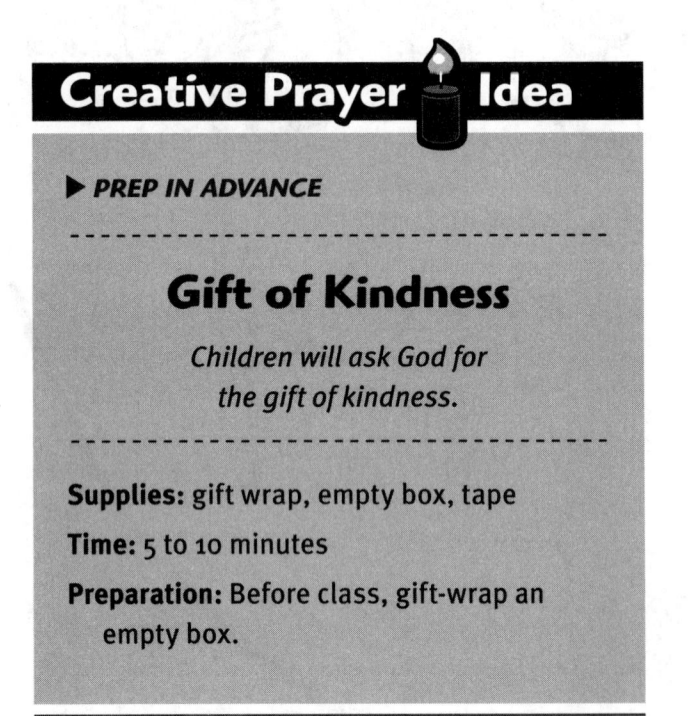

Creative Prayer Idea

▶ ***PREP IN ADVANCE***

Gift of Kindness

Children will ask God for the gift of kindness.

Supplies: gift wrap, empty box, tape

Time: 5 to 10 minutes

Preparation: Before class, gift-wrap an empty box.

Have children sit in a circle. Give one child the gift. Have that child pass the gift to the next person and say the prayer that follows. After praying, have that child suggest a way he or she will be kind this week and then pass the gift to the next person. Continue until each person has prayed.

PRAY: **Dear God, help me give the gift of kindness to others. Amen.**

Life Application

Application Ideas

Children will discover ways to be kind as they participate in these application activities.

Church Service

Have kids brainstorm a list of ways they could show kindness at church. Then work as a group to do some of the things on your list. They could wash car windows in the parking lot, empty the trash, bring treats to other classes, or play with kids in the nursery.

Mission: Kindness

Send kids out on a secret mission to show kindness throughout the week. Brainstorm some ideas, and then deploy kids as secret agents of kindness. Encourage them to find ways to show kindness without getting "caught." The following week, talk about what kids experienced and learned.

Kindness Challenge

Ask kids to think about specific enemies or people they have a hard time with. Then ask them to think of one way they could show kindness to those people during the following week. Set up accountability partners, and encourage kids to check in with one another to encourage each other to show kindness to enemies.

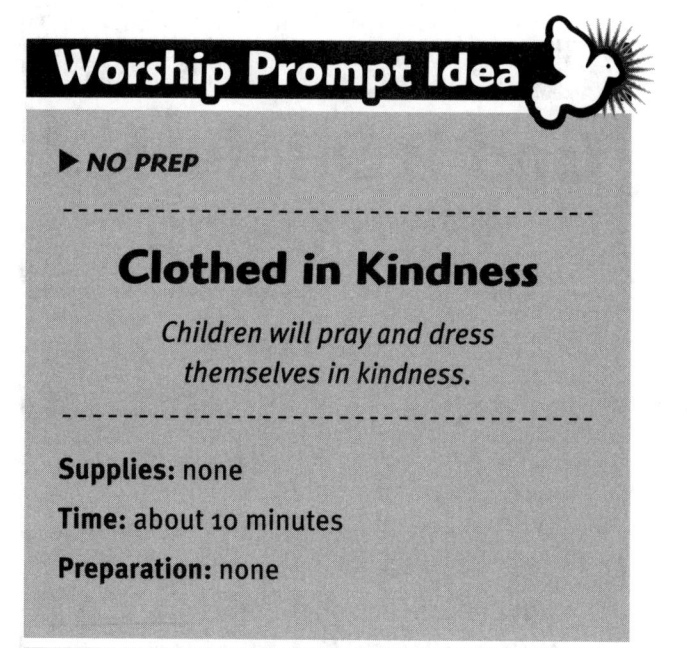

Worship Prompt Idea

▶ *NO PREP*

Clothed in Kindness

Children will pray and dress themselves in kindness.

Supplies: none

Time: about 10 minutes

Preparation: none

SAY: **Worshipping God is something we can do anytime, anywhere, any way. One way to worship God is to show kindness to others. One of the first things we do in the morning to get ready for the day is put on our clothes. Just as our clothes surround and cover our bodies, so kindness can surround us. God wants us to cover ourselves with kindness so we can show kindness to other people. Let's act out this prayer as we "dress ourselves" in kindness.**

Have kids repeat this prayer after you, line by line, pretending to put on each mentioned article of clothing.

PRAY:

Dear God,
My shirt goes right on top.
Let kind deeds never stop.
My pants help me be dressed.
God, help me act my best.
Here are socks for my feet.
Make my words sound sweet.
Last, I'll put on my shoes.
Kindness is what I choose.
Clothe me with kindness and love.
Thank you, God above.
Amen.

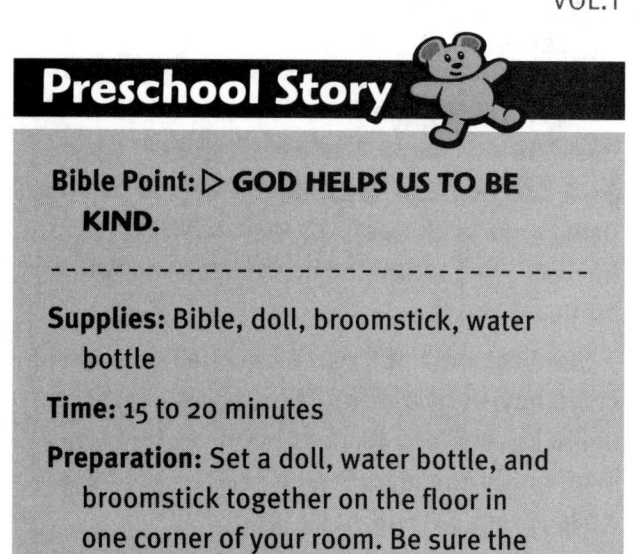

Preschool Story

Bible Point: ▷ **GOD HELPS US TO BE KIND.**

Supplies: Bible, doll, broomstick, water bottle

Time: 15 to 20 minutes

Preparation: Set a doll, water bottle, and broomstick together on the floor in one corner of your room. Be sure the doll is lying down.

The Way of Kindness

Have kids form a circle and sit down around the wall. Open your Bible to 1 Samuel 26, and show children the words. SAY: **King Saul wanted to hurt David. One night King Saul was sleeping in the middle of his army men with a big, long spear and a water jug next to his head.** Point to the doll with the broomstick and bottle of water next to it.

While everyone was sleeping, David and another man went to Saul's camp. Let's pretend to be David and sneak up on Saul. Shh! We have to be very, very quiet. We don't want any of Saul's army to hear us and wake up. Lead children in tiptoeing quietly up to the doll.

The other man wanted to take Saul's sword and hurt him. But David said, "Don't hurt Saul!" David took Saul's water jug and spear and went back to his hiding place. Encourage children to quietly pick up the broomstick and the water bottle and then tiptoe back to where you started.

David yelled from far away to a guard named Abner. David asked, "Abner, why didn't you guard the king?" Abner was scared. He knew he should have guarded the king better.

Saul heard David's voice and asked, "Is that David?" David answered, "Yes, it is." Saul told David he was sorry. David had not hurt King Saul because God had helped David to be kind. David gave back Saul's spear and water jug. Have children return the broomstick and water bottle.

Saul was one of David's enemies, and David could have hurt him while he was sleeping. But David knew that God wanted him to be kind—even to his enemies. ▷ GOD HELPS US TO BE KIND, just as David was kind.

After the story, lead children in singing the following song to the tune of "This Is the Way."

This is the way we're kind to others *(hug each other)*,
Kind to others *(hug each other)*,
Kind to others *(hug each other)*.
This is the way we're kind to others *(hug each other)*:
God helps us each day *(point to God)*.

Repeat the verse several times, changing the action each time. You might want to have kids pretend to share, shake hands, pat each other on the back, or give high fives. ASK:

- **Why didn't David hurt King Saul?**
- **How can God help you be kind to your friends?**

n

o

t

e

s

BIBLE STORY

God Is Displeased With David

For the Leader

After David sinned with Bathsheba and killed her husband, he may have thought he would get away with what he had done. As the king he had the power to cover up his actions and to cause people to look the other way.

But God was displeased with David, and he confronted David's sin through the prophet Nathan. It would have taken tremendous courage for Nathan to obey God and confront David's sin. David had already killed once to cover up his sin with Bathsheba. Nathan had every reason to believe David might kill him as well. But Nathan obeyed God and delivered God's message.

David did repent of his sin, and he proclaimed his remorse in Psalm 51, one of the most beautiful psalms of contrition ever written. His plea for cleansing is an example for us all who, like David, are sinners.

Key Scriptures

2 Samuel 12:1-14

Psalm 51:1-12

Bible Verse

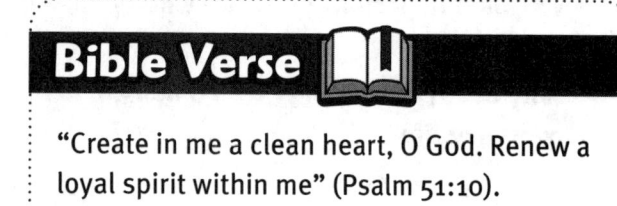

"Create in me a clean heart, O God. Renew a loyal spirit within me" (Psalm 51:10).

Bible Experience

▶ *NO PREP*

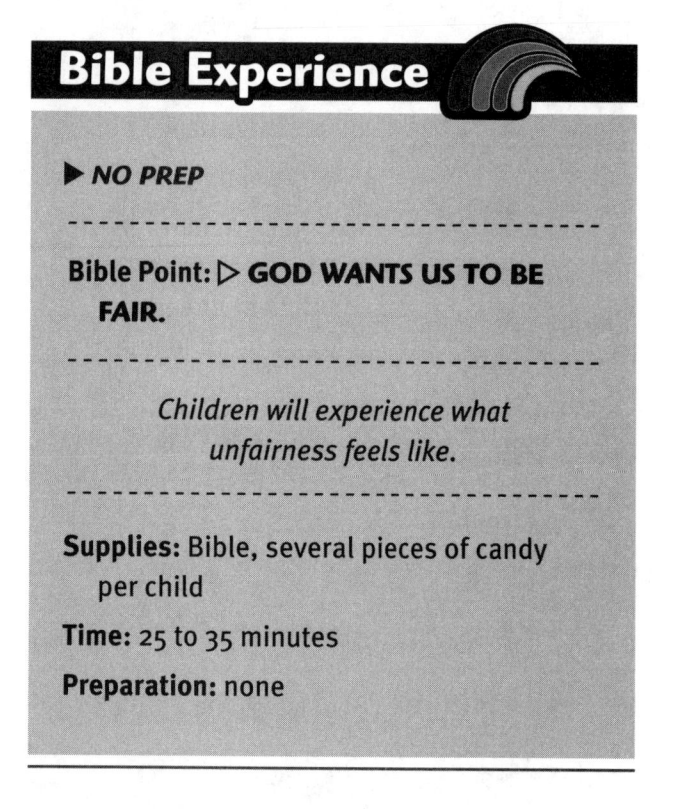

Bible Point: ▷ **GOD WANTS US TO BE FAIR.**

Children will experience what unfairness feels like.

Supplies: Bible, several pieces of candy per child

Time: 25 to 35 minutes

Preparation: none

Give each child a handful of candies. SAY: **The object of this game is to collect as many candies as you can. Tell someone else how many candies you want, such as, "I want three!" If the person has three or more candies, he or she has to give you three candies. If the person has less than three candies, he or she can keep them. But if the person has just one candy, he or she must give you the one piece of candy left in his or her hand and then sit down.**

Play this game for several minutes. Then collect and redistribute the candy.

ASK:

- **How did you feel when someone took away your candy?**
- **If someone who had a lot of candy took yours, how did you feel?**
- **How did you feel if you took someone's last piece of candy?**

Open your Bible to 2 Samuel 12:1-14, and show kids the passage. SAY: **Today's Bible story comes from 2 Samuel 12:1-14. It tells us about a time King David got into trouble because he decided to take another man's wife away from him. Even though he had a lot of things, David wanted something that belonged to someone else. So Nathan, a messenger from God, went to King David to tell him that what he had done was wrong and that God was going to punish him.**

ASK:

- **Why do you think David decided to take what wasn't his?**
- **How do you think God reacted to David's sin?**
- **What should David have done?**

Read aloud Psalm 51:1-12.

ASK:

- **Do you think David was sorry for what he did? Explain.**
- **What did David ask God to do for him?**
- **What do you want God to do for you when you confess your sin?**

SAY: ▷ **GOD WANTS US TO BE FAIR. David wasn't fair when he took another man's wife. When Nathan reminded David that what he had done was wrong, David realized he had done wrong, and he was very sad. He admitted his sins to God, and God forgave him. God will forgive us, too. And he will help us choose to be fair.**

Additional Topics List

This lesson can be used to help children discover... Fairness, Forgiveness, Holy Spirit, Justice, Mercy, and Repentance.

- ◆ **Why is it important to be fair when playing games?**
- ◆ **Why does ▷ GOD WANT US TO BE FAIR in everyday life?**

Game

▶ *PREP IN ADVANCE*
▶ *HIGH ENERGY*

Which Rules?

Children will play an unfair game.

Supplies: copies of the "Rules of the Game" handout (p. 287), balloons, scissors

Time: 10 to 15 minutes

Preparation: Blow up the balloons, and cut apart the sections on the handouts.

Give each child a copy of one section of the "Rules of the Game" handout. Make sure kids don't know that different handouts have different rules. Start the game by tossing several balloons into the air.

After a few minutes of frustration, stop the game and ASK:

- ◆ **What's difficult about this game?**
- ◆ **What would help?**

Play the game again, this time using only one set of rules. Then ASK:

- ◆ **How did the game change when we all played by the same rules?**

Craft

▶ *PREP IN ADVANCE*
▶ *FOR FAMILY MINISTRY*

Doorknob Reminders

Children will create reminders to be fair at home.

Supplies: felt or craft foam; scissors; paints or markers; decorating supplies, such as stickers, glitter, glue, and ribbon; yarn or cord

Time: 15 to 20 minutes

Preparation: Cut a 4x7-inch piece of felt or craft foam and a 12-inch length of yarn or cord for each child. Set out the other supplies.

SAY: **For many of us, it's hardest to be fair when we're at home with our families. Let's make something that will remind us to be fair at home.**

Give each child a piece of felt or craft foam. Allow kids to use paints or markers to write ▷ **"GOD WANTS US TO BE FAIR."** Encourage them to use the other supplies to add decorations. Then show them how to glue yarn or cord on the top corners to create a handle that will fit over a doorknob.

SAY: **Hang your doorknob hanger on the inside of your bedroom door. Every time you leave your room, it can remind you to be fair.**

Rules of the Game

- **Try to keep the balloons up in the air as long as possible.**
- **No one can hit a balloon two times in a row.**
- **After 10 hits, a balloon must touch the floor before the next hit.**
- **Have fun!**

Rules of the Game

- **Try to keep the balloons up in the air as long as possible.**
- **No one can hit a balloon more than three times in a row.**
- **After 15 hits, a balloon must touch the floor before the next hit.**
- **Have fun!**

Bible Application

▶ *NO PREP*

Acting Fair

Children will act out ways to be fair in real-life situations.

Supplies: none
Time: about 30 minutes
Preparation: none

SAY: **Let's think about ways we can be fair in real-life situations.**

Have kids form groups of four to six. Give each group a number. SAY: **I'm going to call out some real-life situations. With each one, I'll also call out a group number. If I call your group number, it will be your turn to show how you could be fair in that situation. Let's get started.**

Read the following scenarios one at a time, along with a group number:

- A friend is trying to cheat off of your paper during a test at school.
- Your teacher accuses you of cheating even though you didn't cheat.
- You see some kids at the park picking on a smaller kid.
- Your cousin wants to play with the new toy you got for your birthday.
- You broke your little brother's favorite toy truck.
- Your mom tells you to share your snack with your sister.

SAY: ▷ **GOD WANTS US TO BE FAIR. And God will help us make fair choices if we follow and obey him.**

Creative Prayer Idea

▶ *NO PREP*

Fairness Prayers

Children will pray a prayer of confession like David's.

Supplies: none
Time: 5 to 10 minutes
Preparation: none

SAY: **David prayed to tell God he was sorry for not being fair. We're going to pray a prayer like David's. In Psalm 51:10 we see the prayer David wrote to show that he was sorry for being unfair. It says, "Create in me a clean heart, O God. Renew a loyal spirit within me."** Let's pray that prayer. I'll say it aloud, and then I'll stop so you can whisper to a friend about one way you want God to help you be fair this week.

PRAY: **"Create in me a clean heart, O God. Renew a loyal spirit within me." Please forgive us for not being fair. Help us to be fair, even when it's hard. We need help when...** Pause for kids to whisper to friends. **Amen.**

notes

Movie Clip

Finding Nemo

Movie Title: *Finding Nemo* (G)

Start Time: 0 hours, 9 minutes, 15 seconds

Where to Begin: Nemo's teacher arrives, singing about the zones of the sea.

Where to End: After Marlin says, "You think you can do these things, but you just can't."

Plot: Nemo has arrived for his first day of school. Because of his "lucky fin," his dad (Marlin) is afraid he can't do what other kids can do. When Marlin learns that Nemo's class is headed toward the edge of the reef, he panics. He finds Nemo at the edge of the open water, where his friends are daring him to swim.

Review: Marlin was unfair in assuming that Nemo was about to disobey. Marlin also put unfair restrictions on Nemo. This frustrated Nemo and drove him to run away.

Discussion

SAY: **Marlin was pretty unfair when he accused Nemo of disobeying.**

ASK:

- **Why was Marlin so afraid to let Nemo do what other kids did?**
- **What should Marlin have done instead of yelling at Nemo?**
- **Why is it important to be fair?**

SAY: **Nemo grew angry and frustrated when his dad was unfair. ▷ GOD WANTS US TO BE FAIR and to treat other people the way God treats us. Being fair helps people instead of hurting them.**

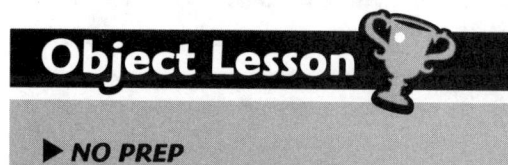

Object Lesson

▶ *NO PREP*
▶ *FOR SMALL GROUPS*

Fair Measurement

Children will compare a scale to being fair.

Supplies: any kind of scale, objects to weigh on the scale

Time: about 15 minutes

Preparation: none

Set out the scale where everyone can see it. SAY: **I've brought a scale with me today so we can practice using it to see how much some things weigh. What do you think this weighs?** Hold up one of the objects you brought. After kids have guessed, weigh the object on your scale and call out the weight. Then allow kids to guess how much the next item will weigh. Do this a few times, and then ASK:

- **How do scales help us?**
- **How did you decide what to guess for the weight of each object?**
- **What if the scale didn't always measure the same way?**
- **How is a scale like being fair in life?**

SAY: **Scales are helpful because they always measure the same way. They help us make comparisons between objects, and they help us understand what we should and shouldn't lift. They even help tell us how healthy we are. But if they didn't always measure the same way, we wouldn't know what to expect. It's the same way with being fair. When we're fair, people know they can count on us.**

Preschool Story

▶ ***NO PREP***

▶ ***ALLERGY ALERT***

Bible Point: ▷ **GOD WANTS US TO BE FAIR.**

Supplies: Bible, bag of cotton candy, 2 paper plates per 2 children

Time: 15 to 20 minutes

Preparation: none

A Sad Story

Have kids form a circle and sit down against a wall in your room. Open your Bible to 2 Samuel 12, and show children the words. SAY: **David was a wonderful king, but he made a bad choice and took something that belonged to another man. Nathan the prophet told King David a sweet but sad story to make the king understand that what King David had done was wrong. This is the story:**

Two men were neighbors. One was rich and one was poor. Set out two paper plates by each pair of children. **The rich man had many, many sheep.** Let the children each pull out some of the cotton candy and put several lumps onto one plate. **The rich man had a whole flock of sheep. But the poor man next door had nothing except one little lamb.** Have one child from each pair put one ball of cotton candy on the other plate. **He raised it from a baby.** Have the other child add more cotton candy to the lamb to make it grow. **His children loved their little lamb. Let's call the lamb Fluffy. Fluffy nibbled from the children's plates and licked milk from their fingers.** Let kids pretend that their lamb is licking their fingers. **Little Fluffy even slept in their arms.** Let kids pick up their cotton candy and make sheep noises—*baa*. **The children loved Fluffy, and Fluffy loved them.**

One day a traveler came to the rich man. He said to the rich man, "I'm hungry. Please cook me a meal of lamb stew."

The rich man said, "You can't have one of *my* sheep." And that rich man who owned all those sheep went next door. He stole Fluffy and gave it to the traveler. Have children put the one ball of cotton candy onto the plate with the many. **That was very mean! But Nathan used this story to show King David how he had also done wrong when he took something that didn't belong to him.**

Let kids snack on the leftover cotton candy. SAY: **God was mad at King David because David had stolen something that wasn't his. ▷ GOD WANTS US TO BE FAIR and to share the things we have.**

ASK:

◆ **Why was God upset with David?**

◆ **How can you choose to be fair with others?**

BIBLE STORY

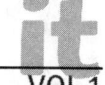

Solomon Asks for Wisdom

For the Leader

Solomon was about 20 years old when he became king of Israel. He knew he was inexperienced and in need of wisdom to rule well, as his father had done.

Solomon's humility and his request for wisdom may reflect the powerful legacy of his father, David. Solomon acknowledged that God had blessed his father because of David's faithfulness and righteousness. This recognition shows that Solomon understood the goodness of his father and presumably had been raised to honor God and seek God's ways. So Solomon asked for wisdom, and he received the promise of God's blessing, as his father had enjoyed.

Key Scriptures

1 Kings 3:1-15

Psalm 37:3

Bible Verse

"Trust in the Lord and do good" (Psalm 37:3).

Bible Experience

▶ ***PREPARE IN ADVANCE***

▶ ***ALLERGY ALERT***

Bible Point: ▷ **LET'S MAKE GOOD CHOICES.**

Children will learn that they can ask God for wisdom.

Supplies: Bible; cordless phone, cell phone, or phone on an extension cord; cookies

Time: 15 to 20 minutes

Preparation: Arrange to call your custodian during the lesson.

SAY: **I brought some cookies for us to enjoy today! But we'd better ask permission from our custodian before we eat the cookies in this room.**

Bring out your phone. Dial and wait for the custodian to answer as arranged. Ask for permission to eat the cookies, and then hang up.

SAY: **Yes, we can have the cookies! All I had to do was let the custodian know what we needed, and I got an answer right away. Before I pass out the cookies, I have some questions.**

ASK:

◆ **Since God already knows what we need, why does he want us to talk to him about what we need, or to thank him?**

◆ **What does God do when lots of people talk to him at once?**

◆ **Does God need an answering machine? Why or why not?**

SAY: **God can listen to everyone's prayers at once! And God always answers our prayers. The**

Bible tells us about King Solomon, who asked God to give him wisdom. He wanted to be a good king, so he asked God to help him be wise and make good choices.

Open your Bible to 1 Kings 3:1-15, and read the passage aloud. Then SAY: **God said yes to Solomon's request. Solomon is now remembered for being very, very wise. God helped him make good choices!**

Read aloud Psalm 37:3.

ASK:

- **How did Solomon show that he trusted in God?**
- **What kinds of things do you trust God to help you with?**
- **How has God answered your prayers?**
- **When has God helped you make good choices?**

SAY: **God gave Solomon wisdom, and God will give us wisdom, too. ▷ LET'S USE THAT WISDOM AND MAKE GOOD CHOICES. As you eat your cookie, remember that God will help us make good choices.**

Additional Topics List

This lesson can be used to help children discover... Blessing, Christ-likeness, Glorifying God, God's Will, Honor and Wisdom.

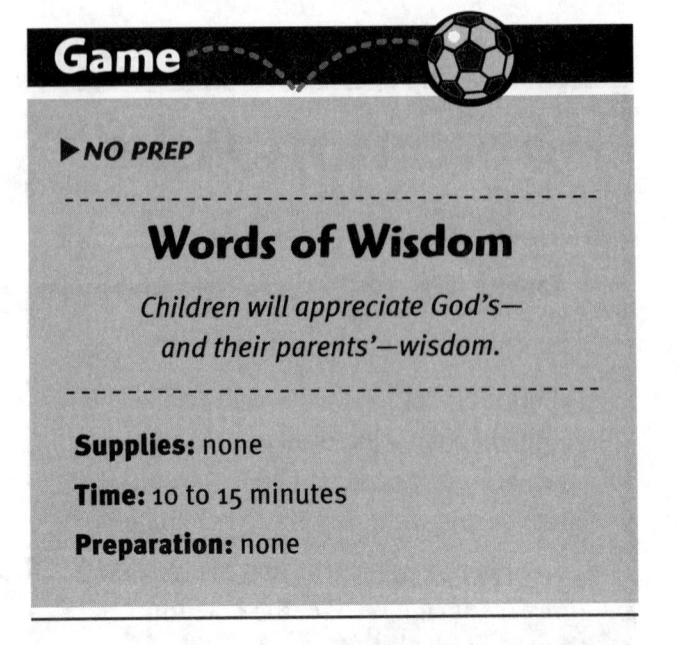

Game

▶ ***NO PREP***

Words of Wisdom

Children will appreciate God's—and their parents'—wisdom.

Supplies: none

Time: 10 to 15 minutes

Preparation: none

Have kids form groups of two to four. SAY: **Let's play a game that will help us get to know each other. Introduce yourself to your group. Tell the group your name plus something wise you've learned from your parents. Please listen carefully because you'll need to remember your friends' names *and* the wisdom they shared.**

After a few minutes, call everyone together and give an example of an introduction, such as "This is my friend John. His father told him not to skate around parked cars." Have kids introduce everyone in their groups.

After the game, have kids discuss these questions:

- **What have you learned from others in the group?**
- **How do we get wisdom to make good choices?**
- **Why did Solomon ask God for wisdom?**

notes

Craft

▶ *PREP IN ADVANCE*

Map It!

Children will see how God helps them make wise choices.

Supplies: copies of "Map It!" handout (p. 294), pencils, tea bags, bowl of warm water, paper towels

Time: about 10 minutes

Preparation: Make one photocopy of the "Map It!" handout (p. 294) for each child.

Give each child a copy of the "Map It!" handout. SAY: **This is your map of choices. Think of three things you know God wants you to choose. Write them in the three blanks on your map (for example, "being patient" or "inviting my friends to church").**

Allow time for children to write down their ideas. SAY: **Have you ever seen pictures of an old map from an adventure movie? Have you noticed how they turn brown and stained? Let's make our maps look like they're old. This will remind us that choosing things God desires and plans has *always* been a good idea.**

Show kids how to wet a tea bag in the warm water and squeeze the excess water out of the bag. Demonstrate how to blot the tea bag on a map to make the map look like an antique. Allow the children to blot their maps until they look authentically weathered. Set them aside to dry. Use the paper towels to dry hands, wipe spills, and blot excess water from the maps.

SAY: **This week, look at your map to remember the good choices God wants you to make.**

▷ **LET'S MAKE GOOD CHOICES!**

Bible Application

▶ *PREP IN ADVANCE*

Real Wisdom Requires Faith

Children will understand and embrace that wisdom comes from God.

Supplies: plastic food container with lid, large bowl of uncooked rice, plastic spoons, wooden cross that will fit inside the food container

Time: about 15 minutes

Preparation: Use a permanent marker to draw a face on your container lid.

SAY: **Raise your hand if you think you're smart. I want to see everyone's hand raised high in the air. God made each and every one of you smart. God gave us wisdom. Sometimes we may be smarter in one area than we are in another area, but you are all very smart.**

God made it so that, other than Jesus, Solomon was the wisest man who ever lived. In the book of Proverbs, Solomon often talked about how knowing and respecting God was the most important part of wisdom. You can fill your head with all sorts of things, but if you don't know God, your knowledge isn't worth too much. Let me show you what I mean.

Let's pretend this container is your head, and the rice is stuff you put in your head, like math, reading, and TV. Let's each put some stuff in here.

Have children each put a spoonful of rice in your container. As children put in the rice, have them name things we put in our heads. Let them continue to add rice until the container is overflowing. Then pull out your cross.

Map It!

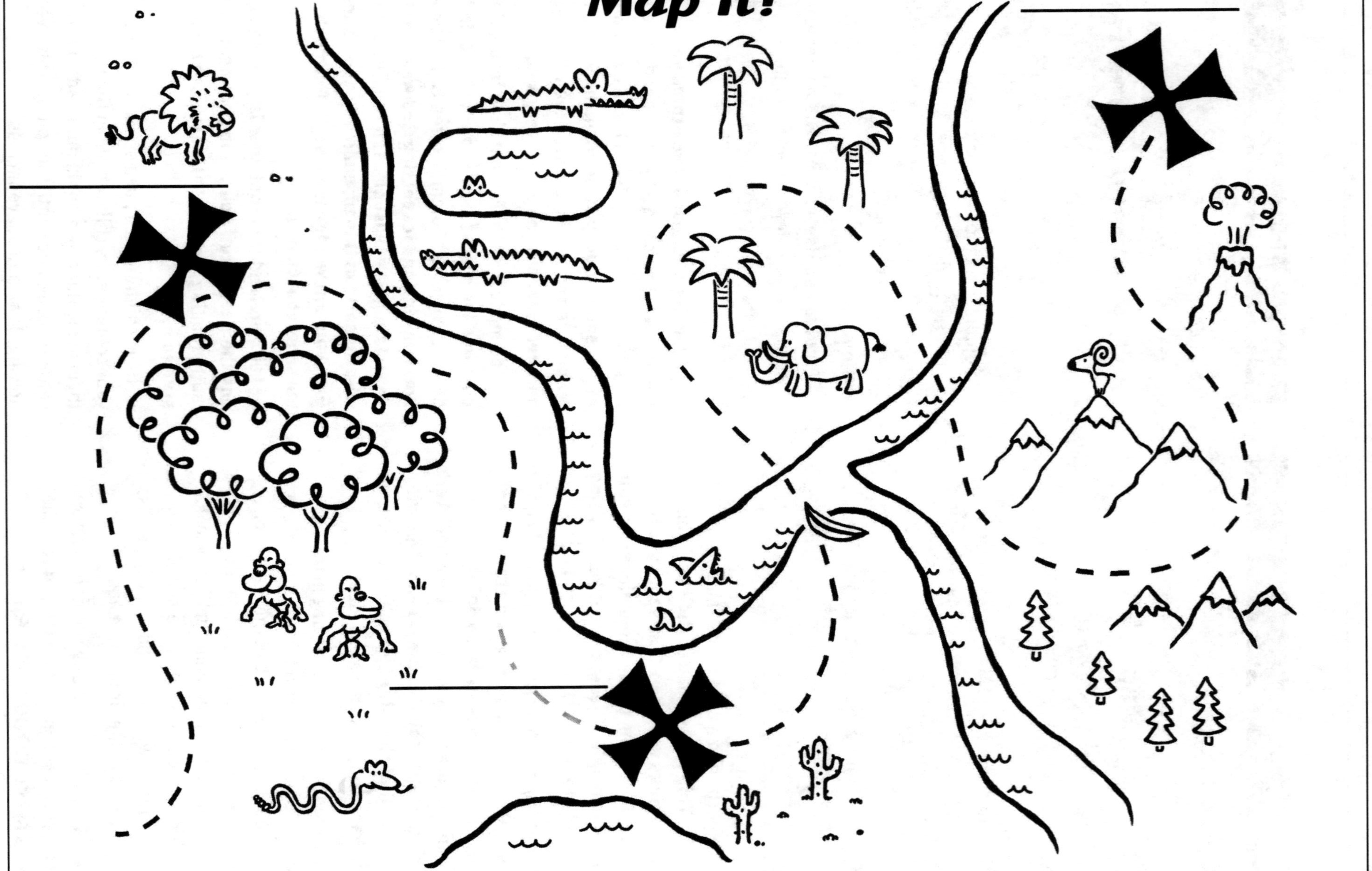

SAY: **Now that we've put all this stuff in here, there's no room for the most important thing of all—faith. Without faith, we can't have real wisdom—we just have a lot of facts and information. Let's start over.**

Dump out the rice and repeat the exercise. This time put the cross into the container before pouring in the rice. SAY: **It's good to learn as much as we can about the world God made and the people in it. But let's remember to put Jesus first in our lives. When he is most important, the things we learn become real wisdom. Jesus is the beginning of all real wisdom.**

Creative Prayer Idea

▶ ***PREP IN ADVANCE***

▶ ***STUDENT LED***

▶ ***ALLERGY ALERT***

Pick a Prayer

Children will pray different prayers, according to the candy they pick.

Supplies: bowl of colorful candies (such as M&M's or Skittles), paper, marker

Time: about 5 minutes

Preparation: Choose candies of any four colors, and place them in a bowl. Make a chart similar to the following example that uses the colors available to you.

Pick-Up Prayers

Red: Pray for the courage to tell a friend about Jesus.

Blue: Ask God to help you to be kind—even to people who aren't kind to you.

Green: Ask God to help you remember to read your Bible this week.

Yellow: Pray that God will help you obey your parents.

SAY: **Let's practice asking God to help us make good choices. We'll pass around the bowl. When it comes to you, close your eyes and pick one piece of candy. Look at the chart to see what you should pray for. Pray aloud as the chart directs you, and then pass the bowl. You can eat the candy as a reminder of how good life is when we make good choices.**

Movie Clip

Decisions, Decisions

Movie Title: *Aladdin* (G)

Start Time: 1 hour, 22 minutes, 16 seconds

Where to Begin: Aladdin apologizes to Jasmine for lying about being a prince.

Where to End: Aladdin wishes for "the Nile" and the Genie says, "No way!"

Plot: Aladdin sacrifices his final wish to set the Genie free, whereas the Genie is willing to sacrifice his freedom to help Aladdin be a prince again.

Review: Use this scene to help children learn about making good choices. Aladdin had to decide whether to keep his promise or break it in order to help himself. We all need to make good choices, and that starts with doing God's will!

After setting up and showing the clip, SAY: **Solomon asked God for wisdom to help him make good choices as king. We all need God's help to make good choices.**

ASK:

◆ **How can we learn to make good choices?**

◆ **Why do we need God's help to make good choices?**

SAY: **We can learn right from wrong and gain wisdom by going to church, listening to Christian adults, praying, and reading the Bible. Following God's rules will help us make good choices.**

Object Lesson

Solomon Asks for Wisdom

Children will learn how to get wisdom from God.

Supplies: Bible, backpack, school supplies

Time: about 10 minutes

Preparation: Place the Bible in the backpack, and then fill the backpack with school supplies.

SAY: **I've brought a backpack similar to those kids use to carry school supplies. Let's see what's inside.** One at a time, bring out each item, and ask the following question. Pull out the Bible last. Remember to hold the items high so everyone can see them.

ASK:

◆ **How does this item help us learn?**

When you've discussed all the items, SAY: **We can use pencils for writing or drawing; we can use an eraser when we make mistakes. We read from books to help us learn. All of these items help us learn lots!**

The *Bible* helps us learn how to live each day. The Bible helps us learn how to make good choices.

ASK:

◆ **How do we learn right from wrong?**

◆ **How does God help us make good choices?**

Preschool Story

▶ ***NO PREP***

Bible Point: ▷ **LET'S MAKE GOOD CHOICES.**

Supplies: Bible

Time: 10 to 15 minutes

Preparation: none

A Sad Story

Have kids form a circle and sit down on the floor. Open your Bible to 1 Kings 3, and show children the words. Students will enjoy acting out this rhyming story. Lead kids in doing the motions as you read the following Bible story.

SAY: **Solomon was the king** *(make a circle with hands, and place them on head)*

And ruled with God in mind *(tap side of head)*,

Obeyed God's rules and laws *(point up)*,

Was fair and good and kind.

Once, while Solomon slept *(rest head on hands)*,

God asked him in a dream,

"Solomon, what do you want? *(Hold hands up and shrug shoulders.)*

I'll give you anything." *(Bring hands forward with palms up.)*

Solomon asked for wisdom *(tap side of head)*,

To be smart and oh, so wise.

He asked to be a good king *(make a circle with hands, and place them on head)*

And always know what's right. *(Show thumbs up.)*

God was pleased with Solomon *(smile big and point to mouth)*

For his unselfish plea. *(Bring hands forward, palms up.)*

God said, "You'll get your wisdom. *(Tap side of head.)*

And much more than that, you'll see." *(Spread hands out, palms up.)*

Solomon ruled God's people *(make a circle with hands, and place them on head)*

And showed them what was right. *(Show thumbs up.)*

He taught them to do good

And be pleasing in God's sight. *(Point up.)*

The people were amazed *(show a surprised look)*

At what Solomon would do. *(Point up.)*

They knew he was of God;

They knew it through and through. *(Show thumbs up.)*

Obey God's rules and laws *(point up)*,

And you'll be richly blessed.

Obey God's rules and laws *(point up)*—

That was Solomon's test.

ASK:

◆ **What good choice did Solomon make?**

◆ **How can you ▷ MAKE GOOD CHOICES?**

BIBLE STORY

Solomon's Wisdom

For the Leader

The story of Solomon's wise ruling is an interesting one. It probably is representative of a host of wise rulings for which Solomon became known throughout the kingdom and even in other nations. It shows Solomon using the wisdom God gave him to quickly and simply solve a problem in his kingdom.

The fact that two prostitutes were brought before the king suggests that Solomon probably was already known for his wisdom in these matters. It also may show that he had great compassion for the people of his kingdom—in the grand scheme of things, this was a small matter between lowly people.

Key Scriptures

1 Kings 3:16-28

Psalm 51:6; 119:99

Proverbs 2:6

Daniel 2:21

1 Corinthians 1:25

James 1:5

1 John 5:14-15

Bible Verse

"Yes, I have more insight than my teachers, for I am always thinking of your laws" (Psalm 119:99).

Bible Experience

▶ *PREP IN ADVANCE*

Bible Point: ▷ **THE BIBLE GIVES US WISDOM.**

Children will act out a skit to learn about Solomon's wisdom.

Supplies: Bible, "Museum of Bible History" handout (p. 299), baby doll, cardboard or plastic sword

Time: about 10 minutes

Preparation: Make a photocopy of the "Museum of Bible History" handout for each person. Assign the following characters: Lindsey (museum curator), King Solomon (wax figure), Mom 1 (wax figure), Mom 2 (wax figure), Guard (wax figure), Group (remaining kids). Cue the wax figures to move whenever Lindsey isn't looking. Instruct the Group to laugh each time the wax figures move.

Read aloud 1 Kings 3:16-28. Then SAY: **Let's do a skit to learn more.** Give kids copies of the "Museum of Bible History" handout, and have them perform the skit.

After the skit, ASK:

- **Why did Solomon threaten to cut the baby in half?**
- **How did Solomon get his wisdom?**
- **How can we get the kind of wisdom Solomon had?**

Read aloud Psalm 119:99.

ASK:

- **What does this verse mean?**
- **Where does this verse say insight (and wisdom) come from?**

SAY: ▷ **THE BIBLE GIVES US WISDOM. If we want the kind of wisdom Solomon had, we can get it from reading and obeying God's Word.**

Additional Topics List

This lesson can be used to help children discover... Holy Spirit, Inspiration, Judgment, Justice, Mercy, and Wisdom.

Game

▶ *NO PREP*
▶ *ALLERGY ALERT*

Remote Controlled

Children will learn to listen to God.

Supplies: clean, soft blindfolds; treats

Time: 5 to 10 minutes

Preparation: none

MUSEUM OF BIBLE HISTORY

Lindsey: *(To the Group)* Welcome to the Museum of Bible History. I'm your tour guide, Lindsey Tells-All. Please walk this way to look at our wax figures depicting wisdom. *(Group follows Lindsey to frozen actors portraying two women holding a baby and kneeling before King Solomon. A "frozen" Guard with a big sword is standing by the king.)*

See how lifelike King Solomon looks as he sits on his throne. This was one wise king. Once God told him he could have whatever he wanted, and King Solomon chose wisdom instead of riches. *(Lindsey turns her back on the display to talk to the Group.)*

King Solomon: *(King Solomon comes to life and waves at the Group.)*

Group: *(Laughs.)*

Lindsey: *(Turns and looks at figures, who freeze.)* I don't see what's so funny about that! Anyway, you're all probably familiar with the story about the two women who came to Solomon because they were having a fight over a baby.

Moms 1 and 2: *(Begin to play Tug of War with the doll.)*

Group: *(Laughs.)*

Lindsey: Honestly, people, this is a serious story! Anyway, both women claimed to be the mother of the baby. They wanted Solomon to settle their argument. Wise Solomon said the baby should be cut in half with a sword.

Guard: *(Poses to cut the baby boy in two with a sword.)*

Lindsey: *(Not noticing)* King Solomon was wise. He knew the real mother would stop him. She did. *(Wax figures act out story as Lindsey's back is turned.)* The real mother told King Solomon to spare the child and give it to the other woman. That's when King Solomon knew which woman was the baby's mother.

King Solomon: *(Acts as if he has an idea. Stands and gives baby to the real mom.)*

Group: *(Applauds and cheers.)*

Lindsey: You act as if this display came to life! *(Wax figures bow.)*

SAY: **Form pairs to try to find treats. The guide gets to see. The other partner has to wear a blindfold and can ask questions such as, "Should I go forward?" or "Should I turn around?" The guide can say yes or no.**

Give each pair a blindfold. Once blindfolds are on, set out treats. Let children find their way to the treats according to the rules. As they find the treats, let the blindfolded child have treats. Then have pairs switch roles and play again.

As children are enjoying their treats, ASK:

- **What was it like to follow the instructions of your guide?**
- **How was listening to your guide like following God's wisdom?**
- **How can we seek God's wisdom?**

Craft

▶ *NO PREP*

Marks of Wisdom

Children will make Bible bookmarks that will remind them that the Bible gives us wisdom.

Supplies: Bibles, large paper clips, craft foam, safety scissors, glue

Time: 10 to 15 minutes

Preparation: none

SAY: **Let's make Bible bookmarks that will help us remember that ▷ THE BIBLE GIVES US WISDOM.**

Give each child a large paper clip and a small piece of craft foam. Help kids use scissors to cut the craft foam into a shape that will remind them of wisdom—such as a crown to remind them of King Solomon.

When the kids have finished cutting their shapes, show them how to glue the back of the craft foam to the top of the paper clip.

As the glue is drying, show kids how they can attach the paper clip to a page in their Bibles. This will mark the page and allow the craft foam shape to stick out of the Bible and remind them to seek God's wisdom in its pages.

Bible Application

▶ *NO PREP*
▶ *FOR FAMILY MINISTRY*

Parents' Wisdom

Children will thank parents for encouraging them to find wisdom.

Supplies: Bibles, poster board, markers, paint, props for skits (optional)

Time: about 30 minutes

Preparation: none

Have children fold the poster board in half and decorate it using markers or paint. Have them write on one side "I love you" and on the other side "I won't forget your wise advice."

Help kids prepare a presentation for their parents. Read aloud the story from 1 Kings 3:16-28. Then ASK:

- **How did the real mother show her love for her baby?**
- **How do your parents show their love for you?**

SAY: **Solomon recognized the real mother because her love was so great that she wanted no harm to come to her child. Your parents love you deeply, too. And by encouraging you to learn about God's Word, they help you find the kind of wisdom Solomon had.**

Allow children to select props and rehearse lines to present this story as a skit for their parents. Use the Bible text for any needed narration. Have kids brainstorm ways their parents help them find wisdom and then prepare skits to show these to their parents following the King Solomon skit. Schedule a time to invite parents to view the skits.

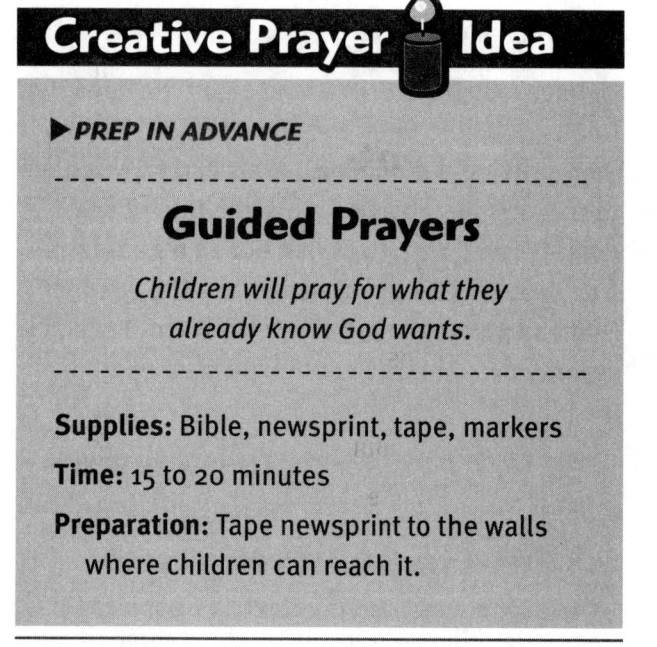

Creative Prayer Idea

▶ ***PREP IN ADVANCE***

Guided Prayers

Children will pray for what they already know God wants.

Supplies: Bible, newsprint, tape, markers

Time: 15 to 20 minutes

Preparation: Tape newsprint to the walls where children can reach it.

Read aloud 1 John 5:14-15, and then SAY: **This verse means that God promises to answer our prayers when we pray for things that are God's desires and plans. ▷ THE BIBLE GIVES US WISDOM. It shows us what God wants for us and what we should pray for. Let's make a list of things we know God wants.**

Have children brainstorm things they know God wants, such as "obeying our parents" or "being kind." Give kids five minutes to brainstorm and write their answers on the newsprint.

Then PRAY: **God, thank you for giving us the Bible and showing us true wisdom. We pray for these things...**Pause while kids call out things listed on the newsprint. **Help us to learn more about your wisdom. Amen.**

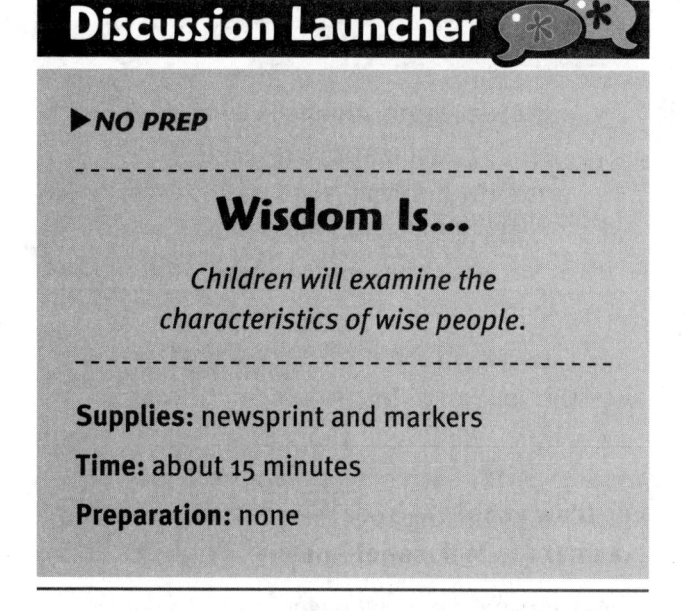

Discussion Launcher

▶ ***NO PREP***

Wisdom Is...

Children will examine the characteristics of wise people.

Supplies: newsprint and markers

Time: about 15 minutes

Preparation: none

Have kids form groups of four. Give each group newsprint and a marker.

SAY: **Have you ever thought about wise people? There are a lot of them on the earth, and I'm sure there are some wise people in your life. I'd like you to make a list in your group of what makes these people wise. What qualities make them wise? Use your ideas to draw the wisest person in the world. What might this person look like? As you draw this person, be sure to have an explanation of each characteristic you give him or her.**

When groups are finished, have them share their wise-person drawings. When all groups have presented, ASK:

- **What makes someone wise?**
- **What kinds of decisions do wise people make?**
- **Why does ▷ THE BIBLE GIVE US WISDOM?**

Worship Prompt Idea

▶ *NO PREP*

Thanks for Wisdom

Children will worship God for giving us wisdom through his Word.

Supplies: Bibles

Time: 5 to 10 minutes

Preparation: none

SAY: **▷ THE BIBLE GIVES US WISDOM. Let's worship God for giving us wisdom through God's Word. We'll read some Bible verses about wisdom. After each one is read, we'll all worship God by saying together, "Thank you, God, for giving us wisdom through the Bible."**

Ask for volunteers who would like to read Scripture verses aloud. Assign each of the following verses to a reader. After each one is read, lead the class in saying, "Thank you, God, for giving us wisdom through the Bible." Psalm 51:6; Proverbs 2:6; Daniel 2:21; 1 Corinthians 1:25; James 1:5.

Close the activity in prayer, thanking God for his Word and his wisdom.

n

o

t

e

s

Preschool Story

▶ *PREP IN ADVANCE*

Bible Point: **▷ THE BIBLE GIVES US WISDOM.**

Supplies: Bible, toys

Time: 15 to 20 minutes

Preparation: Gather enough toys for half the children in your class.

Who Belongs to This Baby?

Have kids form a circle and sit on the floor. Open your Bible to 1 Kings 3, and show children the words. SAY: **Solomon asked God for wisdom to rule wisely, and God gave him lots of wisdom—as well as lots of riches and nice things. One day King Solomon had to use the wisdom God had given him to solve a problem.** Set out several toys, but only enough for about half of the kids.

Oh! I only have enough toys for half of you.

ASK:

- **How do you feel if you got a toy?**
- **How do you feel if you didn't get a toy?**

Help kids solve the problem by sharing the toys or by passing the toys back and forth.

SAY: **Two women came to King Solomon. They were arguing. The women had one baby with them, and both of the women said the baby was theirs.**

ASK:

- **How is this problem like the one that we just had with our toys?**
- **How would you solve this problem if you were Solomon?**

SAY: **Solomon asked to have his sword brought to him, and then he said, "I'll solve this problem. Each of you can have half of the baby."**

ASK:

- **Do you think that was a good idea? Why or why not?**
- **How would you feel if we just cut these toys in half so each of you could have half of a toy?**

SAY: **One of the women stopped Solomon and said to go ahead and give the baby to the other woman instead of hurting him. The other woman said to go ahead and cut the baby in half. Solomon wouldn't really have cut the baby in half; he just wanted to find out who the real mother of the baby was.**

ASK:

- **Who do you think was the real mother?**

SAY: **Solomon knew that the real mother was the woman who didn't want the baby to be hurt. So he gave the baby to the real mother. When all the people heard about how Solomon had solved that problem, they were very excited about his wisdom.** Lead children in clapping and applauding for Solomon's wisdom.

Solomon was wise because God gave him wisdom. Solomon wrote much of his wisdom down in the Bible for us to read. We can get wisdom when we read the Bible. The Bible can teach us many things and help us to be wise.
▷ **THE BIBLE GIVES US WISDOM.**

ASK:

- **How did Solomon use his wisdom?**
- **How can you get wisdom?**
- **When can you use wisdom?**

BIBLE STORY

Solomon Turns From God

For the Leader

It's a sad picture: the wisest man who ever lived, abandoning wisdom on such a grand scale.

Solomon likely married many of his wives for political reasons—to ensure peace with the surrounding nations. But as those wives became part of Solomon's household, they brought their false gods with them. And eventually Solomon was pulled into worshipping those gods.

While Solomon had great wisdom, he failed to obey God. His wisdom meant nothing in the end.

Key Scriptures

Deuteronomy 6:5
1 Kings 11:1-13
Psalms 23:1; 28:1; 42:2
Isaiah 1:24
John 6:45
1 Timothy 6:15
James 1:17
Revelation 1:8; 15:3

Bible Verse

"And you must love the Lord your God with all your heart, all your soul, and all your strength" (Deuteronomy 6:5).

Bible Experience

▶ *NO PREP*

Bible Point: ▷ **WORSHIP GOD ONLY.**

Children will learn how Solomon turned away from God.

Supplies: Bible, heart stickers

Time: 20 to 30 minutes

Preparation: none

Open your Bible to 1 Kings 11:1-13, and show kids the passage.

SAY: **This story is about how King Solomon turned away from God.** Choose one child to be Solomon. Distribute heart stickers to the children.

In his job as king, Solomon met lots of women. Every now and then he would fall in love and get married. One of the women he met might have been named [invite children to call out a girl's name].

Have children stick heart stickers on "Solomon." Then have kids continue to call out girls' names and put stickers on Solomon until he's covered with heart stickers.

SAY: **Solomon got married to seven hundred women. Wow! That's a lot of wives! But this didn't work out so well. Having more than one wife was the custom back in Bible times, but Solomon's wives led him away from God. Solomon's wives got him into trouble—big trouble—with God. That's because not all of Solomon's wives believed in the one true God. Many of them worshipped pretend gods. Solomon loved his wives so much that he started worshipping the pretend gods, too, just to make his wives happy. But that made God sad and angry.**

ASK:

- **Why do you think that made God angry?**

Read aloud 1 Kings 11:1-13.

SAY: **God told Solomon to worship only him. When Solomon started following the false gods, God told Solomon he would tear the kingdom away from Solomon's family because Solomon had decided not to ▷WORSHIP GOD ONLY.**

ASK:

- **Why do you think Solomon turned away from God?**
- **What should Solomon have done instead?**

Read aloud Deuteronomy 6:5.

ASK:

- **What does God want from us?**
- **How can we love God with our heart, soul, and strength?**

SAY: **Having so many wives who wanted Solomon to worship their gods caused Solomon to turn away from the true God. Sometimes in our own lives, things distract us from God. But God wants us to ▷WORSHIP GOD ONLY.**

Additional Topics List

This lesson can be used to help children discover... Choices, Glorifying God, Obedience, Peer Pressure, Righteousness.

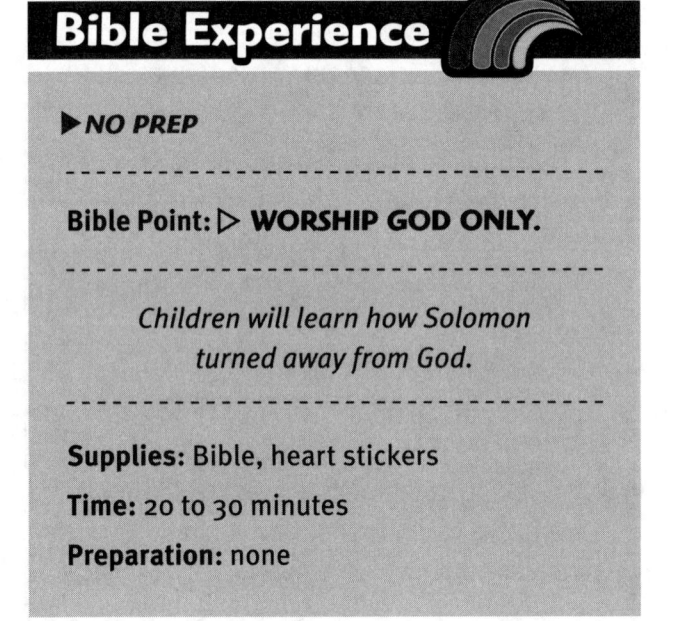

Game

Tag-Along Tag

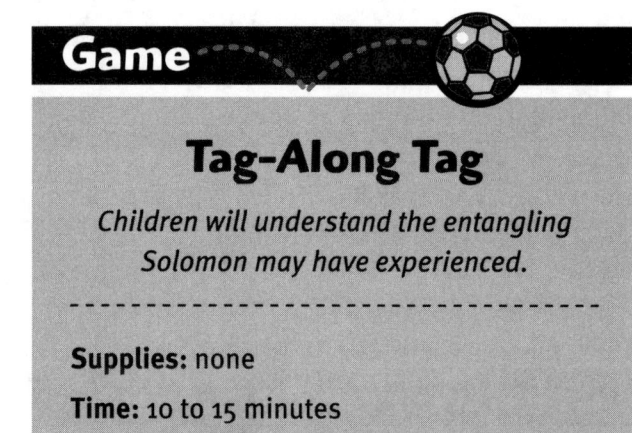

Children will understand the entangling Solomon may have experienced.

Supplies: none

Time: 10 to 15 minutes

Preparation: Find the largest play area you can—the bigger, the better!

Designate one child as "It." Have kids spread out around the play area. Tell kids that It will run around and try to tag them. When someone is tagged, that person must join hands with It and run around with him or her, tagging other kids. Each time someone is tagged, that person must join hands with the It group. Play until everyone has been tagged. Then

ASK:

- **What was it like to run around by yourself?**
- **What was it like to run around holding hands with other people?**
- **How is this similar to what happened when Solomon got married?**
- **What happens when we let things get in the way of ▷WORSHIPPING GOD ONLY?**

n
o
t
e
s

Craft

▶ *PREP IN ADVANCE*
▶ *FOR FAMILY MINISTRY*

One True God

Children will learn that there's only one true God.

Supplies: Bibles, markers, large sheets of newsprint, index cards, CD player and music CDs (optional)

Time: 15 to 20 minutes

Preparation: On separate cards, write the following Scripture references. You'll need one card for each group of three to five students: Psalm 23:1; Psalm 28:1; Psalm 42:2; Isaiah 1:24; John 6:45; 1 Timothy 6:15; James 1:17; Revelation 1:8; Revelation 15:3.

SAY: **King Solomon of Israel was famous for his wisdom. But as he grew older and richer, Solomon did some things that weren't wise at all. Solomon turned away from God and began worshipping fake gods.**

ASK:

- **What did Solomon do wrong?**

SAY: **The Bible teaches us that there is only one God and that we should worship only him. Let's make special banners to remind us how wonderful our one true God is.**

Form groups of three to five to make banners. Give each group markers, a Bible, a sheet of newsprint, and an index card with the Scripture references written on it. On the newsprint, instruct kids to write "The Only 1," making the *1* a large outline that fills most of the paper. Have volunteers in each group look up the Scripture passages that describe God. Kids might write words such as "Shepherd," "Rock," and "King." As kids work, you might want to play songs such as "Great Is the Lord" and "We Will Glorify." Then have kids display the banners around the room as reminders that our God is the one true God.

Bible Application

▶ *FOR SMALL GROUPS*

Commitment to Worship

Children will consider what distracts them from worshipping God.

Supplies: magazines, safety scissors, newsprint, glue, markers or crayons

Time: about 20 minutes

Preparation: Set out the newsprint and art supplies.

Point out the supplies. Encourage kids to find and draw pictures and words to create a collage showing things that may distract or pull them away from worshipping God. When the collage is complete, have kids gather around it and form pairs. Ask pairs to discuss:

- **Why do you think other things often compete with God for our attention?**
- **How can we ▷WORSHIP GOD ONLY and still give time and attention to other important things?**
- **What could you do this week to demonstrate your devotion to God?**

Challenge students to give up one item in the collage this week—something that is distracting them from worshipping God. Have each person turn to his or her partner and make a verbal commitment to do so. Then encourage students to draw an X through the items they've identified on the collage. End in a time of silent prayer as kids discuss their commitments with God.

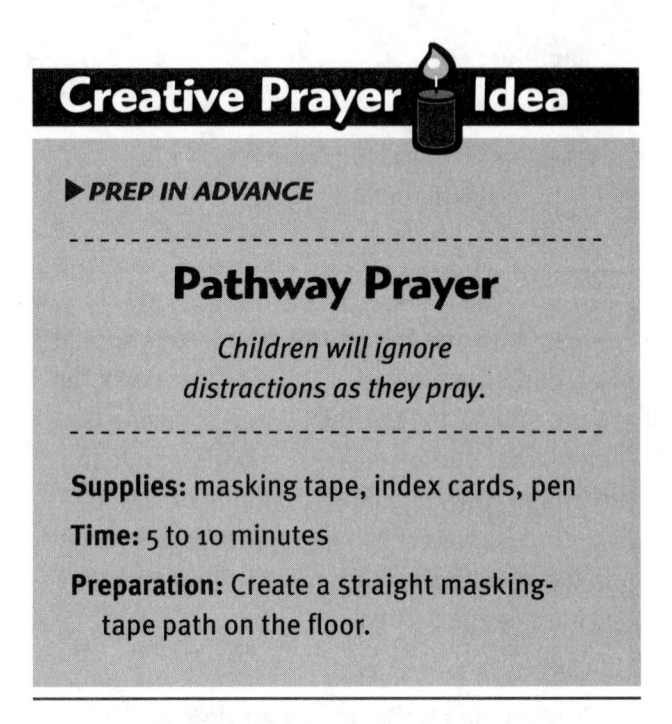

Creative Prayer Idea

▶ *PREP IN ADVANCE*

Pathway Prayer

Children will ignore distractions as they pray.

Supplies: masking tape, index cards, pen

Time: 5 to 10 minutes

Preparation: Create a straight masking-tape path on the floor.

SAY: **If we want to ▷WORSHIP GOD ONLY, we have to ignore the things that might distract us from worshipping him. What are some of the things that might distract us?**

Have kids call out ideas, and write several on cards. Then lay the cards on the floor on both sides of the path you created. Stand at one end of the path, and have kids form a line behind.

SAY: **Let's show God that we want to ignore distractions and ▷WORSHIP GOD ONLY. As we pray, let's walk down this path without looking at the distractions.**

PRAY: **Dear God, we know only you deserve our worship, and we want to worship only you. Help us to ignore the things that distract us. Amen.**

Object Lesson

▶ *NO PREP*

Magnet Turnaround

Children will see a symbol of Solomon turning away from God.

Supplies: at least 2 large magnets (2 small ones for each child if you have them)

Time: about 5 minutes

Preparation: none

Set out two large magnets on a table, where everyone can see them. If you have more magnets, allow kids to use them the same way you do.

SAY: **When Solomon became king of Israel, he and God were close.** Put the two magnets together so they attract and stick together.

God offered Solomon anything he wanted, and he chose wisdom. He relied on that wisdom from God, and he was a great king.

Pull the magnets apart and SAY: **But then Solomon disobeyed God by marrying women who didn't worship God. He married seven hundred women who worshipped false gods!**

Solomon's wives convinced him to worship their false gods. Solomon began to turn away from God and worship them instead.

Turn the magnets around so they repel each other and SAY: **Solomon had turned away from God, and he no longer was a great king. In fact, God told Solomon he would take the kingdom away from his family.**

Worship Prompt Idea

▶ *PREP IN ADVANCE*

Honor to Whom It Is Due

Children create a special document honoring God in worship.

Supplies: paper, pencil, markers, 6-inch lengths of ribbon, self-adhesive stickers in the shapes of stars, hearts, and sunbursts

Time: about 20 minutes

Preparation: Set out supplies, and cut ribbon in 6-inch lengths.

SAY: **Let's practice honoring God through worship.**

ASK:

◆ **What does it mean to honor someone?**

◆ **What are ways we honor other people?**

◆ **Why is it important to honor other people?**

◆ **Why is it important to give honor to God?**

SAY: **One way we honor others is by giving them special papers or certificates that tell why they are so important. We can do the same thing for God. Let's create "honor rolls" that say exactly why we worship God.**

Have kids form groups of four to six. Invite each group to take a sheet of paper and materials to decorate it. Have groups discuss what specific things they would like to worship God for and then create a certificate honoring God for those things. Encourage groups to make their certificates fun and official-looking.

After five to 10 minutes, have groups take turns displaying and explaining their honor rolls to the rest of the group. Then have each group roll up the paper, tie a ribbon around the honor roll, and then "present" it to God in a group prayer.

Preschool Story

▶ *ALLERGY ALERT*

Bible Point: ▷**WORSHIP GOD ONLY.**

Supplies: Bible, classroom toys, coloring books, snacks, girl dolls, age-appropriate worship music, CD player

Time: 15 to 20 minutes

Preparation: Place an age-appropriate worship CD in your CD player.

He's Number One!

Have kids form a circle and sit down on the floor. Open your Bible to 1 Kings 11, and show children the words. SAY: **God made Solomon the wisest person around, and King Solomon loved God. Solomon noticed all the wonderful things God had made, such as trees, plants, animals, and people. Solomon filled his palace with all of these wonderful things. God gave Solomon many things, and Solomon enjoyed the life God had given him.**

ASK:

- **What are some things you enjoy?**

Encourage each child to go and grab one thing in the room that he or she enjoys, such as a toy, coloring book, or snack. Once all the kids have returned with their objects, begin the story again.

SAY: **Solomon had lots of wonderful things, and Solomon also had lots of beautiful wives, and he loved them all.** Set out several girl dolls.

King Solomon had everything he could ever want. But Solomon did something wrong. He chose to love his things and his wives more than God. Solomon's wives wanted him to build temples and worship their pretend gods instead of the one true God. Solomon listened to them and built temples and worshipped these pretend gods, even though God had told King Solomon not to worship other gods. Solomon disobeyed God.

ASK:

- **How do you think God felt when King Solomon chose to worship other gods?**
- **How do you think God would feel if you chose to love those items you have in front of you more than you love God?**

SAY: **God was sad and angry that Solomon had disobeyed him and chose to worship other gods and love his wives more than he loved God. The Bible tells us to ▷WORSHIP GOD ONLY. But Solomon chose to worship other gods and to put others first before God. Solomon let other things become more important to him than God.**

ASK:

- **What are some ways you make God more important than all these items in front of you?**

SAY: **We don't have to be like Solomon. We can put God first and love him more than anything else. God loves us and has given us everything we have. We should ▷WORSHIP GOD ONLY and obey him because God loves us and cares for us.**

Play a favorite worship song, and encourage kids to come up with fun, new ways to worship God together. Then ASK:

- **How did Solomon disobey God?**
- **Why is it important to worship God only?**
- **How can you worship God this week?**

BIBLE STORY

The Kingdom Is Divided

For the Leader

Because Solomon had turned away from God while he was king, God took most of the kingdom of Israel away from his family. In honor of Solomon's father, David, God chose to leave one tribe of Israel in the hands of Solomon's (and David's) family.

Because God had declared he would do this, God pulled 10 tribes away from Rehoboam, Solomon's son (by using Rehoboam's foolish choice), and gave them to Jeroboam. Rehoboam paid the price for his own foolish choice as well as for the sins of his father.

Key Scriptures

1 Kings 12:1-24

Luke 11:28

Bible Verse

"But even more blessed are all who hear the word of God and put it into practice" (Luke 11:28).

Bible Experience

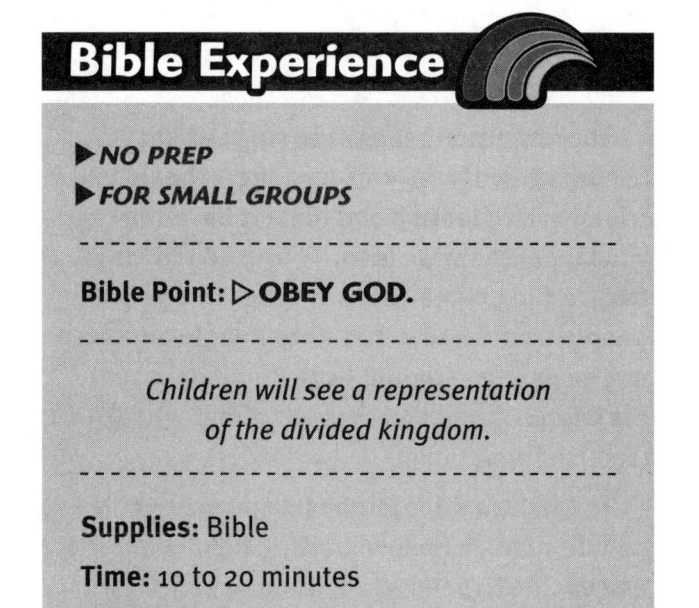

▶ *NO PREP*

▶ *FOR SMALL GROUPS*

Bible Point: ▷ **OBEY GOD.**

Children will see a representation of the divided kingdom.

Supplies: Bible

Time: 10 to 20 minutes

Preparation: none

Designate an open area of your room as a stage. To the left of the stage, have kids form a line that trails around the room. Choose an older child or adult to read the following story adapted from 1 Kings 12, phrase by phrase, as the children perform. Direct the kids onto the stage at the appropriate times.

SAY: **After Solomon died, Rehoboam became king over all of Israel.** (Have one child move onto the stage and act as the king.) **Jeroboam and some of his friends went to the king to talk to him.** (Send three children to the king.) **Jeroboam said, "Your father, Solomon, made us work too hard. He made us build his cities and fight in his armies. It was too much. Give us less work so we can take care of our families, and we will follow you."**

King Rehoboam said, "Come back in three days, and I will give you my answer." (Send the kids offstage, and send the next child onstage.) **King Rehoboam met with his wise men.** (Send three or four kids onstage.) **He asked his wise men if he should give the people less work to do or make them work even harder. The wise men told him to lighten some of the work for**

the people. King Rehoboam sent them away. (Wise men exit.)

The king then brought in some of his friends.(Send three kids onstage.) **These friends were foolish and did not have the wisdom of the wise men. They told the king to give the people twice as much to do so the people would know that King Rehoboam could not be pushed around. King Rehoboam sent his friends away and thought about what to do.** (Foolish friends exit.)

Three days later Jeroboam and many of the people came to hear what King Rehoboam had decided. (Send four kids onstage.) **King Rehoboam treated the people badly. He yelled at them and called them lazy. He told them he would make them work even harder than Solomon had made them work. The people left sad and angry.** (Everyone exits.)

The people decided to fight since they could not possibly work any harder than they already were working. (Send four kids onstage.) **They decided to make Jeroboam their king.** (Send one child onstage.) **They crowned him king and decided not to follow King Rehoboam. They took half the land and started their own country.** (Everyone exits.) **King Rehoboam lost half of his entire kingdom because he listened to foolish friends.**

ASK:

◆ **Why did Rehoboam lose half of the kingdom of Israel?**

◆ **Why do you think Rehoboam decided to listen to his friends?**

Read aloud Luke 11:28.

ASK:

◆ **Who does this verse tell us are blessed? Why?**

◆ **When have you wished you had listened to someone else's advice?**

◆ **When is it hard for you to obey God? Why?**

SAY: **It's important to ▷ OBEY GOD because God is in charge and God always knows what is best for us. When we choose to disobey God, we'll always experience bad consequences. Obeying God is always the wise choice.**

Additional Topics List

This lesson can be used to help children discover... Blessing, Consequences, Following God, God's Will, Obedience, and Submission.

Game

▶ ***NO PREP***

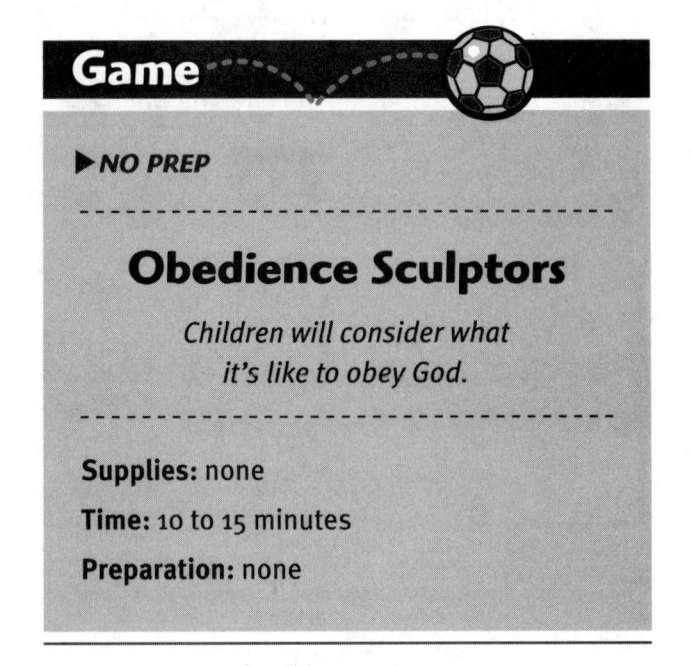

Obedience Sculptors

Children will consider what it's like to obey God.

Supplies: none

Time: 10 to 15 minutes

Preparation: none

Have kids form teams of three to five. Have each team designate their first team sculptor. Tell kids you'll call out a description of a sculpture, and the team sculptor will have 30 seconds to mold the rest of the team into that sculpture. Encourage teams to designate new team sculptors each time.

Call out the following ideas, or come up with your own:

- **a dog being groomed by a team of groomers**
- **a team of mountain climbers just reaching the summit**

- **pizza chefs making the world's biggest pizza**
- **kids eating the world's biggest pizza**
- **people pushing a car up a hill**
- **bodybuilders showing off their muscles**

When kids are finished, have teams discuss these questions:

◆ **What was it like to be the human sculptor?**

◆ **What was it like to obey the human sculptor?**

◆ **How did this compare with what it's like to ▷ OBEY GOD?**

◆ **How can we get better at obeying God?**

Craft

▶ *PREP IN ADVANCE*

Obedience Journals

Children will create journals to use in recording their obedience to God.

Supplies: notebooks or paper; craft supplies, such as markers, crayons, stickers, construction paper, decorative paper, stamps, ink pads, chalk, pens, glue, glitter, scissors, and ribbon

Time: 25 to 30 minutes

Preparation: If you don't want to purchase notebooks, bind a stack of paper for each child, using staples, ribbon, or string.

Give each child a notebook or a stack of paper bound together, and set out craft supplies. SAY: **Let's make obedience journals. You can use your journal to write about times you choose to obey God and to record the consequences of those choices. After a while you'll see many good things that happened because you chose to ▷ OBEY GOD.**

Allow kids several minutes to decorate and personalize their journals. Encourage them to write their names on the journals and to use them at home.

Bible Application

▶ *PREP IN ADVANCE*

Choice and Consequence

Children will consider the consequences of obeying and disobeying God.

Supplies: masking tape, rope or cord

Time: about 20 minutes

Preparation: With masking tape, create a line on the floor down the center of your meeting area.

Have kids form two groups. Give them a rope or cord, and have them play tug of war until one group crosses the line on the floor, or for five to 10 minutes. Then

ASK:

◆ **What was it like to try to pull the other team across?**

◆ **How did you feel when you felt the other team pulling you?**

SAY: **Just as you tried to pull each other across this line, Rehoboam tried desperately to hang on to power over the kingdom of Israel. As he did so, he chose to listen to his unwise friends rather than the wise people who obeyed God. So God took half the kingdom away as a consequence.**

ASK:

- **What kinds of consequences have you faced?**
- **Why does God allow bad consequences for our choices?**

SAY: **Think about a choice you'll make in the next week or month. Think about what might happen if you choose to obey or disobey God.**

Give kids several moments to silently consider the choices they face. Then ask kids to share a few of the consequences they thought about.

SAY: **It's important to always think about the consequences of obeying and disobeying God. It may not always be easy or fun to ▷OBEY GOD, but it's always the best choice.**

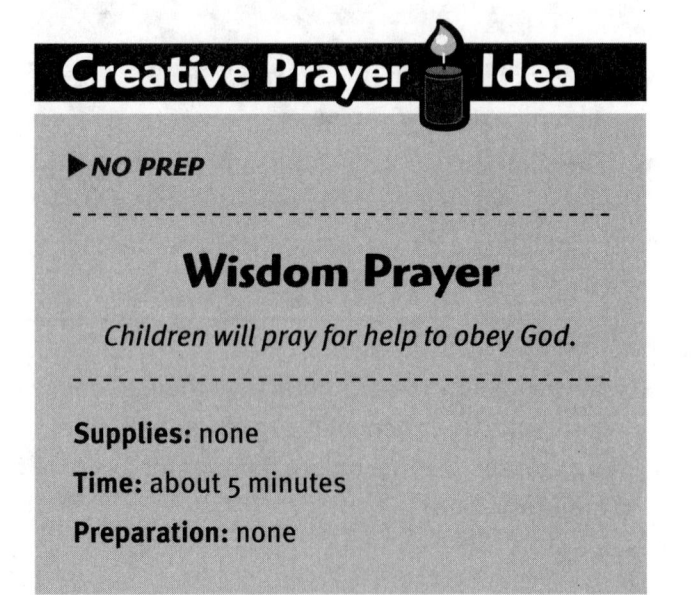

Creative Prayer Idea

▶ ***NO PREP***

Wisdom Prayer

Children will pray for help to obey God.

Supplies: none

Time: about 5 minutes

Preparation: none

Have kids form a large circle, holding hands or linking elbows. Direct kids to take slow, small steps toward the center of the circle as you pray so that by the end of the prayer, kids are standing shoulder to shoulder.

SAY: **As we pray and move toward the center of the circle, think about how obeying God pulls us closer to him.**

PRAY: **Dear God, every day we make choices. Sometimes we choose the right thing, but other times doing wrong seems easier or more fun. Temptations crowd around us, leading us away from your path. Keep us close to you, and give us strength to choose what is right. Amen.**

Life Application

▶ ***FOR LARGE GROUPS***

Children will discover practical ways to obey God as they participate in these application activities.

Obeying Parents

Encourage kids to think of how they can obey God by obeying and honoring their parents at home. Ask kids to help you brainstorm a list of ways to obey and honor their parents, especially by doing chores at home. Then ask each child to commit to doing one item on the list during the next week. Be sure to follow up next week to find out about kids' experiences.

Sharing Faith

Make sure kids understand that one way to obey God is to share their faith with others. They can do so in a variety of ways—such as by making good choices, writing letters, sending e-mails, making phone calls, talking in person, or inviting others to church. Work as a class to come up with a list of ways for kids to share their faith with others, and have each child pick one way to share with a specific person. Then have kids write down the name of the person and the chosen way to share their faith. Seal the paper in an envelope, and mail the envelopes to kids in about a month to serve as reminders.

Time Well Spent

Explain to kids that one way to obey God is to choose wisely how they spend their time—especially free time. Give kids a page from a weekly calendar, and help them think through a typical week by writing down how they usually spend their time. Then have them work with partners to identify ways they could better spend their time in obedience to God. Encourage partners to stay in contact and ask each other about how they follow through on their plans.

Object Lesson

▶ ***NO PREP***
▶ ***FOR SMALL GROUPS***

Toy Obedience

Children will consider why God gives us choices.

Supplies: wind-up toy or remote-control toy

Time: 10 to 20 minutes

Preparation: none

Have kids gather around you, and set a wind-up toy or remote-control toy on the floor. Show kids how the toy works, and then let several students try it themselves. After several minutes of play, SAY: **This toy will do almost exactly what we want it to do. We can control where it goes and what it does. God could have made us like this toy. It would be much easier to obey God if he had—we would just do whatever God wanted us to all the time.**

ASK:

- **Why do you think God didn't make us like this toy?**
- **Why do you think God wants us to be able to choose to obey?**
- **How can we choose to ▷OBEY GOD more often?**

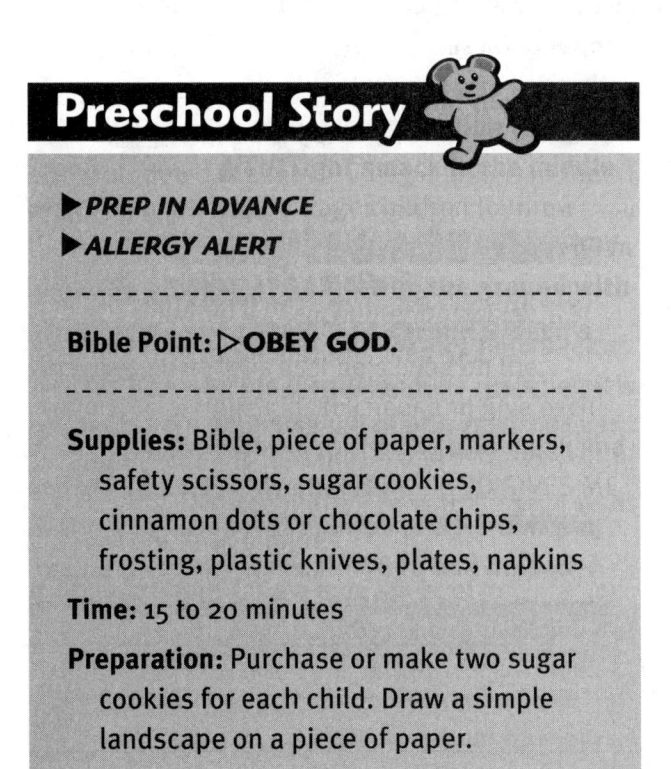

Preschool Story

▶ ***PREP IN ADVANCE***
▶ ***ALLERGY ALERT***

Bible Point: ▷OBEY GOD.

Supplies: Bible, piece of paper, markers, safety scissors, sugar cookies, cinnamon dots or chocolate chips, frosting, plastic knives, plates, napkins

Time: 15 to 20 minutes

Preparation: Purchase or make two sugar cookies for each child. Draw a simple landscape on a piece of paper.

A Split Kingdom

Have kids form a circle and sit down. Open your Bible to 1 Kings 12, and show children the words. SAY: **King Solomon had lots of riches and lots of wisdom, but none of that was enough when he chose to disobey God. God was angry at King Solomon because he had turned against God, so God told Solomon that his kingdom would one day be split apart.**

Show children the picture you drew before class. SAY: **This is the kingdom of Israel. After Solomon died, his son Rehoboam became king.** Encourage one child to draw a picture of King Rehoboam at the top corner of the picture.

Rehoboam was *not* a good king. He didn't listen to God, and he didn't listen to other people who tried to give him wisdom. Rehoboam chose to turn away from God and be mean to the people of Israel.

Encourage kids to stand up and act out the words Rehoboam spoke to his people. SAY: **Rehoboam said he would make the people work very hard and that he would whip them if they didn't work hard enough.**

Have kids pretend to be the Israelites and cross their arms and complain about Rehoboam's words. SAY: **The Israelites were so mad that they ran away and made someone else their king instead. The Israelites made Jeroboam their king instead of Rehoboam.**

Encourage children to pretend to crown one of the other children. SAY: **They thought Jeroboam would be a much better king than Rehoboam was.**

One tiny part of Israel still chose to follow Rehoboam. Help children cut the picture of the land into 12 parts. **Ten parts of Israel chose to follow Jeroboam, and only two tiny parts chose to follow Rehoboam.** Put 10 parts of the picture in one pile and the other two parts in a separate pile. **So the kingdom of Israel was split up, just as God had told Solomon. We can choose to ▷OBEY GOD instead of disobeying him like Solomon did.**

After the story, give each child two sugar cookies and 12 cinnamon dots or chocolate chips. Help kids frost their cookies, and then have them count out 10 cinnamon dots or chocolate chips to put on one cookie and two to put on the other cookie. As children enjoy their snack, remind them that the kingdom of Israel was divided because Solomon chose to disobey God instead of following God.

ASK:

- **Why did God split the kingdom of Israel?**
- **Why is it important to obey God?**
- **How can you choose to obey God this week?**

notes

BIBLE STORY

Elijah and the Prophets of Baal

For the Leader

The emotion reflected in this passage is striking. The prophets of Baal were passionate in their prayers. Elijah was bold—and mocking—in his challenge. The king was angry. The people were desperate. The stakes were high. And Elijah kicked the stakes up another notch when he doused his altar with water. He was not only making it impossible for the altar to light without supernatural intervention; he was also effectively wasting a precious resource that had been in short supply for three years. The land was suffering from drought.

Baal was believed to be the god of fire, storm, vegetation, fertility, and life. When Elijah poured the scarce water all over his altar to God, he was likely further mocking Baal and his followers—pointing out that Baal had not provided water for more than three years.

Key Scriptures

1 Samuel 12:24

1 Kings 18:16-40

Bible Verse

"But be sure to fear the Lord and faithfully serve him. Think of all the wonderful things he has done for you" (1 Samuel 12:24).

Bible Experience

▶ *NO PREP*

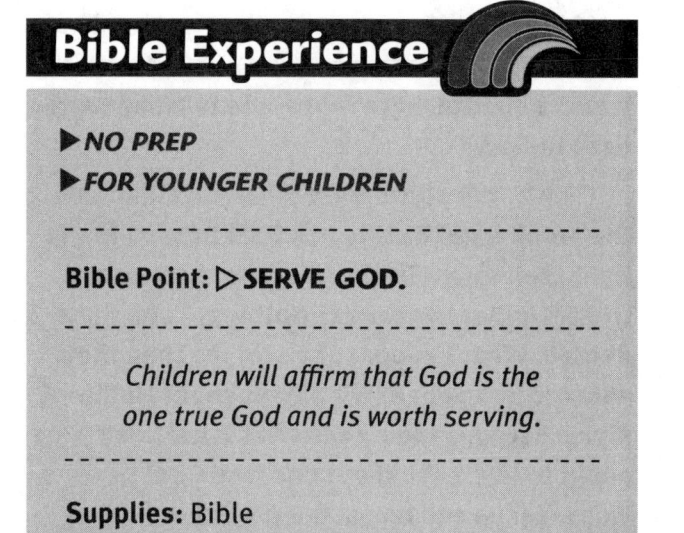

▶ *FOR YOUNGER CHILDREN*

Bible Point: ▷ **SERVE GOD.**

Children will affirm that God is the one true God and is worth serving.

Supplies: Bible

Time: 15 to 20 minutes

Preparation: none

Open your Bible to 1 Kings 18, and show the children the words.

SAY: **Today's Bible story is about the prophet Elijah. A prophet is a person who tells people messages from God. Elijah knew there was one true God.** Hold up one finger, and point up high on each word—*one*, *true*, and *God*. Have kids repeat the motion and the phrase.

But many people in the land where Elijah lived weren't sure if they should follow the one true God (have kids point up and repeat the phrase "one true God") **or if they should worship other gods. You and I know that this is silly. There are no other gods. There's only one true God!** Have kids point up and repeat the phrase.

There were 850 prophets who believed in fake gods with names like *Baal*. But the prophet Elijah believed in the one true God. Have kids point up and repeat the phrase. **The time came for Elijah to prove that the Lord was the one true God.** Have kids point up and repeat the phrase.

Baal's prophets started building an altar; later Elijah built an altar. An altar was made of stone and piled with wood and sticks for a fire. It was a special place for people to make sacrifices to God.

Finally, the altars were finished. Elijah told the prophets of Baal to ask Baal to send fire to light their altar. So the false prophets prayed to Baal. What happened? Nothing! Then they danced. What happened? Nothing! Then they shouted and yelled. What happened? Nothing! It was because their gods were fake! They were about to learn about our one true God! Have kids point up and repeat the phrase.

Then it was Elijah's turn. He built his altar and dug a hole around it. Then he had lots of water poured all over the wood. Not once, but three times! Whoosh! Whoosh! Whoosh! There was so much water, it poured around the altar and into the hole! Then Elijah prayed, "Answer me, O Lord, so these people will know that you are our one true God." Have kids point up and repeat the phrase.

You know what happened? God sent fire! Yes! There was so much fire that it burned up the altar and all that water! Wow! When the people saw this, they believed in our one true God! Point up and repeat the phrase "one true God."

ASK:

- **How do you think the people felt when the altar burned?**
- **Why do you think Elijah was so courageous in serving God?**

Read aloud 1 Samuel 12:24 and ASK:

- **What great things has God done for you?**
- **How can you serve God?**

Additional Topics List

This lesson can be used to help children discover... Glorifying God, God's Will, Honor, Idolatry, Obedience, and Worship.

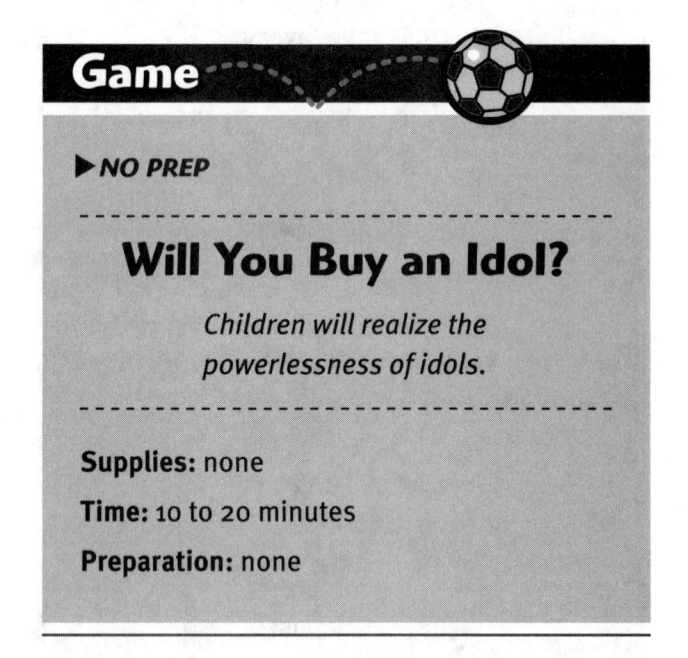

Game

▶ *NO PREP*

Will You Buy an Idol?

Children will realize the powerlessness of idols.

Supplies: none

Time: 10 to 20 minutes

Preparation: none

Have children sit in a circle. Ask two volunteers to go to the center of the circle; they'll be the Idol Seller and the Idol. SAY: **After Elijah's showdown with the prophets of Baal on Mount Carmel, there may have been a lot of people wanting to get rid of their Baal idols.**

The Idol Seller will try to sell the Idol to the children in the circle. The Idol Seller will choose one person and ask, "Will you buy an idol?" That player must answer, "No, thank you," with a straight face. Then the seller will say, "My idol can do cool things like [tap dance, sing a song, do a somersault, and so on]. Will you buy an idol now?"

The Idol should try to do whatever the Idol Seller says he or she can do. Then the player in the circle must answer, "No, thank you," again with a straight face. If the player cracks a smile or laughs, he or she becomes the Idol Seller and the Idol Seller joins the circle. Play until all children have been the Idol or the Idol Seller. After the game, ask students to discuss these questions:

- ◆ **What was the goofiest thing someone just asked an idol to do?**
- ◆ **What did the prophets of Baal ask their idol to do? Why didn't he?**
- ◆ **How did Elijah show everyone that they should ▷ SERVE GOD instead?**

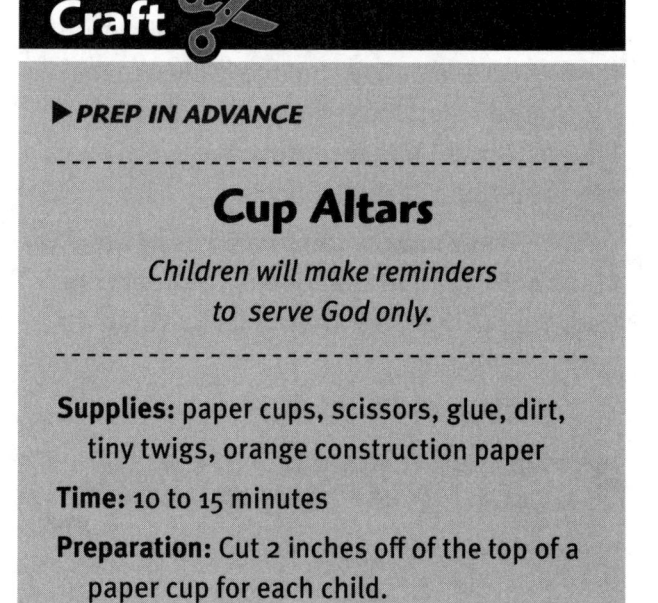

Craft

▶ *PREP IN ADVANCE*

Cup Altars

Children will make reminders to serve God only.

Supplies: paper cups, scissors, glue, dirt, tiny twigs, orange construction paper

Time: 10 to 15 minutes

Preparation: Cut 2 inches off of the top of a paper cup for each child.

Give each child the bottom part of a cup. Have kids cover the outside of their cups with glue and then roll them in dirt. Have kids turn their cups upside down and use tiny twigs and construction-paper flames to build a "fire" on them. Then ASK:

- ◆ **How can this craft remind you of the story of Elijah and the prophets of Baal?**
- ◆ **How can this craft remind you to ▷ SERVE ONLY GOD?**
- ◆ **What do you think Elijah learned about serving God?**

SAY: **As Elijah was reminded, serving God is always the right choice. Sometimes it takes courage, but it's always worth it.**

Have children take their cup altars home as reminders to serve God.

Bible Application

▶ *NO PREP*
▶ *FOR SMALL GROUPS*

Service Skits

Children will consider how they can serve God when it's hard.

Supplies: none

Time: 20 to 30 minutes

Preparation: none

Have kids form groups of three to five.

SAY: **In your group, think of a time it's hard for kids to serve God—just as it was hard for Elijah to serve God when he felt like the only one who loved God. Create a skit that shows how someone your age could serve God in that situation.**

Give groups five to 10 minutes to create their skits, and then have them perform their skits for the entire group. After the skits, ASK:

- ◆ **Why is it so hard to serve God in these situations?**
- ◆ **Why is it important to ▷ SERVE GOD when it's hard to do so?**
- ◆ **How can we help each other serve God?**

Have group members pray for each other, asking for God's help in serving him and in encouraging each other when it's hard to serve God.

Creative Prayer Idea

▶ *NO PREP*

Elijah Challenges the Prophets of Baal

Children will proclaim that there is only one true God.

Supplies: none

Time: about 2 minutes

Preparation: none

As you pray, have children point up with one finger. PRAY: **Dear God, we are so glad that we know you, our one true God. It's sad that some people don't yet know that you're our one true God. Show us who we can tell about you, and give us the courage to share how wonderful and powerful you are. Help us to serve you every day. Amen.**

n

o

t

e

s

Snack

▶ *NO PREP*

▶ *ALLERGY ALERT*

Cheese Altars

Children will make a cheesy snack that will remind them of the altar Elijah built.

Supplies: small cheese cubes, paper plates, toothpicks

Time: 5 to 10 minutes

Preparation: none

Have kids use cheese cubes to build altars like the one Elijah may have built to challenge the prophets of Baal. Toothpicks inserted into the blocks help stabilize the structures, which kids can gobble up after constructing.

SAY: **These snacks can remind us of the altar Elijah built to show that God is the only true God. We can ▷ SERVE GOD, just as Elijah did.**

Worship Prompt Idea

Sticks of Service

Children will worship God by telling him how they will serve him this week.

Supplies: table or 2 chairs, sheet, small sticks, CD player, worship CD

Time: 10 to 15 minutes

Preparation: Build an "altar" in your meeting area by draping a sheet over a table or two chairs.

SAY: **Just as Elijah boldly served God, we can ▷SERVE GOD in many ways every day. Let's worship God now by telling him how we will serve him this week.**

Brainstorm together a few ways kids can serve God this week. Then show kids the "altar" you set up. Give each person a small stick.

SAY: **We're going to sing a few worship songs now. While we're singing, think of a way you will serve God this week. When you're ready, come up and lay your stick on the altar as a way of showing God you will serve him, as Elijah did. Please know that this should be a genuine worship experience, and you don't have to participate if you don't feel you can.**

Sing a few worship songs, allowing kids to lay their sticks on the altar at their own pace. When everyone has had a chance, close in prayer, asking for God's help to serve him this week in the ways your group has committed to doing.

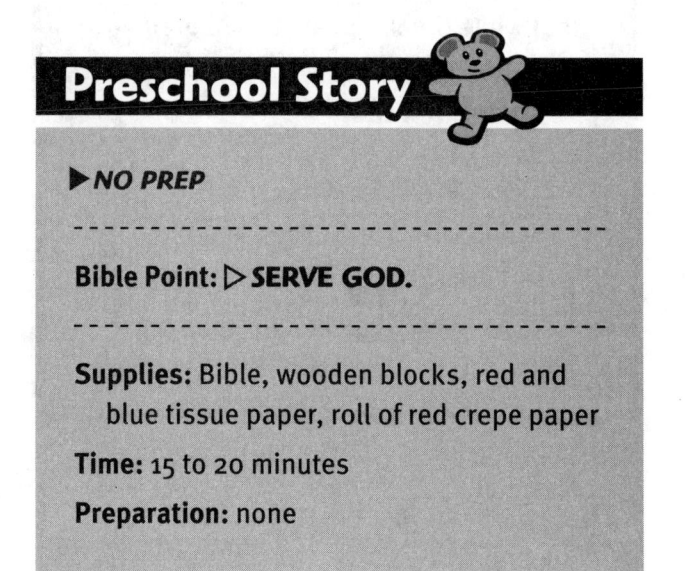

Preschool Story

▶*NO PREP*

Bible Point: ▷**SERVE GOD.**

Supplies: Bible, wooden blocks, red and blue tissue paper, roll of red crepe paper

Time: 15 to 20 minutes

Preparation: none

A Fiery Show

Have kids form a circle and sit on the floor. Open your Bible to 1 Kings 18, and show children the words. Set out wooden blocks, red and blue tissue paper, and a roll of red crepe paper.

SAY: **Elijah was a prophet of God. That meant that God used Elijah to tell people special things God wanted them to know. During Elijah's days, many people worshipped a false god they called Baal. They believed Baal could do things that he really couldn't, so God wanted Elijah to show the people just how wrong they were.**

Elijah dared Baal's followers to see who was the only true God—Elijah's God or Baal. Elijah told the followers of Baal to build an altar. Altars were made of large rocks stacked up in a pile and were used to burn sacrifices and worship gods. The people built an altar to Baal and then called on Baal to light the fire on the altar.

Let children work together to stack the wooden blocks in a pile.

SAY: **Baal didn't answer the people, and no fire came down to light the altar.**

ASK:

- **Hmm. Why do you think Baal didn't send down fire to light the altar?**

SAY: **Now it was Elijah's turn. He built an altar, too.** Let kids stack up wooden blocks to make a second altar.

Elijah knew God could send down fire to burn the sacrifice, so he asked people to pour water all over the altar so that unless God made it happen, the wood couldn't catch on fire. Let children tear blue tissue paper and place it around the wood.

Even though the altar was soaking wet, Elijah knew that God could burn it up anyway. It was Elijah's turn, and he called out to God, "God, please start a fire on the altar." Have children stand up and circle around the altar with praying hands and say, "God, please send your fire." Then ASK:

- **What do you think happened?**

SAY: **A fire came down right away and burned up the sacrifice and even all the water that was**

poured all around! Have kids tear red tissue paper into strips and toss them all over the altar.

The people were so amazed that they fell to the ground. Encourage children to dramatically—but carefully—fall to the ground.

Then the people really believed in God! Have children stand up. Give each child a roughly 3-foot streamer of red crepe paper, and let kids jump up and skip around the altar, waving their streamers and chanting, "There is only one God! There is only God!"

ASK:

- **Was Baal a real god? Why or why not?**
- **How did Elijah serve God and show that God was the only God?**
- **How can you serve God?**

SAY: **Elijah served God when he showed all the other people how powerful God is. We can ▷ SERVE GOD, too, by telling others about him, by loving others, and by obeying our parents.**

notes

BIBLE STORY

God Speaks to Elijah in a Whisper

For the Leader

This event from Scripture takes some children by surprise. They're used to Bible stories where God shows up in a fiery cloud or a descending dove. That the powerful God of Creation would choose to speak in a quiet voice seems odd—out of character.

Yet God seldom speaks from burning bushes into the lives of most believers. As you share today's Bible story, you'll communicate the reality that while God is speaking, children must be willing to listen to hear his voice, too.

Key Scriptures

1 Kings 19:1-18

Matthew 11:15

John 10:26-28

Bible Verse

"Anyone with ears to hear should listen and understand!" (Matthew 11:15).

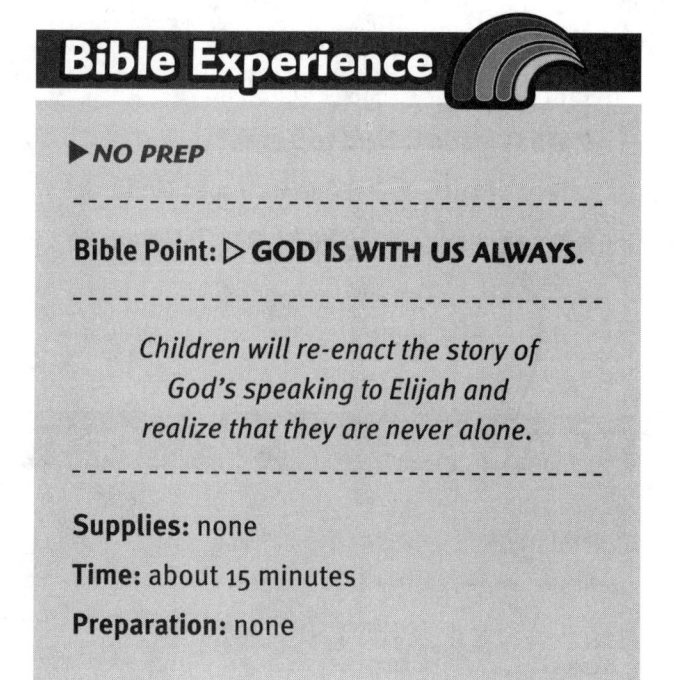

Bible Experience

▶ *NO PREP*

Bible Point: ▷ **GOD IS WITH US ALWAYS.**

Children will re-enact the story of God's speaking to Elijah and realize that they are never alone.

Supplies: none

Time: about 15 minutes

Preparation: none

Ask children to form pairs and sit on the floor, back to back, leaning against each other and linking elbows.

SAY: **Elijah was a prophet, which means he told the people of Israel what God wanted the people to know. And mostly God wanted the people to follow him! Almost all of the people were following a false god.**

Elijah had a showdown with hundreds of false prophets, and with God's help, Elijah won. Unlock your elbows and give each other backward high fives. Aim carefully!

Now lock your elbows again.

Elijah then got a message from the queen, who wanted to *kill* Elijah. Tremble where you're sitting. So Elijah ran away. Pump your feet up and down—you're running.

Elijah hid in the desert. He told God he was ready to die because he was the last one in the whole country serving God. God sent an angel to care for Elijah, and the angel said it was time to go for a hike.

Elijah ended up in a cave on a mountain. God told Elijah to get ready: God was going to reveal his presence.

First, there was a mighty wind. Sway left and right as if you were being blown by the wind. But God's voice wasn't in the wind.

Then there was an earthquake. Move up and down as if there were an earthquake. But God's voice wasn't in the earthquake.

Then there was a fire. Scoot back as if you were getting away from a hot fire. Wait—you're stuck! God's voice wasn't in the fire either.

Then there was a whisper. Unlink your elbows and cup your hands up to your ears so you can listen. Jesus said this: Read aloud Matthew 11:15. **Elijah knew to do this!**

God told Elijah that he wasn't alone—seven thousand people in Israel loved and worshipped God. Then God told Elijah what to do.

Turn to face your partner and discuss:

- **Do you think Elijah was surprised that God whispered? Why?**
- **How does it feel knowing that you're not alone? that God is with you, and so are lots of other people who serve God?**

SAY: **Elijah learned a lesson we need to learn, too. If you follow God, you're never all alone.** ▷ **GOD IS WITH US ALWAYS.**

Additional Topics List

This lesson can be used to help children discover... Faithfulness, God's Love, Obedience, and Rest.

Game

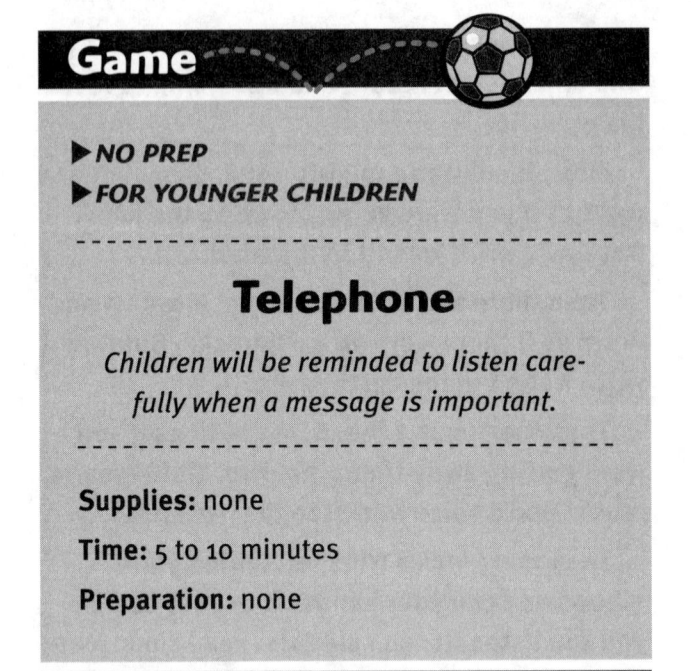

▶ *NO PREP*
▶ *FOR YOUNGER CHILDREN*

Telephone

Children will be reminded to listen carefully when a message is important.

Supplies: none

Time: 5 to 10 minutes

Preparation: none

Have kids sit in a circle. If you have more than 10 students, form more than one circle. Read aloud Matthew 11:15, and then SAY: **If Jesus were talking to *me*, I'd listen to every word he said! If you feel the same way, raise your hand.**

But sometimes it's hard to keep a message straight. I'll show you. I'll whisper one sentence in the ear of the person on my right. That person will whisper it to the person on his or her right, and so on around the circle. Try to repeat the sentence the same way you heard it. While you're not listening or whispering, chant this with me:

"I listen when I'm sitting;
I listen when I'm walking.
Except that I can't listen—
I'm too busy talking!"

Start the chant, and then whisper to the person on your right: **"Which way went the window washer?"** When the message reaches you, repeat what was said. It may be the same—but probably it won't be.

Then start sentences going *both* directions around the circle. Make up your own sentences, and keep the chant going.

After you repeat what you heard,

ASK:

- **What made it hard to listen?**
- **What makes it hard to listen to God?**
- **What can we do to be better listeners to God?**

Craft

▶ *NO PREP*

Elijah Unfolded

Children will make simple Elijah puppets in stages.

Supplies: paper lunch bags, crayons, markers

Time: 10 to 15 minutes

Preparation: none

Give each child a lunch bag. Show children how to place bags so the folded bottom faces up. The flap made by the bottom fold becomes Elijah's mouth. Have markers and crayons available.

SAY: **We're going to each make a hand puppet, but we're going to make them in stages. Ready to get started?**

Elijah was having a tough time. He'd had a showdown with hundreds of false prophets and, with God's help, had won the fight. But instead of getting a medal and a plaque, Elijah got word from Jezebel—the wife of King Ahab—saying, "By this time tomorrow you'll be a dead man."

So Elijah ran for his life. He went into the desert and sat under a tree. He'd had enough. He said, "Lord, take my life."

An angel gave Elijah food and told him to get up and eat because he was going on a hike. A 40-day hike. How do you think Elijah felt?

Draw Elijah's mouth (demonstrate how the edges of the bottom fold become lips when you slip your hand inside and curl your four fingers above the fold and your thumb beneath it) **but *not* Elijah's eyes. You'll draw those later. You'll have two minutes to work.**

After two minutes, ask children to put down their supplies. SAY: **Elijah spent the night in a cave on Mount Sinai. Elijah told God he was the only person serving God. God told Elijah to leave the cave and get ready: God's presence was about to pass by. When Elijah looked, there was a powerful wind that blasted loose large rocks! How do you think Elijah's eyes looked when he saw that? Draw them on your puppet. Work fast—you've got just two minutes!**

After two minutes, ask children to put down their supplies. SAY: **Pull your puppets onto your hands. Next, God sent an earthquake. Make your puppets jump up and down. Great!**

But God wasn't in the wind or the earthquake. And he wasn't in the fire that came next. Then Elijah heard a gentle whisper. He...wait... he doesn't have *ears*. Draw some big ears on Elijah—he needs to hear a whisper! You've got one minute to work.

After one minute, ask children to put down their supplies. SAY: **When Elijah heard the whisper, he stood at the mouth of the cave. God told Elijah that Elijah wasn't alone. There were seven thousand faithful people in Israel!**

Put on your puppet, and give each other puppet high fives! God didn't leave Elijah on his own, and he doesn't leave us on our own either!

Bible Application

▶ *NO PREP*

In Elijah's Shoes

Children will quickly be reminded that, just as Elijah, they're not alone.

Supplies: none

Time: about 5 minutes

Preparation: none

Ask children to stand and to stand apart from others. Ask them to close their eyes as you talk. SAY: **Sometimes we feel all alone. It feels as if we're different from everyone else or that nobody understands how we feel. But God understands, and when we're feeling bad, he wants us to know that he loves us.**

We wish God would shout, "I love you!" at the top of his lungs, but he usually lets us know in softer ways—through his promises in the Bible or through a friend, for instance.

Do this: With your eyes closed, softly whisper, "God loves you."

In a few moments I'm going to tell you to keep whispering, "God loves you." As you do so, listen to what other people are whispering, and slowly move toward another voice. When you bump against another person, open your eyes and say, "God loves you. You are not alone." Then close your eyes and start whispering again, moving toward someone else. Close your eyes and start whispering now.

After children have done this for two minutes, ask them to stop where they are and join you in prayer. PRAY: **Thanks, God, for your love and for never letting us be all alone. You love us always and always know where we are. In Jesus' name, amen.**

Creative Prayer Idea

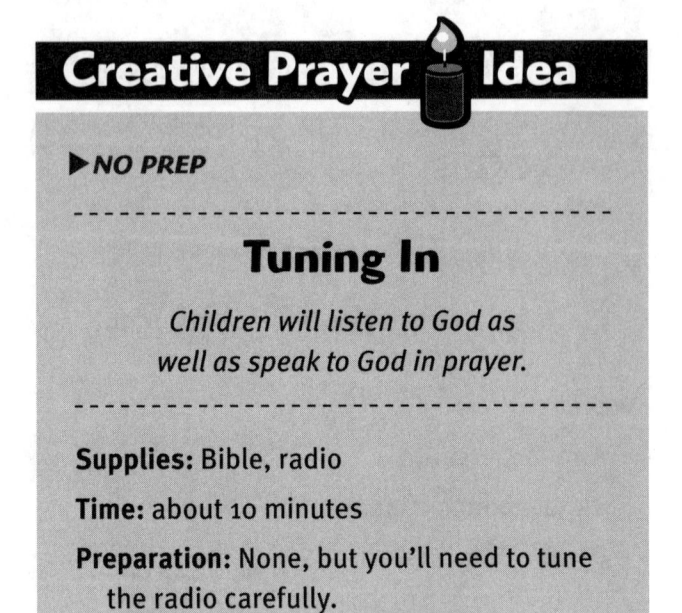

▶ *NO PREP*

Tuning In

Children will listen to God as well as speak to God in prayer.

Supplies: Bible, radio

Time: about 10 minutes

Preparation: None, but you'll need to tune the radio carefully.

Place the radio where children can easily hear it. Tune the radio to a location on the dial where nothing is audible but static. Turn the volume up so children can hear the static, and SAY: **Listen carefully. Can you make out any words or music?**

Almost—but not quite.

Somewhere there's a radio station broadcasting on the frequency we've tuned in to, but the transmitter isn't close enough. There's a station somewhere trying to connect with us, trying to bring us music and commercials...but we can't hear it. We're not close enough.

Now dial in a station that plays gentle, quiet music clearly. SAY: **That's better! The signal is crisp and clear, and we can actually receive it. Sometimes when we pray about things and we don't hear from God, we think he's far away. Or that he doesn't care. But that's not true. God *is* near. He wants you to know him so you can follow in his ways.**

Invite a volunteer to read aloud John 10:26-28. Then read it aloud again yourself, slowly.

SAY: **Jesus wants us to listen for his voice and to follow him. What do you think he's saying to you? Let's pray now—and instead of just talking, we're going to listen, too.**

Go around a circle praying aloud, but instead of just saying "Amen" and moving ahead after you've all prayed, SAY: **Thanks for listening to us, God. We want to listen to you, too. For the next two minutes, as we're silent, please guide our thoughts as we listen for your voice.**

Science Devotion

Can You Hear Me Yet?

Children will discover that volume alone doesn't improve communication.

Supplies: Bible, 2 foam cups per student (waxed paper cups work, too)

Time: about 5 minutes

Preparation: Practice this activity before you try to demonstrate it.

Give each child two empty cups. Ask children to drop their first cup inside their second cup, letting the first nest loosely inside the second.

SAY: **Here's your challenge: Get the top cup out of the bottom one without turning the cups over and without touching the top cup. Start by talking loudly at your cups to see if you can vibrate the top cup out. Use different tones and volumes.**

After children have tried this for a few seconds, suggest that perhaps they should shout instead of talk. After 10 seconds, suggest that the "volume vibrations" aren't yet loud enough, so they should shout louder. This approach will fail, too.

As students catch their breath, do a demonstration. If you blow across the lips of the cups, the cup nested inside the bottom cup you're holding will lift and float upward and out.

SAY: **Shouting at the cup didn't get the cup to jump up and move.**

ASK:

- **Does shouting motivate you to do things? Why or why not?**
- **How do you think God's voice sounds? Describe it.**

Read aloud 1 Kings 19:11-13. Then ASK:

- **What does this passage tell you about God's voice? about God's power and how God uses it?**
- **How was your quietly blowing across the cups like God's speaking to Elijah?**

Worship Prompt Idea

▶ *NO PREP*

Silent Worship

Children will learn to honor God for speaking to us in quiet ways.

Supplies: none

Time: about 5 minutes

Preparation: none

Ask children to gather in a circle for prayer. SAY: **Please be super quiet as you sit here. For 30 seconds I'm not going to say anything, and I want you to simply listen. I'll then guide us in silent prayer and worship. Please get comfortable and close your eyes.**

After 30 seconds, thank God for the things you hear. For instance, you might hear other people nearby and say, "Thank you, God, for giving us other people to be with us." Silently thank God for other people: your family, your friends, the people you know at school, and so on.

You may also hear sounds from nature and sounds of the building in which you're meeting. Thank and worship God for both. Ask children to listen for their own breathing and heartbeats and then worship God for making them.

End with a time of out-loud sentence prayers. Thank God for speaking to us in loud ways that show us his power and in quiet ways that show us his love.

Preschool Story

▶ *PREPARE IN ADVANCE*

Bible Point: ▷ **GOD IS WITH US ALWAYS.**

Supplies: Bible, blanket, table, flashlight, electric fan, large sheet of poster board, red crepe-paper streamers

Time: 15 to 20 minutes

Preparation: Make a "cave" by draping a large blanket over a table. Place the sheet of poster board, the red crepe-paper streamers, and the fan near the cave. Place the flashlight inside the cave.

Wind and Earthquakes and Fire, Oh My!

Have kids form a circle and sit down. Open your Bible to 1 Kings 19, and show children the words. SAY: **Elijah was a prophet of God, which means that he told people about God and about**

God's words. There were a king and a queen named Ahab and Jezebel who didn't like Elijah. They wanted to hurt him because they didn't believe in God. Elijah ran away and hid from Ahab and Jezebel.

Lead children to the "cave" you set up before class, and encourage them to crawl inside. Crawl in after them and turn on the flashlight. SAY: **Elijah hid in a cave on a mountain. He was waiting for God to speak to him.** Sit quietly with children for a minute or two, and then SAY: **I don't hear God, do you? I'm going to go out and check to see if God's there.**

Leave the cave and start the fan. Encourage kids to join you outside. SAY: **Look, there's a strong wind. But God's not in the wind.** Let the fan blow for another minute, and then turn it off and lead kids back into the cave.

God wasn't in the wind, so Elijah continued to wait for God's voice. Sit quietly for another minute, and then SAY: **I don't hear God's voice, do you? I'm going to go out and check to see if God's there.**

Leave the cave and begin shaking the poster board and stomping your feet. Encourage kids to join you outside. SAY: **There's an earthquake!** (Act as if the ground were shaking, and encourage kids to pretend, too.) **But God's not in the earthquake.** Continue to shake the poster board and pretend the ground is shaking for a few more seconds. Then lead kids back into the cave.

God wasn't in the earthquake, so Elijah continued to wait for God's voice. Sit quietly for a minute, and then SAY: **I don't hear God's voice, do you? I'm going to go out and check to see if God's there.**

Leave the cave and begin waving the red crepe paper. Encourage kids to join you outside. Give each child a streamer, and tell students to twirl and wave their red streamers in the air. SAY: **There's a fire out here! But God's not in the fire.** Continue waving the red streamers for a few seconds. Then lead kids back into the cave.

God wasn't in the fire either, so Elijah continued to wait for God's voice. Sit quietly for a minute, and then SAY: **I don't hear God's voice, do you? I'm going to go out and check to see if God's there.**

Leave the cave and begin rubbing your hands together to make a whisper sound. SAY: **Come out, come out! God is here in the sound of a gentle whisper.** Encourage kids to come out and make the whisper sound, too. **Elijah heard God's voice in the sound of a gentle whisper. God told Elijah to go back to Ahab and Jezebel and that God would take care of him.**

Encourage kids to sit down in a circle. SAY: **God was with Elijah on the mountain, and**
▷ GOD IS WITH US ALWAYS, too.

ASK:

- **How was God with Elijah on the mountain?**
- **When are some times you knew God was with you?**
- **How can you trust that God is with you this week?**

n

o

t

e

s

BIBLE STORY

Elijah Taken to Heaven

For the Leader

Elijah's exit from the earth was reminiscent of two similar experiences described in the Bible: Enoch's ascension (Genesis 5:24) and Jesus' return to heaven (Acts 1:9). In such company, and on its own merits, this stands out as a great honor. Obviously God's favor was upon Elijah in such a powerful way that God wanted to honor him in this way.

This incident also apparently served to display God's power and presence to a group of at least 50 other prophets. As witnesses to this event, they no doubt were in awe of God's power as well as the legacy Elijah left as a prophet of God.

Key Scriptures

2 Kings 2:1-11

2 Chronicles 20:20

Bible Verse

"Believe in the Lord your God, and you will be able to stand firm" (2 Chronicles 20:20).

Bible Experience

▶ *NO PREP*

Bible Point: ▷ **WE CAN BE FAITHFUL.**

Children will experience what faithfulness is like.

Supplies: Bible, 2-foot lengths of rope or twine for every 2 children

Time: 20 to 30 minutes

Preparation: none

SAY: **In today's Bible story we'll hear about how Elijah and Elisha were great friends. In fact, Elisha didn't want Elijah to go anywhere without him. So Elisha went with Elijah everywhere.**

Have kids form same-sex pairs. Have partners stand side by side and hold hands. Loosely tie one child's right leg to the other child's left leg, as if you were preparing the children for a three-legged race.

SAY: **I'm going to read the first part of our story. When Elijah and Elisha move on to another city, move with your partner to a different part of the room. You must keep holding hands and keep your feet together. Don't rush—I don't want you to fall!**

Read aloud 2 Kings 2:1-6. Stop at the places that say, "The Lord has told me to go to..." and have pairs move to another area of the room. After you read verse 6, have kids untie their legs, give you the lengths of rope, and then sit together in a large group.

ASK:

- **What was it like to be stuck with your partner during this activity?**
- **What does it mean to be faithful?**
- **How did Elisha show he was a faithful friend to Elijah?**

SAY: **Now let's take a look at what happened when Elijah and Elisha reached the Jordan River.** Read aloud 2 Kings 2:7-11.

God has the power to do all kinds of wonderful things. He helps us when we have problems, comforts us when we're sad, and gives us friends when we're lonely. God is always faithful to us, and because God helps us, ▷WE CAN BE FAITHFUL, too. God rewarded Elijah's faithfulness by allowing him not to die. He simply took Elijah to heaven.

Read aloud 2 Chronicles 20:20.

ASK:

- **Why do you think God rewarded Elijah as he did?**
- **What does it mean to "be able to stand firm"?**
- **How will God reward our faithfulness?**
- **How can we be faithful to God?**

SAY: **It's not easy to be faithful to God or to other people. But God wants us to be faithful, and God helps us so that like Elisha and Elijah, ▷WE CAN BE FAITHFUL.**

Additional Topics List

This lesson can be used to help children discover... Devotion, Following God, Love, Perseverance, and Serving God.

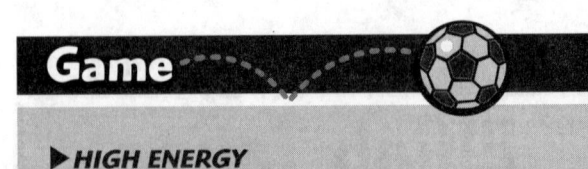

Game

▶ *HIGH ENERGY*

Double-Trouble Kickball

Children will play kickball attached to another person.

Supplies: 2-foot lengths of rope or twine for every 2 children, kickball, bases

Time: 15 to 30 minutes

Preparation: Set up a baseball diamond.

This is a perfect game for a group that's too large to play regular kickball. Have players form two teams, and then have team members form pairs. Give each pair a length of rope or twine, and have partners tie one person's left leg to the other person's right leg as if for a three-legged race.

A kicking pair can opt for either person to kick the ball or to use the pair's "third leg." A pair fielding the ball can use either person's hands to pick up the ball and throw it. Other than these rules, all the rules are the same as regular kickball.

After the game,

ASK:

- **What was it like to play with another person attached to you?**
- **How was this like or unlike being faithful to someone else?**
- **How was this like or unlike being faithful to God?**

SAY: **Elijah and Elisha showed faithfulness both to each other and to God. And God rewarded Elijah's faithfulness by taking him up to heaven in a chariot. Even though God**

probably won't do the same for us, it's important to be faithful to God. Just as in this game, it's not always easy, but with God's help, ▷ WE CAN BE FAITHFUL.

Craft

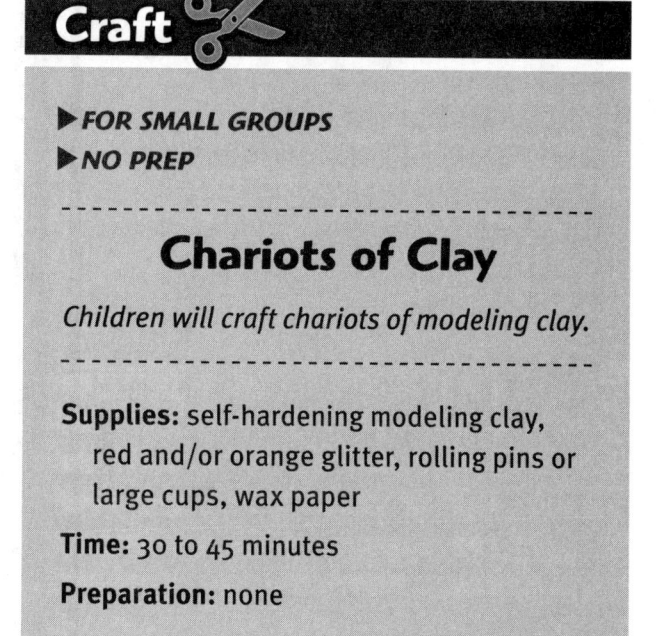

▶ *FOR SMALL GROUPS*
▶ *NO PREP*

Chariots of Clay

Children will craft chariots of modeling clay.

Supplies: self-hardening modeling clay, red and/or orange glitter, rolling pins or large cups, wax paper

Time: 30 to 45 minutes

Preparation: none

SAY: **Let's make our own chariots that can remind us of the chariot that took Elijah up to heaven.**

Give each student three small lumps of self-hardening modeling clay and a sheet of wax paper. Set the red and/or orange glitter and rolling pins or large cups in the middle of the table so everyone can reach them.

Using a cup or a rolling pin, show kids how to roll one lump of clay into a small rectangle. Then have students press their other lumps of clay into the bottom of the rectangles to make wheels.

As children are working, have them discuss the following questions:

- ◆ **What do you imagine the chariot of fire must have looked like?**
- ◆ **How do you think people felt when they saw the chariot?**
- ◆ **How do you think Elijah felt when the chariot swept him up toward heaven?**

Allow kids to sprinkle their chariots with red and/or orange glitter to resemble fire. Allow the clay to dry and harden according to package directions.

Bible Application

▶ *PREPARE IN ADVANCE*

Faithfulness Pictures

Children will draw themselves in faithful situations.

Supplies: "Picture of Faithfulness" handouts (p. 330), crayons or colored pencils

Time: about 15 minutes

Preparation: Make a copy of the "Picture of Faithfulness" handout for each child.

Have children form pairs. Give each child a "Picture of Faithfulness" handout and coloring supplies. SAY: **We've been learning about being faithful. These blank picture frames will give you an opportunity to draw a way to say, "You can count on me!" Write those words in your speech balloon on your picture now.** Pause as children write the words.

Now talk with your partner and decide one way you can be faithful. After you've thought of something, draw a picture of you being faithful. You can both draw the same picture or create different ones.

Picture of Faithfulness

Creative Prayer Idea

▶ *NO PREP*

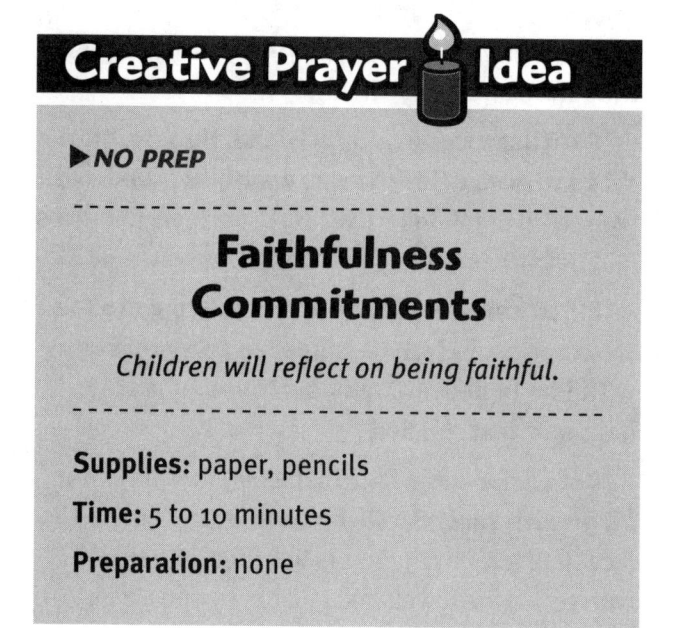

Faithfulness Commitments

Children will reflect on being faithful.

Supplies: paper, pencils

Time: 5 to 10 minutes

Preparation: none

Give each child paper and a pencil. Encourage kids to spread out. SAY: **We're going to write prayers to God. We'll ask God to help us be faithful people.**

PRAY: **Dear God, we praise you that we can read the Bible and see examples of faithfulness in people who are just like us. Faithful people can be counted on. We'll now take a few minutes to write or draw prayers to you, asking you to help us become more faithful in our actions. Let us tell you now that we're going to commit to being people who can be counted on.**

Allow a few minutes of silence for writing or drawing.

PRAY: **Thank you for teaching us that ▷ WE CAN BE FAITHFUL. Please be with us as we go through this next week so that others will see our acts of faithfulness. Amen.**

Discussion Launcher Questions

Ask children to form trios and discuss:

- **When is it hard for you to be faithful to someone else?**
- **When is it hard for you to be faithful to God?**
- **Why do you think God wants to help us be faithful?**
- **What can we do to become more faithful?**

Snack

▶ *ALLERGY ALERT*
▶ *PREPARE IN ADVANCE*

Celery Chariots

Children will make a snack that reminds them of the chariot that took Elijah to heaven.

Supplies: sliced carrots, celery sticks, toothpicks, cream cheese, plastic knives, Keebler E.L. Fudge sandwich cookies, paper plates

Time: about 5 minutes

Preparation: Wash the vegetables and slice the carrots.

Attach carrot-slice "wheels" to the sides of a celery stick using toothpicks. Fill the celery with cream cheese. Place an E.L. Fudge cookie into each celery "chariot."

As kids are eating their snacks, SAY: **This chariot can remind us of the chariot that took Elijah up to heaven. God rewarded Elijah's faithfulness in an unusual way. Like Elijah, ▷ WE CAN BE FAITHFUL, and God will reward us, too.**

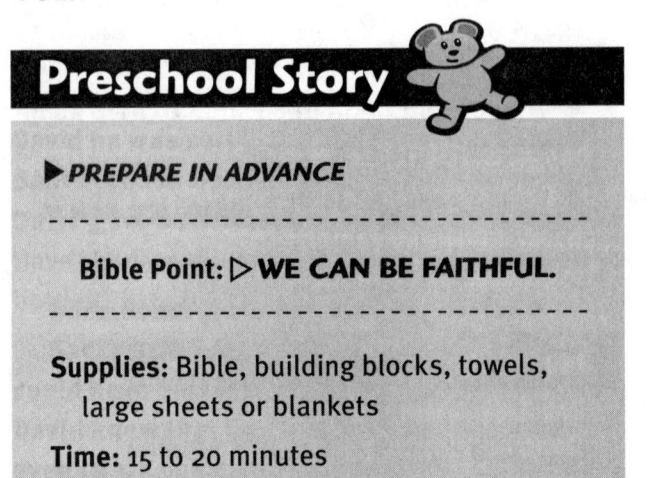

Preschool Story

▶ *PREPARE IN ADVANCE*

Bible Point: ▷ **WE CAN BE FAITHFUL.**

Supplies: Bible, building blocks, towels, large sheets or blankets

Time: 15 to 20 minutes

Preparation: Use building blocks to build two small "towns" in two separate areas of your room. In another area, lay down two towels to make a river.

Best Friends

Have kids form a circle and sit down against a wall. Open your Bible to 2 Kings 2, and show children the words. SAY: **Elijah the prophet grew old. He had a young friend named Elisha who helped him. Elijah and Elisha were good friends.**

Have each child find a partner and link arms. If you have an uneven number of kids in your class, be a partner yourself. Tell partners to pick one person to be Elijah and one person to be Elisha. Tell the "Elijahs" to pretend to talk whenever Elijah is talking in the story and the "Elishas" to pretend to talk whenever Elisha is talking in the story.

SAY: **It was almost time for Elijah to go to heaven and be with God. The good friends would have to leave each other. Elijah said, "Elisha, God wants me to do some things in the town of Bethel before he takes me away to live with him forever. Why don't you just stay here and rest?"**

But Elisha was a faithful friend. Elisha said, "No! I'll go with you!" Elisha was a faithful friend and went with Elijah to Bethel. Have partners link arms and travel with you to the first town you built.

Then Elijah said, "Now God wants me to do some things in Jericho before he takes me away to live with him in heaven. Why don't you just stay here and rest, Elisha?"

But Elisha was a faithful friend. He said, "No! I'll go with you!" Elisha was a faithful friend and went with Elijah to Jericho. Have partners link arms and travel with you to the second town you built.

Elijah said, "Now God wants me to go to the Jordan River before he takes me away to live with him in heaven. Why don't you just stay here and rest, Elisha?"

But Elisha was a faithful friend. He said, "No! I'll go with you!" So Elisha went with Elijah to the Jordan River. Have partners link arms and travel with you to the towels you laid out before class.

When they got to the Jordan River, they needed to cross it. Instead of swimming across, they were going to walk. So Elijah took off his coat and hit the water with it. Encourage the Elijahs to touch the towels and then separate the towels and tell kids to walk through the "river." **Elijah and his faithful friend Elisha walked across the river on dry ground. The two friends got to say goodbye to each other, and then God took Elijah to heaven.** Encourage partners to hug and then throw a blanket or sheet over the Elijahs so the Elijahs can't be seen anymore.

Elisha was sad that his good friend Elijah was gone. But Elisha knew that God wanted him to keep doing the work Elijah had been doing. Have the Elishas cross back over the river and head back to the starting point. Then uncover the Elijahs and have them go back to the starting point, too.

Elisha stayed with Elijah and helped him. Elisha loved Elijah and was faithful to him. God wants us to be faithful, too. ▷ **WE CAN BE FAITHFUL to our friends, our family, and God.**

ASK:

- **How was Elisha a faithful friend?**
- **Why is it important to be faithful?**
- **How can you be faithful this week?**

BIBLE STORY

Elisha and the Widow's Oil

For the Leader

Teaching complete and total trust in God can be a challenge when your students are children who may have suffered abuse, witnessed loss, or experienced poverty.

Introduce kids to Elisha, and they'll soon see how God can perform wonders to help those who trust in God. Help children discover that just as God helped the widow out of a dismal situation, they can trust that God will help them, too.

Key Scriptures

2 Kings 4:1-7

Proverbs 3:5

Psalms 22:4; 28:7; 56:3

Bible Verse

"Trust in the Lord with all your heart" (Proverbs 3:5).

Bible Experience

▶ *PREPARE IN ADVANCE*

The Oil Miracle

Bible Point: ▷ **WE CAN TRUST GOD COMPLETELY.**

Children will experience the miracle of Elisha and the widow's oil.

Supplies: Bible, small paper cups, medicine dropper filled with water

Time: 5 to 10 minutes

Preparation: If you use this experience during a worship service, give each person in the congregation a small paper cup, and tell participants to hold on to the cups until the children ask for them. If you use it during a Sunday-school program, ask another class to give cups to the children when they ask for them.

ASK:

◆ **What are some of the things you need?**

◆ **Who gives you the things you need?**

SAY: **Most of you get the things you need, such as a place to live, food, and clothing, from your parents. But we often don't worry about that stuff because we trust that our parents will take care of us. In today's Bible story, we'll hear about a woman whose husband died, making her a widow with two young boys. She trusted in God to provide for her. Let's listen to their story.** Read aloud 2 Kings 4:1-7.

The widow and her two sons were probably very sad that this man, who loved God, had died. I want you to show me your saddest faces.

Pause for children to show you their saddest faces. **But to make matters worse, there were people who wanted money from the woman, and they were coming to take her sons away to be slaves! What do you think the woman should have done?** Pause. **Well, she turned to Elisha the prophet.**

Elisha asked her how he could help. What do you think Elisha did? Pause. **You might think Elisha offered to give her money to pay her debts or offered to buy her food and clothing, but that's not what he did. Instead, Elisha told the woman to go and collect empty jars from her neighbors.**

Like the widow, I want you to go and collect empty cups from others. You just need to go up to as many adults as you can in one minute and ask them for the empty cups. Give children one minute to collect as many cups as they can, and then have them come back and sit down.

Wow! Look at all of the cups you found! Now let's find out what happened in our story. Elisha told the widow to fill all of the jars with oil. The widow agreed to do what Elisha told her to do, even though she had only a little bit of oil. It would be like trying to fill all of your empty cups with water using only a medicine dropper. Have kids pass around the medicine dropper full of water and try to fill their cups.

We weren't able to fill all of our cups, but the widow was able to fill all of her jars. How do you think she was able to fill all those jars with just a little bit of oil? Pause. **Proverbs 3:5 gives us a clue: "Trust in the Lord with all your heart." God did something miraculous for the widow. He allowed all of her jars to be filled, and once they were filled, the oil stopped flowing. How do you think the widow felt when she saw that she was able to fill all of the jars with just the little bit of oil she had?** Pause.

Elisha told the widow to sell the oil and pay her debts and then live on what was left. The widow learned that ▷ SHE COULD TRUST GOD COMPLETELY.

ASK:

- **How did the widow trust that God would take care of her?**
- **How can we trust in God?**

SAY: **God will take care of everyone, even widows, orphans, and aliens—people who are from other places. God loves each and every one of us so much that he will take care of us even when the situation may seem impossible. That's why ▷ WE CAN ALWAYS TRUST GOD COMPLETELY.**

Song & Connect

Use "Those Who Hope" (track 12, *it: Innovative Tools for Children's Ministry: Old Testament* CD) to help reinforce the Bible Point, **▷ WE CAN TRUST GOD COMPLETELY.**

Help kids understand that God gives us hope even in the toughest of times, which is why we can trust in him completely.

Additional Topics List

This lesson can be used to help children discover... Blessings, Faith, and God's Protection.

n
o
t
e
s

Game

▶ *HIGH ENERGY*

Overflowing Oil

Children will be reminded of God's miraculous care for the widow as they keep gathering "oil."

Supplies: garbage bags, newspaper or scrap paper, watch with a second hand, adult helpers

Time: 5 to 10 minutes

Preparation: You'll need one garbage bag for every three or four children. Recruit several adult helpers, too.

Kids will try to collect as much "oil" (in the form of paper wads) as they can in a short span of time (up to one minute). Have kids form groups of three or four, and give each group one bag. Toss wadded paper all over the room. Tell students they'll have one minute to collect as much "oil" (paper wads) as they can. Shout, "Go!" and start timing. As groups collect, have adult helpers toss out more wadded paper so there's always more to be collected. When time's up, shout, "Stop!" and have teams show how much they collected.

After the game, read aloud Proverbs 3:5. SAY: **▷ WE CAN TRUST GOD COMPLETELY, and he will provide for us what we really need, just as he gave Elisha the power to provide oil for a widow who needed money. Sometimes God gives us even more than we expect!**

Craft

▶ *FOR YOUNGER CHILDREN*

More-Than-Enough Bottles

Children will create bottles that are never empty.

Supplies: 12-ounce plastic bottles with caps, permanent marker, bowl of cooking oil, 1/4-cup measuring cups, funnels, paper towels, craft glue, paint markers

Time: 20 to 30 minutes

Preparation: Set all supplies where children can easily reach them.

Give each child a bottle and cap. Use a marker to write the child's name on the bottom of his or her bottle. Help children dip the measuring cups into the cooking oil and then use funnels to pour the oil into their bottles. Keep paper towels on hand in case of spills. Let children glue on the bottle caps, sealing the bottles shut. Have kids use paint markers to decorate their bottles.

When students have finished painting, set bottles aside to dry. Then

ASK:

- **How can you know that there's always oil in your bottles?**
- **What could your mom or dad do with this little bit of oil?**
- **Why does God give his children more than enough?**

SAY: **When God used Elisha to help the widow, God gave the woman enough oil for her to earn money to pay her bills. That meant that her sons wouldn't have to be slaves! God took**

care of her needs. Then God gave her more than enough! God will take care of our needs, too. He will give us more than enough.

Bible Application

An Abundance of Trust

Children will think of ways their trust results in blessings.

Supplies: Bible, oil lamp, matches

Time: 5 to 10 minutes

Preparation: Set the oil lamp in the middle of the floor.

Gather children in a circle around the oil lamp, and safely light it. Turn out the lights. SAY: **No matter what situation we're in, no matter how scared or alone we feel, we can trust god completely. We may not trust that God will provide us the same kind of blessing he did for the widow who asked Elisha for help. But everything God does for us is a blessing. Let's think a little bit about some of the reasons we can trust him.**

Read aloud Psalm 22:4. ASK:

◆ **What's one way you've seen someone else put his or her trust in God?**

Read aloud Psalm 28:7. ASK:

◆ **What's one way God is your strength? your shield?**

Read aloud Psalm 56:3. ASK:

◆ **What's one way you've trusted God when you were afraid?**

SAY: **God provided an abundance of blessings to the widow, and he provides them for us, too. When we trust in him, our lives are filled with blessings every day.**

Creative Prayer Idea

Shower of Blessings

Children will thank God for all his blessings.

Supplies: Bible, pencils, slips of paper

Time: about 5 minutes

Preparation: This activity requires writing, so pair any younger children in your group with a partner who can write.

Read aloud 2 Kings 4:1-7. SAY: **God provided a miracle for the woman so she wouldn't have to sell her children into slavery. What a blessing!**

ASK:

◆ **What blessings does God give you?**

Have kids form trios. Give each trio pencils and several slips of paper. Have kids write on the slips of paper things God provides for them, such as food, clothing, friends, a church, family, and sunshine. When kids have written on all their slips, have them divide the slips among the trio members and then form a circle with the whole class. Have kids hold their slips in their open palms.

PRAY: **Lord, thank you for all the good things that come from your hand. Thank you for showing us that we can trust you completely to take care of us. Thank you for showering us with your blessings every day.**

Have children toss the slips of paper up into the air as they shout, "Thank you, God!" Have kids scoop up the slips of paper on the floor and toss them again. Keep the "shower of blessings" going for at least 30 seconds.

Snack

▶ ***PREPARE IN ADVANCE***

▶ ***ALLERGY ALERT***

Overflow Cups

Children will make overflowing snack cups to remember that God gave the widow more than enough oil.

Supplies: clear plastic cups (any size), cotton swabs, markers, craft glue, small paper plates, tissue paper, scissors, large plastic bowl, small crackers

Time: 10 to 15 minutes

Preparation: Cut tissue paper into 1- to 2-inch squares. Pour the glue onto several paper plates. Set out all supplies except the crackers.

Give each child a cup and a cotton swab. Have kids write their names on the bottom of their cups. Let children use the cotton swabs to spread glue on the outside of their cups. Then they can press the tissue scraps to the glue in a stained-glass pattern. While the cups dry, have children pour crackers into the large plastic bowl. Ask kids to guess how many crackers will fill each cup. Allow children to fill their cups with crackers until the cups overflow.

After kids have eaten, clear away supplies and leftover crackers. ASK:

- **How did Elisha help the widow?**
- **How is that like the way God helps us today?**
- **Why does God let our lives overflow with so many good things?**

SAY: **We can always trust God to give us what we need. And we can always trust God to love us. Our lives overflow with God's love!**

Object Lesson

Right-Side-Up Trust

Children will discover how to trust God even in impossible situations.

Supplies: Bible, index cards, small drinking cups with mouths narrower than the cards, dishpans of water, paper towels

Time: 15 to 20 minutes

Preparation: If weather permits, plan to do this activity outside.

Form trios and give each trio an index card, a cup, and a dishpan of water. Provide paper towels in case of spills.

SAY: **I want one of you in each trio to dip the cup in the water and fill it to about halfway full. Now place the card over the top of the cup, and hold it there with your pointer finger. Quickly turn the cup upside down over the dishpan. Slowly remove your finger and...look!**

Kids will see that the index card should hold the water in the cup, even when the cup is upside down. Let each person in each trio have a turn. Then gather kids in a circle and

ASK:

- **What surprised you about this experiment?**

SAY: **In our Bible story today, a woman discovered that when she trusted God, remarkable things happened to a jar of oil she had. And as surprised as she was, just like in our experiment, everything turned out all right.**

Read aloud 2 Kings 4:1-7.

ASK:

- **Whose life got turned upside down? What happened?**
- **What good thing happened that seemed impossible?**

SAY: **When things seem impossible and your life seems to turn upside down, your trust in God makes things right side up!**

Preschool Story

Bible Point: ▷ **WE CAN TRUST GOD COMPLETELY.**

Supplies: Bible, clear plastic cups, pitcher of water, table

Time: 15 to 20 minutes

Preparation: Hide a clear plastic cup for each child somewhere in the classroom. Save one cup to show children. Set aside a pitcher with enough water to fill each of the cups halfway.

Trust Me!

Have kids form a circle and sit down. Open your Bible to 2 Kings 4, and show children the words. SAY: **Way back in Bible days, there lived a woman with two sons. The woman was a widow. That means that her husband had died. She had no one to work and make money for her family. She didn't have food to eat. She owed some people money, but she didn't have the money to pay them back. Some of the people the widow owed money to wanted to take away her sons as payment for her bills.**

ASK:

- **How would you feel if you were going to be taken away from your mom and dad?**
- **How do you think the widow's sons might have felt?**

SAY: **The widow trusted God to take care of her. She trusted that God would not allow her sons to be taken from her.**

The widow asked Elisha, one of God's prophets, for help. Elisha told the widow, "Go to all of your neighbors, and ask them to let you borrow all of their empty jars. Borrow lots and lots of jars."

Let's pretend to go to our neighbors' houses and ask for jars. Show children one of the cups so they know what to look for. Have each child hunt for one cup and then come back and sit down in the circle. When all the children have found cups and are sitting down, continue the story.

Elisha told the widow to go home with the jars *and* her sons and then close the doors. Let's pretend to do that. Walk to a table with the children, and pretend to close a door behind you.

Then Elisha told the widow to pour oil into the jars. She kept pouring and pouring, and her oil kept coming. God gave her lots and lots of extra oil. Every empty jar was now filled to the top with oil! Let's pretend to do that with this water. We'll use this water to fill all of your cups.

Pour water into each child's cup, filling it about halfway.

SAY: **Elisha told the woman to sell the oil and use the money to pay the people she owed money to. The widow was so happy! She trusted God and God took care of her! ▷ WE CAN TRUST GOD COMPLETELY, just as the widow did.** Have children say, "We can trust God," and then drink the water from their cups.

ASK:

- **How did God take care of the widow and her sons?**
- **What are some ways God takes care of you?**
- **How can you trust God this week?**

BIBLE STORY

Naaman Healed of Leprosy

For the Leader

He was wealthy, a great leader, a valiant soldier, and highly regarded. But his wealth and status did no good when Naaman contracted leprosy. Only God could save him. And only his humility—his ability to bow before God—could change Naaman's life.

The activities in this lesson show children that humility is not a state of guilt or unimportance. Rather, humility is simply another way for us to place God first in our lives.

Key Scriptures

2 Kings 5:1-16

Philippians 2:3-4

1 Peter 5:6

Bible Verse

"Humble yourselves under the mighty power of God, and at the right time he will lift you up in honor" (1 Peter 5:6).

Bible Experience

▶*NO PREP*

Seven Times

Bible Point: ▷ **BE HUMBLE.**

Children will learn to empathize with Naaman's illness.

Supplies: Bible, miniature sticky notes or dots

Time: 10 to 15 minutes

Preparation: none

ASK:

◆ **When you're sick, how do your parents help you feel better?**

SAY: **Our parents might hug us, fix us soup, or give us vitamins and medicine. In Bible times there were some sicknesses you could never get over, like leprosy. People who got leprosy suffered from horrible sores on their bodies, and eventually they would die.** Pass out the sticky notes, and have the kids stick several on their hands and arms.

Read aloud 2 Kings 5:1-16. SAY: **The Bible tells about a mighty army commander named Naaman who had leprosy. Although Naaman was a powerful soldier, he didn't have enough power to heal himself. One of Naaman's servant girls told him about a prophet of God named Elisha who could heal him.**

Elisha told Naaman to humble himself: God wanted Naaman to wash seven times in the Jordan River. At first Naaman thought that was not good enough for him, an important army commander. Finally, he agreed.

Let's pretend we're going with Naaman to the Jordan River. Have kids march in place. **OK, now we have to wash seven times!** Have kids bend their knees as if they're dipping in a river and count "one"; then have them stand up and bend and count "two," and so forth, all the way to six. **We're coming to the seventh dipping! When you dip down this time, take off your sticky notes!** Have kids bend, take off their notes, and then stand up "clean."

ASK:

- **How do you think Naaman felt when he came out of the water the seventh time and saw that he had been healed?**
- **How did Naaman follow God in the story?**
- **How can we follow God today?**

SAY: **First Peter 5:6 tells us why we should be humble: "Humble yourselves under the mighty power of God, and at the right time he will lift you up in honor." God wants us to ▷ BE HUMBLE. Being humble means understanding how much more important God's will is than yours. Because Naaman humbled himself before God, he was healed! The Bible says his skin was clean, like that of a young child!**

Song & Connect

Use "Walk Humbly" (track 15, *it: Innovative Tools for Children's Ministry: Old Testament* CD) to help reinforce the Bible Point, **▷ BE HUMBLE.**

You may want to use a portable CD player and go on a "humble walk" at a local park with your class. Walk together with kids in quiet reflection. Remind children that humility is not just for times of illness.

Additional Topics List

This lesson can be used to help children discover... God's Compassion, Healing, and Peace.

Game

▶ *FOR YOUNGER CHILDREN*

Close to the Ground

Children will play a crawling game to exemplify humility.

Supplies: Bible, chairs, CD player, CD of praise music

Time: 10 to 15 minutes

Preparation: Set up a simple obstacle course using chairs. Let your students' ages and maturity determine the difficulty of the course.

Read aloud 2 Kings 5:1-16. Then SAY: **Our friend Naaman didn't want to do anything as humbling as going to wash himself seven times in the dirty river. Naaman was proud because he was a very important guy.**

But sometimes God tells us to humble ourselves and do things that we don't want to do. And I've got something for you to do now!

Have children crawl, rather than walk, around the chairs from one end of the room to the other. As kids crawl, play the tape of praise music.

When everyone is finished, discuss how it felt to crawl rather than walk. Ask kids if they could have thought of a quicker way to move from one end of the room to the other.

After children respond, SAY: **The word *humble* comes from a Latin word that means "low" or**

"close to the ground." In this game I invited everyone to crawl through the obstacle course.

In our Bible story Naaman didn't want to do what God wanted him to do. Naaman didn't want to be humble. But when Naaman did as God asked, Naaman was healed. And if we humble ourselves, God takes care of us, too!

Craft

▶ *NO PREP*

Naaman Puppets

Children will make puppets to reenact Naaman's cleansing.

Supplies: markers, paper, plastic or foam cups, safety scissors, glue, craft sticks, blue tissue paper

Time: 15 to 20 minutes

Preparation: none

Help students draw Naaman puppets on paper and then color and cut them out. Make the puppets small enough to fit inside the cups. Glue the puppets onto the top of craft sticks. Using the point of the scissors, carefully make a slit in the bottom of the cups. Have children cut pieces of blue tissue paper and glue them to the outside of the cups to create the Jordan River. Insert the Naaman puppets, sticks first, through the holes in the bottom of the cups.

Introduce or review the Bible story from 2 Kings 5:1-16. Encourage children to move their puppets while you tell the story.

When you're finished with the story, SAY: **When Naaman became humble, he was healed. God wants each of us to be humble, too. Then God can lift us up just as he did Naaman.**

Bible Application

▶ *NO PREP*

The Little Guys

Children will learn about being "smaller."

Supplies: Bible

Time: 10 to 15 minutes

Preparation: none

Pair older children with younger children. Then SAY: **I'd like you to talk to your partner and think together of something really big, like a bear, and then try to make your bodies look that big. For example, if you choose a bear, you could stand on your tiptoes with your arms up and "claws" out and snarl at us.** Give pairs a minute to discuss and assume their postures. Ask each pair what they represent. Then ASK:

- **Can you think of some really important people?**
- **What makes them important?**
- **What kinds of important things would you like to do with your life?**

SAY: **God can use you to do important things. But you'll get into trouble if you start to think you're bigger than you are.**

Second Kings 5 tells us about someone who had that problem. Naaman had a really important job, and the king's appreciation made Naaman feel bigger than he was. He thought he was so big that Elisha should do a great miracle for him. Eventually the little guys—his servants—convinced Naaman to humble himself so God could heal him.

Now I'd like you to talk to your partner and think together of something really small and try to make your bodies look that small. Let children assume their postures, and then ask each pair what they represent.

We can learn something from these little guys. God made them important but not big. And God made you, so you are important. You can do important things for God. But it helps to remember that you're still a little guy, not too big to do little things.

Read aloud 1 Peter 5:6. Tell partners to tell each other seven little things (one for each time Naaman dipped himself in the river) they can do that are important to God.

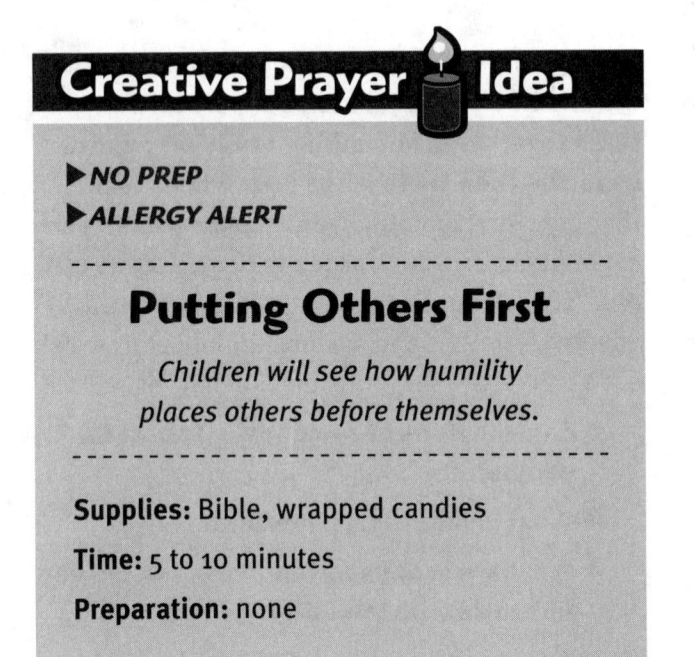

Creative Prayer Idea

▶ *NO PREP*

▶ *ALLERGY ALERT*

Putting Others First

Children will see how humility places others before themselves.

Supplies: Bible, wrapped candies

Time: 5 to 10 minutes

Preparation: none

Have kids sit in a circle. Ask a volunteer to read aloud Philippians 2:3-4. ASK:

- **What does the Bible say about "me bragging"?**
- **What does the Bible say about "you bragging"?**

SAY: **If we chose the most important word in this passage, it would be the word *humble*. When we're humble, we think less of ourselves and more of others. And more importantly, we think more of God.**

Ask children to each select someone near them to be their partners.

Set the wrapped candies on a table, and invite children to choose two pieces of candy each: one for themselves and one for their partners.

Afterward, SAY: **Look at your candy. Do you have big or little pieces? You might have chosen a big piece for yourself—but did you also choose a big piece for your partner? Being selfless and humble means putting others first. It's important to remember that God wants us to be humble. Let's say a prayer asking God to help us be humble. As we do, take your candy and place it in the center of our circle.**

PRAY: **Dear Lord, please help us remember that it's better to put others first in all we do. Because when we do, we are putting you before ourselves, too. In Jesus' name we pray, amen.**

Life Application

▶ *FOR FAMILY MINISTRY*

Children will see the effects of humility with these family application ideas.

Miracles

Encourage children to have their families make notes of every example of God's miracles they see today. Then encourage families to discuss how seeing miracles makes us feel humble.

Problem Solving

Tell kids that the next time they're angry, sad, or frustrated, they should hand their problem over to God. Encourage them to explain to a family member how they felt humbled by God's control.

The Face of Jesus

Encourage kids to look into the face of everyone they see today and imagine they're staring at Jesus. Discuss how humility might change the way we react to other people.

Sacrifice

Ask kids what they can give up today for someone else. A bus seat? a place in line at the store? the bigger piece of cake? time for a friend? How does being humble before God benefit others?

Movie Clip

A Bug's Life

Movie Title: *A Bug's Life* (G)

Start Time: 41 minutes, 20 seconds

Where to Begin: Dot says, "Come on wings!" and then falls and hangs on to the dandelion seed.

Where to End: The bugs escape into the thorn bush.

Plot: Dot, the smallest ant, is in trouble—a hungry bird spies her and envisions lunch. The other bugs go through many obstacles to rescue Dot.

Review: Use this scene to help kids realize that humility is not a state of unimportance but rather a state of greatness.

Discussion

After setting up and showing the clip, ASK:

- **Have you ever done something big that you didn't think you could do? How did you feel about that?**

SAY: **The bugs were much smaller and weaker than the bird, but they managed to rescue Dot. The bugs were very important; if they hadn't been there, Dot surely would have been eaten.**

Read aloud 1 Peter 5:6. SAY: **God wants us to be humble, to think of the importance of others. But that doesn't make us unimportant. Instead, God lifts us up and gives our lives purpose. Our humility gives us the ability to do God's work.**

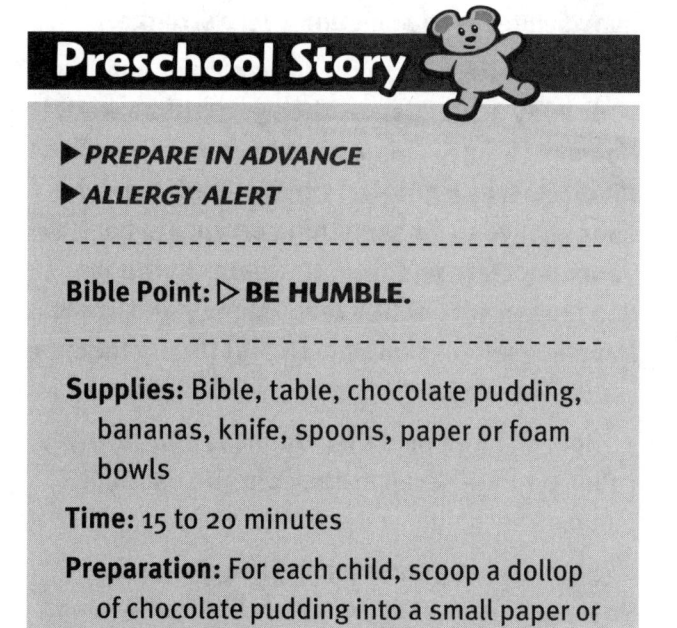

Preschool Story

▶ ***PREPARE IN ADVANCE***

▶ ***ALLERGY ALERT***

Bible Point: ▷ **BE HUMBLE.**

Supplies: Bible, table, chocolate pudding, bananas, knife, spoons, paper or foam bowls

Time: 15 to 20 minutes

Preparation: For each child, scoop a dollop of chocolate pudding into a small paper or foam bowl. Cut unpeeled bananas in half.

A Muddy Bath

Have kids form a circle and sit down around a table. Open your Bible to 2 Kings 5, and show children the words. Give each child a bowl of chocolate pudding and half of an unpeeled banana, preferably one with a few brown spots on the peel.

SAY: **Look at your banana. What does the outside look like? Your banana might have some brown spots on it. We're going to hear a story from the Bible about a man who had lots of spots on his skin. The man's name was Naaman, and he was a captain in the army. Many men worked**

for him, and they saluted him! Lead children in saluting, and then tell them to salute every time they hear Naaman's name during the story.

Naaman's (salute) **sores were all over his body! If someone didn't make Naaman** (salute) **well, he would die from those sores. Naaman's** (salute) **wife had a little servant girl who loved God. One day the little girl said, "Naaman** (salute) **should go talk to the man of God named Elisha. Elisha could make Naaman** (salute) **well." So Naaman** (salute) **went to see Elisha. But Elisha told Naaman** (salute) **to do something very strange.**

Elisha said, "Go to the Jordan River and dip your body seven times. Then you will be well." Naaman (salute) **didn't want to go to the Jordan River! He was a soldier, and he didn't think he should have to do something so yucky! Look at your chocolate pudding; the water in the Jordan looked sort of like that—muddy and brown. Naaman** (salute) **complained, but finally Naaman** (salute) **obeyed.**

Help children peel their bananas and slowly count aloud to seven as they dip and eat their bananas each time you say a number.

SAY: **Just as your bananas are all gone, Naaman's** (salute) **sores were all gone! Naaman** (salute) **was glad that the little servant girl had told him to go to Elisha. And he was glad that he was humble and obeyed God.**

After children finish eating, sing "Who's That Washing?" to the tune of "Clementine."

Who's that washing in the river, *(pretend to wash arms)*

In the Jordan's muddy tide? *(Make a disgusted face.)*

It's the mighty captain Naaman *(salute)*

Humbling his foolish pride. *(Fold hands and bow.)*

Who's that dipping seven times, *(hold up seven fingers, and squat down)*

Like the prophet said to do? *(Stand up and squat down.)*

It's the mighty captain Naaman. *(Stand and salute.)*

Now his skin looks all brand new! *(Rub cheeks and smile.)*

ASK:

- **Why did Naaman need to ▷ BE HUMBLE?**
- **When can you be humble?**

BIBLE STORY

Elisha and the Chariots of Fire

For the Leader

It's not always easy to trust someone whom you can't see, especially in a moment of crisis. So it's understandable that Elisha's servant panicked when he and Elisha were surrounded by the king of Aram's chariots. But Elisha knew that God was working. He had faith that God's work would save him, and it did.

Teach your students that while God may not be visible to them, they can see the evidence of his work everywhere.

Key Scriptures

2 Kings 6:8-23

Romans 1:20

Hebrews 11:1

Bible Verse

"O Lord, open his eyes and let him see!" (2 Kings 6:17).

Bible Experience

▶ *NO PREP*

Invisible Chariots

Bible Point: ▷ **WE CAN'T ALWAYS SEE GOD WORKING, BUT HE IS.**

Children will see how air is like God when we can't see him.

Supplies: Bible, hair dryer with a cool setting, table-tennis ball or balloon

Time: 10 to 15 minutes

Preparation: none

ASK:

◆ **What's something you can't see but you know is there?**

SAY: **Some powerful things that I know of are radio waves, germs, and sound. A gust of wind is invisible, but it can knock a big truck over.**

Turn the hair dryer on the cool setting, and point it straight up. Put the table-tennis ball or balloon in the stream of air until the air holds it up.

ASK:

◆ **If you can't see air, how do you know it's there?**

Read aloud 2 Kings 6:8-23.

ASK:

◆ **How did Elisha know God was there?**

◆ **How did the servant know?**

SAY: **Elisha knew God was there, but the servant didn't. So Elisha prayed, "O Lord, open his eyes and let him see!" and the servant was able to see the heavenly chariots God had sent.**

Take a moment to pray for your group that they may see what God is doing. Then read aloud Romans 1:20.

SAY: ▷ **WE CAN'T ALWAYS SEE GOD WORKING, BUT HE IS. Even though God is invisible, we know he exists because of the things he has made. Just like the servant when he saw the chariots of fire, we can see God's work in his creation and in the good things that happen around us. Just like the air that propped up that ball, God is working, even if we can't see his work right away.**

Song & Connect

Use "The Work of His Hands" (track 3, *it: Innovative Tools for Children's Ministry: Old Testament* CD) to help reinforce the Bible Point, ▷ **WE CAN'T ALWAYS SEE GOD WORKING, BUT HE IS.**

It's easy to take God's work for granted. Help kids remember that they can praise God for the hand he has in everything.

Additional Topics List

This lesson can be used to help children discover... Miracles, Prayer, and Spiritual Warfare.

Game

▶ *PREPARE IN ADVANCE*

Unseen Presence

Children will search through rice for "hidden" things.

Supplies: Bible, blindfolds, bowls full of uncooked rice, paper clips, watch with a second hand

Time: 5 to 10 minutes

Preparation: For each group of four, you'll need a blindfold and a bowl filled with rice mixed with about 25 paper clips.

Have kids form groups of four, and give each group its blindfold and bowl. Have groups choose one person to be the "seeker" and wear a blindfold. Tell seekers they have one minute to find the paper clips in the bowl of rice.

Call time after one minute. Then have kids count the found clips. Let kids remix the paper clips in the rice and choose another seeker.

After everyone has had a chance to be the seeker, ASK:

- **How many paper clips did you find?**
- **How easy or difficult was it to find the paper clips in the rice?**

Read aloud Hebrews 11:1. Then SAY: **Just as we hunted for something we couldn't see, God asks us to believe in things we can't see.**

Read aloud 2 Kings 6:17. Then SAY: **Elisha helped his servant see the chariots of fire that God had sent to save them. Just because we can't see something doesn't mean God isn't working.**

Craft

▶ *FOR SMALL GROUPS*
▶ *PREPARE IN ADVANCE*

Always Alert

Children will make faces with movable eyelids to remind them that even when we can't see God's help, he's always working.

Supplies: construction paper, scissors, crayons, rubber bands, tape

Time: 15 to 20 minutes

Preparation: Set out all the supplies in one area.

Help children cut a large oval shape for a face out of construction paper. Have them draw in the eyes, eyebrows, nose, and mouth with crayons. Then cut two mushroom-shaped pieces (football shapes with a stem on one side) bigger than the eyes on the face. These will act as eyelids.

Cut a small slot above each eye in the eyebrow. Have kids slide the stem of each piece into the slot so that each oval covers an eye. Make sure they draw eyelashes on the bottom portion of each eyelid.

Carefully flip the face over, and fold each stem over the rubber band. Tape the stem to the rubber band without letting excess tape stick to the back of the face. Cut or pinch together excess tape.

Have kids practice holding the faces up and pulling down on the rubber bands to make the eyelids move. Read aloud 2 Kings 6:17 while they make the eyes open. SAY: **Even when ▷ WE CAN'T SEE WHAT GOD IS DOING, HE IS ALWAYS WORKING.**

Bible Application

▶ *PREPARE IN ADVANCE*

God's Garden

Children will see God's work in a garden.

Supplies: Bible; bedding plants, seeds, or bulbs; gardening tools

Time: 60 to 90 minutes

Preparation: Get permission to plant or spruce up flower beds around your church or at the home of an older person from your congregation. Purchase a few bedding plants, seeds, or bulbs, depending on the time of year.

Have kids make up names for some of the plants, based on people or things from the Bible story in 2 Kings 6:8-23. For example, you might have Elisha's Flower, Chariots of Fire (red and orange flowers), or Open My Eyes Iris.

Gather children around the planting area. Talk about the varieties of plants you've gathered, how tall they grow, whether they do well in sunlight or shade, and what kind of soil they need. Explain how important it is to plan a flower bed so the plants will thrive and look good together.

Let children take turns digging and planting. Then gather children around your planted flower bed and read aloud 2 Kings 6:8-23. SAY: **Even though it doesn't look like God is doing anything right now, in a few weeks we'll see God's garden sprout and grow.**

Pray and ask God to bless the garden and help the flowers grow. In the following weeks, point out how the flower bed is doing. Let kids take turns watering and weeding.

Creative Prayer Idea

▶ *FOR YOUNGER CHILDREN*

▶ *PREPARE IN ADVANCE*

See-and-Touch Prayer

Children will be reminded to see God's work and give thanks.

Supplies: colored paper, material scraps, scissors, bag

Time: 5 to 10 minutes

Preparation: Cut scraps of different-colored paper into pieces no smaller than 2-inches square. Collect scraps of material of different textures. Place the paper and the material scraps in a bag.

Let each child pick an item from the bag and say a prayer of thanks to God for something that is the same color or something that feels like what he or she is holding. For instance, he or she might thank God for the blue sky, a fuzzy bunny, a red apple, or a soft doll.

SAY: **God does many things in the world around us. We forget to thank him for all he does. ▷ WE CAN'T ALWAYS SEE GOD WORKING, BUT HE IS! Let's thank God for his wonderful work.**

Discussion Launcher

Follow the Leader

For this activity you'll need a Bible.

Have children form pairs, and have the tallest child in each pair be the leader. Ask the leader to begin walking, with his or her partner following behind. The leader can walk straight, in wavy curves, around obstacles, and while making dancing motions. The follower has to step *exactly* in the leader's footsteps. After a few minutes, allow partners to trade places. Then have pairs play again, this time telling them to speed-walk as they lead their partners on crazy paths. If you have time, have pairs play again, only have a volunteer talk loudly to the follower as he or she tries to follow.

Afterward, have kids discuss these questions:

◆ **Was it hard or easy to follow your partner? Explain.**

◆ **Was it harder or easier when you went faster? when someone was talking to you? Explain.**

◆ **How is this like trying to follow God?**

Read aloud 2 Kings 6:8-23. ASK:

◆ **How hard is it to follow God when you can't see him?**

◆ **As a follower, how are you like Elisha's servant? like Elisha?**

Science Devotion

▶ *PREPARE IN ADVANCE*

An Eclipse and God

Children will explore a solar eclipse as they learn that God is always working, even when he feels far away.

Supplies: Bible, flashlight, basketball, tennis ball

Time: about 10 minutes

Preparation: Practice this experiment ahead of time so you can correctly space the flashlight and the balls.

ASK:

◆ **Can anyone tell me what a solar eclipse is?**

SAY: **Let me show you how an eclipse happens.**

Ask two kids to be your helpers. Give one child the flashlight (representing the sun), and give the other child the basketball (representing the earth). You will be controlling the tennis ball (representing the moon). Have the child holding the "sun" shine it directly onto the "earth." Rotate the "moon" around the earth. Be sure to rotate it in the sun's light.

SAY: **Notice that the moon sometimes blocks out the sunlight and makes the earth dark in the middle of the day! This is called an eclipse. If we didn't know what caused the eclipse, its effect would be frightening, wouldn't it? Now that we know, it is amazing!**

Let kids take turns re-creating an eclipse. Then read aloud 2 Kings 6:8-23.

SAY: **Elisha's servant was pretty scared at first, and he felt that God was far away. But Elisha knew that God was there. That's kind of like our eclipse. During an eclipse, the sky looks dark, but we know that the light is still there. When you have troubles in your life, you may not always be able to sense God there, but you can know that he is always working.**

Preschool Story

▶ *PREPARE IN ADVANCE*

Bible Point: ▷ **GOD IS ALWAYS WORKING.**

Supplies: Bible, transparency sheet, black and red markers, overhead projector, several dolls

Time: 15 to 20 minutes

Preparation: Place a transparency sheet in front of you, horizontally. Use the black marker to draw several chariots and the red marker to draw flames around the chariots on the transparency sheet. When you're finished, place the sheet on an overhead and back the overhead up so the chariots cover an entire wall. Turn off the overhead until you need it during story time.

I Didn't See You There!

Have kids form a circle and sit down on the floor. Open your Bible to 2 Kings 6, and show children the words. Hold up a doll, and tell kids the doll is Elisha.

SAY: **God was with Elisha, and God helped Elisha know when Israel's enemies were attacking them. Elisha would tell the king where the enemies were, and then the king would keep his people safe from the enemies. When the king of the enemies heard about what Elisha was doing, he wanted to stop Elisha and hurt him. So the mean king sent out his army to attack Elisha and hurt him.**

Encourage children to place all the dolls in a row near the wall where you are going to shine the transparency. SAY: **Let's pretend these dolls are the enemies that have come to hurt Elisha.**

Keep the Elisha doll and one other doll near you. Hold up the other doll. SAY: **This is Elisha's servant. When he went outside his tent, he saw all those mean soldiers standing around their camp. "Elisha! Elisha!" he called.** Move the servant doll up and down, and then bring out the Elisha doll.

"Don't be afraid," Elisha told him. "God has sent others to help us." Then Elisha prayed that God would help the servant see all the helpers God had sent. So God helped the servant see. Stand up and turn on the overhead.

The servant saw that the hillsides were filled with horses and chariots of fire! God had sent them to help Elisha! Then God made the mean soldiers blind, and Elisha and the servant led the mean soldiers away from them. God helped Elisha and the servant escape from those mean soldiers!

Even though the servant couldn't see the horses and chariots of fire, they were still there! Sometimes we can't see what God is doing, but we can know that ▷ GOD IS ALWAYS WORKING!

ASK:

- **How did God help Elisha?**
- **How has God helped you before?**
- **How can you trust God even when you can't see him?**

BIBLE STORY

Jonah Flees From God

For the Leader

It may seem like a little thing to children to disobey God. Disobeying God didn't seem that important to Jonah either. All God wanted Jonah to do was visit Nineveh and preach. It took a storm, a near drowning, and three days inside a large fish to change Jonah's mind and turn him toward Nineveh.

Kids today can relate to Jonah's reaction to God's commands. Often they'd like to turn and run from difficulties or uncomfortable situations. The ideas in this section can help kids learn from Jonah's experience and realize that doing what God wants is always the best decision.

Key Scriptures

Deuteronomy 13:4

Jonah 1:1–3:2

Bible Verse

"Serve only the Lord your God" (Deuteronomy 13:4).

Bible Experience

▶ *PREPARE IN ADVANCE*

Jonah Learns a Lesson

Bible Point: ▷ **DO WHAT GOD WANTS.**

Children will re-create Jonah's experience in the sea.

Supplies: Bible, blue sheet, spray bottle filled with water, blanket

Time: 10 to 15 minutes

Preparation: If you have a large group, have three or four older children read each paragraph of Jonah 1:1-17 before you reenact that part of the story.

SAY: **Today we're going to learn about Jonah and how he found out that God's ways are best. You'll all have a part to play in this story.** Choose someone to be Jonah, three kids to be sailors, two kids to hold the blue sheet to be the water, and the rest of the kids to stand in a line behind the sheet to do the wave when the storm hits.

Have a student read Jonah 1:1-3. SAY: **One day God told Jonah, "Go to a city called Nineveh. Tell the people to stop the bad things they're doing." Jonah didn't want to do it.** Have Jonah cross his arms and shake his head "no."

Instead of going to Nineveh, Jonah did the opposite of what God wanted him to do. Jonah ran away to the sea and got on a ship. Have the two kids holding the blue sheet move it gently up and down. Have the three "sailors" stand behind the sheet and pretend to row the boat. Have "Jonah" join in rowing.

Have a student read Jonah 1:4-6. SAY: **At first the water was calm.** Have the two kids gently move the sheet. Have the other kids do a very calm "wave." Starting at one end of the line, have them calmly and slowly stand, raise their hands over their heads, lower their hands, and then sit back down.

Then a storm came. The storm got worse, and the waves got higher. Have kids make their "water" and wave get bigger. SAY: **The storm got so bad that the waves were huge!** Have kids make their water and wave as big as possible. Spray everyone with the spray bottle. **The sailors were afraid and began to pray.** Have sailors look afraid and pray. Then SAY: **But Jonah didn't pay attention to the storm. He went below the deck and fell asleep.** Have Jonah lie on the floor and pretend to sleep.

The captain got mad at Jonah and wanted him to get up and pray. Have a student read Jonah 1:7-12. **The sailors all determined that Jonah was the reason God was mad.** Have one of the sailors wake up Jonah.

Jonah told the sailors that the storm had come because of him. He said, "Throw me in the water and the storm will stop." Have a student read Jonah 1:13-17. Tell Jonah and the sailors to pretend to talk. **So the sailors threw Jonah in the sea.** Have the sailors gently take Jonah and put him out of the boat on the opposite side of the sheet. Have the water and the waves become calm, and have Jonah pretend to swim.

God sent a big fish, and it swallowed Jonah. Throw the blanket over Jonah. **Jonah was inside the fish for three days.**

If you have a small group, have everyone join Jonah under the blanket. If you have a larger group, have Jonah sit on the blanket, and have everyone sit in a circle around Jonah. ASK:

◆ **How do you think Jonah felt when he was swallowed by a big fish?**

◆ **How do you think Jonah felt when God saved him?**

◆ **What do you think it means to do what God wants you to do?**

◆ **How do we know what God wants us to do?**

SAY: **Jonah learned that it's important to do what God wanted him to do. We must also ▷ DO WHAT GOD WANTS. Deuteronomy 13:4 says, "Serve only the Lord your God." Hearing Bible stories, listening to other Christians, going to church, and praying are all ways we can find out what God wants.** Close in prayer, asking God to help everyone know God's will.

Additional Topics List

This lesson can be used to help children discover... Prayer and Respect.

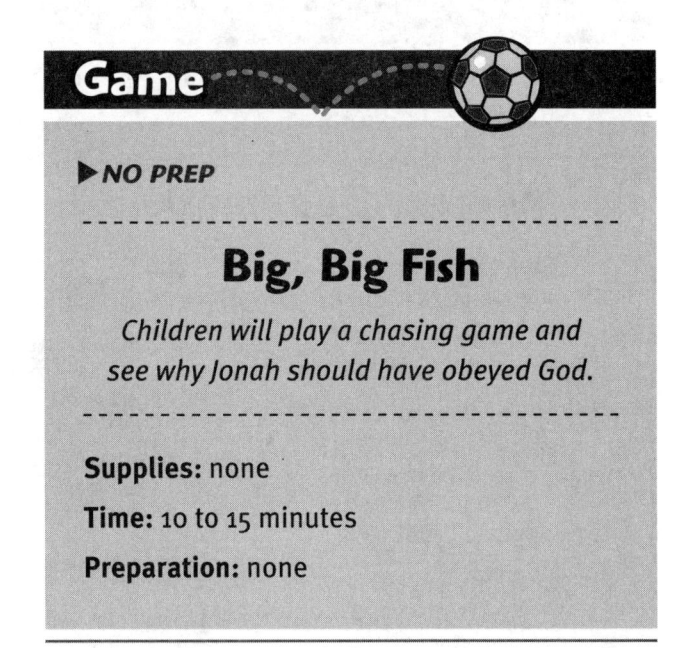

Game

▶ *NO PREP*

Big, Big Fish

Children will play a chasing game and see why Jonah should have obeyed God.

Supplies: none

Time: 10 to 15 minutes

Preparation: none

Ask children to stand in a line, and have each child hold on to the waist of the child in front of him or her. Tell kids to pretend that they're a big fish swishing through the ocean. The person at the head of the fish will try to catch the tail by tagging the person at the back of the line. Encourage all of the children to hold on tightly as the fish twists and turns. When the "tail" is finally tagged, have the first child in line become the new tail. Have the second person in line become the new "head," and start the game again.

Have kids say this rhyme as they play: "Big fish, big fish in the sea, you caught Jonah but you can't catch me!"

After each child has had a chance to be the head of the big fish, ASK:

- **What did God want Jonah to do?**
- **What happened to Jonah because he didn't obey God?**

SAY: **We should always ▷ DO WHAT GOD WANTS. God loves us and wants us to be with him! If we follow God's plans, God will be with us always!**

Craft

▶ PREPARE IN ADVANCE

Memory Bookmarks

Children will make bookmarks that remind them to obey God.

Supplies: card stock, scissors, adhesive-backed magnet strips, markers, fish stickers

Time: 10 to 15 minutes

Preparation: Cut card stock into 2x8-inch strips. Cut the magnetic strips into ½-inch lengths. Set up enough supplies for each child to have one strip of card stock, two magnet pieces, markers, and stickers to decorate his or her bookmark.

Have each child fold the strip of card stock in half. Help kids write on one side the following verse: "Serve only the Lord your God" (Deuteronomy 13:4). On the other side, have kids draw pictures or use stickers to show what happened when Jonah didn't obey God.

On the inside of the strip, have children stick magnetic pieces on each end by the open edge. The bookmarks can be folded around a page in a book, and the magnets will hold it together.

After kids have finished their bookmarks, ASK:

- **What did God want Jonah to do?**
- **Have you ever disobeyed someone? What happened?**

SAY: **When Jonah disobeyed, a big storm came and frightened many people. A big fish swallowed him. When we disobey, consequences often follow, and sometimes they affect other people as well. Good consequences follow when we choose to do what God wants.**

Bible Application

▶ FOR SMALL GROUPS
▶ NO PREP

What God Wants

Children will understand that disobeying God stinks!

Supplies: Bible, tuna in a resealable plastic bag or bowl

Time: 5 to 10 minutes

Preparation: none

ASK:

- **What are some rules or chores your parents expect you to do?**
- **What happens if you don't do what your parents want you to do?**
- **What if we disobeyed our parents, and the consequence was that all we could smell was fish?**

SAY: **That's what happened to a man named Jonah in our Bible story!** Open your Bible to Jonah, and show the children the words. Read aloud Jonah 1:1-17. Then SAY: **Jonah disobeyed and ended up in the belly of a big fish. Maybe it smelled a bit like tuna inside that fish!**

ASK:

- **Why should we obey our parents?**
- **How can we obey our parents?**
- **Why should we obey God?**
- **How can we obey God?**

SAY: **Our parents and people who care for us want to help us ▷ DO WHAT GOD WANTS. We obey them, and we learn how to live life. Even more importantly, God wants us to obey him. He knows what's best for our lives.**

Set the tuna on the floor, and have kids join hands around it. Have each person PRAY: "God, please help me obey you always." Close by PRAYING: **Thank you, God, for showing us how important it is to do what you want. We need to obey you because you know us best. In Jesus' name, amen.**

Creative Prayer Idea

▶ *NO PREP*

A Letter to God

Children will write letters of confession to God.

Supplies: Bible, paper, pens

Time: up to 5 minutes

Preparation: none

Give each child a sheet of paper and a pen. Read aloud Deuteronomy 13:4. SAY: **Today we discovered that we need to work toward doing what God wants us to do. Take a couple of minutes to write a letter to God, first telling him about some times that you have disobeyed him or that you felt yourself moving away from what he would want you to do. Then tell him some ways you can work on better obeying his commands. Be specific in your letter. For example, you might write, "I'll pray every day" or "I'll tell my friends about you."**

Give kids two or three minutes to complete their letters. Then form a circle and have kids fold their letters and place them in the center of the circle. Have children form pairs, and have pairs pray together, asking God to help them follow his commands.

n

o

t

e

s

Movie Clip

Willy Wonka and the Chocolate Factory

Movie Title: *Willy Wonka and the Chocolate Factory* (G)

Start Time: 1 hour, 10 minutes

Where to Begin: Willy Wonka says, "Now over here, if you'll follow me, I have something special to show you."

Where to End: Violet is rolled off to the juicer.

Plot: Willy Wonka has given out five golden tickets for five lucky children to tour his chocolate factory. Violet, one of the children, chews the three-course-dinner gum even though Willy tells her not to. She blows up into a giant blueberry.

Review: Willy is looking for a good, honest, obedient child, but the children who won golden tickets continually show that they are disobedient. Jonah also chose to disobey what God wanted him to do. Use this clip as a reminder to always do what God wants.

Discussion

After setting up and showing the clip, ASK:

- **What happened because Violet disobeyed?**
- **Do you sometimes disobey your parents? What happens?**

SAY: **Let's listen to a story about a man who disobeyed God.** Read or summarize the story from Jonah 1:1–3:2. Then ASK:

- **How did God get Jonah to obey him?**
- **Does God ever need to remind you how to obey him? How does he do that?**

SAY: **We all need to remember to obey. You saw what happened to Violet when she disobeyed. And you heard what happened to Jonah when he disobeyed. We need to obey our parents and our teachers, but above all, we need to obey God and do what he wants.**

Snack

▶ *ALLERGY ALERT*
▶ *OUTREACH*
▶ *PREPARE IN ADVANCE*

Jonah's Sea Snacks

Children will make sacks of snacks that remind them of Jonah's disobedience.

Supplies: blue plastic wrap, fish-shaped crackers, 1/4-cup measuring cup, pretzel sticks, person-shaped cookies, 6-inch lengths of ribbon or yarn

Time: 10 to 15 minutes

Preparation: Tear the blue plastic wrap into 12-inch squares. You'll need one square per child.

Have each child spread the plastic wrap in front of him or her to make a blue sea. Help kids scoop 1/4 cups of crackers into the center of the "sea." Let children count out 10 pretzel sticks to represent the salty sea and add them to the crackers.

Tell children to place one person-shaped cookie in the middle of the sea to represent Jonah. Then help kids gather the edges of the plastic wrap and form the snack into a ball. Students can hold the wrap and have a partner tie the wrap closed with a length of ribbon or yarn.

SAY: **When Jonah disobeyed God, he found himself in the ocean, and God sent a fish to swallow Jonah as a way to teach Jonah to obey. Today give this snack to someone you love, and tell that person the story of Jonah and how we should all ▷ DO WHAT GOD WANTS.**

Preschool Story

▶ *PREPARE IN ADVANCE*

Bible Point: ▷ DO WHAT GOD WANTS.

Supplies: Bible; masking tape; large, clean trash can lined with a clean, black trash bag; construction paper; scissors; glue; can of tuna; can opener

Time: 15 to 20 minutes

Preparation: Put masking tape on the floor in the shape of a boat large enough for the whole class to sit inside. Tip over a large, clean trash can lined with a clean, black trash bag. Cut out eyes and fins from the paper, and glue them to the outside of the trash can so it looks like a fish. For extra effect, put an open can of tuna inside the trash bag!

A Fishy Story

Have kids form a circle and stand near the boat outline. Open your Bible to Jonah 1, and show children the words. SAY: **God told Jonah to go to Nineveh and preach there. God wanted Jonah to tell the people of Nineveh to stop doing wrong things and to do what was right. But Jonah didn't want to go there. He didn't want to obey God. Jonah thought he could hide from God, so he jumped aboard a ship that would sail in the opposite direction.**

Have children join you inside the outline of the boat. SAY: **Let's make the sounds of the ocean with our hands.** Show children how to slide their palms back and forth to make a swishing sound. Have kids softly say, "Swish, swish" each time they rub their hands.

Jonah's boat sailed across the water. Continue making the sounds of the water with your hands. **Let's rock back and forth, just as Jonah's ship is rocking.** Have kids make the swishing noises. **Soon a terrible storm came up! Let's make the thunder sound.** Have children clap their hands loudly. **Now let's make the ocean sounds, louder and faster.** Encourage children to swish their hand faster. **The waves got bigger and bigger!** Encourage children to sway back and forth faster and faster.

The men on the ship were scared, and they didn't know what to do! Jonah knew that God had sent the storm because Jonah had disobeyed God. Jonah told the men to toss him overboard, and then the storm would stop. Have kids pretend to toss something overboard.

Jonah sank down in the water, and then God sent a giant fish to swallow Jonah! Lead kids to the trash can, and tell them to pretend it's the giant fish.

While Jonah was in the fish's belly, he asked God to forgive him and promised to do what God wanted from that time on. Let's take turns being Jonah in the fish's belly. Encourage each child to go inside the trash can and sit for a few seconds. Ask kids what they think it would be like inside a giant fish. As children leave the fish, have them say, **▷ DO WHAT GOD WANTS.**

When Jonah promised to ▷ DO WHAT GOD WANTS, God made the fish spit Jonah out onto the sand. Then Jonah went to Nineveh to do what God wanted him to do.

ASK:

- **Why didn't Jonah do what God wanted at first? What happened?**
- **How can you do what God wants?**

SAY: **Jonah finally did what God wanted him to do. We can ▷ DO WHAT GOD WANTS, too. We can obey God by obeying our parents, by choosing to do the right thing, and by praying to God.**

notes

BIBLE STORY

Jonah Goes to Nineveh

For the Leader

Everyone can fall short when trying to live for God. Accepting God's will is sometimes hard. No one knew that more than Jonah. His story wouldn't be nearly as interesting had Jonah ended up fish food. What makes his story great is that God forgave Jonah. And God's forgiveness led Jonah to do great things.

Teach your students that God is willing to forgive them when they go astray, too. Use these ideas to keep kids moving toward a stronger relationship with God, and let them know that when they wander off course, God can make their paths straight again.

Key Scriptures

Jonah 2:1–3:10

Matthew 6:9-13

1 John 1:9

Bible Verse

"If we confess our sins to him, he is faithful and just to forgive us our sins and to cleanse us from all wickedness" (1 John 1:9).

Bible Experience

▶ *PREPARE IN ADVANCE*

Big Fish

Bible Point: ▷ **GOD FORGIVES US.**

Children will see what it might have been like on Jonah's boat and inside the big fish.

Supplies: 12-foot square of landscaping plastic (larger classes may need a larger square of plastic), duct tape, box fan, green crepe paper (optional)

Time: 40 to 45 minutes

Preparation: Lay the landscaping plastic on the floor in the center of your room.

Tell kids that they're going to help make a whale they can sit inside. Tape down the edges of the plastic with the duct tape. Be sure kids don't stretch the plastic to its full 12 feet. Have them leave the plastic fairly loose in the middle. This may work best if one student cuts long lengths of tape while others use them to tape the edges of the plastic to the floor. Instruct kids to tape the plastic to the floor on two sides. They'll need to tape one end of the plastic securely to the edges of the box fan and tape the opposite end to the floor, leaving an opening for a mouth where everyone can crawl into the belly of the "whale." When the plastic is securely taped down, turn on the fan and allow the whale to "grow." For further fun, have kids tape green crepe paper streamers to the box fan to represent seaweed. When there appears to be enough space inside, have students crawl one by one inside the whale.

SAY: **This story is like the singsong pantomime game Going on a Bear Hunt. You'll repeat everything I say and do.** Have kids repeat line by line your words and actions.

Sit in a chair, and imitate walking by slapping your thighs with open palms. SAY: **I'm going on a Jonah walk.** (Slap your thighs as if you're running.) **Jonah disobeyed 'cause Jonah ran away.** (Pretend to row.) **Jonah boarded a boat.** (Make swimming motions.) **The crew threw him overboard when they'd heard he sinned. Jonah tried to swim.** (Make a loud gulp, and hold cheeks with the palms of your hands.) **But a fish swallowed him!** (Hold up three fingers.) **Jonah sat three days in the belly of that fish.** (Bow your head and clasp your hands in prayer.) **Jonah said, "Forgive me, Lord."** (Hold a thumb up.) **God said, "OK, I'll set you free today!" The whale spit Jonah out.** (Hold your nose.) **Pew-wee, Jonah, you smell like a fish!** (Slap your thighs as if you're walking.) **Going on a Jonah walk.** (Face your palms outward.) **God said, "Stop, Jonah!"** (Shake your finger.) **"Preach in Nineveh today."** (Nod your head.) **Jonah said, "OK!"** (Slap your thighs as if you're running.) **Jonah ran to town.** (Continue to slap your thighs.) **He didn't mess around.** (Shake your finger.) **Jonah told the people,** (Continue to shake your finger.) **"Hear what I say."** (Mime a baseball pitch.) **When you reject your sinful ways,** (Point upward.) **"God will forgive you."**

After the story, ASK:

◆ **What happened when Jonah was in trouble?**

◆ **What happened when he finally obeyed God?**

◆ **Why do you think God forgave Jonah?**

SAY: **1 John 1:9 says about God, "If we confess our sins to him, he is faithful and just to forgive us our sins and to cleanse us from all wickedness." ▷ GOD FORGIVES US no matter what we've done wrong.**

ASK:

◆ **Why do you think God wants to forgive us?**

◆ **What should we do when we do wrong things?**

Additional Topics List

This lesson can be used to help children discover... Discipleship, Grace, and Prayer.

Game

▶ *PREPARE IN ADVANCE*
▶ *HIGH ENERGY*

Big Fish

Children will reenact Jonah's travels.

Supplies: Bible, 3 sheets of construction paper, marker, tape, 2 blankets

Time: 10 to 15 minutes

Preparation: Label one sheet of construction paper "Joppa," another "Tarshish," and the other "Nineveh." Tape the three sheets in three different areas of your room—far enough apart so kids will have to run between the cities. Place one blanket at Tarshish and another one at Joppa.

Review the story of Jonah by reading key verses from Jonah 2:1–3:10; then play this game. Select one player to be the big fish. SAY: **All the rest of you are now Jonahs, and you're in danger of being grabbed by the big fish! When I yell, "Joppa," you must run to Joppa to be safe.** Point to the area with the Joppa sign.

Everyone who makes it safely to Joppa will hide under the blanket until you hear me call another city. When I yell, "Tarshish," you must run to Tarshish to be safe. Point to the area with the Tarshish sign.

Everyone who makes it safely to Tarshish will hide under the blanket. When I call, "Nineveh," you must run to Nineveh to be safe. Point to the area with the Nineveh sign. **You'll have no blanket to hide under there because when Jonah finally went to Nineveh, he obeyed God. So when you get to Nineveh, you'll say, "Obey God." If I call, "Person overboard," you may run to any city you want. Each time I call a new city, you must avoid getting tagged by the big fish. If you do get tagged, you'll become a big fish and help tag others.**

Play several times. Then gather in the Nineveh location, and SAY: **Jonah went to Nineveh after God saved him, and he convinced a city to change its ways. God forgives us because he knows that when we follow him, we can go on to do great things.** Close in prayer, thanking God for his forgiveness.

Craft

▶ *PREPARE IN ADVANCE*

The Belly of a Fish

Children will make Jonah in the belly of a fish.

Supplies: poster board, safety scissors, crayons or markers, string, 10-inch balloons, premixed plaster of Paris, paper plates, blue or gray yarn, wax paper, pencils, construction paper, glue, chopsticks

Time: 30 to 45 minutes

Preparation: Cut the poster board into 2-inch squares. Cut the yarn into 12-inch strands and the string into 7-inch lengths.

Give each child a square of poster board, and have him or her draw a person on it. Have kids cut out their drawings and tie them to the end of lengths of string. Distribute balloons and have kids squeeze their poster board people into the balloons. Then have older children blow up the balloons, mindful that balloons are a choking hazard for younger children. Help kids tie off the balloons so the string hangs out a few inches.

Pour a few cups of the wet plaster of Paris onto several paper plates. Show kids how to dip the yarn into the plaster of Paris and wrap it evenly around the balloons until most of each balloon is covered with yarn. Allow balloons to dry on wax paper. Tie the string to a few of the plaster-yarn pieces.

When the plaster is completely dry, have kids use the tip of a pencil to pop their balloons and remove them from the inside of the plaster casts, making sure they leave the cardboard people inside. Have kids cut fins, eyes, and a spout of water from construction paper and glue them on the plaster whale. Kids can hang their whales (Jonah and all) from the ceiling.

While children are creating their whales, create an extra one. Have kids write affirming notes and slip them inside your balloon. Then give kids chopsticks and have them each pull out a note and read it aloud.

SAY: **When Jonah asked to be forgiven, he was spit out of the fish onto the land. I'm sure he felt much better! God's forgiveness makes us feel better, too. When we realize that God still loves us, even after something bad we've done, life is good!**

n

o

t

e

s

Bible Application

▶ ***PREPARE IN ADVANCE***
▶ ***STUDENT LED***

A Clean Slate

Children will learn that God gives them a clean slate.

Supplies: white card stock, marker

Time: 5 to 10 minutes

Preparation: Write on a piece of card stock "I sank beneath the waves, and the waters closed over me" (Jonah 2:5).

Have children line up next to one another, facing you. You may have more than one line if you have a large group. Hold up the piece of card stock for students to see. SAY: **When Jonah was in the belly of the fish, he realized he'd fallen short of living for God. He was in deep trouble!**

The words written on this piece of paper represent the times you've fallen short of living for God in any area of your life. Think about how Jonah felt when he was engulfed in sin. Think about a time you've fallen short.

Ask each student to turn around in a full circle and face the same spot again. As they turn, flip the paper to reveal the blank side. SAY: **Just as the words on this paper were replaced by a blank sheet, your forgiven sins give you a clean slate to live for God.**

Have children make their own clean slates. Encourage them to teach this simple lesson to family and friends.

Creative Prayer Idea

▶ *PREPARE IN ADVANCE*

Forgiveness Boat Prayers

Children will use boats for confessional prayers.

Supplies: dishpan filled with water, several small rocks, popped popcorn, empty plastic boat or dish

Time: 5 to 10 minutes

Preparation: A plastic banana-split boat works well for this simple prayer. You can find one at a party-supply store or an ice-cream shop.

Have kids gather around the dishpan filled with water. Allow them to float small plastic boats or dishes. ASK:

◆ **How do you feel about yourself when you do something wrong?**

SAY: **We're like this boat that can float on the water. These rocks are like the wrong things we do. Watch what happens to our boat when it gets filled with wrong things.**

As you drop the rocks in the boat, mention wrong things children might do. For instance, you might say, "I hit my brother," "I didn't clean up my room when I was told," or "I wasn't nice to my mom." Continue to add rocks until the boat sinks.

SAY: **Oh, look what happened to our boat! It got filled up with wrong things and sank. The sailors on Jonah's boat thought the boat would sink, so they threw him overboard! But we don't have to jump overboard. God loves us and wants to take away all the wrong things we've done. God wants to hear us say, "I'm sorry." Let's ask God to forgive us right now.** Have kids say the Lord's Prayer (Matthew 6:9-13).

Remove the rocks and boat from the water, and set the boat afloat again. Fill the boat with popcorn. SAY: **When we tell God we're sorry, he forgives us and fills our hearts with good things. Look. When I put good things in our boat, it doesn't sink!** Close in prayer, thanking God for the goodness that his forgiveness brings.

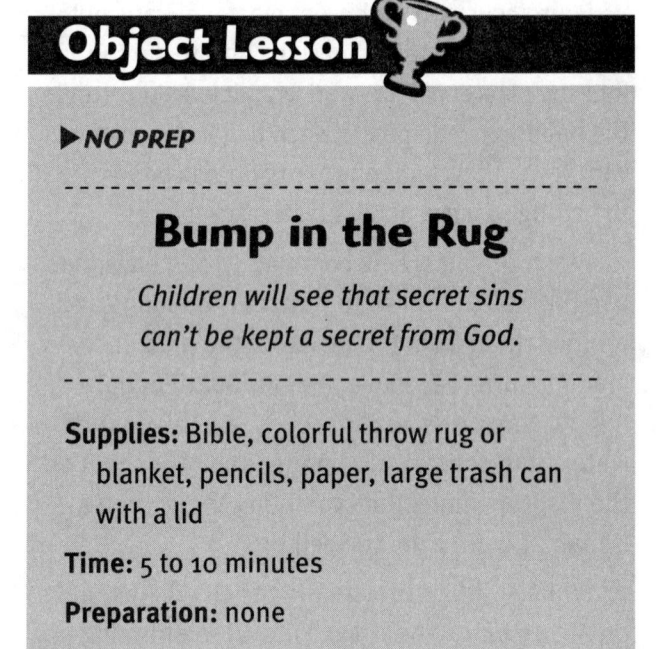

Object Lesson

▶ *NO PREP*

Bump in the Rug

Children will see that secret sins can't be kept a secret from God.

Supplies: Bible, colorful throw rug or blanket, pencils, paper, large trash can with a lid

Time: 5 to 10 minutes

Preparation: none

Place the rug on the floor in the center of the room. Distribute the pencils and sheets of paper. Ask kids to write down something they've done wrong, such as lying, stealing, disobeying, or being unkind. Nonreaders may draw pictures. Reassure children that no one will see what they've drawn or written. Then have kids wad up their papers and put them under the rug. Invite kids to sit in a circle around the rug. Read aloud Jonah 2:6.

SAY: **When we keep secrets about sins, we fall into the "jaws of death" like Jonah did. No one knows what we did. No one knows we've fallen—except God. Then those sins show up, just like all these bumps under the rug.**

ASK:

◆ **When you keep a sin secret, who gets hurt?**

◆ **What does God want us to do when we do something wrong?**

Scoop up the paper wads, and wrap them in the rug. Open the large trash can, shake the paper wads into it, and put the lid back on.

SAY: **Hiding our sins doesn't make them go away. Only God can throw our sins away. He did it for Jonah, and he can do it for us. 1 John 1:9 says about God, "If we confess our sins to him, he is faithful and just to forgive us our sins and to cleanse us from all wickedness." ▷ GOD FORGIVES US no matter what we've done wrong. When we ask him to, God forgives us completely.**

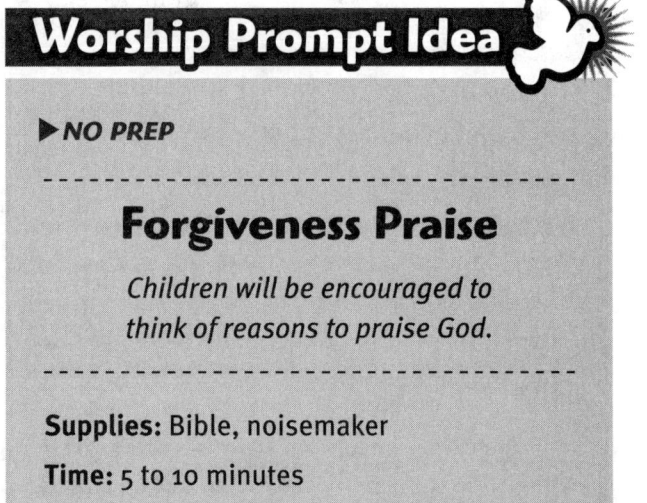

Worship Prompt Idea

▶ *NO PREP*

Forgiveness Praise

Children will be encouraged to think of reasons to praise God.

Supplies: Bible, noisemaker

Time: 5 to 10 minutes

Preparation: none

Have a volunteer read from Jonah's prayer (Jonah 2:2-9) to the rest of the class. Then SAY: **In this passage Jonah praised God and thanked him, and we can praise God, too. Let's give some "up, down, all around" praise!**

Have children sit cross-legged in a circle. Tell them to tap out a rhythm as they say, "Up, down, all around!" Show children how to tap twice on their knees and then clap twice in time to the words. When everyone understands the rhythm, add a twist. As they tap and clap, have children say the phrase in sequence, each child saying one word as the phrase goes around the circle.

Periodically sound the noisemaker. Whoever is speaking when you sound the noisemaker should say, "I'm so glad God forgives me!"

For extra fun, vary the tempo of the praise prayer. Continue until everyone in the circle has had a chance to praise God. Then lead the class in an enthusiastic "hip, hip, hooray" cheer for God!

Preschool Story

▶ *NO PREP*

Bible Point: ▷ **GOD FORGIVES US.**

Supplies: Bible

Time: 15 to 20 minutes

Preparation: none

Another Chance

Have kids form a circle and sit down. Open your Bible to Jonah 2:1-2, and show children the words.

SAY: **While Jonah was still in the fish, he prayed to God and asked God to forgive him for running away. God forgave Jonah and made the big fish spit Jonah onto the beach.** Have kids pretend to be spit out by a whale and land on the beach.

Then God spoke to Jonah again. God told Jonah to go to Nineveh and give God's message to the people who lived there. This time Jonah obeyed God and went to Nineveh. Encourage kids to nod their heads and then walk in place as if they're traveling to Nineveh. After a minute, encourage kids to sit down.

On the day Jonah entered the city of Nineveh, he shouted to the crowds of people in Nineveh. Stand up and shout as you say Jonah's words. **"Forty days from now Nineveh will be destroyed!"** Sit back down. **The people of Nineveh believed what God was saying to them through Jonah. They stopped doing bad things, and they asked God to forgive them.**

ASK:

- **Do you think God forgave the people in Nineveh?**

SAY: **God did forgive the people in Nineveh. God loved the people in Nineveh, and God wanted them to love him, too! God was so glad that the people were sorry that he decided not to destroy the city. God forgave the people of Nineveh because he loved them. God loves us, and ▷ GOD FORGIVES US, too.**

When you finish telling the story, have children gather in a circle for this fun action rhyme:

After three days the fish spat Jonah upon dry, green land. *(Spread out your hands with palms down.)*

After three days the fish spat Jonah, just as God had planned. *(Show a thumbs-up.)*

Jonah told the people to change and stop their wicked ways. *(Hold up a hand, palm out.)*

Jonah told the people to change, and they began to praise. *(Clap your hands and look up.)*

So Nineveh turned away from evil and all their sin. *(Turn around.)*

So Nineveh followed God with a great big grin! *(Smile and point to your mouth.)*

ASK:

- **What happened when the people of Nineveh said they were sorry?**
- **When has God forgiven you?**
- **How can you ask God for forgiveness this week?**

SAY: **When we ask God for forgiveness, we can know that ▷ GOD FORGIVES US because he loves us!**

BIBLE STORY

Jonah's Anger at God's Compassion

For the Leader

Many children live in a melting pot of different cultures, customs, value systems, and faith perspectives. They might identify with Jonah's discomfort with being around people he didn't like. The Assyrians, having gained a reputation for ruthlessness and cruelty, were hated by Jonah and other Israelites. So when God told Jonah to reach out to Nineveh, the capital of Assyria, Jonah ran away. Later, Jonah became angry when God spared the Assyrians.

Use this study to help children see people's universal need for God's love. These activities will help create in children a desire to reach out to people who do not know God.

Key Scriptures

Jonah 4:1-11

James 1:19

1 John 4:7-12

Bible Verse

"Love one another, for love comes from God" (1 John 4:7).

Bible Experience

▶ *NO PREP*

Understanding God's Compassion

Bible Point: ▷ **LOVE PEOPLE WHO DON'T KNOW GOD.**

Children will reenact the story of Jonah's anger.

Supplies: none

Time: 5 to 10 minutes

Preparation: none

Assign one child to be Jonah, one to be the king, one to be the plant, and three to be the fish. All the other children can be the citizens of Nineveh.

Have the king and the citizens of Nineveh stand together on one side of the room. Have the "plant" kneel on another side of the room. Have the children who are playing the fish hold hands and surround "Jonah."

When all the children are in place, start this reenactment from Jonah 4. Have kids do the actions as they are underlined in the story.

SAY: **The story begins with Jonah, who had been inside the fish for three days. Then he prayed to God and promised to obey. So God told the fish to spit out Jonah. After the fish spit Jonah onto the dry ground, God spoke to Jonah: "Get up and go to Nineveh. Tell them what I tell you to say."**

So Jonah got up, dusted himself off, and went to Nineveh. Jonah walked into town and preached to the people. Jonah said, "After 40 days, Nineveh will be destroyed. God is displeased with your sinful ways."

The people of Nineveh listened and believed. Even the king was sorry. He got up from his throne, took off his beautiful robe, and put on itchy, rough cloth. Then he sat down in a pile of ashes to show how upset he was.

The king said, "Everyone must turn away from evil living and kneel in prayer. Maybe then God will stop being angry with us." Everyone did what the king said. When God saw that the people were sorry for their sins, he changed his mind. God decided not to punish them.

But this made Jonah angry. He wanted God to punish the citizens of Nineveh. Jonah said to God, "I knew that if I obeyed you, the people of Nineveh would repent, and you would not punish them. This makes me so angry that it would be better for me to die."

Then Jonah left the city. He built a small shelter for himself and sat in the shade. God made a plant grow very quickly next to the shelter to make Jonah more comfortable. But the next day the plant shriveled up and died.

Jonah became hot, weary, and angry. He pouted and said, "It would be better for me to just die." God said to Jonah, "Do you think it is right for you to be angry about the plant?" Jonah said, "Yes. The plant made me comfortable. Now it's gone and I'm too hot. I'm so angry I could die."

Then God said, "You are so concerned for a plant! If your concern is so great, isn't it right that I should care for the thousands of people?"

After the role play, ASK:

- ◆ **Do you think Jonah was right to be angry? Explain.**
- ◆ **Why do you think God had Jonah talk to people he didn't like?**
- ◆ **Why does God want us to love people who don't know him?**

SAY: **First John 4:7 says, "Love one another, for love comes from God." It's not always easy, but God is pleased when we ▷ LOVE PEOPLE WHO DON'T KNOW HIM. Maybe when we show people God's love, they'll want to know God, too.**

Additional Topics List

This lesson can be used to help children discover... Caring for Others, God's Love, and Kindness.

Game

▶ ***PREPARE IN ADVANCE***
▶ ***FOR SMALL GROUPS***

Crowd Around

Children will show loving actions as they crowd onto different sections of a playing area.

Supplies: Bible, butcher paper (4 colors—such as yellow, red, blue, and orange), scissors, masking tape

Time: 5 to 10 minutes

Preparation: For each group of eight to 10 kids, make a game board as follows: Cut a 4x4-foot section of each color of butcher paper. Tape the four colors to the floor to form a square.

Have kids form groups of eight to 10. Read aloud 1 John 4:7-12. SAY: **Wow! God says we are to love one another because love comes from God! Jonah had a hard time showing God's love to the people of Nineveh. Let's see if we can do better as we play a game and show God's love.**

Ask each group to stand around a game board. Tell kids to stand in a crowd on the color you name and do the loving action you call out:

- **Stand on yellow. Give three people high fives, and say your name.**
- **Stand on red. Give two people a shoulder rub.**
- **Stand on blue. Tell two people what you like about them.**
- **Stand on orange. Give one person a handshake as you say, "God loves you and so do I."**

Continue calling out colors and loving actions, such as, "Pat as many backs as you can until I count to 10." Every now and then, call out a color that kids are already standing on.

At the end of the game, have everyone sit around one of the game boards. Discuss these questions:

- **What loving actions can you show to someone when you go home?**
- **Why does God want us to love people who don't know him?**
- **Why did God want Jonah to show love to the people of Nineveh by telling the people about God?**

SAY: **God wants us to love others, especially people who don't know him. God is love, and he wants people to know about it.** Call out one more action: **Stand any place on this game board, and everyone give me a hug!**

Craft

▶ *PREPARE IN ADVANCE*

A Caring Tree

Children will make trees to remind them of God's compassion.

Supplies: Bible, 9x18-inch sheets of green construction paper, yellow construction paper, paper cutter, safety scissors, tape, black markers or pencils, glue

Time: 10 to 15 minutes

Preparation: Use a paper cutter to cut the green construction paper into 9x18-inch sheets. At each child's place, set out two pieces of green paper, one piece of yellow paper, safety scissors, and a marker.

Have each child tape two green papers together, end to end, so there's one long strip of paper. Starting at one short end, have the child roll up the strip and tape it securely. At one end of the tube, have him or her cut three-fourths of the way down and then make another cut approximately 1 inch from the first one.

Have children continue making cuts until they're all the way around the tube. Tell them to pull the inside layers of paper from the tube to make the tree "grow." Then tell them to cut figs out of the yellow paper. Have children write the names of people who don't know God on each fig. Glue the figs to the ends of the branches.

Bring the group together with their trees. Read the story from Jonah 4. Then ASK:

- ◆ **Why did God care for Jonah?**
- ◆ **Why was Jonah mad?**
- ◆ **Have you ever felt like complaining, like Jonah did? What happened?**
- ◆ **Why did God want Jonah to look out for the people of Nineveh?**

SAY: **God sent Jonah a shade tree to cool him off, but Jonah was still mad that God had forgiven the people of Nineveh. He grumbled, and the tree withered.** Have kids push their trees together and watch them "wither." **Many times we don't want God to be nice to people we don't like. Instead of rejoicing that God cares for them, we grumble. But instead of grumbling, we should love people who don't know God.** Have kids make their trees grow again.

Bible Application

▶ *NO PREP*

Know God, Show God

Children will talk about showing compassion as God does.

Supplies: none

Time: up to 5 minutes

Preparation: none

Read aloud James 1:19. SAY: **Sometimes we, like Jonah, get our quick and our slow mixed up. We sometimes think God moves too slowly. But we need to learn from God to be quick to listen and slow to be angry.** Have kids pantomime what the phrases "quick to listen" and "slow to get angry" might mean to them. **God can show us how to be compassionate, especially to people who don't know him or do what he wants them to do.**

ASK:

- **What are some ways you can show compassion to people who don't know God?**

SAY: **I'd like you to choose one of those ideas and try to do it this week. Remember that God wants you to be slow to get angry and quick to love everyone, even people who don't know him. Let's pray together.**

PRAY: **Dear God, thank you for loving us so much that you show us compassion when we turn away from you. Help us to share your compassion with other people. In Jesus' name, amen.**

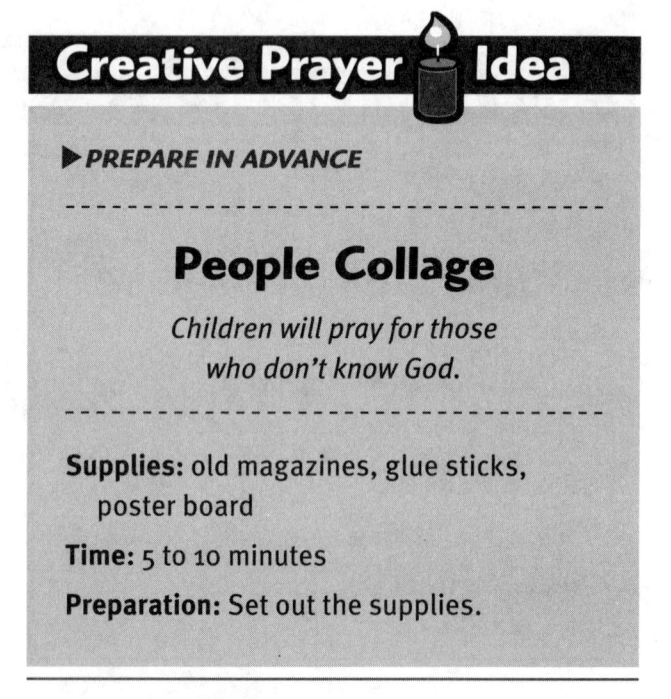

Creative Prayer Idea

▶ *PREPARE IN ADVANCE*

People Collage

Children will pray for those who don't know God.

Supplies: old magazines, glue sticks, poster board

Time: 5 to 10 minutes

Preparation: Set out the supplies.

Form groups of up to four. SAY: **I want you to go through these magazines and tear out pictures of people you would describe as different from you. Work in your groups to create a people collage by gluing the pictures to the poster board.** Give groups about five minutes to complete their collages. Place the collages together on a table or the floor, and have children gather around them.

ASK:

- **Where do you suppose these people live?**
- **Would you want to live there? Why or why not?**

SAY: **It's possible that some of these people may not know God. While they may be different, they have one thing in common with you: God loves them! God wants us to love people who don't know him. Think of the places these people might come from. Say a quiet prayer for those cities or countries.** After a minute, close in a group prayer, asking God to help kids reach out to everyone in his name.

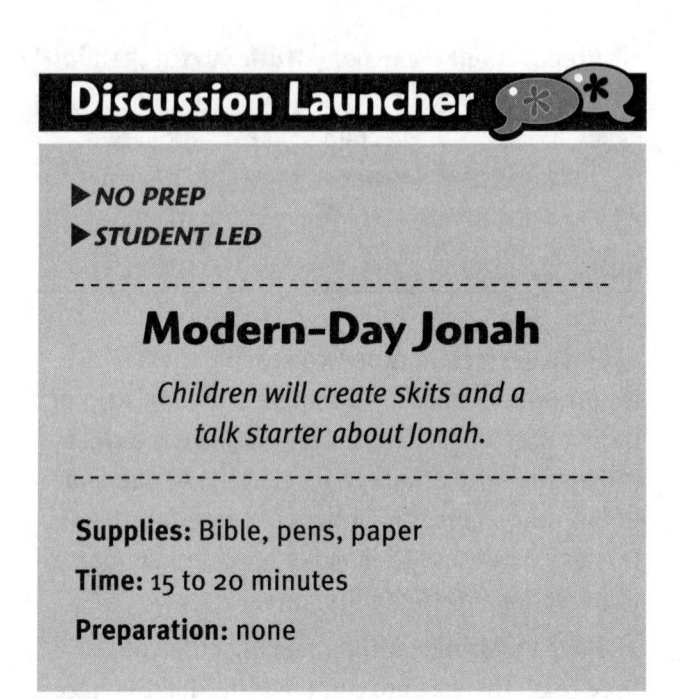

Discussion Launcher

▶ *NO PREP*

▶ *STUDENT LED*

Modern-Day Jonah

Children will create skits and a talk starter about Jonah.

Supplies: Bible, pens, paper

Time: 15 to 20 minutes

Preparation: none

Read aloud the story of Jonah in Jonah 4:1-11. Then form groups of no more than four. Have the kids in each group create and perform a skit telling this story as if it happened to them instead of Jonah. Instead of going to Nineveh, have groups think of something God would want them to do today, such as going to a friend's house or hanging out at a skate park. As groups work on their skits, have them discuss these questions:

◆ **Where would people run to get away from God?**

◆ **How do we get people to return to God?**

When groups are ready, have them perform their skits.

Ask each group to come up with one question for the group, based on its skit. They might ask:

- How are we like Jonah?
- How are people today like the people of Nineveh?
- How do you love people who don't know God?
- What are the needs of the people in your town?
- How can you help meet those people's needs?

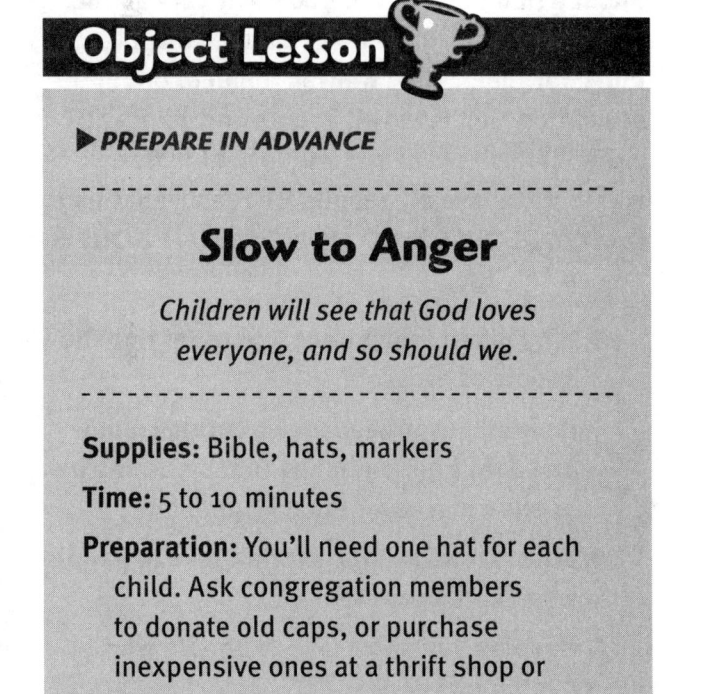

Object Lesson

▶ *PREPARE IN ADVANCE*

Slow to Anger

Children will see that God loves everyone, and so should we.

Supplies: Bible, hats, markers

Time: 5 to 10 minutes

Preparation: You'll need one hat for each child. Ask congregation members to donate old caps, or purchase inexpensive ones at a thrift shop or dollar store.

Hand out hats and markers. SAY: **Sometimes you need to do things quickly, and other times it's important to move slowly. But the Bible tells us that Jonah got mixed up. Jonah should have been quick to obey God. Instead, he was quick to run away. Then Jonah should've been quick to listen to God; instead, he got angry with God for forgiving Nineveh.**

Then God gave Jonah a plant for some shade. And Jonah was happy. Hold up a hat. **Just as this hat gives us relief from the sun, God gave Jonah relief from the sun by giving him some shade. It cooled him down—and cooled his temper, too! Jonah got relief from his anger at God and the people of Nineveh.**

Read aloud James 1:19. Ask kids to write "slow to get angry" on the inside of their caps.

ASK:

◆ **If someone doesn't know God, how do you think your anger will help him or her?**

◆ **How would your love help him or her?**

SAY: **God was compassionate to Jonah and to Nineveh. And he wanted Jonah to be compassionate, too. Sometimes it's hard to reach out to people who don't know God. Sometimes we get angry. Next time you get angry with someone, put on your hat to "cool down," and maybe your compassion for that person can teach him or her about God's love.**

notes

Preschool Story

▶ *PREPARE IN ADVANCE*

Bible Point: ▷ **LOVE PEOPLE WHO DON'T KNOW GOD.**

Supplies: Bible, green construction paper, hair dryer, 1 sock per 2 children, scissors

Time: 15 to 20 minutes

Preparation: Cut large leaves out of the green construction paper.

Love Everyone!

Have kids form a circle and sit down. Open your Bible to Jonah 4, and show children the words. SAY: **Jonah was angry with God for being so nice to the people of Nineveh. Jonah wanted God to punish them for all the wrong things they'd done. Jonah didn't think it was fair that God was going to forgive the people of Nineveh and not punish them at all.** Have everyone pretend to pout as Jonah may have pouted.

So Jonah went outside the city and sat down so he could see what God would do to the city. Choose one child to be Jonah and sit down, and have the other kids gather in a circle around the child. **It was *very* hot outside, and soon Jonah became uncomfortable. God sent a nice leafy plant to shade Jonah from the sun.** Give half of the standing children the green construction paper leaves you made before class. Encourage kids to hold the leaves over "Jonah" and wave them to create a breeze.

Jonah was glad that God sent the plant. But God wanted to teach Jonah a lesson, so he sent a worm to eat the plant. Give the other half of the standing children socks to wear on one of their hands. Encourage children to pretend their sock-covered hand is a worm and to have the worm eat away the plants. After a bit, set the worms and the green construction paper leaves aside.

God also sent a very hot wind to blow on Jonah. Start the hair dryer, and set it on high heat. Blow the hot air toward Jonah and the other kids. **The sun beat down on Jonah's head until he felt very sick. In fact, Jonah felt so sick that he wanted to die!**

Then God said to Jonah, "You are sorry about a plant dying, but you don't care about an entire city dying. I love Nineveh, and I feel sorry for them." God wanted Jonah to understand that God loves all people and wants all people to believe in him and love him. God wants us to love all people. He even wants us to ▷ LOVE PEOPLE WHO DON'T KNOW GOD!

ASK:

- **Why didn't Jonah want God to forgive the people of Nineveh?**
- **Have you ever been upset because someone didn't get punished for something he or she did wrong? What happened?**
- **Why is it important to show love to people who don't know God?**
- **How can you show love to people who don't know God?**

BIBLE STORY

Esther Becomes Queen

For the Leader

The ancient Persian kingdom ruled by Xerxes (486-465 B.C.) was fraught with anti-Semitism. When the king wanted Esther as his queen, the Jewess was afraid of what would happen if her true identity were discovered. Her cousin told her not to say that she was Jewish. So when Esther became queen, she kept her heritage to herself. When the survival of the Jews was in doubt because of Haman's evil plot, God's purpose for Esther was suddenly crystal clear. Although attempting to save her people meant revealing her nationality and risking her life, Esther was brave. Jews still celebrate Purim to honor Esther's bravery.

Children can learn to be brave, too, when they understand that God has a purpose for everything that happens to and around them. God can use any of us to accomplish his purposes "for just such a time as this" (Esther 4:14).

Key Scriptures

Esther 2:1-18; 5:1-8

Ephesians 2:10

Bible Verse

"We are God's masterpiece. He has created us anew in Christ Jesus, so we can do the good things he planned for us long ago" (Ephesians 2:10).

Bible Experience

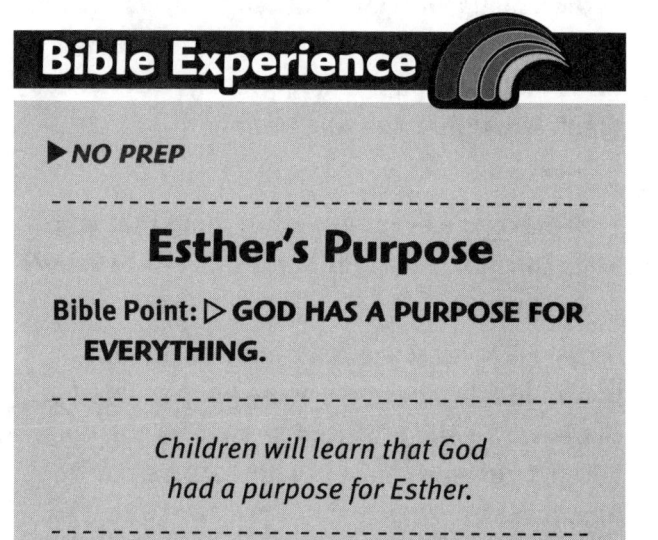

▶ *NO PREP*

Esther's Purpose

Bible Point: ▷ **GOD HAS A PURPOSE FOR EVERYTHING.**

Children will learn that God had a purpose for Esther.

Supplies: Bible, a piece of modeling dough for each child

Time: 10 to 15 minutes

Preparation: none

SAY: **I need help looking for things in this room that are useful. When you see something useful, point at it and freeze. I'll come around and unfreeze you, and then you tell us what you see that's useful and what it does.**

After a few minutes, SAY: **You've pointed to some useful items. But you're useful, too; I asked for help finding things, and you helped me.**

Esther was a helpful woman. She became queen and eventually saved her people. Give each child a small piece of modeling dough, and

SAY: **I'll tell you the story of Esther, and you play with the dough while you listen.**

Many Jews were being forced to live in another country. Esther and her cousin Mordecai were Jews. Mordecai raised Esther like a daughter.

When King Xerxes wanted a new queen, he called for a search throughout his kingdom. Esther, along with many other girls, was taken to the palace. Esther had many attractive features and pleased the king greatly. But Xerxes didn't know that she was Jewish.

ASK:

- **Have you ever done something that you thought was right but it was really scary? Explain.**

SAY: **Mordecai wouldn't let Esther reveal her nationality because many people hated the Jews. So she prepared herself for the king. When a girl was chosen to present herself to him, it took a whole year to prepare! She was given seven maids and had 12 months of beauty treatments. Then Esther presented herself to the king and won his heart. The king of Persia chose Esther as his queen and declared a national holiday.**

After the story, ask children to share what they sculpted with their dough. Follow up with questions about how what they sculpted might be useful.

SAY: **You used modeling dough to create some beautiful things. God used Esther to save the Jews, and God can use you to do good things, too.**

Read aloud Ephesians 2:10. SAY: ▷ **GOD HAS A PURPOSE FOR EVERYTHING, including your life! If you continue to do the good works God has prepared for you to do, he'll take care of you as he took care of Esther.**

Encourage children to take their creations with them as reminders of everyone's purpose for God.

Song & Connect

Use "Let Us Worship" (track 6, *it: Innovative Tools for Children's Ministry: Old Testament* CD) to help reinforce the Bible Point, ▷ **GOD HAS A PURPOSE FOR EVERYTHING.**

Kick off a full celebration of God's purpose. Have kids use noisemakers to get other classes or congregation members to worship with them.

Additional Topics List

This lesson can be used to help children discover... Encouragement, Joy, and Praise.

Game

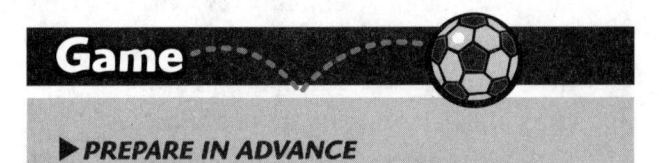

▶ ***PREPARE IN ADVANCE***

▶ ***NO PREP***

Who Will Lead?

Children will follow a leader and then switch and follow new leaders.

Supplies: Bible

Time: 5 to 10 minutes

Preparation: Ask two teenagers or adults to help, and show them ahead of time how to play the game.

Ask children to form a single-file line. Position one leader at the end of the line and another in the middle. Tell children to follow the leader who's holding up his or her hand.

Stand at the head of the line, and hold up your hand. You'll be the first leader, and the line will march behind you. Start walking slowly, and keep holding up your hand. Gradually increase your pace. After a minute of marching, lead kids in forming a circle so you're close to the leader you had placed at the end of the line. When you ask, "Who will lead?" have the leader at the end of the line hold up his or her hand as you take down yours.

Then step out of the line. That adult will become the new leader, and the kids will follow. Rejoin the line anywhere you'd like. After a few laps around the area, the new leader will ask, "Who will lead?" and the adult in the middle of the line will hold up a hand to become the third leader.

Help kids scramble into a line behind the third leader. Direct kids and send them after the new leader. Have kids move into a circle again, and slow the pace to cool down. Then sit in a circle, and discuss the following questions:

- ◆ **How did you know whom to follow in this game?**
- ◆ **What was it like to follow new leaders?**

Open your Bible to Esther 2:1-18. SAY: **The Bible tells us about King Xerxes, who chose a new queen to help him lead.** Briefly tell kids how Queen Esther helped save her people. ASK:

- ◆ **What was Esther's purpose?**
- ◆ **Do you think God has a purpose for everything? Why or why not?**

n

o

t

e

s

Craft

▶ ***PREPARE IN ADVANCE***

Gragers

Note: This is a craft for older children and requires close adult supervision. Children will make colorful noisemakers.

Supplies: flour, sugar, water, measuring cups, large pan or Dutch oven, spoon, pie tins, old newspaper, burned-out light bulbs, tempera paint, paintbrushes, access to a stove

Time: 30 to 35 minutes

Preparation: This craft requires two class sessions. Before this activity, make an easy papier-mâché paste at home. Mix 2 cups flour with ½ cup sugar in a large pan or Dutch oven. Stir in warm water until a paste forms. Then stir in ½ gallon of warm water. Stir over moderate heat until the mixture boils and becomes thick and clear. Remove from heat and stir in 2 cups cold water.

Place a few cups of the paste in several pie tins. Have children tear long, thin newspaper strips and pull the strips through the paste. Have kids cover burned-out light bulbs with four or five layers of wet newspaper strips and set them in a warm, sunny place to dry until your next class.

When the newspaper is completely dry, have children hit the gragers against the floor or a tabletop to break the glass inside. Caution children not to break through the papier-mâché layer, or glass will spill out. Then have kids paint their noisemakers with bright colors.

SAY: **It's hard to find a use for burned out bulbs. Usually we throw them away. But we**

found a use—to make instruments to worship God!

God used Esther to bring honor to himself, too. And God can use us to bring honor to God! We can be instruments of worship!

Have kids use their gragers as worship instruments as you sing together. Choose an upbeat song, and allow kids to accent the music with their gragers.

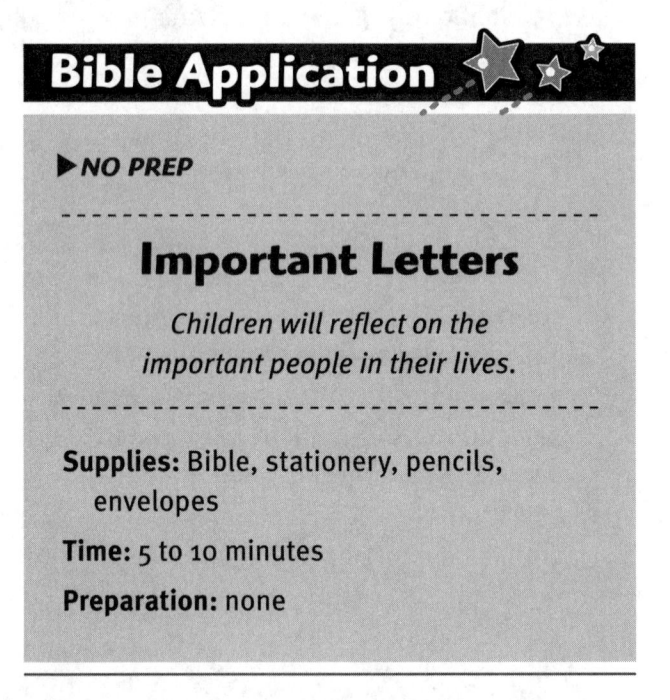

Bible Application

▶ ***NO PREP***

Important Letters

Children will reflect on the important people in their lives.

Supplies: Bible, stationery, pencils, envelopes

Time: 5 to 10 minutes

Preparation: none

Read aloud Esther 2:1-18. SAY: **Because Esther was the queen, she saved her people from death. But without Mordecai's help, Esther might not have been brave enough to be queen. God had a purpose for Esther and Mordecai—he has a purpose for everything. Let's take some quiet time and think about the people we love and who love us.**

Give each child a few sheets of stationery and a pencil. Ask kids to write a letter to someone who loves them, thanking them for carrying out God's work. After they finish, have children sit in a circle and lay their letters in the center. PRAY: **Dear God, we've placed letters to people we love in the center of this circle. Please help those we love and watch over them. Thank you for giving all of us a purpose. In Jesus' name, amen.**

Encourage children to personally deliver their letters.

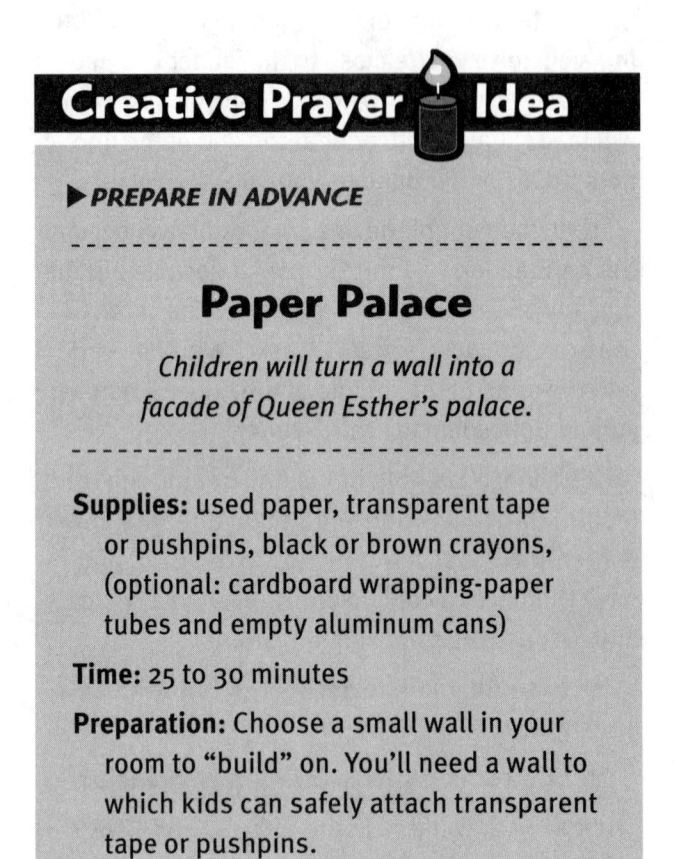

Creative Prayer Idea

▶ ***PREPARE IN ADVANCE***

Paper Palace

Children will turn a wall into a facade of Queen Esther's palace.

Supplies: used paper, transparent tape or pushpins, black or brown crayons, (optional: cardboard wrapping-paper tubes and empty aluminum cans)

Time: 25 to 30 minutes

Preparation: Choose a small wall in your room to "build" on. You'll need a wall to which kids can safely attach transparent tape or pushpins.

Tell kids they'll be working together to build the front of a palace. Remind them that Esther went to live in a huge palace when she became queen. Set out the used paper and several rolls of transparent tape or several pushpins. Have kids lay each sheet against a wall or other rough surface and then rub a black or brown crayon across the paper for a textured look. Show kids how to hold the paper vertically, roll the paper so the ends just overlap, and then secure it with tape.

When kids have a good supply of paper rolls, show them how to tape or pin the rolls to the wall vertically to resemble columns of stone. Have kids plan the palace on a wall where there's a door and use cardboard wrapping-paper tubes as turrets. When kids have finished, they can stack or flatten empty aluminum cans and use them as decorations.

As you read Ephesians 2:10, have children walk through the "palace door" and be affirmed as children of God the king! You can use this as a commissioning service, sending kids into the world with a sense of their purpose.

Snack

▶ *ALLERGY ALERT*
▶ *FOR YOUNGER CHILDREN*

Hamantaschen

Children will celebrate Esther's sweet victory with easy-to-make cookies.

Supplies: margarine, powdered sugar, egg yolks, ice water, flour, apricot jam, mixing bowls, mixing spoon, measuring cups and spoons, rolling pins, baking sheets, oven, colorful tissue paper

Time: 30 to 35 minutes

Preparation: Set out the ingredients for the recipe below. You'll need an area with an oven to bake this snack.

SAY: **We have a lot of different ingredients and kitchen tools here, but each one has a specific purpose in the recipe we're about to make. Plus, each one of you has a part to play, or a purpose, in making our cookies.** Explain that kids will be making cookies to celebrate Esther's purpose. Have a child mix one stick of softened margarine with 4 tablespoons of powdered sugar. Choose another child to mix in two egg yolks and 3 tablespoons of ice water. The mixture will be lumpy; don't worry if the water doesn't mix in well.

Call on someone to measure out and add 1½ cups of flour. Let kids take turns mixing the dough well. Divide the dough into 12 balls, and give one to each child. Have kids roll the dough into 4-inch circles and then spread a spoonful of apricot jam in the center. Show them how to fold up and pinch together three edges of the dough into the center of the cookie. Be sure they pinch the edges tightly; otherwise the cookies will flatten out when baking.

Bake the cookies in a 350-degree oven for 10 to 12 minutes. When done, the cookies should be golden brown. Have kids wrap the cookies in colorful tissue paper and present the sweet gifts to each other. As they give the gifts to each other, have kids say, "God has a purpose for you—rejoice!"

Plan a joyful feast. Sing praise songs, serve Hamantaschen, and share some examples of people and their purpose in life. Then have kids share what they think God's purpose is for them.

Object Lesson

▶ *PREPARE IN ADVANCE*

King's Scepter

Children will carefully watch the king's scepter and develop quick reactions.

Supplies: Bible, baton or stick, paper crown or hat

Time: 10 to 15 minutes

Preparation: Clear a playing area.

Have kids think of something that happened to them this week. Tell them to not say their thoughts aloud yet. Hold the baton and the crown or hat, walk to the other wall, and face the kids.

SAY: **When Queen Esther wanted to talk with the king, she had to wait until he held out his scepter to her; then she could walk over to him. A scepter is like a beautiful, gold stick. Let's pretend I'm King Xerxes.** Place the crown or hat on your head, and SAY: **You can't come talk to me until I hold out my scepter.** Hold up the baton, and SAY: **You can walk forward, not run, only when I hold out my scepter. When I put it down, you must freeze.**

Start by holding up the scepter, and then put it down quickly. If kids keep moving when the scepter is down, have them take three steps back. As kids get closer, hold the scepter high and let all of them come to you for a group hug. Play several times, and let others take turns pretending to be the king. After a few minutes, gather in a circle. Open your Bible to Esther 2:1-18; 5:1-8, and tell kids about Esther. ASK:

- **What was the purpose of the scepter?**
- **What was Queen Esther's purpose?**
- **How do you know what your purpose for God is?**

Pass the scepter and let kids each share what they want to say.

Preschool Story

▶ *PREPARE IN ADVANCE*

Bible Point: ▷ **GOD HAS A PLAN.**

Supplies: Bible, 260 balloons (the kind of balloons used for making balloon animals), bicycle or balloon pump

Time: 15 to 20 minutes

Preparation: Use a bicycle pump or balloon pump to blow up enough 260 balloons for each child to have one. Tie off the balloons.

Good Plan!

Have kids form a circle and sit down. Open your Bible to Esther 2, and show children the words. Distribute balloons to kids. Lead children in the following story, encouraging them to use their balloons to express key parts of the story. (Although balloons are unlikely to pop unless overinflated, be aware that pieces of popped balloon may represent a choking hazard for young preschoolers. If any balloons do pop, pick up pieces immediately, and put them out of children's reach.)

SAY: **A long time ago a king was looking for a special queen.** Use the balloon as a telescope, and peer around the room. **The king found a beautiful woman named Esther and made her his queen.** Touch the ends of the balloon together, and hold it on your head, like a crown. **Esther was one of God's special people—she loved God very much. A bad man named Haman didn't like God's people.** Bend the ends of the balloon down to form a frown, and hold it in front of your face. **Haman made a mean plan to hurt all of God's people. Esther's cousin Mordecai heard about the plan. Mordecai had been like a father to Esther since her parents had died long ago. As quickly as he could, Mordecai went and told Esther about the plan.** Use the balloon as a cane as you hurriedly walk.

Esther wasn't supposed to go to the king without being asked, but she was brave and went to the king. She told him (hold up the balloon as a scepter) **about Haman's bad plan.**

The king was angry at Haman, and the king stopped the plan, so God's people were saved. Wave your balloon in celebration. **There was a great celebration for Esther, the brave queen who saved her people!**

Lead children in singing "Esther's Song" to the tune of "Ten Little Indians."

When Mordecai told me the news *(point to yourself)*
That Haman planned to kill the Jews,
I knew right then that I must choose *(place one palm up and then the other)*
To do a scary thing! *(Place your hands on your cheeks and look scared.)*
I bowed before King Xerxes' feet *(bow down low)*
And asked if he would come and eat *(continue to bow and put both hands out)*
A feast with Haman and with me,
And the king said he would come. *(Stand up straight, looking pleased.)*
I told the king of Haman's plan *(point and shake your index finger)*
To kill the Jews in all the land.
Guards took away the wicked man, *(place your hands behind your back as if they're handcuffed)*
And my people were saved that day! *(Hug a friend.)*

ASK:

- **How did Esther become queen?**
- **How did God use Queen Esther?**
- **How can God use you?**

SAY: **God had a plan for Esther when she became queen. God knew that she would save her people.** ▷ **GOD HAS A PURPOSE FOR EVERYTHING!**

BIBLE STORY

Daniel Trains in Babylon

For the Leader

If there had been a "Who's Who" in the kingdom of Babylon, Daniel and his friends would have been included. They were truly outstanding young men—studious and handsome and training for God. And their faithfulness to God proved to be the one thing that always helped them make the right decision.

Kids can depend on God's presence, too. God's grace can help them avoid or deal with poor choices. Use this study to help children live out this truth in their lives and to help children rely on God to help them make good decisions.

Key Scriptures

Psalms 25:9; 119:105
Proverbs 3:5-6
Daniel 1:1-21

Bible Verse

"He leads the humble in doing right, teaching them his way" (Psalm 25:9).

Bible Experience

▶ *PREPARE IN ADVANCE*

Bible Point: ▷ **GOD HELPS US MAKE GOOD CHOICES.**

Super Daniel

Children will learn how Daniel trained for spiritual strength.

Supplies: Bible; costume items, such as vests, hats, sunglasses, shoes, and coats; pencils; paper; several textbooks; pitcher with water; and various vegetables

Time: 10 to 15 minutes

Preparation: Set out the costume items for kids to choose from.

Have kids form groups of three or four. Give each person one costume item, a pencil, and paper. Explain that kids are to use their costume item to create an imaginary person who has a great power. For example, someone might invent the character who wears sunglasses to protect herself from the flashbulbs of her fans, or one who needs only one shoe because he can jump 50 feet in the air. Have groups share ideas until everyone can write down an imaginary person. Be sure everyone chooses a fun name for his or her character.

ASK:

- **How do powerful people act?**
- **How does their power help them make good choices? bad choices?**

Line up everyone in a row, making sure kids wear their costume items. Read Daniel 1:1-5. Then allow each child to present his or her imaginary character as a person King Nebuchadnezzar might train. After each person presents his or her character, present him or her with a textbook, and tell kids they will be educated and well fed to train for royal service.

Then ask four children to remove their costumes to be Daniel and his friends. Have them take one step out of the line as you read Daniel 1:6-18. Present Daniel and his friends with textbooks, water, and vegetables. After you read the Bible story, ASK:

- **How do you think Daniel's choices gave him and his friends great power?**
- **How did Daniel's good choices show his strength in God?**
- **Do you think Daniel was more super than any superhero? Why or why not?**

SAY: **All the people the king chose were strong, but none of them were stronger than Daniel and his friends. And that's because Daniel made the right choices to make him stronger and smarter. We don't need superhuman powers to help us make the right choice about things. Our power comes from God. Psalm 25:9 tells us this about God: "He leads the humble in doing right, teaching them his way."** ▷ **GOD HELPS US TO MAKE GOOD CHOICES.**

Additional Topics List

This lesson can be used to help children discover... Obedience and Wisdom.

Game

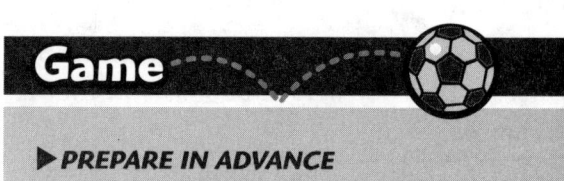

▶ *PREPARE IN ADVANCE*
▶ *HIGH ENERGY*

Peanut-Packing Pass

Children will wear sticky gloves and pass packing peanuts.

Supplies: Bible, latex gloves, four large bowls, foam packing peanuts, spray adhesive, trash bags, tarp

Time: 10 to 15 minutes

Preparation: Place the peanuts in two bowls. Set out a tarp, or play outside.

Form two lines. Have each child put on a pair of latex gloves. Place a giant bowl of packing peanuts at the end of one line. Place a large empty bowl at the other end. Spray thoroughly everyone's gloves with aerosol adhesive.

SAY: **When I say, "Pass the peanuts," the first person will grab peanuts from the bowl and begin passing peanuts down the line. The last person in each row should put the packing peanuts in the empty bowl. Ready? Pass the peanuts!**

Play the game and listen to the laughter! Have trash bags nearby for easy cleanup. At the end of the game, discuss the following questions:

- **Was this game easy or hard? Explain.**
- **How were your sticky gloves like getting stuck in bad habits?**
- **How can God help you choose to avoid unhealthy habits?**

Ask a volunteer to read aloud Psalm 25:9; then SAY: **Just as it was hard to keep the packing peanuts from sticking to your hands, it can be hard to choose healthy habits. But God always helps us make the right choices!**

Craft

▶ *PREPARE IN ADVANCE*
▶ *FOR YOUNGER CHILDREN*

Daily Bread Reminders

Children will make magnetic prayer reminders.

Supplies: mini-toast (found in the deli section of most grocery stores), white poster board, craft glue, magnetic strips, crayons, markers, scissors

Time: 10 to 15 minutes

Preparation: Cut a bread shape from the poster board. The shape should be ½ inch larger than the actual mini-toast. You'll need one bread shape for each child.

Give each child a piece of bread-shaped poster board. Let children color the edges of the poster board in light colors. Then have them write on the rim: "I choose God!" Help each child glue a magnetic strip to the back of the poster-board shape. Direct children to glue a piece of mini-toast to the front of the shape so the words show around it. When children have finished, read aloud Psalm 25:9 and Proverbs 3:5-6.

ASK:

- **Why does God want us to make good choices?**
- **Who are some people God uses to help you make good choices?**

SAY: **We all are hungry for the right choices, and God feeds us with his guidance. God is our daily bread! Put your magnet on your refrigerator to remember that when you choose God, you make the right choice!**

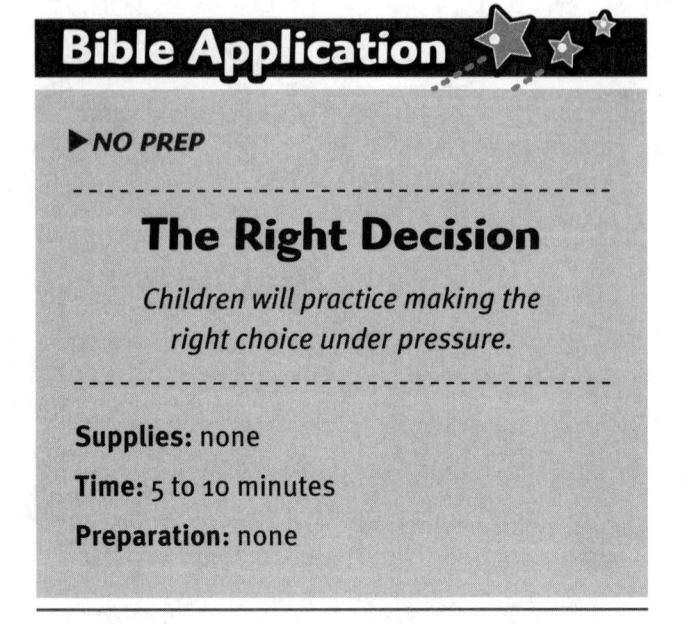

Bible Application

▶ *NO PREP*

The Right Decision

Children will practice making the right choice under pressure.

Supplies: none

Time: 5 to 10 minutes

Preparation: none

Form groups of up to five. Have group members verbally pressure another group member to do one of the following:

- Break a window in someone's house.
- Give someone the answers to a math test.
- Lie to his or her parents.

Have the person resisting pressure use one or more of the following responses to say no to the rest of the group:

- Say "no." Stick with your response.
- Make an excuse. Think of something else you could be doing.
- Change the subject. Pick a topic that interests your friend.
- Suggest a better idea. This will give you a way out.
- Return the challenge. If your friend says, "If you were really my friend, you'd do it," you can say, "If you were really my friend, you wouldn't ask me."

When groups are finished, ASK:

◆ **Which response is most comfortable for you to use? least? Explain.**

Read aloud Psalm 25:9. ASK:

◆ **How can God help you make the right choices?**

Close by reading the story from Daniel 1:1-21, and discuss how God helped Daniel make the right choices.

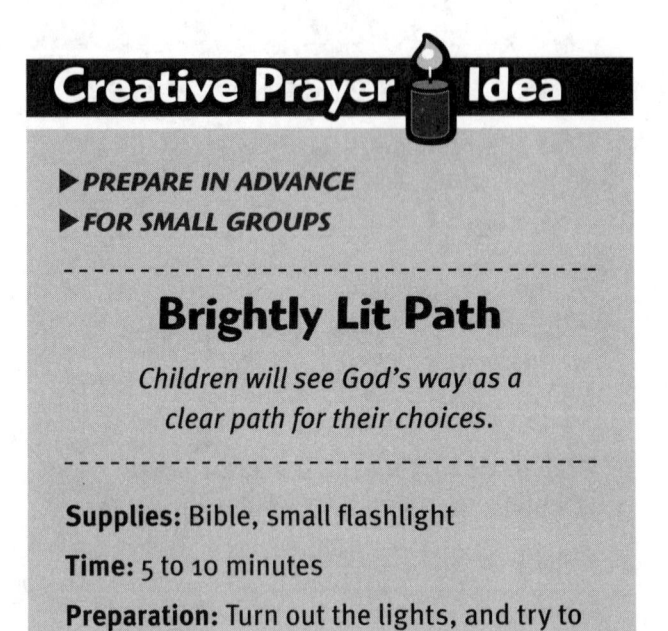

Creative Prayer Idea

▶ *PREPARE IN ADVANCE*
▶ *FOR SMALL GROUPS*

Brightly Lit Path

Children will see God's way as a clear path for their choices.

Supplies: Bible, small flashlight

Time: 5 to 10 minutes

Preparation: Turn out the lights, and try to make the room as dark as possible.

Tell children to close their eyes. ASK:

◆ **When you get up in the morning, what choices do you make?**

◆ **When you're at school, what choices do you make? at home?**

SAY: **Choices, choices. We get up and choose what to wear. We go to school and choose whether to pay attention in class. We go home and choose whether to be kind to our family. So many choices. A bad choice would hurt others and hurt you. Think about a bad choice you've made.** While kids' eyes are closed, open the Bible to Psalm 119:105, turn on the flashlight, and lay it on the opened Bible.

When we need to make difficult choices, God can give us a clear, lighted path to the right choice. Go ahead and open your eyes. Read aloud Psalm 119:105. Have kids hold their hands together, palms up, like a book.

As I shine the light on your hands, think about a decision you need to make today. Then ask God to help you make a good decision. Slowly shine the light on the hands of each child.

Close by shining the flashlight on the Bible and PRAYING: **Dear God, thank you for showing us the right choices to make and the right way to live our lives. In Jesus' name, amen.**

Discussion Launcher

Follow the Beat

Have students form a circle around a volunteer. Have kids begin clapping in unison to a steady beat. Have the volunteer clap to a different beat. Allow everyone to have a chance in the middle. ASK:

- **Which beat was easier to hear? Why?**
- **Do you ever feel as if you're clapping to a different beat? Why or why not?**
- **When friends pressure you to do wrong, what do you do?**
- **How is standing up to pressure like clapping to a different beat?**

Read aloud Psalm 25:9. SAY: **Sometimes friends pressure you into making bad choices. You want to keep your friends, but you also want to do what's right. Always ask God for help—he can help you make the right choices!**

Life Application

Children will help train others to make the right choices as they participate in these application activities.

Seek the Answer in God's Word

Collect used Bibles from thrift stores, and write in them, "Someone else used this book to make the right choice, and so can you!" Add sticky notes to mark Daniel 1:1-13. Have children hand them out at a grocery store.

Choice Prayer

Teach kids this rhyme: **Heavenly Father, up above, show me wisdom, show me love. Help me know just what to do. So I can do it all for you.** Have kids teach it to friends when they have to make tough decisions.

Encouraging Notes

Have children write Psalm 25:9 on business-card-size papers. Tell them to hand the papers to family members when they notice they're angry or confused.

notes

Preschool Story

▶ *ALLERGY ALERT*
▶ *PREPARE IN ADVANCE*

Bible Point: ▷ **GOD HELPS US MAKE GOOD CHOICES.**

Supplies: Bible, books, blank paper, markers, assorted vegetables, 1 cup of water per child

Time: 15 to 20 minutes

Preparation: Clean and cut assorted vegetables, and then place them on a plate for use later in the lesson. You will also need to fill one cup of water per child.

Veggie Delight

Have kids form a circle and sit down. Open your Bible to Daniel 1, and show children the words. SAY: **Daniel and his three friends, Shadrach, Meshach, and Abednego, lived in Babylon. They were training to be servants of the Babylonian king. The king had many young men who were training to be his servants. The king wanted them to be very smart, so he gave them the best teachers, the best food, and the best books.**

Daniel and his three friends probably learned all about math and numbers. Encourage kids to stand up and count to 10 together. **They probably learned how to read and write.** Hand out books, blank paper, and markers. Encourage kids to look through the books and to "write" on the blank paper. **They probably learned about plants and animals.** Encourage kids to act like their favorite animals. **And they probably learned lots of stories about their country.** Encourage kids to tell you their favorite stories.

God helped Daniel and his three friends make good choices and do well in their school. In fact, God helped them do better than any of the other young men!

The king gave the young men lots of good training, and he also gave them lots of good food. The other young men ate all the food the king would give them, but Daniel and his three friends knew that God didn't want them to eat the food of the king.

God helped Daniel and his three friends make a good choice to eat only vegetables and drink water. Pass out the vegetables and water you prepared before class. **That doesn't sound very good, does it? But God made Daniel and his three friends very strong, even though they were eating only veggies and water. In fact, God made Daniel and his three friends stronger than any of the other young men!**

God helped Daniel and his three friends make good choices, and ▷ GOD HELPS US MAKE GOOD CHOICES, too! Encourage kids to eat their veggies and tell each other about a time God helped them make a good choice.

ASK:

- **What did Daniel and his three friends have to do?**
- **How did God help Daniel and his friends?**
- **When have you had to make a good choice?**
- **How can God help you make good choices?**

SAY: **The king was so happy with the results of the good choices Daniel and his three friends made that the king had them come to help him in the royal palace. God continued to help Daniel and his three friends make good choices as they served the king. We can trust God to help us make good choices, too!**

BIBLE STORY

The Flaming Furnace

For the Leader

There's no tougher situation than to find yourself standing in the middle of a fire that's been heated up seven times. But Shadrach, Meshach, and Abednego lived through it—with God's help.

Use these lessons as a training program for your students so your kids remember that the next time they have to stand strong for their faith, they'll do so under God's protection.

Key Scriptures

Daniel 3:1-12, 19-27

Proverbs 14:12

1 Corinthians 16:13

Bible Verse

"Stand firm in the faith. Be courageous. Be strong" (1 Corinthians 16:13).

n
o
t
e
s

Bible Experience

▶ *NO PREP*

No Matter What!

Bible Point: ▷ **GOD HELPS US STAND FOR WHAT IS RIGHT.**

Children will learn how Shadrach, Meshach, and Abednego stood up for God in the face of danger and fear.

Supplies: Bible, handful of play money or real money, toy, bag from a fast-food restaurant, picture of a famous person

Time: 10 to 15 minutes

Preparation: none

Read this story from Daniel 3:1-12, 19-27. Have kids follow your directions. SAY: **A long time ago a king made a golden statue. He wanted people to worship the statue. He had musicians play in its honor, and he told his people to bow to the statue every time they were near it.** Have everyone bow low and "play" musical instruments.

Well, three men named Shadrach, Meshach, and Abednego stood up for God and said, "No way. We won't bow to a statue. We worship God, no matter what!" Have everyone stand tall and say, "Worship God no matter what!" and then sit down again.

We don't bow to golden statues, but we might forget God sometimes. The Bible instructs us to stand up for God as Shadrach, Meshach, and Abednego did. God helped them stand for what was right. And ▷ GOD HELPS US STAND FOR WHAT IS RIGHT, too. First Corinthians 16:13 says, "Stand firm in the faith. Be courageous. Be strong."

Let's see some things people might think of before God. Each time I show you something, stand up tall and say, "Worship God no matter what!" and then sit down again. Bring out a handful of play money, and let kids respond. Do the same with a toy, the bag, and the picture. Affirm kids as they stand up for God.

The king was mad at Shadrach, Meshach, and Abednego, so he threw them into a fire. Have kids all yell out, "Ouch!" **But God protected them, and they didn't get burned. In fact, they didn't even smell like smoke!**

Read aloud 1 Corinthians 16:13. SAY: **These men were strong and courageous and stood firm. We can ask God to help us stand for what's right. He will keep us standing strong, and he will keep us safe as we do so.**

Song & Connect

Use "So Do Not Fear" (track 13, *it: Innovative Tools for Children's Ministry: Old Testament* CD) to help reinforce the Bible Point, ▷ **GOD HELPS US STAND FOR WHAT IS RIGHT.**

Encourage kids to remember this song if they ever have to stand up for what's right in the face of danger or fear.

Additional Topics List

This lesson can be used to help children discover... Armor of God and Temptation.

Game

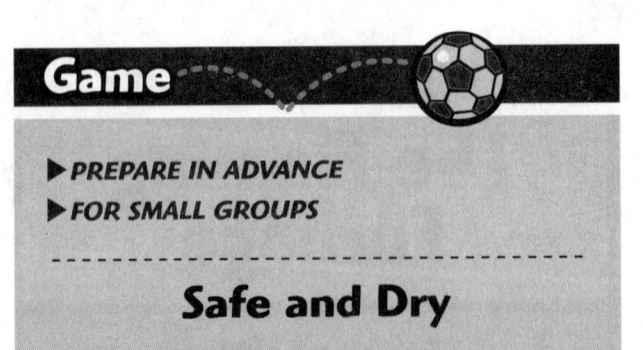

▶ ***PREPARE IN ADVANCE***

▶ ***FOR SMALL GROUPS***

Safe and Dry

Children will relate the protection of umbrellas to the way God protects his children.

Supplies: Bible, water balloons, child-safe umbrellas

Time: 15 to 20 minutes

Preparation: Fill balloons with water, and find an area outside to play this game.

Lead kids outdoors and have them form two groups. Give each member of one group a water balloon, and give each member of the other group an umbrella. Separate the groups by about 20 feet.

SAY: **The team with water balloons will try to get the other team wet. Balloon throwers must toss the balloons *underhand*! The other team will use their umbrellas to try to avoid getting wet. Nobody can move any closer together. Have courage, umbrella holders! Stand strong! The umbrellas will protect you!**

Have teams begin. When half of the water balloons have been thrown, have teams switch roles. Then read aloud 1 Corinthians 16:13. ASK:

- **What was it like to have an umbrella to protect you?**
- **When do you need to have courage in real life?**
- **How does God give you courage to stand for what's right?**

Hold an umbrella over your head, and SAY: ▷ **GOD HELPS US STAND FOR WHAT'S RIGHT. No matter what balloons—er, situations—come our way!**

Craft

▶ PREPARE IN ADVANCE

Escape-the-Heat Potholder

Children will sew potholders as symbols of how God protected Shadrach, Meshach, and Abednego.

Supplies: Bible, cotton scrap material, felt or thicker material, embroidery thread, large-eyed embroidery needles, scissors, fabric paint or permanent markers

Time: 30 to 35 minutes

Preparation: Cut 6x6-inch squares of felt or thicker material, and 7x7-inch squares of scrap material. Each child needs two pieces of felt and two pieces of matching scrap material. Recruit adult volunteers to help with sewing.

Show each child how to center the two pieces of felt on the wrong side of one of the material pieces. Then have him or her place the second piece of material, wrong side down, on top, sandwiching the felt in between.

Help children push the threaded needle down through all four pieces of material, close to one of the corners, and pull the string through, leaving about a 1-inch tail. Then bring the needle back up through the four layers, close to the first entry point. Cut the string and tie the two strings into a firm knot. Do this at all four corners to hold the material together.

Rethread the needle with about 30 inches of thread, and tie a knot at one end. Show kids how to do a simple down-and-up stitch around the outside edge of the cloth to sew the two pieces of material together. Have them tie knots in the strings after they've sewn all four sides. Give children paint or markers to write "God Protects Us!" on the outside of the potholder.

Review the story from Daniel 3 and ASK:

- **Why did the men in the Bible story need protection?**
- **When are some times you might have to stand up for what's right?**
- **How can God protect you in those situations?**

SAY: **If we take something hot from the oven, we trust a potholder to protect us from being burned. Shadrach, Meshach, and Abednego trusted God to protect them when they stood up for what was right.** Close with the song "Trust and Obey" or "Jesus Loves Me" as the prayer for the day.

Bible Application

▶ NO PREP

Forged Faith

Children will discuss times they stand up for what's right.

Supplies: orange and blue construction paper, markers, scissors, tape

Time: 5 to 10 minutes

Preparation: none

Give each child one sheet of orange and one sheet of blue paper and markers. SAY: **Let's think of things that we know are wrong, like worshipping idols, hurting someone, or lying. Write one word that describes that wrong action on your orange paper. Then draw a flame around it and cut it out.** Let kids make their flames and tape them to a wall or bulletin board.

Now think of things that God says are right—something that will help put out that flame! You might think of praising God or reading the Bible. Write one idea on the blue paper. Then draw a raindrop around it and cut it out. Let kids make their raindrops and tape them above the flames.

Shadrach, Meshach, and Abednego knew God would protect them so long as they stood for what was right. And with God's help, they did! Whenever you're in a "flaming furnace," think of God's protection as raindrops that will help you put out the fire.

Let kids add to the flames and raindrops in the coming weeks, as they experience times they have to stand up for what's right.

Creative Prayer Idea

▶ ***NO PREP***

Unison Prayers

Children will learn how to turn to God in tough times.

Supplies: pens, paper

Time: up to 5 minutes

Preparation: none

SAY: **It's not always easy to say what's right when your friends think differently. But God can help you. Let's write prayers about this.** Have each student think of a one- or two-sentence prayer and write it on a piece of paper.

With different voices around us telling us what to do, it's often difficult to make our voices heard. But God hears you, so you can always stand up for what's right.

Form a circle and have students read their prayers aloud at the same time to demonstrate their individuality, followed by "Amen" in unison.

Worship Prompt Idea

▶ ***PREPARE IN ADVANCE***

Stand Up!

Children will reenact the flaming furnace for worship.

Supplies: chairs, CD of a dramatic movie score, CD player

Time: 5 to 10 minutes

Preparation: Choose a dramatic music score from a movie such as *Star Wars* or *Lord of the Rings*.

Pile two or three chairs on top of each other to represent the golden statue. Choose one child to be the king. Have him stand proudly with his arms crossed. He'll point to the statue when you give the signal. Choose two or three children to be musicians and "trumpet" through cupped hands when you signal. Choose three children to be Shadrach, Meshach, and Abednego. Have them stand up straight, link arms, and shake their heads "no" when you signal.

Have the rest of the children kneel in a semicircle to form the flaming furnace. Have them wave their arms in the air like flames when you signal.

When everyone is in place, play the movie score as kids reenact Daniel 3. Point to kids at the appropriate time for their part. When the story is finished, have all kids join you in the flaming furnace and stand up, linking arms. Remind children that ▷ **GOD HELPS US STAND FOR WHAT'S RIGHT.** Turn the music down so it's playing softly, and begin a quiet time of worship for the God who protects us.

Science Devotion

▶ ***PREPARE IN ADVANCE***

Rolling Uphill?

Children will see that God's way is the only right way, even when sometimes it appears otherwise.

Supplies: Bible, 2 stacks of books (1 about 6 inches high and the other about 1 foot high), 2 yardsticks, 2 funnels of the same size, masking tape

Time: 10 to 15 minutes

Preparation: Set the two stacks of books about 30 inches apart on the floor. Make a "track" by taping the two yardsticks together across one end. Put the taped end on the short stack. Spread the other end of the yardsticks apart, and put those ends on the taller stack. Make a "car" by taping the two funnels together at the large end. See the illustration below.

ASK:

◆ **How do you know when to stand up for what's right?**

SAY: **Let's do an experiment that shows us that sometimes wrong decisions might appear to be right.** Have kids gather around the stacks of books, hold up the funnels, and

ASK:

◆ **What do you think will happen when I put my "car" on this track close to the shorter stack of books? Explain.**

Set the car on the track close to the shorter stack of books, and let the car go. It should move toward the taller stack of books.

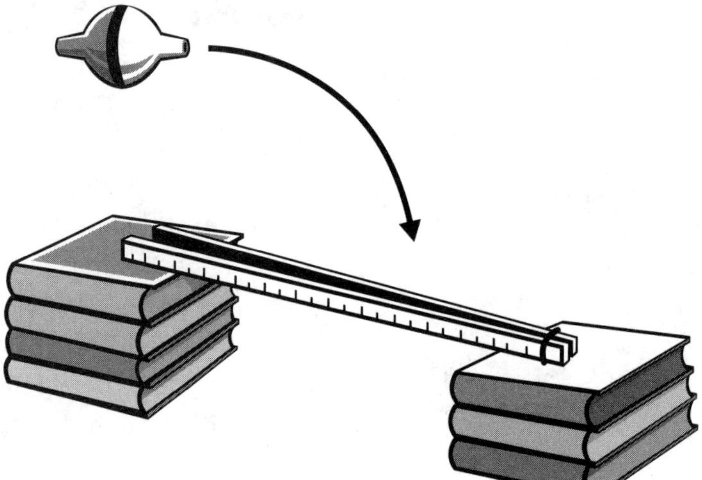

ASK:

◆ **Why do you think the car moved up?**

◆ **Do you think the car really moved up?**

SAY: **Gravity always pulls things down, so it's impossible for the car to move up. Why did the car look like it was rolling uphill?** Roll the car again, letting the kids view the experiment from the side. Set the car on the bottom of the track again, and let it go. **As the track got wider and wider, the center of the car got lower and lower. The car was really moving downhill when it looked like it was going uphill.**

ASK:

◆ **How is this like bad choices in our lives that sometimes seem like the right decisions?**

Read aloud Proverbs 14:12, and SAY: **God's way is the only correct way, no matter what others say. The pressure to do the wrong thing may feel very strong, but remember: Things aren't always as they seem! God will help you stand up for what's right.** Roll the car again as a reminder.

Preschool Story

▶ ***PREPARE IN ADVANCE***

Bible Point: ▷ **WE CAN STAND UP FOR GOD.**

Supplies: Bible, red crepe paper or strips of fabric, hula hoop, table

Time: 15 to 20 minutes

Preparation: Tie the red crepe paper or strips of fabric to the hoop. Save at least one red streamer for each child.

Standing Tall

Have kids form a circle and sit down. Open your Bible to Daniel 3, and show children the words. SAY: **Our story is about three young men who were very brave and stood up for God. These three men were named Shadrach, Meshach, and Abednego.** Ask three volunteers to pretend to be Shadrach, Meshach, and Abednego and to stand next to the table. Ask the rest of the class to sit in front of the table, and give each child a red streamer.

The king told everyone to bow down before a god that wasn't the real, true God. Shadrach, Meshach, and Abednego loved God and said they would bow down and worship only the real God. This didn't make the king happy at all! In fact, he was so angry that he threw the three men into a fiery, hot furnace!

Have the three children step into the hoop and pull it up around their waists. Encourage the other children to stand up and march around the table, waving their "flames." Tell kids to make fire noises, such as "crackle, crackle." As kids march, choose one child to join the three children in the hoop.

SAY: **God took care of Shadrach, Meshach, and Abednego. God even sent someone from heaven to help them! When the king looked into the furnace, he saw an extra person in the fire. Then the king understood that Shadrach, Meshach, and Abednego's God was the only real, true God!**

Play this fun game to help children remember the Bible story. Choose three different children to be Shadrach, Meshach, and Abednego. Have the three children step inside the hoop and hold the hoop at their waists so the "flames" are all around them. Choose one child inside the hoop to be the tagger. The tagger doesn't need to hold on to the hoop. The children inside the hoop must move together to help the tagger tag a fourth child with his or her hands. When the tagger tags someone, that child should climb inside the hoop. Then the four kids should immediately drop the hoop so that it falls around their legs. Then they should shout out this chant (encourage other kids to join in as well):

Nebuchadnezzar threw in three,
But I count four! How can that be?
One, two, three, four!
Come on out,
Let's play some more!

Choose three new children, and repeat the game.

ASK:

- **How do you think the three friends felt when God saved them?**
- **How can you stand up for God like the three friends did?**

SAY: **Shadrach, Meshach, and Abednego would worship only the true God. They did the right thing and stood up for God when they chose not to bow down to the fake god—even though they knew they'd get in trouble with the king. ▷ WE CAN STAND UP FOR GOD, too!**

n
o
t
e
s

BIBLE STORY

Daniel in the Lions' Den

For the Leader

No matter how scared Daniel might've been when he chose certain death over defying God, he did it. No matter how easy it would've been to give up praying, Daniel kept praying. No matter how jealous the others were, Daniel never buckled under their pressure. No matter *what,* Daniel followed God with great strength and great pleasure from his very soul.

Teach kids that when they feel the passion for God that Daniel felt, following God no matter what isn't just a stay in a lions' den—it's a walk in the park!

Key Scriptures

Psalm 19:7
Daniel 6:1-23
3 John 11

Bible Verse

"The instructions of the Lord are perfect, reviving the soul" (Psalm 19:7).

Bible Experience

▶ ***PREPARE IN ADVANCE***

Bible Point: ▷ **FOLLOW GOD NO MATTER WHAT.**

Children will make lion faces as they listen to Daniel's story.

Supplies: Bible, paper plates, colored paper, tape, safety scissors, markers

Time: 15 to 20 minutes

Preparation: Set out supplies to make a paper lion's face.

SAY: **Lions can be pretty scary, and lions play an important role in our Bible story today. As I tell the story, you can make a lion's face. Select some colored paper to cut into strips. Tape them to one side of the paper plate for a mane, and then flip it over and draw a lion's face on the other side. Add to your mane if you still have more paper.** Open your Bible to Daniel 6:1-23, and show children the passage. Let kids start their lion faces.

Daniel was good at being a leader, so King Darius put him in charge of the whole kingdom. The other leaders were jealous of Daniel. They tried to make Daniel look bad, but they didn't succeed. They knew Daniel loved God and prayed every day. So they convinced Darius to make a law saying that no one could pray to any god or man except the king. Anyone found praying would be thrown into the lions' den.

Daniel continued to worship. Tell a partner some ways you can worship God like Daniel did.

After kids have shared, SAY: **When the men saw Daniel praying, they told the king. The king was upset because he couldn't change the law, but he didn't want to punish Daniel. Reluctantly, the king threw Daniel into the lions' den. The king said, "May your God, whom you serve continually, rescue you!" Then men covered the mouth of the den with a stone.**

Find a volunteer to play Daniel. If kids are finished with their lion faces, have them hold up the faces and surround Daniel.

SAY: **Close your eyes and imagine you're all alone in a dark place. You hear the sound of lions' paws walking across the room. You hear the sound of rumbling growls. Then** (pause) **it's very quiet—all—night—long.**

Have kids open their eyes. Tell them that it is now morning, and Daniel has made it through the night. SAY: **Daniel reported to the king that angels had shut the mouths of the lions and that he was unharmed. Daniel had followed God even when it was difficult, and God had protected him! Just like Daniel, we must ▷ FOLLOW GOD NO MATTER WHAT.**

Have kids discuss these questions with partners:

- **Do you think it was hard for Daniel to do what God wanted, even though he knew he'd be thrown to the lions? Why or why not?**
- **Do you think it's hard for you to do what God wants, no matter what? Why or why not?**

SAY: **Daniel did what God wanted, and God protected him in a miraculous way. And you know what? God will protect you, too!**

Additional Topics List

This lesson can be used to help children discover... Armor of God, Faith, Guidance, and Prayer.

Game

▶ *PREPARE IN ADVANCE*

Daniel in the Lions' Den

Children will act like lions creeping up on Daniel and realize that they don't need to fear any danger with God.

Supplies: Bible

Time: 10 to 15 minutes

Preparation: Clear a large playing area.

Open a Bible to Daniel 6, and tell kids about how God protected Daniel in the lions' den. Then choose one child to be Daniel, and have "Daniel" stand on one side of the room. Ask the other children to be lions and stand on the other side of the room.

SAY: **When I say, "Daniel in the lions' den," Daniel, turn your back so you can't see the lions. Lions, quietly creep up and touch Daniel's shoulder before he hears you. Daniel, if you hear a noise, turn around and point to the lion who made the noise. Then that lion will go back to the starting place, and everyone will say, "God protects Daniel!" Daniel, if a lion actually touches you, turn around, give the lion a hug, and say, "God protects me!" Ready? Daniel in the lions' den!**

Play several rounds, and have the hugged lions become the next Daniels. At the end of the game, discuss the following questions:

- **How did Daniel know that God would protect him from the lions?**
- **Why does God protect us?**

SAY: **God protects Daniel, and he protects us, too. That's why we should always follow God. No matter what happens, God protects us.**

Craft

▶ *PREPARE IN ADVANCE*

Daniel's Lions

Children will make lion keepsakes to remind them to follow God no matter what.

Supplies: Bible, craft sticks, low-temperature glue gun, brown felt, safety scissors, paintbrushes, yellow paint, yellow craft foam or yellow construction paper, brown fabric paint

Time: 20 to 30 minutes

Preparation: Set up two separate work stations: the paints and brushes at the first, and all other supplies at the second. Cut a 1x8-inch strip of felt for each child.

Show kids how to lay six craft sticks side by side, horizontally, to create the lion's body. Next, show them how to glue a craft stick onto the back of each end, going vertically, connecting the ends of the six sticks together. The top of each vertical stick should be even with the top of the body, and the remaining end of the stick will make a leg. Have children each break a stick in half to make a tail and then glue it to the backside of the back leg. While the glue dries, have each child use scissors to cut a fringe of brown felt to be fur on the lion, and set it aside.

Let children paint the sticks yellow. While the paint is drying, have them each cut a yellow foam circle about 3 inches in diameter to create the lion's head. Show them how to glue the fringe around the lion's head and cut off the extra to save for the lion's tail. Then have children each paint on the lion's facial features with the brown paint and glue the whole head to the top right-hand corner of the body. Finally, children can glue on the extra fringe to the end of the tail.

Have the children form a circle on the floor. Read aloud Daniel 6:1-23. Then ASK:

- **Why was Daniel thrown in the lions' den?**
- **Besides being protected from the lions, what other good things happened because Daniel followed God?**

Read aloud Psalm 19:7.

ASK:

- **How does following God revive your soul?**

SAY: **Daniel was praying to God because it revived his soul. And God showed favor to Daniel for his loyalty by taming the lions. Just as Daniel followed God no matter what, we can, too. It will revive your soul!**

Bible Application

▶ ***PREPARE IN ADVANCE***

Children will make praying hands and learn about Daniel's prayers.

Supplies: 8½x11-inch pieces of various flesh-colored construction paper, pencils, markers, light-colored paper scraps, glue sticks, sequins (optional)

Time: 10 to 15 minutes

Preparation: Fold each sheet of construction paper in half to make a card. You'll need one card per child. Set all other supplies on a table.

Give each child a card, and demonstrate how to place your hand on the paper so your thumb is flush with the fold. Help kids trace around their hands, with the fingers slightly apart. (Be sure to trace between their fingers, too.) Let kids turn their cards over and repeat the process, tracing the opposite hand.

Allow children to trace over the pencil lines with dark markers. Have children tear light-colored paper into small ovals and then glue them on for fingernails. Children may also want to draw rings and glue on a few sequins.

Have each child open his or her card and draw on the inside a picture of something he or she can pray about. Children might draw things they're thankful for or pictures of prayer requests.

When children have finished, read aloud Daniel 6:1-23. Then ASK:

- **Why did Daniel keep praying to God even when he knew he might get in trouble for doing so?**
- **What's one way that talking to God can help us to follow him?**

Creative Prayer Idea

▶ ***FOR YOUNGER CHILDREN***
▶ ***PREPARE IN ADVANCE***

Prayer Bracelets

Children will make prayer bracelets.

Supplies: construction paper; scissors; markers; small blue, yellow, and black pompoms; shallow containers of glue; stapler or tape

Time: 10 to 15 minutes

Preparation: Cut construction paper into 2x6-inch strips.

Give each child a paper strip, and write his or her name on one side. Let kids dip and glue the pompoms to the paper strip. Direct children to make unique patterns as they use all three colors. Let the bracelets dry. Then wrap each child's bracelet around his or her wrist, and staple or tape it in place. When everyone is finished, read aloud Daniel 6:1-23.

ASK:

- **Why do you think Daniel prayed three times each day?**
- **What kinds of things do you think Daniel talked to God about?**
- **What can you talk to God about?**

Explain that the three colors on the bracelets are reminders to pray three times each day. Yellow is for prayer in the morning, when the sun comes up. Blue is for prayer at noon, when the sky is bright. Black is for prayer at night.

Have children pretend it's first morning, and then noon, and then night, and have them pray three times, just as Daniel did. Remind them that prayer helps us to ▷ **FOLLOW GOD NO MATTER WHAT.**

Worship Prompt Idea

▶ ***NO PREP***

I Will Follow

Children will share ways they can follow God in worship.

Supplies: Bible, a CD player, and worship music

Time: 5 to 10 minutes

Preparation: none

Gather children together, and then read aloud 3 John 11. ASK:

- **Who are the best people to follow? Why are they the best?**
- **What are some ways we can follow God?**

Teach children the words to the worship song you've chosen. Then have children form four groups. Have each group come up with a creative way to move around the room in time to the music. Children might take giant steps, walk sideways, or combine backward and forward steps.

Lead children in singing the song again, but have each group take turns leading others around the room in their chosen manner.

Discussion Launcher

▶ ***STUDENT LED***

Acrostics

For this activity, you'll need paper, pens, and a Bible.

Form groups of four or five, and give each group paper and pens. Have groups write acrostics from the word *LION*. Have them read Psalm 19:7 and base their messages on what Psalm 19:7 says. They might write:

Love God always.

I will follow!

Obey God's rules.

No Matter What!

After groups have written and shared the acrostics, read aloud Daniel 6:1-23. Form different groups of four or five, and have groups discuss these questions:

- **Why did Daniel have such a passion for God?**

- ◆ **How did his passion help him follow God no matter what?**
- ◆ **What are some ways you can have a passion for God?**

Preschool Story

▶*NO PREP*

Bible Point: ▷ **FOLLOW GOD NO MATTER WHAT.**

Supplies: Bible

Time: 15 to 20 minutes

Preparation: none

Hungry Lions

Have kids form a circle and sit down. Open your Bible to Daniel 6, and show children the words. Choose one child to be Daniel, one child to be the king, and two children to be Daniel's enemies. The rest of the children can pretend to be lions. Start the game with "Daniel" on one side of the room, the two "enemies" on the opposite side of the room, and the "king" in between. Encourage the rest of the children to get down on all fours and prowl around the room, roaring and smacking their lips in hunger as you tell the story. Encourage children to say, "Daniel still prayed, and the lions did roar" with you each time.

SAY: **Daniel knew how important it was to pray.** *(Direct Daniel to get on his knees and pray.)*

Daniel still prayed, and the lions did roar.

But some people didn't like Daniel. *(Have the enemies fold their arms on their chests and scowl at Daniel.)*

Daniel still prayed, and the lions did roar.

They planned a way to get rid of Daniel. *(The enemies huddle together and whisper.)*

Daniel still prayed, and the lions did roar.

Three times a day, Daniel got down on his knees and prayed. *(Daniel gets up and then kneels back down three times.)*

Daniel still prayed, and the lions did roar.

The enemies tricked the king with their plan. *(The enemies go to the king and whisper in his ear. Then they return to their side.)*

Daniel still prayed, and the lions did roar.

The king said no one could pray to God for 30 days, *(have the king shake his finger at everyone)* **but**

Daniel still prayed, and the lions did roar.

Daniel's enemies told the king that Daniel didn't obey, *(the enemies go to the king and point to Daniel)* **but**

Daniel still prayed, and the lions did roar.

Daniel's enemies threw him in the lions' den, *(the enemies move Daniel to the middle of the lions and have him sit down)* **but**

Daniel still prayed, and the lions did roar.

Daniel's in the lions' den!

Daniel still prayed, and the lions did roar.

God sent an angel to shut the mouths of the lions so they wouldn't eat Daniel. Daniel followed God even though he knew he would get in trouble. And God took care of Daniel. We can ▷ FOLLOW GOD NO MATTER WHAT, just like Daniel did!

ASK:

- ◆ **Why did Daniel pray even though the king said not to?**
- ◆ **How can you choose to follow God like Daniel did?**

BIBLE STORY

Job Tested

For the Leader

What if Job had known he was being tested? Would he have been as loyal to God had he known the conversation God had with Satan? Perhaps he would've been even stronger. The important part of this story is that Job didn't know fully what was happening to him and why, so he saw no other choice but to rely on God's strength.

Find something silly you can wear around your neck during this lesson, something that represents your reliance on God. Perhaps you can wear a giant plastic frog (to stand for "Fully Relying On God") or an orange juice can (to stand for how God gives you your recommended daily allowance of strength). At the end of your lesson, reveal to kids what the meaning of your necklace is to show them that in *everything*, including the bad things that happen to us, God has plans that we may not fully understand in this lifetime.

Key Scriptures

Job 1:6-22; 42:10-17

Isaiah 40:31

Bible Verse

"Those who trust in the Lord will find new strength" (Isaiah 40:31).

Bible Experience

▶ ***PREPARE IN ADVANCE***

▶ ***ALLERGY ALERT***

Bible Point: ▷ **GOD HELPS US WHEN WE'RE HURTING.**

Children will see how Job depended on God.

Supplies: Bible, small drinking cups, animal crackers

Time: 10 to 15 minutes

Preparation: Recruit a volunteer to take children's cups away from them at the appropriate time and to add 12 more animal crackers to each cup.

SAY: **Our Bible story today is about a man named Job. He is described as being "blameless—a man of complete integrity. He feared God and stayed away from evil" (Job 1:1). Job wanted to please God.**

God had blessed Job with many wonderful things. He had a big family and lots of servants. Job also had a lot of animals. We're going to take a little inventory of what Job had. Give each child a small drinking cup. **Job had seven thousand sheep.** Give each child seven animal crackers, but tell them not to eat them yet. **Job had three thousand camels.** Give children three more crackers. **And Job had hundreds of oxen and donkeys.** Give children two more crackers. **Now that's a lot of animals! God had really blessed him.** Remind children not to eat the snacks yet.

Satan gets jealous that someone would want to obey God and not him. What do you think Satan would try to do with people like Job?

Read aloud Job 1:6-22. SAY: **Satan thought that if Job were to lose everything, he would lose his faith in God, too. But God knew that Job would stand strong. Satan took away almost everything Job had. He took away his children and his livestock.** Have the volunteer take away the cups from the children. **What do you think Job's response was?**

Read aloud Job 1:21-22. SAY: **Job didn't blame God at all! Job knew that it was God who gave him everything to begin with, and God would help him when he was hurting. So Job praised God.**

Job continued to trust God, even though he suffered for a really long time. Job learned what we can know today, too: ▷ GOD HELPS US WHEN WE'RE HURTING.

Read aloud Job 42:10-17. SAY: **God gave back to Job even more than Job had before!** Have your volunteer redistribute the cups with twice as many animal crackers to the children. **At the end of his life, Job had thousands of animals, including sheep, camels, oxen, and donkeys—plus seven sons and three daughters. And Job lived another 140 years!**

God promises that he will help us in hard times, too. Read aloud Isaiah 40:31. **God promises that if we place our hope in him when we're suffering, as Job did, he will help us and give us strength.**

Pray together, asking God to give children the strength of Job when they are hurting. Allow children to eat their crackers.

Song & Connect

Use "All His Promises" (track 9, *it: Innovative Tools for Children's Ministry: Old Testament* CD) to help reinforce the Bible Point, ▷ **GOD HELPS US WHEN WE'RE HURTING.**

Help kids realize that God's promises are valid anytime, not just when we hurt.

Additional Topics List

This lesson can be used to help children discover... Guidance, Prayer, and Sin.

Game

▶ ***NO PREP***

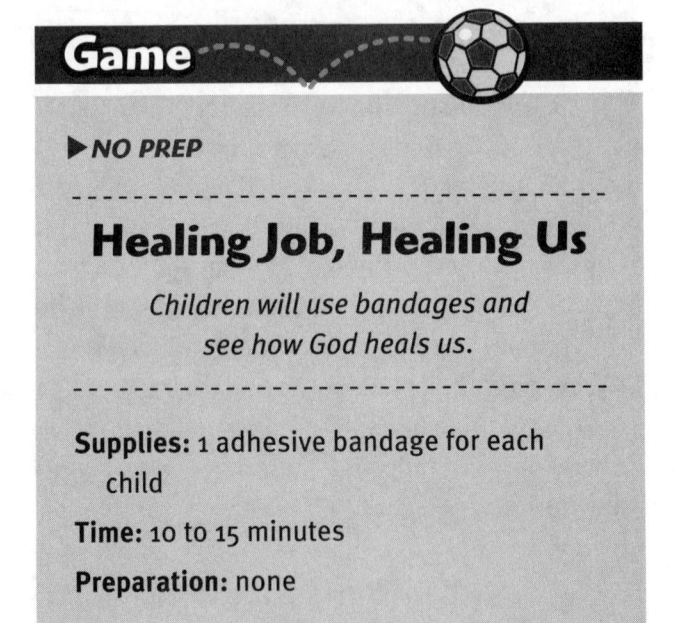

Healing Job, Healing Us

Children will use bandages and see how God heals us.

Supplies: 1 adhesive bandage for each child

Time: 10 to 15 minutes

Preparation: none

Choose one child to be Job. Number off the rest of the children from one to seven. Have "Job" stand at one end of the room and the rest of the class stand at the other end. Place a pile of adhesive bandages next to Job.

Call off a number from one to seven in random order. Every child with that number will run to Job, open a bandage, and place it somewhere on

Job—but not on his face. When all seven numbers have been called, call the numbers at random again, and let children run to remove the bandages. After Job is "healed," let someone else be Job. After the game, ASK:

- **How do you think Job felt when he was suffering?**
- **How do you think Job felt when God cared for him?**
- **How do you feel when God helps you?**

Have children share stories of God healing them or someone they know at a time they were hurting.

Craft

▶ *PREPARE IN ADVANCE*

Comfort Bags

Children will make comfort bags to represent God's comfort.

Supplies: Precut felt squares, permanent markers (Sharpies work best on felt), low-temperature glue gun or fabric glue, uncooked rice

Time: 10 to 15 minutes

Preparation: Set out the supplies. You'll need one felt square per child.

Tell children to fold a piece of felt in half and press it down with their hands. With the felt still folded, have kids use permanent markers to write "God is with me" on them. Then have them turn over the folded felt and write their names on the backs.

Show kids how to glue down two sides of the felt, leaving one end open. Wait until the glue is cool, and then help children carefully fill their bags half or two-thirds full with rice. Help them glue the bags closed. When kids are finished, review the Bible story from Job 1:6-22.

SAY: **Your bag is called a comfort bag because if your mom or dad puts it in the microwave, it will get warm and comforting. You can snuggle with it or put it around your neck and relax. When you feel the warmth, remember that God is with you. When it's hot outside, put your comfort bag in the freezer, and it will cool you off. It will remind you that God helps you when you're hurting, as he helped Job.**

Bible Application

▶ *NO PREP*

Shout It Out!

Children will give their feelings of pain and hurt to God.

Supplies: Bibles, paper plates, markers, tape

Time: 10 to 15 minutes

Preparation: none

Have children form pairs, and give each person a paper plate and a marker. SAY: **Think about a time you faced a difficult or unfair situation. On your paper plate, draw a picture of how you felt.**

Have children read Isaiah 40:31. Encourage kids to write on the blank side of their paper plates how this verse helps their situation.

ASK:

- **What does this verse tell us about God's care during tough times?**
- **Is there any good in the bad things that happen? Explain.**

SAY: **When things are bad, God doesn't desert us. Instead, he offers his listening ear. When we feel like yelling at God, this verse can help us stop and remember how God helps us when we hurt.**

Have kids roll up their paper plates into megaphone shapes and tape the plates. If you can go outside, allow kids to find their own personal space.

SAY: **Let's talk to God like Job did. Yell out your concerns. Be honest with him.**

Let kids yell at the top of their lungs. Close your prayer with kids holding up their megaphones to their ears so they can listen for God's response.

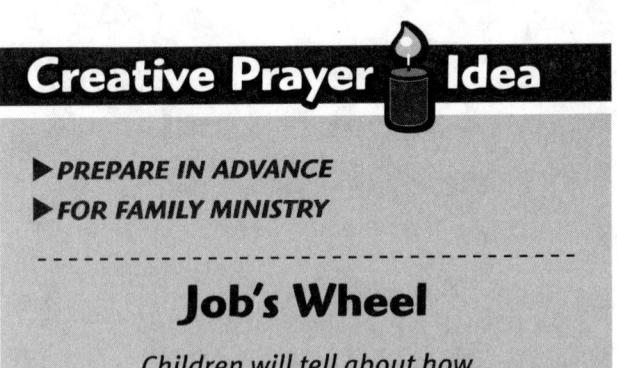

Creative Prayer Idea

▶ *PREPARE IN ADVANCE*
▶ *FOR FAMILY MINISTRY*

Job's Wheel

Children will tell about how God gave Job strength.

Supplies: Bible, paper plates, markers, safety scissors, hole punch, brass fasteners

Time: 10 to 15 minutes

Preparation: For younger children, write the words of Job 1:22 on the plates before class.

Give each child a paper plate, and show kids how to fold them into four equal sections. After folding the plates, have children open up their plates and write in the center the words from Job 1:22.

In the top left section of the plate, have each child write the number 1 and draw oxen and donkeys. In the top right, have the children write the number 2 and draw camels and a servant. In the bottom left part of the plate, have kids write a number 3 and draw a house. And in the bottom right, have them write a number 4 and draw a picture of Job.

After the drawings are complete, have each child cut the plate apart on the folds and place all four sections on top of each other in numerical order. Then, using a hole punch, have each child make a hole ¼ inch from the corner, through all sections of the plate, and place a fastener through the hole.

Have children practice fanning open the plate one picture at a time. As you tell the following story, have kids pray appropriately.

SAY: **Many bad things happened to Job. First, evil people came and stole his oxen and donkeys and killed his servants.** Have children show Section 1 and pray for someone who has experienced loss. **Then his camels were stolen, and the servants caring for them were killed.** Have children open their plates to Section 2 and pray for a victim of crime. **Next, Job's house fell down, and his seven children were killed.** Have children open their plates to Section 3 and pray for a victim of disaster. **After all of that happened, Job got sick and almost died.** Have children open their plates to Section 4 and pray for someone who is sick. **All of these bad things happened to Job. But the Bible tells us:** Have children read the Scripture on their plates.

Have kids take their plates home to tell their parents the story of Job.

Life Application

Children will use these outreach trips to comfort others.

Hope for Hospital Patients

Have children write "Isaiah 40:31" on bandages and hand them out to hospital patients.

Safe-House Friendships

Have kids decorate plain white T-shirts to distribute to kids who live at safe houses. They can write a prayer on the shirt, write "Trust in Jesus," or draw pictures of themselves with "I'm praying for you" written underneath.

Movie Time

Have kids invite to a movie friends who might not otherwise be able to go. Before the movie starts, ask pairs to share a prayer of hope.

Healing Foods

Have children collect cans of chicken soup. Before they donate them to a food bank, have them write "God heals" on the cans.

notes

Science Devotion

▶ ***PREPARE IN ADVANCE***

▶ ***FOR SMALL GROUPS***

Mysterious Ways

Children will experiment with the principle of inertia.

Supplies: Bible, chair with wheels, 3 or 4 large books

Time: 10 to 15 minutes

Preparation: Stack the large books on the seat of the chair with wheels.

Read aloud from Job 1:6-22; 42:10-17. SAY: **This experiment will help us understand some of the amazing ways God displays his power.**

Bring out the wheeled chair stacked with books, and ask for a volunteer. Ask the class:

◆ **What do you think will happen to these books if my volunteer moves the chair forward really fast and then stops it? Why?**

Have the volunteer try this. The books will keep moving after the chair stops, and they'll fall off the chair onto the floor.

ASK:

◆ **Why didn't the books stop when the chair stopped?**

◆ **What stopped them?**

SAY: **Nothing starts moving or stops moving in God's universe unless something makes it move or stop moving. This property of matter is called *inertia*. Everything in the universe is made of matter. If something moves, it's because something else made it move. It will keep moving until something else acts on it, or intervenes, to stop it.**

We push and pull ourselves to get out of bed, to go to school, to kick a ball, to write a sentence, to type on a computer, or to tie our shoes.

God intervened so that Job, who was a faithful servant, could prosper.

ASK:

- **Can you think of a time you saw an example of inertia? Explain.**
- **Can you think of a time you saw God intervene to change inertia?**

SAY: **Something that hurts us can cause inertia in the wrong direction—we might become bitter or angry. But if we follow God, he intervenes and stops the hurt.**

Preschool Story

PREPARE IN ADVANCE

Bible Point: ▷ **GOD HELPS US WHEN WE'RE HURTING.**

Supplies: Bible, several plastic animals, several plastic people figures, adhesive bandage

Time: 10 to 15 minutes

Preparation: Set out several plastic animals and toy people figures. Designate one toy person to be Job.

God Helps Job

Have kids form a circle and sit down. Open your Bible to Job 1, and show children the words.

SAY: **Satan is a bad angel who tried to trick people to make them stop being friends with God. One day Satan decided he would trick Job into being mad at God by hurting Job. Satan thought that maybe Job would be so mad and sad that he would decide God wasn't any good anymore.**

Let's help Job stay true to God and remember that God helps us when we're hurting by shouting, "God helps us when we're hurting!" to Job at different times throughout the Bible story. Practice a few times with the children.

First, Satan tried to hurt Job by sending bad people to come and hurt his oxen and donkeys and the servants who took care of those animals. Take away a third of the plastic animals, and set them behind you so kids can't see them. **Job was sad, but he kept loving God, and God helped him feel better.** Encourage kids to shout, "God helps us when we're hurting!"

Next, Satan tried to hurt Job by sending a fire from the sky that hurt Job's sheep and his servants. Take away another third of the animals and a third of the toy people. **Job was sad, but he kept loving God, and God helped him feel better.** Encourage kids to shout, "God helps us when we're hurting!"

Next, Satan hurt Job by sending mean people to hurt all of Job's camels and servants. Take away the last of the animals and another third of the toy people. **Job was sad, but he kept loving God, and God helped him feel better.** Encourage kids to shout, "God helps us when we're hurting!"

Then Satan saw that he couldn't trick Job into hating God, so he knocked down a house where all of Job's children were eating. All of Job's children died. Take away the last of the toy people—be sure to leave the Job figure. **Job was sad, but he kept loving God, and God helped him feel better.** Encourage kids to shout, "God helps us when we're hurting!"

Satan tried one last time to trick Job into hating God. Satan gave Job painful sores and bumps all over his body. Put an adhesive bandage on the Job figure. **Job was sad, but he kept loving God, and God helped him feel**

better. Encourage kids to shout, "God helps us when we're hurting!"

Even though Satan took away everything Job had and made Job sick, Job kept loving God. God saw that Job kept loving him, even when it was hard.

God helped Job and made Job feel better. God gave Job gold, animals, servants, and best of all, 10 wonderful children for Job to love! Put all of the plastic figures back in front of you. **God helped Job when he was hurting, and Job chose to keep loving God even when it was hard. ▷ GOD HELPS US WHEN WE'RE HURTING, too. And we can always choose to love God!**

ASK:

- **When have you felt sick or sad?**
- **How has God helped you feel better when you were hurting?**

notes

BIBLE STORY

The Birth of John the Baptist

For the Leader

Children know John the Baptist as a friend of Jesus, as someone who taught others to follow him. But they may not grasp fully the significance of John's birth.

Help children see the story of the angel and Zechariah as the beginning of our walk with Jesus, as the first step toward getting ready for Jesus' birthday celebration, for his death, and for his second coming.

Key Scriptures

Isaiah 9:6

Isaiah 40:3

Luke 1:5-25

Bible Verse

"Prepare the way for the Lord" (Isaiah 40:3, NIV).

Bible Experience

▶ *PREPARE IN ADVANCE*

Bible Point: ▷ **GET READY FOR JESUS.**

Children will see Christmas as a time to prepare for Jesus' birth.

Supplies: Bible; small, undecorated Christmas tree; garland; plastic ornaments; treetop angel

Time: 15 to 20 minutes

Preparation: Set out the ornaments around the tree.

Place the Christmas tree on the floor in front of the children. SAY: **This is a Christmas tree, but it seems to be missing some things.**

ASK:

◆ **What do we need to do to get this tree ready for Christmas?**

Let two children wrap the garland around the tree. Give ornaments to several children to hang. Then give the angel to a child to place it on top of the tree.

SAY: **Glad we got our tree ready! Our Bible story today is about getting ready also.** Point to the angel. **See that angel? We put angels on our trees to remind us of the angels who appeared as messengers from God. Zechariah was a man who encountered one of these angels.**

Read aloud Luke 1:5-25.

SAY: **The angel told Zechariah he was going to have a child. And this son was important because he was John the Baptist. John helped people prepare to receive the Messiah. In a way, Zechariah, by preparing for fatherhood, was getting ready for Jesus to come. We can get ready, too.**

Point to the Christmas tree, and SAY: **Decorating trees is one way we can get ready for Christmas.**

ASK:

◆ **What are some other ways you get ready for Christmas?**

◆ **How do you get your heart ready for Jesus?**

SAY: **Getting ready for Christmas can mean decorating or practicing for the class play. But when we prepare our hearts for Jesus, we plan how we will grow our relationship with him. You can do that all year round!**

Isaiah 40:3 says, "Prepare the way for the Lord." John the Baptist prepared the way for the ministry of Jesus. We can ▷ GET READY FOR JESUS still today. Let's get ready!

Song & Connect

Use "Praise the Lord" (track 10, *it: Innovative Tools for Children's Ministry: Old Testament* CD) to help reinforce the Bible Point, ▷ **GET READY FOR JESUS.**

Tell kids they can make the celebration of Christmas last year round. Set aside a few moments once a month to sing with your kids as a way to prepare for Jesus' birthday.

Additional Topics List

This lesson can be used to help children discover... Grace and Joy.

Game

▶ *PREPARE IN ADVANCE*

Decorating Relay

Children will have a party to get ready for Jesus.

Supplies: Bible, poster board, newsprint, construction paper, balloons, crepe-paper streamers, tape, markers, table

Time: 5 to 10 minutes

Preparation: Use this relay for a Christmas party. Place poster board in one corner of the room, newsprint and paper in another, and balloons and streamers in another. Set out tape and markers.

SAY: **We're getting ready for Jesus, but we'd better hurry because he's coming soon! Let's have a decorating race so we can quickly prepare the room for a Christmas party!**

Form three teams. Tell each team that on "go," their mission will be one of the following tasks. One team will use poster board to create a birthday-party banner and tape the finished banner to a wall near your party table. One team will decorate the party table with a tablecloth made of newsprint, draw fun pictures on it, and tear construction paper into small pieces to use as confetti. The last team will blow up and tie off balloons of different colors and then hang the balloons and crepe-paper streamers around the party table.

Start the relay and give teams a minute to complete their tasks. Call time and SAY: **Wow! You were fast! You must really want to get ready for Jesus!** Read aloud Luke 1:5-25. **Zechariah was looking forward to raising a son who would tell everyone about Jesus. And every year, we look forward to Christmas because it is a celebration of the best thing, Jesus' love. We can never prepare too much to receive Jesus' love!**

Craft

▶ *FOR YOUNGER CHILDREN*
▶ *PREPARE IN ADVANCE*

Baby Quilts

Children will make quilts as reminders to get ready for Jesus.

Supplies: Bibles, 9x12-inch sheets of paper, markers, scraps of pastel-colored fabric, scissors, glue

Time: 10 to 15 minutes

Preparation: Cut fabric scraps into 3-inch squares. Draw twelve 3-inch squares on each sheet of paper.

Give each child a sheet of paper. Have kids write the words from Isaiah 9:6 on the back of the paper. Help children set the fabric squares on the paper, in a pattern, creating a "baby quilt." Let children glue their fabric squares in place. When children have finished, collect craft supplies.

ASK:

- **What do people do when they're getting ready for a baby to come?**
- **Why does God want us to be ready for Jesus?**

Read Isaiah 40:3. SAY: **When people are expecting a baby, they make or buy soft blankets that can cover and warm the baby. Keep your blankets in your room to remind you that you can prepare for the baby Jesus, too.**

Bible Application

▶ *PREPARE IN ADVANCE*

Get Ready... Again!

Children will make calendars that symbolize Jesus' return.

Supplies: Bibles, paper cutter, paper, markers, cardboard, rubber bands, rubber cement

Time: 10 to 15 minutes

Preparation: Use a paper cutter to make thirty-one 4-inch squares of paper for each child. Cut one 4x6-inch piece of cardboard and one 4-inch square of cardboard for each child.

Have children count out 31 pieces of paper. Have them use the markers to number the pieces. Have each child stack the paper in order, starting with number one at the top, and then put a 4-inch square of cardboard under the stack.

Have children wrap several rubber bands tightly around their stacks to hold the paper, making sure the bands are as close to the top as possible. Then have them brush rubber cement on the top edge of their stacks. Make sure the tops are completely coated with rubber cement. Let the paper stacks dry.

Have children write the words from Isaiah 40:3 at the top of their other pieces of cardboard. Once the calendar pages have dried, help children use rubber cement to attach the calendar to the cardboard frame.

SAY: **You may not think you need to get ready for Jesus, since he was born a long time ago. But preparing for Jesus includes getting your heart and mind ready for a close relationship with him. And we can also prepare for when he returns to earth a second time.** Give kids a few minutes to mark important Christmas plans on their calendars. Tell them to include several plans that will help them get their hearts and minds ready for Jesus.

Creative Prayer Idea

▶ *OUTREACH*
▶ *PREPARE IN ADVANCE*

Christmas Cradle Prayers

Children will use a nativity scene to serve others and prepare for God.

Supplies: Bible, 2 cardboard boxes, hay or shredded paper, baby gifts, wrapping paper, scissors, tape

Time: 5 to 10 minutes

Preparation: Use this prayer activity over the course of several weeks. Notify parents that kids are encouraged to bring in small baby gifts each week for a needy family. Make a manger from a wooden or cardboard box. Fill it with hay or shredded paper.

Gather kids around the empty manger. Talk about what people do to get ready when a baby is about to be born. Ask kids to bring a small baby gift each week until Christmas. Suggest small items such as pacifiers, knit booties, bibs, rattles, bottles, or cans of formula.

Let children lay their gifts in the manger each week. Ask a child to pray each week, thanking

God for sending Jesus or asking God to protect the needy babies in your city. Remind kids of Zechariah and John the Baptist from Luke 1:5-25. Tell children that reaching out to others is a way they can help others prepare for Jesus. Sometime before Christmas, pack all the baby items in a box, and have the kids wrap and decorate it. Take the box to a local shelter.

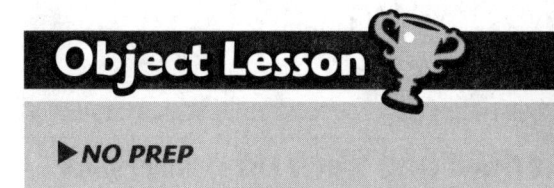

Object Lesson

▶ *NO PREP*

Bubble Lesson

Children will play with bubbles and think about Jesus' coming.

Supplies: bottle of bubble solution, a bubble wand for each child

Time: 5 to 10 minutes

Preparation: none

Blow a bubble from the bubble mixture. Catch it with the bubble wand, and hold it up. If the bubble pops, blow and hold another one on your wand. SAY: **Raise your hand when you think this bubble is going to pop. Let's see who can raise a hand closest to the time it pops.** Allow the children to raise their hands.

I'll blow bubbles, and you catch one with your wand. Just sit still in your spot, and I'll send some bubbles your way. Be careful not to bump the people sitting near you. Just catch one bubble. If it pops, you can't have another, so be careful with your bubble. Blow small bubbles slowly; catch some for smaller children, and hand the bubbles to them. Play for a while, and see whose bubble lasts the longest.

It's hard to wait for these bubbles, and it's hard to wait for other things to happen, too. That's sort of like how we might get ready for Jesus. While we're waiting for him, let's live the way he wants us to, by telling others about him, going to church, being kind to others, and loving each other. Blow bubbles and let kids try to catch more. When they catch a bubble, have them say one way they'll get ready for Jesus.

Worship Prompt Idea

▶ *PREPARE IN ADVANCE*

Advent Worship Band

Children will prepare for Jesus with a homemade worship band.

Supplies: Bible; simple percussion instruments such as spoons, sticks, and empty coffee cans with lids

Time: 10 to 15 minutes

Preparation: Before this activity, make sure the cans and bottles are clean and have no sharp edges. If you have time, let children make their own instruments. Provide materials such as paper cups, dry beans, plastic wrap, tape, empty plastic bottles, and empty soft-drink cans.

Set out the instruments. If you're making instruments, set out bottles, cans, cups, beans, plastic wrap, and tape.

SAY: **Before Jesus was born, God sent a man called John the Baptist to help people get ready for Jesus.** Ask a volunteer to read aloud Luke 1:5-25.

Then <u>SAY</u>: **Jesus was coming, and John the Baptist wanted everyone to be ready! We can ▷ GET READY FOR JESUS, too. Let's follow in John's footsteps and learn a way to share the news that Jesus will come again.**

Read aloud Isaiah 40:3. Teach children this rhythmic message: **Pre-pare-the-way-of-the-Lord! Hal-le-LU-jah!**

Invite each child to choose an instrument. If you're making instruments, help children partially fill the cups, bottles, or cans with dry beans and seal the tops with plastic wrap and tape.

After children have learned the rhythm, practice saying the message while playing the instruments, increasing and decreasing the tempo and volume. Allow children to switch instruments.

Lead a parade during which children repeat the message and play, varying the volume and speed. Have them visit other Sunday school classes or deliver the message as a call to worship at the beginning of the church service.

notes

Preschool Story

▶ ***NO PREP***

Bible Point: ▷ **GET READY FOR JESUS.**

Supplies: Bible, toy musical instruments (optional)

Time: 10 to 15 minutes

Preparation: none

A Welcome Baby

Have kids form a circle and sit down. Open your Bible to Luke 1, and show children the words. Tell children to pretend to rock a baby every time they hear the word *baby*.

<u>SAY</u>: **Back in Bible times, there was a priest named Zechariah and his wife, Elizabeth. Zechariah and Elizabeth loved God and obeyed him, but they were very sad because they couldn't have a baby.** Encourage kids to rock a pretend baby in their arms.

<u>SAY</u>: **One day Zechariah was working in the Temple—which is like a church—and he suddenly saw an angel of God! The angel told Zechariah that God was going to give him and Elizabeth a baby!** Encourage kids to rock a pretend baby in their arms. **That was exciting news! But the angel had even more exciting news. The angel told Zechariah that the baby** (encourage kids to rock a pretend baby in their arms) **would be a boy and that they should name him John. The angel told Zechariah that John would be a special baby** (encourage kids to rock a pretend baby in their arms) **and that he would grow up to help people ▷ GET READY FOR JESUS!**

ASK:

- **What are some ways we can get ready for Jesus?**
- **How do you think John helped people get ready for Jesus?**

SAY: **John helped people get ready for Jesus by telling them about Jesus. He also told people that they needed to get their hearts ready for Jesus by telling God about the wrong things they'd done and asking for his forgiveness. Then John would wash the people in water to show that Jesus would forgive the wrong things they'd done. Let's sing a song now about getting ready for Jesus.**

Give children musical instruments such as bells, tambourines, or toy trumpets. If you don't have any instruments, give them anything they can use to make noise! Sing "Are You Ready?" to the tune of "The Battle Hymn of the Republic":

Christmastime is coming;
It's a special time of year.
We must all get ready;
Jesus' birth is almost here.
We must open up our hearts
For the baby, oh, so dear.
Are you ready for our heavenly king?

Everybody's getting ready.
Everybody's getting ready.
Everybody's getting ready,
Ready for our heavenly king.

BIBLE STORY

The Birth of Jesus Foretold

For the Leader

For those who know Jesus, the preparation for Jesus' birthday brings deep feelings of wonder, joy, and love. The glorious birth of Jesus brings a message of promise to all those who hear and believe. It's that promise that Mary first rejoiced in, a promise that lasts for eternity.

Help children understand that the deep joy they can feel is not simply excitement for a coming holiday—it's their heartfelt connection to the promise that is Christ.

Key Scriptures

Luke 1:26-38, 45

2 Corinthians 1:20

Bible Verse

"All of God's promises have been fulfilled in Christ" (2 Corinthians 1:20).

Bible Experience

▶ *FOR SMALL GROUPS*
▶ *NO PREP*

Bible Point: ▷ **GOD KEEPS HIS PROMISES.**

Children will create backdrops that help them tell the story of the forecast of Jesus' birth.

Supplies: Bibles, newsprint, markers, safety scissors, paper, pencils

Time: 20 to 25 minutes

Preparation: none

Form groups of three or four, and assign each group to read Luke 1:26-38. Give each group a large piece of newsprint, markers, and scissors.

SAY: **In your group, take turns reading the verses from your Bible passage. Then use the markers to turn your paper into the background for a live mural of your story. Draw the background and bodies of the people involved in your story. Then cut out holes for the head and arms. The kids playing the characters in your story will put their heads and arms through the holes and act out the story for the rest of the class.**

Provide paper and pencils for kids to create a script. Encourage them to use as much facial, arm, and hand motions in their script as possible. After several minutes, have groups display their live murals and present their dramas. Give each group a rousing round of applause. Then ASK:

- **What was the message the angel brought to Mary?**
- **Think of a time you were given very important news. Were you surprised? Did you believe the news?**

Ask a child to read aloud Luke 1:45, and then ASK:

- **What did Mary have to do to receive God's promise?**

SAY: **Jesus' birth was the fulfillment of God's promises. The Bible tells us about Jesus, "All of God's promises have been fulfilled in Christ" (2 Corinthians 1:20). Let's repeat that verse together.**

When God promises something, we can believe it! ▷ GOD KEEPS HIS PROMISES. Let's look in the Bible for more of God's promises.

Additional Topics List

This lesson can be used to help children discover... Faith, Heaven, and Joy.

Game

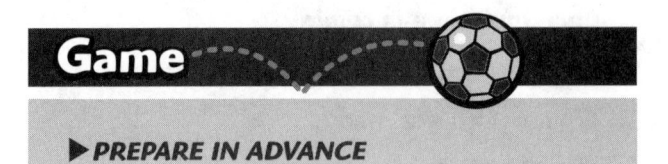

▶ *PREPARE IN ADVANCE*

Toothpick Relay

Children will break toothpicks and discuss broken promises.

Supplies: Bible, table, toothpicks, masking tape

Time: 5 to 10 minutes

Preparation: On a table at one end of the room, set out half of the toothpicks, and at the other end of the room, set out a roll of masking tape for each group on the floor.

Form two groups and have them line up at one end of the room. SAY: **Let's have a relay race. The first person in each line will hop to the table, break a toothpick in two, and hop back to the line. The next person in line will hop to the table, tape the toothpick back together, and hop back to the line. Try to tape the toothpick back together exactly as it was before it was broken. Then continue until everyone has either broken or taped together a toothpick. Ready? Go!**

When all of the toothpicks have been taped back together, have kids sit in a circle. Set the mended toothpicks in the center.

ASK:

- **Are the toothpicks as strong as they were before? Explain.**
- **How are mended toothpicks like broken promises?**
- **How does it feel when someone breaks a promise to you?**

Read Luke 1:45. SAY: **In our race it was hard to tape the toothpicks back together exactly as they were before they were broken. Broken promises are hard to mend. That's why ▷ GOD KEEPS HIS PROMISES. Mary knew that, and we can remember that, too.**

notes

Craft

▶ *PREPARE IN ADVANCE*

Light-to-the-Nations Lantern

Children will make lanterns as symbols of promise.

Supplies: Bible, colored paper, safety scissors, stapler, metallic stickers, baby-food jars, votive candles, matches

Time: 15 to 20 minutes

Preparation: If you have younger elementary kids in your class, draw the cutting lines for them to follow. Set up the supplies in your designated area. Keep matches out of reach until you're ready to use them.

Give each child a piece of paper. Have kids hold their papers horizontally and fold them from top to bottom. Show them how to cut slits in the paper, from the fold to within an inch of the edges. Cuts should be about two finger widths apart. Then have children unfold the paper and wrap it around to form a cylinder. Have them staple the ends that form the seam together and decorate the outside of the lantern with stickers. Place candles inside jars, and have kids set the lanterns over the jars.

Light one lantern to show the children how theirs will look. Turn off the lights to demonstrate the brightness of the lantern. Then ASK:

- **What effect does light have on darkness?**
- **How is Jesus like a light?**
- **How is Jesus' light a promise to all people?**

Read aloud Luke 1:26-38. SAY: **When Jesus came, he showed people—all the nations—that he loved them. That's why the promise of his birth was so important. He is God's promise to his people.**

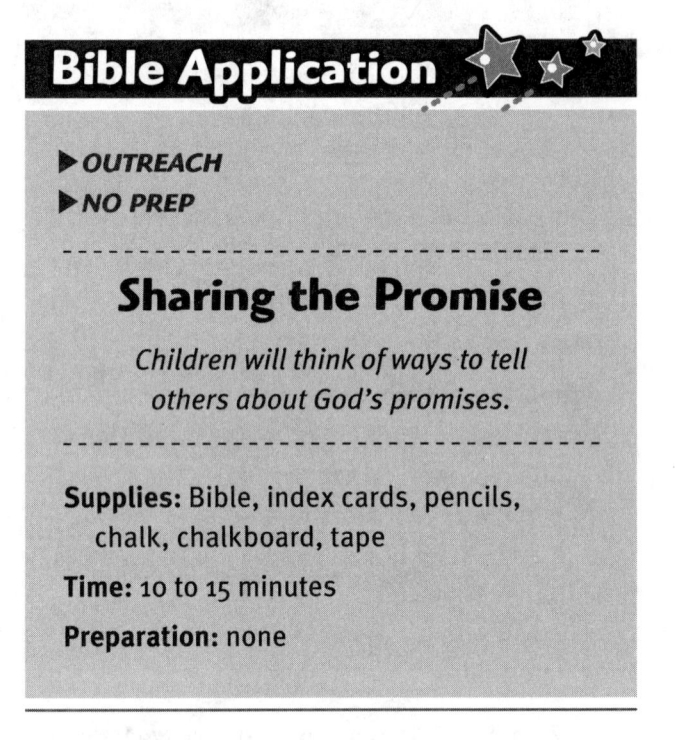

Bible Application

▶ *OUTREACH*
▶ *NO PREP*

Sharing the Promise

Children will think of ways to tell others about God's promises.

Supplies: Bible, index cards, pencils, chalk, chalkboard, tape

Time: 10 to 15 minutes

Preparation: none

Have volunteers take turns reading Luke 1:26-38. Hand out cards and pencils. SAY: **Think of the people you would like to introduce to Jesus. Draw pictures of those people, one picture per card.**

After the children have finished drawing, SAY: **Mary was joyful when the angel said she'd been chosen to raise the Messiah. Though Mary wasn't ready to have children yet, she believed in the extraordinary news that she would be the mother of Jesus. What unusual news!**

Let's think of different ways we can introduce our friends and family members to Jesus. It's OK if our ideas are out of the ordinary. Remember, the message of Jesus began in an extraordinary way.

Write "Jesus" on a chalkboard or piece of newsprint taped to a wall. As a child mentions an idea, have him or her tape one of the drawings under the word *Jesus*. Encourage kids to be creative with their ideas.

After the children finish, SAY: **As Christians, one of our biggest jobs is to introduce others to Jesus. There are lots of ways to do that. We can be creative in helping our friends meet Jesus.**

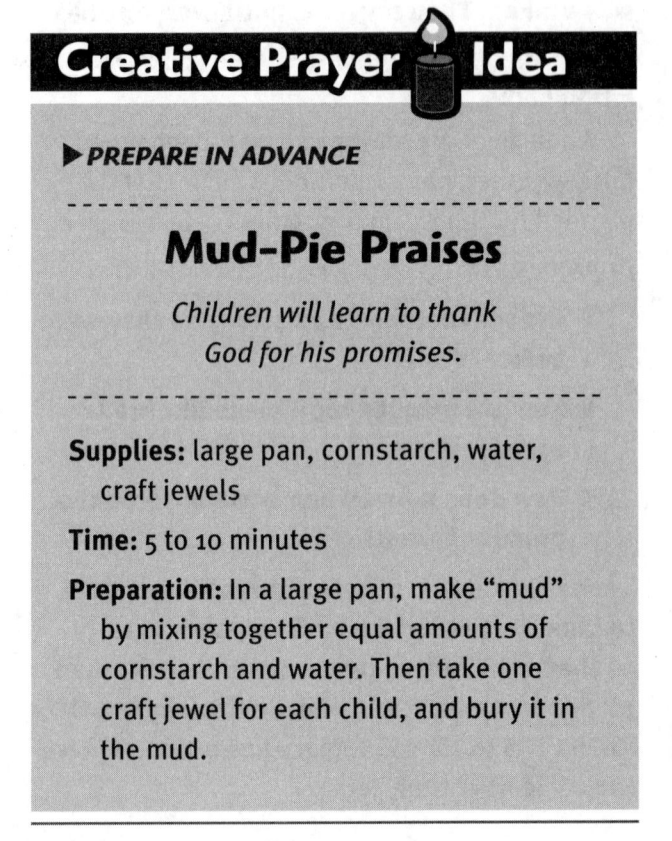

Creative Prayer Idea

▶ *PREPARE IN ADVANCE*

Mud-Pie Praises

Children will learn to thank God for his promises.

Supplies: large pan, cornstarch, water, craft jewels

Time: 5 to 10 minutes

Preparation: In a large pan, make "mud" by mixing together equal amounts of cornstarch and water. Then take one craft jewel for each child, and bury it in the mud.

Invite children to join you in some good, clean fun, playing in the gooey mud. Kids will love squishing and smushing in the mud to find the "treasures."

Let each child choose a jewel to rinse off and keep. Gather kids in a circle, and have them hold their jewels in cupped hands. Have each child mention one promise of God's that is a "gem" to him or her.

Have children hold their gems as they say a prayer of thanks for Jesus. After the first round of prayer, have partners take turns holding each other's hands as they pray that their partners remember God's promises.

Discussion Launcher

Birth Announcements

For this activity you'll need birth announcements and a Bible. Before class, create a simple birth announcement that includes a place to fill in the name, gender, height, weight, date, location, and parent's names. Make one copy for each child, plus one for you, and one extra. Fill out your birth announcement before the meeting.

When kids arrive, SAY: **When families give birth to or adopt babies, they sometimes send out birth announcements. They want to spread their joy at the miracle that's entered their homes!** Show the children the birth announcement. **See here? A birth announcement usually has the name of the baby, whether it's a boy or girl, the date and time of birth, and the baby's length and weight.** Read the information on your announcement. Hand out announcements and have kids fill out as much as they know about their own births.

ASK:

- **Do you think God had a special purpose for your birth? Explain.**
- **How was your birth like a promise from God?**

Read aloud Luke 1:26-38. SAY: **An angel appeared to Mary and had an announcement for her. God sent the angel to declare his promise that Jesus was going to be born.**

ASK:

- **How did Mary know that God would keep his promise?**
- **Why was Jesus an extra special promise from God?**
- **Whom can we tell about God's promise?**

Science Devotion

▶*NO PREP*

The Power of God's Promises

Children will compare the strength of reinforced cardboard to the strength our faith can have when it's reinforced with prayer.

Supplies: Bible, two 4x12-inch strips of corrugated cardboard, one 12-ounce frozen juice can, masking tape or rubber bands, 2 heavy books

Time: 10 to 15 minutes

Preparation: none

ASK:

- **Can you think of any people today who aren't sure they believe God's promises?**

SAY: **This experiment will help us see that God's promises make us strong.** Have a child help you wrap a piece of cardboard around the juice can, and let another child wrap masking tape around the cardboard to keep it firmly in place. Slide the juice can out of the cardboard.

ASK:

- **What are some of God's promises?**
- **How do these promises keep you strong?**
- **How strong do you think this cardboard is? Do you think it's strong enough for a book to sit on?**

Give one volunteer a heavy book and the piece of flat cardboard, and SAY: **Try to hold up your piece of cardboard on one edge on the table (or the floor), and then try to balance the book on top.** Give the child a few seconds to do this.

Give a second volunteer the cardboard tube and the other heavy book, and SAY: **I'd like you to try to balance the book on top of the cardboard tube.**

ASK:

- **Which is stronger: the cardboard piece or the tube? Why?**

SAY: **Cardboard is a strong material. But cardboard is even stronger when we form it in a different shape and reinforce it with masking tape (or rubber bands), as we did with this tube.**

ASK:

- **How is this like God's Word and promises?**

Read aloud 2 Corinthians 1:20. SAY: **The promises of God are strong. And the strongest promise he ever gave us was his Son, Jesus.**

ASK:

- **What can you do to shape your life so your life will thank God for his greatest promise to you?**

Preschool Story

▶ ***NO PREP***

Bible Point: ▷ **GOD KEEPS HIS PROMISES.**

Supplies: Bible, angel and Mary costumes (optional), baby doll

Time: 10 to 15 minutes

Preparation: none

A Surprise Visitor

Have kids form a circle and sit down. Open your Bible to Luke 1, and show children the words. Choose two children to help you tell the story. Dress children in costumes if you have them.

SAY: **In the town of Nazareth, there was a woman named Mary.** Encourage "Mary" to stand up and wave at the group. Tell Mary to act out her part of the story as you speak. **One day Mary was in her house. Maybe she was looking out the window. Or maybe she was cleaning her floor. Or maybe she was washing her dishes. Then, all of a sudden, an angel appeared to Mary!** Encourage "Gabriel" to stand up and wave at the group. Tell Gabriel to act out his part of the story as you speak.

The angel, Gabriel, said, "Greetings! The Lord is with you!" Encourage Gabriel to repeat the words after you. **Mary didn't know what to think. She shrugged her shoulders and wondered what the angel meant.**

"Don't worry, Mary," said Gabriel. Encourage Gabriel to repeat the words. **"God loves you, and he's going to give you a son."** Encourage Gabriel to repeat the words. **"Your son will be named Jesus, and he will be the Son of God."** Encourage Gabriel to repeat the words.

This really made Mary wonder. She shrugged her shoulders and shook her head. Then she asked Gabriel a question. "How can I have a baby? I'm not married?" Encourage Mary to repeat the words.

Gabriel smiled and told Mary not to worry. He told Mary that nothing was impossible with God and that God would give Mary the baby. Mary smiled and smiled and smiled. She said to Gabriel, "I am the Lord's servant, and I will obey him." Encourage Mary to repeat the words.

Reenact the skit again using two different children. Repeat several times so all the kids get a chance to be in the skit.

Once you're finished acting out the story, have children stand in a circle. Choose a child to be the angel Gabriel, and have Gabriel hold a doll to represent baby Jesus. As the class sings "Mary Heard the Angel" to the tune of "The Mulberry Bush," have Gabriel walk around the inside of the circle, getting ready to choose a Mary. At the end of the song, have Gabriel hand the baby Jesus to the Mary of his or her choice. The child chosen then becomes the angel Gabriel.

Sing:

Mary heard the angel say,
Angel say, angel say.
Mary heard the angel say
That Jesus would be born.

Jesus is God's only Son,
God's only Son, God's only Son.
Jesus is God's only Son.
His mother was Mary.

SAY: **A long time before Mary was alive, God told the people that he would send his Son to earth to save everyone. God kept his promise and sent Jesus to earth as the son of Mary.**
▷ **GOD KEEPS HIS PROMISES!**

ASK:

- **How has God kept his promises to you?**
- **How can you trust God to keep his promises?**

BIBLE STORY

An Angel Appears to Joseph

For the Leader

God sent an angel to Joseph to announce the promise of his Son. Oh, the questions that must have entered Joseph's and Mary's minds: "How can this be?" "Why us?" "What will people say?" Scripture tells us that Joseph and Mary believed the angel's promise, humbly trusting God's will for their lives.

You can help instill that same trust in young children. They can trust God's plans through his Word, through others, and through prayer. Use this lesson to encourage your students to trust in God and rely on his plans.

Key Scriptures

Isaiah 7:14
Matthew 1:1-25

Bible Verse

"Look! The virgin will conceive a child! She will give birth to a son, and they will call him Immanuel, which means 'God is with us'" (Matthew 1:23).

Bible Experience

▶ *PREPARE IN ADVANCE*

Bible Point: ▷ **TRUST GOD'S PLANS.**

Children will create new names that reflect ways to serve God.

Supplies: Bible, index cards, markers, tape

Time: 15 to 20 minutes

Preparation: If you like, bring in a book of names and their meanings so all the children can find the meanings of their names.

Have children form trios, and hand everyone a card and a marker. SAY: **All of us have names that we're known by. Most of our names have certain meanings.** Allow children who know the meanings of their names to share them with the class. Read aloud Matthew 1:1-17.

SAY: **That's a lot of names! This history of Jesus' family tells us how Jesus descended from Abraham and David, just as God told the prophets.**

Did you know that Jesus has other names besides *Jesus*? Listen for one of Jesus' other names while I read. When you hear it, put your hand over your heart. Read aloud Matthew 1:18-23. Pause, and then read verse 23 again, asking children to repeat it with you.

ASK:

- **What does *Immanuel* mean?**
- **How did Jesus fulfill the meaning of that name, "God is with us"?**
- **What's so important about having God present with us?**

SAY: **Jesus also has names that tell more about him. Some are "Bread of Life," "Good Shepherd," and "the Way and the Truth." All of his names remind us of the different ways Jesus works in God's plans.**

Read Matthew 1:24-25. SAY: **After Joseph realized what God told him, he changed his plans to divorce Mary. By taking on the role of Mary's husband and Jesus' father, Joseph chose to ▷ TRUST GOD'S PLANS and to serve God. Think of ways you can trust and serve God. Then create a new name for yourself that describes a way you can serve God. On your card, write your new name and the way you can serve God. For example, if I want to serve God by singing, then my new name could be Songster or Tuneful.**

Allow children several minutes to create their new names. Allow them to tape the index cards to themselves and wear the cards as name tags. SAY: **Joseph trusted God, risking his reputation and professional life, because he knew God's plans were more important. We can ▷ TRUST GOD'S PLANS, too.**

Song & Connect

Use "The Plans I Have for You" (track 14, *it: Innovative Tools for Children's Ministry: Old Testament* CD) to help reinforce the Bible Point, ▷ **TRUST GOD'S PLANS.**

Visit the construction site for a home, and have kids draw maps of the house as they would want it built. Discuss how even though their plans may be different, they can trust God's plan for them.

Additional Topics List

This lesson can be used to help children discover... Eternal Life and Grace.

Game

▶ *FOR SMALL GROUPS*
▶ *PREPARE IN ADVANCE*

Guess the Square

Children will try to predict the colors of squares and understand the certainty of God's promises coming true.

Supplies: Bible, red construction paper, white index cards, scissors, small paper bags

Time: 5 to 10 minutes

Preparation: Cut the paper and index cards into same-size squares, and place an even amount of each into two paper bags. You'll need to be able to tell the color of the paper square by the feel of the paper, not by looking at it. Make sure kids can't see the squares.

Have kids form two teams, and tell them that they're going to try to predict the future. Give each team a bag, making sure kids cannot see the squares inside. When you say "Go," teams are to take turns reaching into their bag, guessing a color of the square, and then pulling it out. After a minute, have teams count how many guesses they got correct.

SAY: **How many of you guessed right? You know, I can tell you the right color before I look at it! Watch. I'll even keep my eyes closed.** Close your eyes and choose a paper square. Repeat the process several times, guessing correctly each time. Eventually tell kids how you know the difference between the squares. Then read aloud Isaiah 7:14.

SAY: **Remember the story of when the angel appeared to Joseph and told him that Mary would give birth to Jesus? It was right then that Joseph knew God's plan because he remembered what Isaiah had said.**

You might have been just guessing at the colors in our game. That's kind of like how we try to guess what's in store for us. But when we read the Bible and talk to God in our prayers, those plans become more clear, just like they did for Joseph. The good news is that, no matter what, we are a part of God's plan, and we can trust that our future is safely in his hands.

Craft

▶ *PREPARE IN ADVANCE*

Angel Photo Keepsake

Children will design angel photo keepsakes.

Supplies: poster board; craft foam; safety scissors; 2-inch-wide ribbon; rulers; pencils; glue; black permanent markers; paper; craft supplies, such as measuring tape, alphabet stamps or stickers, smile stickers, and gold glitter

Time: 10 to 15 minutes

Preparation: Cut poster board and craft foam into 5½x7-inch rectangles. Each child will need four rectangles of each material. Cut ribbon into 32-inch lengths.

Have each child measure a 1-inch border around one foam rectangle and cut out the middle. Have kids use these to trace frames on three more foam rectangles and cut out the middles of all of them.

Then have children glue only the bottoms and sides of each foam rectangle onto a poster board rectangle so photos will slide through the top. Tell them to write each of the following words on a separate frame: "Trust," "God's," "Plans." Have kids decorate each of the frames with the appropriate supplies provided. Have children each fold over the top of the ribbon to form a loop, space each frame equally down the length of the ribbon, and glue them in place. Finally, have kids draw and cut out angels on paper and glue one to each end of the ribbon, alongside the frames.

Tell the story in Matthew 1:1-25. Then ask kids to talk about how members of their family demonstrate (or could demonstrate) their trust in God's plans. Encourage kids to use their frames for family photos.

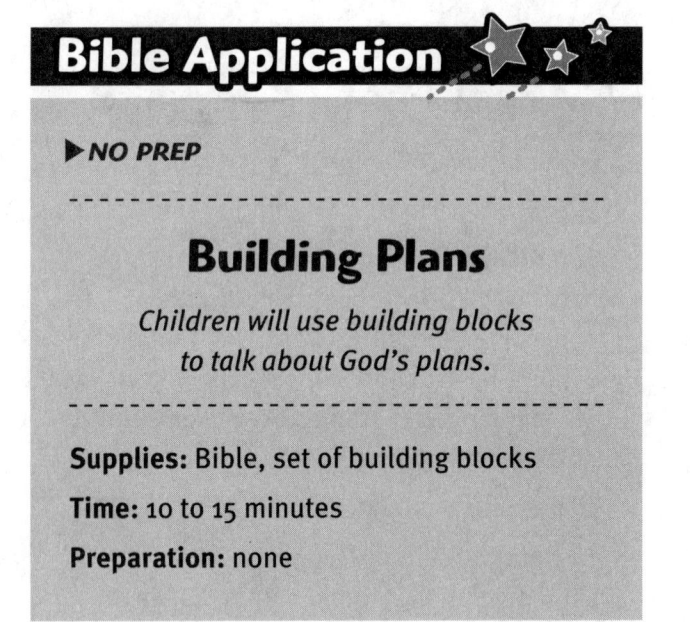

Bible Application

▶*NO PREP*

Building Plans

Children will use building blocks to talk about God's plans.

Supplies: Bible, set of building blocks

Time: 10 to 15 minutes

Preparation: none

SAY: **Joseph was a carpenter. Let's build something along with Joseph. While Joseph sawed and pound-pound-pounded in the woodshop, he was also building a dream.** Hand each child a block. Use one block to create the foundation for a tower. Have one child add his or her block to the tower after each sentence.

SAY: **Perhaps Joseph daydreamed about his bride-to-be, Mary.** Add a block. **He said to himself, "I have a plan. Someday I plan to marry her."** Add a block. **Then we will have children.** Add a block. **Then I plan to build a house for us.** Add a block. **Mary will bake my favorite bread.** Add a block. **I'll hug her every night.** Add a block. **I'll tell stories to all my children.** Add a block. **Joseph would put down his measuring line and give a happy sigh.** Add a block.

Ask kids to think about what they want to be when they grow up, and then add another block.

SAY: **Until one day when Mary came to see him. She said, "Joseph, I'm pregnant."** Push the tower over and leave the blocks lying there. Ask kids what things might keep them from being what they want to be when they grow up.

SAY: **Joseph was confused. His plans were all messed up. He wanted to trust God's plans for his life, but he wasn't sure what they were.**

In the middle of the night, an angel visited him. The angel told Joseph that Mary would give birth to a son and that Joseph was to name the baby Jesus because he would save his people from their sins.

Ask kids to think about a time God might have changed someone's plans.

SAY: **Joseph remembered some Scriptures.** Read aloud Matthew 1:23. SAY: **Immanuel—that means "God is with us."**

Joseph was overjoyed at his call to serve God and fulfill his plans. He jumped up and ran to Mary's house. He took Mary home and married her. She gave birth to God's Son. And Joseph named him Jesus.

Have kids talk about something they'd like to do to serve God.

SAY: **I'd like each of you to take a block. While I say this verse, you can shape the blocks into the best Christmas gift God ever gave the world, the cross of Jesus. That is why Jesus came, to save his people from their sins.** Help children form a cross with the blocks while you repeat Matthew 1:23.

Have kids pray, thanking God for making it easy to trust in his plans.

Creative Prayer Idea

▶ *PREPARE IN ADVANCE*

▶ *FOR YOUNGER CHILDREN*

Prayer Chain

Children will make visual reminders of their answered prayers.

Supplies: construction paper (2 colors), scissors, fine-point markers or pens, transparent tape

Time: 10 to 15 minutes

Preparation: Use scissors to create a supply of 1x6-inch construction paper strips of two colors. Set out the strips, along with the fine-point markers or pens, and the transparent tape. Designate one color of paper strips for prayer requests and the other for answered prayers.

Encourage each child to write a prayer request or a brief description of an answered prayer on a paper strip of the appropriate color. Then have kids loop and tape the paper slips together (with the writing on the outside) to make a prayer chain. Tell kids that colors don't have to alternate in this paper chain. Hang the chain from a corner of your ceiling.

Allow time for kids to add to the prayer chain. As they work, ask them to offer what's on their chain link silently to God and then close by saying aloud, "I trust in God's plans." As the chain grows, hang it festively around the room.

Object Lesson

▶ *PREPARE IN ADVANCE*

Strength in His Plans

Children will see how God's plans can strengthen them.

Supplies: Bible; small, polished stones

Time: 5 to 10 minutes

Preparation: Conceal a stone in one hand before you begin to speak. You'll need one small stone for each child.

SAY: **Hold out both fists. I have something in one of my hands. Can you guess which one?** Let kids guess. Try this a few times, each time putting your hands behind your back to conceal where the stone is.

Hold out the stone in one hand for kids to see. SAY: **God never makes us try to guess the wrong answer.** Read aloud Matthew 1:23. SAY: **He told the prophets that a Savior was coming, and he did! When we trust in God's plans, we strengthen our faith in him. It will be as strong as this rock!**

SAY: **Thanks for your answers! God doesn't play games with his plans.** Give each child a polished stone, and SAY: **Trust in God's plans, and he will be with you always. Hold your shiny stone firmly in your hand as we thank God for his rock-solid promise—his Son, Jesus.** Close in a prayer of thanks for the birth of the Savior.

Discussion Launcher

Who's Watching

For this activity you'll need paper and a pen. Before the meeting, write each child's name on a slip of paper and fold it over.

Have children each draw a name, returning slips only if they get their own names. Have children slowly walk around and watch the person whose name he or she chose. They should keep that child within sight at all times. The object of the game is to discover who's watching you without letting that child know he or she has been discovered and without letting your own person out of sight.

After three minutes, have kids guess who was watching them. Then have children tell who they were watching.

ASK:

- **How did you feel about being constantly watched by someone?**
- **Which was more difficult: watching without being noticed or discovering who was watching you? Explain.**
- **How do you feel about having God watch you constantly?**
- **Why do you think God watches us?**
- **How can you trust God's plans more?**

n
o
t
e
s

Preschool Story

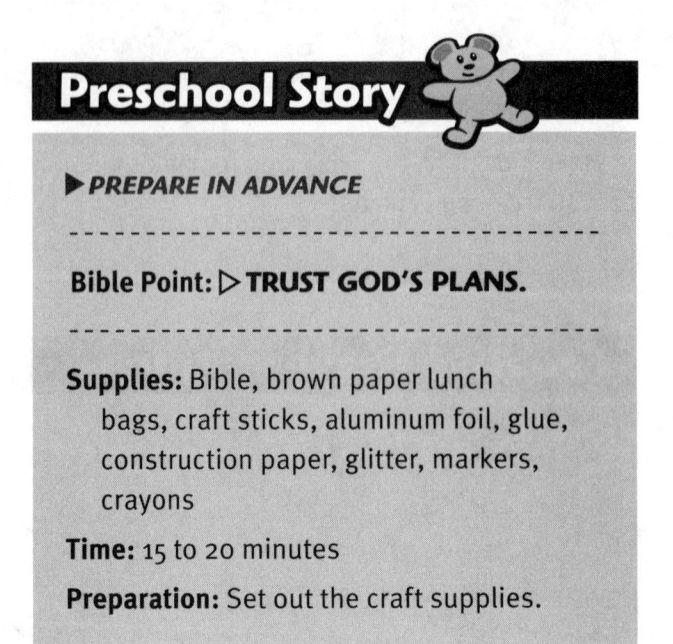

▶ *PREPARE IN ADVANCE*

Bible Point: ▷ **TRUST GOD'S PLANS.**

Supplies: Bible, brown paper lunch bags, craft sticks, aluminum foil, glue, construction paper, glitter, markers, crayons

Time: 15 to 20 minutes

Preparation: Set out the craft supplies.

A Dream Come True

Have kids form a circle and sit down. Give each child three brown paper bags and one small craft stick. Encourage kids to use foil, glitter, and white crayons to decorate one brown paper sack as an angel puppet. Tell kids to use the markers and construction paper to decorate one of the other puppets as Joseph and the other puppet as Mary. Have kids draw a baby on the craft stick. Tell kids to use their puppets to act out the story as you tell it.

Open your Bible to Matthew 1, and show children the words. SAY: **Joseph was planning to be married to Mary. But when Joseph found out that she was going to have a baby, he was a little worried.** Encourage children to make their Joseph puppets shake their heads and mumble. **Joseph didn't know that Mary was going to have God's Son!**

One night Joseph was asleep. Encourage children to make their Joseph puppets sleep. **While he was sleeping, he had a dream. An angel appeared to him in his dream.** Encourage kids to bring out their angel puppet. **The angel said to Joseph, "Don't be afraid to marry Mary. She loves God, and the baby she will have is**

God's Son!" Let children use their angel puppets to repeat the angel's words. **"You should name the baby Jesus because the baby will grow up to save the world."** Encourage kids to have their angel puppets repeat those words. **Then the angel disappeared and Joseph woke up.** Encourage children to have their Joseph puppets wake up. **Joseph believed what the angel said, and he chose to trust God's plans. He married Mary, and when her son was born, they named him Jesus.** Encourage children to bring out their Mary puppets and pretend to have Mary and Joseph get married. Then have kids glue the small craft stick "baby Jesus" to their Mary puppets.

When you're finished with the story, have kids sing the following song to the tune of "London Bridge." Choose two kids to be the bridge, and encourage the other kids to walk under the "bridge." At the end of the song, the bridge should collapse and capture one child. Sing:

Joseph, you can trust God's plans,
Trust God's plans, trust God's plans.
Joseph, you can trust God's plans
Because God loves you!

When kids capture a student in their arms, tell them to sing the song again, using the captured child's name in place of Joseph's name. Then let the captured child choose another child, and those two children will become the new bridge. Continue playing until each child gets a chance to be captured and play the bridge. Remind children that they can always ▷ **TRUST GOD'S PLANS.**

ASK:

- **How did Joseph trust God's plans?**
- **How can you trust God's plans for your life?**

BIBLE STORY

The Birth of Jesus

For the Leader

God entrusted an amazing message to humble, ordinary people—shepherds. They were the ones trumpeting the message in the streets of Bethlehem: The Messiah is born!

Teach children that this message of hope and joy isn't just for an elite few. The shepherds told everyone—they were passionate about the message. We can be, too.

Key Scriptures

Luke 2:1-20

Romans 6:23

Bible Verse

"The Savior—yes, the Messiah, the Lord—has been born today in Bethlehem" (Luke 2:11).

notes

Bible Experience

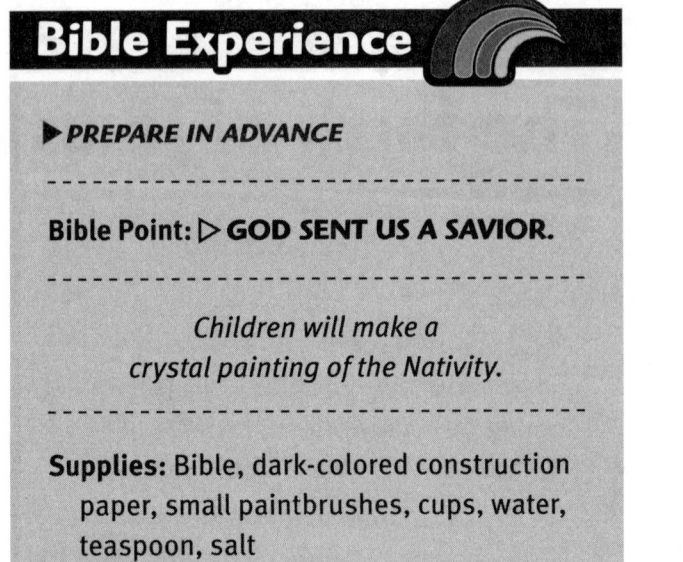

▶ *PREPARE IN ADVANCE*

Bible Point: ▷ **GOD SENT US A SAVIOR.**

Children will make a crystal painting of the Nativity.

Supplies: Bible, dark-colored construction paper, small paintbrushes, cups, water, teaspoon, salt

Time: 10 to 15 minutes

Preparation: You'll need access to an oven.

Read aloud Luke 2:1-20. Then give each child a sheet of paper, a paintbrush, and a cup of water with 3 teaspoons of salt. Have children create a Christmas scene telling the news of Jesus' birth. Tell children to dip and stir with the brush before writing each letter or drawing each image.

As children work, preheat the oven to 150 degrees. Repeat Luke 2:11 several times to remind children of the wonderful good news they're announcing: "The Savior—yes, the Messiah, the Lord—has been born today in Bethlehem." Bake the finished scenes for five minutes or until the papers dry. The images will appear as sparkling crystals on the dark paper.

After the pictures are finished, set them aside and ASK:

- **Were you surprised at how your amazing messages turned out? Explain.**
- **How do you think the shepherds felt when they saw the angels?**
- **If you had been with the shepherds, how would you have reacted?**

SAY: **The angels brought wonderful news: ▷ GOD SENT US A SAVIOR. Although the shepherds were surprised at the message, they went to Bethlehem and found Jesus, just as the angels had said. Everyone who heard the news was amazed.**

We can also share the amazing news that God sent us a Savior. Take home your amazing message, and give it to someone you'd like to tell about Jesus.

Additional Topics List

This lesson can be used to help children discover... Guidance, Heaven, and Joy.

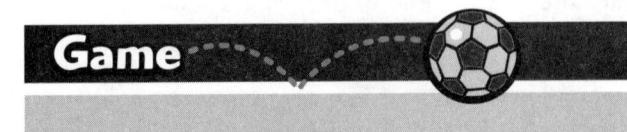

Game

▶ *PREPARE IN ADVANCE*

Bethlehem Balloons

Children will take a census of balloons.

Supplies: Bible, balloons

Time: 5 to 10 minutes

Preparation: You'll need one balloon per child, an equal number of balloons in four colors. Have kids help you inflate and tie balloons before the game (older children can help the younger ones; remember that balloons are a choking hazard for young children), or ask a volunteer to help you. Place the balloons in the center of your room.

Give each child a balloon. Ask kids to scatter around the room so they're equally spaced throughout your playing area, and have them sit down.

Read aloud Luke 2:1-5. SAY: **Joseph had to take Mary to his hometown to be counted in a census. It's time to take a census of the balloons. All our balloons must be counted, and to be counted they must return to their "hometowns."** Designate the corners of your playing area as the hometowns. Assign one color to each corner.

There's one catch with the balloon census: You have to bat the balloons to the correct corners without standing up or moving.

Tell kids to begin, and then stand back and watch the fun! When all the balloons have been batted to the corners, close the game by asking each child to go to a corner, find one balloon, and sit on it to break it. As each child breaks a balloon, help him or her count out "one," "two," and so on until kids have counted all the balloons in each corner. At the end of the game, discuss the following questions:

- **How easy or hard was it for you to get your balloon to its corner?**
- **How is that like how Joseph and Mary might have felt when they had to go to Bethlehem to be counted in a census?**
- **How do you think they felt knowing that God was sending a Savior?**

Read aloud the rest of the story from Luke 2:6-20.

n
o
t
e
s

Craft

▶ *PREPARE IN ADVANCE*

Shepherd Pop-Up Cards

Children will make pop-up cards to share the joy of Jesus' birth.

Supplies: Bible, construction paper, crayons or markers, safety scissors, glue

Time: 15 to 20 minutes

Preparation: Fold a piece of construction paper in half. In the center of the page, draw two vertical lines 2 inches from the fold up and 2 inches from the fold down, and 1 inch apart. Repeat this so that you have one paper ready for each child you expect.

Have children cut slits along the two lines on their papers. Show them how to open their cards, push the centerpieces they just cut in the opposite direction so they are on the inside of the cards, and crease the fold lines. This will be the pop-up part of their cards.

Then have kids each fold another sheet of paper in half. Help kids glue the pop-up paper inside the other whole sheet of paper, being careful not to glue down the pop-up section. With each card's fold on top or on the left-hand side, have kids decorate the outside of their cards. Then they can open the cards. Have children draw shepherd figures (about the size of a finger) on more paper and cut them out. Help students glue the shepherds to the pop-ups in their cards. Then have them write an exciting message for their shepherds to share.

Bring the children together in a circle and SAY: **You've just made cards to share the excitement of Jesus' birth with others. When Jesus was born, the shepherds were the first people to spread the good news that God had sent us a Savior. Like the shepherds, we can share the excitement, too!** Have the kids act out the shepherds' emotions and actions as you read aloud Luke 2:8-20.

Bible Application

▶ *PREPARE IN ADVANCE*
▶ *FOR FAMILY MINISTRY*

The Greatest Gift

Children will learn about the greatest gift of all.

Supplies: Bible, a "baby Jesus" from a Nativity scene, box, gift wrapping, tape, self-sticking bows, fine-point markers

Time: 10 to 15 minutes

Preparation: Wrap up the baby Jesus in a box.

ASK:

- **What's the best Christmas present you've ever given?**
- **What's the best Christmas present you've ever received?**

Have a child open the wrapped box and take out the baby Jesus figure. Show the figure to all the children. Then read aloud Luke 2:11. SAY: **The Bible talks about God's greatest gift to us—a Savior. God sent his Son so we can be free from our sins.**

Read aloud Romans 6:23. SAY: **Here the Bible says that Jesus is a gift from God. Jesus has saved us all from death. That's the best gift of all!**

Give each child several gift bows and a marker. Have kids write the words of Luke 2:11 on the bows. Challenge children to take their bows home and call a family meeting. Encourage families to choose someone who needs to know that God sent us a Savior, purchase gifts for that person, and add their Luke bows on each gift.

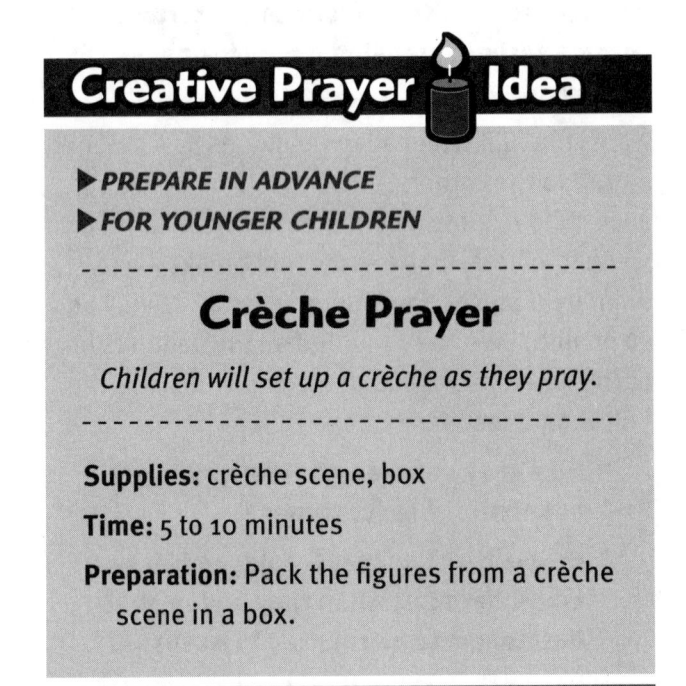

Creative Prayer Idea

▶ *PREPARE IN ADVANCE*
▶ *FOR YOUNGER CHILDREN*

Crèche Prayer

Children will set up a crèche as they pray.

Supplies: crèche scene, box

Time: 5 to 10 minutes

Preparation: Pack the figures from a crèche scene in a box.

Allow kids to take turns unwrapping figures. As they add the figures to the crèche scene, have them give thanks for the role that figure played in Jesus' birth. For instance, the person holding the stable might say, "Thank you that there was at least a stable nearby for Jesus." The person with a shepherd might say, "Thank you that the shepherds went and told lots of people about Jesus."

After all the kids have added their figures and prayed, close with a group prayer, asking God to help everyone remember Jesus' role as their Savior.

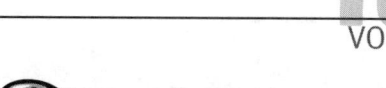

Worship Prompt Idea

Instant Nativity

Children will participate in a Nativity scene as a form of worship.

Supplies: Bible, box, marker, angel halos (sparkling garland), robes, baby doll

Time: 10 to 15 minutes

Preparation: On the outside of the box, write "Instant Christmas Pageant." Fill it with halos and robes. You'll need enough robes for kids to play Mary, Joseph, the shepherds, and the wise men. Try to have one costume prop for each child. Ask an adult to bring a baby doll forward at the appropriate time.

Begin by reading the story of Christmas from Luke 2:1-20. Then put on an instant Christmas Nativity. Have kids each reach into the box and pull out one item to define their role. Ask an adult helper or two to help with the costumes and with positioning the kids in the Nativity scene.

After everyone is dressed, SAY: **Hmm. Everything seems to be in place. But I have a feeling we're forgetting something. What are we forgetting?** Ask the volunteer to bring the baby doll and place him in "Mary's" arms.

We almost forgot Jesus! Sometimes we get so busy with other Christmas stuff that we forget the most important thing—▷ GOD SENT US A SAVIOR. Let's focus on that as we worship God for saving us.

As everyone is in place for the Nativity, sing "Away in a Manger."

Snack

▶ *PREPARE IN ADVANCE*

▶ *ALLERGY ALERT*

Edible Mangers

Children will make edible mangers.

Supplies: frosted shredded-wheat cereal, paper plates, fat pretzel sticks, marshmallow crème, graham crackers

Time: 10 to 15 minutes

Preparation: Set out all the materials.

Give each child a paper plate, and have kids break up several pieces of the frosted shredded-wheat cereal and put it in piles on their plates. Give kids each four pretzel sticks, and instruct them to group their pretzels in pairs. Then show kids how to stick each pair together with marshmallow crème. Show them how to lean one-fourth of a graham cracker on each of the pretzel pairs to form mangers. Have kids "glue" the crackers to the pretzel pairs using the marshmallow crème. Then have kids fill the mangers with the shredded-cereal "hay." Before kids enjoy their manger treats, have them each find one person to show the manager to and say, "This lowly place is where God sent the Savior to be born for everyone to see."

n ______

o ______

t ______

e ______

s ______

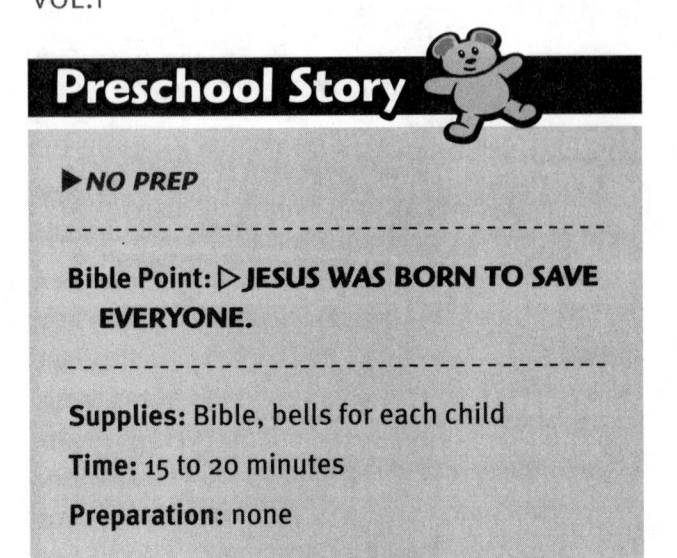

Preschool Story

▶ *NO PREP*

Bible Point: ▷**JESUS WAS BORN TO SAVE EVERYONE.**

Supplies: Bible, bells for each child

Time: 15 to 20 minutes

Preparation: none

Celebration!

Have kids form a circle and sit down. Open your Bible to Luke 2, and show children the words. SAY: **Today's Bible story comes from the book of Luke. There are many angels in this story. An angel is a special messenger from God. Every time you hear me say "angel," I want you to shout out, "Praise God!"**

When Mary was about to have her baby, Mary and Joseph had to go on a long trip back to the town where Joseph was born. When it was time for God to give baby Jesus to Mary and Joseph, they had to find a place to stay for the night. But no one had a room. The only place for Mary to rest was in a stable where farm animals lived—in a barn.

ASK:

- **Can you name an animal that lives in a barn?**
- **What sound does that animal make?**

SAY: **These are some of the animals and sounds that might have filled the place where Jesus was born. Mary wrapped baby Jesus in cloth to keep him warm and laid him in a manger to sleep.** Have the children pretend to wrap a blanket around a baby and rock it back and forth.

Meanwhile, shepherds were taking care of their sheep in the fields. Encourage children to make sheep sounds. **It was late at night when angels** (have children shout, "Praise God!") **appeared to the shepherds. The whole sky was filled with angels.** Have children shout, "Praise God!" **They told the shepherds that baby Jesus was born and that he would take away the bad things people did. The angels** (have children shout, "Praise God!") **told the shepherds that they could find baby Jesus in the city of Bethlehem. So the shepherds ran to find Jesus—the baby King that God had promised for so many years to send.**

When the shepherds saw baby Jesus, they were very happy! They told everyone what the angels (have children shout, "Praise God!") **had said. "Jesus came to take away our sins," they said. The shepherds were very happy that ▷JESUS WAS BORN TO SAVE EVERYONE.**

Give children bells to shake while they sing "Jesus Came" to the tune of "Jingle Bells."

Jesus came.
Jesus came.
Jesus came to show
That he's God's Son and he's the one
God promised long ago.
(Repeat.)

ASK:

- **Why was Jesus born?**
- **How can you thank Jesus for coming to save us?**

BIBLE STORY

Jesus at the Temple

For the Leader

Very little is written in the Bible about Jesus as a boy. The trip to Jerusalem reveals the young boy's love and zeal for his heavenly Father and a great desire to be where people were growing in the knowledge of God. We often focus on Jesus' life as an adult, but we can also learn from his habits as a child.

Children may perceive that the things of God are only for adults to know. Help your students learn a message that even the youngest kids can understand: Jesus is special.

Key Scripture

Luke 2:41-52

Bible Verse

"All who heard him were amazed at his understanding and his answers" (Luke 2:47).

Bible Experience

▶ *NO PREP*

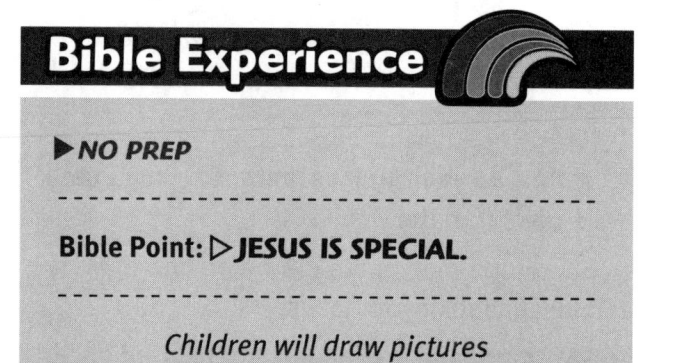

Bible Point: ▷ **JESUS IS SPECIAL.**

Children will draw pictures of Jesus at the Temple.

Supplies: Bible, paper, markers

Time: 10 to 15 minutes

Preparation: none

Give each child a sheet of paper and a marker. SAY: **Listen as I tell the Bible story. I'll stop occasionally and let you draw pictures about the story. You'll have to draw quickly!** Show children Luke 2:41-52. Then begin. **At a certain time each year, all the Jewish people gathered in Jerusalem for Passover: a celebration of song, dance, feasting, and praise.**

When Jesus was 12, he and his family traveled to Jerusalem as usual to celebrate Passover. There was a large group of people because many of Jesus' relatives and neighbors traveled with them. They didn't have cars, so they spent many days walking.

ASK:

- **When you take vacations, what kinds of things do you do to make the time pass more quickly?**

Give kids a moment to draw pictures of Jesus' family traveling.

SAY: **When they finally arrived, they celebrated with food and friends and worshipped God in the Temple. When the feast was over, Jesus' family and friends began the journey**

home. But when Mary and Joseph went to look for Jesus, he was nowhere to be found!

ASK:

- **How do you think parents feel when they can't find their child?**

Give kids a moment to draw a picture of Mary and Joseph looking for Jesus.

SAY: **Mary and Joseph quickly hurried back to Jerusalem. They hunted for Jesus for three days before they finally found him. Mary and Joseph found Jesus in the Temple, listening to the teachers and asking them many questions. Everyone who heard Jesus could tell that he was special. Luke 2:47 tells us: "All who heard him were amazed at his understanding and his answers." His parents said, "Jesus, we couldn't find you anywhere." Jesus replied, "Of course I would have been here, in my Father's house."**

ASK:

- **Why do you think Jesus chose to go to the Temple?**

Give kids a moment to draw Jesus in the Temple.

SAY: **Jesus returned home with his parents and obeyed them. Jesus learned more and more, and God was very pleased with him.**

Give kids time to share their drawings. Then SAY: **We can tell that ▷JESUS IS SPECIAL because early on he had a strong thirst for God's knowledge. Even as a child he understood that we can never know enough about God!**

n
o
t
e
s

Song & Connect

Use "Wonderful" (track 11, *it: Innovative Tools for Children's Ministry: Old Testament* CD) to help reinforce the Bible Point, ▷**JESUS IS SPECIAL.**

Remind children that the word *special* has many meanings when it's used for describing Jesus. Help children know all the special relationships Jesus has in their lives.

Additional Topics List

This lesson can be used to help children discover... Discipleship, Parents, and Praise.

Game

▶ ***NO PREP***

School Moves and Sounds

Children will pantomime and make school sound effects.

Supplies: Bible

Time: 5 to 10 minutes

Preparation: none

Ask kids to sit in a circle. Read aloud Luke 2:40, 46-47. Ask kids to think of ways they're growing in their skills and in wisdom. One at a time, have kids act out skills while the others guess what they're demonstrating. For example, a child could pretend to write, read, do math, kick a ball, or sing.

After each child has had a chance, SAY: **Those are fun things to remember about school! Jesus probably went to a school at his synagogue (a Jewish church). I bet Jesus had some fun school memories, too.**

Ask children to turn to a friend and answer this question:

- **What's special about you at school? Maybe it's that you smile a lot or that you read a lot of books. Share what's special about you with your friend.**

After children talk for a minute or two, ask them to discuss:

- **What's special about Jesus?**

After they talk for a minute or two, SAY: **▷ JESUS IS SPECIAL because he's God's Son. But he's also special because he's our friend!**

Craft

▶ *PREPARE IN ADVANCE*

Jesus Medallions

Children will design medallions to show how special Jesus is.

Supplies: frozen-juice can lids, pencils, scrap wood, nails, hammers, acrylic paints, paint shirts, paintbrushes, colored felt, leather lace

Time: 20 to 25 minutes

Preparation: Collect lids from juice cans (the kind that come off with plastic strips) and one nail for each student. Cut a 20-inch leather lace piece for each child.

Give each child a pencil and a can lid. Instruct kids to draw simple designs on their can lids. Explain that kids will be making medallions for Jesus because **▷ JESUS IS SPECIAL.** Ask children to make their designs symbolize something that's special about Jesus. For instance, they could draw a cross because Jesus died on the cross for us—that's special! Or they could draw a smile because Jesus gives us special joy.

Then show children how to lay the lids on blocks of scrap wood and nail holes in the lids to outline the designs. The nail holes should be about ¼ inch apart. When they've outlined their designs, kids may paint over them with acrylic paints.

While the paint is drying, have kids trace around the can lids on pieces of colored felt. Show them how to cut out the felt circles and glue them to the back of the lids—the side the nails have been punched through. This will cover any sharp edges and allow a bit of color to peek through the holes. Then have kids use the nails to make holes in the top of their medallions and tie leather laces through them.

Have an awards ceremony including each child with his or her medallion for Jesus. Read aloud Luke 2:47, and tell kids that they can wear their Jesus medallions in honor of how special he is.

n
o
t
e
s

Bible Application

▶ *FOR SMALL GROUPS*
▶ *NO PREP*

Whaddya Know?

Children will learn the importance of listening and learning.

Supplies: Bible
Time: 5 to 10 minutes
Preparation: none

Ask kids to talk about some of their favorite things that they've learned so far in school or that their parents have taught them. Then SAY: **What cool things you've learned! Did you know that Jesus was a learner, too?** Read aloud Luke 2:46 and SAY: **The Bible says that Jesus listened to the teachers and asked them questions.**

Let's do a simple activity. Find a partner and try to teach your partner the favorite thing you've learned. When I say "Go!" both of you will try to teach your favorite thing to your partner. But you must talk at the same time. Ready? Go! Give the children a minute to try to teach their partners.

ASK:

- **Did you feel that your partner was listening to you? Explain.**
- **Why is listening an important part of learning?**
- **What's one way you can listen to God?**
- **What's one way you can learn more about God?**

SAY: **The Bible says that when Jesus was a boy, he learned many things. Jesus is special: He was a listener, a learner, *and* a teacher! He learned and taught others at the same time because he set an example of good behavior.**

ASK:

- **What are you learning about God?**
- **In what ways are you teaching others about God because of how you treat people?**

Close in prayer, asking God to help kids to be good listeners and good learners.

Creative Prayer Idea

▶ *PREPARE IN ADVANCE*

Household Hallelujahs

Children will use everyday items to pray.

Supplies: tray, various household items
Time: 5 to 10 minutes
Preparation: Set out on a tray household items, such as a fingernail file, a blunt knife, a pen, an eraser, a spoon, safety scissors, a bar of soap, a flashlight or candle, a crayon, a cookie cutter, a spatula, and salt and pepper shakers.

Have kids form pairs and sit in a circle. Pass the tray around, and have each pair take an item and use it as a way to offer praise for one special thing about Jesus. For instance, if they choose the flashlight, they might pray, "Jesus, thank you for being the light of the world."

When everyone has thought of a prayer, pass the tray around the circle again. Have each pair offer its prayer, place its item back on the tray, and then pass the tray to the next pair. Encourage kids to use this prayer idea with their families.

Movie Clip

Tarzan

Movie Title: *Tarzan* (1999) (G)

Start Time: 9 minutes

Where to Begin: As the male gorilla approaches, Terk hands the baby to Kala and says, "Her's going to be its mother now."

Where to End: The song ends and Tarzan and the mother gorilla go to sleep.

Plot: A mother gorilla's baby is killed, so the saddened gorilla adopts an orphaned human baby as her own. Tarzan becomes a very special baby.

Review: From the moment of Jesus' birth, Mary must have had those same feelings that the mother gorilla had for Tarzan.

Discussion

After setting up the clip, SAY: **When we treasure something, it becomes very special to us. Let's watch a clip from *Tarzan* and see what becomes very special to a gorilla.** Show the clip, and then

ASK:

- **Why was Tarzan so special to this gorilla?**
- **How is that like your being special to your mom or dad?**
- **How is that also like Jesus' being special to his mother, Mary?**
- **How is Jesus special to you?**

SAY: **Jesus was special to his mother, but he's even more special because he's God's Son. God sent Jesus to earth to die for our sins. That very special baby would grow to be the man who would give us eternal life.**

Worship Prompt Idea

▶ ***PREPARE IN ADVANCE***

Joyful Noises

Children will make instruments to help them worship Jesus.

Supplies: paper plates, dry beans, stapler, hole punch, curling ribbon, spoons, bows, markers (optional: wrapping paper, old keys, jingle bells, hard candies, candy canes, glitter glue)

Time: 10 to 15 minutes

Preparation: Set out all of the materials.

Allow children to create their own unique tambourines with the materials provided. Encourage kids with the following ideas:

- Fold a paper plate in half, pour in dry beans, and then staple the edges shut.
- Place two paper plates together, and punch holes around the edge. Weave ribbon through the holes, and then pour in hard candies or dry beans. Finish weaving and tie off the ribbon.
- Punch holes around the edge of a paper plate, and then tie jingle bells or old keys to each hole. Kids can tap this "tambourine" with a candy cane "drumstick."

Allow children to decorate their instruments with any items you've brought in. Have children each come up with their own simple song that's called "Jesus Is Special" and play that song on their instruments.

Preschool Story

▶ *NO PREP*

Bible Point: ▷ **JESUS IS SPECIAL.**

Supplies: Bible

Time: 15 to 20 minutes

Preparation: none

Where Is Jesus?

Have kids form a circle and sit down. Open your Bible to Luke 2, and show children the words. SAY: **This Bible story is about Jesus when he was a 12-year-old boy. Let's act out the story together.** Encourage preschoolers to repeat your words and actions to this fun drama.

I'm Mary, Jesus' mom. *(Pretend to cradle a baby in your arms.)*

I'm Joseph, Jesus' dad. *(Stand with your hands on your hips.)*

We're taking Jesus to Jerusalem for the Passover feast. *(Walk in place.)*

It's time to get some sleep! *(Lay your head on your hands.)*

We must keep traveling to Jerusalem. *(Walk in place.)*

In Jerusalem we celebrate the Passover. *(Clap your hands.)*

It's time to go back home. *(Pretend to pack things up.)*

Where is Jesus? *(Put your hands over your eyebrows, as if searching.)*

We must find him! *(Walk in place.)*

We looked for Jesus for three days! *(Hold up three fingers.)*

Jesus is in God's house, talking to the teachers. *(Make praying hands, and then cup your hands around your mouth.)*

We told him we were worried! *(Put your hands on your cheeks, and shake your head back and forth.)*

Jesus explained he wanted to talk about God. *(Stretch your hands outward.)*

It's time for Jesus to go back home with us. *(Walk in place.)*

Jesus obeyed us, and he grew up to be wise. *(Squat, and then stand up slowly with your finger to your temple.)*

▷ JESUS IS SPECIAL because he is God's Son. When he went to the Temple, he was only 12 years old, but he was teaching the leaders at the Temple, and they were much older than he was! God helped Jesus to be loving and wise. God can help you, too!

ASK:

- **Why was Jesus special?**
- **How can you follow Jesus and be like him?**

notes

BIBLE STORY

Jesus Is Baptized

For the Leader

It's not easy to explain the relationship of Jesus to God, or why Jesus needed to be baptized. But Jesus knew the reasons. He knew he was the Son of God. He knew he had to show others his respect for the Father, just as they should.

Help children know this simple relationship of Father and Son, sealed with baptism. Teach them the joy in having a real relationship with the Father and Son, one that's worthy of sharing with others.

Key Scriptures

Matthew 3:1-17

Mark 16:15

Bible Verse

"A voice from heaven said, 'This is my dearly loved Son, who brings me great joy'" (Matthew 3:17).

n
o
t
e
s

Bible Experience

▶ *PREPARE IN ADVANCE*

Bible Point: ▷ **JESUS IS GOD'S SON.**

Children will recognize Jesus as important above all others.

Supplies: large pictures of famous people, beanbag

Time: 10 to 15 minutes

Preparation: Gather several large pictures of people kids will know, such as George Washington, Tiger Woods, Abraham Lincoln, and your pastor. Make sure you also have a large picture of Jesus.

SAY: **I have some pictures I want to show to you today. As I show you a picture, I want you to tell me who it is.** Show all of the pictures, and allow children time to identify each one. Show kids the picture of Jesus last. **All of these people are important, but Jesus is the Son of God.**

Today we're going to talk about a very special baptism—Jesus' baptism. Ask children if they know what it means to be baptized. **One day John the Baptist was baptizing people, and Jesus wanted to be baptized. John didn't want to do it, but Jesus insisted. When Jesus came up from the water, the heavens opened, and he saw God's Spirit descending like a dove. Let's read from Matthew 3:17 what happened next: "A voice from heaven said, 'This is my dearly loved Son, who brings me great joy.'"**

Yes, that was God talking! ▷ **JESUS IS GOD'S SON.** Hold up the beanbag and SAY: **When I throw this beanbag to you, I'll say, "Whose child are you?" and you'll say, "I'm**

[parent's name]**'s son** [or daughter]**." Then I'll say, "Who's Jesus?" and you'll say, "The Son of God."** Play several times.

Being someone's son or daughter is very important, isn't it? But it's more important that Jesus is God's Son because God sent him to save us from our sins. Close in prayer, thanking God for salvation through his Son.

Additional Topics List

This lesson can be used to help children discover... Faith, Heaven, Holiness, and Obedience.

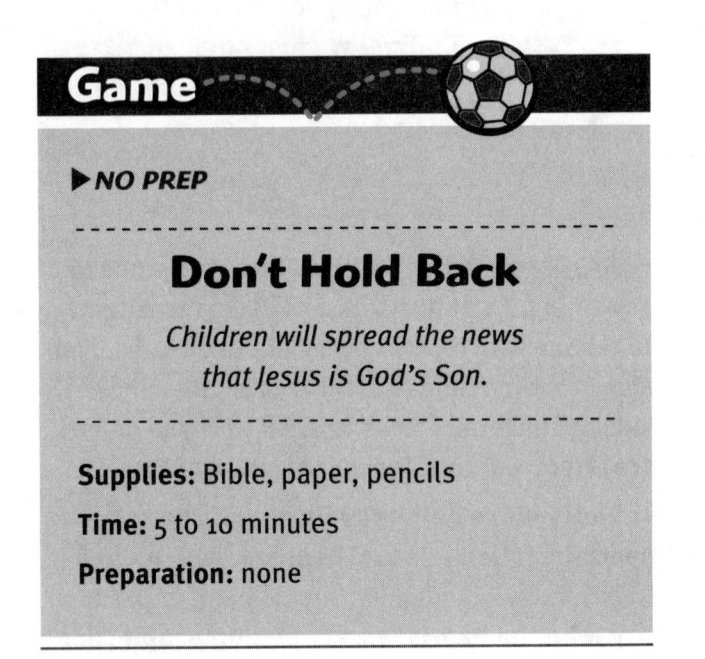

Game

▶ *NO PREP*

Don't Hold Back

Children will spread the news that Jesus is God's Son.

Supplies: Bible, paper, pencils

Time: 5 to 10 minutes

Preparation: none

Have kids form a circle with one "Listener" inside and three "Tellers" outside. The kids who form the circle will be the "Blockers." Give the Tellers paper and pencils, and tell them to write "Jesus is the Son of God."

SAY: **Tellers, try to spread your news to the Listener inside the circle. Blockers, try to keep the Tellers from spreading the news. Ready? Go!**

Allow several kids to be Tellers. After several minutes, call time.

ASK:

- **What obstacles did you have to overcome to spread your news?**
- **What things helped you deliver your news?**

Ask a child to read aloud Mark 16:15. SAY: **God thought it was important that people know Jesus is his Son. Sometimes it's hard for us to tell others that ▷JESUS IS GOD'S SON, but it's important. It's so important that God did it himself!**

ASK:

- **Who is someone you can tell that Jesus is God's Son?**
- **How can you tell this person God's important news about Jesus?**

Craft

▶ *PREPARE IN ADVANCE*

Heavenly Doves

Children will make symbols of God's appearance in Matthew 3:16.

Supplies: Bible, soap clay, wax paper, yarn, vegetable oil, water

Time: 15 to 20 minutes

Preparation: To make soap clay, use a grater to grate white bars of soap until you have approximately 3 cups. Add 1/4 cup of water, and knead until you have the consistency of modeling dough. Store in an airtight bag until ready for use.

At each child's place, lay out a large piece of wax paper and a length of yarn about 8 inches long. Have kids rub a few drops of vegetable oil on their hands, and then give them a portion of the soap clay.

Encourage kids to mold their clay into the shape of a dove. Then show them how to take a piece of yarn, fold it in half, and knot it together. Help kids gently push the knotted ends into the top of their soap doves. Let the doves dry overnight.

After kids wash up, review the story from Matthew 3:1-17. Then

ASK:

- **What happened right after Jesus was baptized?**
- **How do you think the people watching felt when they saw God's Spirit coming down like a dove?**

SAY: **Jesus showed us how important baptism is. When Jesus was baptized, God sent his Spirit like a dove and spoke to Jesus. He reminded the world that Jesus is his Son. As his Son, he washed away our sins! When you take your soap dove home, be sure to tell your family the story of the dove—and then "wash" away your sins together!**

notes

Bible Application

▶ ***NO PREP***
▶ ***ALLERGY ALERT***

Prepare the Way

Children will think about ways to prepare their hearts for Jesus.

Supplies: Bible, 2-quart pitcher of water, sweetened soft-drink mix, paper cups, mixing spoon

Time: 5 to 10 minutes

Preparation: none

Set the pitcher of water on a table, and have kids gather around.

ASK:

- **When was a time you got ready for a special visitor or guest?**
- **What are some ways we could use water to prepare for a visitor?**

SAY: **John the Baptist used water to help people prepare for Jesus.** Read aloud from Matthew 3:1-6.

ASK:

- **What did John the Baptist use water for?**
- **Why did John want people to be ready for Jesus?**
- **How can we prepare our hearts to love Jesus?**

SAY: **John the Baptist wanted people to know that Jesus is the Son of God. And John knew that people needed to be ready to accept Jesus' love into their hearts. We want our hearts to welcome Jesus, too. Let's pray.**

PRAY: **Dear God, thank you for sending John the Baptist to help people get ready for Jesus. Help us prepare our hearts for Jesus, too. Amen.**

SAY: **Now let's use this water to prepare a special treat!** Mix the drink and serve it in paper cups. You may wish to give each child a small packet of soft-drink mix to take home as a reminder to prepare for Jesus.

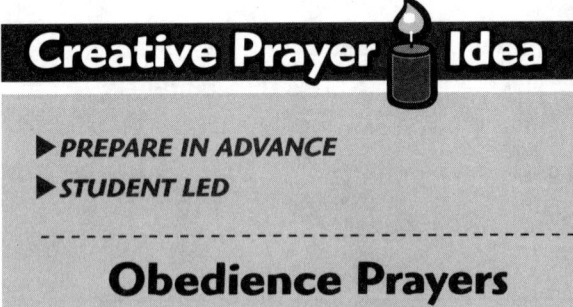

Creative Prayer Idea

▶ *PREPARE IN ADVANCE*
▶ *STUDENT LED*

Obedience Prayers

Children will learn to follow Jesus' act of obedience.

Supplies: Bible

Time: 10 to 15 minutes

Preparation: Arrange for kids to visit the pastor at the pulpit or lectern for this activity.

Gather children in the worship area. Have the pastor or children's minister stand at the pulpit or lectern and SAY: **Most of the time, I stand here to speak to the congregation. I read from the Bible and teach about Jesus, the Son of God. And I lead us all in prayer. But today it's your turn to pray.**

Read aloud Matthew 3:13-17. Explain that even Jesus, the Son of God, obeyed God.

Have children form groups of three, and allow them five minutes to brainstorm about ways to obey God—going to church, honoring their parents, praying, being kind to others, or reading the Bible, for example. Then tell each group to think of a special prayer that asks God to help us with that one way to obey him. They might write a song or poem and each say one line, or conduct a moment of silence. Allow each group to present their prayers from the pulpit.

Snack

▶ *PREPARE IN ADVANCE*
▶ *ALLERGY ALERT*

Locusts and Honey

Children will experience the faith of John the Baptist.

Supplies: Bible, blindfolds, lunch bags, various snacks, Gummi worms, bug stickers (optional)

Time: 5 to 10 minutes

Preparation: Fill 3 or 4 lunch bags with various edible treats children will like, such as cereal, chocolate candy bars, or potato chips. Place the Gummi worms in a bag as well, but set it aside for the end of the activity.

Blindfold several volunteers and have each of them take turns reaching into the bag and selecting a treat. Let them smell, taste, and eat the edible treats. Take off the blindfolds, and ask each one to guess what it was that he or she ate.

ASK:

- **What if, instead of the chocolate bar, I gave you chocolate-covered ants?**

SAY: **Believe it or not, there are some places where that's considered a treat! I'm sure you've all had a time you didn't want to eat something**

on your plate. But here's a secret: You usually don't care about those things when you're focused on something more important. Read aloud Matthew 3:1-6.

ASK:

- ◆ **What did John the Baptist eat?**
- ◆ **What do you think was most important in John the Baptist's life?**
- ◆ **What did John do to show what was most important to him?**

SAY: **John loved God and he loved people. Even Jesus asked to be baptized by John. And John didn't die from eating bugs—God took care of him in the desert. God takes care of those who know that Jesus is the Son of God. So the next time you're tempted to worry about what you're going to eat or wear, change your focus to the Son of God and see how well he takes care of your needs. Now let's focus on Jesus-fand eat worms!**

Pass out Gummi worms to each child. You may want to have bug stickers available for any children with dietary restrictions.

Movie Clip

Toy Story

Movie Title: *Toy Story* (G)

Start Time: 8 minutes, 47 seconds

Where to Begin: Woody says to the army toys, "Sergeant, establish a recon post downstairs."

Where to End: The kids run out of the bedroom, and the closet door opens.

Plot: A new toy threatens to take over the most favored status of Cowboy Woody. In this clip all the toys work together to spy on Andy, their owner, and see what new toys will be joining them in Andy's room.

Review: Many children haven't considered why they should anticipate Christ's return, so this clip provides the emotional connection to help them think about what's in store for them as Christians.

Supplies: Bible

Discussion

After setting up the clip, SAY: **Think of two faces you can make: One is what you look like before vacation, and one is before you take a test at school. Find partners to share your faces. But don't tell them which is which! Let them guess.**

Allow a few minutes for children to interact.

SAY: **Anticipation can be good, and it can be bad! Let's watch how the toys in this movie anticipate and prepare for the arrival of the new toy in the house.**

Show the clip, and then SAY: **I know, you want to see their reaction, don't you? It's hard to wait sometimes. Many people in Jesus' day were waiting for the Messiah, the Son of God. Many people thought John was the Son of God, so they came to follow him. Listen to what John said.** Read aloud Matthew 3:1-11.

ASK:

- ◆ **How do you think the people felt when they heard that John was not the one they were looking for?**

- **What if I told you that at any second, Jesus could come back to meet us? How would you feel?**
- **What would your face look like?**

Allow kids to show their expressions. SAY: **The toys in the movie were afraid. John might have been anxious to know what would happen next! But we can rest assured that ▷JESUS IS GOD'S SON, and he is coming again!**

Preschool Story

▶*NO PREP*

Bible Point: ▷**JESUS IS GOD'S SON.**

Supplies: Bible, large blue sheet or tablecloth, feather

Time: 15 to 20 minutes

Preparation: none

A Proud Father

Spread the sheet on the floor. Have children sit in a circle around the sheet. Open your Bible to Matthew 3, and show children the words. SAY: **Our Bible story takes place at the Jordan River.** Have children hold on to the edge of the sheet and gently make waves up and down.

John the Baptist told many people about God. John told people to get ready for God's Son and to do things that make God happy. Anytime someone said yes to wanting to make God happy, John would wash that person in the river.

Have children grab the sheet with both hands, stand up, and lift it over their heads. Let children make waves for a minute and then set the sheet back on the ground and sit down.

SAY: **Jesus came to where John the Baptist was washing people. Jesus wanted everyone to know that he loved to make God happy, so he asked John to baptize him.**

Have children grab the sheet with both hands, stand up, and lift it over their heads. Let children make waves for a minute and then set the sheet back on the ground and sit down.

SAY: **Then God wanted to let Jesus know how happy Jesus made him. God sent a dove to Jesus and told everyone that ▷JESUS IS GOD'S SON and that Jesus made him very happy.**

ASK:

- **How do you think Jesus felt hearing that he made God happy?**
- **How do you feel when your parents say nice things to you?**

SAY: **Let's all say nice things to each other right now!** Hold up the feather and SAY: **I'll blow this feather. When it lands on someone, I'll tell one thing about that person that makes me happy. Then the person who has the feather will blow the feather to someone else and tell something that has made him or her happy about that person. We'll play until everyone has had the feather.** You may need to help children and prompt them when needed.

That was fun! We all said some very nice things about each other. God wanted to tell the world that ▷JESUS IS GOD'S SON and that Jesus made his Father happy. When we follow Jesus, we can also become children of God, and that makes God happy, too!

BIBLE STORY

Jesus Is Tempted

For the Leader

When children discover that Jesus faced Satan and temptation, their first reaction might be that Jesus could resist because Jesus can do anything. But Jesus didn't resist Satan just to prove to people how superhuman he is. Just the opposite: Jesus wants us to know that he understands our weaknesses and our tendencies toward sin. His successfully overcoming temptation shows us another reason we should focus our lives on God.

With the activities in this lesson, help children understand that this Bible story shows that Jesus understands the struggles we all face. He knows what we're going through. And he showed that God can help us overcome every trial or temptation.

Key Scriptures

Luke 4:1-13

Hebrews 2:18

James 4:7-8

Bible Verse

"Since he himself has gone through suffering and testing, he is able to help us when we are being tested" (Hebrews 2:18).

Bible Experience

▶ *PREPARE IN ADVANCE*

Bible Point: ▷ **WE CAN RESIST TEMPTATION.**

Children will understand the story of Jesus' temptation.

Supplies: Bible, craft sticks, red and green construction paper, safety scissors, tape

Time: 10 to 15 minutes

Preparation: You'll need one craft stick for each child.

Give each child a craft stick and one sheet each of green and red paper. Have kids cut out 3-inch circles from each color and tape one to each end of their sticks to make a stop-go traffic light. Read aloud Luke 4:1-13.

SAY: **Did you know that Satan tempted Jesus? Jesus was in the desert for a very long time without any food. Satan tried to get him to do three things. He tried to get Jesus to turn rocks into bread. He tried to get Jesus to worship him. He tried to get Jesus to prove he was the Son of God. Each time, Jesus thought about what the Bible said to do and said no to Satan.**

ASK:

◆ **Why do you think Jesus was tempted?**

Read aloud Hebrews 2:18. SAY: **Just as Jesus resisted Satan's temptation, ▷ WE CAN RESIST TEMPTATION, too.**

OK, let's put our traffic lights to work. I'll yell out some actions, and you hold a red light or a green light, depending on whether you should do that thing.

Yell out some actions—both good and bad—such as watch six hours of television each day, listen to your parents, eat candy for dinner every night, gossip, pray for homeless people, and hug your little brother.

SAY: **It's not always easy to resist temptation. But Jesus knows what that's like, and we can follow his example and rely on God's Word.**

Additional Topics List

This lesson can be used to help children discover... Friendship, Obedience, Popularity, and Temptation.

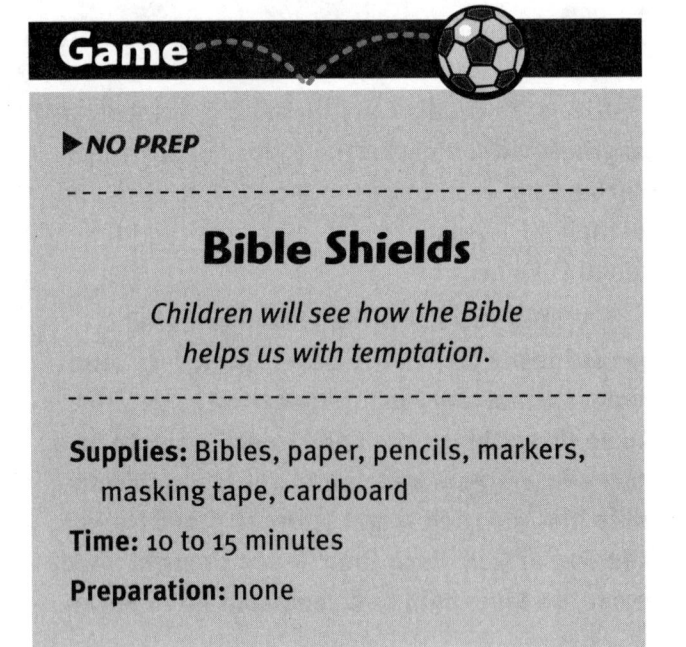

Game

▶ *NO PREP*

Bible Shields

Children will see how the Bible helps us with temptation.

Supplies: Bibles, paper, pencils, markers, masking tape, cardboard

Time: 10 to 15 minutes

Preparation: none

Have children form pairs, nonreaders pairing up with readers. Have the pairs number off from one to two. Have the ones read aloud Luke 4:1-6; then have the twos read aloud Luke 4:7-13. SAY: **Let's play a game to remind us that we can use God's Word to resist temptation.**

Have the ones gather on one side of the room. Give them paper and pencils. Tell them to write down or draw temptations they face every day. Have children crumple each temptation into a paper wad.

As the ones are working, have the twos gather on the other side of the room. Give them markers, paper, masking tape, and large pieces of cardboard. Have them make Bible shields by writing "The Bible" on one side of the cardboard and taping a paper wad to the other side to form a handle.

When you say "go," have the twos try to cross to the other side of the room and back as the ones try to pelt them with the paper-wad temptations. The twos may use their Bible shields as protection. Then have the ones and twos switch roles to play again. After the game,

ASK:

- **How were the paper wads like temptations in real life?**
- **How did the cardboard shields protect you in our game?**
- **How can the Bible protect you from real temptations?**

SAY: **Jesus resisted temptation. And we can resist temptation when we read the Bible for comfort and to learn.** Close with a prayer thanking God for giving us his Word.

Craft

▶ *PREPARE IN ADVANCE*

Desert Drawings

Children will make stained-glass-window pictures.

Supplies: Bible, crayons, fine sandpaper, iron, ironing surface, white paper

Time: 10 to 15 minutes

Preparation: Plug in the iron, and turn it on to medium-high heat. Make sure it's in an out-of-the-way place and is supervised by an adult.

Have kids use the crayons to draw pictures on the sandpaper depicting Jesus' temptation. Tell them to press down firmly and use lots of crayon. Then have them take their papers to the ironing area. Help each child place the sandpaper drawing face up on the ironing surface and lay the white paper on top. Help kids iron the paper until the crayon picture can be seen showing through the paper. Tell children to hold up the finished picture to a window to let the light shine through, giving it a stained-glass effect.

After children have finished their pictures, read aloud Luke 4:1-13.

ASK:

- **How did God help Jesus turn from temptation?**
- **How can God help you when you're tempted?**

SAY: **The sandpaper we drew on reminds us of the time Jesus spent in the desert being tested by Satan. We can use Scripture to fight Satan's temptations. And we can ask for God's help. When Satan is tempting us, we can remember that God is always there to help us resist.**

notes

Bible Application

▶ *FOR LARGE GROUPS*
▶ *PREPARE IN ADVANCE*
▶ *ALLERGY ALERT*

Tempting Maze

Children will learn that temptation takes them away from God.

Supplies: Bible, items to make a life-size maze (blankets, furniture, string, scissors), wrapped candies, paper, pencil, watch with a second hand

Time: 10 to 15 minutes

Preparation: In a large room, arrange the furniture and blankets to form a maze. Create at least three "forks" in the maze that require the kids to choose a path. Make one of the paths for each fork a dead end. Scatter the wrapped candies at the beginning of each dead end.

SAY: **Each of you will get two chances to go through this maze. The object is to complete the maze as quickly as possible. I'll time you to see if you can beat your first time.** Let children take turns going through the maze. Record their times. When everyone is finished,

ASK:

- **What made it easier the second time through the maze?**
- **How many times did you stop the first time?**
- **What made you want to stop the first time?**

SAY: **The candy might have tempted you to turn toward it, but each time it led to a dead end.**

ASK:

- **What are some things in your life that you feel tempted to do?**

SAY: **We all feel tempted sometimes. When your parents say it's time for bed, you might be tempted to stay up. When your teacher blows the whistle to end recess, you might be tempted to pretend you didn't hear it.**

Read aloud Hebrews 2:18. SAY: **The real treat is not to give in to temptation—it's to follow Jesus!** Distribute the candies from the maze, and pray that God helps everyone in your class resist temptation.

Creative Prayer Idea

▶ *PREPARE IN ADVANCE*
▶ *ALLERGY ALERT*

Cupcake Prayer

Children will decorate a snack as they pray.

Supplies: cupcakes, knife, chocolate or rainbow sprinkles, napkins

Time: 5 to 10 minutes

Preparation: You'll need one cupcake for every two children. Set the sprinkles where everyone can reach them.

Have children form pairs. Give each pair a cupcake. SAY: **The cupcake looks mighty tasty, doesn't it? But the question is, who gets it? Take a minute to convince your partner that you deserve to have the cupcake.**

After a few minutes, SAY: **Do you really need the cupcake? Now tell your partner why he or she deserves the cupcake more than you.**

We like to use the word *tempted* when we talk about sweets because eating too many sweets is unhealthy. Cut the cupcakes in half. **We can resist temptation by not having too much. That means sharing!**

Tell kids before they eat their cupcake to think of something they do too much of. Allow each child to put some sprinkles on each other's cupcakes as they ask God to help them cut back on their excess habit. Close by praising God and saying that you can never get enough of him. Allow kids to eat their snack.

Object Lesson

▶ *FOR YOUNGER CHILDREN*
▶ *NO PREP*

Shoo, Satan!

Children will learn that prayer helps them turn away from Satan.

Supplies: Bible, water, paper cups, small containers of black pepper, containers of dishwashing liquid

Time: 5 to 10 minutes

Preparation: none

Have children form pairs, and give each pair a cup of water, a small container of black pepper, and a container of dishwashing liquid.

SAY: **Take turns shaking pepper onto the surface of the water. As you shake the pepper, tell your partner the wrong things Satan wants us to do—lie, steal, disobey our parents, and swear, for example.**

After a few seconds, have children stop shaking the pepper.

ASK:

◆ **How does the water look?**

Read aloud James 4:7-8, and then SAY: **When we pray, we're calling on God's power to take all the sin out of our hearts and to send Satan running. Pray with your partner, and ask God to forgive you for the bad things you've done. When you're both finished, say "Shoo, Satan!"**

After children have prayed, SAY: **Now take the dishwashing liquid and add one tiny drop to your cups.**

ASK:

◆ **What happened to the pepper?**

◆ **How is that like what happens to sin when we pray?**

SAY: **Just as the pepper "ran away" when you added soap, Satan runs away when we pray. Prayer is powerful!**

Close with everyone yelling, "Shoo, Satan!"

Movie Clip

Toy Story 2

Movie Title: *Toy Story 2* (G)

Start Time: 36 minutes, 4 seconds

Where to Begin: The Roundup Gang begins to convince Woody to go with them to Japan.

Where to End: Woody says he will join the gang and go to Japan with them.

Plot: Woody is stolen from his home by a selfish toy collector. The other members of the collection try to convince Woody to join them for display in a Japanese museum.

Review: Use this scene to help children become aware of the hooks Satan uses to bait us and turn our attention away from God. If we follow Jesus' example and look to God's Word, we will be able to overcome temptation.

Supplies: red construction paper, pencils, children's scissors, black or brown chenille wire

Preparation: none

Discussion

After setting up and showing the clip,

ASK:

◆ **What bait was used to hook Woody?**

◆ **Why was it tempting for him?**

◆ **What kinds of things tempt you?**

SAY: **Jesus had made up his mind ahead of time that he would not take Satan's bait. God wants us to resist temptation, too. Think about the things that tempt you. Decide ahead of time not to take the bait. That will make it easier to say no!**

Direct children to draw and cut four 3-inch worms from red construction paper. Allow children to write one thing on each worm that Satan has used in their life as bait. Give each child a chenille wire to bend and form a hook. Have children poke the chenille hooks through their paper worms.

SAY: **Don't take the bait of Satan—he just wants to trap you. God will always be there to help us resist temptation. We just need to call out to God and remember God's Word.**

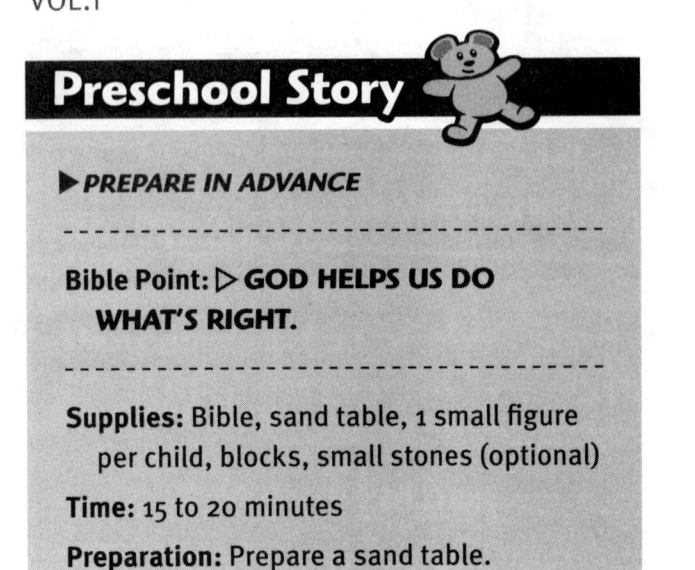

Preschool Story

▶ ***PREPARE IN ADVANCE***

Bible Point: ▷ **GOD HELPS US DO WHAT'S RIGHT.**

Supplies: Bible, sand table, 1 small figure per child, blocks, small stones (optional)

Time: 15 to 20 minutes

Preparation: Prepare a sand table.

In the Desert

Have children gather at the sand table. Give each child one small figure and a pile of blocks. Open your Bible to Luke 4, and show children the words.

SAY: **Today's Bible story tells us that ▷ GOD HELPS US DO WHAT'S RIGHT. Let's find out how God helped Jesus do what's right.**

Jesus had grown to be a man and was about to begin teaching people about God. Before Jesus began, he went to the desert to pray. Encourage children to walk their fingers through the sand.

Jesus stayed in the desert for 40 days. That's a really long time! And the whole time Jesus was in the desert, he didn't eat anything so he could concentrate on talking with and listening to God. On a day when Jesus was very hungry, Satan (who is also called the devil) came to tempt Jesus. Satan told Jesus to turn a stone into bread so Jesus could eat something and feel better. Encourage children to place blocks or stones in front of their figures.

Jesus knew God didn't want him to eat anything yet, and Jesus always obeyed God and did what was right. Even when it's difficult, ▷ GOD HELPS US DO WHAT'S RIGHT.

Jesus told Satan a verse from the Bible that says, "People do not live by bread alone"—Jesus said no to Satan. Encourage children to shout "No!"

Then Satan took Jesus to the top of a very tall mountain. Encourage children to make a "mountain" out of sand and place the figure on top. **Jesus could see for miles in every direction. Satan told Jesus he could have all the land, people, and cities in the world if Jesus would just bow down and worship him instead of God. But Jesus knew that he should worship only God. Jesus told Satan another verse from the Bible: "You must worship the Lord your God and serve only him." God helped Jesus to make the right choice and say no to Satan.** Encourage children to shout "No!"

Then Satan took Jesus to the highest point in the Temple, and they both looked down. Encourage children to build a tall tower with blocks and then place their figure on top of the blocks. **Satan told Jesus to jump off. Satan said that if Jesus was really the Son of God, then God would save Jesus and not let him get hurt. But Jesus knew jumping off the building wasn't a smart choice. Again Jesus told Satan a verse from the Bible: "You must not test the Lord." So Jesus told Satan no again!** Encourage children to shout "No!" as loud as they can.

Finally, Satan left.

God helped Jesus do what's right, and ▷ GOD HELPS US DO WHAT'S RIGHT, too.

ASK:

- **How did God help Jesus do the right thing?**
- **When is it hard for you to do the right thing?**
- **How can you trust God to help you do the right thing?**

BIBLE STORY

Water Into Wine

For the Leader

It wasn't exactly one of Jesus' greatest, life-saving miracles. But it was his first. For the first time, at a wedding in Cana, Jesus revealed his glory to others, and immediately his disciples believed. It was simple and effective. And it was the catalyst that sent a chain reaction of faith all over the world.

Make sure your students don't see Jesus' first miracle as a mere magic trick but rather as a true miracle perfectly timed to give people a reason to follow God.

Key Scriptures

John 2:1-11

Romans 1:20; 8:28

Bible Verse

"For ever since the world was created, people have seen the earth and sky. Through everything God made, they can clearly see his invisible qualities—his eternal power and divine nature. So they have no excuse for not knowing God" (Romans 1:20).

Bible Experience

▶ *PREPARE IN ADVANCE*

▶ *ALLERGY ALERT*

Bible Point: ▷ **JESUS CAN DO MIRACLES.**

Children will drink water that has been turned into a fruit drink and understand that Jesus can do real miracles.

Supplies: Bible; 2 clear pitchers; water; red, sweetened fruit drink mix; spoon; cups; table

Time: 10 to 15 minutes

Preparation: You'll need one cup for each child. Before the meeting, place the red drink mix in the bottom of one pitcher. Fill the other pitcher with water, and then set both pitchers on top of a table.

Open your Bible to John 2:1-11, and show the kids the words. SAY: **Jesus attended a wedding once, and after a while the people ran out of wine. The guests had nothing left to drink, and the party was going to be ruined. So Jesus used his power to turn some large containers of water** (hold up the pitcher of clear water) **into wine.** Pour the water into the other pitcher. The water will turn red as it combines with the drink mix. Hold it up for all to see.

ASK:

◆ **What do you think the people thought when Jesus turned water into wine?**

◆ **What other miracles did Jesus do?**

SAY: **What I showed you wasn't a real miracle. I had red drink mix in a pitcher. When it mixed with water, it turned red. When Jesus turned water into wine, it was a true miracle.**

In fact, the people at the wedding were amazed because the wine Jesus made tasted better than any other wine the host served.

Read aloud Romans 1:20. SAY: ▷**JESUS CAN DO MIRACLES because Jesus is God's Son—the creator of everything! Jesus did a lot of miracles when he lived on earth. Let's tell everyone about Jesus, who is God's Son and the creator of everything.**

Quickly stir the drink mix in the pitcher, and give each child a very small amount in a cup. Ask children to wait until you pray before drinking. PRAY: **Jesus, your miracles show that you are truly God. Please help us to tell others so that they will believe in you. In your name we pray, amen.**

Additional Topics List

This lesson can be used to help children discover... Discipleship and Holiness.

Game

▶ *FOR SMALL GROUPS*
▶ *NO PREP*

Guess Who?

Children will play a guessing game.

Supplies: Bible, blanket

Time: 5 to 10 minutes

Preparation: none

Have children form groups of three or four. Make sure each group includes at least one older child. Choose one group to come forward. Tell the others to turn around. Have the chosen group hold up a blanket in front of them, and then let the others turn around. The other teams have to try to guess the hidden team's identity. Allow each group a chance behind the blanket.

ASK:

- **How did you know who was who?**
- **Do you think you'd know your classmates if you saw them on the street? Explain.**
- **How do you think people knew who Jesus was?**

SAY: **Jesus didn't look any different from other men. But he could do special things called miracles to help us believe that he is God's Son, the Savior God promised.** Read aloud John 2:1-11.

Encourage kids to share their knowledge of Jesus by telling others the story of his miracle.

Craft

▶ *PREPARE IN ADVANCE*

Water to Wine

Children will make pots to remind them of Jesus' miracle at Cana.

Supplies: yogurt cups, white paper, scissors, paintbrushes, sponges cut into strips, paint smocks, glue, purplish-red acrylic paint, black or gray acrylic paint

Time: 20 to 25 minutes

Preparation: You'll need one yogurt cup for each child. Cut white paper into $2\frac{1}{2}$x4-inch strips. Set out one yogurt cup, one paintbrush, two pieces of white paper, and one sponge strip per child. Set out the rest of the supplies, and open your classroom windows for proper ventilation when working with acrylic paints.

Have each child put on a paint smock. Tell kids to glue the white paper around a yogurt cup and paint the inside of the yogurt cups with the purplish-red paint, leaving about 1 inch of white space at the top. Then they can paint the outside of the cups with black or gray paint by dipping the end of the sponge strip into the paint and gently pressing it to the cup all over for a rough, clay-type effect. When their "water pots" are dry, have kids find a partner and take turns telling the story from John 2:1-11 to each other.

ASK:

◆ **Who gave Jesus the power to do miracles?**

SAY: **If we pour clear water into our water pots, it will look like wine because of the purplish-red paint. This will help us tell the story of Jesus' miracle at Cana. Jesus can do miracles, and he can help us with all our problems, no matter how big or how small, if we ask him for help.**

n
o
t
e
s

Bible Application

▶ ***NO PREP***

Signs of God

Children will walk outside and look for God's miracles.

Supplies: Bible, index cards, pencils

Time: 10 to 15 minutes

Preparation: none

Take kids to an outdoor area, and have them spread out and sit down on the grass or a sidewalk. Be sure to bring a Bible with you. Have kids close their eyes and listen quietly for signs of life. They might hear their own breathing, birds chirping, footsteps, or voices in the distance.

Let kids listen for one minute, and then have them open their eyes. Distribute cards and pencils, and ask kids to write down what they heard.

ASK:

◆ **What signs of life did you hear?**

◆ **What sounds did you hear that you don't usually notice? Why don't you hear those sounds all the time?**

SAY: **We can read in the Bible all about how Jesus can perform God's miracles. We can see miracles every day. When we pay attention, we can see and hear signs of creation everywhere. God's Word says creation is a witness to his existence. Let's read what it says.**

Invite a volunteer to read Romans 1:20 aloud.

ASK:

◆ **How did the sounds you heard give witness to God?**

- **What are other things that give witness to God?**
- **How can you help people pay attention to God's miracles?**

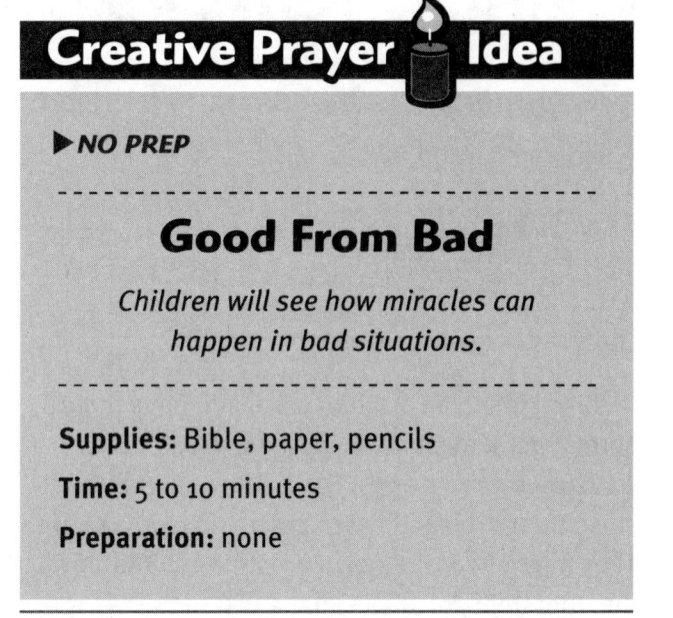

Creative Prayer Idea

▶ *NO PREP*

Good From Bad

Children will see how miracles can happen in bad situations.

Supplies: Bible, paper, pencils

Time: 5 to 10 minutes

Preparation: none

Give each child a sheet of paper and a pencil. SAY: **Let's begin this activity by writing down all the terrible, awful things that might happen to someone your age. Some can be serious things, like falling on ice. And some can be silly things that would probably never happen, like a meteorite crashing into your bedroom.**

Give kids about five minutes to each write about 15 terrible things that might happen. When the time is up, have volunteers read items from their lists to the rest of the class.

Read aloud Romans 8:28. SAY: **It doesn't matter who you are or where you live. At some point, something bad will probably happen to you. But it's just as true that good things will happen to everybody at some time. God has promised us that no matter what happens, he'll be working in our lives.**

Read aloud John 2:1-11. SAY: **Jesus performed a miracle, and he turned a bad situation into a good one. He can do that for you, too.** Give children several minutes to hold their lists over their hearts and quietly think of ways God might turn those situations into good ones. Ask children to pray for God's control over their lives and for a closer relationship with his Son, Jesus.

Worship Prompt Idea

▶ *NO PREP*

The Power of God

Children will celebrate Jesus' power to do miracles.

Supplies: Bibles

Time: 5 to 10 minutes

Preparation: none

Have children form pairs and read John 2:1-11. Then gather everyone in a circle. Lead children in the following song to the tune of the chorus of "Our God Is an Awesome God." After the first verse, have kids share what they've seen Jesus do in the lives of their friends and families. After the second verse, have the children mention ways Jesus will care for them in the future.

VERSE 1

Believe in Jesus' power.

He can do anything.

He brings the dead to life.

Believe in Jesus' power.

VERSE 2

Don't be afraid, my friend.

The Lord will care for you.

Believe in Jesus' love.

Believe in Jesus' power.

Remind children that Jesus still performs miracles in their lives every day.

Movie Clip

Indian in the Cupboard

Movie Title: *Indian in the Cupboard* (PG)

Start Time: 19 minutes, 30 seconds

Where to Begin: Omri pulls a box of toys out from under his bed.

Where to End: Omri closes the cupboard after the toys turn to look at him.

Plot: Omri discovers that his tiny figurines have become real. He shuts the cupboard door when they stop fighting each other to look at him.

Review: Use this clip to teach that Jesus can and still does perform miracles. Jesus' miracle shows his willingness to make the ordinary into something extraordinary.

Discussion

After setting up the clip, SAY: **Let's watch a scene from *Indian in the Cupboard*. Omri has found out that his new cupboard can change things. He wants to see what will happen when he puts toys inside it.** Show the clip, and then ASK:

- **How did Omri feel when he saw his toys change?**

SAY: **We might feel like Omri did when we see God's power—excited, happy, surprised, and even scared. I want you to listen to our Bible story and think about how you would feel if you saw Jesus perform a miracle.**

Read aloud John 2:1-11. Tell kids to imagine that they are the servant who is pouring water as Jesus asked.

SAY: **Jesus turned ordinary water into something extraordinary. It wasn't a trick like the special effects in the movie. It was a real miracle. We can be grateful that miracles are real and still happen today. Jesus loves us enough to change our ordinary lives into something extraordinary.**

Preschool Story

▶ ***PREPARE IN ADVANCE***

▶ ***ALLERGY ALERT***

Bible Point: ▷JESUS CAN DO MIRACLES.

Supplies: Bible, 1-inch-wide sponge brush for each child, 1 small bowl of buttermilk per 2 children, pastel construction paper, colored chalk, powdered drink mix, spoon, opaque pitcher, 1 cup of water per child, craft table, vinyl tablecloth

Time: 15 to 20 minutes

Preparation: Cover the table with a vinyl tablecloth. Pour buttermilk into bowls. Put the powdered drink mix at the bottom of the pitcher. Fill kids' cups with water.

It's a Miracle!

Have children gather at the craft table, and give each child a sponge brush. Have each student dip his or her sponge brush into the buttermilk and smear the buttermilk onto the construction paper, covering the entire page. Then have kids draw a picture with the colored chalk directly onto the wet buttermilk surface. The buttermilk will keep the chalk drawing from smearing or smudging. Allow the drawings to dry.

Have kids form a circle away from the table and sit down. Give each child a cup of water.

Open your Bible to John 2, and show children the words. SAY: **This story tells about the very first miracle Jesus did. Jesus was at a wedding with his mother and some of his followers. Everyone was having a great time at the wedding party, until it happened. All of a sudden they were out of drinks! The special wine they had been drinking was gone.** Have children pretend to hold a glass upside down and look up inside.

Jesus' mother, Mary, told Jesus about it. Then she told the servants to do whatever Jesus said to do. Jesus told the servants to take some empty water jars and fill them up with water. Let's fill up our pitcher with water. Encourage each child to pour his or her cup into the pitcher. Then give the water a little stir.

Then Jesus told them to take a cup of water and give it to the man in charge of the wedding party. When the servants did this, the man in charge couldn't believe what he was tasting. It was the best drink at the entire party! It wasn't water anymore; Jesus had turned the water into a very yummy-tasting drink.

▷**JESUS CAN DO MIRACLES! This was Jesus' very first miracle, and his followers saw that they could trust him. They believed in Jesus. We can believe in Jesus, too. We can also trust Jesus. Let's taste our drink now and see how it tastes.** Give each child a cup filled halfway with the drink.

Tell children to go and get the buttermilk pictures they made before the story.

ASK:

- **Did you think you would be able to draw on the wet buttermilk? Why or why not?**
- **Do you think the people at the wedding believed Jesus could turn water into wine? Why or why not?**
- **Do you think the people believed in Jesus after he turned the water into wine? Why or why not?**
- **What do you believe about Jesus?**

notes

BIBLE STORY

Jesus and Nicodemus

For the Leader

To Nicodemus, what Jesus was saying must have seemed a little crazy. How can you be born *again*? For Jesus, it was simple: Physical birth is for this life, and spiritual birth is for eternal life.

Here are some lessons designed to help children understand that Jesus' sole purpose was to have people follow him to heaven eternally. Help kids realize that when they express their love for Jesus, they are making the commitment for an eternal lifetime.

Key Scriptures

John 3:1-21; 9:5

Bible Verse

"God loved the world so much that he gave his one and only Son, so that everyone who believes in him will not perish but have eternal life" (John 3:16).

Bible Experience

▶ ***PREPARE IN ADVANCE***

Bible Point: ▷**JESUS GIVES US LIFE IN HEAVEN.**

Children will clean dull pennies and talk about eternal life.

Supplies: Bible, dull pennies, plastic tablecloth, salt, water, vinegar, 2 containers, measuring spoons, medicine dropper, moist paper towels

Time: 10 to 15 minutes

Preparation: Spread the plastic tablecloth on a table. In one of the containers, make a solution of 1 teaspoon of salt and 1 tablespoon of water. Place several tablespoons of vinegar into the other container.

Give each child a penny, and tell children to set their pennies on the tablecloth. Have a volunteer use the medicine dropper to put a drop of the salt solution on each penny. Then have another volunteer put a drop of vinegar on each penny. The dark, dull film on the pennies should come off, resulting in bright, shiny pennies.

Open your Bible to John 3:1-17. SAY: **Today we'll learn about a man who wanted to know how he could have eternal life. His name was Nicodemus.**

Nicodemus knew Jesus could only do the miracles he did if God was with him. Jesus told Nicodemus that he could only see the kingdom of God if he was "born again."

ASK:

◆ **What do you think it means to be born again?**

SAY: **When someone believes in Jesus, he or she becomes a new person. When we become new people, it means we've changed. Because we believe in Jesus and become new people, we can have eternal life. ▷JESUS GIVES US LIFE IN HEAVEN. Let's take a look at our pennies and see what has happened to them.**

Have kids go back to the tablecloth and each pick up a penny. Pass out moist paper towels, and have kids wipe off the pennies.

ASK:

- ◆ **What does your penny look like now?**
- ◆ **Why do you think the pennies changed?**

SAY: **Just as the solution we used got rid of the dark, dull stuff on these pennies, Jesus can take away the sin in your life when you believe in him. And that will make you a new person. You will be "born again." Jesus said, "God loved the world so much that he gave his one and only Son, so that everyone who believes in him will not perish but have eternal life" (John 3:16). Let's say that verse together because it's worth remembering. ▷JESUS GIVES US ETERNAL LIFE IN HEAVEN if we'll only believe in him.**

Song & Connect

Use "God So Loved the World" (track 8, *it: Innovative Tools for Children's Ministry: New Testament* CD) to help reinforce the Bible Point, **▷JESUS GIVES US LIFE IN HEAVEN.**

Encourage each child to choose a different family from the church directory to pray for. Have kids write the families' names on index cards, tape them to the floor, and then play the song as you "visit" each family and pray that they all have a living friendship with Jesus.

Additional Topics List

This lesson can be used to help children discover... God's Love and Heaven.

Game

▶ ***NO PREP***

Slap 'n' Clap

Children will experience God's love for them as they receive a running round of standing ovations.

Supplies: Bible

Time: 5 to 10 minutes

Preparation: none

Have kids stand in a line, all facing one direction. Ask each person to hold out his or her right hand, palm up. Explain that the first person in line will run down the line, slapping the hands of others along the way. When a person's hand has been slapped, that person will start applauding the runner and saying over and over, "God loves [name of runner]." As each person's hand gets slapped, he or she will join the others in applauding and cheering for the runner. When the runner has reached the end of the line, the next person will run.

Continue until everyone has had a chance to run, hear affirmations of God's love, and receive a standing ovation from peers.

At the end of the game, discuss the following questions:

- ◆ **How did you feel during this game?**
- ◆ **How do you feel knowing God loves you very much?**

Read aloud John 3:16-17; then

ASK:

◆ **How does Jesus give us life in heaven?**

Ask kids to run the race again. Before kids run, have each runner say one thing he or she loves about God. Then have kids run, clap, and affirm God's love for each runner, applauding as before.

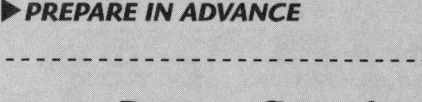

Craft

▶ ***PREPARE IN ADVANCE***

Butterflies Are Beautiful!

Children will create butterfly art to symbolize Jesus' promise of new life.

Supplies: Bible; newspaper; large, white paper; pencils; apple halves; several bright colors of acrylic or tempera paint, plus black, in shallow pans; paintbrushes; markers (optional)

Time: 10 to 15 minutes

Preparation: Cut apples in half horizontally, so the star in the center of the core appears. Cover the work area with newspaper. Put paints into shallow pans.

Give each child a large sheet of white paper and a pencil. Have each child draw the outline of a butterfly (body, head with face, and wings) with a pencil, using up most of the space on the paper. Then have kids go over their outline with black paint or a marker. Help children use the apples to print colors and design the butterfly's wings. Then have kids use another color. Tell them to continue until their butterflies are filled with color.

When children have finished, have them join you. Choose a volunteer to read aloud John 3:1-17. Then

ASK:

◆ **How did God show his love for the world?**

◆ **Why did God send Jesus to our world?**

◆ **How can we have the freedom of eternal life?**

SAY: **Caterpillars make a cocoon around themselves and later burst out in freedom as beautiful butterflies. This is like Jesus' wonderful promise to us: When we die, we will have beautiful new lives in heaven with Jesus forever!** ▷ **JESUS GIVES US LIFE WITH HIM IN HEAVEN.**

Bible Application

▶ ***PREPARE IN ADVANCE***

What Will It Be Like?

Children will write postcards from heaven.

Supplies: Bible, postcards, pens, glue and paper (optional), stamps (optional)

Time: 5 to 10 minutes

Preparation: You may want to see if a local gift shop will donate postcards, or ask congregation members to donate some. Or you can use old ones by gluing blank paper over the writing side. You'll need one postcard for each student.

Hand out postcards and pens. SAY: **Usually people write postcards from a place where they're visiting, but today we'll write postcards to a place where we will be going.** Ask kids to address their postcards to God. Tell them to describe to God what they think heaven will be like. Ask them to tell God about how excited they are to be coming to heaven one day. Then have them tell God about their life on earth and how they are living it so that Jesus will give them a life in heaven. Encourage kids to explain any ways they aren't living for Jesus.

After everyone is finished with their postcards, tell kids to reread what they wrote. Read aloud John 9:5. Challenge kids to write one word in the corner of the postcard that describes a way they can strengthen their relationship with Jesus. Tell kids to keep the postcards in their backpacks and look at them in one week to see if they are holding true to that one word. Option: Give each child a postcard stamp, and have kids address and mail the postcards to themselves!

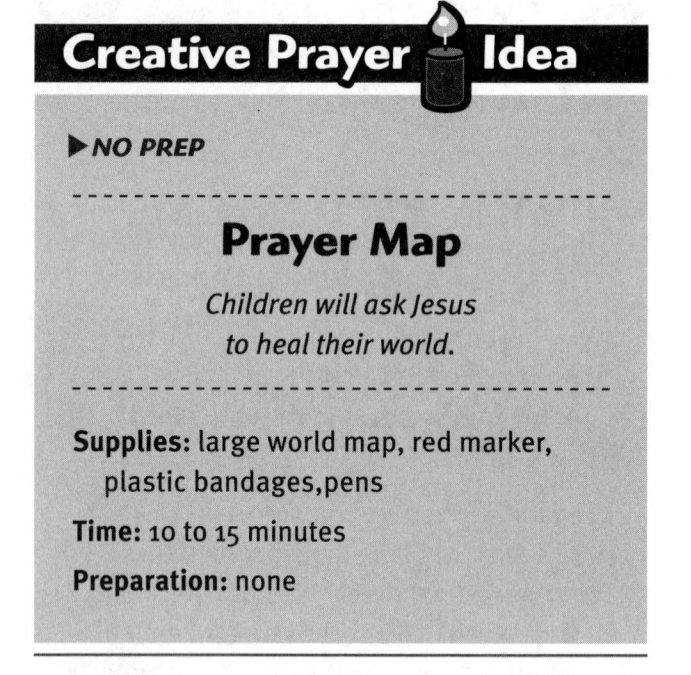

Creative Prayer Idea

▶ *NO PREP*

Prayer Map

Children will ask Jesus to heal their world.

Supplies: large world map, red marker, plastic bandages,pens

Time: 10 to 15 minutes

Preparation: none

Have kids form a circle, and place the map in the middle of the circle. As a group, look at the map and briefly talk about places where poverty, war, violence, oppression, or abuse abound. Use a red marker to put a dot on each country or area you mention.

Distribute plastic bandages and pens. Have each child write a prayer for the world on the bandage. Children may write things such as "God, please help the people in China learn about you" or "Jesus, take away the war in Africa."

Have children take turns praying and then sticking on their bandages. Then join hands around the map and PRAY: **Dear God, we know we live in a broken world. But we also know that Jesus is the light of the world. Please heal the people who experience pain and suffering. Help those who are suffering to know that Jesus gives us all life in heaven. In Jesus' name, amen.**

Worship Prompt Idea

▶ *PREPARE IN ADVANCE*

▶ *FOR LARGE GROUPS*

Heavenly Skies

Children will simulate a starlit sky and worship God in heaven.

Supplies: Bible, flashlight, aluminum pie tin, worship music, CD player, glow-in-the-dark star stickers

Time: 10 to 15 minutes

Preparation: Poke holes in the pie tin.

SAY: **Let's pretend that it's a very dark night and that we're outside looking at the stars.** Darken the room and shine the flashlight through the pie tin to project the "stars" onto the ceiling or a nearby wall.

Look at all those stars! They're bright and twinkling. You know, some people think that heaven is beyond the stars. Sometimes, when people are talking about the sky, they call it the heavens.

ASK:

◆ **Where do you think heaven is?**

◆ **If heaven is God's home, what do you think it's like?**

Read aloud 3:16. SAY: **When we believe in Jesus, he gives us a chance to live in God's home forever. Let's worship God now for providing us a place in heaven. As I play the music, I'll pass around star stickers. Don't stick them anywhere yet! Just listen to the music and praise God for his wonderful creations here on earth. Then praise him for creating heaven for us.**

Turn on the music, and hand each child a star sticker. As the music plays, twirl the pie tin slowly so it looks like the stars are twinkling on the ceiling. Have kids take their stickers home to put in their bedrooms and dream of heaven.

Science Devotion

▶ ***PREPARE IN ADVANCE***

The Light

Children will do an experiment that shows Jesus is the light.

Supplies: Bible, shoe box, construction paper, scissors, tape, flashlight

Time: 10 to 15 minutes

Preparation: Tape a construction-paper cross to the inside of one end of a shoe box. Cut a quarter-size hole opposite the cross. Cut a hole in the lid of the box large enough to insert the end of a flashlight. Cover the top hole with dark paper.

Open your Bible to John 3 and SAY: **Jesus told Nicodemus that the light had come into a dark world. He was trying to get Nicodemus to understand that we need Jesus—who is the Light of the world—so we can live forever with him in heaven. Let's see what Jesus meant.**

Let the children take turns looking in the quarter-size hole inside the box. Ask them what they see. They'll probably say, "Nothing" or "It's too dark." Take the paper off the top hole, and shine a flashlight into the box. Let the kids look through the quarter-size hole. They will be able to see the cross.

ASK:

◆ **Do you think the cross was there the whole time? Explain.**

◆ **What did we need to be able to see it?**

Read aloud John 9:5. SAY: **The cross was there the whole time. But we needed light to see it. The Bible says that we need the Light of the world to have eternal life. We need Jesus!** Shine the flashlight through the hole, and have all kids say with you: **Thank you, Jesus, for being light in the darkness. Amen.**

Preschool Story

▶ ***NO PREP***

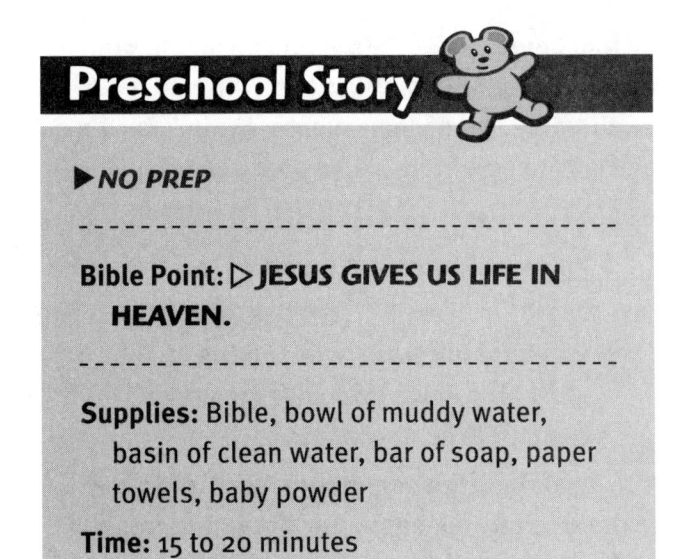

Bible Point: ▷ **JESUS GIVES US LIFE IN HEAVEN.**

Supplies: Bible, bowl of muddy water, basin of clean water, bar of soap, paper towels, baby powder

Time: 15 to 20 minutes

Preparation: none

Fresh and New

Have kids form a circle and sit down near the supplies. Open your Bible to John 3, and show children the words. Tell children they will need to shout, "You can be born again!" when you direct them to. Practice shouting a few times before you tell the story.

SAY: **There once was a man named Nicodemus who was a Jewish teacher. Some people say he might have been afraid to be seen with Jesus, so he sneaked out of his house when it was dark.** Have children stand up, hide their faces as with a cape, and pretend to sneak around the room. After about a minute, direct children back to you.

When he found Jesus, Nicodemus asked him about being God's Son and about the miracles Jesus had performed. Nicodemus also asked how he could get into the kingdom of heaven.

ASK:

- **How do you think you can get into heaven?**

SAY: **Jesus told Nicodemus that to enter God's kingdom, he must be born again.** Have children say, "You can be born again!"

Nicodemus said, "What do you mean, born again? Certainly I can't go back into my mother's tummy and become a baby again." Encourage kids to say, "You can be born again!"

ASK:

- **How would you feel if you were a tiny baby again?**
- **Do you think Jesus was talking about shrinking down into your mommy's tummy? Why or why not?**

SAY: **Babies are something fresh and new. Jesus was talking about our becoming fresh and new.**

When we do bad things, it's kind of like when we get all dirty. Bring out the bowl of muddy water, basin of clean water, bar of soap, paper towels, and baby powder. Invite children to come up, feel the muddy water, and observe how it gets them dirty. Remind children that the bad things we do are like the muddy water and that we need to be made fresh and new. Have children wash their hands and sprinkle a small amount of baby powder on their hands.

When we believe that Jesus is God's Son and ask him to take away the bad things we do, he makes us fresh and new. We start all over, being clean again. That's what Jesus was trying to tell Nicodemus that dark night. But Nicodemus still had a hard time understanding how he could be born again. Encourage kids to shout, "You can be born again!"

Then Jesus told Nicodemus that God loves everyone here on earth so much that he sent Jesus to be born and die for our sins. Now we can have the bad things we do washed away by Jesus. Then someday we'll live forever with him in heaven. ▷JESUS GIVES US LIFE IN HEAVEN with him forever. Jesus wants us to believe in him and be born again. Encourage kids to shout, "You can be born again!"

ASK:

- **How can you be born again?**
- **How does Jesus give us life in heaven?**
- **What do you think heaven will be like?**

notes

BIBLE STORY

The Samaritan Woman

For the Leader

The story of Jesus meeting the Samaritan woman at the well is rich with messages. There are teachable moments in every sentence about sin and redemption, loving others, outreach, God's love, and, of course, knowing Jesus, the Living Water.

Here's a good chance for you to multitask. No matter which direction you go with your teaching sessions, make sure children realize what all these themes add up to: that only Jesus will bring them a new, everlasting life.

Key Scriptures

John 1:12; 4:1-26

1 John 5:12

Revelation 5:11-13

Bible Verse

"Whoever has the Son has life; whoever does not have God's Son does not have life" (1 John 5:12).

Bible Experience

▶ *PREPARE IN ADVANCE*

Bible Point: ▷ **JESUS BRINGS LIFE.**

Children will reenact the story of the Samaritan woman at the well.

Supplies: clean, small plastic trash can or other large container; white grape juice; paper cups

Time: 10 to 15 minutes

Preparation: Empty the white grape juice into the trash can. Make sure you have enough juice for children to fill their cups.

SAY: **Let's pretend that this trash can is a deep well from which people who lived in Jesus' time came to draw water. They didn't have running water in their homes like we do. They brought jars to the well, filled them with water, balanced them on their heads, and carried them home for their drinking, cooking, and washing. Many people around the world still get their water this way. Why don't we try that now?**

Give each child an empty cup, and let kids try to walk with the cups balanced on their heads. SAY: **That's even more difficult than it sounds. Now let's pretend that** [name of an older female child] **is a woman who's come to draw water from the well. Once Jesus met a woman at a well. He was waiting for his disciples to bring some food from the town, and she'd come to draw water.**

She was around people who wouldn't have anything to do with her because she was a woman and because she was from Samaria. She

probably expected that Jesus would ignore her. But he didn't. Instead, Jesus told her all about her life. He talked with her about worshipping God, and he offered her living water—a relationship with God. The woman at the well was so excited about Jesus that she ran to town and told others about him.

Allow your "woman at the well" to fill her cup from the trash can, take a drink, and then describe the "water" to the other children. Guide her with questions such as, "Why should others want a taste of this water?" and "How is this water different from other water you've tasted?" Make sure every child who wants a drink gets one.

SAY: **The woman at the well told people about how ▷ JESUS BRINGS LIFE, and they believed in him. Those people asked Jesus to stay with them. Many more people heard Jesus speak, and they believed in him, too. It's amazing that Jesus loves us so much that he brings us life. The Bible tells us an important truth in 1 John 5:12: "Whoever has the Son has life; whoever does not have God's Son does not have life." Make sure you tell others about the Living Water—Jesus!**

Additional Topics List

This lesson can be used to help children discover... The Bible, Eternal Life, and God's Love.

n ______

o ______

t ______

e ______

s ______

______

Game

▶ *HIGH ENERGY*
▶ *NO PREP*

Runaway Tag

Children will play a "runaway" game and talk about how Jesus embraced those who are often shunned.

Supplies: Bible
Time: 5 to 10 minutes
Preparation: none

Assign each child a number. Explain that you're going to play Tag. When you call out a number, the person with that number becomes "It" and must chase the others. Those who are tagged freeze in place. But every minute or so, you'll call out a new number. When you call out a new number, everyone who is frozen immediately becomes unfrozen and the person who has the number you called becomes the new It. Play for several minutes, calling out new numbers randomly and as often as you like. Then have children sit down.

ASK:

- **How does it feel to be It?**
- **How would you feel if everyone always ran away from you in real life?**
- **Why do we sometimes treat people like that?**

Read aloud John 4:1-26. SAY: **Jesus often approaches those other people run away from. It's because he wants *everyone* to know that he can bring us life.**

ASK:

◆ **Whom do you know whom people run away from?**

◆ **What can you do to let that person know that Jesus won't run away from him or her?**

◆ **What do you think Jesus meant by "living water"?**

SAY: **The woman at the well was sad until she met Jesus. Living water moves and is refreshing. Jesus gives us Living Water.**

Craft

▶ *PREPARE IN ADVANCE*

Water-Drop People

Children will make water-drop people as a reminder of the Living Water.

Supplies: Bible, blue balloons, permanent markers, safety scissors, tape, blue curling ribbon

Time: 10 to 15 minutes

Preparation: Inflate one balloon for each child. Make a few extras for visitors or to replace any balloons that may break. Set out the supplies.

Have kids blow up balloons and use the markers to draw faces and body features on their "water drops." Then have them cut the ribbon and tape it on their water drops to create a watery effect.

When kids have finished their water-drop people, have them join you in a circle. Let kids toss their water drops in the air and watch the living-watery effect come down for a minute. Then have kids say, "Jesus brings life." Read aloud 1 John 5:12. Then

ASK:

◆ **Have you ever felt sad? What happened?**

◆ **What special promise did Jesus give the woman at the well?**

Bible Application

▶ *PREPARE IN ADVANCE*

Living Water

Children will create "living water" and commit to telling others about Jesus.

Supplies: Bible, drinking straws, cups of water

Time: 5 to 10 minutes

Preparation: You'll need a straw and cup of water for each child.

Read aloud John 4:5-42. SAY: **Jesus told the Samaritan woman that if she had asked him for water, he would give her living water.** Give the kids each a straw and a cup of water. Show them how to blow into their cup of water through the straw so the water bubbles.

Jesus was talking about his love being like living water. With Jesus' love in our hearts, it bubbles and bubbles, like when you are blowing into your water. You want to share Jesus' love with others! Jesus brings us life. We want our friends and families and everyone to know so we all can live with Jesus forever. Have kids blow into their water again.

When the woman figured out that Jesus had been sent by God, she was so excited that she told lots and lots of people in her town.

ASK:

◆ **Who is someone you can tell about Jesus?**

SAY: **Let's tell everyone about Jesus and living with him forever.**

Have kids think about one person they can tell this week and then blow bubbles and try to say that person's name at the same time.

Creative Prayer Idea

▶ *FOR YOUNGER CHILDREN*
▶ *NO PREP*

Creature Choir

Children will learn about the creatures that praise Jesus.

Supplies: Bible, marker with washable ink

Time: 10 to 15 minutes

Preparation: none

ASK:

◆ **What do you think heaven will be like?**

Read aloud the description of heaven from Revelation 5:11-13. Have children act out how the angels will praise Jesus.

SAY: **Did you hear that? All of the creatures in heaven and on the earth and under the earth and in the sea will be singing and praising Jesus! Won't that be wonderful? Because Jesus brings life, when we get to heaven, we'll sing along with the whales and the birds and the gophers!**

ASK:

◆ **Why do you think everyone will be praising Jesus?**

◆ **How does Jesus get us into heaven?**

SAY: **Jesus brings us life, both in this world and in heaven forever. That's cool because it means we get to sing with the gophers!**

Have each child choose a creature to imitate. Have the "animal chorus" sing "Jesus Loves Me" together, in their animal voices. PRAY: **Dear God, thanks for making heaven such a fun place to be. We know we'll have fun praising you. Thank you for sending Jesus so that we might have life. In Jesus' name, amen.**

Use a marker with washable ink to draw a musical note on the back of each child's hand. SAY: **Every time you look at this musical note today, remember that we will sing to God in heaven. And don't forget to praise God here, too!**

Object Lesson

▶ *PREPARE IN ADVANCE*
▶ *FOR SMALL GROUPS*
▶ *ALLERGY ALERT*

Angels and Puppies

Children will discuss what they will be when they go to heaven.

Supplies: Bible, baby animal, dog biscuits

Time: 10 to 15 minutes

Preparation: Bring to your meeting a baby animal, such as a bunny, puppy, or kitten. If you don't have access to a baby animal, borrow some stuffed animal toys from the church nursery.

Bring out the baby animal, and give the children each a chance to pet it. Share a little information about the pet.

SAY: **I've been wondering a little bit about this animal—what it's mom and dad look like and what it will look like when it's all grown up. Do you think there's a chance that this animal might grow up to be an elephant?**

That was kind of a silly question. We know that kittens grow up to be cats, not birds or monkeys. The same thing is true for you, too. When you grow up, you'll be an adult person, like your parents. Some people think that when people go to heaven, they'll be angels. But that's not the case.

Read aloud John 1:12. Help kids understand that in heaven, they won't be angels. SAY: **We won't become angels when we die. God loves us so much that when we believe in Jesus, he brings us life again, and we become God's children. And we will remain God's children in heaven.**

Hand out dog biscuits. Tell kids to take them home as a treat for a dog they know. SAY: **Remember that just as our baby visitor here won't turn into an elephant, you won't turn into an angel when you go to heaven. You're God's child, and you always will be!**

Movie Clip

To Kill a Mockingbird

Movie Title: *To Kill a Mockingbird* (not rated)

Start Time: 8 minutes, 54 seconds

Where to Begin: Jem says, "There goes the meanest man that ever took a breath of life."

Where to End: Jem says, "And he drools most of the time."

Plot: Scout and Jem, the children of small-town lawyer Atticus Finch, are afraid of their mostly unseen neighbor, Boo Radley.

Review: Jesus demonstrated his own lack of prejudice with his words and actions to the Samaritan woman. This movie clip helps children see the damage done by prejudice and the hurt that it causes.

Discussion

After setting up the clip, SAY: **In the movie *To Kill a Mockingbird*, Jem and Scout are a brother and sister who meet a new boy in town. They tell him about a man in their neighborhood.** Show the clip.

Boo Radley, Jem and Scout's neighbor, ends up saving Scout's life, and Scout learns not to form an opinion about someone before all the facts are in. We get our word *prejudice* from *prejudge*—to form an opinion before you know for sure. In the Bible the Jews hated the Samaritans, who they felt were not pure or good. They had prejudice against them. But notice what Jesus, who was a Jew, did to this woman he met.

Retell the account from John 4:1-26.

ASK:

- **Why do you think Jesus treated this woman with kindness, even though everyone else kept away from her?**
- **What can we learn from Jesus' example?**

SAY: **Jesus brings life to anyone who asks. And sometimes he wants your help to do that. It's good to try not to prejudge people because then you can share Jesus' life with anyone.**

Preschool Story

▶ *NO PREP*

Bible Point: ▷ **JESUS BRINGS LIFE.**

Supplies: Bible

Time: 15 to 20 minutes

Preparation: none

Living Water

Have kids form a circle and sit down. Open your Bible to John 4, and show children the words. SAY: **Today we're going to act out the story of the woman at the well.** Have kids stand and repeat your actions while you say the words.

One day Jesus was traveling to a place called Galilee. Walk in place. **When he got tired, Jesus passed by a Samaritan city and decided to sit by a well and rest.** Sit down and put your head on your hands. **A Samaritan woman saw Jesus when she came to draw water from the well.** Pretend to pull water out of a well.

Jesus said to the woman, "I would like a drink!" Pretend to drink from a cup.

The Samaritan woman said, "Why are you talking to me? Jewish people, like you, don't even speak to people from Samaria, like me." Raise your hands as if to ask a question.

Jesus said to her, "If you knew who I really am, you would ask me for a glass of water and I would give you special living water." Pretend to peer down the well.

Jesus said, "The water from this well is regular water. If you drink it, you'll get thirsty again. But the water I have will bubble up like a fountain of eternal life—you'll never be thirsty again."

The Samaritan liked the sound of that! Clap your hands. **She said, "Sir, please give me some of this water so that I'll never be thirsty again!"** Shake your head.

Then Jesus told her to get her husband and come back to the well. Point away from yourself, and then beckon with your hand. **The woman said she wasn't married, and Jesus said that he knew she had told the truth.** Shake your head "no," and then smile.

The woman said, "You must be a prophet because you knew I wasn't married even before I told you."

Jesus told the woman that he was the Savior, the Son of God. Make a cross in the air. **Then the Samaritan woman went to the city to tell everyone what had happened.** Run in place with your hands beside your mouth.

Jesus told the woman that he could give her water that would satisfy her forever—she would never be thirsty again. Water brings life, and ▷ JESUS BRINGS LIFE, too. Jesus brings us life forever in heaven. When we believe in Jesus, he promises to bring us life forever!

ASK:

- **What did Jesus promise to give the woman?**
- **What does Jesus promise to give us?**
- **How can you have life that lasts forever?**

notes

BIBLE STORY

Jesus Is Rejected

For the Leader

In Bible times, all someone had to do was run up to a group of people and tell them about Jesus, and they believed...at least, that's how it sometimes seems. Today getting people to believe in Jesus—or believing ourselves—seems like it takes a lot more.

But the story of Jesus being rejected helps us realize that even back then, getting people to believe wasn't always easy. Here Jesus stood before his own friends and neighbors, in flesh and blood, and they still rejected him.

Prepare your students to see that they can never strengthen their faith too much. Help them realize the importance of living for Jesus daily and the need to pursue others relentlessly so that they, too, may one day believe in Jesus.

Key Scriptures

Luke 4:14-30

Acts 16:31

Hebrews 11:1

Bible Verse

"Believe in the Lord Jesus and you will be saved" (Acts 16:31).

Bible Experience

▶ ***PREPARE IN ADVANCE***

Bible Point: ▷ **BELIEVE IN JESUS.**

Children will make paper hearts and talk about Jesus' rejection.

Supplies: Bible, red construction paper, pencils, safety scissors

Time: 10 to 15 minutes

Preparation: Fold paper in half horizontally. You'll need one folded paper for each child, plus one for yourself.

Have kids draw half-a-heart shapes on the folded red construction paper so they can cut out a heart easily. SAY: **Jesus had been preaching to the people throughout the land. He taught the people how much God loves them.**

Hold up one sheet of paper. SAY: **All the people who heard Jesus liked him and said good things about him.** Cut on the line, and then unfold and show the heart and SAY: **But then Jesus went back to Nazareth, to his hometown, where he grew up. He went to the synagogue, or church, and talked to the people there about God. But the people in his town didn't like what he said.** Hold up the heart and SAY: **These people didn't like Jesus at all.** Rip the heart in two.

Read aloud Luke 4:14-30. Have kids make their own hearts. ASK:

◆ **What did these people do that showed they didn't believe Jesus was God's Son?**

SAY: **It's very important that we not be like these people. Instead, we must ▷ BELIEVE IN JESUS. Acts 16:31 tells us why it's so important: "Believe in the Lord Jesus and you will be saved."**

ASK:

- **If Jesus came into our town today, how would you feel? What would you say? How would you treat him?**
- **Would your actions and words show that you believe in Jesus? Explain.**
- **What does it mean to believe in Jesus with all your heart?**
- **Do you think you believe in Jesus with all your heart? Explain.**

Have kids hold their paper hearts to their chests. PRAY: **Dear God, help us to believe in Jesus. When we are having hard times, we want to believe in him. When we are excited or joyful, we want to believe in him. Make our faith strong so we can believe in him always. In Jesus' name, amen.**

Song Connect

Use "I Am the Way" (track 10, *it: Innovative Tools for Children's Ministry: New Testament* CD) to help reinforce the Bible Point, ▷ **BELIEVE IN JESUS.**

Hide the CD player somewhere in your church. Have kids follow the music until they find the player and then celebrate with the yell, "I believe!"

Additional Topics List

This lesson can be used to help children discover... Faith, Friends, and Sin.

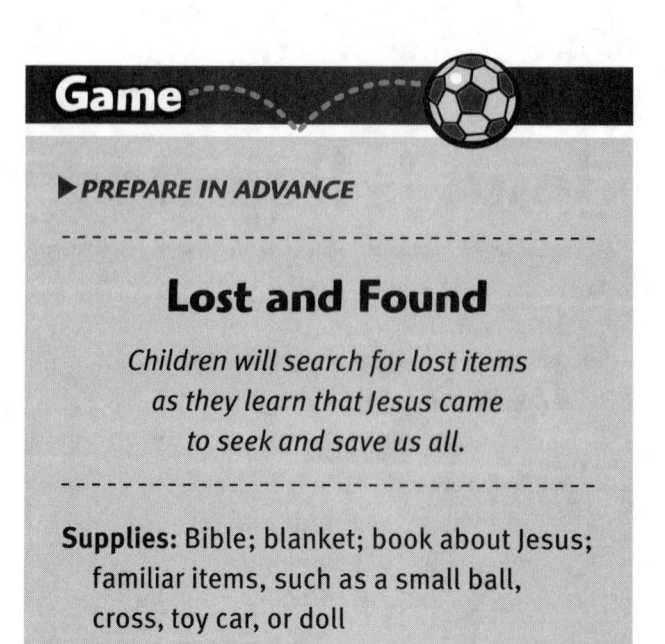

Game

▶ ***PREPARE IN ADVANCE***

Lost and Found

Children will search for lost items as they learn that Jesus came to seek and save us all.

Supplies: Bible; blanket; book about Jesus; familiar items, such as a small ball, cross, toy car, or doll

Time: 10 to 15 minutes

Preparation: Place all the items on the blanket.

Open a Bible to Luke 4:14-21 and SAY: **Jesus said that God doesn't want anyone to be lost—God wants us all to believe in Jesus!**

Bring out the blanket with all the items on it. Ask kids to tell you the names of the items, and then have children close their eyes. Choose one child to take something from the blanket and hide it. Then ask the others to open their eyes, figure out what's missing, and search for the lost item.

Play the game several times, and rejoice with the children over each item they find. At the end of the game, discuss these questions:

- **How did you feel when you found each lost item?**
- **How do you think God feels when one of his lost children is found?**

SAY: **Jesus came for us all, to seek and save what was lost, just as you had to look for and "save" each lost item.**

Craft

▶ *PREPARE IN ADVANCE*

A Light out of Darkness

Children will make pinhole pictures.

Supplies: Bible, paper cutter, white paper, pencils, black construction paper, large and small paper clips, towels, red construction-paper strips, glue, hole punch, suction cups

Time: 10 to 15 minutes

Preparation: Create two work areas: Put all the supplies except the towels on one table. Make the second work area on the floor where you have laid the folded towels. Use a paper cutter to cut two 1x12-inch strips and two 1x9-inch strips from red construction paper for each child.

Have children write "Jesus Shines Through Us" on white paper, leaving at least a 1-inch border around the edge. Then have them draw a picture of something that symbolizes light at the bottom. It could be a sunburst, light bulbs, or something else that shows light. Show kids how to lay the white paper on the sheet of black construction paper and paper-clip the edges. Then tell them to place the papers on a folded towel.

Have each child straighten a large paper clip. Show them how to use the pointed end to poke holes through both papers, outlining the words and the picture. When they finish, have them remove the white paper. Then tell the kids to glue the red strips to the edges of the picture to make a frame. Punch a hole in the top center for hanging with a suction cup.

Read aloud Luke 4:14-30. Then ASK:

- **How can you make it easy to see the picture on your paper?**
- **Why is it hard for people to follow God sometimes?**
- **How can we be like a light showing people the way to God?**

SAY: **When our lives fill with darkness, we need to believe in Jesus more than ever and let the light shine through!**

Bible Application

▶ *PREPARE IN ADVANCE*

Never Die

Children will think about the people they know who don't believe.

Supplies: plastic tub lids, permanent markers, safety scissors, string, erasable markers

Time: 5 to 10 minutes

Preparation: You'll need one plastic tub lid for each child. Plan to give each child an erasable marker to keep.

Give children each a lid, and have them draw a cross on it. Have kids cut out their crosses and then poke a hole in the top to thread a length of string through. Have them decorate the front with permanent markers. Give children erasable markers, and have them write the name of someone whom they want to believe in Jesus on the back of their crosses. As they wear their crosses, have them pray for that person. When that person believes Jesus, kids can thank God and erase the name. They can add several names and erase them as needed.

Creative Prayer Idea

▶ *FOR LARGE GROUPS*
▶ *PREPARE IN ADVANCE*

Prayers on a Cross

Children will see how embracing Jesus' love makes the ugly seem beautiful.

Supplies: scrap lumber, nails, hammer, U-shaped brads or chicken wire, silk flowers, colorful tissue paper

Time: 5 to 10 minutes

Preparation: Make a simple cross from scrap lumber. Attach U-shaped brads to the cross, or cover it with chicken wire.

Gather children in a circle.

ASK:

- **How do you think Jesus felt when he was rejected by people in his own hometown?**

SAY: **Jesus probably felt pretty sad, but he also knew he would be rejected again.** Hold up the cross and SAY: **Crosses are ugly things. The Romans used crosses to execute their worst criminals. But Jesus turned the cross into a beautiful thing.**

We're going to turn this cross into a beautiful thing with our prayers. Let's take turns adding flowers and tissue paper to the cross. When you do, pray, "Thank you, Jesus, for your love."

Let kids decorate the cross. Gather kids around the finished cross and PRAY: **Jesus, thank you for turning the ugly cross into something beautiful. Help our lives to be beautiful as we believe in you. Amen.**

Discussion Launcher

I Believe

For this activity you'll need pencils and scrap paper.

Have kids form pairs, and give each pair a pencil and eight pieces of scrap paper. Have pairs print I-B-E-L-I-E-V-E, writing one large letter on each piece of scrap paper. Then collect the papers from each pair.

Mix all of the scraps of paper together, and then scatter them. SAY: **When I say "Go!" you'll have 30 seconds to work with your partner to find enough letters to spell *I believe*. I'll turn off the lights when time is up. Ready? Go!**

Play several rounds as time permits. Then ASK:

- **How did you feel when the lights went out before you had gathered all your pieces of paper?**
- **How much time do you think you'll have on earth to decide whether you believe in Jesus?**
- **How will you feel if your lights go out before you believe in Jesus?**

SAY: **Look at the papers that spell "I believe." Take away the first two letters of "Believe," B and E. Now you have the words *I live* with an E in the middle. That E stands for "Eternal." *Eternal* means forever, even after your body dies. This is a good way to remember that if you believe in Jesus, you'll live eternally.**

ASK:

- **What do you need to believe in order to have new life?**
- **How will others know that you believe in Jesus?**

Science Devotion

▶ *PREPARE IN ADVANCE*

Invisible but Real

Children will see how air creates an invisible barrier and discuss their faith in Jesus.

Supplies: Bible, newspaper, paper towel, clear drinking glass, deep tub of water

Time: 10 to 15 minutes

Preparation: Spread the newspaper on a table or the floor, and set the tub of water, the drinking glass, and the paper towel on top of it.

Read aloud Luke 4:14-30. ASK:

◆ **Why do you think Jesus' own people rejected him?**

◆ **Why would they have such a hard time believing in Jesus?**

Read aloud Hebrews 11:1, and then SAY: **Let's do an experiment to see that we can believe in Jesus even if we can't really see him physically.** Have kids gather around the newspaper, and have one child wad up the paper towel and put it in the bottom of the glass. ASK:

◆ **What do you think will happen to the paper towel if I put the glass in the tub of water?**

Turn the glass upside down, and push it straight down into the tub of water. Hold the glass completely underwater for a few seconds, and then carefully pull the glass straight up out of the water. Have a volunteer pull out the paper towel. ASK:

◆ **How do think the paper towel stayed dry?**

SAY: **The glass looked empty, but it was actually full of air. When I pushed the glass into the water, a wall of air was pushed back against the paper towel and kept it from getting wet. We can't see the air, but it's still there. We saw evidence of it because the paper towel stayed dry.**

ASK:

◆ **How can you believe in Jesus even though you can't see him?**

◆ **How do you know Jesus works in your life?**

SAY: **By faith we know that Jesus is alive. We can't see him, but we can believe in him and live like him.**

Preschool Story

▶ *PREPARE IN ADVANCE*

Bible Point: ▷ **BELIEVE IN JESUS.**

Supplies: Bible, construction paper, scissors, markers, craft sticks, glue

Time: 15 to 20 minutes

Preparation: Cut 5-inch circles from construction paper. Draw a happy face on one, a sad face on another, and an angry face on the third. Glue a craft stick to the bottom of the faces so you can hold them up during the story.

An Emotional Story

Have kids form a circle and sit down. Open your Bible to Luke 4, and show children the words. Show children the faces you prepared before class, and tell them that when they see you hold up a face during the story, they should act out the emotion on that face.

SAY: **Today's Bible story tells us to ▷ BELIEVE IN JESUS. In our story today, we're going to hear about some people who didn't believe in Jesus, which made Jesus very sad.** Hold up the sad face, and encourage kids to show you their sad faces.

Jesus went from place to place telling people about God. Have kids to stand up and tell one or two other children something about God. **People everywhere spoke nice words about Jesus, and they were happy** (hold up the happy face, and encourage kids to show you their happy faces) **to see Jesus come to their town to do miracles. Then Jesus went to Nazareth, the town where he grew up, to share with his family and friends there. But the people in Jesus' hometown didn't believe Jesus, and that made Jesus sad.** Hold up the sad face, and encourage kids to show you their sad faces. **The people got *angry*** (hold up the angry face, and encourage kids to show you their angry faces) **with Jesus. They didn't like what Jesus told them, so the people didn't want to listen to Jesus. They yelled at Jesus and tried to hurt him, so Jesus went away to find people who wanted to hear about God. Jesus was very sad** (hold up the sad face, and encourage kids to show you their sad faces) **when the people in his town pushed him away. But when we ▷ BELIEVE IN JESUS, it makes him happy!** Hold up the happy face, and encourage kids to show you their happy faces.

ASK:

- **Why do you think the people didn't believe in Jesus?**
- **What makes you believe in Jesus?**
- **How can you help others believe in Jesus?**

SAY: **Jesus loves us, and he wants to be our friend! Even though we can't see or touch him, we can believe in Jesus and he will be our forever friend!**

BIBLE STORY

Disciples Called

For the Leader

It began with a simple command to follow their Savior. Simon, Andrew, James, and John obeyed, and their lives were changed forever. They embarked upon an amazing adventure as the closest companions of the Son of God. Most of the disciples Jesus chose were not highly educated people, renowned speakers, or even extremely powerful men of their time. But the one gift they all had was a passion to follow Jesus and serve God.

Children today can discover that same excitement. Use the ideas in this section to help children experience what it means to follow our Lord.

Key Scriptures

Matthew 4:19; 28:19

Luke 5:1-11

John 8:31

Bible Verse

"Come, follow me, and I will show you how to fish for people" (Matthew 4:19).

Bible Experience

▶ *ALLERGY ALERT*
▶ *PREPARE IN ADVANCE*

Bible Point: ▷ **JESUS WANTS US TO FOLLOW HIM.**

Children will make fishing lures and discuss discipleship.

Supplies: Bible, toothpicks, bags of soft candy

Time: 10 to 15 minutes

Preparation: Set the bags of candy in the center of a table.

Gather kids around the table, and give each child three toothpicks. Caution kids not to run or to poke others with the toothpicks.

ASK:

◆ **Has anyone here ever been fishing?**

SAY: **Four of Jesus' disciples were fishermen by trade—Andrew, Peter, James, and John. Fishermen often use lures to catch fish. A lure is an object that fishermen attach to the end of their fishing lines to attract fish. Use this candy to create your own fishing lures.**

Show kids how to make lures by impaling several types of small candies on a toothpick. Compliment kids on their colorful creations, and then

ASK:

◆ **What makes lures attractive to fish?**

Have kids name some things that are important to know for learning how to catch fish. Then SAY: **Jesus called out to the disciples with a special invitation: "Come, follow me, and I will show you how to fish for people" (Matthew 4:19). When Jesus asked Andrew, Peter, James, and John to follow him, they immediately left their boats and nets behind and followed Jesus.** Have a child read aloud Luke 5:1-11. Then ASK:

◆ **What do you think Jesus meant when he told Peter and Andrew that he would teach them to fish for people?**

◆ **What are ways we can learn more about Jesus?**

SAY: ▷ **JESUS WANTS US TO FOLLOW HIM. Reading the Bible, going to church, praying, and telling others about Jesus are all things to do as Jesus' followers. When we have faith in Jesus, we can be his followers.**

Song & Connect

Use "Go and Make Disciples" (track 6, *it: Innovative Tools for Children's Ministry: New Testament* CD) to help reinforce the Bible Point, ▷ **JESUS WANTS US TO FOLLOW HIM.**

This song works well for a commissioning ceremony at the end of a lesson on discipleship. Award kids with a blank book in which they can record the names of people they introduce to Jesus, and write "Matthew 28:19" on the first page.

notes

Additional Topics List

This lesson can be used to help children discover... Friends and Outreach.

Game

▶ *HIGH ENERGY*

▶ *NO PREP*

Balloon Rally

Children will play a balloon game and learn about following God's path instead of their own.

Supplies: balloons, permanent markers

Time: 10 to 15 minutes

Preparation: none

Clear the middle of your classroom, and have kids stand on one side of the room. Give every student a balloon. Make certain the balloons are easy for children to blow up. Have kids use permanent markers to write their names on their balloons before you begin the game.

Explain that the entire group needs to get to the other side of the classroom by blowing up their balloons, letting them go, going to where they landed, and launching them again. Give the entire group one minute to reach the other side of the classroom. Extend the time period if only one student hasn't made it to the other side of the classroom.

After the game, SAY: **These balloons didn't go where you thought they would, and using the balloons rather than just walking in a straight line made getting to the other side of the room much harder. That's sort of like when we choose to take our lives in a direction that's not focused on God. Jesus wants us to follow him so that we put God first. We need to realize that our own personal desires aren't as important as what God wants.**

Craft

▶ *PREPARE IN ADVANCE*

Followers Footprints

Children will decorate T-shirts with painted footprints.

Supplies: plain white T-shirts (prewashed), cardboard, newspaper, scissors, paper towels, tub of soapy water, 2 or 3 colors of liquid fabric paint, pie tins, markers, masking tape, clothespins, chair, puffy paint

Time: 15 to 20 minutes

Preparation: Cut cardboard rectangles that will fit inside the T-shirts and prevent paint from soaking through from the front to the back. Cover an area of the floor with plenty of newspaper. Set up a washing area nearby by placing paper towels near a basin of warm, soapy water. If weather allows, do this craft outside on the grass. Pour a thin layer of liquid fabric paint into each pie tin.

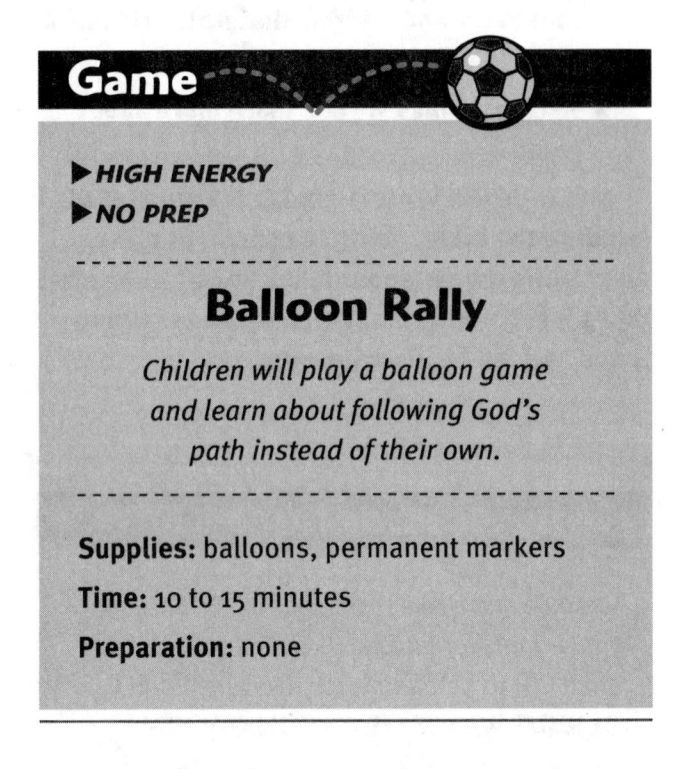

Distribute white T-shirts and have children use markers to print their names on the tags or on pieces of masking tape to temporarily stick to the shirts. Then show kids how to gather the back of the shirts so the front is pulled taut against the cardboard insert. Help them use clothespins to hold the shirts this way. Instruct kids to remove their shoes and socks and go to the newspaper-covered area. Explain that kids will take turns sitting on the chair, placing their T-shirt in front of them, and carefully dipping their feet into the paint. Then they will step on their T-shirts to make footprints. The children may choose to use one or more colors of paint.

As kids finish, move their T-shirts aside and have them wipe their feet with paper towels and then step into the basin of soapy water. Provide more paper towels for drying.

When the footprints have dried, allow children to use puffy paint to write their names or messages, such as, "I Follow Jesus!" or "Will Fish for God" on their shirts. Let the paint on the T-shirts dry completely before you remove the cardboard insert and clothespins.

Bible Application

▶ *PREPARE IN ADVANCE*

Follow the Light

Children will make light-switch plates and discuss ways they can follow God.

Supplies: Bible, light-switch plates, fluorescent or glow-in-the-dark paints, paintbrushes, newspaper

Time: 10 to 15 minutes

Preparation: Cover your workspace with newspaper, and place the fluorescent or glow-in-the-dark paints in the middle.

Give each child a light-switch plate, and instruct kids to design light-switch plates to hang in their bedrooms. Encourage kids to create designs that will remind them of God's power.

When kids finish, set the plates aside to dry. Have kids take them home with notes of simple instructions for installation: Unscrew the current light-switch plate, and replace it with the decorated one, using the same screws.

Read aloud John 8:31.

ASK:

- **According to this verse, what are the requirements of a follower or disciple of Jesus?**
- **How do our attitudes, words, and actions affect what others may think about Jesus?**

SAY: **Those who follow Jesus imitate him. They try to do what he would do, say what he would say, and think what he would think. We can be followers of Jesus by following his example. Then others will see the goodness of God in us and want to become followers, too!**

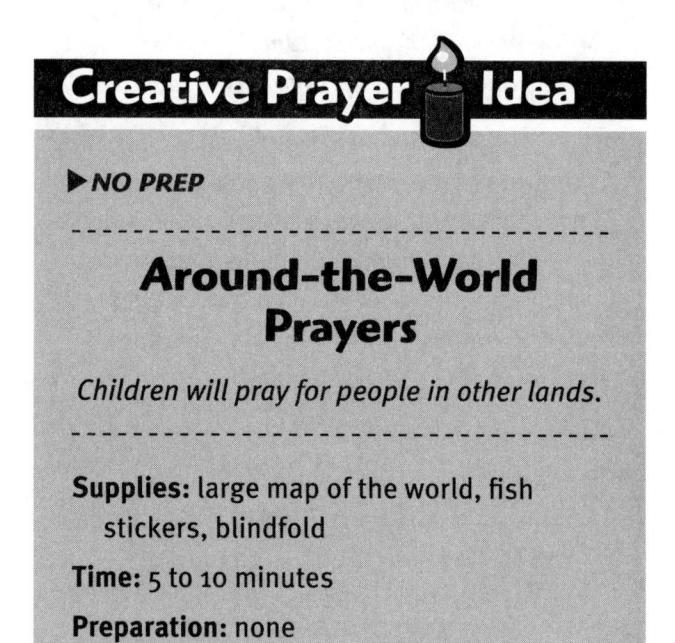

Creative Prayer Idea

▶ *NO PREP*

Around-the-World Prayers

Children will pray for people in other lands.

Supplies: large map of the world, fish stickers, blindfold

Time: 5 to 10 minutes

Preparation: none

Show children the world map. SAY: **This is the world that God made. Jesus wants us to follow him so we can share him with everyone, all over the world.**

Give stickers to the children one at a time, blindfold the children, spin them around, and let them place their stickers on the map. As you spin the children, say this rhyme:

God is here; God is there.

God made our world. God is everywhere!

After a child has placed a sticker, help him or her say this prayer: **God, bless the people in** [name of area] **and help them to follow Jesus.**

Science Devotion

▶ *PREPARE IN ADVANCE*
▶ *FOR SMALL GROUPS*

Feel the Earth Move

Children will use the concept of soil erosion to understand how it's sometimes hard to follow Jesus.

Supplies: newspaper, large aquarium or a clear plastic storage box, potting soil or dirt, sand, bucket, small shovel or large spoon, watering can or a pitcher full of water, plant clippings, dishpan (optional)

Time: 15 to 20 minutes

Preparation: Spread newspaper over a table or on the floor. Place the aquarium, the potting soil, the sand, and the bucket on the newspaper.

Have kids gather around the items on the newspaper, and pour equal parts of soil and sand into the bucket. Ask one student to use a shovel to mix the sand and soil together. SAY: **I'm going to make a hill in the aquarium with this soil mixture.** Pour the soil mixture into the aquarium, keeping the major portion of it at one end. Let kids help you build up this end to make a hill with a flat top.

Let's pretend this hill is the earth. Now it's going to rain!

ASK:

◆ **What do you think will happen to our hill when it rains?**

Gently pour water from the watering can to make it "rain."

ASK:

◆ **What's happening to the hill?**

◆ **What do you think will happen if it rains harder? Why?**

Pour water a little faster from the watering can to make it rain harder. SAY: **The process of water moving the dirt is called *erosion*. Erosion happens when water or wind wears away the earth's surface. If the hill has eroded too much or the dirt is too wet, remake the hill by adding more dirt.** If you need to, carefully drain excess water into a dishpan or bowl. Have several children help you insert the plant clippings into the hillside and on top of the hill. **Let's try making it rain again.** Gently pour water from the watering can over the soil mixture.

ASK:

◆ **Where does the soil go now that there are plants in the hillside?**

◆ **How is this like when our faith in Jesus erodes?**

◆ **How can we stop our faith from eroding so we can follow Jesus?**

SAY: **When we follow Jesus and listen to God's Word, we can feel the peace Jesus offers us. No more faith erosion for us!**

Movie Clip

Toy Story

Movie Title: *Toy Story* (G)

Start Time: 1 hour, 27 seconds

Where to Begin: Sid's alarm goes off.

Where to End: The toys gather around Woody, and he says, "It'll help everybody."

Plot: Toys Woody and Buzz end up in the room of Sid, the sadistic boy next door. Woody pleads with the toys in Sid's room to help him save Buzz from Sid.

Review: Use this clip to remind kids of how Jesus called his disciples. Just as the toys all mobilized to accomplish Woody's mission, the disciples followed Jesus when he called.

Discussion

After setting up and showing the movie clip,

ASK:

- **Why did Woody ask the toys to follow him?**
- **What was unusual about the toys he asked for help?**

SAY: **In this scene the toys in Sid's room were ready to follow Woody and help him accomplish his mission. They responded when Woody called.**

That reminds me of a story about Jesus. When Jesus first began his ministry, he called people to follow him. And they did. These people weren't rich or powerful people—they were just regular, everyday people who left everything behind and followed Jesus. They jumped to follow Jesus! Let's do a little experiment to show us an example of this.

Spread confetti out on a table. Create static by running the comb through your hair several times. Hold the comb about an inch above the confetti, and watch the confetti jump up to the comb. Let children try the experiment.

SAY: **This confetti jumped right up to the comb, just as Jesus' followers left everything and jumped to follow Jesus. Jesus is still calling people to follow him today.** Close by having kids show off their best jumps.

Preschool Story

▶ ***PREPARE IN ADVANCE***

Bible Point: ▷ **JESUS WANTS US TO FOLLOW HIM.**

Supplies: Bible, large blue sheet, 2 laundry baskets, fishing net, construction paper

Time: 15 to 20 minutes

Preparation: Cut simple fish shapes from construction paper. Spread a large blue sheet on the floor, and put the baskets near it.

I Caught You!

Have kids form a circle and sit down. Open your Bible to Luke 5, and show children the words. SAY: **Today we'll learn that ▷ JESUS WANTS US TO FOLLOW HIM.**

One day Jesus was standing by a lake, teaching a large crowd of people. Have children crowd around you. **It got so crowded on the shore that Jesus almost got pushed into the water. Jesus**

saw Peter in his boat, so Jesus told Peter to take him out into the middle of the lake. Push one of the baskets into the "water," and have kids climb in with you.

After Jesus finished teaching the crowd, he told Peter to go out even farther into the water to catch some fish. Peter was very tired because he'd been up fishing all night long, and he hadn't caught a single fish! But Peter followed Jesus' instructions and went out into the water. Encourage kids to get out and push the "boat" farther into the water.

Peter threw his net into the water, and guess what happened? Have kids throw the net over the side of the boat and into the water. **Peter caught so many fish that he couldn't even pull the net back into the water!** Toss the paper fish into the net. **Peter had to call his friends James and John to bring another boat to help him bring in all those fish.**

James and John brought their boat up next to Peter's boat. Encourage half of the kids to push the other basket into the water. **There were so many fish that the boats started to sink!** Pretend to act afraid, and encourage kids to push the boats back to the shore. **The men were surprised by all of the fish they'd caught, but Jesus told them that if they followed him, they could fish for people instead of for fish.**

ASK:

- ◆ **What do you think Jesus meant when he said the men would fish for people?**

SAY: **Jesus was telling Peter, James, and John that they could tell other people about Jesus and "catch" them by helping them believe in Jesus. Let's play a game now in which we'll catch people!**

Have children get into groups of four, and have two of the children form a bridge with their hands so the others can go under. Sing this song to the tune of "London Bridge":

Jesus says to come follow him,
Follow him, follow him.
Jesus says to come follow him,
Catching people. *(Have the pair bring the bridge down and catch the child in the "bridge" between their arms.)*

SAY: **Peter, James, and John left their fishing boats and followed Jesus. ▷ JESUS WANTS US TO FOLLOW HIM, too.**

ASK:

- ◆ **Why did Peter, James, and John choose to follow Jesus?**
- ◆ **Why do you want to follow Jesus?**
- ◆ **How can you follow Jesus in your life?**

SAY: **We can follow Jesus by believing in him, by obeying his words, and by telling others about him. ▷ JESUS WANTS US TO FOLLOW HIM!**

n
o
t
e
s

BIBLE STORY

Jesus Heals and Prays

For the Leader

As Jesus' days on earth progressed, he attracted larger and larger crowds. These crowds weren't rich. The people weren't relaxing in a climate-controlled convention center with concession stands at every turn. These crowds were suffering—physically and spiritually. Jesus knew that helping them would reveal God's love to them in compelling ways.

Jesus had the power to do anything, and he has that same power today. Help children realize the importance of knowing Jesus' power so he can work through their lives and through the lives of those they touch.

Key Scriptures

Mark 1:29-39

Matthew 7:7

John 17:26

Bible Verse

"I have revealed you to them, and I will continue to do so" (John 17:26).

Bible Experience

▶ ***PREPARE IN ADVANCE***

Bible Point: ▷ **JESUS CAN DO ANYTHING.**

Children will shoot rubber bands and discuss how Jesus can do anything through them.

Supplies: Bible, wide rubber bands, fine-point markers, box, masking tape

Time: 10 to 15 minutes

Preparation: Use masking tape to create a starting line on the floor.

Give each student a wide rubber band and fine-tip marker. Caution kids not to shoot the rubber bands yet and never to shoot them at someone else.

SAY: **I've given each of you a rubber band. Write on your rubber band any possessions, attitudes, and abilities that you can share with others. Write as many as will fit.** When kids finish writing,

ASK:

- **What problems did you have thinking of things to share?**
- **How do you think the things you wrote could help others?**

Read aloud Mark 1:29-39. SAY: **Jesus was sent to the earth to heal and pray for God's people. ▷ JESUS CAN DO ANYTHING, and he can help others through us. He gives each of us possessions, attitudes, and abilities, and he wants us to share those things, even though we may not think we have much to offer.**

Set up a box (to use as a target) about 5 to 10 feet away from the line. Have kids hold their rubber bands and line up behind the starting line. Have students take turns shooting rubber bands at the target.

After each child has had a turn, have kids retrieve their rubber bands. SAY: **Jesus will "stretch" his love to others through us. Turn to a partner, and tell that person one thing you wrote on your rubber band and how sharing that thing could change someone's life. Jesus will stretch the gifts we're willing to share. Jesus can use us to show others that ▷HE CAN DO ANYTHING.** Have kids put their rubber bands around one of their wrists as reminders that Jesus can do anything.

Song & Connect

Use "How Wide?" (track 18, *it: Innovative Tools for Children's Ministry: New Testament* CD) to help reinforce the Bible Point, **▷JESUS CAN DO ANYTHING.**

Help kids connect Jesus' ability to do anything with his unconditional love for them. This song will help students understand that of all the things Jesus can do, he chooses first and foremost to love us.

Additional Topics List

This lesson can be used to help children discover... God's Love and Miracles.

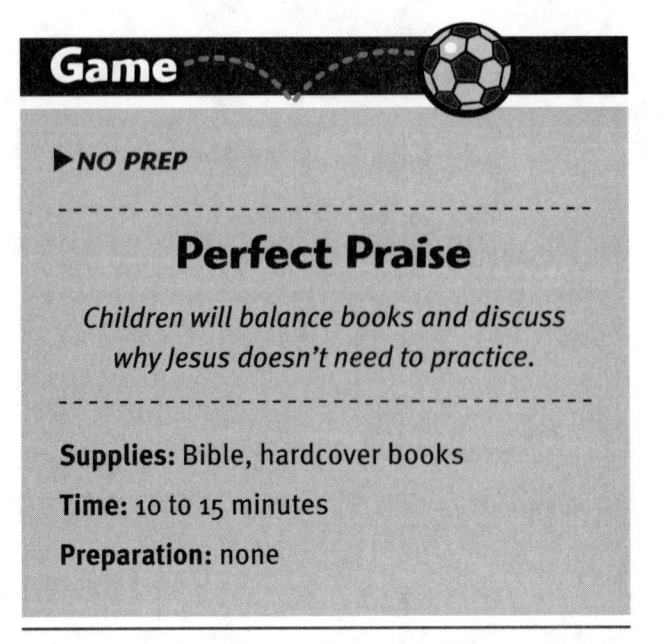

Game

▶ ***NO PREP***

Perfect Praise

Children will balance books and discuss why Jesus doesn't need to practice.

Supplies: Bible, hardcover books

Time: 10 to 15 minutes

Preparation: none

Form two teams and have them line up on one side of your room. Give the first person in each line a hardcover book. Tell kids they have to balance the books on their heads, walk to the other end of the room, touch the wall, and return to the team. If they drop the book, they have to start again at the beginning. Allow time for everyone to take a turn in the relay. After the relay,

ASK:

- **What would make this activity easier?**
- **How important is it to practice when you learn a new skill?**
- **Do you think it's ever possible to be really good at something without practicing? Explain.**
- **What are some things you've learned to do well by practicing?**

Read aloud John 17:26. SAY: **You know what they say: Practice makes perfect. But the good news is that Jesus is already perfect: He doesn't need practice. ▷ JESUS CAN DO ANYTHING. He wants to help you so he can reveal God to you and make your relationship with God stronger. When you're struggling to learn new things, take a minute to ask Jesus for help. Then take an extra minute to remember why he wants to help you!**

Craft

▶ *PREPARE IN ADVANCE*

Prayer Pockets

Children will make prayer pockets as reminders of the many things they can pray for that Jesus can help them with.

Supplies: half sheets of construction paper; markers; staplers; large craft sticks; various craft supplies, such as stickers, shells, or beads; hole punches; yarn

Time: 10 to 15 minutes

Preparation: Clearly print the words from Matthew 7:7, "Keep on asking, and you will receive what you ask for," on paper, and post it for kids to copy. Set out the craft supplies.

Have each child fold up the short end of the half sheet of construction paper three-fourths of the way. Show kids how to staple on two sides to make pockets, and have them copy the words from Matthew 7:7 on the outside. Tell kids to write on each craft stick one thing he or she wants to pray for and then decorate the craft stick with the supplies. Let students make several craft sticks.

Show kids how to place their craft sticks in the pockets. Help them punch two holes at the top of their pockets. Cut pieces of yarn about a foot long, and help kids thread yarn through the holes on their prayer pockets and tie them.

Tell kids to hang their prayer pockets on a bedpost or doorknob. Tell them that each time they pray, they can take out one stick, pray for what is written on it, and then choose another stick and pray for what's written on it.

SAY: **When you pray, remember that ▷ JESUS CAN DO ANYTHING. You may not always get what you want, but you will always get what you need to help you live your life for God.**

Bible Application

▶ *NO PREP*

Savior Bubbles

Children will blow bubbles and pray about how they can share the power of Jesus with others.

Supplies: Bible, bottle of bubble solution

Time: 5 to 10 minutes

Preparation: none

Have kids sit in a circle. Dip the wand in the bubble solution, and hold it up for kids to see. SAY: **This doesn't look like much right now, but what will happen when I blow on the wand?**

Blow a few bubbles, and then read aloud Mark 1:29-39. SAY: **Bubble solution looks like water until you blow a bubble—and then it brings a smile to those who see it. Jesus is like that—he looked like an ordinary man. But he can do anything, and he wants to help us so we can grow closer to God.**

Think of one person you'd like Jesus to help. We'll pass around the bubbles. When it's your turn, fill in this simple prayer: "Jesus, please help [name a person]**. Then you'll blow a bubble and say, "Please show me how I can help** [name a person] **so he or she can grow closer to God."**

When everyone has blown a bubble, close your time by thanking God for sharing his love with everyone in your class.

Creative Prayer Idea

▶ *FOR YOUNGER CHILDREN*
▶ *NO PREP*

Quiet-Time Prayer

Children will take some quiet time to remember Jesus' power.

Supplies: none
Time: 5 to 10 minutes
Preparation: none

Use this prayer to make a transition from play-time to rest time. PRAY:

Thank you for this special day *(fold your hands)*
With time to laugh and eat and play. *(Clap four times in rhythm.)*
There's also time to praise and sing *(hold your hands up, and then hold a "micro-phone")*
To Jesus—who can do anything! *(Hold your arms wide apart.)*
I stretch up high and turn around. *(Stretch your arms overhead and turn around.)*
Now I'm drifting slowly down *(turn around and slowly lie down)*
As I rest so quietly. *(Fold your hands on your chest.)*
Please, dear Lord, watch over me.

Object Lesson

▶ *PREPARE IN ADVANCE*
▶ *ALLERGY ALERT*

Sharing Fruit

Children will taste unusual fruit and discuss the importance of telling others about Jesus.

Supplies: Bible; bag of unusual fruit, such as mango, pomegranate, or papaya
Time: 5 to 10 minutes
Preparation: You'll need enough small pieces of the fruit to serve twice the number of children you expect.

Open your bag and show kids the fruit. Offer a piece of the fruit to each child. It's OK if some don't want any. Take a bite of a piece of fruit yourself.

ASK:

◆ **Why did you decide to take or not take the fruit?**

SAY: **Tasting this unusual fruit is a little bit like believing in Jesus. Some people may be hesitant to eat a fruit they've never tasted before, even if they know it might be good. People sometimes don't choose to believe in Jesus either, even knowing that it might be good.**

Read aloud Mark 1:29-39.

ASK:

◆ **Do you think some people would choose Jesus if they knew that he healed them and prayed for them?**

SAY: **The reasons people don't believe in Jesus may be the same reasons for not trying a new food. Perhaps the person has never heard of the new food! And maybe someone doesn't**

believe in Jesus because he or she doesn't know that ▷ JESUS CAN DO ANYTHING. That's where we can help!

Read aloud John 17:26. SAY: **Jesus healed people so that God would be revealed to them. We can reveal God to people, too. We can tell people in our neighborhood or at school. Sometimes you may need to tell about Jesus more than once, just as I offered you the fruit more than once. The important thing is to keep telling.** Offer kids another taste of fruit as they leave.

Discussion Launcher

The Right Gear

For this activity you'll need flip-flops, sandals, tennis shoes, hiking boots, and a Bible.

SAY: **I believe in having the right equipment for whatever I plan to do! That goes for walking, too. I'll hold up the shoes, and you tell me what they are the right equipment for.**

Hold up the flip-flops and let kids respond. Hold up the sandals and let kids respond. Do the same with the tennis shoes and boots.

ASK:

◆ **What kind of shoes would I need to walk on water?**

SAY: **You're right—I can't walk on water. But ▷ JESUS CAN DO ANYTHING, and Jesus did walk on water! Jesus also healed people, fed those who were starving, and predicted the future. And he prayed for people.**

Read aloud Mark 1:29-39.

ASK:

◆ **Why did Jesus heal people?**

◆ **Why did he pray for them?**

◆ **Does Jesus need special equipment to help others? Explain.**

◆ **Was Jesus able to do anything that people needed? Explain.**

◆ **What about today? Can Jesus *still* do anything? Explain.**

Preschool Story

▶ ***NO PREP***

Bible Point: ▷ **JESUS CAN DO ANYTHING.**

Supplies: Bible

Time: 15 to 20 minutes

Preparation: none

That's Amazing!

Have kids form a circle and sit down. Open your Bible to Mark 1, and show children the words. Tell kids that they are going to help you act out the Bible story. Choose one child to be Peter's mother-in-law, and ask that child to lie down and pretend to be sick. Choose another child to be Jesus, and choose four children to be James, John, Simon, and Andrew. Ask the other children to be the crowd following Jesus. Tell a few people in the crowd to act sick as well.

SAY: **Our Bible story today tells us that ▷ JESUS CAN DO ANYTHING. Let's listen to find out what Jesus did.**

Jesus left the synagogue—like a church—with his friends James and John, and they all went to Simon and Andrew's home. Encourage "Jesus," "James," and "John" to march in place as though traveling. **They walked and walked. Then they arrived at the house and knocked on the door. They knocked and knocked.** Have your Jesus pretend to knock.

Simon answered the door and let them in. Have "Simon" pretend to let the three into a room. **Simon told them that his mother-in-law was very sick with a high fever. Simon showed them his sick mother-in-law.** Encourage Simon to lead Jesus and the others to the sick "mother-in-law."

Jesus took her hand and helped her sit up. Have the child playing Jesus do this. **Then the fever left her, and she was very happy. She was so happy that she may have hugged Jesus.** Encourage the mother-in-law to hug Jesus. **She may have jumped up and down.** Encourage the child to jump up and down. **She may have done all of those things. But we know that she got up and prepared a meal for Jesus and the others.** Encourage the mother-in-law to pretend to cook a meal and serve it to the others. Encourage Jesus and the other disciples to pretend to eat the food.

That evening, after the sun went down, a whole crowd of people gathered at the house. They wanted to hear Jesus teach and see him heal the sick people among them. Encourage the "crowd" to gather near Jesus. **Jesus healed the sick people and made the bad spirits leave other people.** Encourage the child playing Jesus to touch those in the crowd who are pretending to be sick. Then tell the sick kids to act like they're feeling better. **The crowd was so happy that they smiled really big, they jumped up and down, and they hugged each other!** Encourage the crowd to follow these instructions.

Before the sun came up the next morning, Jesus went outside and prayed alone. Encourage your Jesus to go to a different side of the room and kneel. **Later Simon and the others went out to find Jesus.** Direct Simon and the other disciples to go to Jesus. **"Everyone is looking for you," they said to Jesus.** Have them point to the crowd. Encourage the crowd to wave at Jesus. **But Jesus said that he needed to travel to more towns so he could tell even more people about God and help more people feel better. So they all left and traveled to a new town.** Have all the kids march in place together.

ASK:

- ◆ **What are some of the amazing things Jesus did in our story?**
- ◆ **How can you trust that Jesus can do anything in your life?**

SAY: **Jesus did a lot of amazing things in our story: He healed people, he talked about God, and he even made bad spirits leave people. ▷ JESUS CAN DO ANYTHING! We can trust Jesus to do amazing things in our lives, too! Jesus can help us with the hard things we have to do, he can make us feel better when we're sad, and when we believe in him, he can give us life in heaven forever.**

n
o
t
e
s

BIBLE STORY

Jesus Heals a Paralyzed Man

For the Leader

At least two types of roofs were placed on houses in the area of Capernaum at the time of this Bible story. One was built by placing something akin to rafters across the top of the walls and then attaching cross members between them. Then tree branches were laid across the cross members and covered with dirt and mud. Once baked in the sun this became a hardened, reliable roof. The other type consisted of tiles laid across the rafters. Whichever roof was on this house, an opening could not have been made without everyone noticing that *something* was going on.

Everyone in the house (and on the roof!) was likely shocked when Jesus first forgave the paralytic's sins. Evidence that sins are forgiven by God was not immediately visible, but the healing of the man's paralysis was. When Jesus healed the man, he demonstrated that he had the power to do both.

Key Scriptures

Mark 2:1-12

1 John 1:9

Bible Verse

"If we confess our sins to him, he is faithful and just to forgive us our sins and to cleanse us from all wickedness" (1 John 1:9).

Bible Experience

▶ *NO PREP*

Bible Point: ▷ **BRING YOUR FRIENDS TO JESUS.**

Children will play a game and discuss how Jesus wipes away their sins.

Supplies: Bible, stickers, chalkboard, chalk, eraser

Time: about 15 minutes

Preparation: none

Have kids form pairs.

ASK:

◆ **Have you ever wanted to do something so much that you'd give almost anything to be able to do it? Tell your partner what you wanted to do.**

After partners discuss this with each other, invite a few volunteers to share their answers with rest of the group. Then open your Bible to Mark 2:1-12, and show kids the passage.

SAY: **The Bible tells a true story about five men who found a creative way to do something they really wanted to do. Here's what happened. Jesus was at a house teaching people. But there were so many people in the house**

that these men couldn't get inside. Still, the five men really, really wanted to see Jesus because one of the men was paralyzed. He couldn't use his arms or legs, and he knew Jesus could help him.

Let's play a game. I have a sticker for each of you, but you have to come get it from me. The catch is, you can't use your arms or legs in any way. Everybody try!

Pause for only a few moments, and then SAY: **Nice try. You can imagine how hard it was for the paralyzed man to get to Jesus. Four of the man's friends carried him to see Jesus, but they couldn't get inside the house. Yet that didn't stop them! They climbed onto the roof and cut a hole in it, and then they lowered the man down to Jesus!**

ASK:

- **What do you think the people in the house thought when they saw a man being lowered through the roof?**
- **What do you think Jesus said when he saw the man?**

SAY: **When Jesus saw that the men believed he could heal their paralyzed friend, Jesus said to him, "My child, your sins are forgiven."**

ASK:

- **What is sin?**

SAY: **Let's write some things we've done that we think are sins.** Let each child write a sin on the board; then SAY: **When Jesus forgave the paralyzed man, he erased his sins. When we believe in Jesus and ask him to forgive us, he erases our sins, too. Just like this!** Let each child erase his or her sin from the board.

You know, this story reminds me of a verse in the Bible. Read aloud 1 John 1:9. If kids have their own Bibles, let them read it with you. Then SAY: **This verse says that when we confess, or tell, our sins to God, he forgives us and erases our sins. In our Bible story, Jesus forgave the sins of the paralyzed man.**

But that's not the end of our story! To show that Jesus could forgive the man's sins *and* heal him, he told the man to get up and walk. And the man did! Jesus healed him! Those four men wanted to bring their friend to Jesus. God wants you to ▷ BRING YOUR FRIENDS TO JESUS, too!

ASK:

- **How can you bring your friends to Jesus this week?**
- **What can you tell your friends about Jesus?**

SAY: **This week, see how many of your friends you can tell about Jesus!**

Song & Connect

Use "I Will Be Your Friend" (track 23, *it: Innovative Tools for Children's Ministry: New Testament* CD) to help reinforce the Bible Point, **▷ BRING YOUR FRIENDS TO JESUS.**

Additional Topics List

This lesson can be used to help kids discover... Courage, Determination, Faith, and Friendship.

notes

Game

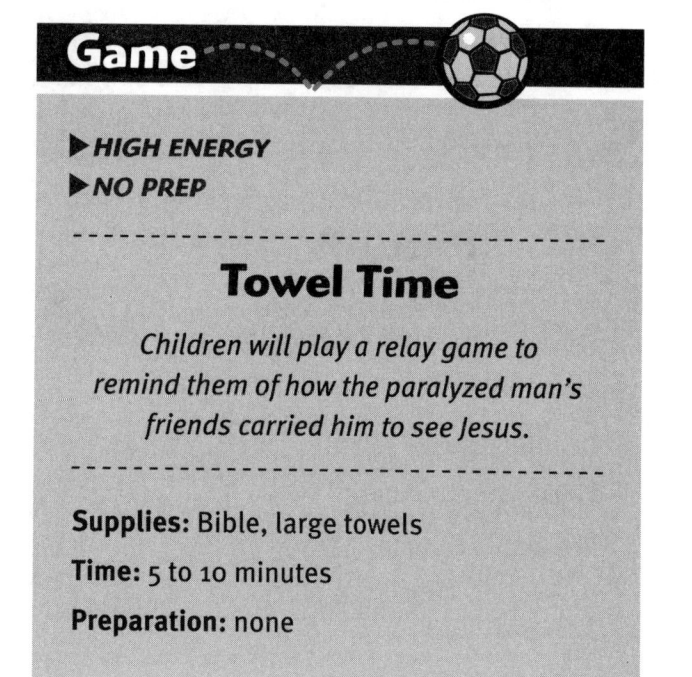

▶ *HIGH ENERGY*
▶ *NO PREP*

Towel Time

Children will play a relay game to remind them of how the paralyzed man's friends carried him to see Jesus.

Supplies: Bible, large towels

Time: 5 to 10 minutes

Preparation: none

Open your Bible to Mark 2:1-12, and briefly summarize the story of Jesus' healing a paralyzed man. Then have kids form teams of equal number. Give each team a large towel.

Have each team line up single file on one side of the room. Have the first person in each line sit on a towel. Have the next person in line hold the towel and, at your signal, *slowly* pull the towel—with the child sitting on it—across the room and back.

Then the first child will go and sit at the back of the line. The child who did the pulling will sit on the towel while the next person in line pulls him or her across the room and back. Continue until everyone is sitting. Then have kids answer the following questions with their team members.

ASK:

- **What was it like to pull your friend across the room?**
- **How did it feel to be pulled on the mat?**
- **How do you think the paralyzed man felt when he knew his friends were taking him to Jesus?**
- **Why is it important to help our friends know Jesus?**

SAY: **The paralyzed man's friends knew how important it is to know Jesus. They knew that Jesus could heal their friend. It's important for you to ▷ BRING YOUR FRIENDS TO JESUS because Jesus is the only one who can forgive their sins.**

Craft

▶ *PREPARE IN ADVANCE*

Wonderful Weaving

Children will weave mats to remind them that the paralyzed man's friends carried him on a mat.

Supplies: Bible, construction paper, ruler, pencils, safety scissors, glue sticks

Time: about 15 minutes

Preparation: Create a sample of the craft to show kids.

Read aloud (or summarize) Mark 2:1-12. Show kids how to fold a sheet of paper in half so the short ends are together. Use a ruler to draw a light line opposite the fold, about an inch from the edge. At 1-inch intervals, cut from the fold to the pencil line. Then open the paper. This will be your weaving base.

Cut colorful strips of paper to weave through the base. The strips should be at least as wide as the opened base. Demonstrate how to weave the strips over and under, from one side of the base to the other. When the base has been filled in with woven strips, trim the edges and glue the ends of the strips down. Encourage kids to use their mats to tell how Jesus healed the paralyzed man.

Bible Application

▶*NO PREP*

Picture This!

Children will be encouraged to tell their friends about Jesus.

Supplies: Bible, index cards, pencils, marker and newsprint or chalk and chalkboard, tape

Time: about 5 minutes

Preparation: none

Read aloud or summarize Mark 2:1-12. Then hand out 3x5-inch cards and pencils. SAY: **The paralyzed man's friends brought him to Jesus. You can ▷ BRING YOUR FRIENDS TO JESUS, too. Think of people you'd like to introduce to Jesus. Draw pictures of those people, one picture per card.**

After kids finish drawing, SAY: **The paralyzed man's friends went out of their way to make sure he got to see Jesus. Let's think of ways we can introduce people to Jesus. It's OK if our ideas are unusual! For example, maybe you could plant a flower garden that spells out, "Jesus loves you," and then invite a friend over to see it when it blooms.**

Write the word *JESUS* on a chalkboard or sheet of newsprint taped to a wall. As each child mentions an idea, have him or her tape a picture under the word *JESUS*. After all of the pictures have been taped, have kids each choose one idea they want to follow through on.

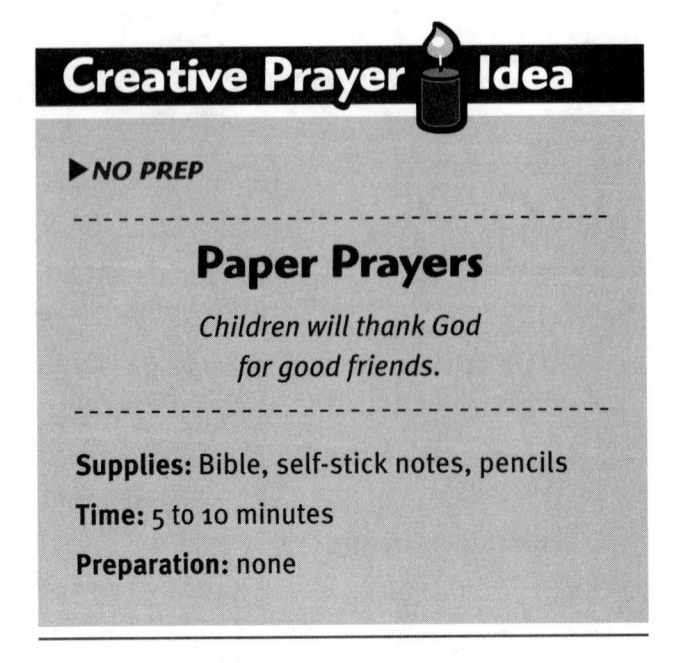

Creative Prayer Idea

▶*NO PREP*

Paper Prayers

Children will thank God for good friends.

Supplies: Bible, self-stick notes, pencils

Time: 5 to 10 minutes

Preparation: none

Read aloud or summarize Mark 2:1-12. Have kids form a circle, and give each person as many self-stick notes as there are other kids in class. Have each person write the name of one classmate on the top of each note. Beneath the name, have each child write a simple prayer for that person. Then have kids stick their paper prayers on the appropriate people.

Remind kids that the paralyzed man was probably grateful to his friends for taking him to Jesus. Close with a prayer, thanking God for the good friends your kids have and asking him to help them bring their friends to Jesus, too.

Discussion Launcher Questions

Have kids form trios to discuss the following questions. After each question, invite volunteers to share their answers with the rest of the class.

ASK:

- **Why do you think Jesus was more concerned with forgiving the paralyzed man's sins than with healing his body?**
- **What do you think would have happened if the paralyzed man's friends had given up when they saw the crowd?**

- ◆ **Who first told you about Jesus? How has knowing Jesus changed your life?**
- ◆ **How many of your friends have you told about Jesus? If you haven't told all of your friends, why not?**
- ◆ **Whom can you tell about Jesus this week?**

As kids eat the rest of the roofs, have them discuss how the paralyzed man and his friends must have felt when Jesus healed the man. Remind kids that God wants them to ▷**BRING THEIR FRIENDS TO JESUS,** just as the paralyzed man's friends did.

Snack

▶*PREPARE IN ADVANCE*

▶*ALLERGY ALERT*

Raise the Roof

Children will make edible roofs to remind them of today's story.

Supplies: Bible, bread, small paper plates, plastic knives, softened cream cheese, chow-mein noodles, Gummi bears

Time: about 10 minutes

Preparation: Have kids wash their hands.

Read aloud or summarize Mark 2:1-12. Then SAY: **The roofs in Bible times were often made of a thatchlike substance, kind of like layers of dried branches and grass. Let's make our own roofs to remind us of this story.**

Give each child a plastic knife and a slice of bread on a small paper plate. Let kids spread the bread with softened cream cheese and then sprinkle chow-mein noodles over the spread to look like thatch. SAY: **There—we have our roofs. Then what happened in the story?**

Let kids use the knives to cut holes in their roofs. (Kids can eat the cut-out sections.) Then have students form pairs, and give each pair a few Gummi bears. Let partners take turns lowering their Gummi bears through the holes in their roofs.

Preschool Story

▶*PREPARE IN ADVANCE*

Bible Point: ▷ **BRING YOUR FRIENDS TO JESUS.**

Supplies: Bible, butcher paper, pencil, scissors, tape, beach towel, chairs

Time: 10 to 15 minutes

Preparation: Make a paper outline of a man, and attach it to the beach towel with tape. Also, make a square house out of chairs by setting the chairs side by side with the seats facing out. Make the "house" large enough for your class to sit inside but small enough to be crowded while they're in it.

A Crowded Room

Have kids form a circle and sit down. Open your Bible to Mark 2:1-12, and show children the words. SAY: **Jesus had gone to Capernaum and was talking to a group of people in a house.** Choose a child to be Jesus, and place him or her in the house. **The house was very crowded.** Have all but four children go into the house with Jesus.

Everyone was listening to Jesus talk when, all of a sudden, four people came carrying a crippled man on a mat. These friends wanted to bring their sick friend to Jesus. Give the four remaining children the beach-towel "mat" with the paper man placed in the center, and have them carry it to the door of the house. **But there was no way they would be able to get in through the door. So they came up with a better plan: They would lower their friend down through the roof!** Help the four children with the mat climb up on the chairs and lower the mat down into the house. Have the children inside the house make room for the mat to be placed on the floor.

The people inside were very surprised! Have the children inside the house make surprised faces. Then look up at the ceiling and

ASK:

- **How would you feel if someone started coming through our ceiling?**

SAY: **When Jesus saw them, he did something amazing. He told the crippled man that his sins were forgiven. Well, some of the important teachers who were there didn't like that.** Have children cross their arms and make grouchy faces. **"How can you forgive this man's sins? Do you think you're God?" they asked. Jesus said to the grouchy men, "I will show you that I am the Son of God. I can forgive his sins and tell him to get up and walk." So Jesus turned to the crippled man and said, "Stand up, pick up your mat, and go home!"** Have one child pick up the paper man from the mat and pretend to walk him out of the house.

Wow! The friends were very excited to see that Jesus had healed their crippled friend. They were glad they had brought their friend to Jesus.

ASK:

- **How would you feel if you were one of those friends?**
- **How would you feel if you were the man who could walk again?**

SAY: **Those four friends brought their crippled friend to Jesus. Jesus healed the man, and he forgave the man's sins. You can ▷BRING YOUR FRIENDS TO JESUS, too. When you ▷BRING YOUR FRIENDS TO JESUS and help them believe in Jesus, then Jesus will forgive their sins, too!**

notes

BIBLE STORY

Jesus Walks on Water

For the Leader

Evening was approaching when Jesus sent his disciples toward the other side of the Sea of Galilee by boat, dismissed the crowd, and retired alone to pray. He must have prayed for several hours because the Bible says he didn't approach the disciples' boat until about three o'clock in the morning.

The disciples' terror at seeing a figure walking on the water was understandable. They assumed the figure must be a ghost. Their cries of fear prompted Jesus to respond with compassion.

Hearing Jesus' voice, Peter had the impetuous idea that maybe Jesus could help *him* walk on water, too. Jesus took him up on it. Peter's success and then his failure hinged on his focus on Jesus. When his focus wavered from Jesus, Peter faltered and almost drowned.

Key Scriptures

Matthew 14:22-33

2 Timothy 2:13

Bible Verse

"If we are unfaithful, he remains faithful" (2 Timothy 2:13).

Bible Experience

▶ ***NO PREP***

Bible Point: ▷ **HAVE FAITH IN JESUS.**

Children will use storytelling to help them have faith in Jesus.

Supplies: Bible, sheets of paper

Time: about 10 minutes

Preparation: none

You'll need one child to be Jesus, one to be Peter, and two to be followers. Everyone else will be the waves. Have the "waves" sit in a wide circle, and give each one a sheet of paper. Have the two "followers" sit together inside the circle and pretend to row a boat. Have "Jesus" stand outside the circle. Have the children join you in doing the motions indicated as you read the following story.

SAY: **Let's pretend we're there the night Jesus walked on water.** Read aloud Matthew 14:22-33; then SAY: **We're rowing across the lake.** (Followers continue to row.) **It sure is dark out here.** (Followers shield their eyes and then continue to row.) **At least the waves are gentle and the breeze is light.** (Waves slowly fan the papers up and down and make gentle whooshing sounds. Followers slowly row.)

What's that noise? The wind seems to be picking up. (Waves fan papers faster and make louder whooshing sounds. Followers row harder.)

Oh, no! It looks like a storm! It's getting harder and harder to row! (Followers row harder as waves fan faster and make more noise.) **This is terrible! I'm so scared! What if we drown? I wonder if Jesus knows what's happening to us?** (Jesus puts his hand over his eyebrows and looks toward the boat; then he steps into the "lake" and walks toward the followers.)

What's that? I can barely see through the rain, but...but it looks like someone walking toward us! On the water! Help, it must be a ghost! No human could do that! (Followers crouch in fear as waves continue fanning.)

Wait! I know that voice! Could it really be Jesus? (Jesus says, "Don't be afraid. Take courage. I am here!" Followers peer into the storm. Waves continue fanning.) **It is! It's Jesus! Then Peter calls out, "Lord, if it's really you, tell me to come to you, walking on water."**

"Yes, come," Jesus says. So Peter goes over the side of the boat and walks on the water toward Jesus. But when he looks around at the high waves, he's terrified and starts to sink. "Save me, Lord!" he shouts.

Instantly Jesus reaches out his hand and grabs him. "You have so little faith," Jesus says. "Why did you doubt me?" And when they climb back into the boat, the wind stops. (Waves stop fanning. Jesus steps into the boat. Followers hold their arms up toward him.)

We're safe! Jesus made the storm stop! Thank you, Jesus! You can do anything! (Everyone claps.)

Peter learned how important faith is. When he had faith, he could walk on water. When he took his eyes off Jesus, he began to sink.

Ask a volunteer to read aloud 2 Timothy 2:13, and then have kids repeat it. SAY: **Even when the winds and waves of circumstances shake our confidence in God's power, he remains faithful and worthy of our trust. He has power to save us. It's important to ▷ HAVE FAITH IN JESUS.**

Additional Topics List

This lesson can be used to help kids discover... Facing Fear, Faith, Jesus' Power, and Trust.

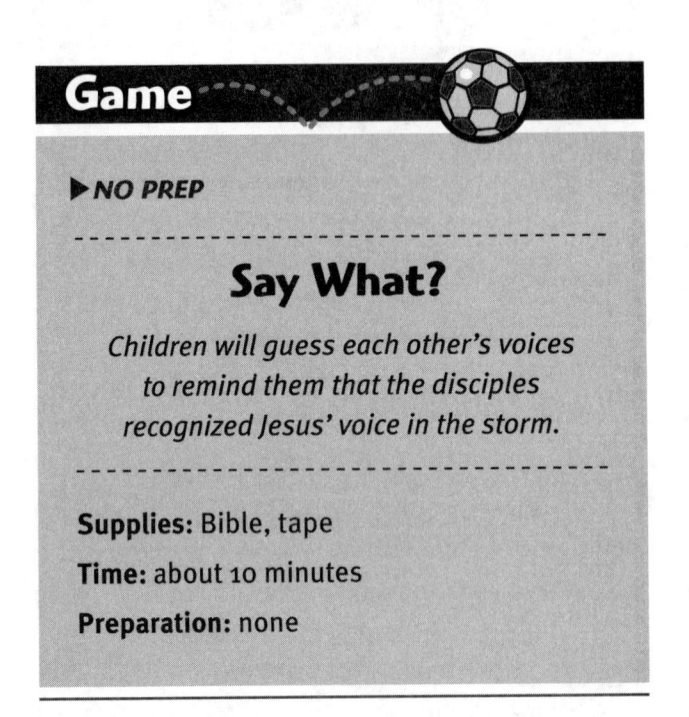

Game

▶ *NO PREP*

Say What?

Children will guess each other's voices to remind them that the disciples recognized Jesus' voice in the storm.

Supplies: Bible, tape

Time: about 10 minutes

Preparation: none

Open your Bible to Matthew 14:22-33, and briefly summarize the story of Jesus walking on water. Explain that the disciples recognized Jesus' voice in the storm. Tell kids that in this game, they'll try to guess each other's voices.

Have everyone sit on the floor, side by side but not touching each other. Tell kids that they are to close their eyes and keep them closed. You'll walk behind the line and tap one person on the shoulder. That child will carefully stand behind the line and say something in a disguised voice. (For example, kids could sing a preschool song, recite the alphabet, or count to 10.) The rest of the class will try to guess who's speaking.

Play a few rounds with different speakers. (If you have time, let everyone have a turn.) Then have kids form trios to discuss the following questions. Invite volunteers to share their answers with the class.

ASK:

- **What was it like trying to guess who was speaking?**
- **How do you think the disciples felt when they recognized Jesus' voice in the storm?**
- **How does Jesus speak to you during the stormy times in your life?**

Lead children in a brief prayer thanking Jesus for being with us during the scary times we face. Remind children to ▷ **HAVE FAITH IN JESUS,** no matter what stormy times they're facing.

Craft

▶ *PREPARE IN ADVANCE*

Stormy Seas

Children will make stormy pictures to remind them that Jesus saved the disciples during a storm.

Supplies: Bible, black foam board (found in office-supply stores), scissors, white poster board, sponges, clothespins, brown and blue tempera paint, shallow dishes, gel pens, glitter-glue pens

Time: about 15 minutes

Preparation: Cut the black foam board into 8-inch squares. Cut several simple boat templates out of white poster board. The boats should be about 5 inches long. Cut sponges into small pieces, and attach the clothespins as holders to keep mess to a minimum. Pour paint into shallow dishes.

Read aloud Matthew 14:22-33 (or summarize the story for the kids). SAY: **It's important to ▷ HAVE FAITH IN JESUS. Jesus can help us through all of the stormy times in our lives. Let's make stormy-sea pictures to remind us of this Bible story.**

Help kids follow these instructions: Place a boat template on a black foam square. Using a sponge, paint the boat with brown paint to a few inches from the bottom. Use the blue paint to paint the water around the boat. Then use gel pens and glitter-glue pens to paint the disciples in the boat, Jesus walking on the water toward the boat, and other details, such as the waves and night sky. As pictures dry, have kids discuss these questions. ASK:

- **What's one word that describes how you would have felt if you had been one of the disciples and had seen someone walking on the water?**
- **What's one thing you're afraid of?**
- **How can having faith in Jesus help you with that fear?**

SAY: **When we ▷ HAVE FAITH IN JESUS, we can ask him to help us when we're afraid. And he will!**

Bible Application

▶ *PREPARE IN ADVANCE*

Stay Focused

Children will learn to keep their eyes on Jesus.

Supplies: masking tape, blindfold

Time: about 10 minutes

Preparation: Use masking tape to make a meandering path on the floor.

SAY: **When Peter climbed out of the boat, he was able to walk on the water. That is, as long as he kept his eyes on Jesus! As soon as he lost his focus on Jesus, he started to mess up. It's like that in life, too.**

Have a volunteer stand at the start of your tape path. Blindfold the volunteer and SAY: **Walk along this path, keeping your feet on the tape the whole time. I'll let you know if you stray off the path. Ready? Go!**

The volunteer won't be able to stay completely on the path for long. As soon as he or she strays off the tape, call time and choose another volunteer. (If you have time, give everyone a turn.)

ASK:

- **Was this game easy or difficult? Why?**
- **What would make this game easier?**

Play again without blindfolding the volunteers.

ASK:

- **How was the game different the second time we played?**
- **How is that like keeping your eyes on Jesus?**
- **In our game, the blindfold kept us from seeing where to go. What kinds of things keep us from staying focused on Jesus in real life?**

SAY: **When we ▷ HAVE FAITH IN JESUS and keep our eyes on him, it's easy to follow the right path. This week, let's not allow anyone or anything to blind us. Let's keep our eyes on Jesus!**

Creative Prayer Idea

▶ PREPARE IN ADVANCE

Floating Fears

Children will tell Jesus something that scares them and then watch their fears float away.

Supplies: fish bowl, water, sponge, scissors

Time: 5 to 10 minutes

Preparation: Partially fill a fish bowl with water. Cut a sponge into as many small pieces as you have kids in class.

Have children sit in a circle on the floor. Place the fish bowl in the center of the circle. Give each person a sponge piece. SAY: **These sponge pieces float on water. They can remind us of how Jesus walked on the water in today's Bible story. In the story the disciples were afraid, but Jesus calmed their fears. Think of one thing you're afraid of right now.** Pause. **We'll go around the circle. When it's your turn, place your sponge piece on top of the water and say, "Jesus, I give my fear to you."**

After everyone has placed a sponge piece in the bowl, close with a prayer to thank Jesus for always being with us, even during scary times.

n
o
t
e
s

Science Devotion

▶*NO PREP*

The Eyes Have It

Children will see that just as the pupils of their eyes dilate automatically, they can choose to have faith in Jesus even in scary situations.

Supplies: Bible, small flashlights, large mirror that several kids can look into at the same time (or enough hand mirrors for each child to have one)

Time: about 10 minutes

Preparation: none

Open your Bible to Matthew 14:22-33, and show kids the passage. Read or summarize the story of Jesus walking on water. SAY: **We all have scary times in our lives. But we can ▷ HAVE FAITH IN JESUS and know that he's always there with us.**

Have kids form pairs. SAY: **Look into your partner's eyes, especially watching the black circle, or the pupil, in the middle of the eye. When we're in normal light, the pupils of our eyes are a certain size that lets in just the right amount of light so we can see clearly. If we're in bright light, the pupils get smaller to keep the light from hurting our eyes. If we turn off the lights, our pupils get bigger to let in more light so we can see better.**

Give each child (or group of children) a small flashlight, and have kids stand in front of a mirror (or give each child a hand mirror). SAY: **Quickly turn on your flashlight and shine it across your face while you look in the mirror. Can you see your pupils change in response to the light? We can't choose to make our eyes do this; it's an automatic response.**

In the same way, we can choose to automatically have faith in Jesus, even when we're feeling afraid. We can remember that Jesus is always with us, just as he was with the disciples in our Bible story. This experiment can remind us that although we can't always choose what situations we're in, we can choose to ▷ HAVE FAITH IN JESUS.

Snack

▶ *ALLERGY ALERT*
▶ *PREPARE IN ADVANCE*

Water Walking

Children will make a jiggly snack to remember that Jesus walked on water.

Supplies: gelatin mix, blue food coloring, knife, small plastic bowls, graham crackers, jellybeans, teddy-bear crackers

Time: about 5 minutes

Preparation: Clean the surface where you and your kids will be creating your boats. Follow package directions to make a pan of gelatin. Tint the gelatin blue. When it's ready, cut the gelatin into squares, and place a square in a small plastic bowl for each child.

SAY: **It must have been amazing to see Jesus walking on the water. Let's make a snack to remind us not only of the Bible story but also to ▷ HAVE FAITH IN JESUS. Remember, Jesus can do anything!**

Give each child a bowl containing a gelatin square. Explain that the blue gelatin represents the sea. Show kids how to take two graham-cracker rectangles and angle them together to form an open V shape in the center of the bowl. This will be the "boat." Let kids place jellybeans inside the boat to be the disciples, and place the teddy-bear crackers outside the boat to represent Jesus walking on the water. As kids enjoy their snacks, have them discuss these questions with partners:

- ◆ **How would you have felt if you had seen Jesus walking toward you on top of the water?**
- ◆ **How can your faith in Jesus help you the next time you face a tough situation?**
- ◆ **Of all the amazing things you know that Jesus has done, what do you think is the most amazing?**

Preschool Story

▶ *ALLERGY ALERT*
▶ *PREPARE IN ADVANCE*

Bible Point: ▷ **HAVE FAITH IN JESUS.**

Supplies: Bible, teddy-bear crackers, muffin cup-sized portions of blueberry finger gelatin, candy orange slices, napkins

Time: 15 to 20 minutes

Preparation: Prepare blueberry finger gelatin according to the package instructions. Pour the liquid gelatin into a muffin pan. After the gelatin is firm, pop it out of the muffin pan. Serve the gelatin on napkins. Make four slits crosswise in each orange slice.

Miracle at Sea

Have kids form a circle and sit down. Open your Bible to Matthew 14:22-33, and show children the words. SAY: **This is the story of Jesus walking on water. We're going to act out the story as we make a special snack.** Give each child one portion of the finger gelatin and five teddy-bear crackers.

Jesus told his disciples to get into the boat while he prayed. Encourage each preschooler to put four teddy-bear crackers into the slits of his or her orange-slice "boat" and place the boat in the gelatin, which is the "water.")

The wind blew and blew, and the boat moved far away from the shore! Have kids imitate wind by blowing on the gelatin. **The next morning Jesus came to the disciples by walking across the water! Jesus didn't sink—he walked right on top of the water.** Encourage children to take the remaining teddy-bear cracker and "walk" it on the gelatin.

When Peter saw Jesus, he wanted to try it, too! Jesus said, "Peter, come to me!" Peter had faith that Jesus could help him walk on water, too! Have kids take one teddy bear cracker out of their boat and walk it toward the Jesus cracker. **The wind started to blow, and Peter was afraid! Peter forgot to have faith in Jesus, and he started to sink.** Encourage children to blow on the gelatin and then push the Peter cracker down into the gelatin. **"Save me!" Peter cried out to Jesus. Jesus reached out his hand and helped Peter.** Have children lift the Peter cracker back up onto the gelatin. **The disciples said to Jesus, "Truly, you are the Son of God!"** Encourage children to say, "You are the Son of God!"

Enjoy eating the snack together. When children are finished eating, teach them this song to the tune of "Did You Ever See a Lassie?" As you sing the song, have kids pretend to walk on water.

Jesus walked upon the water,
The water, the water.
Jesus walked upon the water.
He is God's Son.

Peter walked upon the water,
The water, the water.
Peter walked upon the water.
He had faith in God.

ASK:

- **How did Peter have faith in Jesus?**
- **Why did Peter lose faith in Jesus?**
- **How did Jesus help Peter?**
- **When can you have faith in Jesus?**

SAY: **Peter had faith in Jesus to help him walk on water at first, but when the wind began to blow, Peter was afraid and lost his faith in Jesus. But Peter should have continued to have faith in Jesus; Peter should have trusted Jesus to help him even when he was scared. We can always ▷HAVE FAITH IN JESUS, no matter what—even when we're scared or worried! Jesus will always be there to help us and take care of us.**

n
o
t
e
s

BIBLE STORY

Jesus Calms a Storm

For the Leader

Jesus' suggestion to go to the other side of the Sea of Galilee sounds simple. But few Galileans ever ventured across the lake. The boats Jesus' disciples used were small fishing boats not intended for crossing the lake, which was 14 miles long and six miles wide. Finally, the geography surrounding the lake made it susceptible to sudden storms.

Although many of the disciples were experienced fishermen and expert sailors, the fact that they turned to Jesus for help during the storm likely meant that they were at the end of their means. When Jesus awoke, he immediately demonstrated that he was in control. He simply said "Silence!" Then he said, "Be still!" a term which literally means "muzzle yourself and continue to be silent." The disciples came to learn that no matter how bad a situation seemed, the first thing they needed to do was turn to Jesus.

Key Scriptures

Mark 4:35-41

1 Peter 5:7

Bible Verse

"Give all your worries and cares to God, for he cares about you" (1 Peter 5:7).

Bible Experience

▶ ***PREPARE IN ADVANCE***

Bible Point: ▷ JESUS IS BIGGER THAN FEAR.

Children will use a dramatic reading to discover that Jesus is bigger than fear.

Supplies: Bible, blue and green crepe paper

Time: about 10 minutes

Preparation: Cut crepe paper into 1-foot lengths.

Have a volunteer read aloud Mark 4:35-41, or summarize the story for your class. Then SAY: **Today we're going to act out the story of Jesus calming the storm.** Have kids form two groups, the Waves and the Disciples. Give each Wave a blue streamer and a green streamer made of foot-long crepe paper. **These will be your waves.**

Give each Disciple a long streamer of either color of crepe paper. SAY: **These will be your rain hats.** Have each Disciple wrap the streamer around his or her head like a scarf and carefully tie it under the chin.

Have the Disciples sit together in the center of the floor, as if huddled together in a boat. Have the Waves stand on one side of the room.

SAY: **OK, Waves, let's practice being wild waves.** Have the Waves crouch down. When you point from one end of the line to the other, have kids stand, stretch their arms and wave their streamers in the air, and then crouch back down. **Great job! As I tell the story and you hear the storm really get going, I want you to do the wave. But I also want you to move back and forth across the room so the waves go *over* the disciples in the boat. Let's practice that.** Have the Waves move across the room and back, letting the streamers flow up and down over the Disciples.

Now, Disciples, let's practice rowing that boat. Have the kids practice rowing in unison. **OK, I think we're ready to start. Listen carefully and act along with what the story says. Ready? Here we go!**

Jesus and his disciples had gotten into a boat to go across a big lake, and Jesus was sleeping. At first the wind was low, so the waves were tiny. Have the Waves make a gentle wave motion as they walk across the room and back. **The disciples had no trouble rowing their boat.** Have the Disciples row in a leisurely way. **But then the wind picked up, and the waves got bigger. The disciples had to row harder.** Pause to let kids respond with the appropriate actions. **Finally, the storm got so big that the water was crashing over the boat and the disciples could barely row against the wind.** Pause so kids can respond. **The waves kept crashing, and the disciples kept struggling, but the boat was filling up with water!** Pause.

They woke Jesus up, crying, "Teacher, don't you care that we're going to drown?" Jesus did an amazing thing. Have everyone freeze. **Jesus said to the wind and the water, "Silence! Be still!" Suddenly, the wind and the waves stopped, and everything was calm.** Have the Waves crouch down and the Disciples stop rowing. **The disciples couldn't believe it—even the wind and the waves obeyed Jesus!**

Have kids throw away their crepe paper and sit in their groups to answer these questions:

- **What were the disciples afraid of during the storm?**
- **What are you afraid of sometimes?**
- **How can Jesus help you when you're afraid?**

SAY: **▷JESUS IS BIGGER THAN FEAR. He's bigger than anything that scares us. He's in control, so we don't have to be afraid. He'll always be with us, no matter what situation we face.** Close with a prayer thanking Jesus for being bigger than our fears and for always being with us.

Song & Connect

Use "He Cares for You" (track 22, *it: Innovative Tools for Children's Ministry: New Testament* CD) to help reinforce the Bible Point, **▷JESUS IS BIGGER THAN FEAR.**

Additional Topics List

This lesson can be used to help kids discover... Anxiety, Faith, and Trust.

notes

Game

▶ *NO PREP*

Stormy Seas

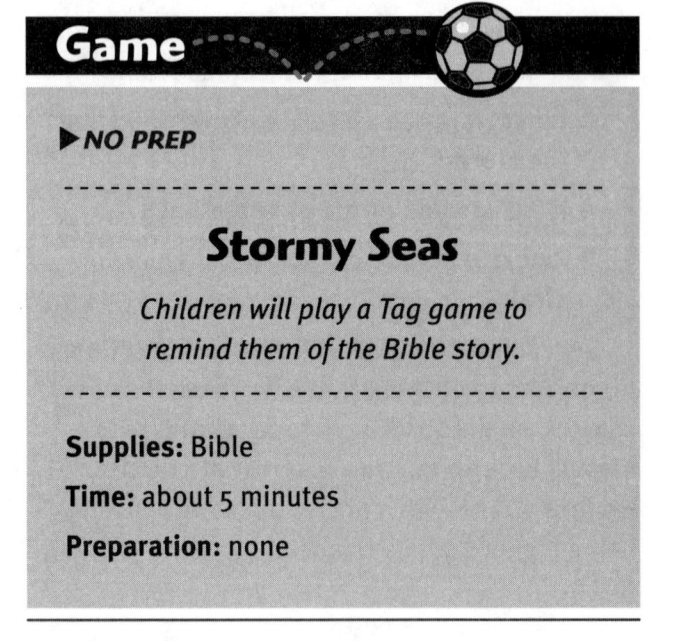

Children will play a Tag game to remind them of the Bible story.

Supplies: Bible

Time: about 5 minutes

Preparation: none

Open your Bible to Mark 4:35-41, and summarize the story of Jesus calming the storm. SAY: **Jesus' followers must have been scared!**

ASK:

- **Have you ever been in a scary storm? What was it like?**
- **When are some other times you've been afraid?**

SAY: **We're all scared sometimes, but it's great to know that Jesus is always taking care of us. Let's play a game to remind us of the Bible story.**

Form two groups, the Followers and the Stormy Seas. At your signal, have the Followers pretend to row across the room to the opposite wall. To do so the Followers will have to walk backward. The Stormy Seas will try to tag the Followers as they row. Encourage the Stormy Seas to move their arms up and down and make wind and thunder noises.

A Stormy Sea can't tag a Follower if the Follower first says, "Be still!" If a Follower is tagged first, though, he or she becomes a Stormy Sea and joins in the tagging.

Play for a few minutes, and then call time. Have kids switch roles and play again. Then let everyone sit down to rest. SAY: **Jesus can calm all the storms in our lives. Let's thank him for that right now!** Close with a prayer thanking Jesus for being bigger than the fears and storms in our lives.

Craft

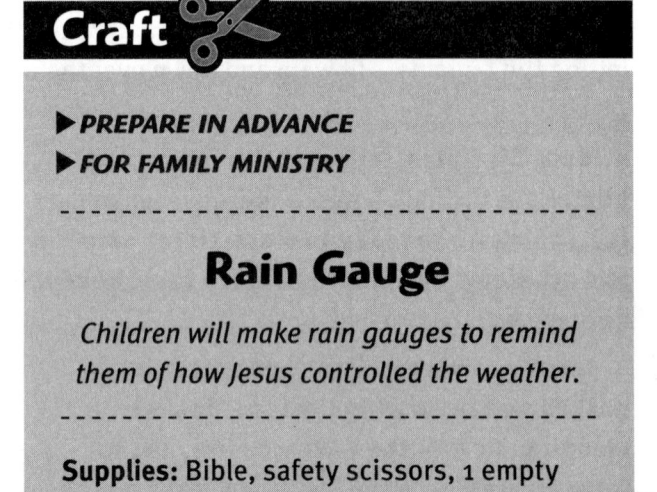

▶ *PREPARE IN ADVANCE*
▶ *FOR FAMILY MINISTRY*

Rain Gauge

Children will make rain gauges to remind them of how Jesus controlled the weather.

Supplies: Bible, safety scissors, 1 empty 2-liter bottle, 1 clear jar for each child

Time: about 10 minutes

Preparation: Make a sample craft to show your class.

Read aloud Mark 4:35-41. SAY: **Let's make a craft to remind us of how Jesus calmed the storm. We'll make rain gauges to remind us of the rain in the storm.**

Show kids how to carefully cut the top from the bottle. (If you have mostly young children, do this step before class.) Place the bottle top upside down in the clear jar to serve as a funnel. Explain that kids can place their rain gauges in a safe place outside at home or as a class outside the church. Each day (or week) they can check to see how much it rained by pouring the contents of the jar into a measuring cup that measures milliliters. (You could also print a measuring guide and tape it to the side of the jar.) Encourage kids to record their measurements and try to observe weather patterns.

SAY: **In our story the disciples were surprised by a big storm.**

ASK:

- **Do you think people can predict the weather today?**
- **Who's in control of the weather?**
- **Who's in control of your life?**

SAY: **Scientists can sometimes predict what the weather will be, but sometimes they can't. And they certainly can't control the weather like Jesus did in the Bible. God is in control of the weather, and he's in control of your life. You can trust God to take care of all of your situations—even the scary ones like storms—because he loves you. Every time you measure the rain in your rain gauge, remember that God is in control!**

Bible Application

▶ *FOR FAMILY MINISTRY*
▶ *NO PREP*

Super Sailing

Children will make pictures to remind them that Jesus is bigger than their fears.

Supplies: Bible, construction paper, pencils, safety scissors, small paper plates, stapler, markers, gel pens, glitter glue, cotton balls, glue sticks, scrap paper

Time: 10 to 15 minutes

Preparation: none

Read aloud Mark 4:35-41. SAY: **Let's make something to remind us that ▷JESUS IS BIGGER THAN FEAR.** Have kids hold a sheet of construction paper horizontally and draw water and waves at the bottom. Show kids how to cut a paper plate in half and staple it, rounded side down, on the "water" for the boat. Let kids decorate their pictures by coloring the boat, drawing rain and lightning in the sky, and adding lots of waves to the water. Show them how to pull cotton balls apart and glue "whitecaps" at the tips of their waves.

When everyone has finished drawing, gather kids together in a circle. Set out the scrap paper and pencils. Read aloud 1 Peter 5:7, and then SAY: **In our story the disciples were worried about drowning in the storm.**

ASK:

- **What kinds of things do you worry about?**
- **What does the Bible say we should do with our worries and fears?**

SAY: **God cares for us so much that he wants us to give him all of our fears and worries. Let's try that. Think of one thing that's worrying or scaring you today, and write a word or two about it on a piece of scrap paper.** Pause as kids write, and then SAY: **Now we'll go around the circle, and each person can say, "Jesus, I give you my fear," as you put the paper inside the boat on your drawing.** Go around the circle.

Take your pictures home, and every time you're worried or scared, write down your fear and put it in your boat. Ask Jesus to take away your fear, just as he did for the disciples.

n
o
t
e
s

Creative Prayer Idea

▶ *NO PREP*

Storm Sounds

Children will tell God their fears and trust him to care for them.

Supplies: none

Time: about 5 minutes

Preparation: none

Have kids sit in a circle on the floor. SAY: **Today we heard about Jesus' calming a scary storm. Think of something that scares you. We'll go around the circle and tell God what we're afraid of as we make a storm right here.** Explain that you'll name something you're afraid of, such as getting sick or losing your job. Then you'll start patting your hands on the floor to sound like rain. Then the person on your left will do the same, and so on, until everyone in the circle has named a fear and is patting the floor. By the time the prayer goes around the circle, it will sound like a pounding rainstorm.

Explain that you'll then name one thing you're thankful to God for, such as your family or something in nature. Then you'll stop patting your hands. That part of the prayer will go around the circle, too, quieting the stormy sounds.

Give kids a moment to think of what they'll say, and then begin the prayer. After the storm sounds quiet, close the prayer by thanking God for calming the storms in our lives and handling all of our fears.

Discussion Launcher

Storm Stories

For this activity, gather pictures of actual storms. Weather books and posters are one source, or you can print pictures from storm sites on the Internet.

Pass the pictures around to children, or hang them in your classroom. Let kids examine the pictures and discuss their reactions. Then have kids form trios to discuss these questions:

- **Which of these pictures do you think most resembles the storm the disciples were in?**
- **How would it feel to be in one of these storms?**
- **What do you think would have happened if Jesus hadn't been in the boat during the storm?**
- **When is it hard for you to remember that Jesus is there to help you when you're scared?**
- **How can this Bible story help you the next time you face a stormy time in your life?**

Snack

▶ *PREPARE IN ADVANCE*

▶ *ALLERGY ALERT*

A-Sailing We Will Go

Children will make snack boats to remind them of how Jesus saved the disciples during a storm.

Supplies: oranges, knife, fruit leather, small foam bowls, markers, gel pens, coffee stirrers

Time: about 15 minutes

Preparation: Cut the oranges in half, and cut fruit leather into squares.

SAY: **It must have been scary to be in the middle of a storm at sea. Let's make a snack to remind us of the Bible story and to have faith in Jesus the next time *we're* facing a storm.**

Give each child a foam bowl, and explain that this will be the sea. Let kids use markers and gel pens to paint waves on the outside of the bowls to represent a stormy sea. Then give each person an orange half to place in his or her bowl. The orange halves will be the boats.

Give each person a square of fruit leather, and demonstrate how to weave a coffee stirrer several times through one side of the leather square. Kids can stick the coffee stirrer in the middle of the orange to form a sail.

As kids are enjoying their snacks, discuss these questions:

- **How does it feel to know that Jesus will be with you during the next stormy time you face?**
- **What are some scary things you face right now?**
- **How can your faith in Jesus help you help someone else facing a tough time?**

Preschool Story

▶ *PREPARE IN ADVANCE*

Bible Point: ▷**JESUS IS BIGGER THAN FEAR.**

Supplies: Bible, blindfold, blue tissue paper, scissors, fan, spray bottle, water

Time: 15 to 20 minutes

Preparation: Cut two narrow strips of tissue paper per child. Fill a spray bottle with water, and set a fan near your story area.

Larger Than Life

Before you begin the Bible story, play this game. Blindfold one child. Have the other children walk in a circle around the blindfolded student. Tell the blindfolded child to try to walk out of the circle without running into anyone. When the child is about to run into someone, yell, "Stop, kids! Don't be afraid." Then have the other students squeeze together and hug the blindfolded child. Remove the blindfold and give it to another child to continue the game.

SAY: **Jesus tells us the same thing when we're afraid: "Stop, kids! Don't be afraid. I'm here to help you." When we're afraid, we can always remember that ▷JESUS IS BIGGER THAN FEAR. In our Bible story today, we'll see how Jesus helped the disciples when they were afraid.**

Have kids form a circle and sit down. Open your Bible to Mark 4:35-41, and show children the words. Then give each child two strips of blue tissue paper.

SAY: **During the Bible story, you'll get to help me be the storm. When I say "wind," I want you to blow like the wind. When I say "waves," hold your papers above your heads and gently wave them. When I say "afraid," show me what your face looks like when you're afraid.** Practice a few times, and then begin the Bible story.

Jesus had been traveling and teaching during the day. In the evening Jesus and his disciples got into a boat to go across to the other side

of the lake. Jesus was very tired and went to sleep. All of a sudden, the wind began to blow. Turn on the fan to a low setting, and have children blow. **The wind blew harder!** Turn up the fan, and have children blow harder. **The wind blew even harder!** Turn the fan on high, and encourage kids to blow their hardest.

Then the waves started splashing into the boat. Have children wave their strips of paper above their heads. Use the water bottle to gently spray kids. **The disciples were afraid.** Have children show you what they look like when they feel afraid. **The wind and the waves were about to make the boat sink.** Encourage kids to blow and wave their papers more. Spray the water into the fan so it sprays out to the children. **Finally, the disciples woke Jesus and said, "Teacher, don't you care that we're going to drown?" The wind and the waves continued to grow.** Tell kids to blow hard and wave their papers. Spray more water into the fan. **Jesus woke up and ordered the wind and the waves to stop.** Stop the fan and have children stop blowing and waving their papers.

Everything got quiet, and everything was calm. Have kids put one finger in front of their mouths and say "Shh." **Then Jesus said, "Why are you afraid?"**

The disciples couldn't believe their eyes. Even the wind and the waves obeyed Jesus! Everything was still. Everything was quiet. And Jesus had made it all happen. Jesus was bigger than the wind and the waves. ▷ JESUS WAS BIGGER THAN THEIR FEAR. The disciples knew they could believe that Jesus was the Son of God. Jesus was amazing!

ASK:

- **Why were the disciples afraid?**
- **When have you been afraid?**
- **How can Jesus help you when you're afraid?**

BIBLE STORY

Jesus Feeds 5,000

For the Leader

Jesus and the disciples withdrew from the crowds to "a quiet place, where they could be alone." Unfortunately for them, the crowds followed. Jesus, instead of slipping away to have his privacy, showed that he cared more about the needs of the curious crowd than about his own needs.

When you think about the size of the fish and the small loaves (probably only a few ounces each) compared with the size of the crowd (probably more than 10,000 people, including women and children), this was an amazing miracle. Even after all the people had eaten, the food that remained was many times more than had originally been given.

Key Scriptures

Mark 6:30-44

Philippians 4:19

Bible Verse

"This same God who takes care of me will supply all your needs from his glorious riches" (Philippians 4:19).

Bible Experience

▶ *FOR SMALL GROUPS*
▶ *PREPARE IN ADVANCE*
▶ *ALLERGY ALERT*

Bible Point: ▷ **WE CAN COUNT ON GOD.**

Children will share a group meal to celebrate the Bible story.

Supplies: Bible; tablecloths; plates; silverware; carving knife; a pan with only one cooked fish stick and one tortilla; pizza, ice cream, and toppings hidden away somewhere where kids can't see or smell the food

Time: about 20 minutes

Preparation: Have the kitchen or dining room "overprepared." Have tablecloths, plates, and silverware for everyone. Make it look as though you're going all out for this meal.

Have kids come in and be seated. Bring out your pan with a flourish. Empty the fish stick and tortilla onto a serving platter in the middle of the table. Get out a carving knife, and make a big show of cutting the food so small that everyone gets a piece. Play this up so kids think that's all they're getting. Distribute the food and invite kids to eat.

After everyone has eaten, read aloud Mark 6:30-44. Have kids discuss these questions:

◆ **Is it possible to feel full on what you've just eaten?**

◆ **Did anyone here bring food to share?**

◆ **How would you have felt if you had been one of the people that day who saw that there was no food at first and then suddenly saw 12 baskets of leftovers?**

SAY: ▷ **WE CAN COUNT ON GOD. The Bible tells us that God will provide everything we need.** Read aloud Philippians 4:19, and then SAY: **Jesus took what could have been a disastrous event and turned it into a great picnic that the world would remember. We can't do that, but we can have a picnic of our own!**

Bring out the pizza, ice cream, and toppings, and let kids eat until they're full. Say a prayer, thanking God for all of the blessings he pours out on us every day.

Additional Topics List

This lesson can be used to help kids discover... Faith, Miracles, Thankfulness, and Trust.

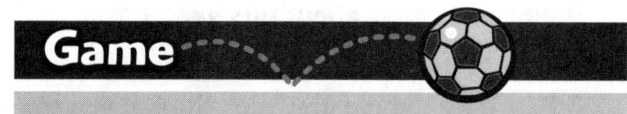

Game

▶ *PREPARE IN ADVANCE*
▶ *ALLERGY ALERT*

Feeding Fun

Children will play a feeding-frenzy game to get an idea of how they can count on God to provide for them.

Supplies: Bible; furniture; masking tape; bag of bagels; carton of goldfish crackers; shallow, rectangular laundry basket (not the vertical kind); napkins

Time: 10 to 15 minutes

Preparation: Arrange furniture or other objects to create a simple obstacle course. Include things for kids to safely step over, around, or past. Create tape arrows on the floor to show the direction of the course. Place the carton of crackers and bag of bagels in the laundry basket, and place the basket at the starting point of the course.

Read or briefly summarize the story of Jesus feeding the 5,000 from Mark 6:30-44. Have kids form groups of four. Explain that each group will get a turn to balance the basket on their heads and move together through the obstacle course to the other end. Have students do the obstacle course one group at a time, while the other groups cheer them on.

After the game, pass out napkins and some of the crackers and bagels to the kids. Have them discuss these questions in their groups:

- **What was easy about this game? What was hard?**
- **How hard did the disciples think it would be to feed all those people? Explain.**
- **How did Jesus show all those people that he cared for them?**
- **How has God shown his care for you?**

SAY: ▷**WE CAN COUNT ON GOD. He knows exactly what we need, and he will never let us down.**

Craft

▶ ***PREPARE IN ADVANCE***

You Can Bank on It

Children will create banks to help them remember that they can count on God.

Supplies: Bible, construction paper, safety scissors, shoeboxes with lids, tape, markers, 2 colors of craft foam, large paper brads, pin, poster board

Time: about 15 minutes

Preparation: Create a sample of the craft to show kids. Make several 2-inch fish-shaped and 3-inch bread-shaped stencils out of poster board for kids to trace. Cut a 1½-inch slit in each lid.

Read aloud Mark 6:30-44. SAY: **The disciples and the people listening to Jesus that day had no idea where they could get enough food to feed everyone. But Jesus took care of them. Let's make something to help us keep track of how God meets all of our needs.**

Have kids cover the sides of their boxes with construction paper and tape it in place. Let kids use markers to decorate their boxes. Let kids trace the stencils onto craft foam and cut out the shapes. Demonstrate how to place the fish shape on top of the bread shape and poke a brad through both pieces. Using the pin, poke a hole in each child's lid, just above the slit. Place the brad, with foam pieces, through the hole and secure it. Both pieces can be swung to the side, revealing the slit. (See the illustration on the next page.)

<u>SAY</u>: **Keep your shoeboxes as reminders that ▷WE CAN COUNT ON GOD. Every time you see God providing a need for you or your family, write what happened on a scrap of paper and slip it into your box. Every so often, open the box and read all the things you've written. You'll be amazed at how much God does for you!**

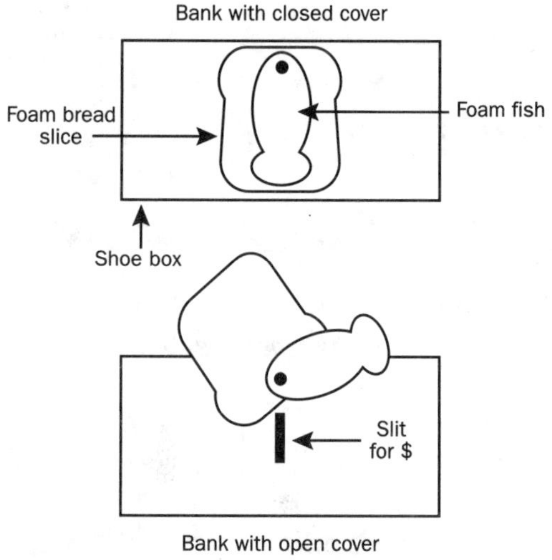

Bible Application

▶ ***PREPARE IN ADVANCE***
▶ ***FOR FAMILY MINISTRY***

Feed the Hungry

Children will collect food to give to the needy.

Supplies: Bible, nonperishable food, poster board, markers, pens, paper

Time: about 15 minutes

Preparation: Find a local organization that will accept your donations.

Read aloud Mark 6:30-44. <u>SAY</u>: **In this story Jesus fed thousands of hungry people. We probably can't feed that many, but we can feed some. We already know that ▷WE CAN COUNT ON GOD. Let's share that good news as we share some food!**

Have kids work together to make a poster advertising your food drive. (The poster can be a reminder for kids or an outreach for the whole church.) After all of the food has been collected, have kids compose a letter to the recipients and sign the letter. If possible, let kids accompany you as you deliver the food.

Creative Prayer Idea

▶ ***NO PREP***

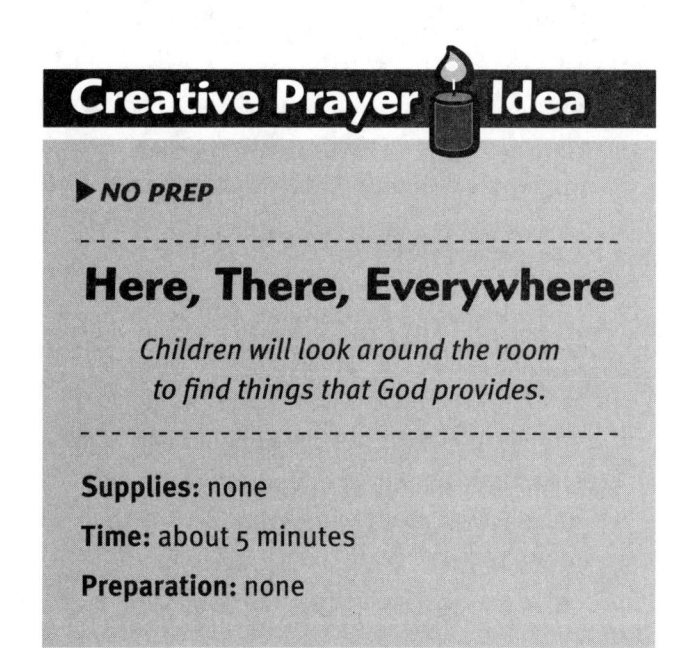

Here, There, Everywhere

Children will look around the room to find things that God provides.

Supplies: none

Time: about 5 minutes

Preparation: none

Have kids sit in a circle on the floor. <u>SAY</u>: **Our Bible story of Jesus feeding 5,000 people helps us know that ▷WE CAN COUNT ON GOD. But sometimes it's easy to overlook everything God does for us and gives to us. Let's say a circle prayer to thank God for everything we can see in this room that he gives to us. We'll keep going around until we can't think of anything else. You may keep your eyes open during this prayer so you can look for things that remind you that ▷WE CAN COUNT ON GOD.**

If kids run out of ideas, suggest things like sunshine, light, heat, friends, teachers, Bibles, a church building, sight, voices, laughter, and so on.

Movie Clip

It Really Is Wonderful!

Movie: *It's a Wonderful Life* (not rated)

Start Time: 55 minutes, 6 seconds

Where to Begin: George steps up to hear the crowd's concerns.

Where to End: The clock strikes, closing the Building and Loan for the day.

Plot: After learning that the bank has closed, panicked clients crowd into the Building and Loan to withdraw money. George explains that their money is invested in each other's property, but some clients insist on having cash.

Review: Jesus meets our needs in amazing ways. In the movie, George has limited cash on hand, yet he loans to everyone and ends with two dollars to spare. Jesus stretched a very limited amount of fish and bread to feed more than 5,000 people and had baskets of leftovers to spare. God is never limited; he's able to provide for all our needs, both physical and spiritual.

Discussion

After setting up and showing the clip, SAY: **George was able to stretch his own money—two thousand dollars—to meet the needs of all who turned to him for help. Jesus multiplied a few loaves and fish to feed more than 5,000 people! Unlike George, though, Jesus is never limited. He is able to provide above and beyond what we need.**

ASK:

- **Can you think of ways Jesus is already meeting your needs?**
- **How do you think Jesus might use *you* to meet someone else's needs?**

SAY: **Remember that Jesus is able to meet your needs in amazing ways. ▷ WE CAN COUNT ON GOD!**

Object Lesson

▶ *PREPARE IN ADVANCE*
▶ *FOR FAMILY MINISTRY*
▶ *ALLERGY ALERT*

A Little Goes a Long Way

Children will learn that God can meet their needs.

Supplies: Bible, unpopped popcorn, glass measuring cup, electric popcorn popper, napkins, large bowl

Time: about 10 minutes

Preparation: Prepare the popcorn popper for use.

Read aloud or summarize the story from Mark 6:30-44. Gather kids around a table, and give each child a small handful of popcorn kernels. SAY: **This amount of popcorn ought to keep the hunger away, right?** Kids will probably say they'd like more. **It doesn't look like much, that's true. Maybe if we put all of our kernels together, it'll be enough.**

Ask each child to put his or her kernels into the measuring cup. SAY: **Hmm. It still doesn't look like much, but let's give it a try.**

Empty the measuring cup into the popcorn popper. As the corn pops, pour enough kernels into the measuring cup to reach the same level you had before. When the popcorn is ready, pour it into a bowl. Hold up the bowl and the measuring cup of kernels and SAY: **Wow! Look at the difference! A little bit of popcorn goes a long way.** As kids enjoy the snack,

ASK:

◆ **Did you think that little bit of popcorn would be enough to feed all of us? Explain.**

◆ **What do you think Jesus' followers thought when they saw that they had only two fish and five loaves of bread to feel all those people?**

◆ **How would you have felt if you had seen Jesus' miracle that day?**

SAY: **Jesus took care of the people's needs that day, and he'll do the same for us. ▷WE CAN COUNT ON GOD!**

Preschool Story

▶ ***PREPARE IN ADVANCE***

▶ ***ALLERGY ALERT***

Bible Point: ▷ **WE CAN COUNT ON GOD.**

Supplies: Bible, fish-shaped crackers, round crackers, paper lunch bag, bread basket

Preparation: Place two fish-shaped crackers and five round crackers in a paper lunch bag. Place the remaining crackers in a bread basket, and set it aside for later.

5 + 2 =...5,000?

Have kids form a circle and sit down. Open your Bible to Mark 6:30-44, and show children the words. SAY: **Let's pretend that we're going to hear Jesus teach. He's way up on a hillside. Let's climb up the hill to Jesus.** Pretend to climb a steep, long hill.

Look at all the people! One, two, three, four...there are too many to count! But where is Jesus? Have children shield their eyes with their hands and look one way and then the other. **There he is, on top of the hill.** Point away.

Shh! Let's sit down and listen to what Jesus is saying. He's telling everyone about God's power and love. He will give them food (pretend to eat) **and clothes** (point to clothes) **and love** (hug yourself).

Jesus has taught all day, and everyone is getting very hungry. Encourage children to rub their tummies and lick their lips. **I think I might even hear some tummies growling.** Encourage children to make growling sounds. **I'll bet Jesus can hear them, too. He wants to give everyone something to eat. Look, he's sending his disciples in search of food. Do you see any food around here?** Let kids look around a bit. **The disciples are coming back to Jesus. All they can find is five loves of bread and two fish.** Hold up and shake the lunch bag. Let children see what's inside. **Well, that's not enough food for all the people here—that's only one small lunch!**

Look what Jesus is doing now. He's telling everyone to sit down. Have kids join you in sitting down. **He's praying and thanking God for the food. Let's pray with Jesus.**

Lead children in saying the following prayer with you: **Thank you, God, for this bread and fish. Amen.**

SAY: **Jesus' disciples are passing the small lunch around, and all the people are being fed. How is that possible? That's amazing!** Pass around the lunch bag, and pretend to eat. **Only God can make one small lunch feed lots and lots of people! Look!** Bring out the basket of extra crackers, and let children have some. **There's even food left over!**

The people could count on God to provide them with food on that day. ▷ WE CAN COUNT ON GOD to provide for and take care of us, too!

Let's do a finger play now to help us remember our Bible story and to remind us that ▷ WE CAN COUNT ON GOD! SAY:

Five loaves, *(hold up five fingers on one hand)*

Two fish—*(hold up two fingers on the opposite hand)*

Look at all the people. *(Wiggle all 10 fingers.)*

Five loaves, *(hold up five fingers on one hand)*

Two fish—*(hold up two fingers on the opposite hand)*

Many hungry people. *(Wiggle all 10 fingers.)*

Five loaves, *(hold up five fingers on one hand)*

Two fish—*(hold up two fingers on the opposite hand)*

God fed all the people! *(Wiggle all 10 fingers.)*

ASK:

- **What amazing things did God do in the story?**
- **Why can you count on God?**
- **When can you count on God to help you?**

notes

BIBLE STORY

Wise and Foolish Builders

For the Leader

Jesus used everyday images to drive home his truths to people he spoke to—in Bible times and throughout the ages, including us! Everyone needs shelter, so everyone can relate to wanting a sturdy shelter that's able to withstand the forces of nature. A house built on a firm foundation won't wash away when the storms come.

Likewise, a life built on the firm foundation of faith in Jesus won't fall apart when life's crises arrive. When life is calm, foundations don't seem so important. But when trouble hits, only the rock-solid foundation of Jesus can help us survive the storm.

Key Scriptures

Luke 6:46-49

John 14:15

Bible Verse

"If you love me, obey my commandments" (John 14:15).

Bible Experience

▶ *NO PREP*

Bible Point: ▷ **DO WHAT JESUS SAYS.**

Children will use an object lesson to learn about wise and foolish builders.

Supplies: Bible, pan of sand, pan of stones, plastic blocks, container of water

Time: about 10 minutes

Preparation: none

Set out the pan of sand and the pan of stones. Let kids help create a mound of sand and a mound of stones. Then have kids place plastic blocks on top of each of the mounds.

SAY: **Let's pretend these blocks are houses—*your* houses!**

ASK:

- **What do you think will happen if the wind blows on these houses?**

Let a few volunteers blow on the houses. Some sand may blow around a bit, but the houses on both mounds should stand. Then

ASK:

- **What do you think will happen if a rainstorm hits these houses? Why?**

Pour water on the houses. The houses on the sand should shift. SAY: **The Bible tells us about houses just like these.** Have a volunteer read aloud Luke 6:46-49.

ASK:

- **How is sand different from rocks?**
- **Why do you think Jesus compared himself to a strong rock?**

SAY: **Jesus said that believing in him and obeying him is like building a house on strong rock. Though everything else may be shaky, like sand, we know that Jesus is our solid rock. If we ▷ DO WHAT JESUS SAYS, our lives will be rock solid. In the Bible Jesus gives us all the information we need to decide whether to be wise or foolish builders in our lives. Let's be wise builders!**

Additional Topics List

This lesson can be used to help kids discover... Consequences of Sin, Obedience, and Wisdom.

Game

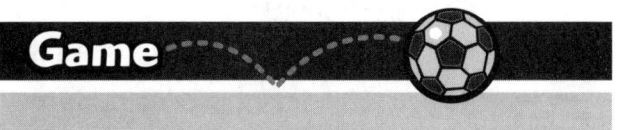

▶ *PREPARE IN ADVANCE*
▶ *FOR SMALL GROUPS*

Traffic Jam

Children will play a game about obeying to remind them to do what Jesus says.

Supplies: Bible; 3 blankets, towels, or sheets—one red, one yellow, and one green

Time: about 10 minutes

Preparation: Lay the blankets side by side on the floor.

Read aloud Luke 6:46-49; then SAY: **Jesus said that if we don't obey, our lives could end up in a big mess. Let's play a game to remind us of that.** Tell kids the three blankets represent the colors on a traffic light. Have everyone stand on the yellow (middle) blanket. When you shout out another color, have kids move quickly to the appropriate blanket. The last child to get both feet on the blanket is eliminated.

To make the game more challenging, occasionally call out the color of the blanket on which kids are already standing. Anyone who steps off the blanket is eliminated. For a change of pace, call out, "Traffic accident!" and have everyone vacate all blankets. The last child to get off is eliminated.

Keep the pace fast, and vary the colors. Play until only one child is left on the traffic light. Play several rounds if you have time. Then have kids sit together on one of the blankets. SAY: **In this game you had to listen carefully and follow all the directions.**

ASK:

- **What would happen in real life if no one obeyed traffic signals?**
- **Why is it important to do what Jesus says?**
- **Why do you think Jesus gave us rules to follow?**

SAY: **Jesus tells us what to do because he loves us and knows what's best for us. He knows that if we don't do what he says, our lives could end up like a big traffic accident.**

Craft

▶ ***PREPARE IN ADVANCE***

Rock Solid

Children will make textured drawings to remind them of the Bible story.

Supplies: Bible, copy paper or newsprint, bricks or large stones, crayons, blocks of wood, safety scissors, glue, construction paper

Time: about 15 minutes

Preparation: Set up one table with copy paper, large stones or bricks, and a few blocks of wood. Set up another table with scissors, glue, and construction paper. Have crayons available at both tables. Remove the paper from the outside of the crayons if necessary.

Open your Bible to Luke 6:46-49, and briefly summarize the story of the wise and foolish builders. SAY: **Jesus said that when anyone hears his teaching and does what he says, it's like building a house on a rock-solid foundation. Let's make a reminder of that.**

Lead kids in following these directions: Place your paper over the stone or brick. Rub the side of a crayon over the paper and watch the texture appear. Then place your paper over a block of wood, and do the same thing. Do this several times so you have a large area of wood texture. Go to the next table.

Draw the outline of a house over your wood rubbing, and cut it out. Cut a section of your stone rubbing to use as ground. Glue the stone rubbing near the bottom of a sheet of construction paper, and then glue on the house so it looks like the house is built on stone. Draw a picture of yourself near the house. Add other details like trees, pets, and people. Somewhere on the picture, write "Do what Jesus says!"

Encourage kids to hang their pictures at home as a reminder to build their lives on the rock-solid foundation of Jesus.

Bible Application

▶ *NO PREP*

Rock in My Sock

Children will make reminders to do what Jesus says that they can carry with them during the week.

Supplies: Bible, smooth stones (available at craft stores), fine-tipped permanent markers

Time: about 5 minutes

Preparation: none

Briefly summarize the story of the wise and foolish builders from Luke 6:46-49. Have kids form pairs to answer these questions.

ASK:

- **When is it hard for you to obey Jesus?**
- **Why is it hard for you to obey Jesus?**

SAY: **In John 14:15, Jesus said, "If you love me, obey my commandments." Let's repeat that verse together. As Christians we love Jesus and want to obey him. Sometimes we all need a little reminder—a little nudge in the right direction—to keep us on the right path. Let's make something we can carry with us this week to remind us to ▷ DO WHAT JESUS SAYS.**

Give each child a smooth stone and a fine-tipped marker. Tell kids to write on their stones something that represents when they have the most trouble obeying Jesus. For example, a child might write "brother" if he or she has trouble getting along with a sibling. Another child might write "spelling" if he or she is tempted to cheat on spelling tests. Explain that kids won't have to show their stones to anyone.

When kids have finished writing, SAY: **Take your stones home with you, and carry them in your pocket this week. If you don't have a pocket, put your stone in your shoe! Every time you feel or touch your stone, remember that Jesus knows what's best for us and that it's always best to ▷ DO WHAT JESUS SAYS. Remember—you don't want to wind up like the foolish builder!**

Creative Prayer Idea

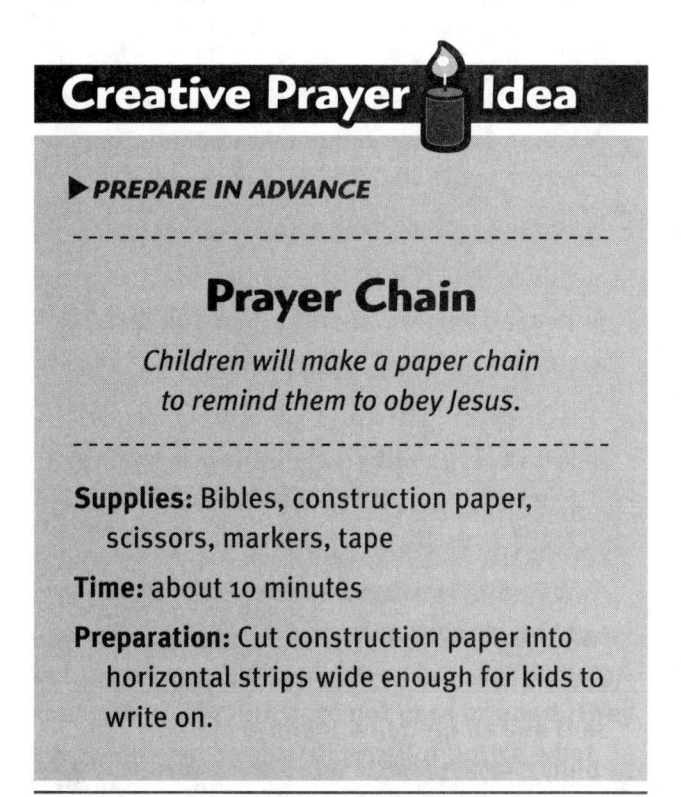

▶ *PREPARE IN ADVANCE*

Prayer Chain

Children will make a paper chain to remind them to obey Jesus.

Supplies: Bibles, construction paper, scissors, markers, tape

Time: about 10 minutes

Preparation: Cut construction paper into horizontal strips wide enough for kids to write on.

Read aloud Luke 6:46-49. SAY: **We all disobey sometimes. But we also know how important it is to ▷ DO WHAT JESUS SAYS. Let's make a prayer reminder to help us remember what Jesus said to do.**

Let kids write on each paper strip something Jesus said to do. Have Bibles handy for reference. For example, kids might write "Love your Enemies," "Pray," and "Be nice." Have kids write as many ideas as they can think of. Have kids loop their paper strips together to make a paper chain, words facing out.

Then have kids sit in a circle on the floor. Say a circle prayer, letting each child take the chain and read what's written on one of the loops.

Close the prayer by asking God to help each of you ▷ **DO WHAT JESUS SAYS during the coming week.** Then hang the chain in your meeting room as a visual reminder to obey Jesus.

Discussion Launcher Questions

Read aloud Luke 6:46-49. Then have kids form trios and discuss these questions:

- **When is a time you disobeyed your parents? What were the consequences?**
- **When is a time you disobeyed Jesus? What happened?**
- **How do you feel inside when you disobey?**
- **When and where are you most likely to disobey? Why?**
- **When Jesus talked about floods hitting the houses, what do you think he meant by "floods"?**
- **Why do you think it's important to do what Jesus says?**

Movie Clip

Better to Obey!

Movie Title: *Pinocchio* (not rated)

Start Time: 59 minutes, 59 seconds

Where to Begin: Pinocchio and Lampwick are riding the wagon to Pleasure Island. Lampwick is telling Pinocchio how fun it will be to be disobedient.

Where to End: Jiminy Cricket and Pinocchio run to escape Pleasure Island. Jiminy and Pinocchio jump over a cliff and into the water below.

Plot: Pinocchio and other boys are taken to Pleasure Island, where children can do whatever they want. However, their disobedience causes them to turn into donkeys. Once the boys become donkeys, they're sold to the salt mines to work. Jiminy Cricket rescues Pinocchio before he is completely transformed into a donkey.

Review: Use this scene to reinforce the importance of obedience to Jesus. Pinocchio learned the lesson of obedience the hard way. Through his story about the wise and foolish builders, Jesus teaches us that obeying his words will lead to a life built on a firm foundation that won't give way with life's hardships.

Discussion

After setting up and showing the movie clip,

ASK:

- **Why did Pinocchio want to go to Pleasure Island?**
- **What happened to Pinocchio at Pleasure Island?**

SAY: **Pinocchio went to Pleasure Island because he wanted to disobey. But it almost cost him his life. Jesus told us about the consequences of disobeying him. Listen to what Jesus said.** Read aloud Luke 6:46-49.

ASK:

- **How was Pinocchio's going to Pleasure Island like building a house on sand?**
- **What happens when we obey Jesus?**

SAY: **It's important to ▷ DO WHAT JESUS SAYS because Jesus knows what's best for us. Just like Pleasure Island was bad for Pinocchio, disobeying Jesus is bad for us.**

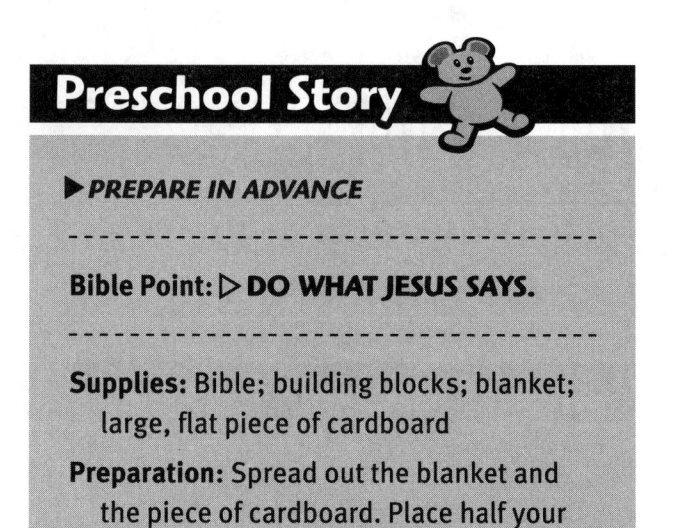

Preschool Story

▶ ***PREPARE IN ADVANCE***

Bible Point: ▷ **DO WHAT JESUS SAYS.**

Supplies: Bible; building blocks; blanket; large, flat piece of cardboard

Preparation: Spread out the blanket and the piece of cardboard. Place half your building blocks on the blanket and the other half on the piece of cardboard.

Solid Rock

Have half of your group sit down around the blocks on the blanket. Encourage the other half to sit down around the blocks on the cardboard. Open your Bible to Luke 6:46-49, and show children the words.

SAY: **One day Jesus was teaching about two men who were building their houses. Let's build some houses right now!** Encourage one group to begin building a block house on top of their blanket. Encourage the other group to begin building a block house on top of the cardboard.

One of the men built his house on the sand. The other man built his house on the rock.

ASK:

- **Which do you think is better to build on: sand or rock? Why?**

SAY: **One day a big storm came and flooded the houses. Let's see what happens to the houses we built when a storm comes.** Encourage kids to finish building their houses. Once they've finished, tell them to carefully slide the blanket or the sheet of cardboard and work together to move their house across the room. ASK:

- **What happened to our houses?**

SAY: **The house we built on the blanket fell apart right away when we tried to move it! That's what happened to the house that was built on sand in Jesus' story. When the storms and the flood came, the house fell apart. But the house that was built on a sturdy foundation—like the cardboard—stood strong against the storms and the flood.**

Encourage kids to begin building new houses on the floor or on the cardboard.

SAY: **Then Jesus said something amazing. He said that the man who had built his house on the strong, solid rock is just like someone who obeys Jesus! When you obey Jesus and ▷DO WHAT JESUS SAYS, then when something bad happens, you'll be OK. But Jesus said that when you don't listen to him and don't obey him, then you're like the man who built his house on sand—when something bad happens, you won't be able to make it.**

Let's sing a song now to help us remember to ▷ DO WHAT JESUS SAYS. Then we can be like the man in the story who built his house on rock.

Sing this song to the tune of "This Is the Way":

This is the way we build our house, *(pretend to stack bricks)*

Build our house, build our house. *(Continue stacking bricks.)*

This is the way we build our house. *(Continue stacking bricks.)*

We build on solid rock. *(Stomp your feet on the ground.)*

This is the best way to live our lives, *(march in place)*

Live our lives, live our lives. *(March in place.)*

This is the best way to live our lives. *(Continue marching in place.)*

When we do what Jesus says. *(Point up to the sky.)*

ASK:

- **Why is it best to build on solid ground?**
- **Why is it important to do what Jesus says?**
- **How can you ▷ DO WHAT JESUS SAYS in your life?**

TOPIC

Ten Healed of Leprosy

For the Leader

The disease called leprosy in the Bible is generally thought to be the same as what we call Hansen's disease today. That disease often results in rotting flesh, which can be repulsive. That would at least partially explain why lepers were outcasts, forced to live outside the village. As seen in today's passage, they weren't even allowed to get close to other people.

It's interesting that Jesus didn't heal the 10 lepers on the spot. Before they could be healed, they had to act on what Jesus told them to do. They had to respond to Jesus in faith by heading toward town to see the priest. If they hadn't trusted Jesus, they probably wouldn't have gone—they would have looked foolish showing up before the priest still having leprosy. But when they demonstrated their faith, they were healed.

Key Scriptures

Luke 17:11-19

1 Thessalonians 5:18

Bible Verse

"Be thankful in all circumstances" (1 Thessalonians 5:18).

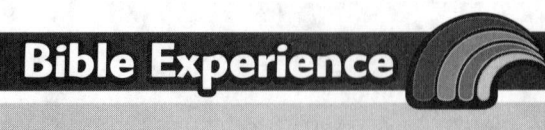

Bible Experience

▶ *NO PREP*

Bible Point: ▷ **BE GRATEFUL TO JESUS.**

Children will use a drawing race to think of things to be grateful for.

Supplies: Bible, 2 easels (or a chalkboard), newsprint, markers

Time: 10 to 15 minutes

Preparation: none

Have a volunteer read aloud Luke 17:11-19. Have kids form two groups. Place an easel equipped with newsprint at either end of the room. Have markers handy. SAY: **Jesus showed his power when he healed 10 men of leprosy. One of the men came back to thank Jesus. In this activity, you'll each get to draw two pictures—one that shows Jesus' power and one that shows something you're grateful to Jesus for. Think of what you can draw. Then let's see how fast we can think of, draw, and guess your ideas!**

Assign one easel for the "power" pictures and one easel for the "thanks" pictures. Place one group at each easel, and have both groups begin at the same time. One child from each group will draw while others in the group try to guess what the picture is. As soon as a picture is guessed, the artist will move to the other easel and join the other group. Gradually all players will switch groups. Play until kids have each drawn two pictures. Then have kids answer these questions in their original groups.

ASK:

◆ **What were some things you learned about Jesus' power in this activity?**

◆ **Why is it important to take time to thank Jesus?**

◆ **How do you think Jesus feels when we thank him? when we don't thank him?**

◆ **Why do you think Jesus keeps blessing us even when we forget to thank him?**

SAY: **Jesus loves us and wants to do good things for us. First Thessalonians 5:18 says, "Be thankful in all circumstances." This week, look for times you should ▷ BE GRATEFUL TO JESUS—and then be grateful! Don't be like those nine lepers—remember to thank Jesus!**

Additional Topics List

This lesson can be used to help kids discover... Healing, Miracles, Sharing Faith, and Thankfulness.

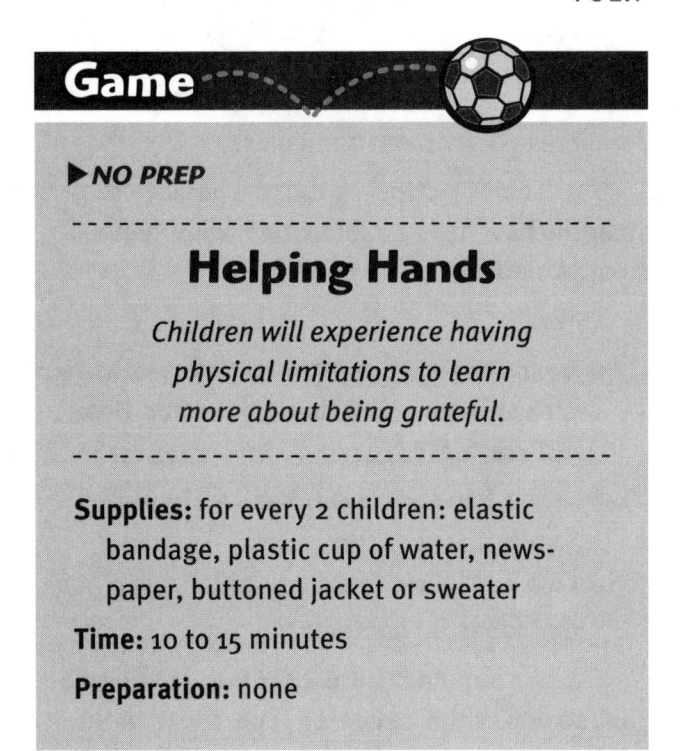

n
o
t
e
s

Game

▶ *NO PREP*

Helping Hands

Children will experience having physical limitations to learn more about being grateful.

Supplies: for every 2 children: elastic bandage, plastic cup of water, newspaper, buttoned jacket or sweater

Time: 10 to 15 minutes

Preparation: none

Form pairs. Have one partner from each pair wrap up the other's hands in an elastic bandage so the partner can't use any fingers. (If you have disabled kids in class, you may want to skip this game or ask their permission first. Perhaps they would welcome sharing information about what life is like with disabilities.) Have the bandaged partners try to drink a cup of water, page through a newspaper, and put on a buttoned jacket or

sweater and button all the buttons. Then have partners switch roles. Finally, let kids each perform the tasks without bandages.

SAY: **Leprosy cripples those who have it. Imagine how happy a leper was when Jesus healed him!**

ASK:

- **Describe to your partner a time you were sick or in pain and then got better. How did you feel?**
- **When have you seen healing in your family?**
- **How do you think we should respond to God when he heals us?**

SAY: **We should ▷BE GRATEFUL TO JESUS, just as one of the 10 healed lepers was in the Bible. Let's try to remember to thank Jesus for all he does for us.**

Craft

▶ *PREPARE IN ADVANCE*

Praise Sticks

Children will make praise sticks to praise Jesus as the leper did.

Supplies: Bibles, dowel sticks, brightly colored chenille wires, jingle bells

Time: 10 to 15 minutes

Preparation: Cut dowels into sticks at least 6 inches long. Each child will need one stick and at least three jingle bells.

Have kids turn to Luke 17:11-19 in their Bibles, and ask a volunteer to read the passage aloud while others follow along. SAY: **When Jesus healed the 10 lepers, one of them came back to praise him. Let's make praise sticks to remind us to ▷BE GRATEFUL TO JESUS!**

Lead kids in making praise sticks by following these directions: Weave jingle bells onto several chenille wires. Twist the ends of the wires in loops so the bells don't fall off. Wrap the wires around the dowel stick from one end of the stick to its center. Shake the praise stick to hear the bells jingle.

When everyone has made a praise stick, gather kids in a circle.

ASK:

- **How would you feel if you were one of the 10 lepers Jesus healed?**
- **What would you tell people if you had just been healed? How would you act?**

SAY: **One leper came back and praised Jesus for healing him. We made praise sticks to remind us to be like that leper and ▷BE GRATEFUL TO JESUS.** Encourage kids to use their praise sticks to create a cheer to thank Jesus for all he has done for them.

Bible Application

Airborne Thanks

Children will quietly reflect on reasons they should be grateful to Jesus.

Supplies: Bible, newsprint, marker, tape, paper, pens

Time: 5 to 10 minutes

Preparation: Draw a large cross on a sheet of newsprint, and tape the newsprint to a wall so the bottom of the cross touches the floor.

Read aloud Luke 17:11-19.

ASK:

◆ **Why do you think only one person returned to thank Jesus for what he had done?**

◆ **Are there things in your life lately that you've forgotten or neglected to thank Jesus for?**

Give kids sheets of paper and pens. Have them write on the paper anything that comes to mind that is a blessing from God. After a few minutes, help kids make paper airplanes out of their papers. Then SAY: **After we pray, one by one we'll fly our planes to the foot of the cross. Until then, hold on to your plane and bow your head with me.**

PRAY: **Lord, there are times we're guilty, just like those nine lepers, of not saying thank you. Forgive us as we come before you now with gratitude for all you do for us. Just as the leper returned and threw himself at your feet, we throw our airplanes as symbols of our thanks.**

Have kids quietly line up and sail their airplanes, one at a time, toward the bottom of the cross. (If anyone's plane misses, let that person keep trying until the plane lands near the cross.) Close by encouraging kids to ▷ **BE GRATEFUL TO JESUS every day in the coming week.**

Creative Prayer Idea

▶ ***PREPARE IN ADVANCE***

Paper-People Prayer

Children will create a paper-people chain to thank Jesus for what he's done for them.

Supplies: Bible, gingerbread-person cookie cutters, pencil, colorful construction paper, scissors, tape, pens

Time: about 10 minutes

Preparation: Cut construction paper into gingerbread-person shapes, all the same size.

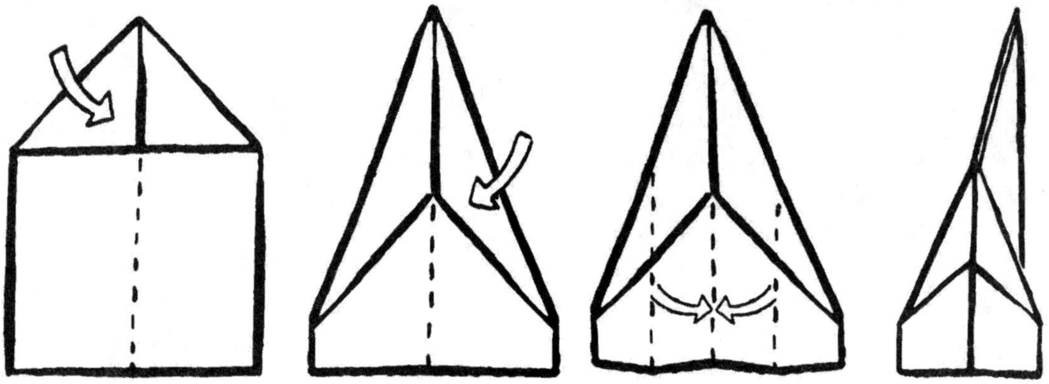

Have a volunteer read aloud Luke 17:11-19. SAY: **One of the lepers in this passage remembered to ▷BE GRATEFUL TO JESUS. Let's make a paper-people chain to remind us to be grateful, too.**

Set out pens and the paper people shapes. Have kids write on each paper person something they're grateful to Jesus for. Tell kids to write on as many paper people as they can. Then gather kids in a circle with their paper people.

SAY: **As we go around and around the circle, we'll each tape a paper person to the chain. As you tape your person to the chain, say aloud what you wrote on the shape.** When kids have finished taping all their paper people to the chain, have kids help you hold up the chain for all to see. **Wow! We have lots of reasons to ▷BE GRATEFUL TO JESUS! Let's thank Jesus for all he does for us!** Lead kids in a prayer praising and thanking Jesus for all he does for us.

Movie Clip

Miracles of Mercy

Movie Title: *Gordy* (G)

Start Time: 58 minutes, 22 seconds

Where to Begin: Hanky and Gordy are entering the barn.

Where to End: Hanky and Gordy are picked up by their traveling friends.

Plot: Hanky is helping his pig friend, Gordy, find his family. After traveling for many miles, they realize they will need a miracle to reach their destination. Hanky explains to Gordy how miracles help us, and then they experience one.

Review: It seemed impossible for Gordy and Hanky to find Gordy's family. But a miracle happened when their traveling friends came by to give them a lift. The 10 lepers were outcasts of society—they would need a miracle to change their lives, and that's exactly what happened when they cried out to Jesus for mercy.

Discussion

After setting up and showing the movie clip, ASK:

- **How do you think Gordy and Hanky felt after talking with the big pig?**
- **How do you think they felt when their friends picked them up?**
- **How is that like how the lepers must have felt when Jesus healed them?**

SAY: **Gordy and Hanky were discouraged about finding Gordy's folks. Lepers in Bible times had to live all by themselves, away from other people. They probably felt discouraged, too. But Jesus healed them! And at least one of the lepers had the good sense to ▷BE GRATEFUL TO JESUS!**

notes

Science Devotion

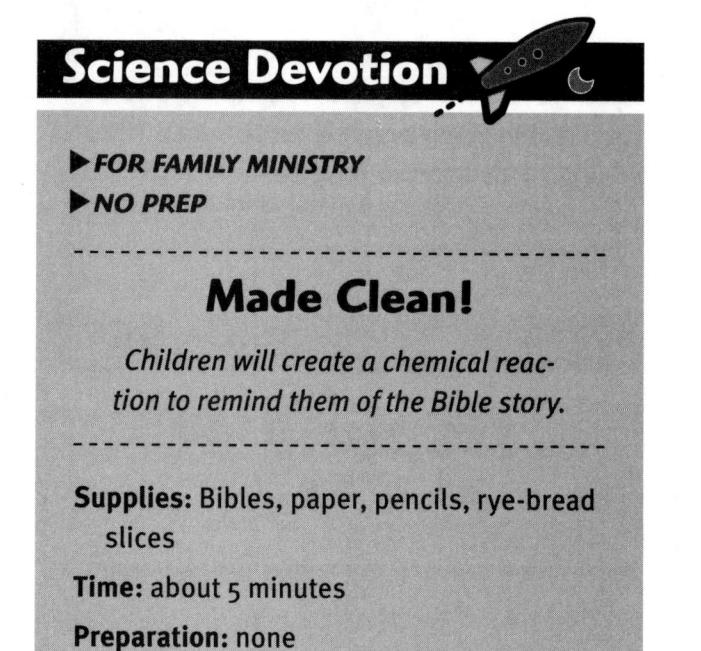

▶ *FOR FAMILY MINISTRY*
▶ *NO PREP*

Made Clean!

Children will create a chemical reaction to remind them of the Bible story.

Supplies: Bibles, paper, pencils, rye-bread slices

Time: about 5 minutes

Preparation: none

Read aloud Luke 17:11-19 while kids follow along in their Bibles. SAY: **Jesus performed a miracle and dramatically changed the lives of 10 lepers. He removed their leprosy spots and their illness altogether—they were clean! Let's do an experiment to remind us of this Bible story. It won't be a miracle by any means, but maybe it will help us remember the story and tell it to someone else.**

Have kids form groups of four. Give each group a sheet of paper, a pencil, and a slice of rye bread. Have kids each lightly scribble a small line on the paper. Then let kids tear off a piece of the rye bread and rub it hard across the scribbled lines. The bread will work like an eraser and clean the paper.

SAY: **Wow! The bread cleaned the paper! OK, so it's not a miracle. I warned you. But still, it can remind us of how Jesus removed the lepers' spots in the Bible story. Do this experiment at home for your family members and friends, and tell them the story of how Jesus healed the 10 lepers. But don't forget the part about how one leper came back to thank Jesus. That important part of the story can remind us to ▷ BE GRATEFUL TO JESUS!**

Preschool Story

▶ *PREPARE IN ADVANCE*

Bible Point: ▷ **SAY THANK YOU TO JESUS.**

Supplies: Bible; large sheet of poster board; laminate; scissors; washable marker; warm, soapy water; bucket; washcloth; 11 craft sticks; tape

Time: 10 to 15 minutes

Preparation: Draw 11 gingerbread-shaped people on the large sheet of poster board. Laminate the poster board. Then cut out each of the people. Tape a craft stick to the bottom of each of the figures to make puppets. With a washable marker, draw spots on 10 of the people. Fill a bucket with warm, soapy water.

Thank You! Thank You! Thank You!

Have kids form a circle and sit down. Open your Bible to Luke 17:11-19, and show children the words. Give 10 children each one of the 10 spotted puppets—but hang on to the puppet without spots. This is the Jesus puppet.

SAY: **One day 10 men came up to Jesus.** Encourage the children with the 10 puppets to make them "walk" up to your Jesus puppet. **These 10 men were very sick. They had a disease called leprosy. Leprosy makes you have spots all over and turns your skin white. These men had been sick for a long time, and because they had leprosy, other people wouldn't talk to them or go near them. The men were very sad, and all they wanted was not to have leprosy anymore.**

The men thought maybe Jesus could heal them and get rid of their leprosy. Encourage the kids with the 10 puppets to ask the Jesus puppet to heal them. **Jesus loved the men, and he wanted them to be better. So Jesus healed them and got rid of their leprosy!** Let children dip the puppets in the warm, soapy water and use a cloth to wipe off the spots on their puppets. If some of your children don't have puppets, let them wash off the spots. ASK:

- **What would you have done if Jesus had healed you from leprosy?**
- **What do you think these men did?**

SAY: **After Jesus had healed the 10 men, they ran away to celebrate. But one man came back to Jesus. Do you know why he came back? The man wanted to thank Jesus for healing him!** Encourage one child to have his or her puppet run back to Jesus and say thank you. Jesus was very happy that the man had come back to say thank you. But Jesus wondered where the other nine men were. None of the other men came back to tell Jesus thank you for healing them.

Jesus did an amazing thing for those men, and Jesus does amazing things for us, too. Jesus wants us to ▷SAY THANK YOU TO HIM when he does amazing things for us. Let's say thank you to Jesus right now!

Walk around to each child and use the washable marker to draw a spot on his or her arm. Remind children that the men with leprosy were covered with spots. Once each child has a spot, ask kids to come up one by one and name one reason they are thankful to Jesus. As children give their reasons, use a washcloth and the warm, soapy water to wash the spot off their arms. If children need help, suggest thanking Jesus for their food, for their families, for taking care of them when they're afraid, for loving them, or for coming to earth to help them.

ASK:

- **What are some more things Jesus has done for us?**
- **How can we thank Jesus for all the wonderful things he does?**

SAY: **Jesus helps us in all sorts of ways. We can always count on Jesus to help us, but we should also always remember to ▷SAY THANK YOU TO JESUS for helping us.**

BIBLE STORY

Healing at the Pool

For the Leader

Jesus had returned to Jerusalem for one of the Jewish holy days. Jewish males were required to come to Jerusalem for three festivals: the Festival of Passover and Unleavened Bread, the Festival of Pentecost, and the Festival of Shelters.

The paralyzed man had been afflicted for 38 years. His problem had become a way of life, and he likely felt without hope that his situation would ever change. But Jesus sought him out and healed his body. More importantly, Jesus told him how to heal his spirit—he told the man to stop sinning.

Key Scriptures

John 5:1-15

Philippians 4:6

Bible Verse

"Tell God what you need, and thank him for all he has done" (Philippians 4:6).

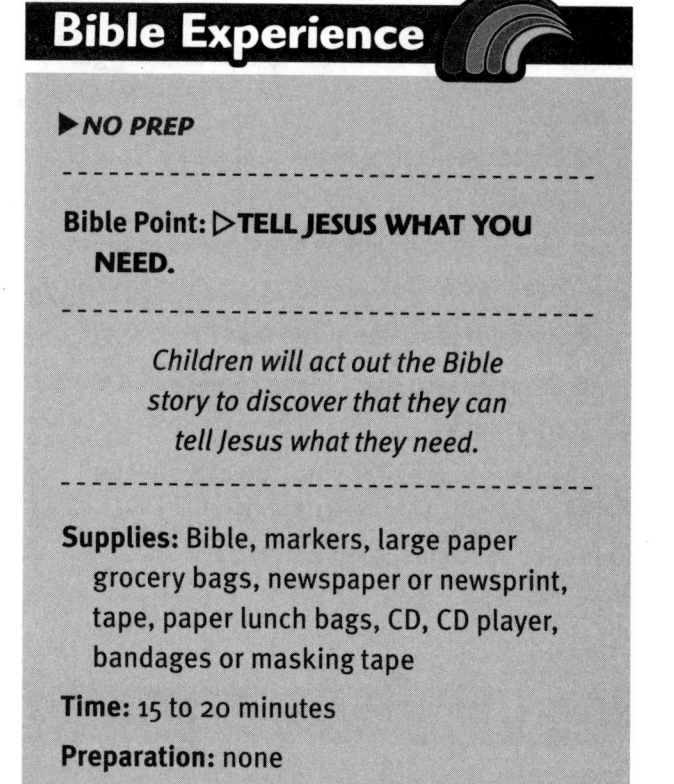

Bible Experience

▶ *NO PREP*

Bible Point: ▷**TELL JESUS WHAT YOU NEED.**

Children will act out the Bible story to discover that they can tell Jesus what they need.

Supplies: Bible, markers, large paper grocery bags, newspaper or newsprint, tape, paper lunch bags, CD, CD player, bandages or masking tape

Time: 15 to 20 minutes

Preparation: none

Read aloud John 5:1-15 or summarize the story of the healing at the pool. SAY: **Wow, that poor man by the pool really was in a bad way before Jesus came along. Let's see what that was like.** (Be sensitive to any children with disabilities. If you have a disabled child in class, skip making the paper person and use a large red poster-board heart to put the bandages on at the end of the activity.)

Have kids work together to create a person from the paper bags. Children can draw a face on one side of a large bag and then stuff the bag with newspaper or newsprint, taping it closed. Then they can draw buttons down one side of another large bag, stuff it, and tape it closed. Let kids use tape to attach the head to the torso. Kids can then stuff the lunch bags to use as arms and legs.

Place the paper person at one side of the room, and have kids sit on the floor all around it. SAY: **The Bible tells us that the lame man sat on his mat by the pool of Bethesda. He was surrounded by other sick and hurting people. They all went there because they believed that when the water in the pool bubbled, anyone who was able to get into the water right away would be healed. But the lame man was never able to be the first into the water.**

I'm going to play a song. When the music stops, race to the other side of the room. Ready? Here goes. Play "He Cares for You" (track 22, *it: Innovative Tools for Children's Ministry: New Testament* CD). After a minute or so, stop the song and wait for kids to race across the room. Have kids sit down. Point to the paper person left behind.

ASK:

◆ **How would you feel right now if you were that person left behind?**

◆ **How would you feel about your chances of getting well if you were the lame man in the story?**

SAY: **The lame man didn't have a chance of getting into the water first. He probably felt frustrated and hopeless.** Have kids answer these questions in pairs.

ASK:

◆ **When have you felt frustrated or hopeless because of your situation?**

◆ **What did you do?**

SAY: **The Bible tells us what to do when we need help.** Have a volunteer read aloud Philippians 4:6. **Jesus cares about you. You can always ▷TELL JESUS WHAT YOU NEED. The lame man told Jesus his problem, and Jesus healed him. Jesus will help with your problems, too.**

Distribute bandages and markers. Let kids write needs they have on the bandages and place the bandages on the paper person. Close by gathering kids around the paper person. PRAY: **Lord, we all have needs. And we all need your help. We thank you for caring about us. We're grateful that we can tell you our needs. Thank you for loving us. In Jesus' name, amen.**

Song Connect

Use "He Cares for You" (track 22, *it: Innovative Tools for Children's Ministry: New Testament* CD) to help reinforce the Bible Point, ▷**TELL JESUS WHAT YOU NEED.**

Additional Topics List

This lesson can be used to help kids discover... Faith, Healing, Miracles, and Prayer.

Game

▶***HIGH ENERGY***
▶***NO PREP***

Stay Away

Children will play a game of Keep Away and then tell Jesus their needs.

Supplies: Bible

Time: about 5 minutes

Preparation: none

Read aloud or summarize the story in John 5:1-15. SAY: **In our Bible story, the lame man couldn't get into the water. Let's play a game to see what that must have felt like.**

Have half of the group link arms and form a tight circle, facing in. Tell kids to pretend that the pool of Bethesda is inside the circle. The rest of the kids will try to get to the pool, just as the lame man did. The goal of the game is to keep anyone from getting to the pool. (Caution kids not to push hard or shove during the game.) Play for a minute or two, and then let kids switch roles. After the game,

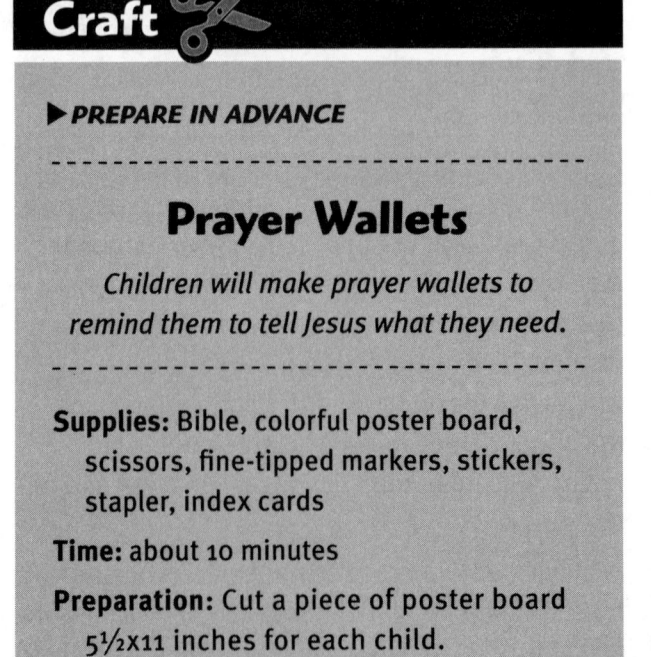

ASK:

- **What was it like to be kept away from the pool?**
- **How is that like how the lame man must have felt?**
- **How did Jesus help the man?**
- **What do you need Jesus to help you with this week?**

SAY: **Jesus cares for you. You can always ▷TELL JESUS WHAT YOU NEED.** Close by having kids silently tell Jesus what they need.

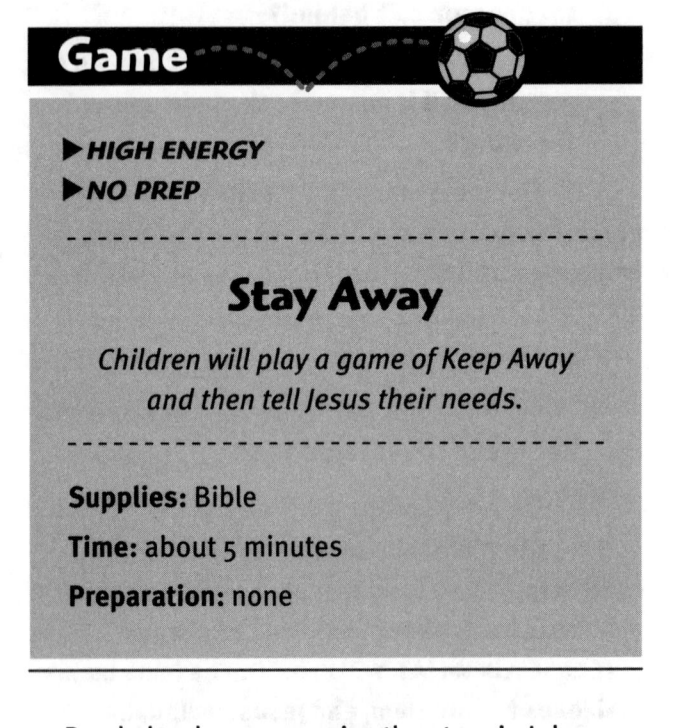

Craft

▶***PREPARE IN ADVANCE***

Prayer Wallets

Children will make prayer wallets to remind them to tell Jesus what they need.

Supplies: Bible, colorful poster board, scissors, fine-tipped markers, stickers, stapler, index cards

Time: about 10 minutes

Preparation: Cut a piece of poster board 5½x11 inches for each child.

Read aloud John 5:1-15. SAY: **Jesus reached out to the lame man, and the man told Jesus his problem. Jesus solved the problem, didn't he? Jesus wants to solve our problems, too. Let's make prayer wallets as reminders that we can always ▷TELL JESUS WHAT WE NEED.**

Give each child a piece of poster board cut to size. Have kids fold the poster board in half to create a square. Then demonstrate how to open the square and make a 2-inch fold on each end to create pockets. Staple the sides of the pockets close to the edges. Let kids use markers and stickers to decorate the outside of their wallets.

Give each child several index cards. Explain that they can tell Jesus what they need by writing a prayer request on each card and inserting the cards into one pocket of the wallet. When the prayer is answered, they can transfer that card to the other pocket as a reminder that Jesus cares about us and answers our prayers.

Bible Application

▶ *PREPARE IN ADVANCE*

Wants or Needs?

Children will make posters differentiating needs from wants and then tell Jesus their needs.

Supplies: Bible, magazines, safety scissors, poster board, tape

Time: about 10 minutes

Preparation: Gather a variety of magazines containing lots of advertisements. At the top of one large sheet of poster board write "Needs." At the top of the other, write "Wants." Hang the posters on the wall where kids can reach them. Set out tape by both posters.

Read aloud or summarize the story of Jesus healing the lame man at the pool in John 5:1-15. SAY: **The lame man told Jesus what he needed, and Jesus helped him. It's important to remember that you can ▷TELL JESUS WHAT YOU NEED, too. But sometimes it's hard to tell the difference between what we actually need and what we just want. This next activity might help.**

Form trios, and give each trio several magazines. Have kids look through the magazines and cut out pictures of things people want and things people need. Have kids tape their pictures to what they think are the appropriate posters. Then gather everyone together and let students look at the collages. Have kids point out any pictures they think are on the wrong poster and explain their decisions. Have kids stand in front of the posters and close in prayer, asking God to help know the difference between needs and wants, and thanking God that kids can always tell Jesus what they need.

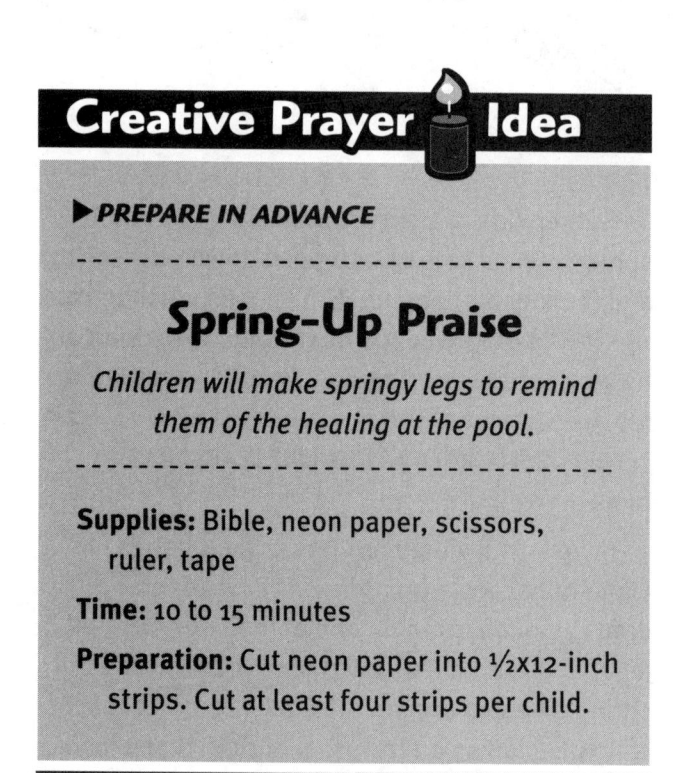

Creative Prayer Idea

▶ *PREPARE IN ADVANCE*

Spring-Up Praise

Children will make springy legs to remind them of the healing at the pool.

Supplies: Bible, neon paper, scissors, ruler, tape

Time: 10 to 15 minutes

Preparation: Cut neon paper into ½x12-inch strips. Cut at least four strips per child.

Read aloud John 5:1-15. SAY: **The lame man at the pool didn't think he could ever get well. But Jesus cared about the man, and Jesus cares about us, too. This story can remind us that we can ▷TELL JESUS WHAT WE NEED. Let's make something to help us praise Jesus!**

Give each child two paper strips. Help kids make praise strips by following these directions: Lay the end of one strip over the end of the other strip to make an L shape. Alternate folding the first strip on top of the second and the second on top of the first until the strips are completely folded into one square. Tape each end of the square to make a spring. Let each child make two springs.

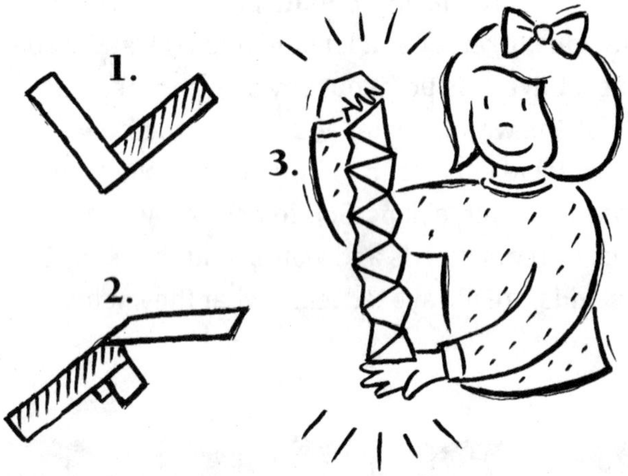

Gather kids in a circle on the floor with their springs. Show kids how to push down on a spring and then let it spring up. SAY: **These springs can remind us of how Jesus healed the lame man so he was able to "spring up." He told Jesus what his problem was, and Jesus healed him. You can ▷TELL JESUS WHAT YOU NEED, just as the lame man did.**

Have kids lay their springs in their hands. Explain that you'll go around the circle. Children can push down on one of their springs, tell Jesus something they need, and then release the spring. Then go around the circle again. Let each child push down on the other spring, thank Jesus, and release it. Close the prayer by thanking Jesus for letting us tell him what we need.

Discussion Launcher Questions

Ask kids to form pairs and discuss:

- **Why do you think Jesus approached the lame man at the pool?**
- **The lame man said, "I can't," when Jesus asked if he'd like to get well. What kinds of things do you say, "I can't," about instead of asking Jesus for help?**
- **What's the difference between a need and a want?**
- **How do you think God feels about us asking for wants? for needs?**
- **What sometimes keeps you from telling Jesus what you need?**

Movie Clip

Helping Hands

Movie Title: *The Secret of Roan Inish* (PG)

Start Time: 22 minutes, 17 seconds

Where to Begin: A woman is walking on the beach collecting food.

Where to End: The young man's eyes are opening.

Plot: A grandfather tells a tale of village women stumbling upon a half-drowned boy on the beach while they were searching for food. The women nurse the young man back to health.

Review: Use this scene to help children understand that Jesus wants to help us with our needs, just as he helped the lame man by the pool.

Discussion

After setting up and showing the movie clip, ASK:

- **How do you think the boy felt when he opened his eyes?**
- **How has someone cared for you when you were hurt or sick?**

SAY: **Everywhere Jesus went, he healed the hurt and sick. One time he healed a man who had been sick for 38 years! Here's what happened.** Open your Bible to John 5:1-15, and read or summarize the story of Jesus healing the lame man at the pool. ASK:

- **How do you think the lame man felt when he could stand and walk?**
- **How do you think the man felt about Jesus after Jesus healed him?**

SAY: **In the movie clip we just watched, the boy didn't ask to be helped—the women knew he needed help and just did it. Jesus knew what the lame man needed, and he healed him on the spot. The man hadn't even asked Jesus to help him. It was Jesus who reached out to the man first. You never have to be afraid to ▷TELL JESUS WHAT YOU NEED. Jesus already knows what we need, and he wants to help us. You can always count on Jesus!**

n
o
t
e
s

Preschool Story

▶*ALLERGY ALERT*

Bible Point: ▷**TELL JESUS WHAT YOU NEED.**

Supplies: Bible, wading pool or large dishpan, 2-liter bottle filled with small candies, paper, pencils, safety scissors (1 pair for each child), crayons, craft sticks, tape or glue

Time: 10 to 15 minutes

Preparation: Fill the wading pool or dishpan with water. Select an outside spot to place the wading pool or dishpan.

Talk to Jesus!

Have kids form a circle and sit down. Open your Bible to John 5:1-15, and show children the words. SAY: **In this Bible story, a man who couldn't walk wanted to get to the water in this pool as soon as it started swirling. He thought that if he got into the pool, the water would heal him.**

When you see me swirl the water in the pool with the bottle, get to the pool as quickly as you can without using your feet. You can crawl, wriggle, roll, or scoot; but you can't stand on your feet. When you get to the pool, put one hand in the water and hold the other hand up to me.

Swirl the pool water with the bottle. When all the children have gotten to the pool, pour one of the treats from the bottle into each child's hand.

ASK:

- **Which hand got the treat, the one in the water or the one reaching out to me?**
- **How did it feel to get a treat? Why?**

SAY: **It was Jesus who healed the man, not the water in the pool. Just like you got the candy by reaching out to me, the man was healed when he reached out to Jesus and told Jesus what he needed.**

Repeat the activity several times, encouraging children to use different movements to get to the pool each time. Close in prayer, thanking Jesus that he is here for us when we need him.

ASK:

- **How do you think the man felt when Jesus healed him?**
- **How do you think Jesus feels when we reach out to him and ▷TELL HIM WHAT WE NEED?**

SAY: **Jesus wants us to ▷TELL HIM WHAT WE NEED, and then he will take care of us. Let's make a craft now to help us remember to ▷TELL JESUS WHAT WE NEED.**

Give each child a piece of paper, a pencil, and a pair of safety scissors. Encourage kids to trace each of their hands on a piece of paper. Then help kids cut out the hand outlines. (If you have younger kids in your class, you may want to trace and cut out their hands before class.) Once kids are finished cutting, set out crayons and encourage kids to draw one thing that they need on the inside (palm) of each paper hand. Then help kids glue or tape a craft stick to the bottom of each hand. Show kids how they can hold the two hands as though in prayer. Remind kids that they can pray and tell Jesus what they need and that Jesus will care for them.

ASK:

- **When do you like to pray?**
- **What do you like to talk to Jesus about?**

SAY: **Jesus always likes to hear our prayers. We can pray to Jesus anytime. When we pray, we can ▷TELL JESUS WHAT WE NEED.**

BIBLE STORY

Jesus Heals a Blind Man

For the Leader

The Pharisees were trying to find a way to trap Jesus. To the Pharisees, healing was "work" that should not be done on the Sabbath, as this healing had been. The Pharisees brought the man in and grilled him about the healing and whether he truly had been born blind. They just couldn't accept that Jesus could perform such a miracle!

After the formerly blind man's testimony that Jesus must be from God since he could heal blindness, the Pharisees threw the man out. Later Jesus looked for the blind man. After the second encounter with Jesus, the blind man understood that he had experienced the healing power of a God who cares.

Key Scriptures

John 9:1-15, 24-34

1 Peter 5:7

Bible Verse

"Give all your worries and cares to God, for he cares about you" (1 Peter 5:7).

Bible Experience

▶ *NO PREP*
▶ *ALLERGY ALERT*

Bible Point: ▷**JESUS CARES FOR US.**

Children will use an object lesson to discover that Jesus cares for us.

Supplies: Bible, bag of wrapped candy
Time: about 10 minutes
Preparation: none

SAY: **Before we talk about today's Bible story, let's try an experiment. Everyone, close your eyes and cover them with your hands. Tell me what you see.** Pause as children respond. **Keep your eyes closed and covered, and tell me how many fingers I'm holding up.** Hold up some fingers.

ASK:

- **How do you like seeing nothing but darkness?**

SAY: **OK, you can take your hands down and open you eyes.**

ASK:

- **Now what do you see?**
- **How many fingers am I holding up?** Hold up some fingers.
- **Which do you like better: darkness or light?**

Read aloud John 9:1-15, 24-34. SAY: **This Bible story is about a man who had been born blind. Jesus healed him, even though it was the Sabbath. No one was supposed to work on the Sabbath, so the Pharisees tried to get Jesus in trouble for healing the man.** Hold up the bag of candy.

ASK:

- **Why do you think the Pharisees wanted to get Jesus in trouble?**
- **Why do you think Jesus healed the man on the Sabbath anyway?**

Have a volunteer read aloud 1 Peter 5:7. SAY: ▷**JESUS CARES FOR US. He loves us and wants to help us. He didn't worry about what the Pharisees thought when he healed than man. It's kind of like this.** Hold up the bag of candy.

ASK:

- **What if I told you that if I gave you some candy, I'd get in trouble with the pastor? Would you still want me to give you the candy?**
- **What if I could even go to jail for giving you the candy? Do you think I'd still give it to you?**

Give each child a piece of candy. SAY: **I'm giving you the candy because I care for you. Of course, I won't get fired or go to jail for giving you candy. But I wanted you to think about what Jesus was willing to risk when he healed the blind man. Jesus cared for that man, and** ▷**JESUS CARES FOR US!** Say a prayer thanking Jesus for caring for us, and then let kids enjoy the candy.

Song & Connect

Use "He Cares for You" (track 22, *it: Innovative Tools for Children's Ministry: New Testament* CD) to help reinforce the Bible Point, ▷**JESUS CARES FOR US.**

Additional Topics List

This lesson can be used to help kids discover...
Faith, God's Power, Healing, and Miracles.

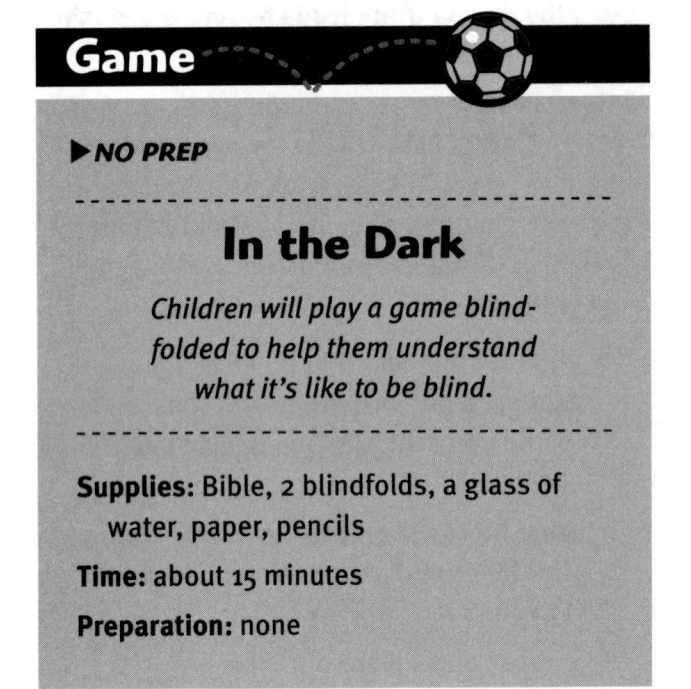

Game

▶ *NO PREP*

In the Dark

Children will play a game blindfolded to help them understand what it's like to be blind.

Supplies: Bible, 2 blindfolds, a glass of water, paper, pencils

Time: about 15 minutes

Preparation: none

Open your Bible to John 9:1-15, 24-34, and briefly summarize the story of Jesus healing the blind man. Have kids form two teams of equal size. Have children from each team come forward to a table one at a time. Blindfold one child from each team. Have teammates cheer as the two blindfolded children perform these tasks: Pour water into a glass, write their names on pieces of paper, and then walk back to the team to tag the next teammate to come forward.

After everyone has had a turn,

ASK:

- ◆ **How did it feel to do the tasks in this game without being able to see?**
- ◆ **What do you think the blind man told his friends about Jesus?**
- ◆ **What will you tell your friends about Jesus this week?**

Craft

▶ *FOR FAMILY MINISTRY*

I See the Light

Children will decorate switch-plate covers to help them remember the Bible story.

Supplies: Bible, switch-plate covers, fine-point permanent markers, tape

Time: about 10 minutes

Preparation: Tape the screws to the back of each switch plate cover.

Briefly summarize the story in John 9:1-15, 24-34 about Jesus healing the blind man. Give each child a switch-plate cover and some markers. SAY: **Using a marker, write your name on the back of the cover and write "I Want to See" on the front. Then decorate your cover by drawing things you'd want to see if you had been blind and could suddenly see.**

When kids have finished, let them show their artwork to others. Then

ASK:

- ◆ **What would you want to see if you had been blind?**
- ◆ **What is one truth that you can see—that you know about Jesus?**

SAY: **When you get home, ask your parents to help you put your cover on a light switch. Each time you turn on the light, think about how Jesus cared for the blind man by healing him and about how ▷ JESUS CARES FOR US.**

Bible Application

Air Traffic Control

Children will guide each other in a game and learn that Jesus is in control of their lives.

Supplies: Bible, blindfolds

Time: about 10 minutes

Preparation: Place a few chairs around the room.

Read aloud John 9:1-15, 24-34, or briefly summarize the story of Jesus healing the blind man. SAY: **The blind man in our Bible story was in the dark, literally, before Jesus healed him. Before we discuss that, let's play a game called Flying in the Dark.**

Have kids form pairs. Tell partners to choose who will be the airplane and who will be the air-traffic controller. SAY: **Airplanes, you'll need guidance through a foggy night. So put on your blindfolds and pretend it's foggy and that you can't see.** Pause as partners help their airplanes put on blindfolds. **Airplanes, your air-traffic controllers will walk beside you and guide you around the room, using their voices only. Trust your air-traffic controllers and do what they say. They'll bring you through the fog safely!**

Let partners walk around the room, and then have kids switch roles and play again.

ASK:

- **What was it like to be the airplane? the air-traffic controller?**
- **What do you think it was like to be blind in Bible times?**

SAY: **In our game your air-traffic controller was in control as you navigated through the room. In life, God is like our air-traffic controller. He sees the big picture and guides us through life.**

ASK:

- **Why was the man in the story born blind?**
- **Have you ever wondered why something bad or difficult happened to you? Tell a partner about it.**

SAY: **The man in the story was born blind so people could see the power of God. Sometimes, when bad things happen to us, they actually happen so God can use the situation for his glory. Think about something bad that has happened to you.** Pause. **Now let's pray and ask God to use that bad thing to show his power and glory.** Close with a prayer asking God to show his power in the difficult times kids face.

Creative Prayer Idea

Color Coded

Children will discover that everything they see can remind them that Jesus cares for them.

Supplies: different-colored paper, scissors, paper bag

Time: about 5 minutes

Preparation: Cut the paper into pieces no smaller than 2 inches square. Put the paper slips in the bag.

SAY: **In our Bible story the man couldn't see, just like you can't see what's in the bag.** Let each child pick a slip of paper from the bag. **But Jesus healed the man, and then he could see! Now that you can see what was in the bag, let's**

each say a prayer of thanks to God for something that's the same color as the paper you're holding. Let each child add to the prayer, and then close by thanking Jesus for caring for each of the children in class.

Discussion Launcher Questions

Have kids form pairs to discuss the following questions. After each question, invite volunteers to share their answers with the rest of the class.

ASK:

- **How do you think the blind man felt about Jesus after the man was healed?**
- **What do you think the blind man's friends said to each other when they saw what Jesus did?**
- **Why do you think Jesus performed miracles?**
- **How does Jesus show he cares for you and your family?**

Movie Clip

The Real King

Movie: *The Sword in the Stone*, 1983 revised version (rated G)

Start Time: 1 hour, 15 minutes, 15 seconds

Where to Begin: The crowd walks with Arthur back to the stone.

Where to End: The crowd shouts, "Long live the king!"

Plot: No one believes that Arthur pulled the sword from the stone, so they go back to see him do it again. The people witnessing the feat proclaim Arthur king.

Review: Connect this scene to the Bible by talking about how the miracles Jesus performed were one way Jesus showed that he is the Son of God, just as Arthur's feat showed he was the rightful king.

Discussion

After setting up and showing the clip, have kids form pairs to discuss these questions:

- **Why was Arthur the only one able to pull the sword from the stone?**
- **Why was Jesus able to heal the blind man?**

SAY: **In our movie Arthur showed that he was the rightful king by the things he was able to do. Like Arthur, Jesus revealed who he was by what he did. But Jesus didn't have to show his power to become God's Son. He performed miracles, such as healing the blind man, to help people. Jesus' miracles can help us remember that ▷ JESUS CARES FOR US, just as he cared for the blind man.**

notes

Preschool Story

▶PREPARE IN ADVANCE
▶ALLERGY ALERT

Bible Point: ▷**JESUS CARES FOR US.**

Supplies: Bible, old magazines or pieces of paper and markers, glue, scissors, mud (optional), chocolate pudding, teddy-bear cookies, 2 bowls, spoons, paper plates, napkins

Time: 10 to 15 minutes

Preparation: Draw or cut out (from magazines) one of each of the following pictures: Jesus, a blind man, a pool or lake, a happy crowd, and an angry crowd. Glue or draw a star on the back of each picture. Hide the pictures around the room, with the star facing out—be sure these are placed where kids can easily find them. You will also need a little bit of mud or chocolate pudding in a small bowl.

At your snack table, set out a bowl of chocolate pudding and several teddy-bear cookies for each child. Set out plates and napkins.

A Muddy Mix

Have kids form a circle and sit down. Open your Bible to John 9:1-15, 24-34, and show children the words. SAY: **In our Bible story today, we're going to learn about an amazing thing that Jesus did. But first we need to find some pictures hidden in this room.** Encourage children to find all the pictures you hid before class. Once all the pictures are found, have kids hand the pictures to you. **We're going to use these pictures to help us tell the Bible story.**

Hold up the picture of Jesus and SAY: **One day Jesus was walking along, and he saw a man who had been born blind.** Hand the picture of the man to one child, and have the child hold up the picture. **Jesus saw the man and wanted to help him. So Jesus spit in the sand and made mud.** Encourage children to pretend to spit on the ground, pick up some mud, and rub it between their fingers. **Then Jesus took the mud and rubbed it on the man's eyes.** Take a dab of the mud or chocolate pudding and rub it on the eyes of the man in the picture.

Jesus told the man to go to the pool of Siloam and wash off his eyes. Hand the picture of the lake or pool to another child, and have the child hold it up. **The man went to the pool and washed the mud off his eyes. As soon as he washed off the mud, the man could see for the first time in his life! Jesus had healed him! Show me how you would feel if Jesus had done this for you.** Encourage children to show you happy faces and to celebrate by jumping up and down.

The man was so happy that he ran to tell others about what Jesus had done. Hand the picture of the happy crowd to a different child, and encourage the child to hold it up. **The people were very happy to hear about how Jesus had healed the man! But soon the Pharisees heard about what Jesus had done for him.** Hand the picture of the angry crowd to a new child, and encourage the child to hold up the picture. **The Pharisees were jealous that Jesus could heal the man, and they didn't believe that Jesus was the Son of God. They thought Jesus was just another ordinary person. So they asked the man who had healed him. The man told the Pharisees that Jesus had healed him. But the Pharisees still didn't believe that Jesus was the Son of God.**

ASK:

- **Why didn't the Pharisees believe in Jesus?**
- **How did Jesus care for the man?**
- **How has Jesus cared for you?**

Gather children at your snack table. Give each child a spoonful of chocolate pudding and several teddy-bear cookies on a paper plate. Encourage kids to rub a bit of chocolate pudding over each teddy-bear cookie's eyes. Let kids use their snacks to retell the story.

SAY: **Jesus did an amazing thing when he helped the blind man to see. Jesus cared for the blind man, and ▷JESUS CARES FOR US, too.** Encourage each child to name one way Jesus has cared for him or her. Then pray and thank Jesus for all the ways he has cared for the children in your class.

notes

BIBLE STORY

Lazarus Raised From the Dead

For the Leader

Martha, distraught over Lazarus' death, had trouble fully understanding what Jesus was capable of doing, even though she had great faith in him. Jesus' comment to her in John 11:25 indicates that he was trying to teach her that he is more than a great teacher and healer. He's in control of life itself!

We don't know exactly why Jesus wept when approaching Lazarus' tomb, knowing that Lazarus was going to be raised. Perhaps it was because of the unbelief of the crowd. More likely, he was hurting with his friends, feeling the pain they were experiencing.

The hope we have in Jesus hinges on belief or unbelief. Jesus divides those who believe from those who don't.

Key Scripture

John 11:17-44

Bible Verse

"Jesus told her, 'I am the resurrection and the life. Anyone who believes in me will live, even after dying'" (John 11:25).

Bible Experience

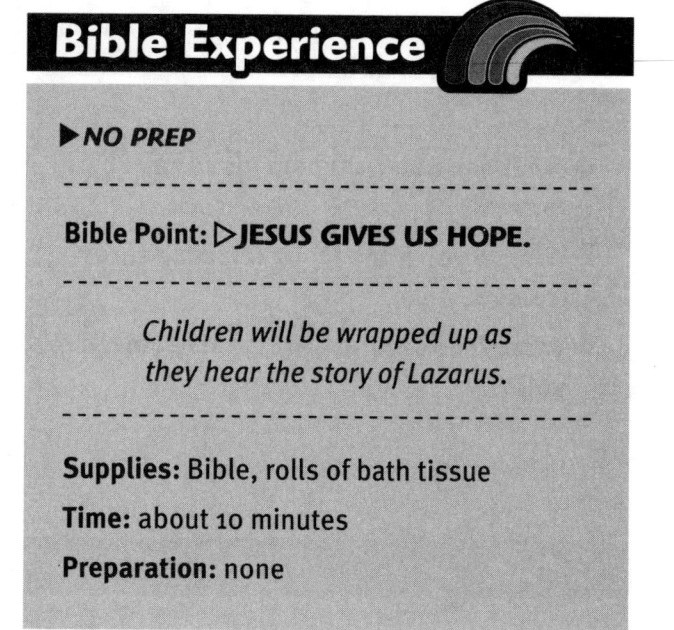

▶ *NO PREP*

Bible Point: ▷**JESUS GIVES US HOPE.**

Children will be wrapped up as they hear the story of Lazarus.

Supplies: Bible, rolls of bath tissue

Time: about 10 minutes

Preparation: none

Open your Bible to John 11:17-44, and show kids the passage. SAY: **Our Bible story today is about Jesus raising his friend Lazarus from the dead. Before I tell you more of the story, I'll need to wrap you up. You'll see why in just a minute.**

Have an adult or teen volunteer help you quickly wrap each child in bath tissue. (An easy way to accomplish this is to have the child hold the end of the bath tissue and then turn round and round as you hold the roll.) Say that you'll tell the story and explain what kids should do.

SAY: **In Jesus' day, when people died and were buried, they were wrapped in strips of cloth. That's why I had to wrap you up like I did. Jesus' friend Lazarus had died, and they had wrapped him up and put him in a tomb. So all you Lazarus impersonators need to come over here to a tomb.** Motion to one corner of the room. Tell kids they should hop across the room so as not to break the bath-tissue wrapping. When everyone is in the corner you indicated, continue with the story.

Lazarus' two sisters, Mary and Martha, were crying because they were sad that their brother had died. Jesus cried, too. Jesus came to the tomb and asked that the stone in front of the tomb be taken away. Then he said, "Lazarus, come out!"

Everyone was surprised because Lazarus had been dead for four days. But that's what Jesus said: "Lazarus, come out!" And guess what happened? Out came Lazarus! Have all the kids hop back across the room. **Jesus brought Lazarus back to life. He broke the bonds of death!** Have all the kids break free of their bath-tissue grave clothes.

After kids clean up the bath tissue and throw it away, have them form trios to discuss these questions:

- **How did Mary and Martha feel at the beginning of the story? How do you think they felt at the end?**
- **What would you have said that day if you had seen Jesus raise Lazarus from the dead?**
- **What does this story tell you about Jesus' power?**

SAY: ▷**JESUS GIVES US HOPE because Jesus has power over death! He gave Mary and Martha hope because he raised their brother from the dead. But that's not the end of the story. Jesus said that anyone who believes in him will live forever. Listen to what he said.** Have a volunteer read aloud John 11:25; then SAY: **That means that if you believe in Jesus, you'll live with him forever in heaven. That's great news! Let's thank God for sending Jesus.**

Close in prayer, thanking God for giving Jesus power over death.

Song & Connect

Use "I Am the Resurrection and the Life" (track 9, *it: Innovative Tools for Children's Ministry: New Testament* CD) to help reinforce the Bible Point, ▷**JESUS GIVES US HOPE.**

Additional Topics List

This lesson can be used to help kids discover... Death, Eternal Life, Grief, and Heaven.

Game

▶ *NO PREP*

Mummy Making

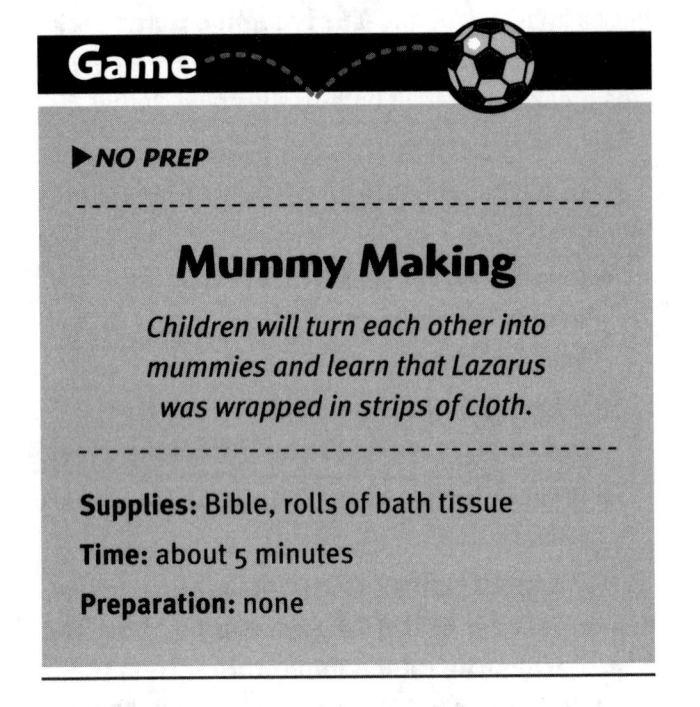

Children will turn each other into mummies and learn that Lazarus was wrapped in strips of cloth.

Supplies: Bible, rolls of bath tissue

Time: about 5 minutes

Preparation: none

Open your Bible to John 11:17-44, and briefly summarize the story of Jesus raising Lazarus from the dead.

Have kids form trios, and give each trio a roll of bath tissue. Tell each trio that they'll have about four minutes to turn one child into a mummy. The first step is for each trio to decide who will be the mummy and who will be the mummy makers. After kids have decided, SAY: **Ready...set...make a mummy!**

As children work, give updates about how much time is left to work. When time has elapsed, have children step back and applaud each others' handiwork. Then have all the "mummies" burst forth from their wrapping. Ask trios to clean up the bath tissue and throw it away. Then have kids sit in their trios. SAY: **If we had really been wrapped in linen cloths, like Lazarus was, it wouldn't have been easy to get out. We would have needed big-time help!**

ASK:

- **What's the biggest help Jesus gave Lazarus?**
- **Why do you think Jesus raised Lazarus from the dead?**
- **What does Lazarus' being raised mean to you?**

Craft

▶ *NO PREP*

Dry Those Eyes

Children will make tissue-box covers to remind them that in times of sadness, Jesus gives us hope.

Supplies: Bibles, 1 box of tissues per child, newsprint, tape, safety scissors, fine-tipped markers, glitter-glue pens, gel pens, stickers

Time: about 15 minutes

Preparation: none

Read aloud John 11:17-44. SAY: **In today's Bible story, Mary and Martha cried because they were sad that their brother had died. Even Jesus cried.**

ASK:

- **What kinds of things make you cry?**
- **How can this story help you the next time you're sad and feel like crying?**

SAY: **We all get sad sometimes, and we all cry sometimes. But we need to remember that ▷JESUS GIVES US HOPE.** Give each child a box of tissues. **Let's make covers for these tissue boxes. The covers can remind us of today's Bible story.**

Have children wrap their tissue boxes in newsprint. Help them tape the wrapping in place and cut an opening where the tissues are dispensed. Then let them use the supplies you brought to draw pictures of the Bible story all around the box and to decorate the box. Have Bibles handy so kids can also write the words to John 11:25 on the boxes.

When kids finish, let them admire each other's work. Encourage kids to take their decorated tissue boxes home with them so that the next time they or someone in their family feels like crying, they can remember that **▷JESUS GIVES US HOPE.**

Bible Application

▶NO PREP

Practice Makes Perfect

Children will guess sad situations and then practice telling each other about the hope Jesus brings.

Supplies: Bible

Time: 5 to 10 minutes

Preparation: none

Read aloud or summarize the story in John 11:17-44. SAY: **We all have opportunities to comfort other people when they're feeling sad. It doesn't have to be because someone has died. People get sad for all kinds of reasons.**

ASK:

- **What makes your friends or family members feel sad?**
- **What makes you feel sad sometimes?**
- **How can knowing that ▷JESUS GIVES US HOPE help us when we're sad?**

Have kids form pairs. SAY: **Let's practice telling each other about the hope Jesus brings. I'll ask a volunteer to come up and silently act out a sad situation. Then the volunteer will sit down, and partners can tell each other what they'd say about Jesus to the person in that sad situation.**

Have a volunteer come to the front. Whisper a sad situation for him or her to act out. Examples might be a sick pet, a broken toy, or having to move away. (You might also want to use examples kids gave when they answered your questions a few moments ago.) After the volunteer performs, let kids guess the situation. Then have the volunteer sit down, and let partners practice telling each other about the hope Jesus could bring in that situation.

Play several rounds. Then close with a prayer thanking Jesus for bringing us hope, even in sad situations.

notes

Creative Prayer Idea

▶ *NO PREP*

In the News

Children will search out and pray for people who need hope.

Supplies: several recent newspapers

Time: 5 to 10 minutes

Preparation: none

Set out several recent newspapers. Let kids scan the papers for stories of people who need the hope Jesus brings. After each child has chosen an article, gather kids in a circle and invite them to summarize their news stories. After each person shares a story, invite that person to pray for the people in the story. (If a child feels too uncomfortable to pray aloud, lead the prayer yourself.)

Discussion Launcher Questions

Have kids form pairs to discuss the following questions. After each question, invite volunteers to share their answers with the rest of the class.

ASK:

- **Why do you think Jesus cried, even though he knew he was going to raise Lazarus from the dead?**
- **What would it be like to see Jesus crying?**
- **What things do you think make Jesus sad?**
- **How do you feel, knowing that Jesus cares if you're sad?**
- **How does Jesus give you hope when you're sad?**

Snack

▶ *FOR YOUNGER CHILDREN*

▶ *ALLERGY ALERT*

Sad to Glad

Children will make a snack to remind them that Jesus gives us hope, even when we're sad.

Supplies: English muffins, small plates, plastic knives, softened cream cheese, apple slices, lemon juice, knife, string licorice, grapes, raisins

Time: about 10 minutes

Preparation: Cut the apples into slices, and then dip the slices in lemon juice to keep them from browning. Be sure to place the knife out of children's reach. Clean the surface where you and your kids will be creating your snacks.

SAY: **Let's make a snack to remind us that ▷JESUS GIVES US HOPE, just as he gave hope to Mary and Martha.** Have kids wash their hands. Give each child half of an English muffin on a small plate. Let kids spread the muffins with the cream cheese. Then let kids use the supplies you set out to make a sad face on each muffin. Kids can use an apple slice for a down-turned mouth, string licorice for hair, grapes for the eyes and nose, and raisins for tears.

When Lazarus died, everyone's faces were sad, just like these sad faces we made. But when Jesus raised Lazarus from the dead, everyone's faces were happy! Let's turn our sad faces into glad faces.

Let kids eat the raisin tears and turn the apple slices into smiles.

Preschool Story

▶ *NO PREP*

Bible Point: ▷ **JESUS GIVES US HOPE.**

Supplies: Bible, bathroom tissue or white crepe paper, craft sticks, paper, crayons

Time: 15 to 20 minutes

Preparation: none

Hope Is on the Way

Before you begin the story, set out bathroom tissue or white crepe paper and encourage kids to wrap each other in the paper. Once a child is wrapped up, encourage him or her to break free of the wrapping. This fun game will get children ready to hear the Bible story and help them understand that Jesus gave everyone hope when he brought Lazarus back to life.

Have kids form a circle and sit down. Open your Bible to John 11:17-44, and show children the words. Give each child four craft sticks and a wadded up piece of paper. Have kids draw a sad face on one side of each craft stick and a smiley face on the other. Tell kids that one puppet is Lazarus, one is Mary, one is Martha, and one is Jesus. If you have time, let kids decorate their puppets to look like the characters. Tell kids to use the sad side of their puppets for now.

SAY: **A man named Lazarus was very sick. His sisters, Mary and Martha, were worried about their brother, so they sent a message to their good friend Jesus. Mary and Martha knew that Jesus could help their brother.** Have children lay their Lazarus puppet down and stand their Mary and Martha puppets nearby. Tell kids to put their Jesus puppet far away.

Jesus was sad that his friend Lazarus was sick, but Jesus wanted to do something very special for Lazarus. So Jesus waited a few more days before he went to see Lazarus. During that time, Lazarus died.

Mary and Martha were very sad that their brother had died. Encourage children to make their Mary and Martha puppets cry. **Lots of friends and relatives came to be with Mary and Martha after Lazarus died. They wrapped Lazarus in grave clothes and placed him in a tomb, which is like a cave.** Have kids wrap their Lazarus puppet in tissue paper. **They rolled a very heavy stone in front of the tomb.** Have kids place their paper stone in front of Lazarus.

Lazarus was in his tomb for four days before Jesus came. When Jesus came, Martha came running out to greet him. She was very sad. She asked Jesus why he hadn't come sooner. She knew that Jesus could have saved him. Encourage kids to move their Jesus puppet close to the other puppets. Kids can pretend that the three puppets are talking.

Mary was also sad that Jesus hadn't come sooner. She knew that Jesus was powerful and that he could have done something to help her brother.

Jesus went to Lazarus' tomb. He asked that the heavy stone be rolled away from the tomb. Encourage kids to roll the paper stone away from Lazarus.

When the stone was rolled away, Jesus called out, "Lazarus, come out!" And then Lazarus came out of the tomb! Encourage kids to make Lazarus stand up and "walk" toward Jesus. Tell kids to show the smiling side of Lazarus now. **Jesus had brought Lazarus back to life! Lazarus was still wrapped in his grave clothes, so Jesus told the people to unwrap him and let him go.** Encourage kids to unwrap their Lazarus puppet.

Everyone was excited and happy that Jesus had brought Lazarus back to life! Jesus had

brought hope to Mary, Martha, Lazarus, and all their friends and family. Encourage kids to turn all their puppets to the smiling side and make their puppets celebrate.

Jesus did an amazing thing for them, and he gave them all hope. We can have hope also because Jesus does amazing things for us, too!

ASK:

- **What amazing things has Jesus done for you?**
- **How can you have hope in Jesus?**

SAY: ▷**JESUS GIVES US HOPE, just as he gave hope to Mary, Martha, and Lazarus!**

notes

BIBLE STORY

Jesus Eats With Sinners

For the Leader

The tax collector named Levi (also called Matthew) is the same Matthew who became Jesus' disciple and one of the four Gospel writers. Levi left what was probably a lucrative tax-collecting business to follow Jesus. Then he gave a reception so his friends could meet Jesus.

Jesus chose to spend time not with people who were proud of their good deeds and so-called spirituality but rather with people who sensed their own sinfulness.

Key Scriptures

Luke 5:27-32

Romans 3:23

Bible Verse

"Everyone has sinned; we all fall short of God's glorious standard" (Romans 3:23).

Bible Experience

▶ *ALLERGY ALERT*

Bible Point: ▷**EVERYONE IS WELCOME.**

Children will have a party and celebrate Jesus' love.

Supplies: Bibles, party supplies and decorations (If possible, make the party supplies fancy, and serve something special, such as a decorated cake that says "Everyone Is Welcome!"), snacks, dress-up clothes (If possible, use dress-up clothes that are out of style.), face paint

Time: about 15 minutes

Preparation: Decorate your room for a party.

As kids arrive, welcome them enthusiastically. Gather everyone together and ask a volunteer to read aloud Luke 5:27-32. SAY: **In this passage the Pharisees couldn't believe that Jesus would associate with unpopular, sinful people like tax collectors. They didn't understand that with Jesus, ▷EVERYONE IS WELCOME!**

Invite kids to use the clothes and face paints to dress up for a party. Explain that people who are poor, unpopular, poorly dressed, or strangers are welcome at this party. As kids are dressing up, SAY: **It's good news that ▷EVERYONE IS WELCOME with Jesus! He came to save sinners—and that means everyone, including you and me. Listen to what the Bible says:** Have a volunteer read aloud Romans 3:23. **See? We're all sinners. None of us deserves God's love, but he gives it to us anyway. I'm glad that ▷EVERYONE'S WELCOME with Jesus! Let's celebrate!**

Play games that involve someone being left out, such as Musical Chairs or Monkey in the Middle. Then serve your special snack, and treat everyone like royalty. End the party by thanking Jesus for welcoming all of us into his kingdom.

Additional Topics List

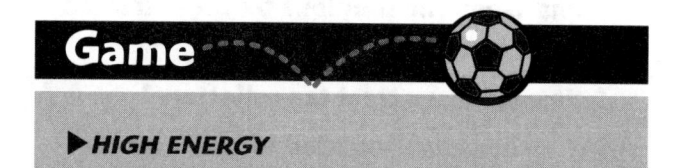

This lesson can be used to help kids discover... Acceptance, Grace, and Prejudice.

Game

▶ *HIGH ENERGY*
▶ *PREPARE IN ADVANCE*

Stay Away

Children will play a version of Keep Away to help them realize that with Jesus, everyone is welcome.

Supplies: Bible, balloons, markers

Time: about 5 minutes

Preparation: Blow up and tie off a bunch of balloons, approximately one per child. (The number doesn't have to be precise, however.)

Have kids draw faces on the balloons. Then have kids scatter around the room. Explain that the object of the game is for kids to keep batting the balloons away from themselves. Encourage children to shout, "Stay away from me!" "Get away!" and

"I don't want you near me!" each time they bat a balloon. Have kids bat the balloons for a few minutes, and then call time and collect the balloons.

ASK:

- ◆ **What was it like to try to keep all those balloons away from you?**
- ◆ **Are there certain kinds of people you try to keep away from you in real life? Explain.**

SAY: **In Jesus' day, certain kinds of people were looked down on. But those were the kind of people Jesus wanted to be with. I'll show you what I mean.** Have a volunteer read aloud Luke 5:27-32.

ASK:

- ◆ **How was our balloon game like how the Pharisees and religious teachers treated tax collectors?**
- ◆ **How did Jesus treat tax collectors?**

SAY: **In our game we tried to keep the balloon people away from us. That's how the Pharisees looked down on and tried to stay away from tax collectors and people like them. But Jesus came to save all people, including the people no one else wants to hang out with. With Jesus, ▷ EVERYONE IS WELCOME!**

notes

Craft

You're Invited!

Children will make invitations to their church.

Supplies: Bible, construction paper, pencil, safety scissors, crayons and markers, glue sticks

Time: 10 to 15 minutes

Preparation: For each child, fold a sheet of construction paper in half. In the center of the page, draw two vertical lines 2 inches from the fold up and 2 inches from the fold down, and 1 inch apart.

Have a volunteer read aloud Luke 5:27-32.

SAY: **In this story Jesus ate a special dinner with people the Pharisees didn't like. The Pharisees thought they were better than people like tax collectors, and they wouldn't even eat with them! But Jesus loves sinners—that's who he came to save. With Jesus, ▷ EVERYONE IS WELCOME! Let's make special invitations to invite people to our church so they can learn about Jesus.**

Help kids follow these steps to make pop-up invitations: Use scissors to cut slits along the two lines on the paper. Open the card, push the centerpiece you just cut in the opposite direction so it's on the inside of the card, and crease the fold line. This will be the pop-up part of the card.

Take another sheet of paper and fold it in half. Glue the first sheet inside the second sheet, being careful not to glue down the pop-up section. Decorate the outside of the invitation. Then open the card. On another sheet of paper, draw a figure or a heart (about the size of your finger)

and cut it out. Glue it to the pop-up. Inside the card, write a message inviting someone to your church.

Encourage kids to give their invitations to a friend or family member this week and to tell them that ▷**EVERYONE IS WELCOME with Jesus!**

Bible Application

▶ ***NO PREP***

Stick With Jesus!

Children will make stickers to remind them that everyone is welcome with Jesus.

Supplies: Bible, large self-adhesive labels (available at office-supply stores), fine-tipped markers

Time: about 5 minutes

Preparation: none

Have a volunteer read aloud Luke 5:27-32. SAY: **With Jesus, ▷EVERYONE IS WELCOME.**

But that's not always the case with people, is it? In this Bible passage, the Pharisees couldn't believe that Jesus would hang out with tax collectors. Remember what they said? "Why do you eat and drink with such scum?" Those are pretty harsh words!

At your school there are probably people no one wants to eat lunch with or hang out with. Some of them are the unpopular kids, some are kids no one really knows, and some of them may be troublemakers. No matter who they are, they all need Jesus because they're all sinners. But guess what? So are you. So am I. We're all sinners, and we *all* need Jesus! Thankfully, Jesus welcomes everyone.

Distribute the labels and set out markers to share. SAY: **I want you to make a sticker to put on a book or backpack that you'll see every day at school. Decorate your sticker in a way that will remind you that ▷EVERYONE IS WELCOME with Jesus and that everyone needs Jesus. When you look at your sticker, pray for the outcasts at your school. Ask God to help them find Jesus. Ask God how you can help.**

Creative Prayer Idea

Pray Away!

Children will use newspapers to identify people they normally wouldn't pray for.

Supplies: Bibles, newspapers

Time: 5 to 10 minutes

Preparation: Gather several national newspapers.

Read aloud Luke 5:27-32. Then SAY: **With Jesus, ▷EVERYONE IS WELCOME. He loved all people. Let's try to be like Jesus and keep love in our hearts for all kinds of people, not just the people we like or agree with.**

Have kids form trios, and give each trio a section of newspaper. Tell kids to look for groups of people (not specific people) they might not normally be inclined to pray for. After each trio has identified one or more groups of people to pray for, have kids pray in their trios. Close by asking God to help kids welcome everyone the way Jesus does.

Discussion Launcher

Welcome Mats

For this activity you'll need a Bible, construction paper, markers, gel pens, glitter glue, and tape.

Read aloud Luke 5:27-32. Then SAY: **It's easy to look down on people and not welcome them as Jesus would. Sometimes we don't even realize we're doing it.**

ASK:

- **When have you felt left out or unwanted?**
- **When have you felt welcomed and appreciated?**

SAY: **Sometimes when you go somewhere new, like a new school or a new church, you might feel scared and awkward because you don't know anyone. Let's not let that happen at our church! Let's make welcome mats to let everyone know that because of Jesus, ▷EVERYONE IS WELCOME at our church!**

Set out the supplies, and let kids make as many welcome mats as you think your church can handle. (Be sure to get permission before hanging them on the walls in your church entrance. If necessary, hang them in the hallways instead.)

Snack

▶*FOR SMALL GROUPS*
▶*NO PREP*
▶*ALLERGY ALERT*

Welcome Wedges

Children will break bread together to remind them of Jesus' eating with tax collectors.

Supplies: Bible, loaf of unsliced bread, various dips

Time: about 5 minutes

Preparation: none

Read or have a volunteer read aloud Luke 5:27-32. Then SAY: **In Bible times breaking bread and eating together held special significance. People broke bread together to seal an agreement and as a symbol of peace, goodwill, and friendship.**

We know from our Bible story that ▷EVERYONE IS WELCOME with Jesus. Let's celebrate that fact by breaking bread together, just as Jesus broke bread with the tax collector and his friends.

Have kids sit around a table. Set out various dips for kids to share. Pass around a loaf of unsliced bread, and let each child break off a few hunks. Before kids enjoy the bread and dip, say a prayer thanking Jesus for welcoming everyone with his love.

Preschool Story

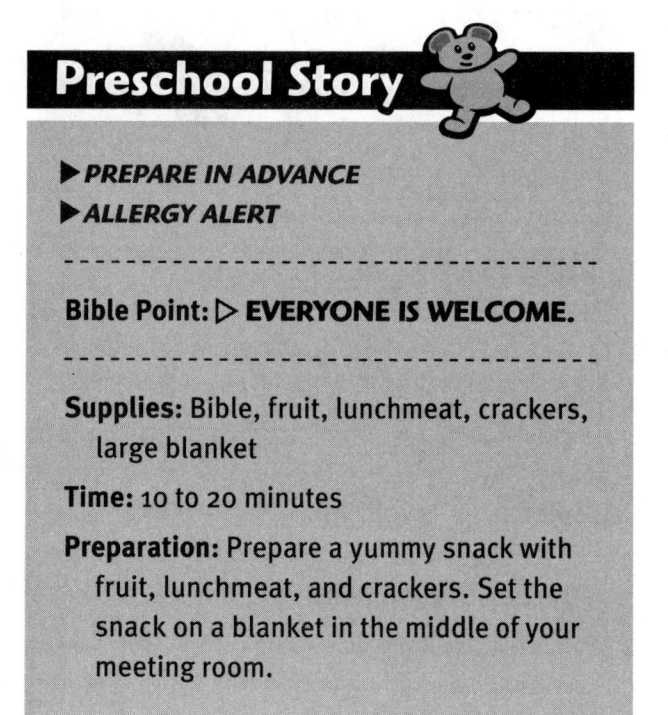

▶ ***PREPARE IN ADVANCE***
▶ ***ALLERGY ALERT***

Bible Point: ▷ **EVERYONE IS WELCOME.**

Supplies: Bible, fruit, lunchmeat, crackers, large blanket

Time: 10 to 20 minutes

Preparation: Prepare a yummy snack with fruit, lunchmeat, and crackers. Set the snack on a blanket in the middle of your meeting room.

Potluck

Have kids form a circle and sit down around the picnic blanket. Open your Bible to Luke 5:27-32, and show children the words. SAY: **One day Jesus went to have dinner with a tax collector named Levi. Many other tax collectors and friends of Levi came to the dinner to see Jesus. Let's pretend that we're at that dinner, too.** Encourage children to gather near the picnic blanket. Begin passing out some of the snacks.

Isn't it nice of Levi to invite us to this delicious dinner? I'm having such a nice time. It's wonderful to see Jesus and hear him speak. Continue talking about the dinner, and encourage children to join in the "table talk." After a little while, pause and look up.

Oh no! Did you hear what that Pharisee said? He said it's wrong for Jesus to be eating with all of us. He said that some of us shouldn't be here. Let's pretend he said that all the people with green shirts on have to leave. Have all children with green shirts on go and stand away from the picnic blanket. **Oh no! Now let's pretend he said that all the people with purple on have to leave.** Have kids with any purple on go and stand with the green-shirt kids. Continue naming colors until all the kids—and you—are standing away from the picnic blanket.

I'm so sad that we can't be with Jesus anymore. I wish we were still over there at the dinner. Point longingly at the picnic blanket.

Wait! What's Jesus saying? He's saying that we can come back. Jesus is saying that he wants us to go over there with him. It doesn't matter what we're wearing—he wants us to be with him! Lead kids back over to the blanket. **This is so exciting! Jesus told the Pharisee that ▷ EVERYONE IS WELCOME. Jesus said that he came to help every single person—not just the good people. The Pharisee thought Jesus should hang out only with certain people—people who are just like him. But Jesus said that he wants to be with all people, no matter what they've done or who they are. Jesus came for every person in the world. With Jesus, ▷ EVERYONE IS WELCOME!**

Encourage kids to eat the food and discuss the story.

ASK:

◆ **Why didn't the Pharisees want some of the people to have dinner with Jesus?**

◆ **Why was it important to Jesus that everyone be included?**

◆ **What can you do to help other people know that Jesus loves them?**

SAY: **The Pharisees thought that Jesus should hang out only with "good" people. But Jesus knew that no one is perfect. Everyone needs Jesus' help, and Jesus came for everyone. We need to remember that Jesus loves every single person in the world. We can tell others about Jesus' love, and we can tell them that with Jesus, ▷ EVERYONE IS WELCOME!**

BIBLE STORY

The Cost of Discipleship

For the Leader

When Jesus used the illustration of his disciples taking up their cross to follow him, his listeners knew what he meant. Crucifixion was a common method of execution, and condemned criminals had to carry their own crosses through the streets.

Following Jesus meant a real commitment—not one to be taken lightly but a commitment from which there was no turning back.

Key Scripture

Matthew 16:24-26

Bible Verse

"Jesus said to his disciples, 'If any of you wants to be my follower, you must turn from your selfish ways, take up your cross, and follow me'" (Matthew 16:24).

n

o

t

e

s

Bible Experience

▶ *NO PREP*

Bible Point: ▷ **SAVE YOUR LIFE.**

Children will count the cost of following Jesus.

Supplies: Bibles, paper, pencils, tape, newsprint, markers

Time: about 10 minutes

Preparation: none

Have kids form pairs. Give each pair a sheet of paper and pencils. SAY: **Pretend that you want to buy a new bicycle that costs 90 dollars. Your parents agree to pay half. So you need to come up with 45 dollars. Unfortunately, you haven't saved any of your allowance, and you have no money. You need to earn the whole 45 dollars. With your partner, come up with a plan to earn the money.**

Give kids several minutes to develop plans. Then ask the following questions, and have partners share their answers with the class:

ASK:

- **How did you decide to come up with the money?**
- **What will you have to give up to make your plan work?**
- **Do you think buying a new bike will be worth the extra work and time it would take to earn the money? Explain.**
- **How do you decide whether something is worth doing?**

SAY: **People set all kinds of goals for themselves. Often they have to give up things to**

reach those goals. If your goal is buying a new bike, you may have to give up some things to reach your goal. Jesus talked about giving up things to reach a certain goal. Let's read about it. Have a volunteer read aloud Matthew 16:24-26.

ASK:

◆ **What goal was Jesus talking about?**

SAY: **Let's consider the costs and rewards of following Jesus, just as we considered buying a bike.** Tape a sheet of newsprint to a wall. With a marker, divide the paper into two columns titled "Costs" and "Rewards." Write kids' responses to the following questions in the appropriate columns. Encourage kids to refer to the Bible passage.

ASK:

◆ **What do you have to give up to follow Jesus?**

◆ **What are the rewards of following Jesus?**

◆ **Is following Jesus worth it? Explain.**

Give each child a sheet of paper and a pencil. SAY: **On your paper, write or draw the cost of following Jesus that's hardest for you. Then write or draw the reward that means the most to you.**

After kids finish writing or drawing, invite them to spend a few moments in silent prayer, thanking Jesus for making the rewards of following him worth the costs. Close by SAYING: **The reward of following Jesus is that you ▷SAVE YOUR LIFE. When you believe in Jesus, you can have eternal life with him. There's no greater reward than that!**

Additional Topics List

This lesson can be used to help kids discover...
Faith, Obedience, and Sacrifice.

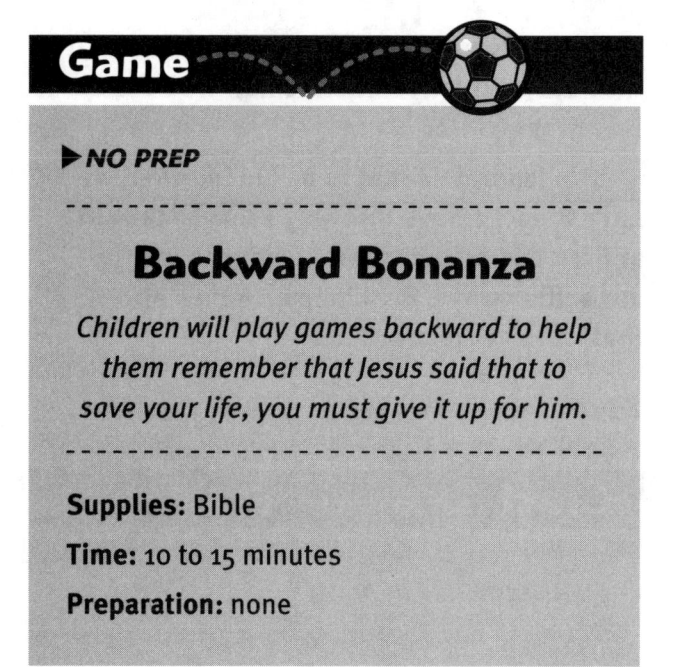

Game

▶ *NO PREP*

Backward Bonanza

Children will play games backward to help them remember that Jesus said that to save your life, you must give it up for him.

Supplies: Bible

Time: 10 to 15 minutes

Preparation: none

SAY: **You've all been selected to compete in an unusual event—the Backward Bonanza. Every game we play will be played backward!**

Form groups of four, and let kids try these backward events:

- Say the alphabet as quickly as they can—backward!
- Run a relay race—backward!
- Walk a line without looking behind them—backward!
- Toss and catch balls to each other—backward!

After the events,

ASK:

◆ **What did it feel like to play these games backward?**

SAY: **It felt a little weird playing games backward, right? Sometimes, in real life, the things we're asked to do may seem backward at first. Listen to what Jesus said.** Read aloud Matthew 16:24-26.

ASK:

◆ **What do you think Jesus meant when he said that to save your life, you must give it up to him?**

◆ **How does what Jesus said to do feel a little backward in relation to how we usually want to act?**

SAY: **Jesus said that to be his follower, we have to act in ways that may seem backward at first. But he'll be there to help us give up our selfish ways. He'll help us follow him. And that's not backward at all!**

Craft

▶ *PREPARE IN ADVANCE*

Wanted!

Children will create Wanted posters to remind them of what it means to be a disciple of Jesus.

Supplies: Bibles, newspaper want ads, paper cutter, black construction paper, glue, gel pens

Time: 10 to 15 minutes

Preparation: Cut newspaper want ads with a paper cutter to measure 9x13 inches (you'll need one per child).

Read aloud Matthew 16:24-26. SAY: **Jesus wants you to be his disciple. Let's make old-fashioned Wanted posters to remind us of what it means to be a disciple of Jesus. Here's what we'll do.**

Demonstrate the following steps: Tear the edges of a sheet of black paper to make it look a little old-fashioned, and glue it onto the newspaper. Use gel pens to create a Wanted poster. Tell kids to describe on the poster what Jesus wants in a disciple, sort of like what employers do to describe whom they want to have as an employee. Have Bibles handy so kids can refer to the Bible passage for ideas. When kids have finished making their posters, let them display their artwork for each other. Then ASK:

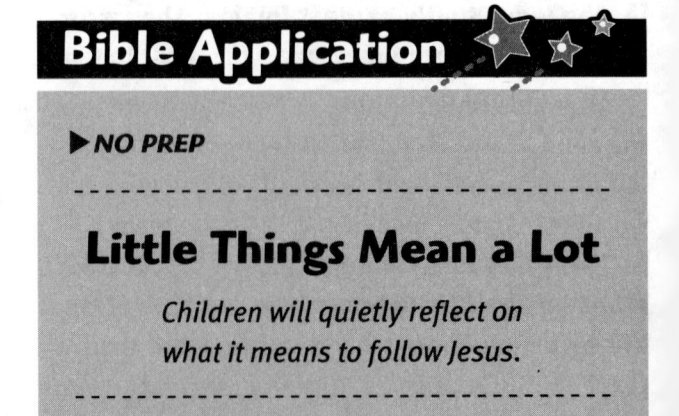

◆ **What do you think it means to be a disciple?**

◆ **What did Jesus say we have to do to be his disciples?**

SAY: **Jesus said that to be his disciple, you have to turn from your selfish ways. To ▷SAVE YOUR LIFE, you have to give it up for him. Hang your poster in your room to remind you of what it means to be a disciple of Jesus.**

Bible Application

▶ *NO PREP*

Little Things Mean a Lot

Children will quietly reflect on what it means to follow Jesus.

Supplies: Bibles

Time: 5 to 10 minutes

Preparation: none

Read aloud Matthew 16:24-26.

ASK:

◆ **What do you think this passage means?**

◆ **Which part of this passage seems hardest for you to obey? Why?**

SAY: **It's not always easy to be a follower of Jesus. We have to make tough decisions that sometimes go against what everyone else thinks is OK. And those decisions aren't always earth-shattering ones—they can be little decisions that may not seem like a big deal at the time. But when you add up all those little decisions, that's the way you've lived your whole life!**

For example, let's say you forgot to study for a test. But then the teacher leaves the room during the test, and everyone starts sharing answers. It would be easy to cheat, and you'd pass the test. But what's the cost? You wouldn't be following Jesus. Would it be worth it?

Form pairs and give each pair a Bible. SAY: **With your partner, read the passage again. Then think of a little decision that you face every day. Think of a way to silently act out the decision. The rest of the class will guess the situation, and then we'll discuss what decision to make based on this Bible passage.**

Let pairs act out their situations, and then lead the class in a discussion based on the Bible passage. (If you have a large class, just have a few pairs act.) Then SAY: **The little things mean a lot in terms of following Jesus. We need to try to follow him every day and in every way. With your partner, pray for help in doing that this week.**

notes

Creative Prayer Idea

▶ ***NO PREP***

Give It Up!

Children will write prayers asking Jesus to help them be his followers.

Supplies: Bible, index cards, pens

Time: about 5 minutes

Preparation: none

Read aloud Matthew 16:24-26. SAY: **Following Jesus means trying to become more like him and giving up our selfish ways. Jesus said that to ▷ *SAVE YOUR LIFE*, you have to give it up to him. Think of something you need to give up to follow Jesus more closely.**

Distribute cards and pens. SAY: **Maybe you need to give up thinking selfishly about your belongings. Maybe you're having trouble giving up a certain sinful behavior. On your card, write a prayer asking Jesus to help you give up those thoughts or behaviors so you can follow him more closely.** When kids have finished writing, gather everyone together in a circle. Close with a prayer asking Jesus to help each student with his or her request. Encourage kids to take their cards home and pray the same prayer each day.

Discussion Launcher

Follow the Leader

Before class, write a series of instructions for a mini-scavenger hunt in your classroom. For example, you might write "Find a piece of yellow paper," "Make a quick sketch of our room," and "Find a pencil with a worn eraser." You may repeat the same task on more than one card. On only one card, write: "Walk up to everyone you see and say, 'Leave your task and follow me.' "

Have a scavenger hunt. Put one card in the basket for each child, including the "Follow me" card. Instruct kids to complete their tasks within two minutes and not to tell anyone else what their tasks are. After two minutes, call time. Ask who had the "Follow me" card, and ask that person:

- **How did people react when you asked them to abandon their tasks and follow you?**

Ask everyone:

- **What did you feel like when you were asked to stop what you were doing and follow** [name]**?**
- **Did you want to wait until you had finished your task? What did you say?**

Have a volunteer read aloud Matthew 16:24-26. SAY: **Jesus said in this passage that we have to give up our own ideas and schedules to follow him. If you want to ▷SAVE YOUR LIFE, you need to give your life to Jesus. In the game, you were asked to stop what you were doing to follow the leader. In life Jesus wants us to stop trying to live our own selfish way and follow him.** Lead kids in a discussion of how they could change their lives to follow Jesus more closely.

n

o

t

e

s

Snack

▶ ***ALLERGY ALERT***

Recipe for Success

Children will follow a recipe and learn to follow Jesus' recipe of discipleship.

Supplies: Bible, English muffins, pizza sauce, cheese, pizza toppings, cookie sheets, oven, newsprint, tape, marker

Time: about 20 minutes

Preparation: Split the English muffins in half. Set out all your pizza supplies. (If you don't have access to an oven, make "cookie pizzas" instead, using frosting for sauce and candies and raisins for toppings.) Tape two sheets of newsprint on a wall.

Gather kids together near your supplies. SAY: **Today we're going to make little pizzas, using English muffins for crusts. Let's write a recipe of how you think we should make them. What do we have to do?** On one sheet of newsprint, write kids' answers. Emphasize the order in which kids should use the ingredients. After you've written the recipe, SAY: **This looks like a good plan for making pizzas. But I wonder if it's the only way.**

ASK:

- **What would happen if we put the sauce on the cookie sheet first?**
- **What if we put the cheese on the bottom?**

SAY: **We could mix up the toppings a little, but there really is only one way to make these pizzas turn out right. This is a recipe for success!** Let kids each make a pizza, and then have an adult take the pizzas to the kitchen to bake.

While the pizzas are baking, SAY: **In the Bible Jesus tells us how to follow him and be his disciples.** Read aloud Matthew 16:24-26; then ASK:

- ◆ **What does this mean to you? How can you take up your cross?**
- ◆ **What do you think Jesus meant when he talked about giving up your life for his sake?**

SAY: **Jesus meant that we have to be willing to give up everything to follow him. We have to turn from our sins and let him be in charge of our lives. That's the only way we'll really be happy and really be following him. Let's write Jesus' advice about how to follow him in recipe form.** Write kids' responses as a recipe on the second sheet of newsprint. **We must follow certain steps to be Jesus' disciples. Just as in making the pizzas, if we try to change the order, it won't work. We can't keep being selfish and hope to be a disciple of Jesus. You can't ▷SAVE YOUR LIFE if you don't give it up and let Jesus guide you.**

Pray with kids that each one would be willing to give up control of their lives to Jesus. Then enjoy fellowship time as you eat the pizzas.

Preschool Story

▶ ***PREPARE IN ADVANCE***

▶ ***ALLERGY ALERT***

Bible Point: ▷SAVE YOUR LIFE.

Supplies: Bible; picture of Jesus; several pieces of poster board or cardboard; marker; supplies such as a basketball, fake money, and toys; large box; treats

Time: 5 to 10 minutes

Preparation: Set up a maze in the classroom by laying out poster board or cardboard in various paths. Create one center path, and draw arrows on each of those pieces. Create side paths off of the center path, but make sure the side paths don't go anywhere—they are to be dead ends. Place a basketball at the end of one side path, fake money at the end of another, toys at the end of another, and other supplies at the end of each side path. At the end of the center path, place a picture of Jesus and a box full of toys, treats, and other goodies.

It Was Worth It!

Have kids form a circle and sit down. Open your Bible to Matthew 16:24-26, and show children the words. SAY: **One day, when Jesus was talking to his disciples, he said, "If you try to hang on to your life, you will lose it. But if you give up your life for my sake, you will save it"** (Matthew 16:25). **Let's play a game now to help us know what that means.**

Lead children to the beginning of the maze you created before class. SAY: **We're going to go down this path. Before we go, though, let's listen to what Jesus said again: "If you try to hang on to your life, you will lose it. But if you give up your life for my sake, you will save it." This means that if we follow Jesus, we'll find true life. Let's see if we can figure out how to follow Jesus through this maze.**

Point out the arrows in the maze and SAY: **I think if we follow these arrows, then we're following Jesus through this maze.** Lead kids down the arrows. Stop when you reach a side path. SAY: **Look, if we go down that path, we'll get a** [name of item at end of path]. **That would be fun. I'd like to have one of those.** ASK:

◆ **Does anyone think we should go down that path?**

SAY: **Well, maybe we should stay on this center path and follow Jesus. I guess we'll have to give up that** [name of item].

Lead kids down the arrows until you reach another side path. SAY: **Look, if we go down that path, we'll get a** [name of item at end of path]. **That would be fun. I'd like to have one of those.**

ASK:

◆ **Does anyone think we should go down that path?**

SAY: **Well, maybe we should stay on this center path and follow Jesus. I guess we'll have to give up that** [name of item].

Continue down the path, hesitating at each side path but each time choosing to continue down the center path. Stop when you reach the picture of Jesus. SAY: **We followed Jesus all the way down the path. And look! There are all sorts of fun treats at the end!** Let kids look through the "treasure" chest. Let kids eat the treats and play with the toys.

SAY: **We gave up all those other things on the side paths in order to follow Jesus. But since we chose to follow Jesus the whole way, we found all sorts of wonderful things at the end of the path!**

ASK:

◆ **Was it easy or hard to follow Jesus' path through the maze? Why?**

◆ **Did you ever really want to follow one of the side paths? Why?**

◆ **What did we gain by following Jesus' path through the maze?**

SAY: **Jesus told the disciples that they'd have to give up some things to follow him, but he also told them that they'd receive much more than they gave up—just like we did when we followed Jesus through the maze. Jesus said that he would ▷*SAVE YOUR LIFE* if you follow him—what a wonderful promise!**

BIBLE STORY

The Greatest!

For the Leader

From Mark's Gospel we learn that Jesus precipitated the conversation in Matthew 18 by asking the disciples what they had been discussing among themselves earlier. Jesus used a child to help his disciples understand that we are not to be childish (like the disciples, arguing over petty issues) but childlike, with humble hearts.

The disciples had become preoccupied with their place in the organization of Jesus' earthly kingdom and had lost sight of its divine purpose. Instead of seeking positions of service, they sought positions of advantage.

Key Scriptures

Matthew 18:1-5

James 4:10

Bible Verse

"Humble yourselves before the Lord, and he will lift you up in honor" (James 4:10).

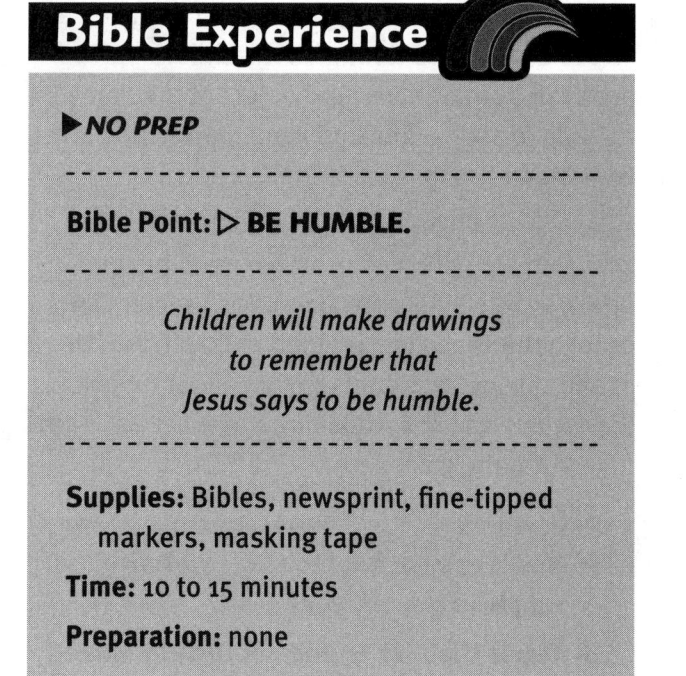

Bible Experience

▶ ***NO PREP***

Bible Point: ▷ **BE HUMBLE.**

Children will make drawings to remember that Jesus says to be humble.

Supplies: Bibles, newsprint, fine-tipped markers, masking tape

Time: 10 to 15 minutes

Preparation: none

Have kids form groups of four, and give each group a Bible. Have kids read Matthew 18:1-5 in their groups. SAY: **In this passage Jesus said we need to humble ourselves like little children. But what does that mean? Let's think about it!**

Give each group a large sheet of newsprint. Tell groups to each draw an outline of a little child and an outline of an adult. Then have groups write as many characteristics of little children as they can think of inside the child's outline, and then have them do the same for the adult.

When groups have finished writing, have them tape their pictures to a wall. Let each group explain what it wrote for the child and the adult.

SAY: **Wow! I can tell from what you wrote that there are big differences between little children and adults. As you look at what everyone wrote, answer these questions in your groups:**

- **Which characteristics of little children do you think Jesus wants us to have? Why?**
- **What characteristics of adults keep them from being humble like little children?**
- **What does it mean to be humble?**
- **Why do you think little children are naturally more humble than adults?**

SAY: **Little children have childlike faith. They don't question everything; they don't argue over every detail. They don't tell others that they're wrong. They just believe that Jesus loves them, and that's that.**

ASK:

- **How could you be more humble in your attitude toward God?**

SAY: **Jesus often talked about the need to ▷ BE HUMBLE. We shouldn't worry about being the greatest. If we keep our faith simple, like little kids do, we'll end up being the greatest anyway. Listen to what the Bible says about that.** Read aloud James 4:10. **See? If we're humble, God will notice. Let's pray for help in being humble.** Close with a prayer asking God to help you and your students be humble like little children and have childlike faith this week.

notes

Additional Topics List

This lesson can be used to help kids discover... Faith, Pride, and Repentance.

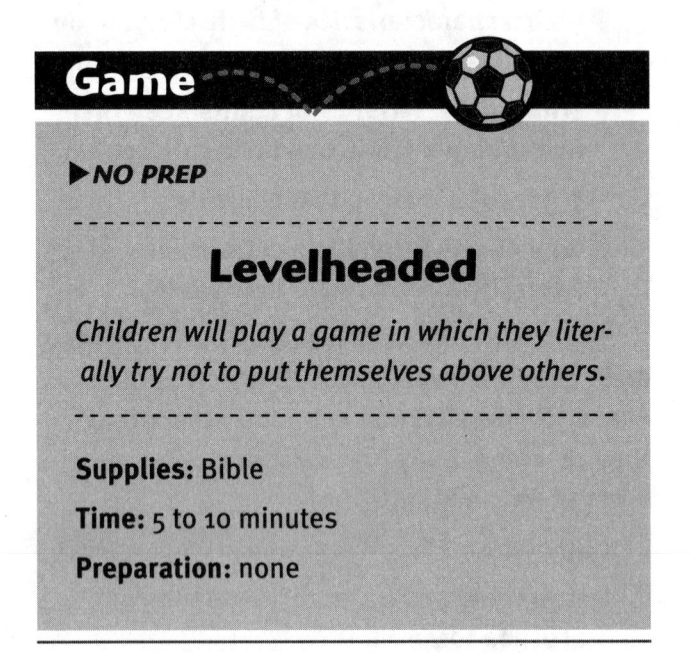

Game

▶*NO PREP*

Levelheaded

Children will play a game in which they literally try not to put themselves above others.

Supplies: Bible

Time: 5 to 10 minutes

Preparation: none

Open your Bible to Matthew 18:1-5, and read aloud or summarize what Jesus said about entering the kingdom of God.

ASK:

- **What does it mean to be humble?**
- **When is it hard for you to be humble?**

SAY: **To be humble means not to put yourself above anyone else. Sometimes that's hard to do. But practice makes perfect, they say, so let's play a game to practice not putting ourselves above others.**

Choose a volunteer to be the Leveler, and have kids line up behind him or her. Have kids try to position themselves so their heads are level with the children's heads in front of them. The object of the game is for kids to stay in line and keep their heads level with the heads in front of them.

Ask the Leveler to walk around the room and change the position of his or her head (up and down, side to side, and so on). The Leveler can change the speed and method of travel, too. He or she can jog, hop, and even go under tables! Play several rounds, choosing a new Leveler each time. After the game,

ASK:

- **Was it easy or hard to stay level with the people in front of you?**
- **How is that like trying not to put yourself above others in real life?**

SAY: **Jesus wants us to ▷BE HUMBLE. He said that's the way we can enter the kingdom of heaven. This week practice not putting yourself above others.**

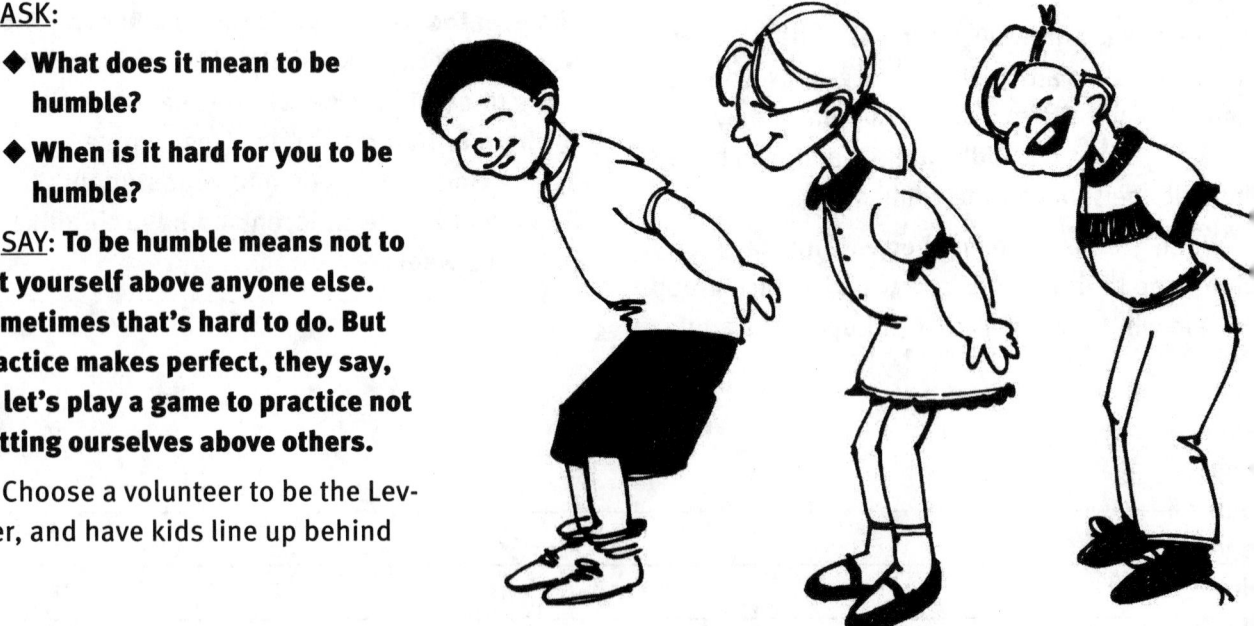

Craft

▶ PREPARE IN ADVANCE

God's the Greatest!

Children will make trophies to remind them to be humble.

Supplies: Bible, paper cutter, heavy aluminum foil, paper plates, pens, 3-ounce paper cups, 7-ounce paper cups, paper fasteners, glue pens, gel pens

Time: 10 to 15 minutes

Preparation: Use a paper cutter to cut 10 pieces of foil measuring 1x8 inches for each child. Put the 10 pieces on a paper plate for each child. Set out the rest of the supplies.

Read aloud Matthew 18:1-5, or summarize what Jesus said about entering the kingdom of God. Then SAY: **Jesus wants us to ▷ BE HUMBLE. We're going to make something that's not usually associated with being humble, but I'll explain as we go along.**

Lead kids through the following steps in making a trophy: Use a pen to poke a small hole in the bottom of a small cup and a larger cup. Use a paper fastener to attach the bottoms of the two cups together. Glue the foil pieces to the outside of the cups, with the smaller cup on top. Let each piece slightly overlap the next. Fold the excess foil into the top and bottom of the cups. Use your fingers to smooth out wrinkles.

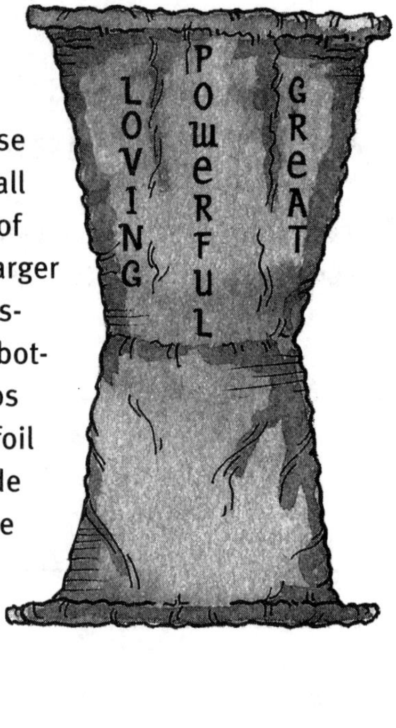

After kids have finished making their trophies, SAY: **We usually give trophies to people who are the best at something. But instead of giving *ourselves* trophies today, we're going to be humble and give God our trophies instead! That's because one way to be humble is to recognize how awesome God is.**

Have kids use gel pens to write compliments to God and attributes of God all over their trophies. Then let kids display their trophies for all to see. Close in prayer, thanking God for being all the great things he is.

Bible Application

▶ NO PREP

Turn Away

Children will think of sins they need to turn from.

Supplies: Bible, paper, pens

Time: about 5 minutes

Preparation: none

Read aloud from Matthew 18:1-5 what Jesus said about entering the kingdom of God. SAY: **Jesus wants us to ▷ BE HUMBLE. From reading this passage, it looks as though one of the things we need to do before we can be humble is to turn from our sins.**

ASK:

- **What does it mean to turn from our sins?**

SAY: **To turn from a sin means to try not to do that bad thing anymore. We may not always be successful in never committing that sin again, but it means that we set our minds to trying to stop doing it. If we're honest, though, we admit that we need God's help in turning away from our sins. By ourselves, we don't do a very good job of it. But that's part of being humble—admitting that we need God!**

Distribute paper and pens, and have kids form pairs. SAY: **Think of one sin you need to turn away from. On your paper, write the sin or something that only you know represents the sin, like a code word or letter. We're going to exchange papers with our partners and pray for each other.**

You may not want your partner to know what your sin is, and that's OK. But part of being humble means admitting our faults to each other. It's actually very powerful to let another person know what you're struggling with and to have that person pray for you. But it's up to you what you want to write on your paper.

Caution kids that whatever they read on their partners' papers is to remain completely confidential. Praying for someone else is an intimate gesture, and gossip has no place there.

When kids have finished writing, have them exchange papers and pray for each other. Even if kids have written code words, partners can still pray for God to help their partners turn away from whatever sin they're dealing with. Close with a class prayer thanking God for helping us turn away from sin and be humble. Encourage kids to take the papers home with them and continue praying for their partners during the week.

Creative Prayer Idea

▶ *NO PREP*

Back in Time

Children will sing a favorite childhood song as a prayer.

Supplies: none

Time: about 5 minutes

Preparation: none

SAY: **Jesus said that to enter his kingdom, we have to ▷ BE HUMBLE like little children. Let's go back in time and pretend that we're little kids for this prayer.**

Teach kids this simple song to the tune of "Jesus Loves Me":

Thank you, God, that we have fun
With family, friends, and everyone.
Help us always to obey
And be humble every day.
Help us be humble.
Help us be humble.
Help us be humble.
And do the things you say.

If you have extra time, let kids make up more prayers to favorite childhood songs.

notes

Discussion Launcher Questions

Read aloud Matthew 18:1-5. Then have kids form trios to discuss these questions.

ASK:

- **What does it mean to be humble?**
- **What does it mean to repent?**
- **Can you repent without being humble? Can you be humble without repenting? Explain your answers.**
- **How do you think little children are more humble than adults?**

Movie Clip

Give It Away

Movie Title: *The Rainbow Fish* (Not Rated)

Start Time: 7 minutes, 38 seconds

Where to Begin: The Rainbow Fish gives a scale to the Little Blue Fish.

Where to End: The Rainbow Fish begins to sing a song about sharing.

Plot: The Rainbow Fish was the most beautiful fish in the ocean, but he wasn't happy. When the Rainbow Fish was willing to give away his scales and no longer be the most beautiful fish, he found true happiness.

Review: The Rainbow Fish didn't find happiness until he humbled himself and gave away his scales to the other fish in the ocean. Jesus said that in order for us to enter the kingdom of heaven, we must humble ourselves and become like children in our faith.

Discussion

After setting up and showing the clip,

ASK:

- **Did the Rainbow Fish want to give away his scales at first? Why or why not?**
- **Why do you think he changed his mind?**
- **How did the Rainbow Fish feel after he gave away his scales?**

Read aloud Matthew 18:1-5. SAY: **Jesus wants us to be like the Rainbow Fish. He wants us to give up our pride, stop thinking we're better than others, and ▷BE HUMBLE. Just as being humble was the only way the Rainbow Fish could find happiness, being humble is the only way we can enter the kingdom of heaven.**

Preschool Story

▶*NO PREP*

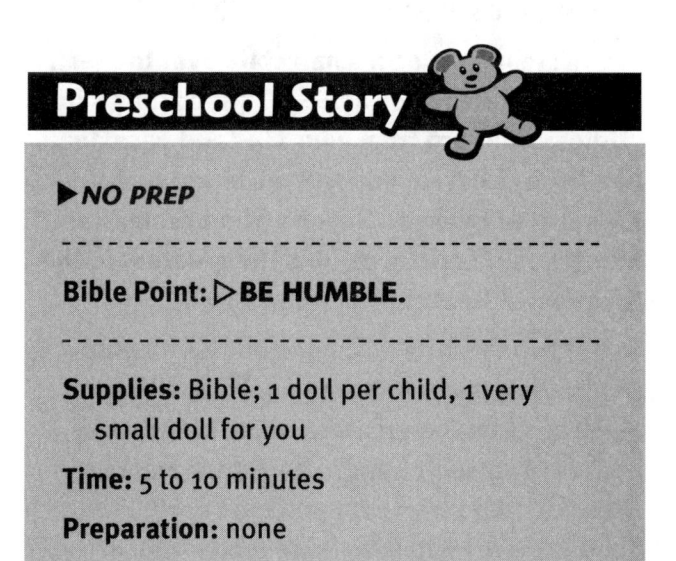

Bible Point: ▷BE HUMBLE.

Supplies: Bible; 1 doll per child, 1 very small doll for you

Time: 5 to 10 minutes

Preparation: none

Childish Behavior

Have kids form a circle and sit down. Open your Bible to Matthew 18:1-5, and show children the words. Give each child a doll, but save the smallest doll for later. Tell children that each of them should think of a way that his or her doll is great, such as, "My doll can run really fast" or "My doll is very smart." Give children a few moments to come up with an idea. Then ask each child to tell the others the way his or her doll is great.

ASK:

◆ **Which doll do you think is the greatest out of all the dolls? Why do you think that?**

◆ **Who do you think is the greatest or most important person in the world? Why?**

SAY: **The talents of our dolls are all great things, but let's listen to our Bible story to hear who Jesus said is the greatest in the kingdom of heaven.**

Encourage kids to use their dolls to act out the story as they listen. SAY: **The disciples came up to Jesus and asked him, "Who is greatest in the Kingdom of Heaven?"**

ASK:

◆ **What do you think Jesus said?**

SAY: **Jesus called a small child over to them.** Hold up the small doll and SAY: **Then Jesus said, "Unless you turn from your sins and become like little children, you will never get into the Kingdom of Heaven...anyone who becomes as humble as this little child is the greatest in the Kingdom of Heaven"** (Matthew 18:3-4).

Hold up the little doll again and SAY: **Jesus was saying that you have to become like little children to be the greatest in the kingdom of heaven! You don't have to be able to run really fast or be the smartest person on earth. You don't have to be able to jump really high or swim really far. You don't have to have a lot of money or be really powerful. Jesus said that none of those things are the most important. Jesus said that being humble like a little child is the most important thing!**

ASK:

◆ **What does it mean to be humble?**

SAY: **To be humble means that you don't think you're better than everyone else. When a person is humble, he or she believes that others are great, too. God wants us to ▷BE HUMBLE and put others' needs above our own.**

Let's do an action prayer right now and ask God to help us ▷BE HUMBLE like little children.

Dear God,

Help us remember that we don't have to be great *(shake your head)*

in order for you to love us. *(Hug yourself.)*

We don't have to jump really high *(jump up, and then shake your head)*

or swim really far. *(Make a swimming motion, and then shake your head.)*

We don't have to have lots of money and toys *(pretend to count all the wonderful things you have, and then shake your head)*

or be really smart. *(Tap your head, and then shake your head.)*

Help us remember that the greatest in your kingdom *(point up)*

Are those who are humble *(squat down low)*

Like little children. *(Hug yourself.)*

Help us to ▷ BE HUMBLE *(squat down low)*

Like little children. *(Hug yourself.)*

In Jesus' name, amen.

notes

BIBLE STORY

Sheep and Goats

For the Leader

At the final judgment God will separate his true followers from the imposters. Jesus used sheep and goats to illustrate the difference between believers and nonbelievers. Sheep and goats often grazed together but were separated when it was time to shear the sheep.

The true evidence of what we believe is seen in our actions. The acts of mercy Jesus described can be done by all—they don't depend on wealth or status. We all have the ability to reach out and help a person in need.

Key Scripture

Matthew 25:31-46

Bible Verse

"When you did it to one of the least of these my brothers and sisters, you were doing it to me!" (Matthew 25:40).

notes

Bible Experience

▶ ***ALLERGY ALERT***

Bible Point: ▷**TREAT OTHERS LIKE YOU'D TREAT JESUS.**

Children will use a skit to learn to treat others like they'd treat Jesus.

Supplies: Bibles, 2 hats, 2 necklaces, 2 dresses, baseball caps, 4 chairs, 2 books, "homework" supplies, hymnal, newspaper, toy cat, bowl of popped popcorn

Time: 10 to 15 minutes

Preparation: Photocopy the skit for your actors.

Children who don't have assigned parts in the following skit can be the audience, design simple sets, cue the other actors, or make sound effects. Kids can also take turns being the Reader. Be sure to involve everyone in the production.

CHARACTERS

The Gimme Family: Father Gimme (older boy with hat); Mother Gimme (older girl wearing a dress and necklace); Sister Gimme (younger girl); Brother Gimme (younger boy wearing baseball cap).

Reader: Slowly reads the story from offstage as the actors pantomime their roles. (Kids can take turns being the Reader.)

The Itsmine Family: Father, mother, and any number of children, all dressed similar to the Gimme family.

SCRIPT

(Father Gimme is sitting in a chair reading the newspaper and eating popcorn. Mother Gimme is sitting next to him, eating from the same popcorn bowl and petting the cat. Sister Gimme is sitting on the floor reading a book. Brother Gimme is lying on the floor doing homework.)

Reader:

Once upon a time there lived a family named the Gimmes. They were an average family except for one thing: They couldn't share. The parents fought over the popcorn, each grabbing the bowl and trying to hold it. The kids fought over their books and over who would sit where on the floor. They couldn't share anything! Pretty soon they would all get mad and each go off to sulk.

Each Sunday the Gimmes went to church. When they got there, they pushed and shoved because they all wanted to sit next to the aisle. Then they fought over who would hold the hymnal. They really couldn't share at all.

But one Sunday the pastor said something that made the Gimmes think. They stopped fighting and turned their heads so they could listen better. The pastor said that people should treat each other the way they'd treat Jesus. The Gimmes looked surprised. They all nodded their heads as they realized that they would never fight with Jesus and that they would always share with him. Hmm. Maybe they should share with each other!

They decided to give it a try. They shook hands to seal the deal. They smiled and hugged happily. The Gimmes had learned a lesson. And just in time, too, because soon they heard the new neighbors knocking at their door. They peeked out and saw the neighbors pushing and shoving to stand right in front of the door. It was the Itsmine family!

After the skit, lead kids in a round of applause for everyone's participation. Then form groups of four. Give each group a Bible, and have kids read Matthew 25:31-46 in their groups. Then have kids answer these questions in their groups. Invite groups to share their answers with the class.

ASK:

- **What was the difference between the sheep and the goats in this parable? What did they do differently?**
- **In our skit, do you think the Gimmes would be sheep or goats? Why?**

SAY: **The point of this parable is that we should ▷TREAT OTHERS LIKE WE'D TREAT JESUS. That's hard to do when we're always thinking about ourselves, like the Gimme family was in the beginning. But we can change, just like they did.**

ASK:

- **What is one thing you can do this week to treat others like you'd treat Jesus?**

Read aloud Matthew 25:40. Pray, asking God to help kids remember that whatever they do to others, they're doing it to Jesus.

Song & Connect

Use "Work" (track 19, *it: Innovative Tools for Children's Ministry: New Testament* CD) to help reinforce the Bible Point, **▷TREAT OTHERS LIKE YOU'D TREAT JESUS.**

Additional Topics List

This lesson can be used to help kids discover... Compassion, Love, and Service.

Game

▶*NO PREP*

Not I!

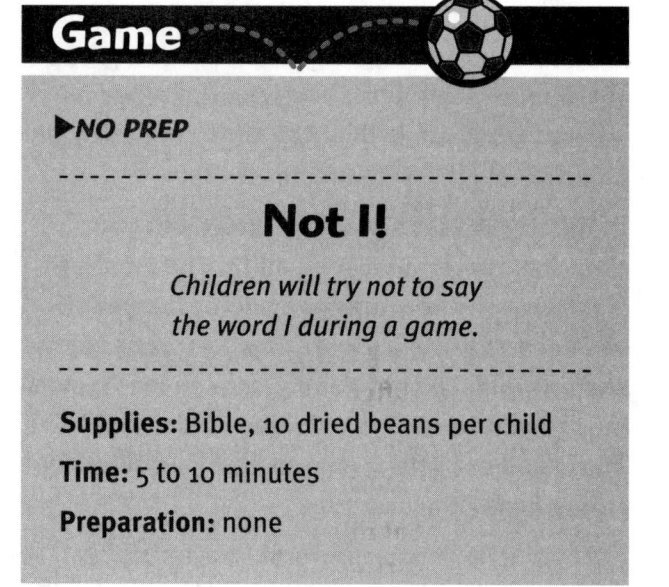

Children will try not to say the word I during a game.

Supplies: Bible, 10 dried beans per child

Time: 5 to 10 minutes

Preparation: none

Give each child 10 dried beans. Have kids mingle and talk about their week. Explain that whenever someone says "I," any listener who hears it gets a bean. At the end of five minutes, have kids count their beans.

ASK:

- ◆ **Was it hard not to say "I" in this game? Why or why not?**
- ◆ **Were you surprised at how many times you almost said "I"? Explain.**

SAY: **It's hard not to focus on ourselves, isn't it? But Jesus wants us to focus on others. In fact, he wants more than that. Listen to what the Bible says.** Read aloud or summarize Matthew 25:31-46. **The Bible says to ▷TREAT OTHERS LIKE WE'D TREAT JESUS. We can't do that if we're constantly thinking of ourselves. This week try to avoid the "I" syndrome, and concentrate on Jesus instead!**

Craft

Reminder Bracelets

Children will make bracelets to help them remember to treat others as they would treat Jesus.

Supplies: Bible, craft foam, safety scissors, fine-tipped markers of various colors, stapler, two 1-foot lengths of yarn per child

Time: about 15 minutes

Preparation: Cut the craft foam into ¼x8-inch strips. You'll need three strips per child.

Read aloud or summarize Matthew 25:31-46.

SAY: **The Bible says we should ▷TREAT OTHERS LIKE WE'D TREAT JESUS. Let's make bracelets to help us remember that every day!**

Give each child three foam strips. Set out the markers for kids to share. Tell kids to write, "Treat others like you'd treat Jesus," on each foam strip so the strip is filled with writing. Then have kids stack the three strips on top of each other, words facing up. Help them staple one end of each stack together.

Have kids form pairs. Demonstrate how to braid the three strips. One partner can hold the stapled end of the strips steady while the other partner braids. Tell kids to keep the words facing up as they braid. When kids finish braiding, staple the other end of the strips together. Have kids wind a length of yarn around each end of the bracelet and tie it off tightly. The yarn will cover the staples and make the tie for the bracelets. Cut off the excess ends. Have kids put on their bracelets and sit on the floor with their partners.

ASK:

◆ **When in the last week have you treated someone in a way that you wouldn't have treated Jesus? Tell your partner about it.**

◆ **How can these bracelets help you next week to treat others like you'd treat Jesus?**

Encourage kids to wear their bracelets throughout the week to remind them to ▷**TREAT OTHERS LIKE THEY'D TREAT JESUS.**

Bible Application

What Would You Do?

Children will compare how they'd react in various situations.

Supplies: newsprint, tape, markers

Time: about 10 minutes

Preparation: Hang three sheets of newsprint on a wall at kids' eye level.

Have kids form pairs, and give each pair a marker. SAY: **Let's play a game called What Would You Do? I'll give you a situation, and you and your partner will have one minute to decide what you'd do and write your answer on the newsprint. Be completely honest—don't say what you think you *should* do. Say what you would really do. Ready?**

Here's the first situation: A new kid has just started at your school, and he looks kind of tough. You've never even talked to him, but he asks to borrow lunch money from you. What would you do? After a minute, call time and have kids write their answers on the first sheet of newsprint.

Here's the next situation: The nerdiest kid in class trips and falls right in front of a group of the most popular kids in school. Everyone laughs. What would you do? After a minute, call time and let kids write their answers.

Here's the last situation: One kid in your class has real trouble with math. The teacher picks on her, and she might fail for the year if she doesn't bring her grade up. Everyone thinks she's stupid. You get good grades in math, even though you barely have time to study. What would you do? After a minute, call time and have kids write their answers.

Thanks for those answers! Now let's play again, but this time pretend that the person I talked about in each situation is Jesus. Talk with your partner about how your reactions might differ. Read each situation again, but substitute Jesus' name for the child in the scenario. Then ASK:

◆ **How were your reactions different the second time we played?**

◆ **Why would you treat Jesus differently than you'd treat others?**

SAY: **The Bible says to ▷TREAT OTHERS LIKE YOU'D TREAT JESUS. Try to keep that in mind this week as you interact with people at school and at home. Jesus wants us to treat everyone like we'd treat him!**

notes

Creative Prayer Idea

▶ *NO PREP*

Let Me See Jesus

Children will use a responsive prayer to remind them to treat others like they'd treat Jesus.

Supplies: none

Time: about 5 minutes

Preparation: none

SAY: **The Bible says to ▷ TREAT OTHERS LIKE YOU'D TREAT JESUS. To do that, we need to try to see Jesus in everyone we meet. This prayer might help.** Explain that after you speak a line, kids should respond by saying, "Lord, let me see you."

When I see someone who needs a hand,
(Lord, let me see you.)
When a friend needs me to understand,
(Lord, let me see you.)
When someone's in pain, and feels so sad,
(Lord, let me see you.)
When my temper is short and I'm getting mad,
(Lord, let me see you.)
When someone is scared and turns to me,
(Lord, let me see you.)
When every day everyone I see.
(Lord, let me see you.)

Close by praying that kids will try to treat everyone like they'd treat Jesus.

Discussion Launcher Questions

Read aloud Matthew 25:31-46; then

ASK:

- **Why is it hard to treat others like you'd treat Jesus?**
- **When is it hardest to treat others like you'd treat Jesus? Why?**
- **How would life improve if others treated you as they'd treat Jesus?**
- **How would the world improve if everyone treated others that way?**
- **What three steps can you take this week to treat others like you'd treat Jesus?**

Movie Clip

Fair Treatment

Movie Title: *The Hunchback of Notre Dame* (G)

Start Time: 25 minutes, 40 seconds

Where to Begin: Quasimodo is handed a scepter.

Where to End: Esmeralda calls for justice.

Plot: When the crowd attacks Quasimodo, Esmeralda stands up to the crowd to stop them.

Review: Use this scene to help children understand that we should try to see Jesus in everyone and treat them accordingly. Esmeralda stood up for Quasimodo and demanded that he be treated fairly and kindly. We should treat others in the same way that we would treat Jesus.

Discussion

After setting up and showing the clip,

ASK:

- **Why did Esmeralda stop the crowd?**
- **How is the way Esmeralda treated the hunchback like how we should treat others?**
- **When have you treated someone like you'd treat Jesus? When has someone treated you that way?**
- **Why is it important to treat others like you'd treat Jesus?**

Preschool Story

Bible Point: ▷**TREAT OTHERS LIKE YOU'D TREAT JESUS.**

Supplies: Bible, 7 dolls (or 6 dolls and a picture of Jesus), fake food, doll clothes, empty glass, doll bed, blocks

Time: 5 to 10 minutes

Preparation: Set six dolls around the classroom. Place food near one doll, take the clothes off another doll, place an empty glass near another doll, place one doll just outside the door to your classroom, place another doll in bed, and another in a block prison.

A Helpful Journey

Have kids form a circle and sit down. Open your Bible to Matthew 25:31-46, and show children the words. SAY: **If you look around the room, you'll find several dolls that need your help. Let's walk around the room together and help these dolls.** Lead children to the hungry doll.

ASK:

- **What does this doll need?**

SAY: **This doll needs some food. Let's help it.** Encourage each child to pretend to feed the doll. Then lead kids to the naked doll.

ASK:

- **What does this doll need?**

SAY: **This doll needs some clothes. Let's help it.** Encourage children to help each other put clothes on the doll. Then lead kids to the thirsty doll.

ASK:

- **What does this doll need?**

SAY: **This doll needs some water. Let's help it.** Encourage each child to pretend to give the doll a drink. Then lead kids to the doll outside your classroom.

ASK:

- **What does this doll need?**

SAY: **This doll is cold and needs to come inside. Let's help it.** Encourage kids to pretend to invite the doll inside. Then lead kids to the sick doll.

ASK:

- **What does this doll need?**

SAY: **This doll is sick and needs someone to care for it. Let's help it.** Encourage kids to care for the sick doll. Then lead kids to the doll in prison.

ASK:

- **What does this doll need?**

SAY: **This doll is in jail. This doll is lonely and needs someone to visit it while it's in jail. Let's help it.** Encourage children to talk to the doll. Then lead children to the Jesus doll or the Jesus picture. **Let's pretend this doll** (or picture) **is Jesus. Let's listen to what Jesus has to say.**

Encourage kids to sit down around you. Hold up the doll, and begin speaking in a different voice than you usually use.

As Jesus, SAY: **Hi, children. It's good to see you. I just wanted to say thank you. Thank you for feeding me when I was hungry. Thank you for giving me clothes when I didn't have any. Thank you for giving me water when I was thirsty. Thank you for inviting me inside when I was cold and lonely outside. Thank you for taking care of me when I was sick. Thank you for visiting me when I was in jail.**

As yourself,

ASK:

- **Kids, did we do any of those things for Jesus?**

SAY: **We didn't do those things for you, Jesus. We did them for all those other dolls.** Encourage kids to agree with you and tell Jesus whom they helped.

As Jesus, SAY: **When you helped those other dolls, you were helping me! What you did for those others, you did for me! I love everyone in the world, and I want you to ▷TREAT OTHERS LIKE YOU'D TREAT ME.**

Put down the Jesus doll, and begin talking normally again.

SAY: **In the Bible Jesus tells us that whenever we help someone in need or show love to someone, we are really doing that for Jesus!**

ASK:

- **How would you treat Jesus if you saw him?**
- **How can you treat other people as you'd treat Jesus?**

SAY: **Jesus loves every single person in the world, and he wants us to ▷TREAT OTHERS AS WE'D TREAT HIM.**

BIBLE STORY

Lord of the Sabbath

For the Leader

Jesus and his disciples were not stealing when they picked grain. Old Testament law said that farmers were to leave the edges of their fields unharvested so that some of their crops could be picked by travelers and by the poor. The Pharisees interpreted the actions of Jesus and his disciples as harvesting on the Sabbath, so they judged Jesus to be a lawbreaker.

Jesus rebutted them by proving not only that he was not a lawbreaker but also that he is Lord of the Sabbath. Rather than admitting Jesus was the Messiah, the Pharisees looked for ways they could be rid of him.

Key Scriptures

Mark 2:23–3:6

John 1:1

Bible Verse

"In the beginning the Word already existed. The Word was with God, and the Word was God" (John 1:1).

Bible Experience

▶ ***HIGH ENERGY***

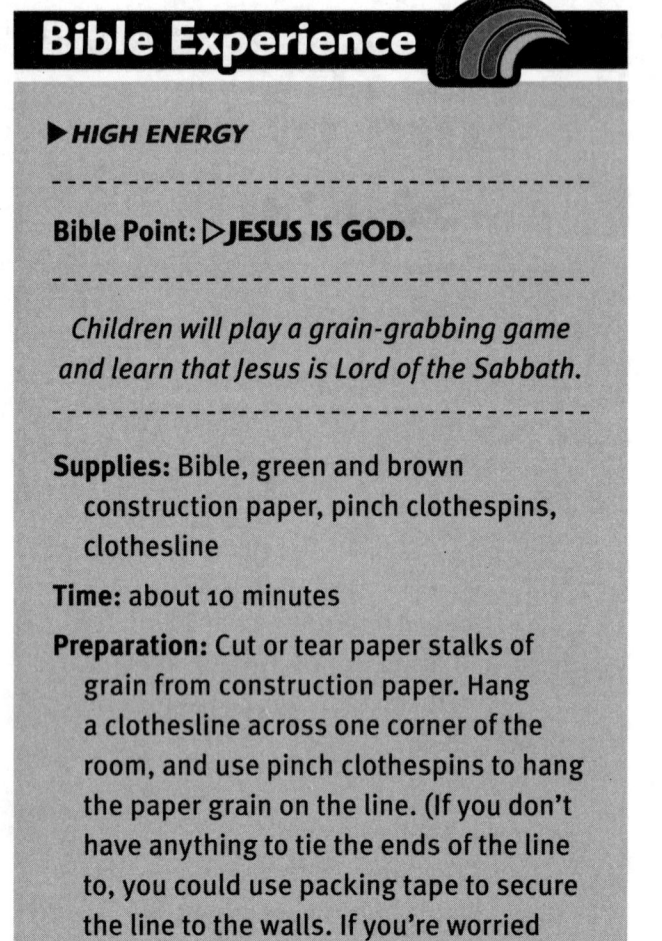

Bible Point: ▷**JESUS IS GOD.**

Children will play a grain-grabbing game and learn that Jesus is Lord of the Sabbath.

Supplies: Bible, green and brown construction paper, pinch clothespins, clothesline

Time: about 10 minutes

Preparation: Cut or tear paper stalks of grain from construction paper. Hang a clothesline across one corner of the room, and use pinch clothespins to hang the paper grain on the line. (If you don't have anything to tie the ends of the line to, you could use packing tape to secure the line to the walls. If you're worried about marring the paint, just lay the paper grain on the floor in one corner.)

Have kids form two equal groups, the Pharisees and the Disciples. Gather everyone in a line on the side of the room opposite the grain. Explain that the object of the game is for the Disciples to "harvest" as much of the grain as possible in two minutes by grabbing a stalk of grain and taking it back to the starting line. The object for the Pharisees is to prevent the Disciples from harvesting the grain without using physical contact. Once a Disciple has picked up a piece of grain, he or she is "safe" until leaving the starting line again.

Play for two minutes, and then have kids switch roles. After another two minutes, call time. Have kids each find a partner from the opposite team to answer these questions.

ASK:

- **What was it like trying to harvest grain while the Pharisees were trying to stop you?**
- **What was it like trying to stop the Disciples from getting to the grain?**

SAY: **In today's Bible story the Pharisees didn't think that Jesus and his disciples should be picking and eating grain on the Sabbath. Jesus didn't see a problem with it. Let's find out why.** Read aloud or summarize Mark 2:23–3:6.

ASK:

- **Why did Jesus say it was OK to pick the grain and heal on the Sabbath?**
- **Why do you think the Pharisees were looking for a reason to say Jesus was breaking the law?**
- **What do you think it means that Jesus is Lord of the Sabbath?**

SAY: **Jesus is Lord of the Sabbath—and of every other day, for that matter.** ▷**JESUS IS GOD. Listen to what the Bible says about him.** Have a student read aloud John 1:1. **Jesus was God right from the beginning. Jesus has always been God and always will be.**

Jesus didn't break the law when he and his disciples picked grain or when he healed on the Sabbath. Jesus said the Sabbath was created for our benefit. God set aside the Sabbath so we could rest and focus on him. The Pharisees were just looking for a way to get rid of Jesus because they felt jealous and threatened by Jesus. ▷**JESUS IS GOD, but the Pharisees didn't want to admit that. Let's say a prayer to thank Jesus for being Lord over every area of our lives.**

Have partners pray together, thanking Jesus for being Lord over specific areas of their lives.

Additional Topics List

This lesson can be used to help kids discover...
God's Sovereignty, The Sabbath, and The Trinity.

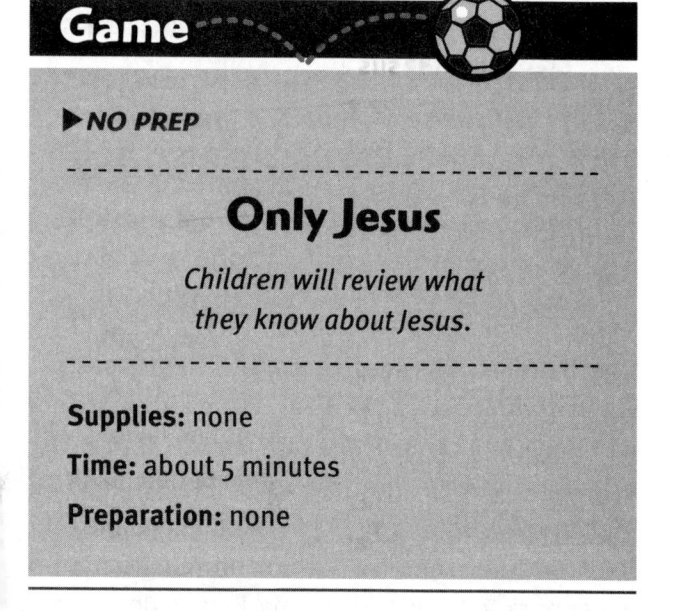

Game

▶ *NO PREP*

Only Jesus

Children will review what they know about Jesus.

Supplies: none

Time: about 5 minutes

Preparation: none

Have children sit in a circle. SAY: **Let's play a game in which we share things we know about Jesus.** Have one child start by turning to the person on his or her left and saying one thing that only Jesus could do. For example, the child might say, "Jesus can walk on water." The child on the speaker's left should then say, "Only God can do that, and Jesus is God."

Keep going around the circle. If a child can't think of anything new to say about Jesus, let the other kids offer suggestions. Keep going until every child has added a new fact about Jesus. Then ASK:

- **Why was Jesus able to do so many amazing things?**
- **What's your favorite thing that Jesus did? Why?**

SAY: **Jesus was able to do all those amazing things because ▷JESUS IS GOD. Let's tell Jesus how special we think he is.** Go around the circle again and have kids each say thank you to Jesus.

Craft

▶ *PREPARE IN ADVANCE*

Pop-Up Cross

Children will make a pop-up picture to remind them that Jesus is God.

Supplies: Bible, cross patterns, 9x12-inch sheets of construction paper, 8x11-inch sheets of paper, glitter, markers, glue, rulers, safety scissors

Time: 10 to 15 minutes

Preparation: Create a cross pattern about 4 inches tall. Photocopy a pattern for each child.

Read aloud or summarize Mark 2:23–3:6. SAY: **We know from this passage that Jesus is Lord over the Sabbath. Jesus is Lord over everything because ▷JESUS IS GOD! Let's make something to help us remember that.**

Lead kids in the following steps: Cut out a cross, and decorate it with glitter. Set it aside to dry. Fold the smaller sheet of paper in half like a card. From the fold, cut two 2-inch slits 1 inch apart. Turn the slit inside out, creating a pop-up. Across the front edge of the paper, write "Jesus is God."

Fold a sheet of construction paper in half like a card that opens from the bottom, rather than the side. Draw a church on the front of the card.

Glue the paper with the pop-up inside the construction-paper card, being careful not to glue down the pop-up section. Glue the cross onto the pop-up section so that when you open the card, the cross pops up. Encourage kids to give their cards to someone else this week and tell that person about Jesus.

Bible Application

▶ *NO PREP*
▶ *FOR FAMILY MINISTRY*

Calendar Reminders

Children will create calendars to remind them every day that Jesus is God.

Supplies: pencils, rulers, white paper, markers, construction paper, glue

Time: about 10 minutes

Preparation: none

SAY: **Jesus is Lord over the Sabbath and over every other day, too! Jesus is Lord over every day because ▷JESUS IS GOD.**

ASK:

◆ **Why is it important to live in a way that shows that Jesus is God?**

◆ **What are some ways to show others that Jesus is God?**

SAY: **Let's make calendars to remind us to live in a way that shows that ▷JESUS IS GOD and that he is Lord over every day.**

Have kids use pencils and rulers to divide a sheet of white paper into seven sections or "days." (Kids could make a monthly calendar if they'd prefer.) Let kids use markers to title each section with a day of the week. Have kids write a way they can acknowledge that Jesus is God each day of the week. Kids might write "Praise Jesus," "Tell others about Jesus," and "Read my Bible." Have kids glue the white papers on construction-paper backgrounds and use markers to decorate their calendars.

Encourage kids to hang their calendars at home to remind them that **▷JESUS IS GOD.** Kids could also make calendars at home and work with their families to think of more ways to acknowledge Jesus as God every day.

notes

Creative Prayer Idea

▶ *NO PREP*

Jesus Is God When...

Children will use a responsive rhythm to remember that Jesus is God.

Supplies: none

Time: about 5 minutes

Preparation: none

SAY: **Jesus is Lord over every day because ▷JESUS IS GOD. Let's thank Jesus for being there for us each and every day.**

Have kids sit in a circle on the floor. Explain that kids will acknowledge that Jesus is God by using a responsive prayer. Ask kids to think of things they do every day, such as riding the school bus, eating dinner, playing with friends, and so on. Remind kids that Jesus is God and is with them every day, everywhere they go. Have kids each think of an activity during which they're glad that Jesus is with them.

Explain that each child will get a turn to say that Jesus is God during the activity they thought of. Everyone else will respond by saying, "Jesus is God! Jesus is God!" The rhythm rhyme will sound like this:

Child: Jesus is God when I'm playing with my friends.

Class: Jesus is God! Jesus is God!

Child: Jesus is God when I'm riding on the bus.

Class: Jesus is God! Jesus is God!

For extra fun, let kids hit their palms twice on the floor and then clap once each time they say, "Jesus is God!" After everyone has had a chance to name an activity, lead kids in a cheer to shout, "Jesus is God!" one last time.

Discussion Launcher Questions

Ask children to form trios and discuss these questions:

- **Why do you think the Pharisees were trying to get Jesus in trouble?**
- **How do you think they felt when Jesus said he was Lord, even over the Sabbath?**
- **Why do you think Jesus healed people on the Sabbath even though he knew it would make the Pharisees mad?**
- **How does knowing that Jesus is God make a difference in your life?**

Science Devotion

Always on Top

Children will experiment with oil and water.

Supplies: Bible, food coloring, water, tablespoon, light cooking oil, narrow jar or soda bottle with lid

Time: 5 to 10 minutes

Preparation: Use food coloring to color 2 tablespoons of water.

Read aloud or summarize Mark 2:23–3:6. SAY: **Jesus is Lord over the Sabbath because ▷JESUS IS GOD. No matter what day it is, no matter what the situation, Jesus is Lord. It's kind of like this.**

Pour 2 tablespoons of oil and 2 tablespoons of colored water into the jar. Cover and shake hard. Then set the jar down.

ASK:

◆ **What happened to the water and oil?**

◆ **Do you think the oil will be on top if we shake it again? Why or why not?**

Do the experiment again. The oil will always rise to the top. SAY: **No matter how many times you shake the jar, the oil will always rise to the top. That's kind of like what we learned from this Bible passage. Jesus is always Lord, no matter what day it is and no matter what situation you're in. You can always count on Jesus because ▷JESUS IS GOD!**

Preschool Story

▶ ***NO PREP***

Bible Point: **▷JESUS IS GOD.**

Supplies: Bible

Time: 5 to 10 minutes

Preparation: none

A Special Day

Have kids form a circle and sit down. Open your Bible to Mark 2:23–3:6, and show children the words. SAY: **Today we're going to hear that ▷JESUS IS GOD, but I'm going to need your help to tell the story.**

Tell kids that when you say "Jesus," they should point up to heaven; when you say "disciples," they should rub their tummies and say that they're hungry; when you say "Pharisees," they should cross their arms, look mad, and say, "No, no, no"; when you say, "the hurt man," they should cradle one hand in the other as if it's hurt. Practice this with children several times before you begin the story.

SAY: **One day Jesus** (point up to heaven) **was walking along with his disciples** (rub tummy and say you're hungry). Encourage kids to march in place.

The disciples (rub tummy and say you're hungry) **were very hungry, so when they passed a field of grain, they began to pick the grain and eat it.** Encourage kids to pretend to pick some grain and eat it.

But the Pharisees (cross arms, look mad, and say, "No, no, no") **didn't like that. They said that Jesus'** (point up to heaven) **disciples** (rub tummy and say you're hungry) **were doing something wrong by picking the grain. You see, it was the Sabbath day, which meant no one was supposed to work all day long. The Pharisees** (cross arms, look mad, and say, "No, no, no") **thought that picking the grain and eating it was work. But Jesus** (point up to heaven) **said that if you're hungry, then you should be able to eat. Jesus** (point up to heaven) **said that the Sabbath was meant to help people rest, but it wasn't meant to rule over people. Then Jesus** (point up to heaven) **told the Pharisees** (cross arms, look mad, and say, "No, no, no") **that he was master of the Sabbath. Jesus** (point up to heaven) **said this because ▷JESUS** (point up to heaven) **IS GOD.**

Another day Jesus (point up to heaven) **was in the synagogue—which is like a church—and noticed a hurt man** (cradle one arm in the other). **This man's hand was hurt very badly. Jesus** (point up to heaven) **wanted to help the man, but he knew it was the Sabbath again. He knew that**

the Pharisees (cross arms, look mad, and say, "No, no, no") **would think he was doing work on the Sabbath if Jesus** (point up to heaven) **healed the man.**

ASK:

◆ **What do you think Jesus did?**

SAY: **Jesus** (point up to heaven) **called the hurt man** (cradle one arm in the other) **over to him. Jesus** (point up to heaven) **turned to the Pharisees** (cross arms, look mad, and say, "No, no, no") **and asked them, "Is it best to do the right thing on the Sabbath, or is it a day for doing wrong?" But the Pharisees** (cross arms, look mad, and say, "No, no, no") **wouldn't answer him.**

ASK:

◆ **What do you think?**

SAY: **Jesus** (point up to heaven) **was angry because he knew they didn't understand. Then Jesus** (point up to heaven) **said to the hurt man** (cradle one arm in the other)**, "Hold out your hand." The man held out his hand.** Encourage kids to hold out their hands. SAY: **The man's hand became normal again! He was healed!**

Jesus (point up to heaven) **knew that it was best to do the right thing on the Sabbath, and the right thing was to heal the man's hand. Jesus** (point up to heaven) **is Lord of the Sabbath because ▷JESUS** (point up to heaven) **IS GOD.**

ASK:

◆ **Why were the Pharisees angry at Jesus?**

◆ **Why is it important to always do the right thing?**

SAY: **▷JESUS IS GOD, and he tells us to always do the right thing, even when others might be mad at you for doing the right thing.**

BIBLE STORY

Jesus Teaches About Loving Enemies

For the Leader

The Jews knew what enemies were, and when Jesus talked about people who cursed them, struck them, and stole from them, the Jews likely thought of the Romans. It would have been tough for Jews to accept the concept that they should love their oppressors. But Jesus wasn't saying they should have warm feelings toward their enemies. He was saying to love their enemies as a conscious act of will, to behave toward them as a merciful God would.

Jesus also pointed out the emptiness of loving only those who love us. Our love shouldn't be based on the expectation of being loved in return; instead, we should look forward to a heavenly reward because we have treated people the way God wants us to. When people watch us, they should see our merciful God in our attitudes and actions.

Key Scripture

Luke 6:27-38

Bible Verse

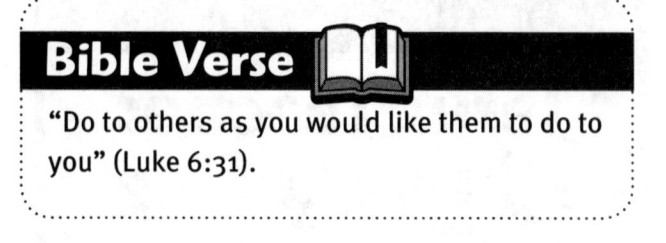

"Do to others as you would like them to do to you" (Luke 6:31).

Bible Experience

▶ *NO PREP*

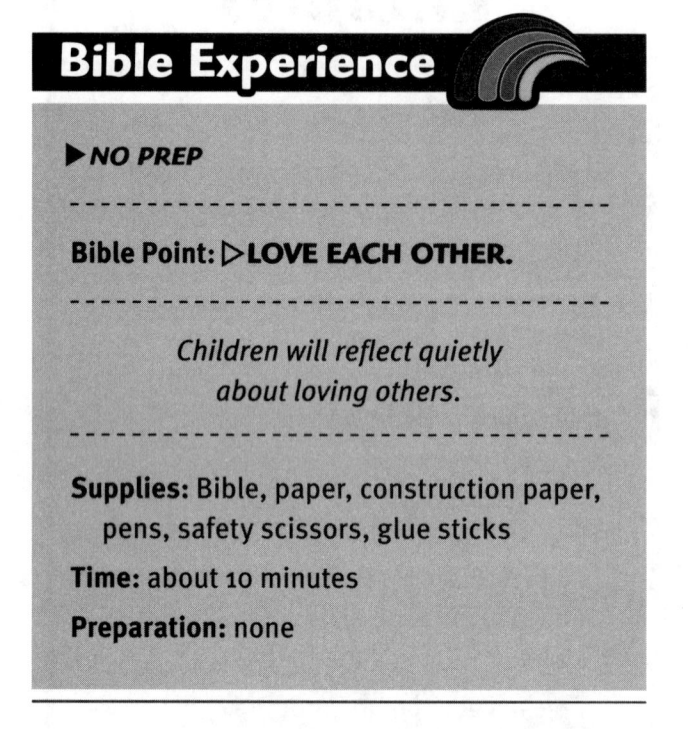

Bible Point: ▷ **LOVE EACH OTHER.**

Children will reflect quietly about loving others.

Supplies: Bible, paper, construction paper, pens, safety scissors, glue sticks

Time: about 10 minutes

Preparation: none

Begin your time together by briefly discussing what enemies are.

ASK:

◆ **What is an enemy?**

◆ **How do we usually treat enemies?**

SAY: **Let's see what Jesus had to say about how we should treat enemies.** Have a volunteer read aloud Luke 6:27-38.

ASK:

◆ **Why do you think Jesus would ask us to love our enemies?**

◆ **What do you think might happen if we love our enemies?**

Set out paper, construction paper, pens, scissors, and glue sticks. Demonstrate how to cut a backward, upside-down L, starting at the bottom middle of the construction paper so the L can be folded back like a door. Next, have kids glue a piece of paper to the back of the construction paper they've just cut, leaving the flap unglued.

Ask kids to leave the flap closed for a moment as they quietly think about the feelings they have for their enemies. Have them write as many of those feelings as possible on the front of their doors.

Ask a child to read aloud Luke 6:31. SAY: **Often, when we have enemies, we close the door to relationships with them. We shut them out so they can't hurt us. But Jesus said to ▷ LOVE EACH OTHER, and that includes enemies! We need to open the door to others and try to treat them as we'd like to be treated.**

n
o
t
e
s

Have kids fold back the paper flap, opening the door. On the paper underneath, have them write words that represent how Jesus wants us to treat our enemies. Close with a prayer, asking God to help students love each other and their enemies.

Song & Connect

Use "Do to Others" (track 7, *it: Innovative Tools for Children's Ministry: New Testament* CD) to help reinforce the Bible Point, ▷**LOVE EACH OTHER.**

Additional Topics List

This lesson can be used to help kids discover... Compassion, Forgiveness, Obedience, and Perspective.

Game

▶ ***NO PREP***

Friendship Fun

Children will explore how to love each other.

Supplies: Bible, bubble wands, containers of bubble solution

Time: 5 to 10 minutes

Preparation: none

Open your Bible to Luke 6:27-38, and briefly summarize the story of Jesus teaching about loving enemies. SAY: **Jesus wants us to ▷LOVE EACH OTHER and do to others as we'd like them to do to us. Let's play a game to help us do that!**

Have kids form pairs, and give each pair a container of bubble solution and a bubble wand. Explain that they're going to tell each other about a time someone hurt them or upset them. As they talk, they'll blow a bubble. The partner will suggest one way to forgive and treat that person as Jesus wants us to and will then pop the bubble.

Have kids switch roles often. When everyone has had a few turns, call time and gather everyone together.

ASK:

- **How was popping the bubbles like loving each other, even our enemies?**
- **How can we help each other ▷LOVE EACH OTHER?**

Craft

Love-ly Decorations

Children will make beaded window decorations.

Supplies: thin jewelry wire, scissors, clear beads, wide craft sticks, red beads, glue, fine-tipped markers, ribbon or string

Time: about 15 minutes

Preparation: For each child, cut nine strips of wire about 5 inches long.

Explain that kids will be making window decorations to remind them that Jesus wants us to ▷**LOVE EACH OTHER.**

Demonstrate the following steps: Thread a clear bead on a wire. Bend and twist the wire so the bead won't fall off. Thread 10 more clear beads on the wire so there are 11 beads total. Firmly wrap the end of the beaded wire around a craft stick. You'll be securing the end of each wire around the stick from left to right. Do the same for the remaining eight wires, following the bead lineup below.

Second wire: 11 clear beads. Third wire: seven clear beads, and then one red bead, and then three more clear beads. Fourth wire: same as third wire. Fifth wire: 11 red beads. Sixth wire: same as third wire. Seventh wire: same as third wire. Eighth and ninth wires: 11 clear beads on each.

Glue two craft sticks on each side of the one that has the wires wrapped around it to cover up the wires. On one craft stick, write, "Love each other." Tie ribbon or string around each end so the craft can be hung in a window.

SAY: **Jesus was the perfect example of how to ▷LOVE EACH OTHER. Let your beaded cross remind you that Jesus gave his life because he loves us, and he wants us to love others—even our enemies.**

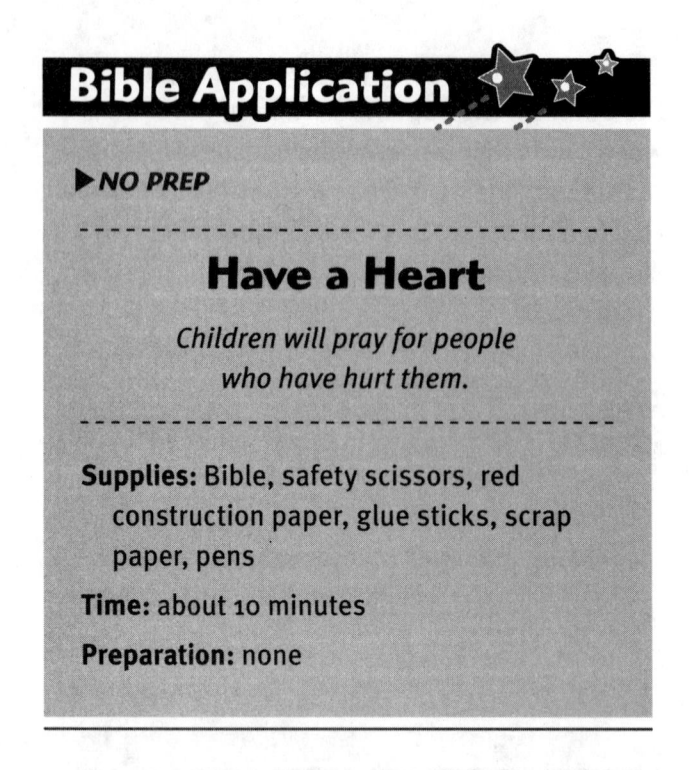

Bible Application

▶ ***NO PREP***

Have a Heart

Children will pray for people who have hurt them.

Supplies: Bible, safety scissors, red construction paper, glue sticks, scrap paper, pens

Time: about 10 minutes

Preparation: none

Open your Bible to Luke 6:27-38, and briefly summarize Jesus' teaching about loving enemies.

SAY: **Jesus wants us to ▷LOVE EACH OTHER. He even wants us to love our enemies, the people who have hurt us. And he wants us to pray for them, too! That may seem like a tough assignment, but let's think it through.**

ASK:

- **Have you ever hurt someone? Turn to a partner and tell what happened.**
- **How do you feel when you know you've hurt someone else?**
- **Think of someone you've hurt. Would you want that person to give you another chance? Explain.**

SAY: **We all mess up and hurt other people. When that happens, it's great when those people forgive us and give us another chance. That's what Jesus wants us to do for the people who have hurt us. Let's make something to help us do that!**

Have kids each cut a heart shape from red construction paper. Then let them each cut a smaller heart and glue it to the first one, leaving the top open to form a pocket. On pieces of scrap paper, have kids write the initials of people who have hurt them. Give them a few minutes to do this quietly.

Close with a time of silent prayer, asking kids to pray for the people whose initials they wrote. As they pray for each person, they can put the person's initials inside the heart pocket. Encourage kids to take their hearts home and continue to pray for their enemies. Explain that in that way, they'll be obeying Jesus' instruction to ▷**LOVE EACH OTHER!**

Creative Prayer Idea

▶***NO PREP***

Prayerful Reminders

Children will make reminders to pray for their enemies.

Supplies: Bible, thorny weeds, lightweight jute twine

Time: about 5 minutes

Preparation: none

Ask a volunteer to read aloud Luke 6:27-38. SAY: **Praying for our enemies is a lot harder than praying for people we love. But Jesus tells us to ▷LOVE EACH OTHER—even our enemies!**

Hand each child a thorny weed. SAY: **Let this thorn represent people you have a hard time getting along with—people who aren't nice to you. Let's pray for those people. As we do, let's think of Jesus as our example. He prayed for God to forgive the people who put him on the cross.**

Allow about a minute of silent prayer; then begin passing out 12-inch lengths of jute twine. SAY: **Tie your weed in the middle of your twine. Then knot the ends of the twine together to form a necklace. Hang the necklace somewhere in your room at home as a reminder of Jesus' command to pray for our enemies.**

Discussion Launcher Questions

Ask kids to form pairs and discuss:

- **How would you define the word *enemy*?**
- **Can kids your age have enemies? Explain.**
- **Which part of Luke 6:27-38 is the hardest for you to obey? Why?**
- **Why do you think Jesus said to love our enemies?**
- **How did Jesus set an example for loving our enemies?**

notes

Movie Clip

To the Rescue!

Movie Title: *The Land Before Time V: The Mysterious Island* (not rated)

Start Time: 1 hour, 15 seconds

Where to Begin: Chomper's mother battles another dinosaur.

Where to End: Littlefoot's friends cheer for Chomper's rescue.

Plot: While Littlefoot and his friends look for food on an island inhabited by enemy Sharptooth dinosaurs, they become reacquainted with their friend Chomper. During a battle Chomper falls over a cliff and into the sea. Littlefoot endangers his own life diving into the sea to rescue Chomper.

Review: Littlefoot and Chomper are members of enemy dinosaur camps. In Luke 6:27-38, Jesus said to love our enemies and do good to them, treating them as we'd like to be treated. In the movie, Littlefoot treats Chomper as he'd like to be treated—he helps him and rescues him from harm.

Discussion

After setting up and showing the clip,

ASK:

- **What do you think was going through Littlefoot's mind before he decided to rescue Chomper?**
- **How do you think Chomper's mom felt about Littlefoot?**

SAY: **Even though they were enemies, Littlefoot decided to help Chomper. In real life that's exactly what Jesus says we should do. Listen to what Jesus said.** Have a volunteer read aloud Luke 6:27-38.

ASK:

- **When is it hard for you to be nice to people you don't like?**
- **How can this movie clip remind you to love your enemies?**

Say: **Jesus said to ▷LOVE EACH OTHER. That means he wants us to love even our enemies. Sometimes that's hard to do, but we should try. The next time you're trying to decide how to treat someone—especially a person you have trouble liking—remember how Littlefoot treated Chomper!**

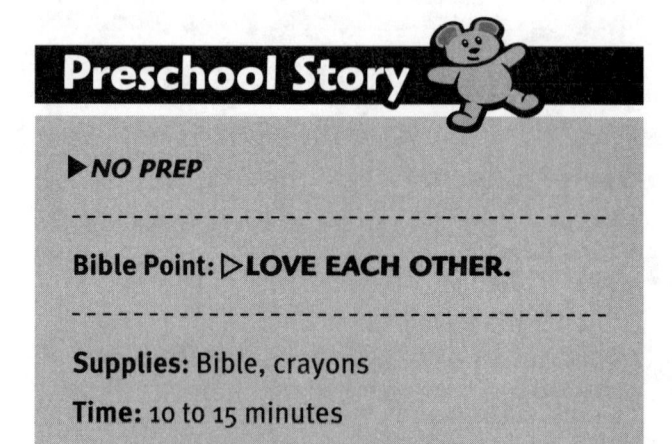

Preschool Story

▶*NO PREP*

Bible Point: ▷**LOVE EACH OTHER.**

Supplies: Bible, crayons

Time: 10 to 15 minutes

Preparation: none

No Fighting!

SAY: **We're going to talk about fighting and hurting each other. We're going to discover better, peaceful ways to solve problems instead of hurtful ways of doing it.**

Form pairs. Give each pair a crayon, and ask the partners to both hold it. On the count of three, have kids pretend to fight over the crayon. One child can say, "It's mine!" and pull it; the other child can say,

"No! It's mine!" and pull it back. Let kids keep going back and forth like this until you say stop.

After children have pretended for a while, tell them to stop.

ASK:

- ◆ **How did it feel to fight over a crayon?**
- ◆ **Have you ever fought over toys or clothes or food before? When?**
- ◆ **Instead of fighting over the crayon, how could you solve the problem?**

SAY: **One way to solve that kind of problem is to share. Take turns. Jesus wants us to think of others and help them. Let's listen to his words.**

Open your Bible to Luke 6:27-31, and show children the words. SAY: **Jesus said, "Love your enemies! Do good to those who hate you... Pray for those who hurt you. If someone slaps you on one cheek, offer the other cheek also. If someone demands your coat, offer your shirt also. Give to anyone who asks; and when things are taken away from you, don't try to get them back. Do to others as you would like them to do to you."**

ASK:

- ◆ **What do you think Jesus meant when he said this?**

SAY: **Jesus was saying that we shouldn't fight with others, but we should love them instead. Even when people aren't nice to us, we should be nice to them. Jesus was saying that we should ▷LOVE EACH OTHER.**

ASK:

- ◆ **What are some things that make you so mad that you want to fight?**
- ◆ **What can you do instead of fighting?**

SAY: **There are lots of peaceful and loving ways to solve problems instead of fighting. We can share, say we're sorry, take turns, or give hugs. Jesus wants us to ▷LOVE EACH OTHER instead of fighting. Let's sing a song now to help us remember to ▷LOVE EACH OTHER.**

Sing this song to the tune of "Mary Had a Little Lamb." Sing through the two verses several times to help kids learn it:

If a person makes you mad,
Makes you mad,
Makes you mad,
If a person makes you mad,
Turn the other cheek.

Jesus tells us, do not fight,
Do not fight,
Do not fight,
Jesus tells us, do not fight,
Be a peacemaker.

Tell kids that a peacemaker is someone who loves other people and chooses not to fight.

ASK:

- ◆ **How can you show love to others?**

SAY: **Jesus wants us to ▷LOVE EACH OTHER instead of fighting with each other.**

notes

BIBLE STORY

John Beheaded

For the Leader

Herod was ruler over Galilee. His brother Philip was married to Herodias, but she left Philip to marry Herod. When John the Baptist confronted the two for committing adultery, Herodias began plotting a way to get rid of John.

Herod arrested John the Baptist under pressure from his wife and advisers. Although Herod respected John, in the end he had John killed so as not to be embarrassed in front of his friends and family.

Key Scriptures

Mark 6:14-29

Philippians 4:13

Bible Verse

"I can do everything through Christ, who gives me strength" (Philippians 4:13).

n

o

t

e

s

Bible Experience

▶ *NO PREP*

Bible Point: ▷**WE CAN BE FAITHFUL.**

Children will make clay sculptures as reminders to be faithful to God.

Supplies: Bible, clay

Time: 10 to 15 minutes

Preparation: none

Gather the children, and then ASK:

- **What does it mean to be faithful?**
- **When have you been faithful to someone or had someone be faithful to you?**
- **Why do you want to be faithful to God?**

SAY: **In the Bible is a story about a man who remained faithful to God even though it meant losing his life.** Read aloud Mark 6:14-29, or summarize the story.

ASK:

- **How far was John the Baptist willing to go for his faith?**
- **How have you stood up for your faith?**
- **How can we show our faithfulness to God?**

Encourage kids to name ways such as praying, learning about Jesus, sharing their faith, and loving others as Jesus loves us. SAY: **Jesus will always help us remain faithful to him. Listen to what the Bible says.** Read aloud Philippians 4:13. Then give each child a lump of clay. Ask kids to form the clay into something that will remind them to be faithful. For example, kids might form a cross, a heart, or praying hands. Encourage children to take their clay creations home to remind them that ▷**WE CAN BE FAITHFUL to God.**

Song & Connect

Use "Persevere!" (track 21, *it: Innovative Tools for Children's Ministry: New Testament* CD) to help reinforce the Bible Point, ▷**WE CAN BE FAITHFUL.**

Additional Topics List

This lesson can be used to help kids discover... Faith, Perseverance, and Strength.

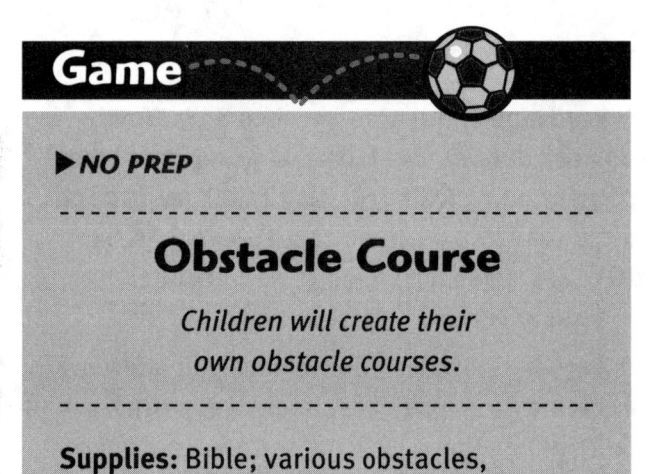

Game

▶*NO PREP*

Obstacle Course

Children will create their own obstacle courses.

Supplies: Bible; various obstacles, such as chairs, tables, boxes, ropes, athletic equipment, hymnals, blankets; newsprint; markers

Time: 15 to 20 minutes

Preparation: none

Have children form groups of three to five. Explain that groups will take turns creating an obstacle course for the rest of the class to follow. Show kids the items available for use as obstacles. Each group can plan to use all of the items available. (You could also have kids work together to form one obstacle course.)

Give each group a sheet of newsprint and markers. Have each group design its own obstacle course and draw a diagram of the course on the newsprint. For each obstacle on the course, have group members think of something that is an obstacle to remaining faithful to God. (Kids might say things like anger, gossip, fear, and temptation.)

Have groups take turns setting up their obstacle courses and leading other groups in completing the courses. Have each group describe what real-life things the obstacles represent. After each group has had a turn, lead everyone in a round of applause.

SAY: **In the Bible is a story about a man who remained faithful to God despite some pretty big obstacles.** Read aloud Mark 6:14-29, or summarize the passage. Then

ASK:

◆ **What obstacles did John the Baptist face?**

◆ **How can you remain faithful to God this week despite the obstacles you might face?**

◆ **How can you encourage and help each other to be faithful to God?**

SAY: ▷**WE CAN BE FAITHFUL to God no matter what obstacles we face. God will help us, and we can help each other, too.** Close in prayer, asking God to help each person remain faithful to him in the coming week. Pray also that children will encourage and help each other as they face obstacles to their faith.

n ______

o ______

t ______

e ______

s ______

Craft

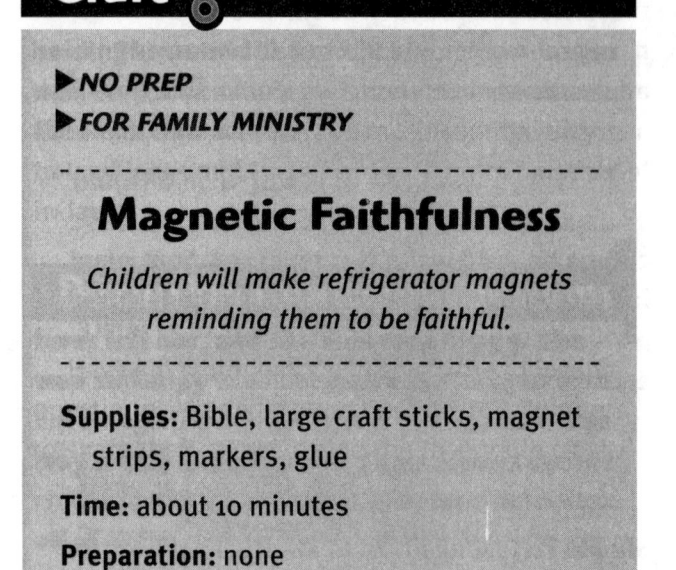

▶ *NO PREP*
▶ *FOR FAMILY MINISTRY*

Magnetic Faithfulness

Children will make refrigerator magnets reminding them to be faithful.

Supplies: Bible, large craft sticks, magnet strips, markers, glue

Time: about 10 minutes

Preparation: none

Read aloud Mark 6:14-29; then SAY: **John the Baptist remained faithful to God, even to the point of being killed for his faith. That's real faithfulness! Let's make something to remind us every day that ▷WE CAN BE FAITHFUL to God, too.**

Give each child one large craft stick and a magnet strip. Set out markers and glue for kids to share. Direct children to color the craft stick with a light-colored marker for background. Then have them write, "We can be faithful," on the stick with a dark-colored marker. Have kids glue their magnet strips to the back of their craft sticks.

SAY: **Put this magnet on your refrigerator at home. Tell your family that it can be a reminder to all of you that ▷WE CAN BE FAITHFUL to God, just as John the Baptist was.**

Bible Application

Tough-Times Faithfulness

Children will think of times it's hard to be faithful to God and then pray for each other.

Supplies: Bible, old magazines, pair of safety scissors for every 2 children, tape, newsprint

Time: 10 to 15 minutes

Preparation: Hang a sheet of newsprint on a wall at kids' eye level.

Read aloud Mark 6:14-29; then SAY: **Wow! John the Baptist was faithful to God even when it meant being killed for his faith. Even though we're not faced with the same trials John had, there are times it's tough to be faithful. Let's talk about that.**

Have kids form pairs. Give each pair a few old magazines and a pair of scissors. Let partners look through the magazines and each cut out one or two pictures that remind them of when it's hard to be faithful. For example, a child might cut out a picture of expensive jeans because it's hard not to put material things before God. Another child might cut out a picture of a school bus because school is where he or she is tempted to cheat on a test.

Have kids tape their pictures on the newsprint and explain the significance of the pictures. Then gather everyone in front of the newsprint and SAY: **▷WE CAN BE FAITHFUL even when it's tough. God will help us be strong, and we can pray for and encourage each other, too.** Pray together, asking God to help your students remain faithful to him in the coming week, even as they face challenges.

Creative Prayer Idea

Faithful Acrostic

Children will create acrostics to help them remember to be faithful.

Supplies: Bible, newsprint, marker, tape, paper, pencils

Time: 10 to 15 minutes

Preparation: On a sheet of newsprint, use a marker to write the letters of the word *FAITHFUL* vertically on a sheet of newsprint. Hang the newsprint on a wall.

Read aloud Mark 6:14-29; then SAY: **John the Baptist remained faithful to God, and ▷WE CAN BE FAITHFUL, too.**

Distribute paper and pencils, and have kids copy the letters as they're printed on the newsprint. Explain that the letters spell *faithful*. For each letter in the word, ask kids to write a way or a time to be faithful. For example, for the letter F, a child might write, "Find a friend to pray for me." For the letter I, a child might write, "In school." Give kids several minutes to write.

Have kids sit in a circle. Then pray, saying each letter of the word *faithful* and letting each child read what he or she wrote for that letter. Close by asking God to help each child be faithful to him during the coming week.

n

o

t

e

s

Discussion Launcher

Bible Shields

For this activity you'll need a Bible, scrap paper, pencils, tape, markers, and pieces of cardboard.

Read aloud or summarize Mark 6:14-29. SAY: **▷WE CAN BE FAITHFUL to God, just as John the Baptist was. One way to stay faithful to God is by knowing and following the Bible, his Word. Let's see how that works.**

Form two groups. Give kids in the first group scrap paper and pencils. Have them write on the paper things that tempt them to be unfaithful to God, such as cheating or fighting. Have children crumple each temptation into a paper wad.

Give the other group scrap paper, tape, markers, and the cardboard. Have kids write, "The Bible," on one side of the pieces of cardboard. On the other side, let kids tape paper-wad handles to the cardboard to make shields. At your signal, have kids in the second group try to cross the room by using their Bible shields as kids in the first group pelt them with paper temptations. Have kids switch roles and play again. Then

ASK:

- **How did the cardboard shields protect you in our game?**
- **How does the Bible help us to be faithful in real life?**

SAY: **God's Word is powerful and true! Knowing what the Bible says is one way ▷WE CAN BE FAITHFUL to God. Let's think of other ways.** Have kids brainstorm other ways to be faithful to God, such as praying for each other and encouraging each other. Close in prayer, asking God to help your students remain faithful to him in the coming week.

Movie Clip

Stand Strong

Movie Title: *Peter Pan* (1953) (not rated)

Start Time: 1 hour, 2 minutes, 35 seconds

Where to Begin: The pirates are dancing a circle around the Lost Boys and Wendy, who are tied up.

Where to End: Captain Hook mocks Wendy as she says that Peter Pan will save them.

Plot: Captain Hook has captured the Lost Boys and orders them to become pirates or walk the plank. Wendy challenges them to hold fast and trust Peter Pan to help them.

Review: Use this scene to help children understand that although it's sometimes hard to remain faithful to God, we can encourage each other to do just that. The Lost Boys were scared and in a bad situation. Wendy reminded them that they could trust Peter Pan to help them be strong. John the Baptist was in a bad situation, but he remained faithful to God.

Discussion

After setting up and showing the clip, have children discuss these questions.

ASK:

- **How do you think the Lost Boys felt when Captain Hook captured them?**
- **Why would it have been hard for Wendy and the Lost Boys to trust Peter Pan to help them?**

SAY: **With God's help, ▷WE CAN BE FAITHFUL. We can trust God to always be with us and help us be strong. John the Baptist remained faithful to God even when it meant being in jail and eventually losing his life.**

Preschool Story

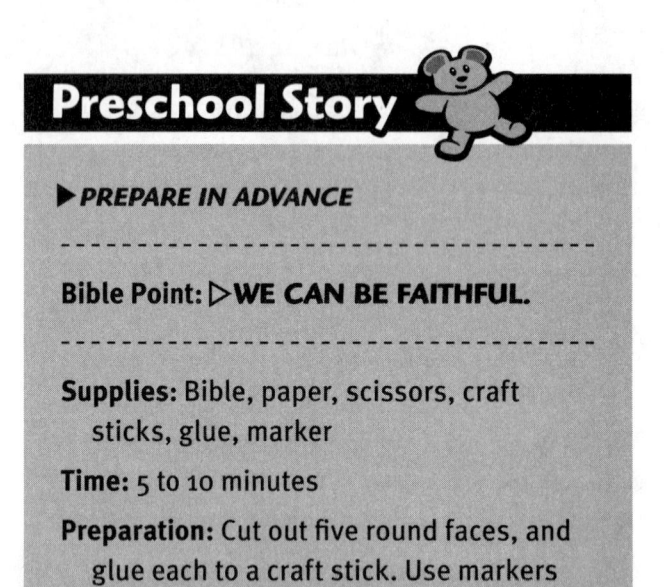

▶ ***PREPARE IN ADVANCE***

Bible Point: ▷WE CAN BE FAITHFUL.

Supplies: Bible, paper, scissors, craft sticks, glue, marker

Time: 5 to 10 minutes

Preparation: Cut out five round faces, and glue each to a craft stick. Use markers to give each face a different expression. You will need one happy face, one sad face, one mad face, one excited face, and one worried face.

An Emotional Story

Have kids form a circle and sit down. Open your Bible to Mark 6:14-29, and show children the words. Show students the emotion faces you made before class. Explain that you're going to hold up the emotion faces during the story; when they see you hold up an emotion face, they should mimic the emotion on that face.

SAY: **John the Baptist was Jesus' cousin and friend. John traveled around telling others about Jesus. John told people that Jesus was the Son of God. Some people were very happy to hear what John had to say.** Hold up the happy face, and encourage children to show you their happiest faces. **But some other people were mad to hear what John had to say.** Hold up the mad face, and encourage children to show you their mad faces. **These people were mad because they were doing wrong things and John wanted them to stop doing those wrong things.**

One person who was happy to hear John was a king named Herod. Hold up the happy face, and encourage children to show you their happiest faces. **Even though John told Herod to stop doing wrong things, Herod still liked to listen to John, and Herod respected John's teachings. But one person who was mad to hear what John had to say was Herodias, the king's wife.** Hold up the mad face, and encourage children to show you their mad faces.

Herodias didn't like to hear John's teachings because John kept telling her that she needed to change and stop doing bad things. But Herodias liked doing bad things, and she didn't want to listen to John's teachings. In fact, John made her so mad that she wanted to hurt him very badly. Hold up the mad face, and encourage children to show you their mad faces.

Herod worried about how much his wife hated John. Hold up the worried face, and encourage children to wring their hands and show you what they look like when they're worried. **Herod liked to listen to John, and he didn't want to hurt John.**

On Herod's birthday there was a big party, and everyone came to celebrate the king's birthday. Everyone was excited to celebrate in the king's palace. Hold up the excited face, and encourage children to act excited and to celebrate. **One young girl came out and danced for the king. The king was so happy to see her dance and liked her dance so much that he promised to give her anything she wanted.** Hold up the happy face, and encourage children to show you a happy face. **But the girl tricked Herod, and she told Herod's wife about the king's promise.**

When Herodias heard this, she told the girl to ask the king to hurt John the Baptist. When the girl asked the king to do this, the king was very sad because he liked John the Baptist a lot. Hold up the sad face, and encourage children to act sad. **The king should not have made such a silly promise to the girl, but he chose to keep his promise and hurt John the Baptist.**

When Jesus and John's friends heard about what happened to John the Baptist, they were very, very sad. Hold up the sad face, and encourage children to act sad.

Herod the king should have been faithful to his friend John. He shouldn't have let his wife trick him like that.

ASK:

◆ **Why is it important to be faithful to our friends?**

◆ **When can you be faithful to your friends?**

SAY: ▷**WE CAN BE FAITHFUL to each other and to Jesus.**

n
o
t
e
s

BIBLE STORY

The Transfiguration

For the Leader

Jesus took only three of his disciples with him up the mountain. Jesus wanted these disciples to experience what he knew was to come so they could describe it later. (An account was considered reliable if established by two or three witnesses.)

Why were Moses and Elijah the ones to appear with Jesus? A likely explanation is that Moses represented the law, and Elijah represented the prophets. Jesus was the fulfillment of both.

Key Scripture

Mark 9:2-13

Bible Verse

"This is my dearly loved Son. Listen to him" (Mark 9:7).

Bible Experience

▶ ***NO PREP***

Bible Point: ▷**JESUS IS GOD'S SON.**

Children will act out the Bible story to discover that Jesus is God's Son.

Supplies: Bible, pair of sunglasses for each child

Time: about 10 minutes

Preparation: none

Open your Bible to Mark 9:2-13. SAY: **Today we're going to learn about an amazing thing that three of Jesus' disciples saw. You can help me tell the story. You'll be the disciples, OK? Just follow my actions.**

One day Jesus took Peter, James, and John along with him as he started walking. Let's walk! Lead kids in marching around the room a time or two. **Then they came to the foot of a tall, tall mountain. The disciples looked up and thought, *Uh-oh, I wonder if we're going to be climbing that tall, tall mountain.*** Shield your eyes and look straight up. **Sure enough, they started climbing up that tall, tall mountain. Up and up they went.** Pretend to climb a steep mountain. **And up and up some more.** Keep pretending to climb. **Yep, you guessed it—up and up some more.** Keep pretending to climb. **Soon they were way above the path they had been on.** Shield your eyes and look down. **Just then, when they looked up, they saw the amazing thing I told you about.**

Jesus was standing in front of them, but he was different—he was transformed! His clothes were dazzling white, whiter than any earthly

bleach could ever make them. It was so white and bright that the disciples could barely look at it. Have everyone put on sunglasses. **And that's not all: Elijah and Moses appeared with Jesus and began talking to him!** Put your hands to your cheeks and look surprised. **The disciples were amazed, and to tell you the truth, they were pretty scared. After all, Elijah and Moses had been dead for a long time! The disciples were terrified!** Crouch down and pretend to be terrified. **And even *that's* not all!**

Then a cloud overshadowed them, and a voice from the cloud said, "This is my dearly loved Son. Listen to him." Cup your hand to your ear as if listening. **Suddenly, Elijah and Moses were gone, and only Jesus was with them. The disciples didn't know what to think.** Take off the sunglasses, and shake your head in bewilderment.

Thank kids for their participation. Have them form pairs to answer these questions.

ASK:

◆ **Who can tell us who Moses was? Elijah?**

SAY: **Moses was the person God gave the Ten Commandments to. Elijah was a prophet in the Old Testament. They both had been dead for a long time.**

ASK:

◆ **What do you think you would have done if you had seen Moses and Elijah appear on the mountain with Jesus?**

◆ **Why do you think Jesus' appearance changed?**

◆ **What did God say about Jesus?**

◆ **How do we know ▷JESUS IS GOD'S SON?**

SAY: **We know that ▷JESUS IS GOD'S SON because God said so!** Read aloud Mark 9:7; then ask students to repeat God's words with you: **"This is my dearly loved Son. Listen to him."**

This story in the Bible is called the Transfiguration because Jesus was transfigured. For just a few minutes, those three disciples got a glimpse of Jesus' true glory as God's Son. That must have been amazing! Let's thank God for telling us about Jesus.

Pray, asking God to help kids remember that Jesus is his Son.

Additional Topics List

This lesson can be used to help kids discover... Faith, Heaven, Salvation, and Sharing Faith.

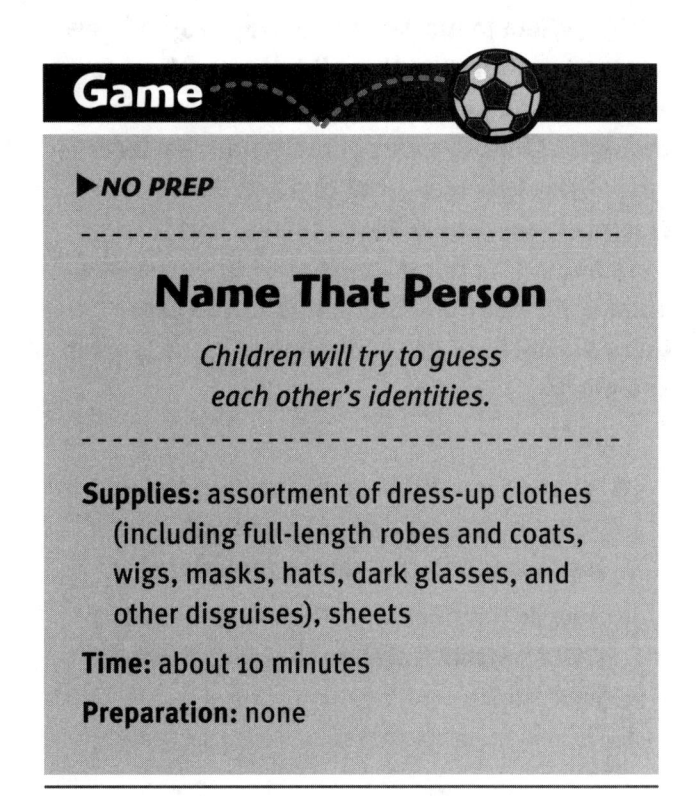

Game

▶ *NO PREP*

Name That Person

Children will try to guess each other's identities.

Supplies: assortment of dress-up clothes (including full-length robes and coats, wigs, masks, hats, dark glasses, and other disguises), sheets

Time: about 10 minutes

Preparation: none

Have kids form four teams. Explain that each team should disguise one member from head to toe. Keep teams separate while they're disguising their teammates.

SAY: **Let's play Name That Person. When a disguised player from another team comes forward, other teams will take turns guessing the player's true identity.**

Give each group a sheet, and have all team members hide behind the sheet. Have groups take turns sending their disguised team member from behind the sheet while others guess who he or she is. After all mystery team members have been guessed, lead kids in a round of applause for everyone's participation.

ASK:

- **What was it like trying to guess the disguised team members' identities?**
- **Have you ever known someone who turned out to be different from what you thought he or she was like at first? Explain.**

SAY: **When Jesus came to earth, people knew he was a person, but they didn't know he was also God. The people who saw him grow up thought of him as a carpenter's son, and later others saw him as a great teacher. Some of his disciples, especially Peter, James, and John, were beginning to realize that while Jesus was human, he was also God. God allowed those three disciples to get a glimpse of Jesus' power and glory.**

ASK:

- **What do you think went through the minds of Peter, James, and John when they saw Jesus transfigured on the mountain?**
- **How do you feel knowing that ▷JESUS IS GOD'S SON? How has that fact changed your life?**

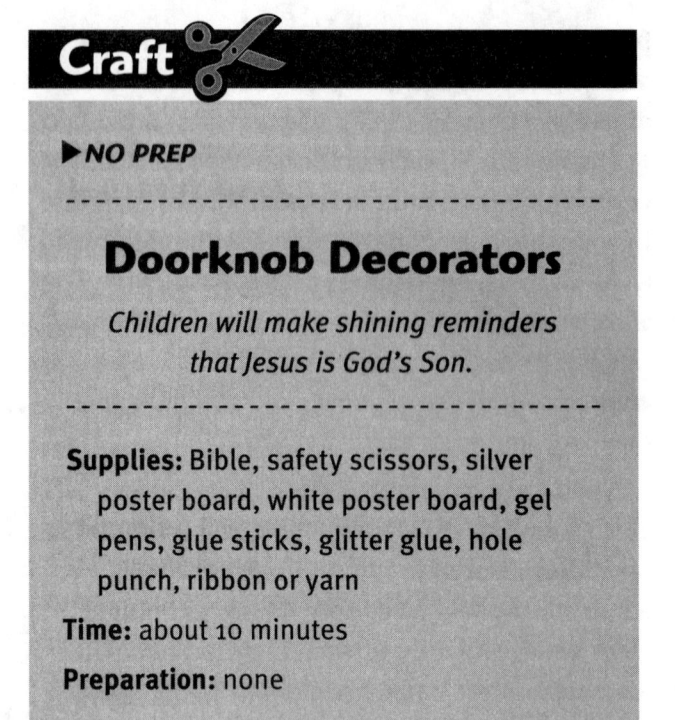

notes

Craft

▶ *NO PREP*

Doorknob Decorators

Children will make shining reminders that Jesus is God's Son.

Supplies: Bible, safety scissors, silver poster board, white poster board, gel pens, glue sticks, glitter glue, hole punch, ribbon or yarn

Time: about 10 minutes

Preparation: none

Read aloud or summarize Mark 9:2-13. SAY: **In this story, which is often called the Transfiguration, Jesus changed appearance. His clothes took on a dazzling brightness. Let's make reminders of this story to hang on our doorknobs at home.**

Explain that kids can cut starbursts out of the silver poster board to represent the dazzling light the disciples saw when Jesus was transfigured. On a smaller, white starburst, they can write, **▷"JESUS IS GOD'S SON!"** Have kids glue the white starburst on the silver one and then decorate both with the supplies you set out. Punch a hole in the top of the craft, and thread and loop ribbon or yarn as a hanger.

Encourage kids to use their Doorknob Decorators to tell someone else that **▷JESUS IS GOD'S SON.**

Bible Application

▶ *PREPARE IN ADVANCE*

Make a Change in Me

Children will quietly contemplate who Jesus is.

Supplies: Bible, photocopies of gingerbread-person outline, pens

Time: about 5 minutes

Preparation: Draw a simple gingerbread-person shape on a sheet of paper. Draw an arrow to the head, and in the margin, write: "Change my thinking by..." Draw an arrow to the chest, and in the margin, write: "Change my heart by..." Draw an arrow to the feet, and in the margin, write: "Change my actions and steps by..." Make a photocopy of the sheet for every child in class.

Read aloud Mark 9:2-13, or summarize the story of Jesus' transfiguration. SAY: **In this story the three disciples saw an amazing change in Jesus. And then God announced who Jesus is—God's Son. Knowing that ▷JESUS IS GOD'S SON and that he came to die for our sins should create a change in us, too.**

Give each child a pen and a photocopy of the sheet you made before class. SAY: **Think of three ways you'd like to change to be more like Jesus. Write your thoughts in the margin.** Give kids several minutes to write. Invite volunteers to share what they wrote. Then encourage kids to take the papers home and look at them during the week as a prompt to pray for God's help in changing to be more like Jesus.

Creative Prayer Idea

Name-Tag Prayer

Children will create a giant name tag for Jesus.

Supplies: poster board, markers, tape

Time: 5 to 10 minutes

Preparation: Draw a border around the edges of a sheet of poster board so it looks like a big name tag. In the middle, write: "Hi, I'm Jesus, God's Son."

SAY: **Sometimes when people go to events where they won't know anyone, they wear name tags to let people know who they are. Let's pretend that this is a name tag for Jesus and that we have a chance to introduce Jesus to others. Think of all the things you could tell people about Jesus. Then write your ideas all over the name tag.**

When kids have finished writing, hang the poster on the wall. Gather kids in front of the poster, and ask them to hold hands. Close with this PRAYER: **Dear God, thank you for sending your Son, Jesus, into the world. We thank you for all of his wonderful qualities and deeds that we've written here. Help us to learn more about him every day. In Jesus' name, amen.**

notes

Movie Clip

Mistaken Identity

Movie Title: *The Prince and the Pauper* (animated) (G)

Start Time: 19 minutes, 55 seconds

Where to Begin: The real prince escapes from prison.

Where to End: The real prince is crowned.

Plot: Disguised as an executioner, Goofy comes to rescue the prince from jail. Together Goofy and the prince burst into the coronation ceremony where the prince confronts his own evil guard, Captain Pete. A zany battle ensues before the prince is finally crowned.

Review: Though the prince was disguised as a beggar for a while, he never ceased being the prince. To many of his followers, Jesus was "disguised" simply as a carpenter's son. Though he was fully human, Jesus never ceased being God. At the transfiguration, Peter, James, and John glimpsed the majesty and glory of Jesus' kingliness.

Discussion

After setting up and showing the clip,

ASK:

- **What were other people's reactions when the real prince entered the ceremony?**
- **How do you think it would feel to be mistaken for a beggar when you were really a prince?**
- **How do you think it felt for the disciples to finally understand Jesus' true identity?**

Science Devotion

Now You See It...

Children will use foil to help them remember the Bible story.

Supplies: Bible, scissors, aluminum foil

Time: about 5 minutes

Preparation: Use scissors to cut a square of aluminum foil for each child. Don't tear the foil from the roll. Cut it to avoid wrinkles.

Read aloud or summarize the story in Mark 9:2-13. SAY: **In this story three of the disciples saw an amazing sight. Just as suddenly, they saw it disappear. Let's do a little experiment to see what that might have been like. OK, this obviously won't be anything like Jesus' transfiguration, but it can help us remember the story.**

Give each child a square of foil. SAY: **Look at your reflection on the shiny side of the foil. It won't be perfect, but you'll see yourself pretty clearly.** Pause for kids to look at their reflections. **Now crinkle the foil into a loose wad. Don't crinkle it too tightly because you'll have to smooth it out again.** Pause as kids loosely crinkle their foil. **Open your foil square back up. Now look for your reflection.**

Kids won't be able to see their reflections, no matter how they angle the foil.

ASK:

- **What happened to your reflection?**
- **How is that like what happened when the disciples were looking at Moses and Elijah?**

SAY: **Moses and Elijah disappeared, just like your reflections on the foil disappeared. Your reflections disappeared because the light rays bounce off a smooth surface differently than they do off a crinkled surface. Jesus' appearance changed, and Moses and Elijah appeared and disappeared because that was part of God's plan to tell who Jesus is and show a glimpse of his glory. You can use this foil experiment to remind you of this Bible story and how you learned that ▷JESUS IS GOD'S SON.**

Preschool Story

▶ ***PREPARE IN ADVANCE***

Bible Point: ▷**JESUS IS GOD'S SON.**

Supplies: Bible, blocks, 6 wide craft sticks, marker, white crayon or white paint, foam cup, knife, white paper, scissors

Time: 10 to 15 minutes

Preparation: Draw faces on all the craft sticks to make puppets. On one puppet, draw a face on both sides. Use a white crayon or white paint to color one side of this puppet white—this puppet represents Jesus. On two of the puppets, color the face side white—these are the Elijah and Moses puppets. The other three puppets represent Peter, James, and John. Cut three slits in the bottom of a foam cup—be sure the slits are wide enough for the craft sticks to fit through. Hide the Elijah and Moses craft sticks under the cup. Cut a cloud shape from white paper.

On the Mountain

Have kids form a circle and sit down. Open your Bible to Mark 9:2-13, and show children the words. Ask children to help you build a mountain out of blocks. At the top of the mountain, place the foam cup upside down, with the Elijah and Moses craft sticks hidden underneath. Give one child the paper cloud, another child the Peter craft stick, another child the James craft stick, and another child the John craft stick. Keep the Jesus craft stick.

SAY: **One day Jesus took Peter, James, and John to the top of a mountain. No one else was there.** "Walk" your Jesus puppet up to the top of the block mountain. Encourage the children with the other three puppets to walk them up the mountain behind your puppet. **As Peter, James, and John watched, Jesus' appearance changed. His clothes became dazzling white—far whiter than anything they'd ever seen before.** Turn the Jesus puppet around so his white side is showing. Then stick him in the middle slot of the foam cup.

Pick up the cup and poke the Elijah and Moses puppets up through the other two slots so they are on either side of the Jesus puppet. SAY: **Suddenly Elijah and Moses appeared and began talking with Jesus. This was amazing because both Elijah and Moses had gone to heaven a long, long time ago—no one had seen them on earth for hundreds of years!**

Have the child with the paper cloud stand up and hold the cloud above the mountain. SAY: **Then a cloud came over them, and a voice from the cloud said, "This is my beloved Son. Listen to him"** (Mark 9:7). **The voice was God's voice! God was telling everyone that ▷JESUS IS HIS SON.**

Suddenly, Peter, James, and John looked around. Moses and Elijah were gone, and only Jesus was with them. Pull the Elijah and Moses puppets back under the foam cup. Pull the Jesus puppet out from the top of the cup, and walk it back to the Peter, James, and John puppets.

Peter, James, John, and Jesus walked back down the mountain. Walk your puppet back down the mountain. Encourage the kids to have their puppets follow yours. **Jesus told the disciples not to tell anyone what they had seen until Jesus had risen from the dead. So the disciples kept it a secret, but they often wondered what Jesus had meant when he talked about rising from the dead.**

ASK:

- **What do you think Jesus meant when he said he would rise from the dead?**
- **How would you have felt if you'd been on the mountain that day?**

SAY: **If I had been on that mountain, I would have wanted to celebrate and worship Jesus because ▷JESUS IS GOD'S SON. You can worship Jesus, too. We can worship Jesus by singing to him, praying to him, telling others about him, and loving him. It's important for us to worship Jesus because ▷HE IS GOD'S SON.**

If you have extra time, let kids make their own set of puppets to help them retell today's story.

notes

BIBLE STORY

Rich Young Man

For the Leader

Jesus knew the rich young man's problem—the man's possessions were too important to him. So Jesus confronted him by suggesting that the rich man do the one thing that would be hardest for him to do: sell his possessions and give the money to the poor.

Jesus' example of a camel going through the eye of a needle caught his disciples' attention. His disciples likely looked on earthly riches as a sign of God's blessing. But Jesus wanted them to see that riches and possessions can be a barrier to truly following God.

Key Scriptures

Matthew 6:19-21

Mark 10:17-31

Bible Verse

"Don't store up treasures here on earth, where moths eat them and rust destroys them, and where thieves break in and steal. Store your treasures in heaven, where moths and rust cannot destroy, and thieves do not break in and steal. Wherever your treasure is, there the desires of your heart will also be" (Matthew 6:19-21).

Bible Experience

▶ ***ALLERGY ALERT***

Bible Point: ▷**GOD IS NUMBER ONE!**

Children will use an active object lesson to help them remember that God is number one!

Supplies: Bible, 2 plastic 1-gallon milk cartons, scissors, duct tape, small toys, wrapped candy

Time: about 10 minutes

Preparation: Before class, cut off the tops of the two cartons so the hole is just large enough for a small child to get his or her hand into it. Cover the edges of the holes with duct tape. Fill one carton with small toys and the other with wrapped candy.

Show students the two prepared cartons of goodies. Invite kids, if they choose, to come forward and get a treasure or treat. Several things might happen. Some children may be too shy to come forward. Some might reach into a carton, grab lots of goodies, and not be able to get their hands out of the hole with all the bounty. Others' hands might not fit through the holes in the first place.

After everyone who wants a turn has had one,

ASK:

◆ **What did you do when I asked you to come get a treasure or treat? Why was that your decision?**

◆ **Who had trouble getting the treats out of the carton? What did you have to do?**

SAY: **Just like in our class, if I asked any group of kids to do this same activity, some wouldn't want to try. Others wouldn't be able to get their hands into the cartons. And others would grab too much and would have to let go. That's like life. Some people don't have any treats. Some are content with a little. And some have so much, they can't let go. That reminds me of a Bible story I want to share with you.**

Have a volunteer read aloud Mark 10:17-31.

SAY: **Jesus wanted this rich young man to realize that ▷GOD IS NUMBER ONE in our lives—or at least he should be! The man walked away sad because he had lots of riches. Jesus doesn't want us to be like that rich young man. He wants to be number one in our lives, above everything else. Listen to what the Bible says about filling our lives with riches.** Read aloud Matthew 6:19-21. **Jesus wants our treasures to be about faith in him, not earthly riches.** Ask kids to hold out their hands, palms up. Tell them that each time you pause, they should say, "Jesus, we give it to you."

- **Our hands may be full of activities, like baseball, soccer, or music lessons.** Pause for kids to say, "Jesus, we give it to you."
- **Our hands may be full of friends who may influence us to do things you don't want us to do.** Pause for kids to say, "Jesus, we give it to you."
- **Our hands may be full of fears that keep us from doing the right thing or following you.** Pause for kids to say, "Jesus, we give it to you."
- **Our hands may be full of stress that we can't seem to handle.** Pause for kids to say, "Jesus we give it to you."
- **Our hands may be full of expectations that make us try to be somebody we aren't.** Pause for kids to say, "Jesus, we give it to you."

PRAY: **Jesus, we have empty hands right now. Fill our empty hands with your love and purpose. Help us to make you number one in our lives. In Jesus' name, amen.**

Song & Connect

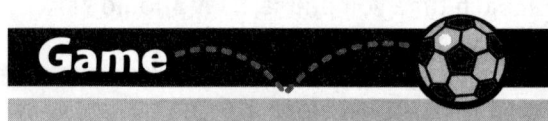

Use "Treasures" (track 3, *it: Innovative Tools for Children's Ministry: New Testament* CD) to help reinforce the Bible Point, ▷**GOD IS NUMBER ONE!**

Additional Topics List

This lesson can be used to help kids discover... Faith, Greed, and Obedience.

Game

▶ ***FOR YOUNGER CHILDREN***

Eye of a Needle

Children will discover how difficult it would be for a camel to go through the eye of a needle.

Supplies: Bible, 4 adult-sized folding chairs

Time: about 10 minutes

Preparation: Line up the chairs so they're touching each other, side by side, with the seats all facing the same direction. This will create a tunnel, which represents the eye of the needle, between the legs of the chairs.

Open your Bible to Mark 10:17-31, and briefly summarize the story of the rich young man.

ASK:

- ◆ **Why do you think Jesus used the image of a camel going through the eye of a needle to make his point?**

SAY: **Let's play a game to remind us of this Bible passage. These chairs will be the eye of the needle, and all of you can be "camels."**

Have children line up and take turns crawling through the eye of the needle. They'll probably end up on their bellies. Make sure the second child doesn't start through the tunnel until the first child is all the way through. If you have more than eight children, set up two tunnels. (If you have girls in class wearing dresses, they can be cheerleaders.)

SAY: **Well, we were able to crawl through this pretend eye of a needle, but just barely! A real camel could never go through the eye of a needle. Jesus used that image to emphasize how important it is to make sure that ▷GOD IS NUMBER ONE in our lives. Remember this game the next time you feel your focus shifting from Jesus to possessions.**

Craft

God Is Number One!

Children will make spinners to help them remember that God is number one.

Supplies: Bible, poster board, ruler, scissors, hole punch, rubber bands, markers

Time: about 10 minutes

Preparation: Cut a 3-inch poster-board circle for each child. Punch a hole near one edge of each circle.

Open your Bible to Mark 10:17-31, and briefly summarize the story of the rich young man. SAY: **The rich young man had so many treasures that he didn't want to give them up to follow Jesus. In our lives there are lots of things that take up all of our time when we should be trying to make God number one. In fact, our lives can get so busy and filled with possessions that it makes our heads spin! So let's make spinners that will help remind us to make God number one in our lives.**

Give each child a prepared poster-board circle. Demonstrate how to thread the rubber bands through the holes and pull the rubber bands back through themselves. Tighten the rubber bands until they're tightly fastened to the circles. Let kids use markers to decorate their circles. Have them write "God Is" on one side and "#1" on the other side.

Show kids how to put their fingers through the rubber bands and wind the rubber bands tight. When they let go, the circles will spin and the words "God Is #1" will appear. Encourage kids to use their spinners to tell someone else the story of the rich young man and to explain that it's important to make sure that ▷**GOD IS NUMBER ONE!**

Bible Application

▶ *PREPARE IN ADVANCE*

Keep God Number One

Children will encourage each other to keep God number one throughout the week.

Supplies: Bible, poster board, safety scissors, pens, tape

Time: about 10 minutes

Preparation: Create a template for a giant "#1" hand, the kind worn at sporting events. (If you have a large class, make several templates.)

Open your Bible to Mark 10:17-31, and briefly summarize the story of the rich young man. SAY: **The rich young man had trouble keeping his priorities straight. We sometimes have the same trouble. It's important for Christians to help each other remember that ▷GOD IS NUMBER ONE! So let's make something to help us remember!**

Let kids take turns tracing the hand template onto poster board. Each person will need to cut out two copies. Let kids each tape the two copies together to make a "#1" glove. Have kids write their names on their gloves. Then have students sit in a circle, and set out pens for them to use. Have kids pass the gloves around the circle. Each person will write a note of encouragement on everyone's glove about making God number one. When the gloves come back to their owners, close with a prayer asking God to help kids keep their priorities straight this week by making him number one.

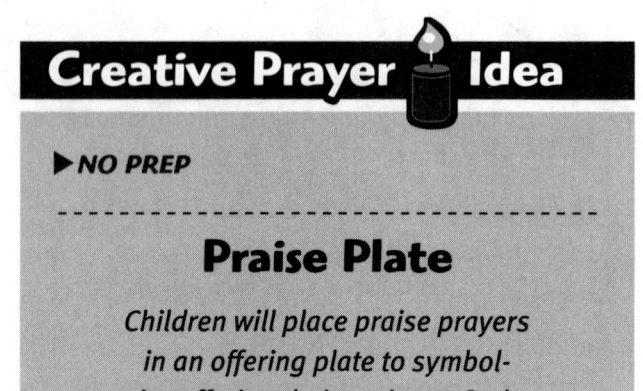

Creative Prayer Idea

▶ *NO PREP*

Praise Plate

Children will place praise prayers in an offering plate to symbolize offering their praise to God.

Supplies: Bible, paper scraps, pens, offering plate

Time: about 5 minutes

Preparation: none

Have kids sit in a circle on the floor. Open your Bible to Mark 10:17-31, and briefly summarize the story of the rich young man. SAY: **In this story the young man didn't want to give up his riches to follow Jesus. I'm sure there are things we all need to give up to make sure we ▷ MAKE GOD NUMBER ONE! Let's offer those things up to God right now. Think of something that's keeping you from following Jesus as closely as you could. Write your thought on a scrap of paper.**

After kids finish writing, begin a prayer asking God to help kids give up whatever they need to in order to follow Jesus and make him number one in their lives. Then pass the offering plate around the circle, and let kids place their papers in the plate. Close the prayer by thanking God for sending Jesus and for helping kids give up the specific things that hinder them from making Jesus number one.

Discussion Launcher Questions

Ask kids to form pairs and discuss:

- **Why do you think it's hard for rich people to enter the kingdom of God?**
- **Is it wrong to have money? Why or why not?**
- **How would having more money and possessions than you do now change your relationship with Jesus?**
- **What can you do this week to make sure you ▷ MAKE GOD NUMBER ONE?**

Object Lesson

▶ *HIGH ENERGY*

Balloon Bonanza

Children will try to keep balloons in the air to see what it's like to have lots of things competing for their attention.

Supplies: Bible, balloons, trash bag

Time: 5 to 10 minutes

Preparation: Blow up and tie off a balloon for each child in class. Make sure all of the balloons are the same color. Then blow up another balloon of a different color to represent Jesus. Place the balloons in one or more trash bags. Keep the balloon representing Jesus on top.

Open your Bible to Mark 10:17-31, and briefly summarize the story of the rich young man. SAY: **The man in the story had lots of riches. Let's play a game to see what it's like to have lots of riches and treasures competing with Jesus for attention in our lives.**

Have kids join you in forming a tight circle. Place the bag of balloons in the center. Explain that the different-colored balloon represents Jesus and that all of the other balloons represent things we own or want to own and activities that take up our time. The goal of the game is to try to keep all of the balloons in the air at the same time, much like trying to juggle all of our possessions and activities. If a balloon hits the ground, the nearest person should pick it up and put it back into play.

Take out one balloon, and tap it to the child next to you. Keep adding balloons. As kids bat the balloons, encourage them to call out possessions they have or would like to have as well as activities that keep them busy during a typical week. See how many balloons the kids can keep going before the game reaches total chaos. Then call time and have kids sit down.

ASK:

- **What was it like trying to keep all of the balloons in the air?**
- **How is that like trying to juggle all of our activities and possessions in life?**
- **What happened to the single balloon representing Jesus?**

SAY: **With all of the activities we do in a week and all of the possessions we own or want, it's easy to lose sight of Jesus in the chaos. Just like the rich young man, it's hard to put Jesus first. But we need to make sure that ▷GOD IS NUMBER ONE in our lives—every day.**

Close in prayer, asking God to help kids keep their focus on Jesus.

Preschool Story

▶ ***NO PREP***

Bible Point: ▷**GOD IS NUMBER ONE!**

Supplies: Bible, large doll, classroom toys clothes, fake money

Time: 5 to 10 minutes

Preparation: none

Number One!

Set the doll in the center of your room. SAY: **Our story today is about a very rich young man. Let's pretend this doll is the rich young man. He doesn't look very rich right now. Let's make him look rich!**

Encourage children to go through the room and pick out lots of toys, clothes, fake money, and anything else appropriate to give to the doll to make him look rich. Have kids pile all the stuff near or around the doll. Encourage kids to keep going back and getting more things—tell them to be sure and bring their favorite classroom toys to the doll. Once the doll has a very tall pile of stuff, have kids sit down.

Open your Bible to Mark 10:17-31, and show children the words. SAY: **One day, as Jesus was**

starting out on a trip, a rich young man came to talk to him. Point to the doll. **This rich young man asked Jesus a very important question: "What should I do to live forever?"**

Jesus answered, "You know the commandments: Do not murder. Do not take another man's wife. Do not steal. Do not lie. Be good to your father and mother."

The rich young man was very happy because he had done all of those things!

Jesus loved the man very much, so he told the man that he needed to do only one more thing: "Go and sell all you have and give the money to the poor...Then come, follow me" (Mark 10:21).

When the rich young man heard this, he was very sad. He had lots and lots of things. He didn't want to give up all of those things. Point to the doll. **He loved all of his stuff and wanted to keep it. So the man walked away. He chose not to give away his stuff and follow Jesus.**

This made Jesus very sad. Jesus said that it's very hard for people to put God first, before all their stuff. But that's what he wants us to do. Jesus wants us to know that ▷GOD IS NUMBER ONE. God is above all the things we have.

ASK:

- ◆ **Why is it hard to put God first, over our stuff?**
- ◆ **How can you ▷MAKE GOD NUMBER ONE?**

As children answer your questions, encourage them to put away all the stuff they gave to the doll. Remind them that God is above all of those fun things.

SAY: **Let's do a cheer now to help us remember that ▷GOD IS NUMBER ONE!**

Lead children in the following cheer. Encourage them to respond using the italicized words. Hold up your index finger each time you ask who is number one. SAY:

Who is number one?

(God is number one!)

Are toys number one?

(No!)

Who is number one?

(God is number one!)

Is food number one?

(No!)

Who is number one?

(God is number one!)

Is money number one?

(No!)

Who is number one?

(God is number one!)

Continue with the cheer, substituting new words each time.

n

o

t

e

s

BIBLE STORIES

Children and Jesus

For the Leader

The disciples saw it as their job to keep the masses away from Jesus—especially those as insignificant as children. But as he did many times during his ministry, Jesus challenged the status quo. He ignored what the disciples considered politically important—appeasing the religious leaders of the day—and spent time blessing children.

Another theme winds through this passage: to make it to heaven, we must become like one of these small children. Jesus' message is that, just as children place their trust in their parents, we must be humble and willing to place our trust in God.

Key Scripture

Mark 10:13-16

Bible Verse

"[Jesus] said to them, 'Let the children come to me. Don't stop them! For the Kingdom of God belongs to those who are like these children' " (Mark 10:14).

Bible Experience

Bible Point: ▷**JESUS LOVES CHILDREN.**

Children will use magnets to learn that Jesus loves them.

Supplies: Bible, safety scissors, thin cardboard, tape, crayons, paper, large paper clips, at least 2 magnets

Time: about 10 minutes

Preparation: Cut a cardboard figure of Jesus. (Or you could tape a flannel-board figure of Jesus to cardboard.)

Have children form pairs. Supply several crayons for each pair, and give each child a sheet of paper. Have kids draw pictures of themselves, and then let them cut out the pictures. As they work, read aloud Mark 10:13-16.

Show kids how to make a triple accordion fold along the bottom of their finished pictures and then paper-clip the folds together at each end. The pictures should now stand upright.

Place the figure of Jesus on one end of the cardboard. Let the children stand their pictures on the other end. Let kids take turns holding the magnets on the underside of the cardboard. They can use the magnets to make the pictures move closer to Jesus. After everyone has had a turn, ASK:

- **Why do you think the parents wanted their children to be with Jesus?**
- **How did Jesus react to the children?**
- **Why does Jesus love children?**
- **How does Jesus feel about you?**

SAY: **▷JESUS LOVES CHILDREN. Let me read a special verse again about that.** Read aloud Mark 10:14; then SAY: **Jesus wanted the children of his time to come to him, and he wants the children of today to come to him, too. And that's you!** Put two magnets together, and show kids how the magnets are drawn to each other. Pass the magnets around so kids can feel the magnetic pull. **Jesus' love is like a magnet. It draws us to him. Let's thank Jesus for wanting to have a special relationship with us.** Close with a prayer thanking Jesus for drawing us toward him.

Song & Connect

Use "Let All the Children" (track 5, *it: Innovative Tools for Children's Ministry: New Testament* CD) to help reinforce the Bible Point, **▷JESUS LOVES CHILDREN.**

notes

Additional Topics List

This lesson can be used to help kids discover... Acceptance, Faith, Friendship, and Love.

Game

▶*NO PREP*

Let Them Through

Children will play a variation of Tag to simulate the Bible story.

Supplies: Bible

Time: about 10 minutes

Preparation: none

Open your Bible to Mark 10:13-16, and read or briefly summarize the story of Jesus blessing the children. Then choose one child to be "Jesus" and six children to be "disciples." The rest of your students will play the part of...children!

Instruct Jesus to walk, heel to toe, from one point in the room to another that's about 20 feet away. The disciples should surround the child playing Jesus and try to keep the other children from touching him. Here's the catch: All kids must keep their hands at their sides. No using hands to touch Jesus or keep people away!

Play for a few minutes, and then call time and have kids switch roles. Play several rounds, and then gather kids together. ASK:

- **Why do you think the disciples tried to keep children away from Jesus?**
- **Why do you think Jesus liked to be with children?**

SAY: **▷JESUS LOVES CHILDREN, and Jesus loves you!**

Craft

▶ *NO PREP*

Jesus Loves You!

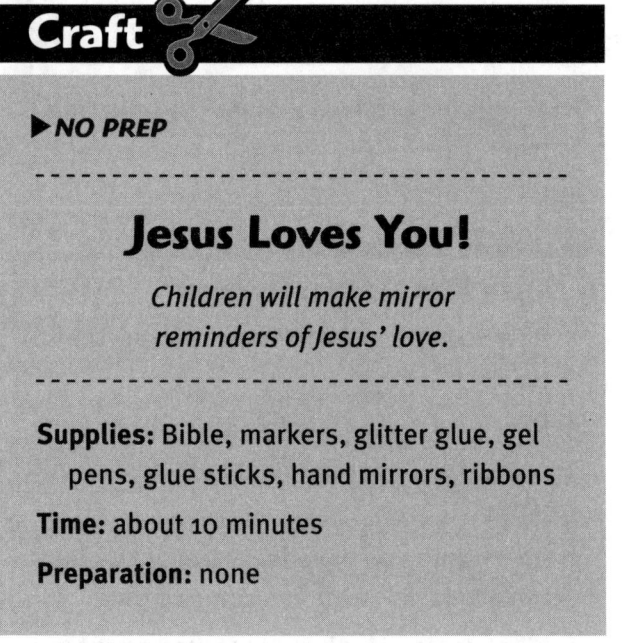

Children will make mirror reminders of Jesus' love.

Supplies: Bible, markers, glitter glue, gel pens, glue sticks, hand mirrors, ribbons

Time: about 10 minutes

Preparation: none

Read aloud Mark 10:13-16 (or summarize the story of Jesus blessing the children). Give each child a hand mirror, the bigger the better. These can usually be purchased inexpensively at dollar stores. (If you'd rather, cover cardboard squares with aluminum foil instead of using mirrors.)

SAY: **Jesus didn't just love the children back in Bible times. ▷JESUS LOVES CHILDREN today, too.** Have kids look in their mirrors. **And Jesus loves you! Decorate your mirror any way you want to. Then take it home with you. Every time you look in it, remember how much Jesus loves you!**

Encourage kids to write "Jesus loves children" on their mirrors, festoon them with ribbons, draw pictures of the Bible story on them, and think of any other ideas they can to personalize this Bible story.

____

____

____

____

____

____

Bible Application

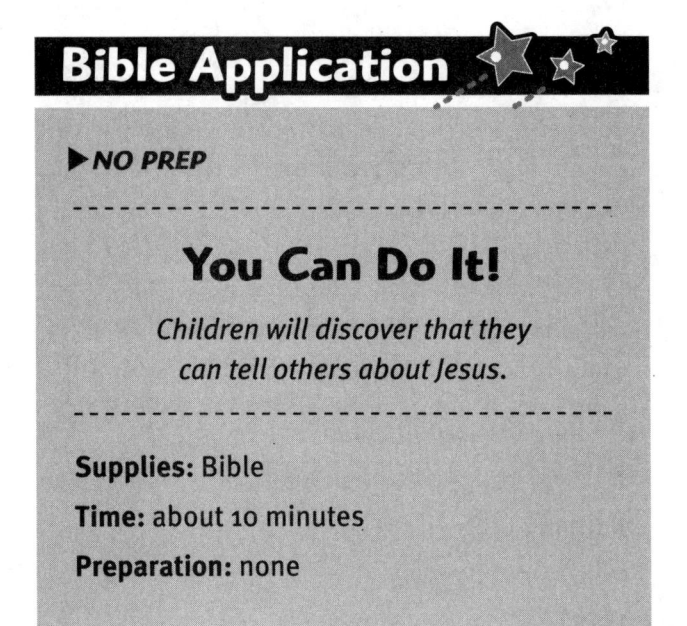

▶ *NO PREP*

You Can Do It!

Children will discover that they can tell others about Jesus.

Supplies: Bible

Time: about 10 minutes

Preparation: none

Read aloud Mark 10:13-16. SAY: **At some point in your life, you've likely heard someone say, "You can't do that; you're too young." Turn to a partner and tell about a time you heard something like that.** Pause.

Some of Jesus' disciples thought that children were too young and unimportant to talk to Jesus. OK, I know that there are *some* things kids really are too young to do. But kids can do tons of things and are really good at lots of things. Think of something you're really good at. Silently act it out for your partner.

Give kids a few moments to think, and then have partners take turns silently acting out their skills for each other. Partners can try to guess what's being acted out. After everyone has had a turn, SAY: **I knew it—you're good at lots of things! And you can be good at something you may not have thought of. Jesus not only told his disciples not to turn away the children, but he even said that children can show others how to believe in him. Turn to your partner and tell one thing you can do this week to help someone believe in Jesus.**

Invite volunteers to share their ideas with the rest of the class. Then encourage kids to follow through on their ideas during the coming week. Check back next week to see how kids did.

Creative Prayer Idea

Welcome!

Children will add to a prayer poster.

Supplies: poster board, markers, tape

Time: about 5 minutes

Preparation: On the top of a large sheet of poster board, write "Jesus Welcomes YOU!" Then draw a large heart outline on the rest of the sheet. Hang the poster at kids' eye level, and set out markers nearby.

SAY: ▷**JESUS LOVES CHILDREN, and that means that Jesus loves you! Jesus knows your name and everything else about you. He wants you to come to him, just as he wanted the children in the Bible story to come to him. Let's do an active prayer that can remind you of how much Jesus loves you.**

Point to the prayer poster you hung up. Explain that each child in turn will go up to the poster and write his or her name inside the heart. After children have each written their name, gather kids in front of the poster and close in a prayer thanking Jesus for loving and welcoming each person in class.

After the prayer, let kids add to the poster handprints, favorite Bible verses, and notes of thanks to Jesus. Keep the poster on your wall to remind kids that ▷**JESUS LOVES CHILDREN.**

Discussion Launcher Questions

Have kids form trios to discuss the following questions.

ASK:

- **Why do you think the children in this story were important to Jesus?**
- **How do you know that you're important to Jesus?**
- **How would you have felt if you had been one of the children being kept away from Jesus?**
- **How would you have felt when Jesus told the disciples to let you come to him?**
- **What do you think Jesus talked about with the children that day?**

Movie Clip

Hooked on Kids

Movie: *Hook* (PG)

Start Time: 19 minutes, 23 seconds

Where to Begin: Peter is addressing an audience at a banquet to honor Granny Wendy for her work with orphaned children.

Where to End: Peter, at the end of his speech, says, "We're all orphans."

Plot: Peter and his family have come to visit Grandma Wendy and are attending a banquet held in her honor. Just about everyone in attendance was once a child that Wendy "saved."

Review: Grandma Wendy loved all children. She found lost children who had no homes or families and gave them love and care. Her kindness to children can be likened to that of Jesus. At a time children were thought of as less important, Jesus took time to love them.

Discussion

After setting up and showing the clip, have kids form pairs to discuss these questions:

- **How do you think Wendy felt about the children she helped?**
- **How did all the people she helped as children feel about her?**
- **How is what Wendy did for the orphaned children like what Jesus has done for us?**
- **How does it make you feel knowing that Jesus loves all children, including you?**

Preschool Story

▶ ***NO PREP***

Bible Point: ▷**JESUS LOVES CHILDREN.**

Supplies: Bible

Time: 5 to 10 minutes

Preparation: none

I'm Important to Jesus!

Have kids form a circle and sit down. Open our Bible to Mark 10:13-16, and show children the words. SAY: **The Bible tells us that Jesus loves everyone.** Have kids give high fives to children sitting next to them. Then speak in a deep voice, stand up tall, and SAY: **Jesus loves tall, strong people.** Speaking in a soft, sweet voice, SAY: **He loves nice, kind people.** Tap your head and SAY: **He loves smart, wise people.**

ASK:

- **Who else does Jesus love?**

SAY: **That's right! Jesus loves all those people.** Speak in a higher voice, crouch down low, and SAY: **And Jesus loves little children, too!**

Resume your normal voice and SAY: **Whenever Jesus was in town, people would walk to see him.** Have kids walk in place. **As they walked, the tall, strong people might have said, "Jesus loves me."** Speak in a low voice and stand up tall. **The nice, kind people might have said, "Jesus loves me."** Speak in a soft, sweet voice. **The smart, wise people might have said, "Jesus loves me."** Tap your head. **And the little children might have said, "Jesus loves me, too."** Speak in a higher voice and crouch down low.

The people would sit and listen to Jesus tell about God. Have kids sit down. **They would stand and watch him make a sick person well.** Have kids stand up. **Sometimes they just wanted Jesus to touch them and tell them they were special to God.** Have kids pat a friend's shoulder.

One day many children were coming to Jesus. Have kids come in close to you. **This made the disciples mad.** Have kids put their hands on their hips and look mad.

"Go away," they growled. Growl, "Go away!" **They didn't think Jesus wanted the children there. They thought Jesus was too busy for little kids.** Have kids walk around the room telling everyone, "Go away. Jesus is too busy." **But Jesus said, "Don't send them away. See how they believe in me? Let them come. I want them here with me."** Form a group hug.

As they walked home that day, the tall, strong people might have said, "Jesus loves me." Speak in a low voice and stand up tall. **The nice, kind people might have said, "Jesus loves me."** Speak in a soft, sweet voice. **The smart, wise people might have said, "Jesus loves me."** Tap your head. **And the little children might have said, "Jesus loves me, too—he told me so!"** Speak in a higher voice and crouch down low.

ASK:

- **Why do you think Jesus wanted the children to come to him?**
- **What would you tell Jesus if you could sit on his lap?**

SAY: **Jesus wanted the disciples to see that children were important to him and that he loved them. Always remember that ▷JESUS LOVES CHILDREN.**

Let's sing a song to help us remember the Bible story. Sing the following song to the tune of "Jesus Loves Me":

Jesus loves me! This I know, *(hug yourself)*
For the Bible tells me so; *(make a book with your hands)*
Little ones to him belong, *(point to yourself)*
They are weak, but he is strong. *(Hug yourself.)*
Yes, I'm important! *(Point to yourself.)*
Yes, I'm important! *(Point to yourself.)*
Yes, I'm important! *(Point to yourself.)*
The Bible tells me so! *(Make a book with your hands.)*

BIBLE STORY

Taxes to Caesar

For the Leader

The Jews hated paying taxes to Rome because the money supported their oppressors. In addition, much of the money went to maintain the pagan temples and rich lifestyles of the upper Roman class. But anyone who avoided paying taxes was in lots of trouble with the Roman government.

The Pharisees and supporters of Herod hoped to catch Jesus in a statement that would incriminate him. If he said that people should pay taxes, he would seem to be supporting Rome. If he said people shouldn't pay taxes, he could be accused of treason. But Jesus answered wisely and in a way that thwarted his detractors.

Key Scripture

Mark 12:13-17

Bible Verse

"Give to Caesar what belongs to Caesar, and give to God what belongs to God" (Mark 12:17).

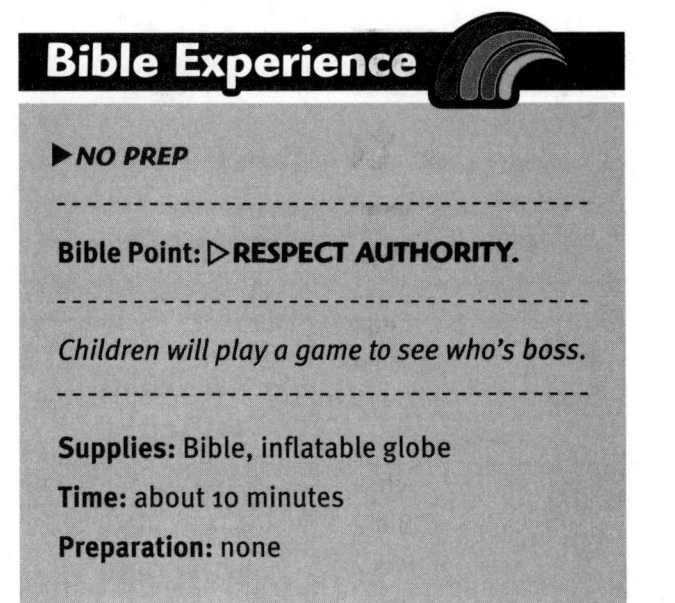

Bible Experience

▶ *NO PREP*

Bible Point: ▷**RESPECT AUTHORITY.**

Children will play a game to see who's boss.

Supplies: Bible, inflatable globe

Time: about 10 minutes

Preparation: none

SAY: **We're going to talk today about who's the boss in our lives. Let's play a quick game to get started. I'm going to be the boss and tell you what to do. And you have to do what I ask you to! I'll ask a question and then toss the globe ball to someone. Whoever catches it will answer the question and then toss it back to me so I can ask another question. Ready? Remember—do what I tell you because I'm the boss!** Ask questions such as:

- **Who's the boss at your school?**
- **Who's the boss in your house?**
- **Who's the boss on a soccer team?**
- **Who's the boss at church?**

Get the ball back, and open your Bible to Mark 12:13-17. SAY: **There are all kinds of bosses and authority figures in our lives. Sometimes it can be hard to know whom and when to obey. Listen to something Jesus said about authority.** Have a volunteer read aloud Mark 12:13-17.

ASK:

- **What do you think Jesus was saying about authority in this passage?**

SAY: **We all have authority figures in our lives. And unless those authority figures are trying to make us go against what God says, we should respect them. Sometimes that might be hard, but it's important to ▷RESPECT AUTHORITY.**

Let's toss the globe again. Each time you catch it, name one kind of authority figure we can pray for. Maybe it's a parent, teacher, coach, or even the president. Begin a prayer for those in authority. Toss the globe again, and let kids add authority figures to the prayer. Close by thanking Jesus for being the ultimate authority in all areas.

Additional Topics List

This lesson can be used to help kids discover... Discernment, Obedience, and Respect.

Game

Hurry Up and Lead!

Children will take turns being in charge.

Supplies: Bible, marker, small paper plates, CD player, CD of fast-paced praise music

Time: about 10 minutes

Preparation: Use the marker to draw a simple crown shape on the back of one of the paper plates.

Gather kids in a circle.

ASK:

- **How do you feel about authority?**

SAY: **Listen to what Jesus says about authority.** Have a volunteer read aloud Mark 12:13-17. **The Bible says to ▷RESPECT AUTHORITY. Let's play a game and see who's an authority here!**

Explain that you'll play a song on the CD. You'll also pass several paper plates around the circle. Kids should pass them quickly as the music plays. When the music stops, whoever is holding the plate with the crown on the back should stand and lead the class around the room once doing an action of choice, such as hopping on one foot or quacking like a duck.

Start the music and begin passing plates. Pause the song several times to give different children a chance to lead the class in an action. (If you have a small class, let everyone have a turn.) Then

ASK:

◆ **What was it like to be the authority and to lead everyone else?**

◆ **What was it like to obey what the authority said to do?**

SAY: **Unless an authority figure tries to get us to go against God, we should ▷RESPECT AUTHORITY. Let's close with a prayer for all of the authority figures in our lives.** Lead a prayer asking God to help your students show respect for the authority figures in their lives.

Craft

An Encouraging Word

Children will make cards for those in authority.

Supplies: Bible, card stock, craft scissors, hole punches, stampers, ink pads, ribbons, colored pens

Time: about 10 minutes

Preparation: Select a community leader to send the cards to. Ideas may include a pastor, mayor, or teacher. Write a few sample messages for younger children to copy.

Read aloud Mark 12:17. SAY: **Jesus wants us to ▷RESPECT AUTHORITY. Let's make cards to do just that!** Have kids follow these card-making steps: Fold a piece of card stock in half. Use the remaining supplies to decorate the outside and inside of the card. Use the craft scissors and hole punch to make unique borders around the card.

Then have kids each write an encouraging note inside the card and sign their first names.

ASK:

◆ **Why should we respect and encourage our leaders?**

◆ **How else can we support our leaders?**

SAY: **It's important to ▷RESPECT AUTHORITY. By writing to and praying for our leaders, we can encourage them to continue doing their best.** Close in prayer for the leader kids wrote to. Collect the cards and mail them together in one envelope, including a short explanatory note.

notes

Bible Application

▶ *NO PREP*

Give Back

Children will learn that they should give back to God.

Supplies: Bible, a variety of coins

Time: 5 to 10 minutes

Preparation: none

Read aloud Mark 12:13-17.

ASK:

◆ **What do you think this passage means?**

SAY: **Maybe these coins will give us a clue.** Have kids form trios, and give each trio a coin. **Look at these coins. They may have different faces on them, but they're all coins issued by the government. When Jesus said to give to Caesar what is Caesar's, he essentially was saying to give to the government what is the government's. These coins bear the image of the government. So we should ▷RESPECT AUTHORITY and pay taxes to the government with the coins bearing the government's image.**

ASK:

◆ **But whose image do we bear?**

SAY: **The Bible says that we're made in the image of God. We bear God's image. Jesus said we should give to God what is God's.**

ASK:

◆ **What do you have that you could give to God?**

SAY: **Because we're made in God's image, we all have certain gifts and talents that God has given us to use in his service. And we should give those gifts and talents to God. Think of one gift or talent that God has given you that you can give back to him.**

Have kids form a circle, and let each person name the gift or talent he or she thought of. Close by thanking God for equipping each person with ways to serve and praise him. Encourage kids this week to give back to God the gifts and talents he has given them.

Creative Prayer Idea

▶ *NO PREP*

Prayergrams

Children will create prayergrams.

Supplies: Bible, colorful postcards, pens

Time: about 5 minutes

Preparation: none

Read aloud Mark 12:13-17. SAY: **It's good to ▷RESPECT AUTHORITY. One way to show respect for those in authority is by praying for them.**

Have children make a list of authorities in the church, community, nation, or world to pray for. Set aside a few minutes each week for children to pray for the people they've chosen. Then have children fill out "prayergram" postcards to send to the people they prayed for, encouraging them and letting them know they were prayed for. Mail the postcards on your way home from church.

Discussion Launcher

My Heart Belongs to God

For this activity, you'll need paper, crayons, and coins.

Read aloud Mark 12:13-17. SAY: **Let's make something to help us remember to ▷RESPECT AUTHORITY, both God's and man's.**

Give kids paper and crayons. Have kids draw a heart in the center of their papers. Inside the heart, have kids write "My Heart Belongs to God." Around the outside of the heart, let kids make coin rubbings by placing coins under the paper and rubbing over them with a crayon. Have children join you in a circle with their papers.

SAY: **Jesus said that we should give to Caesar, or the government, what belongs to Caesar. The pictures on the Roman coin had a picture of Caesar, so Jesus was saying to give back to the Roman government what belonged to it—the money with Caesar's picture on it.**

ASK:

- **Whom do you consider an authority figure in your life?**
- **How can you show respect for the authorities in your life?**
- **Why do you think Jesus wants us to respect authority?**

SAY: **Jesus also said that we should give to God what is God's.**

ASK:

- **What do you have that belongs to God?**
- **What can you give to God to show that you respect his authority?**

SAY: **Just as coins are made with the image of someone from the government, we're made in the image of God. All of our blessings and gifts and talents come from God, and we should give them back to him for his glory. Let's ask God to help us do that.** Close in prayer, asking God to help kids respect his authority and the authority of those in government. Ask his guidance in giving back to each in kind. Encourage kids to take their papers home to remind them to **▷RESPECT AUTHORITY.**

Snack

▶*NO PREP*
▶*ALLERGY ALERT*

Coin Capers

Children will make edible coins.

Supplies: Bible, round crackers, frosting, small paper plates, plastic knives, toothpicks, napkins

Time: 5 to 10 minutes

Preparation: none

Read aloud Mark 12:13-17. SAY: **Jesus used a coin to say that we should ▷RESPECT AUTHORITY when it comes to the government. Let's make some coins that we can eat!**

Set out the supplies. Let kids each frost some cracker "coins" and then use toothpicks to draw faces on the coins, like real coins have. As kids enjoy their snacks, have them answer these questions.

ASK:

- **What image do real coins have on them?**
- **Whose image are we made in?**
- **Why should we show respect for the authority figures in our lives?**
- **How can we show that we respect them?**
- **Why should we show respect for God?**
- **How can we show that we respect God?**

Preschool Story

▶ ***PREPARE IN ADVANCE***

Bible Point: ▷**RESPECT LEADERS.**

Supplies: Bible, construction paper, marker, scissors, tape, basket

Time: 10 to 15 minutes

Preparation: Cut out one 5-inch circle from light-colored construction paper for each child in your class. Draw a simple face on the circle—you may want to put a crown on the face to show that it's Caesar. Draw the same face on a piece of paper, and tape it to a wall. Place a basket underneath the picture. Hide the circles around the room, with Caesar's face showing. You will also need to cut out one 5-inch cross per child.

Coin Collection

Have kids form a circle and sit down. Open ur Bible to Mark 12:13-17, and show children the ords. SAY: **Some men, who were called Phari-es, didn't like Jesus very much. These Phari-es thought that Jesus' teachings were wrong, and they wanted him to stop teaching people. So one day the Pharisees decided to try to trick Jesus into saying something bad. They thought that if Jesus said the wrong thing, he might get arrested and thrown into jail. Then he'd stop teaching other people.**

So the Pharisees asked Jesus, "Is it right to pay taxes to the Roman government or not? Should we pay them, or shouldn't we?" (Mark 12:14-15). **Taxes are money that people pay to the government. That money helps build roads and pay for schools. But in those days the Romans made the Israelites pay too much money for taxes, and that made the Israelites angry.**

Jesus knew they were trying to trick him, but it didn't matter because Jesus had a very good answer. Jesus said, "Show me a Roman coin, and I'll tell you."

Can any of you find me a Roman coin? If you look around, you'll find a bunch of them. Encourage kids to go and find the Roman coins in the room. Once each child has a coin, have kids come back to your circle. **Show me the coins you found.**

ASK:

- **What is special about these coins?**

SAY: **When the Pharisees showed Jesus one of the Roman coins, he asked them whose picture was on the coin. "Caesar's" they said. Caesar was the king and ruler of the Romans.**

"Well then," Jesus said, "Give to Caesar what belongs to him." Jesus knew that the coins were made by the Roman government and that the coins belonged to the Romans. Let's give our coins to Caesar. Encourage kids to walk over to the picture of Caesar and drop their coins in the basket under his picture. Then have kids come back to the circle.

Jesus said that they should pay taxes to Caesar. Jesus knew that it was important for them to respect their leaders—and Caesar was their

leader. Jesus also wants us to ▷RESPECT OUR LEADERS.

ASK:

- **Why is it important to ▷RESPECT OUR LEADERS?**
- **Who are your leaders?**
- **How can you ▷RESPECT YOUR LEADERS?**

SAY: **Jesus said one more thing to the Pharisees after he told them to give to Caesar what was Caesar's. Jesus told them that they should also give to God what belongs to God.**

ASK:

- **What do you think belongs to God?**

SAY: **Let's find some things in this room that belong to God. When you find something, you can bring it back to our circle.** Encourage kids to look around the room to find things that belong to God. Kids might find a Bible, pictures of Jesus, songbooks, or even other kids! Once all the kids are back in the circle, distribute the paper crosses.

We know that the cross reminds us of God. Let's put crosses on all these things to show that they belong to God. Encourage kids to tape a cross to their item and then lay it in the center of the circle.

Jesus told us that it's important to ▷RESPECT OUR LEADERS. Jesus also told us that it's important to respect God.

n

o

t

e

s

BIBLE STORY

Widow's Offering

For the Leader

While Jesus—and presumably some of his disciples—sat in the Temple watching, numerous rich people gave large amounts of money. The disciples, who were from lower economic classes, were probably amazed at some of the fortunes offered by these wealthy Jews. They may not have even noticed the poor widow who dropped her two coins into the collection box.

These were the smallest coins in the Roman Empire. It took 40 of these to make up a day's wages. In terms of today's wages, they would have been worth no more than a couple of dollars each. Yet Jesus knew how big the widow's gift truly was.

Key Scriptures

Mark 12:41-44

2 Corinthians 9:7

Bible Verse

"God loves a person who gives cheerfully" (2 Corinthians 9:7).

Bible Experience

▶*NO PREP*
▶*ALLERGY ALERT*

Bible Point: ▷**GIVE YOUR ALL TO JESUS.**

Children will learn to give their all to Jesus.

Supplies: Bible, 2 pieces of gum per child
Time: about 10 minutes
Preparation: none

SAY: **I'm going to give each of you a piece of gum. Please hold on to it without chewing it.** Distribute the gum and SAY: **I'd like you to think about the gum you're holding. Imagine that every person needs one piece of gum each day to live and that you're holding your last piece of gum.** Have kids form pairs. **Now imagine that your best friend asks you for your piece of gum. Remember, it's your last piece, and you need it to live. Talk with your partner about what you'd do.** Give kids a short time to discuss the scenario. Then ask volunteers to share their answers with the rest of the class.

It might be hard to give up your gum, huh? The Bible tells us a true story of a very poor widow who was in a similar situation. Open your Bible to Mark 12:41-44, and show kids the passage. **The woman in the story had almost no money. And since she was a widow, she didn't have a husband to help take care of her. One day, in the Temple, which is like a church, she put two small coins in the collection box, even though that was all she had to live on. Jesus noticed what she'd done. Listen to what Jesus told his disciples.**

Read aloud Mark 12:43-44. SAY: **Jesus said that even though the widow had given only a little bit of money, it was as if she had given more than anyone else because she had given all she had, something she really needed. That would be like giving up your last piece of gum.**

The widow gave her all, and you can ▷GIVE YOUR ALL TO JESUS, too. God loves it when we cheerfully give what we have. Listen to what God's Word says. Read aloud 2 Corinthians 9:7; then SAY: **Now you can try it. I want you to give your piece of gum to someone else today and tell that person the story of the poor widow's offering. Tell your partner whom you're going to give your gum to.** Pause for kids to do this, and then SAY: **And because you're such cheerful givers, I'm going to give you each another piece of gum! Thanks for being cheerful givers!** Distribute the rest of the gum.

Additional Topics List

This lesson can be used to help kids discover... Faith, Greed, and Reliance.

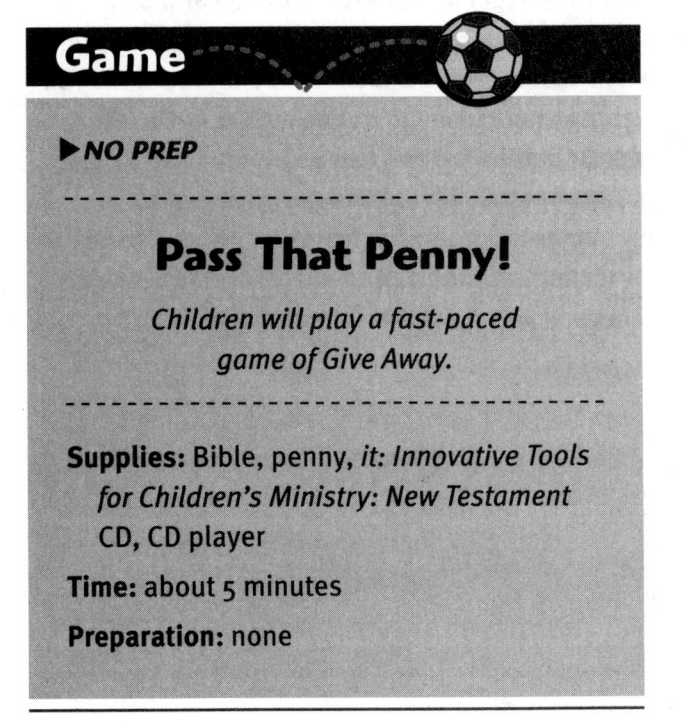

Game

▶*NO PREP*

Pass That Penny!

Children will play a fast-paced game of Give Away.

Supplies: Bible, penny, *it: Innovative Tools for Children's Ministry: New Testament* CD, CD player
Time: about 5 minutes
Preparation: none

Read aloud Mark 12:41-44. Have kids sit in a circle on the floor. SAY: **The widow in this story gave everything she had to the Temple, which is like a church. It's good to ▷GIVE YOUR ALL TO JESUS.**

ASK:

- **What do you think it means to ▷GIVE YOUR ALL TO JESUS?**
- **What kinds of things can you give to Jesus in addition to money?**

SAY: **Let's play a game in which we try to give away this penny as fast as we can. I'll play a song from the CD. When the music stops, whoever is holding the penny can tell one thing we can give to Jesus to give him our all. Ready? Let's pass that penny!** Have kids quickly pass the penny around the circle as you play "Treasures" (track 3, *it: Innovative Tools for Children's Ministry: New Testament* CD). Periodically pause the song to let the holder of the penny say something we can give to Jesus. (If kids seem stumped, suggest things such as our time to help others, kind words, Bible stories they can tell others, and things they know about Jesus.)

After the game, collect the penny and SAY: **Thanks for all of those ideas! There are lots of ways we can ▷GIVE OUR ALL TO JESUS. Maybe we can give money, like the widow in the story did. Or maybe we can use our talents and time to serve Jesus. Maybe we can give our all to him by helping others. However we go about it, remember that God loves it when we ▷GIVE OUR ALL TO JESUS!**

n

o

t

e

s

Craft

▶ *FOR FAMILY MINISTRY*

Cheerful-Giving Cups

Children will make cups to collect loose change.

Supplies: Bible, knife, clean deli containers with lids, round stickers, fine-tipped permanent markers

Time: 5 to 10 minutes

Preparation: Use the knife to cut a slit large enough for a coin to pass through in each plastic lid.

Read aloud Mark 12:41-44. SAY: **The widow gave her all to Jesus, and we should, too. Let's make banks to remind us of this Bible story.** Give each child a container and a prepared lid. Set out the stickers and markers for kids to use. **We know from 2 Corinthians 9:7 that God loves a cheerful giver. You can use these round stickers to make bunches of smiley faces all over your Cheerful-Giving Cup. Just draw smiley faces on the stickers, and you're ready to go! Then you can decorate the cups anyway you want with the markers. Be sure to write ▷"GIVE YOUR ALL TO JESUS" somewhere on your cup.**

When kids have finished, let them admire each other's handiwork. SAY: **Take your cups home, and use them to collect loose change. Maybe you can even use your cup as a family change container. When the cup is filled with money, decide as a family what organization or person you'd like to give it to.**

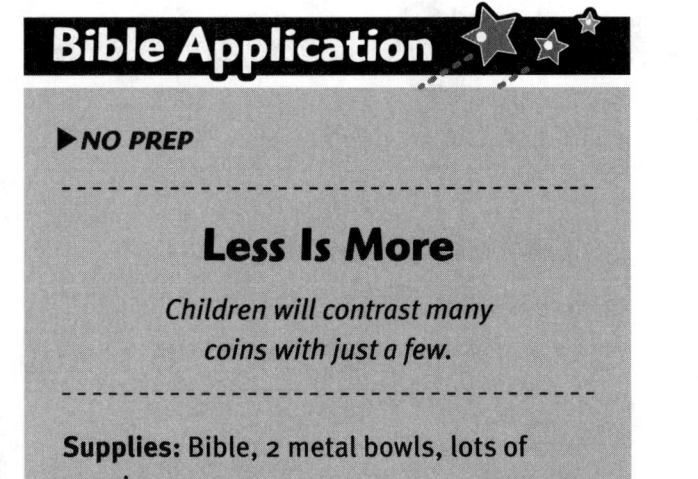

Bible Application

▶ *NO PREP*

Less Is More

Children will contrast many coins with just a few.

Supplies: Bible, 2 metal bowls, lots of coins

Time: about 5 minutes

Preparation: none

Read aloud Mark 12:41-44. SAY: **The Bible tells us that one day Jesus was watching what people were doing with their offerings.** Motion to the table with the two metal bowls and coins. Set two coins aside. **Lots of rich people were giving lots of money. It was kind of like this.** Let kids take turns adding coins to one of the metal bowls—the more racket, the better! **Wow! Lots and lots of money! Then Jesus noticed a poor widow as she gave her offering.** Slowly drop the two coins into the other bowl so kids hear, *clink,clink.* Shake the two bowls and SAY: **Jesus said the widow gave the most.**

ASK:

◆ **Why did he say that?**

SAY: **The widow gave the most because she gave all she had to live on. The other people had lots of money, so it wasn't a big deal for them to give some of it away. Think of either something you don't have much of or something of yours that you really like. Turn to a partner, and tell one thing that it would be really hard for you to give away.** Pause, and then invite volunteers to share their answers.

We don't always have to give up our favorite things. There are lots of ways to give our all for Jesus. Think of a way you can give your time to serve Jesus. Tell your partner your idea. Pause.

Now think of a talent you have that you could use to serve Jesus. Tell your partner about your idea. Pause.

We can serve Jesus and give our all to him in lots of ways. Choose one thing you'll do this week to ▷ GIVE YOUR ALL TO JESUS. Tell your partner what you'll do. Pause, and then SAY: **Let's pray and ask God to help us ▷ GIVE OUR ALL TO JESUS this week.**

Close in prayer, asking God to help all of your students follow through on their ideas and **▷ GIVE THEIR ALL TO JESUS this week.**

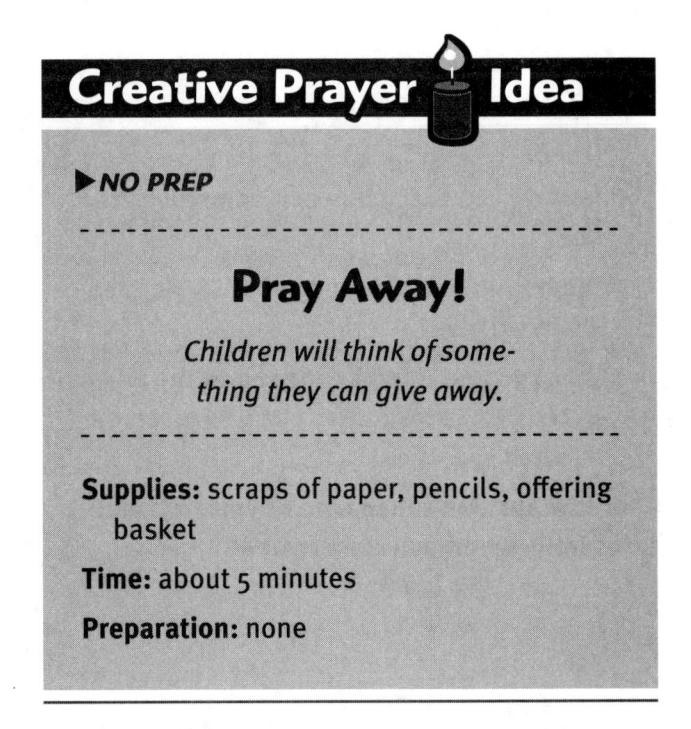

Creative Prayer Idea

▶ *NO PREP*

Pray Away!

Children will think of something they can give away.

Supplies: scraps of paper, pencils, offering basket

Time: about 5 minutes

Preparation: none

SAY: **In today's Bible story the widow gave all she had. Think of something you have that you could give away. It doesn't have to be money, although it could be. Or maybe you have extra time that you could give away by visiting a neighbor who can't get out much. Or maybe you have an old toy that you like but that you**

know someone else might like, too. As you're thinking, I'll pass out some paper and pencils. Write your idea on the paper.

When kids have finished writing, gather everyone together in a circle. Pass around your offering basket, and let each child place his or her paper in the basket. Have kids say, "Lord, I give my all to you," as they place the paper in the basket. When the basket comes back to you, close the prayer by thanking God for all the cheerful givers in your class. Then encourage kids to follow through on their giving intentions.

Discussion Launcher Questions

Have kids form pairs to discuss these questions:

ASK:

- **How do you feel when you give something?**
- **How do you feel when someone gives to you?**
- **What kind of an attitude should we have when we give?**
- **What do you think happened to the widow in the Bible story after she had given all she had to live on?**
- **How has God taken care of you and your family when you were in need?**

n
o
t
e
s

Snack

▶ ***ALLERGY ALERT***

Good to Go and Give

Children will make snacks for each other.

Supplies: Bible, yellow food coloring, softened cream cheese, English muffins, small paper plates, plastic knives, M&M's chocolate candies, raisins

Time: about 10 minutes

Preparation: Use food coloring to tint the cream cheese yellow. Split the muffins in half. Set out all your snack supplies on a table.

Read aloud Mark 12:41-44. Have kids wash their hands. SAY: **In today's Bible story we heard how a poor widow gave away her two small coins—all the money she had to live on. We're going to make snacks to remind us of the story.**

Tell kids they can make English-muffin coins. Then they can make smiles on their coins because the Bible says that God loves a cheerful giver. Caution kids not to eat their snacks until you tell them to. Let kids spread the yellow cream cheese on muffin halves and then make smiley faces with the candies and raisins.

When everyone has finished making a snack, SAY: **I'll bet you're ready to eat the yummy snack you created, right? In today's story, the widow gave what she had away, and that's just what we're going to do! Give your snack to someone else!**

Have kids exchange snacks. SAY: **I know you weren't expecting to give your snack away, but we should always be ready to share what we have with others.** Before kids eat, thank God for his provision and ask him to help kids ▷ **GIVE THEIR ALL TO JESUS.**

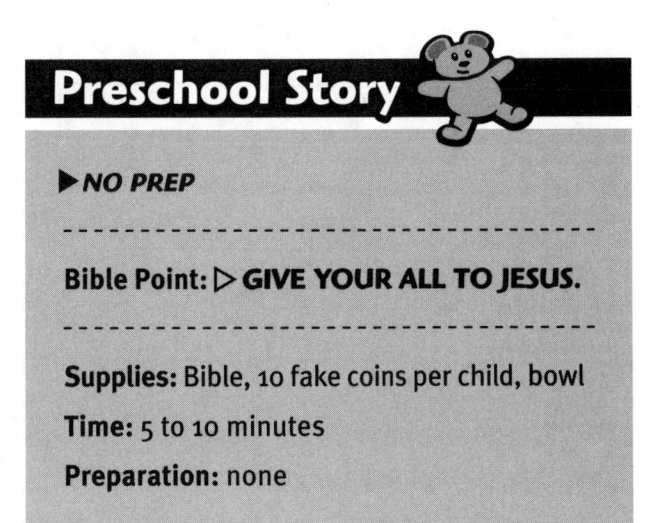

Preschool Story

▶ ***NO PREP***

Bible Point: ▷ **GIVE YOUR ALL TO JESUS.**

Supplies: Bible, 10 fake coins per child, bowl

Time: 5 to 10 minutes

Preparation: none

A Beautiful Gift

Have kids form a circle and sit down. Open your Bible to Mark 12:41-44, and show children the words. SAY: **The Bible tells us that Jesus was sitting at a place in the Temple where people brought their gifts to God. One by one the rich people brought their coins and dropped them into the money box. As the coins fell in, they made a lot of noise.** Have children count and set out two coins. Then let kids take turns slowly dropping the rest of their coins into the bowl. As children drop their coins, ooh and aah at all the noise they make.

Jesus watched as the rich people gave money to God. Those people thought they were pretty good for being rich and having lots of money to give to God. After all, they had lots more coins at home.

Jesus continued to watch and listen as coin after coin was dropped into the money box. Then Jesus saw a very poor woman walk up to the money box. She didn't have very much money at all. She had only two coins and nothing more at home.

ASK:

- **What would you do if you had only two coins?**
- **What do you think the poor woman did with her coins?**

SAY: **The poor woman had only two coins to give to God. She didn't have any more money at home. Even though it wasn't much, she dropped the coins into the money box. They barely made a sound.** Let children take turns dropping their last two coins into the bowl.

Jesus watched as the woman gave her money to God. He heard the tiny sound the two coins made as they dropped into the money box. And Jesus knew that the woman was giving to God all the money she had in the world. He told the disciples that this poor woman's gift was worth more than all the money the rich people had given because it was everything she had.

God wants us to give gifts to him, too. Little gifts can be big when they're given to God. He sees what you give, and he says thank you.

ASK:

- **What do you have that you can give to God?**
- **Why do you think it's important to give to God?**

SAY: **God wants us to ▷ GIVE OUR ALL TO JESUS, just like the woman in the story did. Let's do an action rhyme to help us remember to cheerfully give to Jesus.**

I'll share a little secret that's hardly ever told. *(Place your hands around your mouth and pretend to whisper.)*

Some people think the way to get is to grab and hold. *(Pretend to grab air.)*

But God loves a cheerful giver who gives his love and gold. *(Hold your hands out.)*

If we start now, we'll learn to give as we're growing old. *(Pretend to lean on a cane.)*